The
Informed Argument

A Multidisciplinary Reader and Guide

The
Informed Argument

A Multidisciplinary Reader and Guide

Robert K. Miller
University of Wisconsin/Stevens Point

Harcourt Brace Jovanovich, Publishers

San Diego   New York   Chicago   Atlanta   Washington, D.C.

London   Sydney   Toronto

Preface

Behind *The Informed Argument* is the belief that students resent being asked to write on topics that seem trivial or contrived, but welcome the opportunity to discuss serious subjects. The readings in this book are assembled into eight separate casebooks, seven of which are focused on large issues of the sort that students often want to write about, although they may lack sufficient information to do so effectively. Instructors are free to treat each section either as a self-contained unit or as a springboard to further reading. In order to facilitate class discussion, every essay has its own editorial apparatus and every section ends with a list of suggestions for writing—some of which direct students exclusively to material within the book, while others ask them to incorporate their own experience or research. This allows instructors much flexibility. They can assign readings in whatever sequence they deem appropriate. And there is plenty of material so that instructors can vary the readings they choose to assign, passing over any that seem inappropriate for a particular class.

The 71 selections are drawn from a variety of disciplines in order to help students master different types of writing and reading. Among the fields represented are biology, business, history, journalism, medicine, law, literature, philosophy, physics, political science, psychology, and sociology. In selecting these readings, I have been guided by two concerns: to include different points of view within each section and to provide students with both model arguments and adequate data for composing essays of their own.

Although I believe in the importance of writing across the curriculum, I also believe that literature should be a part of the curriculum being written across. Consequently, the book includes some poetry and a section on literary criticism as a type of argumentation. The thematically organized sections are followed by "Some Classic Arguments," a ninth section that is not focused on a particular issue. Increasing the variety of readings made available to students, this section includes such well-known essays as "A Modest Proposal," "Politics and the English Language," and "Letter from Birmingham Jail," as well as excerpts from several important works in the history of ideas.

The readings are the heart of this book. But *The Informed Argument* is more than an anthology. Because books have become so expensive, I have tried to design a text that would satisfy all the needs of students in a semester-long course and be useful to them long afterward. Part One introduces students to the rhetorical principles that they will need to understand in order to write argumentative essays of their own and profit from the readings in Part Two. I have tried to keep the explanations as simple as possible, avoiding complex terminology. Examples are provided for each of the concepts discussed, and student essays illustrate both inductive and deductive reasoning. In addition to introducing students to the fundamentals of logical reasoning, Part One also explains the nature and importance of summary and paraphrase.

Part Three, "A Guide to Research and Documentation," teaches students how to find material that has not been already gathered for them. In keeping with the book's multidisciplinary approach, I emphasize a search strategy that can be used to locate material for assignments in many different courses. All of the major documentation styles in use across the curriculum are discussed— not only the styles of the Modern Language Association (MLA) and the American Psychological Association (APA), which are discussed in detail, but also the use of documentary footnotes and of a numbered system favored in much scientific and medical writing. The 1984 MLA style is illustrated by a student essay in Part Three. The other systems, including two that are recommended by *The Chicago Manual of Style*, are all illustrated by one or more of the essays in Part Two (for a list, see page 573).

In completing this book, I have contracted many debts. I would like to thank my colleagues in the English department at the University of Wisconsin at Stevens Point, especially Ruth Dorgan, Steve Odden, Don Pattow, and Al Young. I would also like to thank the staff of the Albertson Learning Resource Center, especially John Gillesby, Kathleen Halsey, Mary Louise Smith, and Margaret Whalen. For generous help with word processing, I want to thank Jean Kewer, Eleanor Ligman, and Lorraine Swanson. For encouragement and support without fail, I want to thank Dr. Warren Garitano. At Harcourt Brace Jovanovich, Lynn Edwards, Eleanor Garner, Barbara Girard, Ann Marie Mulkeen, Cheryl Solheid, and Ellen Wynn deserve many thanks for their expert help. Finally, I want to thank Tom Broadbent, the talented and ever-patient editor whose help was essential in every stage of finishing this book.

R.K.M.

Contents

PART 3
A Guide to Research and Documentation   539

PART 1

An Introduction to Argument

Many people assume that writing arguments must be difficult—perhaps because the word *argument* can have such disagreeable connotations. It may remind us of anger, loud voices, maybe even violence. If you believe that "arguing" is the same as "quarreling"—that "having an argument" is only a polite way of saying "having a fight"—then it would be understandable if you decided that argument is something best avoided. It is important to realize that written arguments have nothing to do with slamming doors or calling names. Written arguments require that we think clearly, without letting our feelings dominate what we have to say. A good argument is both well thought out and carefully organized, making it possible for us to persuade others that our ideas deserve to be taken seriously. We may not always succeed in converting others to our point of view. But we can win their respect. This, in a way, is what argument is all about. When we argue for what we believe, we are asking others to believe in *us*. We must prove to our audience that we are worth listening to. If we succeed this far, we may have won the argument even if we lose the vote on the particular issue at hand. Argumentation is intellectual self-assertion designed to secure the consideration and respect of our peers.

Bearing this in mind, you should always be careful to treat your opponents with respect. Few people are likely to be converted to your point of view if you treat them as if they were fools and dismiss their beliefs with contempt. Reason is the essence of effective argumentation, and an important part of being reasonable is demonstrating that you have given consideration to beliefs that are different from your own and have recognized what makes them appealing. You should not be narrow-minded or contentious. Don't make the mistake of assuming that you have a monopoly on truth. Remember that nobody likes a know-it-all.

Similarly, you should avoid the temptation of arguing all things at all times. Most points can indeed be argued. But you won't be taken seriously if you seem to argue automatically and routinely. Argument should be the result of reflection rather than reflex. And argumentation is a skill that should be practiced selectively.

finesse ; style ; the classics

1

CHOOSING A TOPIC

The first step in written argumentation, as in all forms of writing, is choosing a topic. In doing so, you should be careful to avoid subjects that could be easily settled by referring to an authority, such as a dictionary or an encyclopedia. There is no point in arguing about how to spell "separate," or how many people live in San Diego, because questions of this sort can be settled quickly and absolutely, allowing only one correct answer. Argument assumes the possibility of more than one position on any important issue. When you disagree with someone about anything that could be settled by simply checking the facts, you would be wasting your time to argue, even if you are sure you are right.

Almost all intelligent arguments are about *opinions*. But not all opinions lead to good written arguments. There is no reason to argue an opinion with which almost no one would disagree. An essay designed to "prove" that puppies are cute, or that vacations can be fun, is unlikely to generate much excitement. Don't belabor the obvious. Nearly everyone welcomes the arrival of spring, and you will be preaching to the converted if you set out to argue that spring is a nice time of year. If you've been reading T.S. Eliot, however, and want to argue that April is the cruelest month (and that you have serious reservations about May and June as well) then you may be on to something. You should not feel that you suddenly need to acquire strange and eccentric opinions. But you should choose a topic which is likely to inspire at least some controversy.

In doing so, you should be careful to distinguish between opinions that are a matter of taste, and those that are a question of judgment. Some people like broccoli, and some people don't. You may be the world's foremost broccoli-lover, dreaming each night of broccoli crops to come, but no matter how hard you try, you will not convince someone who hates green vegetables to head quickly to the produce department of the nearest supermarket. A gifted stylist could probably write a familiar essay on broccoli, in the manner of Charles Lamb or E.B. White, that would be a delight to read. But it is one thing to describe our tastes, and quite another to insist that others share them. We all have likes and dislikes that are so firmly entrenched that persuasion in matters of taste is usually beyond the reach of what can be accomplished through the written word—unless you happen to command the resources of a major advertising agency.

Taste is a matter of personal preference. Whether we prefer green to blue, or iris to tulips, is unlikely to affect anyone but ourselves. Questions of judgment are more substantial than matters of taste because judgment cannot be divorced from logic. Our judgments are determined by our beliefs, behind which are basic principles to which we try to remain consistent. These principles subsequently lead us to decide that some judgments are correct and others are not, so judgment has greater implications than taste. Should a university require freshmen to live in dormitories? Should men and women live together before getting married? Should parents spank their children? All these are questions of judgment.

✱ In written argumentation, questions of judgment provide the best subjects. They can be argued because they are complex, giving you more angles to pursue. This does not mean that you must cover every aspect of a question in a single essay. Because good subjects have so many possibilities, the essays that are written on them will take many different directions. Good writers sound like individuals, not committees or machines, and it is easier to sound like an individual when you address a subject about which many different things can be said. Moreover, in making an argument the writer always hopes to surprise his audience with information—or an ingenious interpretation of information—that is not usually considered. If your audience consists of people who know almost nothing about your subject, then you may be able to build a convincing case by simply outlining a few basic points. But an educated audience will be converted to your view only if you move beyond the obvious and reveal points that are often overlooked. And this is most likely to happen when the subject itself is complex.

It is important, therefore, to choose subjects which you are well-informed about or willing to research. This may sound like obvious advice, and yet it is possible to have an opinion with nothing behind it but a few generalizations that are impossible to support once we begin to write. We may have absorbed the opinions of others without thinking for ourselves. We may even be prejudiced, which is to say we have prejudged a particular subject without knowing much about it. Nobody is going to take us seriously if, when we are asked to explain ourselves, we can produce nothing more sophisticated than, "Well, isn't that what everybody thinks?"

The readings that form the core of this book were chosen to make you better informed on some of the major questions of our time. After you have read six or seven intelligent essays on the same subject, you should be able to compose an argument of your own that will consider the various views you have encountered. But you should remember that being "better informed" does not always mean being "well informed." Well-educated men and women recognize how little they know in proportion to how much there is to be known. Don't think that you've become an expert on abortion simply because you have spent a week or two reading about it. What we read should influence what we think. But as we read more, we should realize that controversial subjects are controversial because there is so much that could be said about them—much more than we may have realized at first.

In learning to write arguments, you will be mastering a skill that will be important beyond the world of the classroom. In the years ahead, you will need to argue many questions. You may very well have the occasion to argue, and argue seriously, about political and ethical concerns. Someone you love may be considering an abortion, or the school board in your own community may begin to censor books. A large corporation may try to bury its chemical wastes on the property that adjoins your own. Or you may be suddenly deprived of a benefit to which you feel entitled. Arguments are not limited to the sort of issues that are reported in newspapers and magazines. When you apply for a job, propose a marriage, or recommend any change that involves someone besides yourself, you are putting yourself in a position that requires effective argumentation. And whatever the subject, be it large or small, you should know what you are talking about.

DEFINING YOUR AUDIENCE

Argumentation demands a clear sense of audience. Good writers remember whom they are writing for, and their audience helps shape their style. It would be a mistake, for example, to use complicated technical language when writing for a general audience. But it would be just as foolish to address an audience of experts as if they knew nothing about the subject. The writer should always be careful not to confuse people. On the other hand, he or she must also be careful not to insult the readers' intelligence. Although awareness of audience is important in all types of writing, it is especially true in written arguments. A clear sense of audience allows us to choose the points we want to emphasize in order to be persuasive. Just as importantly, it enables us to anticipate the objections our readers or listeners are most likely to raise if they disagree with us.

[In written argumentation, it is usually best to envision an audience that is skeptical.] Unless you are the keynote speaker at a political convention, rallying the members of your party by telling them exactly what they want to hear, there is no reason to expect people to agree with you. If your audience already agrees with you, what's the point of your argument? Whom are you trying to convince? Remember that the immediate purpose of an argument is almost always to convert people to your point of view. Of course, an audience may be entirely neutral, having no opinion at all on the subject that concerns you. But by imagining a skeptical audience, you will be able to anticipate the opposition and offer counterarguments of your own, thus building a stronger case.

Before you begin to write, you should list for yourself the reasons why you believe as you do. Realize that you may not have the space, in a short essay, to discuss all of the points you have listed. You should therefore rank them in order of their relative importance, considering, in particular, the degree to which they would probably impress the audience for whom you are writing. Once you have done this, compose another list—a list of reasons why people might disagree with you. Having considered the opposition's point of view, now ask yourself why it is that you have not been persuaded to abandon your own beliefs. You must see a flaw of some sort in the reasoning of your opponents. Amend your second list by adding to it a short rebuttal to each of your opponent's arguments.

You are likely to discover that the opposition has at least one good argument, an argument which you cannot answer. There should be nothing surprising about this. We may like to flatter ourselves by believing that Truth is on our side. In our weaker moments, we may like to pretend that anyone who disagrees with us is either ignorant or corrupt. But serious and prolonged controversies almost always mean that the opposition has at least one valid concern. Be prepared to concede a point to your opponents when it seems appropriate to do so. Nothing is to be gained by ignoring their point of view. You must consider their views and respond to them, but your responses do not always have to take the form of rebuttals. When you have no rebuttal, and recognize that your opponent's case has some merit, be honest and generous enough to say so.

By making concessions to your opposition, you demonstrate to your audience that you are trying to be fair-minded. Far from weakening your own case, an occasional concession can help bridge the gulf between you and your opponents, making it easier for you to reach a more substantial agreement. It's hard to convince someone that your views deserve to be taken seriously when you have belligerently insisted that he or she is completely wrong and you are completely right. Life is seldom so simple. And human nature being what it is, most people will listen more readily to an argument that offers some recognition of their views.

You must be careful, of course, not to concede too much. If you find yourself utterly without counterarguments, and ready to concede a half dozen points, you had better reconsider the subject you have chosen. In a short essay, you can usually afford to make only one or two concessions. Too many concessions are likely to confuse readers who are uncertain about what they think. Why should they be persuaded by you, when you seem half-persuaded by your opponents?

Having a good sense of audience also means illustrating your case with concrete examples your audience can readily understand. It's hard to make people care about abstractions; good writers always try to make the abstract particular. Remember that it is often easy to lose the attention of your audience, so try to address its most probable concerns.

There is, however, a great difference between responding to the interests of your audience by discussing what it most wants to know, and twisting what you say in order to please an audience with whatever it wants to hear. You should remember that the foremost responsibility of any writer is to tell the truth as he or she sees it. What we mean by "truth" often has many dimensions, and when limited space forces us to be selective, it is only common sense to focus on those facets of our subject that will be the most effective with the audience we are attempting to sway. But it is one thing to edit, and quite another to mislead. Never write anything for one audience that you would be compelled to deny before another. Hypocrites are seldom persuasive, and no amount of verbal agility can compensate for a public loss of confidence in a writer's character.

ORGANIZING YOUR ARGUMENT

If you have chosen your subject carefully and given sufficient thought to your audience and its concerns (paying particular attention to any objections that could be raised against whatever you wish to advocate), then it should not be difficult to organize an argumentative essay. The lists discussed in the previous section will provide you with what amounts to a rough outline, but you must now consider two additional questions: "Where and how should I begin my argument?" and "How can I most efficiently include in my argument the various counterarguments that I have anticipated and responded to?" The answers to these questions will vary from one essay to another. But while arguments can take many forms, formal arguments usually employ logic, of which there are two widely accepted types: inductive and deductive reasoning.

Inductive Reasoning   *specific evidence*

[When we use *induction*, we are drawing a conclusion based upon specific evidence. Our argument rests upon a foundation of details that we have accumulated for its support. This is the type of reasoning that we use most frequently in daily life. We look at the sky outside our window, check the thermometer, and may even listen to a weather forecast before dressing to face the day. If the sun is shining, the temperature high, and the forecast favorable, we would be making a reasonable conclusion if we decided to dress lightly and leave our umbrellas at home. We haven't *proved* that the day will be warm and pleasant, we have only *concluded* that it will be. And this is all we can usually do in an inductive argument: arrive at a conclusion which seems likely to be true.] Ultimate and positive proof is usually beyond the writer's reach, and the writer who recognizes this, and proceeds accordingly, will usually arrive at conclusions that are both moderate and thoughtful. He or she recognizes the possibility of an unanticipated factor undermining even the best of arguments. A lovely morning can yield to a miserable afternoon, and we may be drenched in a downpour as we hurry home on the day that began so pleasantly.

Inductive reasoning is especially important in scientific experimentation. A research scientist may have a theory which he or she hopes to prove. But in order to work towards proving this theory, hundreds, thousands, and even tens of thousands of experiments may have to be conducted in order to eliminate variables and gather enough data to justify a generally applicable conclusion. Well-researched scientific conclusions sometimes reach a point where they seem uncontestable. It's been many years since Congress required the manufacturers of cigarettes to put a warning on every package stating that smoking can be harmful to your health. Since then, additional research has supported the conclusion that smoking can indeed be dangerous, especially to the lungs and the heart. That "smoking can be harmful to your health" now seems to have entered the realm of established fact. But biologists, chemists, physicists, and physicians are usually aware that the history of science, and the history of medicine in particular, is an argumentative history, full of debate. Methods and beliefs established over many generations can be overthrown by a new discovery. Within a few years, that "new discovery" can also come under challenge. So the serious researcher goes back to the lab, and keeps on working—ever mindful that truth is hard to find.

Induction is also essential in law enforcement. The police are supposed to have evidence against someone before making an arrest. Consider, for example, the way a detective works. A good detective does not arrive at the scene of a crime with his or her mind already made up about what happened. If the crime seems to be part of a pattern, the detective may already have a suspicion about who is responsible. But a good investigator will want to make a careful study of every piece of evidence that can be gathered. A room may be dusted for fingerprints, a murder victim photographed as found, and if the body is lying on the floor, a chalk outline may be drawn around it for future study. Every item within the room will be catalogued. Neighbors, relatives, employers, or employees will be questioned. The best detective is usually the detective with the best eye for detail, and the greatest determination to keep searching for the details that will be strong enough to bring a case to court. Similarly, a first-rate detective will also be honest enough never to overlook a fact that does not fit in with the rest of the evidence. The significance of every loose end must be examined in order to avoid the possibility of an unfair arrest and prosecution.

In making an inductive argument, you will reach a point at which you decide that you have offered enough evidence to support the thesis of your essay. When you are writing a college paper, you will probably decide that you have reached this point sooner than a scientist or a detective might. But whether you are writing a short essay, or conducting an investigation, the process is essentially the same. When you stop citing evidence and move on to your conclusion, you have made what is known as an *inductive leap*. In an inductive essay, you must always offer interpretation or analysis of the evidence you have introduced; there will always be at least a slight gap between your evidence and your conclusion. It is over this gap that the writer must leap; the trick is to do it agilely. Good writers know that their evidence must be in proportion to their conclusion: The bolder your conclusion, the more evidence you will need to back it up. Remember the old adage about "jumping to conclusions," and realize that you'll need the momentum of a running start to make more than a moderate leap at any one time.

If you listen closely to the conversation of the people around you, the chances are good that you'll hear examples of faulty inductive reasoning. When someone says, "I don't like Chinese food," and reveals, under questioning, that his only experience with Chinese food was something called "hamburger chow mein" in a high school cafeteria, we cannot take the opinion seriously. A sweeping conclusion has been drawn from flimsy evidence. People who claim to know "all about" complex subjects often reveal that they actually know very little. Only a sexist claims to know all about men and women, and only a racist is foolish enough to generalize about the various racial groups that make up our society. Good writers are careful not to overgeneralize.

When you begin an inductive essay, you might cite one particular piece of evidence that strikes you as especially important. You might even begin with a short anecdote. A well-structured inductive essay would then gradually expand as the evidence accumulates, so that the conclusion is supported by numerous details. Here is an example of an inductive essay written by a student.

In Defense of Hunting

I killed my first buck when I was fourteen. I'd gone deer hunting with my father and two of my uncles. I was cold and wet and anxious to get home, but I knew what I had to do when I sighted the eight-point buck. Taking careful aim, I fired at his chest, killing him quickly with a single shot.

I don't want to romanticize this experience, turning it into a noble rite of passage. I did feel that I had proved myself somehow. It was important for me to win my father's respect, and I welcomed the admiration I saw in his eyes. But I've been hunting regularly for many years now, and earning the approval of others no longer seems very important to me. I'd prefer to emphasize the facts about hunting, facts that must be acknowledged even by people who are opposed to hunting.

3   It is a fact that hunters help to keep the deer population in balance with the environment. Since so many of their natural predators have almost died out in this state, the deer population could quickly grow much larger than the land can support. Without hunting, thousands of deer would die slowly of starvation in the leafless winter woods. This may sound like a self-serving argument (like the words of a parent who beats a child and insists, "This hurts me more than it does you; I'm only doing it for your own good"). But it is a fact that cannot be denied.

4   It is also a fact that hunters provide a valuable source of revenue for the state. The registration and licensing fees we pay are used by the Department of Natural Resources to reforest barren land, preserve wetlands, and protect endangered species. Also there are many counties in this state that depend upon the money that hunters spend on food, gas, and lodging. "Tourism" is our third largest industry, and all of this money isn't being spent at luxurious lakeside resorts. Opponents of hunting should realize that hunting is the most active in some of our poorest, rural counties—and realize what hunting means to the people who live in these areas.

5   It is also a fact that we have one of the highest unemployment rates in the country. There are hundreds of men and women for whom hunting is an economic necessity and not a sport. Properly preserved, the meat that comes from a deer can help a family survive a long winter. There probably are hunters who think of hunting as a recreation. But all the hunters I know—and I know at least twenty—dress their own deer and use every pound of the venison they salt, smoke, or freeze. There may be a lot of people who don't have to worry about spending $3.00 a pound for steak, but I'm not one of them. My family needs the meat we earn by hunting.

6   I have to admit that there are hunters who act irresponsibly by trespassing where they are not wanted and, much worse, by abandoning animals that they have wounded. But there are many different kinds of irresponsibility. Look around and you will see many irresponsible drivers, but we don't respond to them by banning driving altogether. An irresponsible minority is no reason to attack a responsible majority.

7   I've listened to many arguments against hunting, and it seems to me that what really bothers most of the people who are opposed to hunting is the idea that hunters *enjoy* killing. I can't speak for all hunters, but I can speak for myself and the many hunters I personally know. I myself have never found pleasure in killing a deer. I think that deer are beautiful and incredibly graceful, especially when in movement. I don't "enjoy" putting an end to a beautiful animal's life. If I find any pleasure in the act of hunting, it comes from the knowledge that I am trying to be at least partially self-sufficient. I don't expect other people to do all my dirty work for me, and give me my meat neatly butchered and conveniently wrapped in plastic. I take responsibility for what I eat.

8   So the next time that you hear someone complaining about hunters, try to be fair-minded before going along with the usual stereotypes. The men and women who hunt are no worse than anyone else. Lumping us all together as insensitive beer-drinking thugs is an example of the mindless stereotyping that logic should teach us to avoid.

This writer has drawn upon his own experience in order to make an articulate defense of hunting. He begins with an anecdote that helps to establish that he knows something about the subject he has chosen to write about. The first sentence in the second paragraph helps to deflect any skepticism his audience may feel at this early stage in his argument, and the last sentence in this paragraph serves as a transition into the facts that will be emphasized in the next three paragraphs. In the third paragraph, the writer introduces the evidence that should most impress his audience, if we assume that his audience is unhappy about the idea of killing animals. In paragraphs 4 and 5, the writer defends hunting on economic grounds. He offers a concession in paragraph 5 ("There probably are hunters who think of hunting as a recreation") and another concession in paragraph 6 ("I have to admit that there are hunters who act irresponsibly"). But after each of these concessions he manages to return smoothly to his own thesis. In paragraph 7 the writer anticipates an argument frequently made by people who oppose hunting and offers a counterargument that puts his opponents on the defensive. The concluding paragraph is a little anticlimatic, but within the limitations of a short essay, this student has made a fairly strong argument.

Deductive Reasoning *right, value, belief*

Sometimes it is best to rest an argument on a fundamental truth, value, or right rather than on specific pieces of evidence. You should try to be specific within the course of such an essay, giving examples to support your case. But in deductive reasoning, evidence is of secondary importance. Your first concern is to define a commonly accepted value or belief that will prepare the way for the argument you want to make.

The Declaration of Independence, written by Thomas Jefferson (page 477), is a classic example of deductive reasoning. Although Jefferson cited numerous grievances, he rested his argument on the belief that "all men are created equal" and that they have "certain unalienable Rights" which King George III had violated. This was a revolutionary idea in the eighteenth century, and even today there are many people who question it. But if we accept the idea that "all men are created equal" and have an inherent right to "Life, Liberty, and the pursuit of Happiness," then certain conclusions follow.

The right, value, or belief from which we wish to deduce our argument is called our *premise*. Perhaps you have already had the experience, in the middle of an argument, of someone saying to you, "What's your premise?" If you are inexperienced in argumentation, a question of this sort may embarrass you and cause your argument to break down—which is probably what your opponent had hoped. But whether we recognize it or not, we almost always have a premise lurking somewhere in the back of our minds. Logical deductive argument requires that we think about values we have automatically assumed and get them up front as a crucial part of our case.

A good premise satisfies two requirements. In the first place, it is general enough that your audience is likely to accept it, thus establishing a common ground between you and the audience you hope to persuade. On the other hand, the premise must still be specific enough so that it prepares the way for the argument that will follow. It usually takes a lot of careful thought in order to frame a good premise. Relatively few people have their values always at their fingertips. We usually know what we want, or what our conclusion is going to be—but it takes time to realize the fundamental beliefs that we have automatically assumed. For this is really what a premise amounts to: the underlying assumption that must be agreed upon before the argument can begin to move along.

Because it is difficult to formulate an effective premise, it is often useful to work backwards when you are outlining a deductive argument. You should know what conclusion you expect to reach. Write it down, and assign to it number 3. Now ask yourself why you believe statement 3. This should prompt a number of reasons which you can group together as statement number 2. And now that you can look both at your conclusion and at the immediate reasons that seem to justify it, ask yourself if there's anything you've left out—something basic that you skipped over, assuming that everyone would agree with that already. When you can think back successfully to what this assumption is, knowing that it will vary from argument to argument, you have your premise, at least in rough-draft form.

This may be difficult to grasp in the abstract, so let us consider an outline for a sample argument. Suppose that the forests in your state are slowly dying because of the pollution known as acid rain—one of the effects of burning fossil fuel, especially coal. Coal is being burned by numerous industries not only in your own state, but in neighboring states as well. You hadn't even realized that there was a problem with acid rain until last summer, when fishing was prohibited in your favorite lake. You are very upset about this and declare, "Something ought to be done!" But as you begin to think about the problem, you recognize that you'll have to overcome at least two obstacles in deciding what that something should be. Only two years ago, you participated in a demonstration against nuclear power, and you'd also hate to see the United States become dependent upon foreign oil. So if you attack the process of burning coal for energy, you'll have to be prepared to recommend an acceptable alternative. The other question you must answer is "Who's responsible for a problem that seems to be springing from many places in many states?" Moreover, if you do decide to argue for a radical reduction in coal consumption, you'll have to be prepared to anticipate the opposition: "What's this going to do to the coal miners?" someone might well ask. "Will you destroy the livelihood of some of the hardest working men and women in America?"

You realize that you have still another problem. Your assignment is for a 500-word deductive argument, and it's due the day after tomorrow. You feel strongly about the problem of acid rain, but you don't think that you should have to become an energy expert to pass freshman English. Your primary concern is with the effects of acid rain, which you've witnessed with your own eyes. And while you don't know much about industrial chemistry, you do know that acid rain is caused principally by public utilities burning coal that has a high percentage of sulfur in it. Recognizing that you lack the expertise to make a full scale attack upon coal consumption, you decide that you can at least go so far as to argue on behalf of using low-sulfur coal. In doing so, you will be able to reassure your audience that you want to keep coal miners at work, recognize the needs of industry, and do not expect the entire country to go solar by the end of the semester.

Taking out a sheet of paper, you begin to write down your outline in reverse:

3. Public utilities should not burn coal that is high in sulfur content.
2. Burning high-sulfur coal causes acid rain, and acid rain is killing American forests, endangering wildlife, and spoiling local fishing.

Before going any farther, you realize that all of your reasons for opposing acid rain cannot be taken with equal degrees of seriousness. As much as you like to fish, recreation does not seem to be in the same league with your more general concern for forests and wildlife. You know that you want to describe the condition of your favorite lake at some point in your essay, because it gave you some firsthand experience with the problem and some vivid descriptive details. But you decide that you'd better not make too much of fishing in order to avoid the risk of sounding as if you care only about your own pleasure.

You now ask yourself what lies behind the "should" in your conclusion. How strong is it? Did you say "should" when you meant "must"? Thinking it over, you realize that you did mean "must," but now you must decide who or what is going to make that "must" happen. You decide that you can't trust industry to make this change on its own because you're asking businessmen to spend more money than they have to. You know that as an individual you don't have the power to bring about the change you believe is necessary, but you also know that individuals become powerful when they band together. Individuals band together in various ways, but the most important—in terms of power—is probably the governments we elect to represent us. You should be careful with a term like "government," avoiding statements like "The government ought to do something about this." Not only is the "something" hopelessly vague, but we don't know what kind of government is in question. Most of us are subject to government on at least three levels: municipal, state, and federal. Coming back to your topic, you decide to argue for *federal* legislation, since acid rain is being generated in several different states—and then carried by air to still others.

You should now be ready to formulate your premise. Since your conclusion is going to demand federal regulation, you need, at the very beginning of your argument, to establish the principle which supports this conclusion. You realize that the federal government cannot solve all problems; you therefore need to define the nature of the government's responsibility so that it will be clear that you are appealing legitimately to the right authority. Legally, the federal government has broad powers to regulate interstate commerce, and this may be useful to you since most of the industries burning coal ship or receive goods across state lines. More specifically, ever since the creation of Yellowstone National Park in 1872, the U.S. government has undertaken a growing responsibility for protecting the environment. Acid rain is clearly an environmental issue, so you would not be demanding anything new, in terms of governmental responsibilities, if you appealed to the type of thinking that led to the creation of a national park system in 1916, and of the Environmental Protection Agency in 1970.

You know, however, that there are many people who distrust the growth of big government, and you do not want to alienate anyone by appealing to Washington too early in the essay. A premise can be a single sentence, a full paragraph, or more—depending upon the length and complexity of the argument. Since its function is to establish a widely accepted value which even your opponents should be able to share, it would probably be wise to open this particular argument with a fairly general statement. Something like: "We all have a joint responsibility to protect the environment in which we live and preserve the balance of nature upon which our lives ultimately depend." As a thesis statement, this obviously needs to be elaborated in the paragraph that follows. In the second paragraph you might cite some popular examples of joint action to preserve the environment, pointing out, for example, that most people are relieved to see a forest fire brought under control, or an oil slick cleaned up before it engulfs half the Pacific coastline. Once you have cited examples of this sort, you could then remind your audience of the role of state and federal government in coping with such emergencies, and emphasize that many problems are too large for states to handle. By this stage in your essay, you should be able to narrow your focus to acid rain, secure in the knowledge that you have laid the foundation for a logical argument. *If* the U.S. government has a responsibility to help protect the environment, and *if* acid rain is a serious threat to the environment of several states, then it follows logically that the federal government should act to bring this problem under control. A brief outline of your argument would look something like this:

1. The federal government has the responsibility to protect the quality of American air, water, soil, and so on—what is commonly called "the environment."
2. Acid rain, which is caused principally by burning high-sulfur coal, is slowly killing American forests, endangering wildlife, and polluting lakes, rivers, and streams.
3. Therefore, the federal government should restrict the use of high-sulfur coal.

Once again, this is only an *outline*. An essay that made this argument, explaining the problem in detail, anticipating the opposition, and providing meaningful concessions before reaching a clear and firm conclusion, would amount to at least several pages.

By outlining your argument in this way, you have followed the pattern of what is called a *syllogism*, a three-part argument in which the conclusion rests upon two premises, the first of which is called "the major premise" because it is the most general and therefore the premise from which we begin to narrow ourselves down to a specific conclusion. Here, for example, is a simple example of a syllogism:

MAJOR PREMISE: All people have hearts.
MINOR PREMISE: John is a person.
CONCLUSION: Therefore, John has a heart.

If the major and minor premises are both true, then the conclusion we have reached should be true. Note that the minor premise is much more specific than the major premise. In an argumentative essay, the "minor premise" would usually involve concrete evidence that helps support the more abstract generalization with which the essay began.

A syllogism such as the one just cited may seem very simple. And it is simple—if you're thinking clearly. On the other hand, it's even easier to write a syllogism (or an essay) that breaks down because of faulty reasoning. Consider the following example:

MAJOR PREMISE: All women like to cook.
MINOR PREMISE: Elizabeth is a woman.
CONCLUSION: Therefore, Elizabeth likes to cook.

Technically, the form here is *valid*. The major premise is broader than the minor premise, and if we accept both the major and minor premises, then we will have to accept the conclusion. But someone who thinks along these lines may be in for a surprise, especially if he's married Elizabeth confidently expecting her to cook his favorite dishes every night just as his mother used to do. Elizabeth may *hate* to cook, preferring to go out bowling at night, or read the latest issue of the *Journal of Organic Chemistry*. You should realize, then, that while a syllogism may be valid in terms of its organization, it can also be *untrue*, because it rests upon a premise that can be easily disputed. Always remember that your major premise should inspire widespread agreement. Someone who launches an argument with the generalization that "all women like to cook," is likely to find he's lost at least half of his audience before he even makes it to his second sentence. Some generalizations make sense, and some do not. Don't make the mistake of confusing generally accepted truths with privately held opinions. You may argue effectively on behalf of your opinions, but you cannot expect your audience to accept an easily debatable opinion as the foundation for an argument on behalf of yet another opinion. You may have a lot of important things to say, but nobody is going to read them if alienated by your major premise.

Deductive reasoning, which begins with a generalization and works to a specific conclusion, is therefore the opposite of *inductive reasoning* which begins with specific evidence and ends with a conclusion that is broader than any single piece of the evidence that led up to it. So that you can see what a deductive essay might look like, here is a short argument written a few years ago by one of my students.

The Weaker Sex

National responsibilities should be equally shared by all citizens, especially during   1
a world crisis, when unity plays a vital role. And there is no reason why these
duties should not be shared by everyone.

Women make up a large percentage of the United States population. They are   2
becoming more and more a major influence in the social, economic, and political
aspects of our country. And yet, in certain areas, they are still dealt with as frail,
over-emotional, and super-sensitive creatures. This is most obvious in the recent
debate on reinstating the draft, or more importantly, in the question of drafting
women.

It has been argued that drafting women would be immoral, illogical, and even   3
unconstitutional. (Females just aren't tough enough to handle the rigors of military life.) It appears to make little difference to legislators and the public that
women have survived experiences equal to if not more strenuous than any wartime
conditions. There have been female explorers, dictators, and warriors. In Israel
women play a major role and take an active part in warfare.

Granted, not all women have the physical strength of most men. And not all   4
women have the mental capacity to deal capably with the atrocities of battle.
However, not all men can cope with these pressures either. For example, consider
the debilitating effect the Viet Nam War had on many of its veterans.

I am not trying to present participation in a war as a glorious objective that   5
should be sought after. On the contrary, war is a horrifying experience, especially
in the nuclear age. What I am attempting to point out is that American women
have a responsibility to do their share—typing reports and rolling bandages is not
enough.

If a person has to risk his life on the battlefield because he is a man, there is no   6
reason why a woman should be exempt from the same risk because she is a
woman. I feel that if the draft is reinstated, females should not only be inducted
but should be involved in active, front-line duty. How can women expect equality if they are not willing to give up their special privileges and accept their
responsibilities?

This is not a perfect essay. In her opening paragraph, for example, the author
should have been more cautious in writing of "all citizens." One might ask if she
intended to imply that the physically and mentally handicapped should also be
drafted in the event of a national emergency. Nonetheless, the argument is
clearly deductive. The premise with which it opens ("National responsibilities
should be shared equally by all citizens . . . .") is broader than the minor premise
("Women make up a large percentage of the United States population.") and
both are considerably broader than the conclusion they join to support: "I feel
that if the draft is reinstated, females should not only be inducted but should
be involved in active, front-line duty."

The strength of this argument lies in its careful organization. I have read the
essay to several classes, and students almost always agree with the opening
paragraph, finding it a reasonable generalization. Many of these students are
subsequently disturbed to see where the logic of this argument eventually takes
them. But the conclusion is implied by the premise. Anyone who agrees with

the first paragraph has been led halfway down the road towards agreeing with the last.

As you can see from this example, deduction allows a writer the chance to prepare the way for a controversial argument by strategically opening with a key point that draws an audience closer, without immediately revealing what exactly is afoot. With a genuinely controversial opinion, one must always face the risk of being shouted down—especially with a potentially hostile audience. Deductive reasoning increases our chance of gaining a fair hearing. Logic may be difficult, but it is essential to effective argumentation.

Before turning away from "The Weaker Sex," you should note that, within the limitations of a short assignment, the author was still able to demonstrate good audience awareness. She anticipates opposition at the beginning of the third paragraph ("It has been argued that drafting women would be immoral ....") and in the next two paragraphs concedes that "not all women have the physical strength of most men," and that some women lack "the mental capacity to deal capably with the atrocities of battle." These are concessions that deserve to be taken seriously; they are especially likely to appeal to the men and women who would be most opposed to drafting young women. But the author was too sophisticated to let these concessions simply sit on the page and possibly fester. She immediately returns to her thesis by claiming that many men also lack the physical strength and mental stamina that war demands. Having made this generalization, she then backs it up: "For example, consider the debilitating effect the Viet Nam War had on many of its veterans." This is a strong comeback, and should show you that concessions need not weaken an argument. On the contrary, they can strengthen an argument by making it more subtle and complex.

Since this essay was originally written for an audience of college freshmen, the author was also wise to emphasize that "war is a horrifying experience, especially in the nuclear age." College students frequently criticize the military and oppose whatever legislation seems likely to add to its already formidable power. A student audience might easily dismiss an argument on behalf of drafting women if the writer herself seemed especially eager to get her hands on a submachine gun and march off to Central America. But after reassuring us about the importance of avoiding war whenever possible, the author once again ends her paragraph by reaffirming her thesis that women need to do more than "typing reports and rolling bandages."

The moment at which writers choose to anticipate the opposition will usually vary; it depends upon the topic, how much the author knows about it, and how easily he or she can deal with the principal counterarguments that others might raise. But whether one is writing an inductive or a deductive argument, it is usually advisable to recognize and respond to the opposition fairly early in the essay. You will need at least one or two paragraphs to launch your own thesis, but by the time you are about one third into your essay, you may find it useful to defuse the opposition before it grows any stronger. If you wait until the very end of your essay to acknowledge that there are points of view different from your own, your audience may have already put your essay aside, dismissing it as "one-sided" or "narrow-minded." Also, it is usually a good idea to put the opposition's point of view at the beginning of a paragraph. By doing so, you can devote the rest of that paragraph to your response. It's not enough to recognize the opposition and include some of its arguments in your essay. You are a writer, not a referee, and you must always try to show your audience why it should not be persuaded by the counterarguments you have acknowledged. If you study the organization of "The Weaker Sex," you will see that the author begins her third, fourth, and fifth paragraphs with sentences which acknowledge other sides to the question of drafting women. But in each case, she was able to end these paragraphs with her own argument still marching clearly forward.

Logical Fallacies

An apparently logical argument may reveal serious flaws if we take the trouble to examine it closely. Mistakes in logic are commonly made—and, as in mathematics, a single error in reasoning can lead to a faulty conclusion. We have already seen how a deductive argument may break down if the premise *over-generalizes*, as in the syllogism which began with the claim "All women like to cook." A deductive argument can also fall apart if the minor premise is as broad as the major premise:

MAJOR PREMISE: The French are Europeans.
MINOR PREMISE: The Italians are Europeans.
CONCLUSION: The French are Italian.

Although this example may seem ridiculous, it is not unusual to find people arguing along these lines when the subject is more abstract. The minor premise should always be narrower and more specific than the major premise if you want your argument to work like a funnel rather than a shaft.

On the other hand, you must also be careful not to narrow your argument too quickly—writing a minor premise that relates to only a small part of your major premise, as in this example:

MAJOR PREMISE: Good citizens are well-informed.
MINOR PREMISE: Richard is well-informed.
CONCLUSION: Richard is a good citizen.

It's possible that Richard may be keeping "well-informed" from a carefully guarded compound on a Caribbean island—to which he retreated after embezzling seven million dollars from the Bank of America. Most people would immediately recognize that being a "good citizen" involves more than just being "well-informed," although being well-informed is certainly a part of good citizenship. The problem here is twofold. The major premise offers a reasonable generalization but an inadequate definition. And the minor premise then takes advantage of that definition's inadequacy. The elements of this syllogism would be acceptable only if we slowed down the movement from the general to the particular:

MAJOR PREMISE: Good citizens are well-informed.
MINOR PREMISE: Richard is a good citizen.
CONCLUSION: Richard is well-informed.

Mistakes in reasoning are called *logical fallacies*. Here is a list of common fallacies which you should be careful to avoid in your own arguments and which you should be alert to in the arguments of others.

Ad Hominem Argument   An ad hominem argument is an argument that attacks the personal character or reputation of one's opponents while ignoring what he or she has to say. "Ad hominem" is Latin for "to the man." Although an audience may often consider the character of a writer or speaker in deciding whether it can trust what he or she has to say, most of us realize that good people can make bad arguments, and even a crook can sometimes tell the truth. It is always better to give a logical response to an opponent's arguments, than to ignore those arguments and indulge in personal attacks. *Brand X*

Ad Populum Argument   An ad populum argument, which means "argument to the crowd," excites the prejudices of an audience so that reasonable discussion is no longer possible. The orator who incites a mob to loot and kill, or the newspaper that creates a patriotic frenzy through exaggerated reports of enemy "atrocities," will often rely on ad populum arguments. A logical argument should appeal to the mind, not to the emotions. *use this to be popular*

Argument by Analogy   An analogy is a comparison that works on more than one level. A political campaign may be analogous to a football game in that both involve planning, teamwork, and ultimately a winner and a loser. But politics and football are not identical. An analogy can be very useful in helping an audience understand a complex idea. But illustration should not be confused with proof. Writers can easily carry an analogy too far and thus reach a faulty conclusion. Someone who helped win the Super Bowl by knocking people down should not assume that the same technique will necessarily get him elected to Congress. An argument that relies entirely upon analogy proves nothing except that the author is not thinking clearly.

Begging the Question   In the fallacy of "begging the question," a writer begins an argument with a premise which is acceptable only to those who will agree with the conclusion that is subsequently reached—a conclusion that is often very similar to the premise itself. When a writer begs the question, the argument may go around in a circle. Someone might begin an essay by claiming, "Required courses like freshman English are a waste of time" and end with the conclusion that "Freshman English should not be a required course." It might indeed be arguable that freshman English should not be required, but the author who begins with the premise that freshman English is a waste of time has assumed what the argument should be devoted to proving. Because it is much easier to claim that something is true than to prove it is true, you may be tempted to beg the question you set out to answer. This is a temptation that should always be avoided.

Equivocation   Someone who equivocates uses vague or ambiguous language in order to mislead an audience. In argumentation, equivocation often takes the form of using one word in several different senses, without acknowledging that this has been done. It is especially easy to equivocate if you are addicted to abstract language. Watch out in particular for the abuse of terms like "society," "right," "natural," "liberal," "radical," "revolutionary," "freedom," "law," "moral," and "real." When you use words like these, make sure you make your meaning clear. And make double sure your meaning doesn't shift when you use the term again.

Guilt by Association   This is a fallacy which is frequently made in politics, especially towards the end of a close campaign. A candidate who happens to be religious, for example, may be maneuvered by opponents into the false position of being held accountable for the actions of all the men and women who hold to that particular faith. Nothing specific has been *argued*, but a negative association has been either created or played upon through hints and innuendos. Guilt by association may take the form of an ad hominem argument, or it may be more subtle. A careless writer may simply stumble into using a stereotype in order to avoid the trouble of coming up with a concrete example. But whatever its form, guilt by association is a fallacy in which prejudice takes the place of thought.

Ignoring the Question   When someone says, "I'm glad you asked that question!" and then promptly begins to talk about something else, he or she is guilty of ignoring the question. Politicians are famous for exploiting this technique when they don't want to be pinned down on a subject. But students (and teachers) sometimes use it too, when asked a question which they want to avoid. Ignoring the question is also likely to occur when friends or lovers have a fight. In the midst of an emotional quarrel, criticism is likely to evoke remarks like, "What about you!" or "Never mind the budget! I'm sick of worrying about money! We need to talk about what's happening to our relationship!"

Jumping to Conclusions   This fallacy is so common that it has become a cliché. It means that the conclusion in question has not been supported by an adequate amount of evidence. Because one green apple is sour, it does not follow that all green apples are sour. Failing one test does not mean that you will necessarily fail the next. An instructor who seems disorganized the first day of class may eventually prove to be the best teacher you ever had. You should always try to have more than one example to support an argument. Be skeptical of arguments that seem heavy on opinion but weak on fact.

Non Sequitur   This is Latin for "it does not follow." Although this phrase can be applied to almost any faulty argument, it is usually used more precisely. The most common type of non sequitur is a complex sentence in which the subordinate clause does not clearly relate to the main clause, especially in terms of causation. An example of this type of non sequitur would be "Because the wind was blowing so fiercely, I passed the quiz in calculus." This is a non sequitur because passing calculus should not be dependent on the weather. A cause and effect relationship has been claimed but not explained. It may be that the wind forced you to stay indoors, which led you to spend more time studying than you usually do, and this in turn led you to pass your quiz. But someone reading the sentence as written could not be expected to know this. A non sequitur may also take the form of a compound sentence: "Mr. Blandshaw is young, and so he should be a good teacher." Mr. Blandshaw may indeed be a good teacher, but not just because he is young. On the contrary, young Mr. Blandshaw may be inexperienced, anxious, and humorless. He may also give you unrealistically large assignments because he lacks a clear sense of how much work most students can handle. So watch out for non sequiturs the next time you register for classes.

Non sequiturs sometimes form the basis for an entire argument: "William Henderson will make a good governor because he is a friend of the working-man. He is a friend of the workingman because he was a plumber before he became a millionaire through his contracting business." Before allowing this argument to go any further, you should realize that you've been already asked to swallow two non sequiturs. Being a good governor involves more than being "a friend of the workingman." And there is no reason to assume that Henderson is "a friend of the workingman" just because he used to be a plumber. It may be over thirty years since he last saw the inside of a union hall, and he may have acquired his wealth by taking advantage of the men and women who work for him.

Post Hoc, Ergo Propter Hoc   If you assume that an event is the result of something that merely occurred before it, you have committed the fallacy of post hoc, ergo propter hoc. This is a Latin phrase which means "after this, therefore because of this." Superstitious people offer many examples of this type of fallacious thinking. They might tell you, "Everything was doing fine until the lunar eclipse last month; *that's* why the economy is in trouble." Or personal misfortune may be traced back to spilling salt, stepping on a crack, or walking under a ladder.

This fallacy is often found in the arguments of writers who are determined to prove the existence of various conspiracies. They often seem to amass an impressive amount of evidence—but the "evidence" is frequently questionable. Or to take a comparatively simple example, someone might be suspected of murder simply because of being seen near the victim's house a day or two before the crime occurred. This suspicion may lead to the discovery of evidence, but it could just as easily lead to the false arrest of the meter reader from the electric company. Being observed near the scene of a crime proves nothing by itself; in court, it would be unacceptable even as circumstantial evidence. A prosecuting attorney who would be foolish enough to base a case on such a flimsy piece of evidence would be guilty of post hoc, ergo propter hoc reasoning. Logic should always recognize the distinction between *causes* and what may simply be *coincidences*. Sequence is not a cause since every event is preceded by an infinite number of other events, all of which cannot be held responsible for whatever happens today.

This fallacy can be found in more subtle forms in essays on abstract social problems. Writers who blame contemporary problems on such instant explanations as "the rise of television" or "the popularity of computers" are no more convincing than the parent who argues that all the difficulties of family life can be traced to the rise of rock and roll. It is impossible to understand the present without understanding the past. But don't isolate at random any one event in the past, and then try to argue that it explains everything.

A final caution: Be careful not to accidentally imply a cause-and-effect relationship where you did not intend to do so. Trying to be concise, you might find yourself writing something like "Castro took over Cuba in 1959, and Hemingway killed himself only two years later." If you really believe that Hemingway killed himself *because* of the Cuban revolution, then you'll need to work hard to prove it. To simply link these two events together in one sentence is to fall into the fallacy of post hoc, ergo propter hoc.

Other Forms of Persuasion

Of the various forms of persuasive writing, logical argument is the most honorable. Its object is truth, not manipulation—although logic, like any other tool, can be abused. It appeals to the mind and works only to the extent that it moves ahead with mathematical clarity and precision. This is why logic is difficult: Whether we are writing a logical argument or simply trying to understand one, we have to be actively involved with ideas. To put it simply, we have to *think*. And behind any logical argument is the assumption that reasonable men and women should agree with its outcome—not so much because it is gracefully written (although it may be that) but because it is *true*.

There are other types of writing which rely upon an indirect appeal to the mind, exploiting what is known about the psychological makeup of an audience, or its most probable fears and desires. Successful advertising is *persuasive* in that it encourages us to buy one product or another, but there is nothing logical about it. Few people have the money, time, or inclination to sample every product available for consumption. When we buy a particular mouthwash, toothpaste, soap, or soft drink—and even when we make purchases as large as a car—we may simply choose the cheapest product available. But bargain hunting aside, we are frequently led to purchase brands that advertising has taught us to associate with health, wealth, and happiness. A prominent greeting card company insists that we send their cards if we really and truly care about someone. Love is also used as the justification for piling up extravagantly high phone bills. (After all, who wants to worry about money when doing something as noble as "reaching out to touch someone"?) One popular cigarette is associated with the masculinity of mounted cowboys, and another implies a dubious

link with the women's movement. Even in an age that pretends to have outgrown sexual stereotyping, Detroit continues to suggest that beautiful women
can be acquired through the purchase of a beautiful car. Almost no one really
believes this sort of thing when forced to stop and think about it. But we often
act without thinking, and this is one of the reasons why advertising has been
able to grow into a billion dollar industry: Through the clever use of language
and visual images, advertisers can lead people into a variety of illogical and
possibly ruinous acts.

This, then, is the principle distinction between argument and persuasion:
Argument seeks to clarify thought, while persuasion often seeks to obscure it.
Argument is dependent on facts, and does not necessarily dictate any one
particular course of action. Persuasion, on the other hand, can work altogether
independent of the facts as we know them (such as how much money we can
afford to spend before the end of the month) and it is almost always designed
to inspire action—whether it be buying a new kind of deodorant or voting for
the candidate with the nicest teeth. Persuasion is thus a form of domination.
Its object is to make people agree with the will of the persuader, regardless
of whether the persuader is "right" or simply selling his or her services by
the hour.

In addition to utilizing psychology, persuasion often works by appealing to
our emotions. A persuasive writer or speaker knows how to evoke feelings
ranging from love, loyalty, and patriotism to anger, envy, and xenophobia. An
audience may be deeply moved even when nothing substantial has been said.
With a quickened pulse or tearful eyes, we may find ourselves convinced that
we've read or heard something wonderfully profound. But a few days later, we
may realize that we've been inhaling the intoxicating fumes of a heavily scented
gasbag, rather than digesting genuine "food for thought."

Although you may often find it useful to appeal to the heart as well as to the
head, you should try to avoid appealing to the heart alone. People can be fickle,
and the audience you move on Friday may have forgotten your name by Monday. An argument or speech that works primarily by inspiring an emotional
response can succeed only when an audience can be called upon for immediate
action. If a senator can inspire his colleagues moments before a critically important vote, or an evangelist move a congregation to generosity just as the
collection plate is about to be passed, then the results of such persuasion may
be significant. But opportunities of this sort are rare for most writers. Almost
everything we write can be put aside and reconsidered at another time. Irre-
spective of the ethical importance of arguing what is true, and not just what is
convenient, there is therefore a very practical reason for trying to argue logically: The arguments that carry the greatest weight are usually the arguments
that are capable of holding up under analysis. They make more sense as we
think about them, not less. Whereas persuasion relies upon impulse, argument
depends upon conviction. Our impulses may determine what we do this afternoon, but our convictions shape the rest of our lives.

In addition to the various types of fallacious reasoning which we have already discussed, persuasive writing sometimes becomes dishonest—which is worse than being illogical. When analyzing persuasion, you should be especially on guard against the following three tricks:

Bogus Claims   A claim can be considered "bogus," or false, whenever a persuader promises more than he or she can prove beyond dispute. If a Chicago restaurant offers "fresh country peas" in the middle of January, you might want to ask where these peas were freshly picked. And if a large commercial bakery advertises "homemade pies," try asking whose home they were made in. You'll probably get some strange looks, because many people don't really expect words to mean what they say. But good writers become good writers in part because they have eyes and ears—eyes that see, and ears that hear.

If a toothpaste promises to give your mouth "sex appeal," you'd still better be careful about who you try to kiss. A claim of this sort is fairly crude, and therefore easily recognizable. But bogus claims can take many forms, some more subtle than others. A television advertisement for a new-improved designer laxative may star an unnamed man in a white coat, with a stethoscope around his neck. The advertisement implies—without necessarily saying so—that the product in question is endorsed by physicians. Ads of this sort are also likely to speak vaguely of "recent studies," or better yet, "recent *clinical* studies," which are declared to prove a product's value. The product may indeed have value; on the other hand, it may be indistinguishable from its competition except in price and packaging. You might like it when you try it. But well-educated men and women should always be a little skeptical about promises from strangers.

When writing an essay, it is easy to fall into the habit of making bogus claims when reaching for generalizations to support your point of view. Imitating the style of the advertisements with which they grew up, careless writers like to refer to those ever popular "recent studies," especially in conjunction with the passive voice: "Recent studies *have shown*," whatever the writer happens to be arguing. The use here of the passive voice enables the writer to avoid identifying who did the study. A recent study may provide the evidence to prove a point, but a good writer should be prepared to cite it, especially when the claim is surprising. It is one thing to write "Recent studies have shown that nutrition plays an important role in maintaining good health," for the generalization in this case enjoys wide acceptance. It would be something else altogether to toss off a claim like, "Recent studies have shown that chocolate can cure cancer." This example is only a slight exaggeration of the type of unsupported claims that can be made by sloppy writers who are desperate to complete an assignment.

Writers who like to refer to "recent studies" are also fond of alluding to unspecified statistics, as in "Statistics have shown," or "according to statistics." If you look hard enough, you can find statistics to prove almost anything, so don't make the mistake of assuming the word itself is filled with such dazzling appeal that further documentation is unnecessary. Similarly, you should turn a critical eye on claims like "It is a well-known fact that . . ." or "Everybody knows that ..." If the fact *is* well-known, why is the writer boring us with what we already know? And if the fact is *not* well-known, as is usually the case when lines of this sort are thrown about, then the writer had better explain how he or she knows it.

In short, if you want to avoid bogus claims never claim anything that would leave you speechless if called upon to explain or defend what you have written.

Loaded Terms   Good writers have good diction; they know a lot of words and, just as important, they know how to use them accurately. They know that most words have positive or negative *connotations*—associations with the word that go beyond its standard definition or *denotation.* "Placid," "tranquil," or "serene" might all be used to describe someone who is "calm," but each word points towards a slightly different impression. An experienced writer is likely to pause before choosing the adjective which best suits his or her subject.

A term becomes *loaded* when it is asked to carry more emotional weight than its context can legitimately support. A loaded term is a word or phrase that goes beyond connotation into the unconvincing world of the heavy-handed and narrow-minded. To put it simply, it is *slanted* or *biased.*

Loaded terms may appeal to the zealous, but they mislead the unwary reader and offend the critically-minded. For example, when a Young Democrat denounces the Reagan "regime" in the school newspaper, he is taking what many men and women would consider a cheap shot—regardless of their own politics. "Regime" is a loaded term because it is most frequently used to describe military dictatorships. Even someone who is opposed to everything that Reagan stands for should still be clearheaded enough to speak of the Reagan "Administration," which is the term best suited for a political discussion of the U.S. Presidency.

Like "regime," many words have such strong connotations that they can become loaded terms very easily. In the United States, for example, "Marxist" is almost always used as a type of rebuke. (And in communist countries, "capitalist" is used in a similar way.) When most Americans hear that an idea is "Marxist," they become immediately hostile toward it. Nevertheless, when Salvador Allende became the democratically elected president of Chile in 1970, American newspapers seemed unable to report news from Chile without repeated references to "Marxist President Salvador Allende," as if "Marxist" was part of his job title. Even now, so many years after his assassination, "Marxist President Salvador Allende" can still be found making occasional appearances in the American press.

Within a particular context, a seemingly inoffensive word may become a loaded term. In order to manipulate reader response, a writer may sneak unnecessary adjectives into his or her work. A political correspondent may write, "Mr. D'Arcy, the wealthy candidate from Park Ridge, spoke today at Meryton High School." The candidate's income has nothing to do with the news event being reported, so "wealthy" is a loaded term. It's an extra word that serves only one function: to divide the candidate from the newspaper's audience, very few of whom are "wealthy." It would not be surprising if some readers began to turn against this candidate, regardless of his platform, simply because they had been led to associate him with a background that is alien to their own.

Do not make the mistake of assuming that loaded terms occur only in political discourse. They can be found almost anywhere, if you take the trouble to read critically and intelligently. You may even find some in your textbooks.

Misrepresentation   Misrepresentation can take many forms. Someone may come right out and lie to you, telling you something you know—or subsequently discover—to be untrue. In the course of writing a paper, someone may invent statistics or alter research data that points to an unwelcome conclusion. And then, of course, there is *plagiarism*—which means taking someone else's words or ideas without acknowledgment, and passing them off as your own (see pages 553–55).

There are always going to be people who are tempted to lie, and there isn't much we can do about this except to keep our eyes open, read well, and choose our friends with care. As for research—how to do it and how to document the results—we will discuss this subject separately in Part Three of this book. There is another type of misrepresentation which must be understood as part of our introduction to the principles of argument and persuasion: Dishonest writers will often misrepresent their opponents by twisting what others have said.

The most common way in which writers misrepresent opposing arguments is to oversimplify them. The ability to summarize what others have said or written is a skill that cannot be taken for granted, and we will turn to it shortly. There is always the possibility that someone may misrepresent an opponent accidentally—having failed to understand what has been said, or having confused it in reporting it. But it is also possible to misreport others *deliberately*. A complex argument can be reduced to ridicule in a slogan, or an important element of such an argument could be entirely overlooked—creating a false impression.

Political campaigns are especially likely to inspire deliberate misrepresentation. Republicans are said to favor the rich, and Democrats are blamed for excessive spending. Biologists are accused of tampering with life, and physicists with trying to destroy it. Catholics have been accused of mind-control, and Jews with profiteering. Feminists have been said to favor single-sex toilets, and homosexuals accused of corrupting children. And so forth. A list of misrepresented realities would be very long indeed. *Don't add to it*. What's more, have the courage to ask for evidence whenever someone seems drifting off into an ideological fantasy.

Also, if you ever find it necessary to quote someone, make sure you do so not only correctly but also *fairly*. The concept of "quoting out of context" is so familiar that the phrase has become a cliché. But clichés sometimes embody fundamental truths, and here is one of them: Quotations should be more than accurate; they should also reflect the overall nature of the quoted source. When you select a passage that truly represents the thesis of another's work, you can use it in good conscience—so long as you remember to put it in quotation marks and reveal to your readers where you got it. But if you fasten upon a minor detail and quote a line that could be misunderstood if lifted away from the sentences that originally surrounded it, then you are guilty of a type of misrepresentation as dishonest as oversimplification.

Whether you are writing persuasion, or simply trying to defend yourself against it, it is important to be aware of the ways in which the techniques of persuasive writing can be abused. And they are abused—frequently. As a result, many people automatically distrust anyone who seems unusually persuasive, convinced that smooth-talkers will always prove to be con-men of one sort or another. In *Gulliver's Travels*, Jonathan Swift defined lawyers as "a society of men among us, bred up from their youth in the art of proving by words multiplied for the purpose, that white is black, and black is white, according as they are paid." Lawyers are still regarded skeptically by many people, even if they've never read Swift. Advertisers, actors, and public relations experts also have reputations that often suffer because people question the integrity of anyone who uses language too glibly.

There is nothing new about this. Over two thousand years ago, there was a group of philosophy teachers in ancient Greece known as the Sophists. They were smart, and they were articulate. But they were a little too slick. The Sophists could argue anything—and do so eloquently. They were famous for ingenuity rather than wisdom or honesty. Their name lives on in the word *sophistry*, which means "a clever and tricky argument that makes sense only superficially." If you make a genuinely logical argument, you may make some people angry with you, but you will not be accused of dishonesty. When you abandon logic for the techniques of persuasion, make sure that this is simply a change in writing strategy. Never write anything that you don't believe. This does not mean that there's anything wrong with writing fiction or satire. But it does mean that good writers shouldn't tell lies.

SUMMARIZING

In the last section, we briefly considered the importance of being able to summarize what others have said and written. There are many occasions in which you will be called upon to summarize—possibly to summarize what you yourself have written in a report, or even a memo. But this skill is especially important in argumentation. You have to be able to summarize the main arguments of your opponents if you want to write a convincing argumentative essay. And research papers will become ridiculously long, obscure, and unwieldy if you lack the ability to summarize your reading.

Equipped with a yellow felt pen, some students make the mistake of "highlighting" nearly everything that they read. Unable to distinguish the main points from the supporting details, such students end up with yellow-coated pages that offer little help when it's time to study. When you are reading material for a college class, and especially when you think that you may need to summarize this material, you should assume that you will probably need to read it at least twice. Instead of marking haphazardly in ink, you might find it useful simply to make a small check ($\sqrt{}$) in the margin whenever a line seems important the first time you are reading something (assuming, of course, that the book is your own). Use a pencil so that you can erase these marks later if you wish to do so. It's hard to erase ink, and almost impossible to erase highlighting, and you don't want to be distracted by permanent marks that you later decide you don't need.

There is no clear rule to determine what passages are more significant than others. Every piece of writing must be judged on its own merits, and this means that you must consider every paragraph individually. The first sentence of a paragraph may be important if it introduces a new idea. Unfortunately for writers of summary (but fortunately for readers, who would be easily bored if every paragraph followed the same mechanical pattern) the first sentence may simply be a transitional sentence, linking the paragraph with whatever has preceded it. The *topic sentence* (also called the *thesis sentence*) is the single most important sentence in most paragraphs—the exception being the very short paragraphs that serve only as transitions. (Transitional paragraphs do not advance a new idea, but simply link together longer paragraphs devoted to ideas that are related, but not closely enough so that the paragraphs can flow smoothly together.) And it is important to realize that *the topic sentence can occur anywhere in the paragraph.*

As you read the material you want to summarize, limit yourself to marking no more than one or two sentences per paragraph. You should identify the topic sentence, and you may want to mark a line that contains an important supporting detail. At this point, you may choose to copy all the material you have underscored onto a separate sheet of paper. But do not think that this means you have completed a summary. What you have are the notes for a summary: a collection of short quotations that are unlikely to flow smoothly together. A good summary should always be easy to read. So you must now take your notes and go to work shaping them into a clear, concise piece of writing.

Writers of summary must be prepared to *paraphrase,* which means to restate something you've read or heard into your own words. There are many different reasons for paraphrasing, and you've probably been practicing this skill since you were a child. We frequently paraphrase the words of others in order to soften unpleasant truths. Sometimes we may even be tempted to restate a relatively mild statement more harshly, in order to make trouble for someone we don't like. But in writing summary, we should paraphrase only in order to make complex ideas more easily understandable. A paraphrase can be as long as the original material; under some circumstances, it may even be longer. So don't confuse paraphrase with summary. Paraphrasing is simply one of the skills that we call upon in order to write a coherent summary.

Reading over the quotations you have compiled, look for lines that seem longer than they have to be and ideas that seem unnecessarily complicated. Lines of this sort are likely subjects for paraphrase. As you restate these ideas more simply, you may also be able to include details that appeared elsewhere in the paragraph and seem too important to leave out. You should not have to restate everything that someone else has written, although there's nothing necessarily wrong in doing so. A summary can include direct quotation, so long as the quotations are relatively short and have the sort of clarity that you yourself cannot surpass.

∗You should now reread your paraphrasing and any quotations that you have included. Look for gaps between sentences, where the writing seems awkward or choppy. Rearrange any sentences that would flow more smoothly once you have done so. Eliminate any repetition, and add transitional phrases wherever they can help smooth the way from one idea to the next. After you have made certain that your sentences follow in a clear and easily readable sequence, and have corrected any errors in grammar, spelling, or syntax, you should have an adequate summary of the material you set out to cover. But you would be wise to read over what you have written at least one more time, making sure that the content accurately reflects the nature of whatever is being summarized. And be absolutely sure that any direct quotations are recognizable as such by being placed within quotation marks.

Writing summary requires good judgment. A writer has to be able to distinguish what is essential and what is not. But the judgment that summary demands should be editorial only. If the material being summarized has a particular bias, then a good summary should indicate that that bias is part of the work in question. But *writers should not interject their own opinions into a summary of someone else's work*. The tone of summary should be neutral. You may choose to summarize someone's work in order to be able to criticize it later on, but do not confuse summary with criticism. When summarizing, you are taking the role of helping another writer to speak for him- or herself. Don't let your own ideas get in the way.

Good summaries vary in length, depending upon the length and complexity of the original material, and how much time or space is available for summarizing it. It's unusual, however, to need more than 500 words to summarize most material, and you may be required to summarize an entire book in less than half that. When summary is being used as a preliminary to some other type of work—such as argument or analysis—it is especially important to be concise. For example, if you are summarizing an argument before offering a counterargument of your own, you may be limited to a single paragraph. The general rule to follow is to try to do justice to whatever you are summarizing in as few words as possible, and to make sure that you have a legitimate reason for writing any summary that goes on for more than a page or two.

Experienced writers know that summary is a skill worth practicing. The selections in the following nine units will provide you with many opportunities for mastering this skill. If you find summary difficult, remind yourself that it combines two skills of fundamental and inescapable importance: reading and writing. Well-educated men and women must be proficient in both. Summarizing tests not only your ability to write simply and clearly, but also your ability to comprehend what you read.

By reading several selections in each unit, you should begin to recognize that some writers make stronger arguments than others. You will find that some essays make sense to you and others do not. But when you find yourself inclined to reject a particular selection, ask yourself why you want to do so. Is it because your own point of view is prejudiced? Is it because the style is more difficult than you are used to? Or is it because you have carefully analyzed the piece in question and identified a faulty premise, an overly large inductive leap, or one or more of the logical fallacies described in this introduction? If you are reading attentively, and working toward improving your own ability in argumentation, then you should always have specific reasons for citicizing anything you read in this book. The flaws you cite should be on the page, not in your mind.

Moreover, the readings that follow should help you to clarify your own thinking on several major issues. By analyzing, summarizing, and comparing the arguments of others, you should become better able to formulate an argument of your own. You may find yourself siding with one writer and rejecting another. You may find that every writer makes at least one good point and that you want to draw these points together in a single essay. Or you may discover that none of the essays are persuasive and that you want to argue an entirely different thesis.

Whatever the case, the readings collected in this book are meant to provide you only with a starting point. Part Three of the book discusses ways to do further research, not only on the issues in Part Two but on almost any subject that would bring you to draw upon the resources of a library. But whether you are evaluating selected essays on gun control or researching a term paper on Aztec courting rituals, the process will require the skills that you will be perfecting in the weeks ahead. The quality of your writing will depend upon the quality of your reading and, most importantly, how carefully you think about what you read.

PART 2

The Arguments

Section 1
Gun Control: Triggering a National Controversy

JEANNE SHIELDS
Why Nick?

When people discuss controversial issues, they sometimes lose sight of how these issues affect individual lives. Gun control has been the subject of national debate for so many years that it may seem of interest only to men and women who are directly involved with guns: those who either own them, sell them, or work with them. But the abstract can become painfully real to anyone who becomes the victim of handgun violence, as this essay by Jeanne Shields reveals. After her son was murdered, Shields became active in the movement to control handguns. Her essay, which originally appeared in Newsweek, *is both a tribute to the memory of her son and an argument on behalf of stricter laws regulating the sale and possession of guns.*

If the telephone rings late at night, I always mentally check off where each   1
child is, and at the same time get an awful sinking feeling in the pit of my
stomach.

Four years ago, April 16, we had a telephone call very late. As my husband   2
answered, I checked off Pam in Long Beach (California), Nick in San Francisco,
David in New Brunswick (New Jersey) and Leslie outside Boston. The less my

29

husband spoke, the tighter the knot got in my stomach. Instinctively, I knew it was bad news, but I wasn't prepared for what he had to tell me. Our eldest son, Nick, 23, had been shot dead on a street in San Francisco.

Nick was murdered at about 9:30 p.m. He and a friend, Jon, had come from   3
lacrosse practice and were on their way home. They stopped to pick up a rug at the home of a friend. While Jon went in to get the rug, Nick rearranged the lacrosse gear in the back of their borrowed Vega. He was shot three times in the back and died instantly, holding a lacrosse stick.

Nick was the fourteenth victim of what came to be called the "Zebra killers."   4
Between the fall of 1973 and April 16, 1974, they had randomly killed fourteen people and wounded seven others—crippling one for life. Four men were subsequently convicted of murder in a trial that lasted thirteen months.

My son was tall, dark and handsome, and a good athlete. He was particularly   5
good at lacrosse and an expert skier. Nick was an ardent photographer and wrote some lovely poetry. He was a gentle and sensitive man with an infectious grin and the capacity to make friends easily. It was hard for me to believe he was gone.

The generous support and love of our friends gave us the strength to go on   6
during those days. The calls and letters that poured in from those who knew Nick were overwhelming. In his short life, Nick had touched so many people in so many ways. It was both heartwarming and very humbling.

But always, running through those blurred days was the question. Why? Why   7
Nick? My deep faith in God was really put to the test. Yet, nothing that I could do or think of, or pray for, was ever going to bring Nick back.

Because Nick was shot two days after Easter, the funeral service was filled   8
with Easter prayers and hymns. Spring flowers came from the gardens of friends. The day was mild, clear and beautiful, and a kind of peace and understanding seeped into my aching heart.

No matter how many children you have, the death of one leaves a void that   9
cannot be filled. Life seems to include a new awareness, and one's philosophy and values come under sharper scrutiny. Were we just to pick up the pieces and continue as before? That choice became impossible, because a meaning had to be given to this vicious, senseless death.

That summer of 1974, the newspapers, magazines and television were full of   10
Watergate. But I couldn't concentrate on it or anything else. Instead I dug hard in the garden for short periods of time, or smashed at tennis balls.

On the other hand, my husband, Pete, immersed himself in a study of the   11
gun-control issue. Very near to where Nick had died, in a vacant lot, two small children found a gun—*the* gun. It was a .32-caliber Beretta. Police, in tracing it, found that initially it had been bought legally, but then went through the hands of seven different owners—most of whom had police records. Its final bullets, fired at close range, had killed my son—and then it was thrown carelessly away.

Pete's readings of Presidential commission recommendations, FBI crime   12
statistics and books on the handgun issue showed him that our Federal laws were indeed weak and ineffective. He went to Washington to talk to politicians and to see what, if anything, was being done about it. I watched him wrestle

with his thoughts and spend long hours writing them down on paper—the pros and cons of handgun control and what could logically be done about the proliferation of handguns in this nation.

Through friends, Pete had been introduced in Washington to the National   13
Council to Control Handguns, a citizens' lobby seeking stricter Federal controls over handguns. As Pete became more closely associated with the NCCH as a volunteer, it became increasingly obvious that he was leaning toward a greater involvement.

Consequently, with strong encouragement from me and the children, Pete   14
took a year's leave of absence from his job as a marketing executive so that he could join NCCH full time. A full year and a half later, he finally resigned and became the NCCH chairman.

The main adversaries of handgun control are members of the powerful and   15
financially entrenched National Rifle Association, macho men who don't understand the definition of a civilized society. They are aided by an apathetic government which in reality is us, because we citizens don't make ourselves heard loud and clear enough. How many people are in the silent majority, who want to see something done about unregulated sale and possession of handguns? Why do we register cars and license drivers, and not do the same for handguns? Why are the production and sale of firecrackers severely restricted—and not handguns?

I now work in the NCCH office as a volunteer. One of my jobs is to read and   16
make appropriate card files each day from a flood of clippings describing handgun incidents. The daily newspapers across the country recount the grim litany of shootings, killings, rapes and robberies at gun point. Some of it's tough going, because I am poignantly aware of what a family is going through. Some of it's so appalling it makes me literally sick.

Some people can no longer absorb this kind of news. They have almost   17
become immune to it, because there is so much violence. To others, it is too impersonal; it's always something that happens to somebody else—not to you.

But anybody can be shot. We are all in a lottery, where the likelihood of your   18
facing handgun violence grows every day. Today there are 50 million handguns in civilian hands. By the year 2000, there will be more than 100 million.

So many families have given up so much to the deadly handgun. It will take   19
the women of this country—the mothers, wives, sisters and daughters—to do something about it. But when will they stand up to be counted and to be heard? Or will they wait only to hear the telephone ringing late at night?

QUESTIONS FOR MEANING

1. Why is Shields especially interested in working for stronger *federal* controls on handguns? Does she present any evidence that such controls would save lives? Would gun control have saved the life of her son?

2. Describe the Shields family as they are presented in this essay. What sort of marriage do the parents seem to have? What are the children like? What type of home do you think they live in? How can you tell?

3. What is the National Council to Control Handguns, and what sort of work does the author of this essay do there? What is the object of this work?
4. Why does Shields believe that it will take "the women of this country—the mothers, wives, sisters and daughters" to control handgun violence? Is this a reasonable observation on the nature of violence in America? Or is it a simple case of sexual stereotyping? Does Shields support her conclusion, or does she contradict herself?
5. Vocabulary: ardent (5), proliferation (12), apathetic (15), litany (16), poignantly (16), and appalling (16).

QUESTIONS ABOUT STRATEGY

1. Why does Shields begin her essay with a description of her son's murder? And why does she repeat such small details as the specific car he was driving, and what he was holding in his hand when he died?
2. Shields writes lovingly of her son in paragraph 5, describing him as athletic, gentle, sensitive, friendly, and "tall, dark and handsome." How do you respond to this description when you read it? Does the description make Nick come alive for you? Does it make you more or less sympathetic to a mother's grief?
3. Shields acknowledges in paragraph 11 that the gun that killed her son was originally bought legally. What effect does this have upon her argument?
4. Does Shields ever say anything likely to offend the people she most needs to convince? Is this essay really designed to make an audience come to favor gun control, or does it have some other purpose?
5. How would you characterize the tone of this essay? Is there any evidence to suggest that Shields may have been too close to her subject to write about it effectively?

ADAM SMITH
Fifty Million Handguns

Adam Smith is the pseudonym of George J. Goodman (b. 1930). A magna cum laude graduate of Harvard and a former Rhodes Scholar, Goodman has written several novels and screenplays. He is best known for the work he has published as "Adam Smith," the name he borrowed from a great eighteenth century economist. A well-respected journalist, "Adam Smith" writes about business and finance for magazines like Esquire, Fortune, *and* New York. *He is also the author of several bestselling books on money management:* The Money Game *(1968),* Supermoney *(1972), and* Paper Money *(1980). He was moved to write about gun control after a good friend was murdered in 1981. Smith alludes to this murder, and also to the death of John Lennon, which occurred only a few days later. But he does not dwell upon these deaths, preferring to show how they are part of a large and complex problem.*

"You people," said my Texas host, "do not understand guns or gun people." By "you people" he meant not just me, whom he happened to be addressing, but anyone from a large eastern or midwestern city. My Texas host is a very successful businessman, an intelligent man. "There are two cultures," he said, "and the nongun culture looks down on the gun culture." 1

My Texas host had assumed—correctly—that I do not spend a lot of time with guns. The last one I knew intimately was a semi-automatic M-14, and, as any veteran knows, the Army bids you call it a weapon, not a gun. I once had to take that weapon apart and reassemble it blindfolded, and I liked it better than the heavy old M-1. We were also given a passing introduction to the Russian Kalashnikov and the AK-47, the Chinese copy of that automatic weapon, presumably so we could use these products of our Russian and Chinese enemies if the need arose. I remember that you could drop a Kalashnikov in the mud and pick it up and it would still fire. I also remember blowing up a section of railroad track using only an alarm clock, a primer cord, and a plastic called C-4. The day our little class blew up the track at Fort Bragg was rather fun. These experiences give me some credibility with friends from the "gun culture." (Otherwise, they have no lasting social utility whatsoever.) And I do not share the fear of guns—at least of "long guns," rifles and shotguns—that some of my college-educated city-dweller friends have, perhaps because of my onetime intimacy with that Army rifle, whose serial number I still know. 2

In the gun culture, said my Texas host, a boy is given a .22 rifle around the age of twelve, a shotgun at fourteen, and a .30-caliber rifle at sixteen. The young man is taught to use and respect these instruments. My Texas host showed me a paragraph in a book by Herman Kahn in which Kahn describes the presentation of the .22 as a rite of passage, like a confirmation or a bar mitzvah. "Young persons who are given guns," he wrote, "go through an immediate maturing experience because they are thereby given a genuine and significant responsibility." Any adult from the gun culture, whether or not he is a relative, can 3 admonish any young person who appears to be careless with his weapon. Thus, says Kahn, the gun-culture children take on "enlarging and maturing responsibilities" that their coddled upper-middleclass counterparts from the nongun culture do not share. The children of my Texas host said "sir" to their father and "ma'am" to their mother.

I do not mean to argue with the rite-of-passage theory. I am quite willing to   4
grant it. I bring it up because the subjects of guns and gun control are very emotional ones, and if we are to solve the problems associated with them, we need to arrive at a consensus within and between gun and nongun cultures in our country.

Please note that the rite-of-passage gifts are shotguns and rifles. Long guns   5
have sporting uses. Nobody gives a child a handgun, and nobody shoots a flying duck with a .38 revolver. Handguns have only one purpose.

Some months ago, a college friend of mine surprised a burglar in his home in   6
Washington, D.C. Michael Halberstam was a cardiologist, a writer, and a contributor to this magazine. The burglar shot Halberstam, but Halberstam ran him down with his car on the street outside before he died, and the case received widespread press. I began to work on this column, in high anger, right after his death. A few days later, John Lennon was killed in New York. These two dreadful murders produced an outpouring of grief, followed immediately by intense anger and the demand that something be done, that Congress pass a gun-control law. The National Rifle Association was quick to point out that a gun-control law would not have prevented either death; Halberstam's killer had already violated a whole slew of existing laws, and Lennon's was clearly sufficiently deranged or determined to kill him under any gun law. The National Rifle Association claims a million members, and it is a highly organized lobby. Its Political Victory Fund "works for the defeat of antigun candidates and for the support and election of progun office seekers." Let us grant the National Rifle Association position that the accused killers in these two recent spectacular shootings might not have been deterred even by severe gun restrictions.

In the course of researching this column, I talked to representatives of both   7
the progun and the antigun lobbies. Anomalies abound. Sam Fields, a spokesman for the National Coalition to Ban Handguns, is an expert rifleman who was given a gun at age thirteen by his father, a New York City policeman. The progun banner is frequently carried by Don Kates Jr., who describes himself as a liberal, a former civil rights worker, and a professor of constitutional law. Fields and Kates have debated each other frequently. Given their backgrounds, one might expect their positions to be reversed.

Some of the progun arguments run as follows: 8

Guns don't kill people, people kill people. Gun laws do not deter criminals.   9
(A 1976 University of Wisconsin study of gun laws concluded that "gun control laws have no individual or collective effect in reducing the rate of violent crime.") A mandatory sentence for carrying an unlicensed gun, says Kates, would punish the "ordinary decent citizens in high-crime areas who carry guns illegally because police protection is inadequate and they don't have the special influence necessary to get a 'carry' permit." There are fifty million handguns

out there in the United States already; unless you were to use a giant magnet, there is no way to retrieve them. The majority of people do not want guns banned. A ban on handguns would be like Prohibition—widely disregarded, unenforceable, and corrosive to the nation's sense of moral order. Federal registration is the beginning of federal tyranny; we might someday need to use those guns against the government.

Some of the antigun arguments go as follows: 10

People kill people, but handguns make it easier. When other weapons   11
(knives, for instance) are used, the consequences are not so often deadly. Strangling or stabbing someone takes a different degree of energy and intent than pulling a trigger. Registration will not interfere with hunting and other rifle sports but will simply exercise control over who can carry handguns. Ordinary people do not carry handguns. If a burglar has a gun in his hand, it is quite insane for you to shoot it out with him, as if you were in a quick-draw contest in the Wild West. Half of all the guns used in crimes are stolen; 70 percent of the stolen guns are handguns. In other words, the supply of hand-guns used by criminals already comes to a great extent from the households these guns were supposed to protect.

"I'll tell you one thing," said a lieutenant on the local police force in my town.   12
"You should never put that decal in your window, the one that says THIS HOUSE IS PROTECTED BY AN ARMED CITIZEN. The gun owners love them, but that sign is just an invitation that says 'Come and rob my guns.' Television sets and stereos are fenced at a discount; guns can actually be fenced at a premium. The burglar doesn't want to meet you. I have had a burglar tell me, 'If I wanted to meet people, I would have been a mugger.' "

After a recent wave of burglaries, the weekly newspaper in my town pub-   13
lished a front-page story. "Do not buy a gun—you're more likely to shoot yourself than a burglar," it said. At first the police agreed with that sentiment. Later, they took a slightly different line. "There is more danger from people having accidents or their kids getting hold of those guns than any service in defending their houses; but there was a flap when the paper printed that, so now we don't say anything," said my local police lieutenant. "If you want to own a gun legally, okay. Just be careful and know the laws."

What police departments tell inquiring citizens seems to depend not only on   14
the local laws but also on whether or not that particular police department belongs to the gun culture.

Some of the crime statistics underlying the gun arguments are surprising. Is   15
crime-ridden New York City the toughest place in the country? No: your chances of being murdered are higher in Columbus, Georgia, in Pine Bluff, Arkansas, and in Houston, Texas, among others. Some of the statistics are merely appalling: we had roughly ten thousand handgun deaths last year. The British had forty. In 1978, there were 18,714 Americans murdered. Sixty-four percent were killed with handguns. In that same year, *we had more killings with handguns by children ten years old and younger than the British had by killers of all ages.* The Canadians had 579 homicides last year; we had more than twenty thousand.

H. Rap Brown, the Sixties activist, once said, "Violence is as American as   16
apple pie." I guess it is. We think fondly of Butch Cassidy and the Sundance
Kid; we do not remember the names of the trainmen and the bank clerks they
shot. Four of our Presidents have died violently; the British have never had a
prime minister assassinated. *Life* magazine paid $8,000 to Halberstam's ac-
cused killer for photos of his boyhood. Now he will be famous, like Son of Sam.
The list could go on and on.

I am willing to grant to the gunners a shotgun in every closet. Shotguns are   17
not used much in armed robberies, or even by citizens in arguments with each
other. A shotgun is a better home-defense item anyway, say my police friends,
if only because you have to be very accurate with a handgun to knock a man
down with one. But the arguments over which kinds of guns are best only
demonstrate how dangerously bankrupt our whole society is in ideas on personal safety.

Our First Lady has a handgun.   18

Would registry of handguns stop the criminal from carrying the unregistered   19
gun? No, and it might afflict the householder with some extra red tape. However, there is a valid argument for registry. Such a law might have no immediate
effect, but we have to begin somewhere. We license automobiles and drivers.
That does not stop automobile deaths, but surely the highways would be even
more dangerous if populated with unlicensed drivers and uninspected cars.
The fifty million handguns outstanding have not caused the crime rate to go
down. Another two million handguns will be sold this year, and I will bet that
the crime rate still does not go down.

Our national behavior is considered close to insane by some of the other   20
advanced industrial nations. We have gotten so accustomed to crime and violence that we have begun to take them for granted; thus we are surprised to
learn that the taxi drivers in Tokyo carry far more than five dollars in cash, that
you can walk safely around the streets of Japan's largest cities, and that Japan's
crime rate is doing *down*. I know there are cultural differences; I am told that
in Japan the criminal is expected to turn himself in so as not to shame his
parents. Can we imagine that as a solution to crime here?

In a way, the tragic killings of Michael Halberstam and John Lennon have   21
distracted us from a larger and more complex problem. There is a wave of grief,
a wave of anger—and then things go right on as they did before. We become
inured to the violence and dulled to the outrage. Perhaps, indeed, no legislation
could stop murders like these, and perhaps national gun legislation would not
produce overnight change. The hard work is not just to get the gunners to join
in; the hard work is to do something about our ragged system of criminal justice,
to shore up our declining faith in the institutions that are supposed to protect
us, and to promote the notion that people should take responsibility for their
own actions.

What makes us so different from the Japanese and the British and the   22
Canadians? They are not armed, as we are, yet their streets and houses are far
safer. Should we not be asking ourselves some sober questions about whether
we are living the way we want to?

QUESTIONS FOR MEANING

1. In his opening paragraph, Smith introduces the idea that there are two separate cultures in the United States—the "gun culture" and the "nongun culture." Describe these different cultures in your own words. What sort of people belong to the gun culture? How can you identify them? How do they differ from people who have nothing to do with guns?

2. Smith tells us that the army wants its soldiers to use the word "weapon" rather than "gun." What's the difference? Do the words we use to describe objects affect how we see them—and therefore how we use them? What reason is there for teaching men and women that guns are "weapons"?

3. What are the "anomalies" that Smith reports in paragraph 7?

4. Why has gun culture remained so strong in the United States—compared to England, Canada, and Japan? Does Smith provide any explanation why our country is so much more violent than other industrial nations?

5. According to a lieutenant on the police force in Smith's home town, "Television sets and stereos are fenced at a discount; guns can actually be fenced at a premium." What does this mean?

6. What is Smith saying about Mrs. Reagan in paragraph 18? Taken by itself, "Our First Lady has a handgun" seems like a simple observation. But what is the implication of this sentence when set in a separate paragraph and juxtaposed against the paragraph that immediately precedes it?

7. Many people who oppose gun control also believe that it's important to "support your local police." Although he recognizes that some police departments belong to the gun culture and others do not, Smith emphasizes reasons why police do not like private citizens to own guns. Explain why the police may feel this way.

8. How committed is Smith to the importance of gun control? Does he see gun control as a way to insure public safety, or does he see it only as a first step in working toward that goal? Is there anything else that he wants?

QUESTIONS ABOUT STRATEGY

1. At what point in the essay does it first become clear that Adam Smith is in favor of gun control?

2. What is the importance of paragraph 2? Why does Smith devote so much space to describing his experience with a variety of weapons when he was in the army? What is this supposed to prove about him?

3. In paragraphs 9 and 11, Smith summarizes the leading arguments of both sides. Is he fair to each or does he allow his own opinion to influence his summaries in any way?

4. Comment on the use of italics in paragraph 15. Is this sentence worth emphasizing? Why this sentence and not another? Is this a genuinely disturbing sentence, or does putting it in italics give it prominence artificially, making it seem more disturbing than it really is?

5. Smith argues that "we need to arrive at a consensus between gun and nongun cultures in our country." How has he tried to do this? What concessions has he offered, and what sort of compromise has he proposed?

EDWARD ABBEY
The Right to Arms

*Edward Abbey (b. 1927) lives in Wolf Hole, Arizona. A former ranger for the
National Park Service, Abbey now describes himself as an "Agrarian anarchist." He
writes frequently about the beauty of the American west and the ways in which that
beauty has been spoiled by government, business, and tourism. His many books
include such novels as* Fire on the Mountain *(1963),* The Monkey Wrench Gang
(1975), and Good News *(1980), and several collections of essays, such as* Desert
Solitaire *(1968),* Abbey's Road *(1979), and, most recently,* Beyond the Wall: Essays
from the Outside *(1984). As the following essay reveals, Abbey values the
importance of the individual in a world in which individuals are at risk.*

If guns are outlawed
Only outlaws will have guns
(True? False? Maybe?)

Meaning weapons. The right to own, keep, and bear arms. A sword and a
lance, or a bow and a quiverful of arrows. A crossbow and darts. Or in our time, a
rifle and a handgun and a cache of ammunition. Firearms.

In medieval England a peasant caught with a sword in his possession would   2
be strung up on a gibbet and left there for the crows. Swords were for gentlemen only. (*Gentlemen!*) Only members of the ruling class were entitled to own
and bear weapons. For obvious reasons. Even bows and arrows were outlawed—see Robin Hood. When the peasants attempted to rebel, as they did in
England and Germany and other European countries from time to time, they
had to fight with sickles, bog hoes, clubs—no match for the sword-wielding
armored cavalry of the nobility.

In Nazi Germany the possession of firearms by a private citizen of the Third   3
Reich was considered a crime against the state; the statutory penalty was
death—by hanging. Or beheading. In the Soviet Union, as in Czarist Russia, the
manufacture, distribution, and ownership of firearms have always been monop-
olies of the state, strictly controlled and supervised. Any unauthorized citizen
found with guns in his home by the OGPU or the KGB is automatically suspected of subversive intentions and subject to severe penalties. Except for the
landowning aristocracy, who alone among the population were allowed the
privilege of owning firearms, for only they were privileged to hunt, the ownership of weapons never did become a widespread tradition in Russia. And Russia
has always been an autocracy—or at best, as today, an oligarchy.

In Uganda, Brazil, Iran, Paraguay, South Africa—wherever a few rule   4
many—the possession of weapons is restricted to the ruling class and to their
supporting apparatus: the military, the police, the secret police. In Chile and
Argentina at this very hour men and women are being tortured by the most up-
to-date CIA methods in the effort to force them to reveal the location of their
hidden weapons. Their guns, their rifles. Their arms. And we can be certain that

the Communist masters of modern China will never pass out firearms to *their* 800 million subjects. Only in Cuba, among dictatorships, where Fidel's revolution apparently still enjoys popular support, does there seem to exist a true citizen's militia.

There must be a moral in all this. When I try to think of a nation that has   5 maintained its independence over centuries, and where the citizens still retain their rights as free and independent people, not many come to mind. I think of Switzerland. Of Norway, Sweden, Denmark, Finland. The British Commonwealth. France, Italy. And of our United States.

When Tell shot the apple from his son's head, he reserved in hand a second   6 arrow, it may be remembered, for the Austrian tyrant Gessler. And got him too, shortly afterward. Switzerland has been a free country since 1390. In Switzerland basic national decisions are made by initiative and referendum—direct democracy—and in some cantons by open-air meetings in which all voters participate. Every Swiss male serves a year in the Swiss Army and at the end of the year takes his government rifle home with him—where he keeps it for the rest of his life. One of my father's grandfathers came from Canton Bern.

There must be a meaning in this. I don't think I'm a gun fanatic. I own a   7 couple of small-caliber weapons, but seldom take them off the wall. I gave up deer hunting fifteen years ago, when the hunters began to outnumber the deer. I am a member of the National Rifle Association, but certainly no John Bircher. I'm a liberal—and proud of it. Nevertheless, I am opposed, absolutely, to every move the state makes to restrict my right to buy, own, possess, and carry a firearm. Whether shotgun, rifle, or handgun.

Of course, we can agree to a few commonsense limitations. Guns should not   8 be sold to children, to the certifiably insane, or to convicted criminals. Other than that, we must regard with extreme suspicion any effort by the government—local, state, or national—to control our right to arms. The registration of firearms is the first step toward confiscation. The confiscation of weapons would be a major and probably fatal step into authoritarian rule—the domination of most of us by a new order of "gentlemen." By a new and harder oligarchy.

The tank, the B-52, the fighter-bomber, the state-controlled police and mili-   9 tary are the weapons of dictatorship. The rifle is the weapon of democracy. Not for nothing was the revolver called an "equalizer." *Egalité* implies *liberté*. And always will. Let us hope our weapons are never needed—but do not forget what the common people of this nation knew when they demanded the Bill of Rights: An armed citizenry is the first defense, the best defense, and the final defense against tyranny.

If guns are outlawed, only the government will have guns. Only the police,   10 the secret police, the military. The hired servants of our rulers. Only the government—and a few outlaws. I intend to be among the outlaws.

QUESTIONS FOR MEANING

1. Do you recognize the italicized lines with which the essay opens? If so, where have you seen them?

2. In paragraph 4, Abbey moves from "weapons," to "guns" to "rifles" and finally, in a separate sentence, to "arms." Is he playing with the meaning of the word "arms"? What are the connotations and denotations of this particular word?

3. What allusion is implicit in Abbey's mention of "egalité and liberté"?

4. How does Abbey seem to feel about "gentlemen"? In what particular sense does he use this term? How does the question of differences in social class relate to the question of gun control?

5. Vocabulary: autocracy (3), oligarchy (3), and referendum (6).

QUESTIONS ABOUT STRATEGY

1. Abbey uses numerous sentence fragments. Why does he do so? How do they affect the rhythm of his essay if you read it out loud. Is there any particular pattern that determines what ideas are conveyed in fragments? Is Abbey's style suitable for the subject he is writing about?

2. In paragraph 7 Abbey claims that he's not "a gun fanatic." Can you identify any other concessions Abbey offers in order to make his case seem reasonable?

3. Abbey describes himself as a "liberal." What advantage is there in making this claim? What does his essay reveal about his political beliefs beyond the issue of gun control?

4. Why does Abbey introduce into his argument references to Robin Hood, William Tell, Nazi Germany, and the B52? How do these allusions help to advance the point of this argument?

DON B. KATES, JR.
Against Civil Disarmament

A graduate of Yale Law School, Don B. Kates, Jr., has worked as an Office of Educational Opportunity poverty lawyer and taught both criminal and constitutional law. During the last ten years, he has emerged as one of the most articulate opponents of gun control, a subject on which he has written for numerous magazines. In the following essay, which originally appeared in Harper's, *Kates argues that conventional attitudes toward gun control need to be rethought. He tries to show that the controversy over gun control has confused the traditional distinction between liberal and conservative views.*

Despite almost 100 years of often bitter debate, federal policy and that of 44 states continues to allow handguns to any sane adult who is without felony convictions. Over the past twenty years, as some of our most progressive citizens have embraced the notion that handgun confiscation would reduce violent crime, the idea of closely restricting handgun possession to police and those with police permits has been stereotyped as "liberal." Yet when the notion of sharply restricting pistol ownership first gained popularity, in the late nineteenth century, it was under distinctly conservative auspices.

In 1902, South Carolina banned all pistol purchases, the first and only state ever to do so. (This was nine years before New York began requiring what was then an easily acquired police permit.) Tennessee had already enacted the first ban on "Saturday Night Specials," disarming blacks and the laboring poor while leaving weapons for the Ku Klux Klan and company goons. In 1906, Mississippi enacted the first mandatory registration law for all firearms. In short order, permit requirements were enacted in North Carolina, Missouri, Michigan, and Hawaii. In 1922, a national campaign of conservative business interests for handgun confiscation was endorsed by the (then) archconservative American Bar Association.

Liberals at that time were not necessarily opposed in principle to a ban on handguns, but they considered such a move irrelevant and distracting from a more important issue—the prohibition of alcohol. To Jane Addams, William Jennings Bryan, and Eleanor Roosevelt (herself a pistol carrier), liquor was the cause of violent crime. (Before dismissing this out of hand, remember that homicide studies uniformly find liquor a more prevalent factor than handguns in killings.) Besides, liberals were not likely to support the argument advanced by conservatives for gun confiscation: that certain racial and immigrant groups were so congenitally criminal (and/or politically dangerous) that they could not be trusted with arms. But when liberalism finally embraced handgun confiscation, it was by applying this conservative viewpoint to the entire populace. Now it is all Americans (not just Italians, Jews, or blacks) who must be considered so innately violent and unstable that they cannot be trusted with arms. For, we are told, it is not robbers or burglars who commit most murders, but average citizens killing relatives or friends.

It is certainly true that only a little more than 30 percent of murders are   4
committed by robbers, rapists, or burglars, while 45 percent are committed
among relatives or between lovers. (The rest are a miscellany of contract killings, drug wars, and "circumstances unknown.") But it is highly misleading to
conclude from this that the murderer is, in any sense, an average gun owner.
For the most part, murderers are disturbed, aberrant individuals with long
records of criminal violence that often include several felony convictions. In
terms of endangering his fellow citizen, the irresponsible drinker is far more
representative of all drinkers than is the irresponsible handgunner of all hand-
gunners. It is not my intention here to defend the character of the average
American handgun owner against, say, that of the average Swiss whose government not only allows, but requires, him to keep a machine gun at home. Rather
it is to show how unrealistic it is to think that we could radically decrease
homicide by radically reducing the number of civilian firearms. Study after
study has shown that even if the *average* gun owner complied with a ban, the
one handgun owner out of 3,000 who murders (much less the one in 500 who
steals) is not going to give up his guns. Nor would taking guns away from the
murderer make much difference in murder rates, since a sociopath with a long
history of murderous assault is not too squeamish to kill with a butcher knife,
ice pick, razor, or bottle. As for the extraordinary murders—assassins, terrorists, hit men—proponents of gun bans themselves concede that the law cannot
disarm such people any more than it can disarm professional robbers.

The repeated appearance of these facts in studies of violent crime has   5
eroded liberal and intellectual support for banning handguns. There is a growing consensus among even the most liberal students of criminal law and criminology that handgun confiscation is just another plausible theory that doesn't
work when tried. An article written in 1968 by Mark K. Benenson, longtime
American chairman of Amnesty International, concludes that the arguments
for gun bans are based upon selective misleading statistics, simple-minded non
sequiturs, and basic misconceptions about the nature of murder as well as of
other violent crimes.

A 1971 study at England's Cambridge University confounds one of the most   6
widely believed non sequiturs: "Banning handguns must work, because England does and look at its crime rate!" (It is difficult to see how those who
believe this can resist the equally simple-minded pro-gun argument that gun
possession deters crime: "Everybody ought to have a machine gun in his house
because the Swiss and the Israelis do, and look how low their crime rates are!")

The Cambridge report concludes that social and cultural factors (not gun   7
control) account for Britain's low violence rates. It points out that "the use of
firearms in crime was very much less" before 1920 when Britain had "no controls of any sort." Corroborating this is the comment of a former head of Scot-
land Yard that in the mid-1950s there were enough illegal handguns to supply
any British criminal who wanted one. But, he continued, the social milieu was
such that if a criminal killed anyone, particularly a policeman, his own confed-
erates would turn him in. When this violence-dampening social milieu began to
dissipate between 1960 and 1975, the British homicide rate doubled (as did the

American rate), while British robbery rates accelerated even faster than those in America. As the report notes, the vaunted handgun ban proved completely ineffective against rising violence in Britain, although the government frantically intensified enforcement and extended controls to long guns as well. Thus, the Cambridge study—the only in-depth study ever done of English gun laws— recommends "abolishing or substantially reducing controls" because their administration involves an immense, unproductive expense and diverts police resources from programs that might reduce violent crime.

The latest American study of gun controls was conducted with federal fund-   8
ing at the University of Wisconsin. Advanced computerized techniques allowed a comprehensive analysis of the effect of every form of state handgun restriction, including complete prohibition, on violence in America. Published in 1975, it concludes that "gun-control laws have no individual or collective effect in reducing the rate of violent crime."

Many previous studies reaching the same conclusion had been discounted   9
by proponents of a federal ban, who argued that existing state bans cannot be effective because handguns are illegally imported from free-sale states. The Wisconsin study compared rates of handgun ownership with rates of violence in various localities, but it could find *no correlation.* If areas where handgun ownership rates are high have no higher per capita rates of homicide and other violence than areas where such rates are low, the utility of laws designed to lower the rates of handgun ownership seems dubious. Again, the problem is not the "proliferation of handguns" among the law-abiding citizenry, it is the existence of a tiny fraction of irresponsible and criminal owners whom the law cannot possibly disarm of these or other weapons.

Far from refuting the Wisconsin study, the sheer unenforceability of hand-   10
gun bans is the main reason why most experts regard them as not worth thinking about. Even in Britain, a country that, before handguns were banned, had less than 1 percent of the per capita handgun ownership we have, the Cambridge study reports that "fifty years of very strict controls has left a vast pool of illegal weapons."

It should be emphasized that liberal defectors from gun confiscation are no   11
more urging peopled to arm themselves than are those who oppose banning pot or liquor necessarily urging people to indulge in them. They are only saying that national handgun confiscation would bring the federal government into a confrontation with millions of responsible citizens in order to enforce a program that would have no effect upon violence, except the negative one of diverting resources that otherwise might be utilized to some effective purpose. While many criminologists have doubts about the wisdom of citizens trying to defend themselves with handguns, the lack of evidence to justify confiscation requires that this remain a matter of individual choice rather than government fiat.

Nor can advocates of gun bans duck the evidence adverse to their position   12
by posing such questions as: Why should people have handguns; what good do they do; why *shouldn't* we ban them? In a free country, the burden is not upon the people to show why they should have freedom of choice. It is upon those who wish to restrict that freedom to show good reason for doing so. And when

the freedom is as deeply valued by as many as is handgun ownership, the evidence for infringing upon it must be very strong indeed.

If the likely benefits of handgun confiscation have been greatly exaggerated,   13
the financial and constitutional costs have been largely ignored. Consider the various costs of any attempt to enforce confiscation upon a citizenry that believes (whether rightly or not) that they urgently need handguns for self-defense and that the right to keep them is constitutionally guaranteed. Most confiscationists have never gotten beyond the idea that banning handguns will make them magically disappear somehow. Because they loathe handguns and consider them useless, the prohibitionists assume that those who disagree will readily turn in their guns once a national confiscation law is passed. But the leaders of the national handgun prohibition movement have become more realistic. They recognize that defiance will, if anything, exceed the defiance of Prohibition and marijuana laws. After all, not even those who viewed drinking or pot smoking as a blow against tyranny thought, as many gun owners do, that violating the law is necessary to the protection of themselves and their families. Moreover, fear of detection is a lot more likely to keep citizens from constant purchases of liquor or pot than from a single purchase of a handgun, which, properly maintained, will last years.

To counter the expected defiance, the leaders of the national confiscation   14
drive propose that handgun ownership be punished by a nonsuspendable mandatory year in prison. The mandatory feature is necessary, for otherwise prosecutors would not prosecute, and judges would not sentence, gun ownership with sufficient severity. The judge of a special Chicago court trying only gun violations recently explained why he generally levied only small fines: The overwhelming majority of the "criminals" who come before him are respectable, decent citizens who illegally carry guns because the police can't protect them and they have no other way of protecting themselves. He does not even impose probation because this would prevent the defendants, whose guns have been confiscated, from buying new ones, which, the judge believes, they need to live and work where they do.

These views are shared by judges and prosecutors nationwide; studies find   15
that gun-carrying charges are among the most sympathetically dealt with of all felonies. To understand why, consider a typical case that would have come before this Chicago court if the D.A. had not dropped charges. An intruder raped a woman and threw her out of a fifteenth-floor window. Police arrived too late to arrest him, so they got her roommate for carrying the gun with which she scared him off when he attacked her.

Maybe it is not a good idea for this woman to keep a handgun for self-defense.   16
But do we really want to send her to federal prison for doing so? And is a mandatory year in prison reasonable or just for an ordinary citizen who has done nothing more hurtful than keeping a gun to defend herself—when the minimum mandatory sentence for murder is only seven years and most murderers serve little more?

Moreover, the kind of nationwide resistance movement that a federal hand-   17
gun ban would provoke could not be broken by imprisoning a few impecunious

black women in Chicago. Only by severely punishing a large number of respectable citizens of every race and social class would resisters eventually be made to fear the law more than the prospect of living without handguns in a violent society. At a very conservative estimate, at least half of our present handgun owners would be expected to defy a federal ban.* To imprison just 1 percent of these 25 million people would require several times as many cells as the entire federal prison system now has. The combined federal, state, and local jail systems could barely manage. Of course, so massive an enforcement campaign would also require doubling expenditure for police, prosecutors, courts, and all the other sectors of criminal justice administration. The Wisconsin study closes with the pertinent query: "Are we willing to make sociological and economic investments of such a tremendous nature in a social experiment for which there is no empirical support?"

The argument against a federal handgun ban is much like the argument   18
against marijuana bans. It is by no means clear that marijuana is the harmless substance that its proponents claim. But it would take evidence far stronger than we now have to justify the enormous financial, human, institutional, and constitutional costs of continuing to ferret out, try, and imprison even a small percentage of the otherwise law-abiding citizens who insist on having pot. Sophisticated analysis of the criminalization decision takes into account not only the harms alleged to result from public possession of things like pot or guns, but the capacity of the criminal law to reduce those harms and the costs of trying to do so. Unfortunately most of the gun-control debate never gets beyond the abstract merits of guns—a subject on which those who view them with undifferentiated loathing are no more rational than those who love them. The position of all too many gun-banning liberals is indistinguishable from Archie Bunker's views on legalizing pot and homosexuality: "I don't like it and I don't like those who do—so it ought to be illegal."

The emotionalism with which many liberals (and conservatives as well)   19
react against the handgun reflects not its reality but its symbolism to people who are largely ignorant of that reality. A 1975 national survey found a direct correlation between support for more stringent controls and the inability to answer simple questions about present federal gun laws. In other words, the less the respondent knew about the subject, the more likely he was to support national confiscation. Liberals advocate severely punishing those who will defy confiscation only because the liberal image of a gun owner is a criminal or right-wing fanatic rather than a poor black woman in Chicago defending herself against a rapist or a murderer. Contrary to this stereotype, most "gun nuts" are

---

*I reach this estimate in this fashion: Surveys uniformly find a majority of gun owners support gun registration—in theory. In practice, however, they refuse to register because they believe this will identify their guns for confiscation if and when a national handgun ban eventually passes. In 1968, Chicago police estimated that two-thirds of the city's gun owners had not complied with the new state registration law; statewide noncompliance was estimated at 75 percent. In Cleveland, police estimate that almost 90 percent of handgun owners are in violation of a 1976 registration requirement. My estimate that one out of two handgun owners would defy national confiscation is conservative indeed when between two out of three and nine out of ten of them are already defying registration laws because they believe such laws presage confiscation.

peaceful hobbyists whose violence is exclusively of the Walter Mitty type. Gun owners' views are all too often expressed in right-wing terms (which does nothing for the rationality of the debate) because twenty years of liberal vilification has given them nowhere else to look for support. If only liberals knew it, handgun ownership is disproportionately high among the underprivileged for whom liberals traditionally have had most sympathy. As the most recent (1975) national demographic survey reports: "The top subgroups who own a gun *only* for self-defense include blacks (almost half own one for this reason alone), lowest income group, senior citizens." The average liberal has no understanding of why people have guns because he has no idea what it is like to live in a ghetto where police have given up on crime control. Minority and disadvantaged citizens are not about to give up their families' protection because middle-class white liberals living and working in high-security buildings and/or well-policed suburbs tell them it's safer that way.

A final cost of national gun confiscation would be the vast accretion of   20
enforcement powers to the police at the expense of individual liberty. The Police Foundation, which ardently endorses confiscation, recently suggested that federal agencies and local police look to how drug laws are enforced as a model of how to enforce firearms laws. Coincidentally, the chief topic of conversation at the 1977 national conference of supporters of federal confiscation was enforcement through house searches of everyone whom sales records indicate may ever have owned a handgun. In fact, indiscriminate search, complemented by electronic surveillance and vast armies of snoopers and informers, is how handgun restrictions are enforced in countries like Holland and Jamaica, and in states like Missouri and Michigan.* Even in England, as the Cambridge report notes, each new Firearms Act has been accompanied by new, unheard-of powers of search and arrest for the police.

These, then, are the costs of banning handguns: even attempting an effective   21
ban would involve enormous expenditures (roughly equal to the present cost of enforcing all our other criminal laws combined) to ferret out and jail hundreds of thousands of decent, responsible citizens who believe that they vitally need handguns to protect their families. If this does not terrorize the rest of the responsible handgun owners into compliance, the effort will have to be expanded until millions are jailed and the annual gun-banning budget closely seconds defense spending. And all of this could be accomplished only by abandoning many restraints our Constitution places upon police activity.

What would we have to show for all this in terms of crime reduction? Terror-   22
ists, hit men, and other hardened criminals who are not deterred by the penalties for murder, robbery, rape, burglary, et cetera are not about to be terrified by the penalties for gun ownership—nor is the more ordinary murderer, the disturbed, aberrant individual who kills out of rage rather than cupidity.

---

*According to the ACLU, St. Louis police have conducted 25,000 illegal searches in the past few years under the theory that any black man driving a late-model car possesses a handgun.

Michigan court records indicate that almost 70 percent of all firearms charges presented are thrown out because the evidence was obtained through unconstitutional search.

What we should have learned from our experience of Prohibition, and En- 23
gland's with gun banning, is that violence can be radically reduced only through
long-term fundamental change in the institutions and mores that produce so
many violent people in our society. It is much easier to use as scapegoats a
commonly vilified group (drinkers or gun owners) and convince ourselves that
legislation against them is an easy short-term answer. But violence will never
be contained or reduced until we give up the gimmicky programs, the scape-
goating, the hypocritical hand-wringing, and frankly ask ourselves whether we
are willing to make the painful, disturbing, far-reaching institutional and cultural changes that are necessary.

QUESTIONS FOR MEANING

1. What states were the first to initiate gun control legislation, and what
   motivated them to do so? Who were the supporters of these early laws, and
   who were they trying to control? Why does Kates believe that it is important to remember the history of the movement for gun control as we argue
   about the possibility of additional legislation?
2. What does Kates mean by "company goons" in paragraph 2?
3. In paragraph 6, Kates summarizes two simple arguments and describes
   them as non sequiturs. Explain why the reasoning is faulty in both the
   examples he cites.
4. What types of people are the most likely to own handguns? Why do these
   people feel that they need guns? Why is it, according to Kates, that the
   average liberal cannot understand this?
5. According to this essay, what is the main reason why gun control cannot
   work?
6. Proponents of gun control have frequently advocated a mandatory year in
   prison for anyone illegally possessing a handgun. Why do such people insist that the penalty be mandatory? Why does Kates oppose this idea in
   particular?
7. Vocabulary: congenitally (3), aberrant (4), felony (4), milieu (7), dissipate
   (7), loathe (13), impecunious (17), pertinent (17), empirical (17), vilification (19), demographic (19), and cupidity (22).

QUESTIONS ABOUT STRATEGY

1. Why does Kates quote a chairman of Amnesty International in paragraph
   5? Why is this more effective than quoting the president of the National
   Rifle Association? Similarly, why does he describe the poor black woman in
   Chicago? What does this tell us about his audience? What type of people is
   Kates trying to convince, and what is his basic strategy in doing so?
2. What basic values does Kates assume in making this argument? What does
   he think of "law"—what it can and cannot do?

3. Why does Kates compare gun legislation with laws designed to control marijuana? Why is he then able to argue that gun laws are even harder to enforce?
4. Does Kates ever resort to ridiculing his opponents, or does he consistently treat them with respect?
5. Does Kates offer any alternatives to gun control as a way of making America less violent? Is it his responsibility to do so in order to make a good argument?

EDWARD M. KENNEDY
The Need for Handgun Control

The senior senator from Massachusetts, Edward M. Kennedy (b. 1932) is the youngest and only surviving son of Joseph and Rose Kennedy. He graduated from Harvard in 1956, attended International Law School in the Hague, and began to practice law after receiving his L.L.B. from the University of Virginia in 1959. First elected to the Senate in 1962, Kennedy has chaired subcommittees on administrative practice and procedure, refugees and escapees, health care, and the judiciary. He is also a trustee of Brown University, the Boston Symphony, Children's Hospital in Boston, and the John F. Kennedy Center for the Performing Arts. For many years he has been considered one of the leaders of the Democratic Party. A strong advocate of gun control, Kennedy published the following essay in 1981, shortly after John Hinkley tried to kill President Reagan.

The wounding of President Reagan has stunned the world and stirred a vast reaction. Yet he is only the most famous casualty of an endless guerrilla war inside this country waged with a growing arsenal of handguns in the wrong hands. Every day others less famous are wounded or killed; their families worry and suffer. They weep and, too often, they mourn.   1

Every 50 minutes an American is killed by a handgun; 29 Americans who are alive today will be shot dead tomorrow. In the streets of our cities, the arms race of Saturday-night specials and cheap handguns will take 10,000 lives this year and will threaten or wound another 250,000 citizens. In the past year alone, we have seen a 13 percent rise in violent crime, the greatest increase in a decade.   2

Today the clear and present danger to our society is the midnight mugger and the deranged assassin. And their weapons are as close as the nearest pawnshop. There are 55 million handguns in circulation. The lethal number rises by two and a half million each year. By the year 2000, there will be 100 million handguns in America.   3

The shooting of President Reagan was frightening, but not surprising. Are   4 we now too accustomed to the repeated carnage of our national leaders? Are we ready to accept the neighborhoods of our cities as permanent free-fire zones? That sort of fatalism insures more fatalities.

But handgun control is hardly the whole answer to lawlessness. That is why 5 we must adopt other measures as well.

We can, and we must, set more stringent conditions on bail, because no 6 suspect charged with violent crime should be free to rape or to rob again. We can, and we must, demand that juveniles who shoot, stab and assault should not be allowed to misuse their youth as an automatic excuse for their offenses. We can, and we must, provide sufficient resources for law enforcement. No police officer should ever have to jeopardize his life for a subsistence salary that cannot support his family.

All of this is important—but none of it is enough. In the truest sense, law 7 enforcement is part of our national defense. And in the effort to defend ourselves, we must not duck the question of gun control. No sane society should stand by while its enemies arm themselves—whether those enemies are adversaries abroad or criminals and assassins at home.

For America in 1981, crime control means gun control. This is not an easy 8 issue for any officeholder or candidate. In 1980, in the presidential primaries, I constantly met voters who opposed me because they thought I favored confiscation of hunting rifles, shotguns and sporting pistols. It was not true, but it was believed—because the gun lobby had repeated it over and over.

Other senators and representatives faced a similar assault in 1980. The 9 political action committees opposing gun control spent $2.2 million for their candidates, while those on the other side had less than a tenth as much to contribute. That is why we cannot control the plague of handguns, even though two-thirds of the American people have favored such control ever since 1963.

Perhaps this latest tragedy will challenge us to put away past apprehensions 10 and appeals which have treated handgun control as a sinister plot or a subversion of civil liberties. I hope we can now agree that the first civil liberty of all citizens is freedom from fear of violence and sudden death on the streets of their communities.

In this session of congress, I will join again with Rep. Peter Rodino (D-N.J.) 11 to introduce a bill to control handguns. It will be a moderate bill. It will be a sensible bill. It is all I will seek on this issue—and it is something all Americans should be able to support.

All Americans, including sportsmen and hunters, should be able to support 12 a ban on Saturday-night specials and cheap handguns. Those guns are not accurate beyond a range of 10 or 15 feet. They are meant to maim or kill another human being. Saturday-night specials can be purchased now because of a loophole in the law that allows their lethal parts to be imported from abroad, to be assembled and sold in this country. And last week, one of those weapons almost killed our President.

All Americans, including all liberals, should be able to support a mandatory 13 minimum prison sentence for any felon who commits a crime with a handgun.

And all Americans, including the National Rifle Assn., should be able to support a waiting period for the purchase of handguns to prevent them from falling into the hands of criminals and psychopaths.

The question is not whether we will disarm honest citizens, as some gun   14
lobbyists have charged. The question is whether we will make it harder for those who break the law to arm themselves.

Gun control is not an easy issue. But, for me, it is a fundamental issue. My   15
family has been touched by violence; too many others have felt the same terrible force. Too many children have been raised without a father or a mother. Too many widows have lived out their lives alone. Too many people have died.

We all know the toll that has been taken in this nation. We all know the   16
leaders of our public life and of the human spirit who have been lost or wounded year after year: My brother, John Kennedy, and my brother, Robert Kennedy; Medgar Evers, who died so that others could live free; Martin Luther King, the apostle of nonviolence who became the victim of violence; George Wallace, who has been paralyzed for nearly nine years, and George Moscone, the mayor of San Francisco who was killed in his office. Last year alone, we lost Allard Lowenstein and we almost lost Vernon Jordan. Four months ago, we lost John Lennon, that gentle soul who challenged us in song to "give peace a chance." We had two attacks on President Ford and now the attack on President Reagan.

It is unacceptable that all these good men have been shot down. They all   17
sought, each in their own way, to make ours a better world. And, too often, too soon, their own world came to an end.

It is unacceptable that a man who has been arrested before, who has been   18
apprehended carrying loaded guns through an airport security check, who apparently has psychiatric problems as well as a criminal record should be able to go to a pawnshop and buy a cheap handgun imported because of a loophole in the law, and then use that gun to attempt murder against the President of the United States.

It is unacceptable that there are states in the American union where the   19
accused attacker of President Reagan could today buy another Saturday night special.

The day after Martin Luther King's assassination, Robert Kennedy said: "The   20
victims of violence are black and white, rich and poor, young and old, famous and unknown. They are, most important of all, human beings whom other human beings loved and needed. No one, no matter where he lives or what he does, can be certain who next will suffer from some senseless act of bloodshed. And yet it goes on, and on, and on, in this country of ours. Why?"

Thirteen years later, that same tragic question must be raised again.   21

It is for us to answer it. We must resolve that the next generation of Ameri-   22
cans will not have to witness the carnage next time and ask—"Why?"

QUESTIONS FOR MEANING

1. Why does Kennedy single out "Saturday-night specials and cheap hand-guns" for his attack? If an opponent asked him if he'd prefer criminals to carry more expensive weapons, how do you think he would respond?

2. Can you identify Medgar Evers, Martin Luther King, and George Wallace? Kennedy pauses after each of these names to offer additional information, but he does not do so after mentioning Allard Lowenstein and Vernon Jordan. Why do you think he decided that it was not necessary to say anything about these men? Do you know who they were? If you don't, how could you find out?

3. Why does Kennedy claim that the shooting of President Reagan was "frightening, but not surprising"?

4. Vocabulary: guerrilla (1), lethal (3), carnage (4), fatalism (4), stringent (6), apprehensions (10), and subversion (10).

QUESTIONS ABOUT STRATEGY

1. What is Kennedy's purpose in paragraph 6? What part of his audience was this paragraph meant to satisfy?

2. Why does Kennedy associate gun control with "law enforcement" and "our national defense"?

3. In paragraph 11, Kennedy begins three sentences in a row with "It." Similarly, paragraphs 17–19 all begin with the same words. Is this careless or deliberate writing?

4. Why does Kennedy, a liberal Democrat, begin his argument with a reference to the attempted assassination of President Reagan? Why does he mention his own brothers only toward the end of the essay?

5. In paragraph 2, Kennedy cites the rise in violent crime as evidence that guns are too easily obtainable. Does he clearly establish the relationship between this cause and its effect?

BARRY GOLDWATER
Why Gun Control Laws Don't Work

The son of a wealthy department store owner, Barry Goldwater (b. 1909) first entered politics in 1949 when he ran successfully for a seat on the Phoenix City Council. Four years later, he was elected as a U.S. senator from Arizona. With the 1960 publication of his book The Conscience of a Conservative, *Goldwater emerged as an important spokesman for the conservative wing of the Republican Party. He was the Republican nominee for president in 1964, but, widely perceived as an extremist, he carried only six states in a frequently bitter campaign with Lyndon Baines Johnson. Goldwater returned to the Senate in 1968, and many of his former opponents have come to respect his candor and integrity. He wrote the following argument for* Reader's Digest *in 1976.*

Let me say immediately that if I thought more gun-control laws would help   1
diminish the tragic incidence of robberies, muggings, rapes and murders in the
United States. I would be the first to vote for them. But I am convinced that
making more such laws approaches the problem from the wrong direction.

It is clear, I think, that gun legislation simply doesn't work. There are already   2
some 20,000 state and local gun laws on the books, and they are no more
effective than was the prohibition of alcoholic beverages in the 1920s. Our most
recent attempt at federal gun legislation was the Gun Control Act of 1968,
intended to control the interstate sale and transportation of firearms and
the importation of uncertified firearms; it has done nothing to check the availability of weapons. It has been bolstered in every nook and cranny of the nation
by local gun-control laws, yet the number of shooting homicides per year has
climbed steadily since its enactment, while armed robberies have increased 60
percent.

Some people, even some law-enforcement officials, contend that "crimes of   3
passion" occur because a gun just happens to be present at the scene. I don't
buy that. I can't equate guns with the murder rate, because if a person is angry
enough to kill, he will kill with the first thing that comes to hand—a gun, a
knife, an ice pick, a baseball bat.

I believe our *only* hope of reducing crime in this country is to control not   4
the weapon but the user. We must reverse the trend toward leniency and
permissiveness in our courts—the plea bargaining, the pardons, the suspended
sentences and unwarranted paroles—and make the lawbreaker pay for what
he has done by spending time in jail. We have plenty of statutes against killing
and maiming and threatening people with weapons. These can be made effective by strong enforcement and firm decisions from the bench. When a man
knows that if he uses a potentially deadly object to rob or do harm to another
person he is letting himself in for a mandatory, unparolable stretch behind bars,
he will think twice about it.

Of course, no matter what gun-control laws are enacted—including national   5
registration—the dedicated crook can always get a weapon. So, some people
ask, even if national registration of guns isn't completely airtight, isn't it worth

trying? Sure, it would cause a little inconvenience to law-abiding gun owners. And it certainly wouldn't stop all criminals from obtaining guns. But it might stop a few, maybe quite a few. What's wrong with that?

There are several answers. The first concerns enforcement. How are we 6 going to persuade the bank robber or the street-corner stickup artist to register his means of criminal livelihood? Then there is the matter of expense. A study conducted eight years ago showed a cost to New York City of $72.87 to investigate and process one application for a pistol license. In mid-1970 dollars, the same procedure probably costs over $100. By extrapolation to the national scale, the cost to American taxpayers of investigating and registering the 40 to 50 million handguns might reach $4 billion or $5 billion. On top of that, keeping the process in operation year after year would require taxpayer financing of another sizable federal bureau. We ought to have far better prospects of success before we hobble ourselves with such appalling expenditures.

Finally, there are legal aspects based on the much-discussed Second Amend- 7 ment to the Bill of Rights, which proclaims that "A well regulated Militia, being necessary to the security of a free State, the right of the people to keep and bear Arms, shall not be infringed." The anti-gun faction argues that this right made sense in the days of British oppression but that it has no application today. I contend, on the other hand, that the Founding Fathers conceived of an armed citizenry as a necessary hedge against tyranny from within as well as from without, that they saw the right to keep and bear arms as basic and perpetual, the one thing that could spell the difference between freedom and servitude. Thus I deem most forms of gun control unconstitutional in intent.

Well, then, I'm often asked, what kind of gun laws *are* you for? I reply that I 8 am for laws of common sense. I am for laws that prohibit citizen access to machine guns, bazookas and other military devices. I am for laws that are educational in nature. I believe that before a person is permitted to buy a weapon he should be required to take a course that will teach him how to use it, to handle it safely and keep it safely about the house.

Gun education, in fact, can actually reduce lawlessness in a community, as 9 was demonstrated in an experiment conducted in Highland Park, Mich. City police launched a program to instruct merchants in the use of handguns. The idea was to help them protect themselves and their businesses from robbers, and it was given wide publicity. The store-robbery rate dropped from an average of 1.5 a day to none in four months.

Where do we go from here? My answer to this is based on the firm belief that 10 we have a crime problem in this country, not a gun problem, and that we must meet the enemy on his own terms. We must start by making crime as unprofitable for him as we can. And we have to do this, I believe, by getting tough in the courts and corrections systems.

A recent news story in Washington, D.C., reports that, of 184 persons con- 11 victed of gun possession in a six-month period, only 14 received a jail sentence. Forty-six other cases involved persons who had previously been convicted of a felony or possession of a gun. Although the maximum penalty for such repeaters in the District of Columbia is ten years in prison, half of these were not jailed at all. A study last year revealed that in New York City, which has about the most prohibitive gun legislation in the country, only one out of six people convicted of crimes involving weapons went to jail.

This sorry state of affairs exists because too many judges and magistrates   12
either don't know the law or are unwilling to apply it with appropriate vigor. It's time to demand either that they crack down on these criminals or be removed from office. It may even be time to review the whole system of judicial appointments, to stop weakening the cause of justice by putting men on the bench who may happen to be golfing partners of Congressmen and too often lack the brains and ability for the job. In Arizona today we elect our judges, and the system is working well, in part because we ask the American and local bar associations to consider candidates and make recommendations. In this way, over the last few years, we have replaced many weaklings with good jurists.

We have long had all the criminal statutes we need to turn the tide against   13
the crime wave. There is, however, one piece of proposed legislation that I am watching with particular interest. Introduced by Sen. James McClure (R., Idaho), it requires that any person convicted of a federal crime in which a gun is used serve five to ten years in jail automatically on top of whatever penalty he receives for the crime itself. A second conviction would result in an extra ten-year-to-life sentence. These sentences would be mandatory and could not be suspended. It is, in short, a "tough" bill. I think that this bill would serve as an excellent model for state legislation.

And so it has in California which, last September, signed into law a similar   14
bill requiring a mandatory jail sentence for any gun-related felony.

Finally, it's important to remember that this is an area of great confusion; an   15
area in which statistics can be juggled and distorted to support legislation that is liable to be expensive, counter-productive or useless. The issue touches upon the freedom and safety of all of us, whether we own firearms or not. The debate over gun control is an adjunct to the war against crime, and that war must be fought with all the intelligence and tenacity we can bring to it.

QUESTIONS FOR MEANING

1. What are "crimes of passion," and why does Goldwater believe that they will not be eliminated by gun control?
2. Do you understand the analogy in paragraph 2 between gun control and Prohibition? Is this a fair comparison?
3. Is Goldwater opposed to all gun laws?
4. What does Goldwater mean by "weaklings" in paragraph 12? Are there any risks in requiring judges to run for election?
5. Vocabulary: contend (3), infringed (7), perpetual (7), mandatory (13), adjunct (15), and tenacity (15).

QUESTIONS ABOUT STRATEGY

1. Is it logical to imply that new laws won't work because old laws have failed? How effective is paragraph 2?

2. At what points in his argument does Goldwater reveal that he is aware of his opponents?
3. In paragraph 6, Goldwater argues against gun control on the grounds that it costs too much to process an application for a pistol license. In paragraphs 8–9 he argues on behalf of mandatory gun education for anyone who wants to buy a gun. Is he contradicting himself?
4. Both Kennedy and Goldwater favor mandatory prison sentences for crimes in which a gun is used. Do you think this is a good idea? Do you think there may be problems in carrying it out?

United States Conference of Mayors Policy Statement on Handgun Control

American mayors convene annually in order to discuss areas of common concern. They adopted the following resolution at their meeting in 1972.

WHEREAS, over 8,000 Americans were felled by handguns in 1970 and nationally 80% of all homicide victims knew killers as a relative or friend; and   1

WHEREAS, 95% of the policemen killed in the line of duty between 1961 and 1970 were felled by handguns; and   2

WHEREAS, gun dealers today sell to the mentally ill, criminals, dope addicts, convicted felons, juveniles, as well as good citizens who kill each other; and   3

WHEREAS, those who possess handguns cannot be divided into criminals and qualified gun owners; and   4

WHEREAS, handguns are not generally used to sporting or recreational purposes, and such purposes do not require keeping handguns in private homes; and   5

WHEREAS, the United States Supreme Court ruled in 1939 that firearms regulation is not unconstitutional unless it impairs the effectiveness of the State militia,   6

NOW THEREFORE BE IT RESOLVED that the United States Conference of Mayors takes a position of leadership and urges national legislation against the manufacture, importation, sale and private possession of handguns, except for use by law enforcement personnel, military and sportsmen clubs; and   7

BE IT FURTHER RESOLVED that the United States Conference of Mayors   8 urges its members to extend every effort to educate the American public to the dangerous and appalling realities resulting from the private possession of handguns, and that we urge the Congress to adopt a national handgun registration law; and

BE IT FURTHER RESOLVED that (i) effective legislation be introduced and approved by the states not having adequate legislation to that effect; (ii) the proposed legislation shall provide for the registration of all firearms; (iii) state legislation shall require all citizens interested in carrying a weapon to obtain a license after showing just cause and good conduct; (iv) federal legislation shall provide, in addition to existing restrictions, that any person not having a state license to carry a firearm shall commit an offense for transporting such in interstate commerce.   9

QUESTIONS FOR MEANING

1. Is there a difference between "criminals" and "convicted felons" in article 3?
2. Why is it that "those who possess handguns cannot be divided into criminals and qualified gun owners?"
3. Can you define "just and good conduct" in article 9? Do you think your definition would satisfy government officials?

QUESTIONS ABOUT STRATEGY

1. Although this is only a short "policy statement," it is arranged in argumentative form. What type of reasoning have the mayors employed?
2. In article 7, the mayors oppose "the private possession of handguns." Would Shields, Smith, and Kennedy agree with this resolution? Could Abbey, Kates, and Goldwater use this statement to reinforce their own arguments?

SUGGESTIONS FOR WRITING

1. Shields, Smith, Abbey, and Kates all describe members of what Smith calls "the gun culture." Summarize and compare these descriptions determining which, if any, seem fair and accurate.
2. Shields, Smith, and Abbey all draw upon personal experience in making their arguments. If you have ever used a gun, write an essay on gun control that begins with an account of your experience.
3. Kates argues that "liberals" should oppose gun control but recognizes that many liberals are in favor of it. Addressing yourself to a liberal, college-educated audience, write a deductive argument for or against control. Your premise should define either the rights of citizens or the responsibilities of government.
4. Goldwater argues that the rise in violent crime cannot be explained by the absence of gun control. Consider this argument and write an essay that

will either support it or reveal its shortcomings. Do library research if necessary.

5. What is your own opinion of gun control? Were you influenced by your reading in this unit? Summarize at least two of the arguments you have read and use these summaries as the foundation for a short essay of your own. Be sure to summarize the argument of at least one writer with whom you disagree—carefully explaining why the "opposition" did not convince you.

6. Regardless of your own opinion on gun control, which essay in this unit is the most persuasive? Write an essay in defense of this writer, evaluating the techniques he or she has used.

7. Regardless of your own opinion on gun control, which essay in this unit is the weakest? Reveal the flaws you perceive in the essay, and do not indulge in ad hominem attacks.

8. Write an essay explaining why advocates of gun control object especially to handguns. Draw support from Adam Smith, Edward Kennedy, and the U.S. Conference of Mayors.

9. Do a research paper comparing the rate of violent crime in two states with significantly different gun laws.

Section 2
Capital Punishment: Justice or Vengeance?

CLARENCE DARROW
The Futility of the Death Penalty

Specializing in labor and political cases, Clarence Darrow (1857–1938) was one of the most famous lawyers in American history. He was especially prominent in the 1920s, a decade that witnessed his two most celebrated cases. In 1925, he was the defense attorney for John L. Scopes, a high school biology teacher who was charged with violating a Tennessee law that prohibited teaching any theory that suggested man may have evolved from a lower species. Although Charles Darwin had published The Origin of Species *more than a half century earlier, evolution was still regarded as a dangerous doctrine that would undermine the moral authority of the Bible. The Scopes trial attracted worldwide attention as a major test of civil liberties, especially freedom of thought. Darrow lost the case, but his forceful defense of Scopes almost certainly saved teachers in other states from being prosecuted under similar laws.*

A year earlier, Darrow had undertaken an even more difficult case when he defended Nathan Leopold and Richard Loeb in a notorious murder case. Although his clients had confessed to an unusually cold-blooded murder and popular feeling demanded that they be executed, Darrow managed to win prison terms for them by arguing persuasively against the death penalty. His objections to capital punishment are best summarized in the following essay, first published in 1928.

Little more than a century ago, in England, there were over two hundred 1
offenses that were punishable with death. The death sentence was passed upon
children under ten years old. And every time the sentimentalist sought to lessen
the number of crimes punishable by death, the self-righteous said no, that it
would be the destruction of the state; that it would be better to kill for more
transgressions rather than for less.

Today, both in England and America, the number of capital offenses has 2
been reduced to a very few, and capital punishment would doubtless be abolished altogether were it not for the self-righteous, who still defend it with the
same old arguments. Their major claim is that capital punishment decreases

58

the number of murders, and hence, that the state must retain the institution as its last defense against the criminal.

It is my purpose in this article to prove, first, that capital punishment is no   3
deterrent to crime; and second, that the state continues to kill its victims, not so much to defend society against them—for it could do that equally well by imprisonment—but to appease the mob's emotions of hatred and revenge.

Behind the idea of capital punishment lie false training and crude views of   4
human conduct. People do evil things, say the judges, lawyers, and preachers, because of depraved hearts. Human conduct is not determined by the causes which determine the conduct of other animal and plant life in the universe. For some mysterious reason human beings act as they please; and if they do not please to act in a certain way, it is because, having the power of choice, they deliberately choose to act wrongly. The world once applied this doctrine to disease and insanity in men. It was also applied to animals, and even inanimate things were once tried and condemned to destruction. The world knows better now, but the rule has not yet been extended to human beings.

The simple fact is that every person starts life with a certain physical struc-   5
ture, more or less sensitive, stronger or weaker. He is played upon by everything that reaches him from without, and in this he is like everything else in the universe, inorganic matter as well as organic. How a man will act depends upon the character of his human machine, and the strength of the various stimuli that affect it. Everyone knows that this is so in disease and insanity. Most investigators know that it applies to crime. But the great mass of people still sit in judgment, robed with self-righteousness, and determine the fate of their less fortunate fellows. When this question is studied like any other, we shall then know how to get rid of most of the conduct that we call "criminal," just as we are now getting rid of much of the disease that once afflicted mankind.

If crime were really the result of wilful depravity, we should be ready to   6
concede that capital punishment may serve as a deterrent to the criminally inclined. But it is hardly probable that the great majority of people refrain from killing their neighbors because they are afraid; they refrain because they never had the inclination. Human beings are creatures of habit; and, as a rule, they are not in the habit of killing. The circumstances that lead to killings are manifold, but in a particular individual the inducing cause is not easily found. In one case, homicide may have been induced by indigestion in the killer; in another, it may be traceable to some weakness inherited from a remote ancestor; but that it results from *something* tangible and understandable, if all the facts were known, must be plain to everyone who believes in cause and effect.

Of course, no one will be converted to this point of view by statistics of crime.   7
In the first place, it is impossible to obtain reliable ones; and in the second place, the conditions to which they apply are never the same. But if one cares to analyze the figures, such as we have, it is easy to trace the more frequent causes of homicide. The greatest number of killings occur during attempted burglaries and robberies. The robber knows that penalties for burglary do not average more than five years in prison. He also knows that the penalty for murder is

death or life imprisonment. Faced with this alternative, what does the burglar do when he is detected and threatened with arrest? He shoots to kill. He deliberately takes the chance of death to save himself from a five-year term in prison. It is therefore as obvious as anything can be that fear of death has no effect in diminishing homicides of this kind, which are more numerous than any other type.

The next largest number of homicides may be classed as "sex murders." Quarrels between husbands and wives, disappointed love, or love too much requited cause many killings. They are the result of primal emotions so deep that the fear of death has not the slightest effect in preventing them. Spontaneous feelings overflow in criminal acts, and consequences do not count. 8

Then there are cases of sudden anger, uncontrollable rage. The fear of death never enters into such cases; if the anger is strong enough, consequences are not considered until too late. The old-fashioned stories of men deliberately plotting and committing murder in cold blood have little foundation in real life. Such killings are so rare that they need not concern us here. The point to be emphasized is that practically all homicides are manifestations of well-recognized human emotions, and it is perfectly plain that the fear of excessive punishment does not enter into them. 9

In addition to these personal forces which overwhelm weak men and lead them to commit murder, there are also many social and economic forces which must be listed among the causes of homicides, and human beings have even less control over these than over their own emotions. It is often said that in America there are more homicides in proportion to population than in England. This is true. There are likewise more in the United States than in Canada. But such comparisons are meaningless until one takes into consideration the social and economic differences in the countries compared. Then it becomes apparent why the homicide rate in the United States is higher. Canada's population is largely rural; that of the United States is crowded into cities whose slums are the natural breeding places of crime. Moreover, the population of England and Canada is homogeneous, while the United States has gathered together people of every color from every nation in the world. Racial differences intensify social, religious, and industrial problems, and the confusion which attends this indiscriminate mixing of races and nationalities is one of the most fertile sources of crime. 10

Will capital punishment remedy these conditions? Of course it won't; but its advocates argue that the fear of this extreme penalty will hold the victims of adverse conditions in check. To this piece of sophistry the continuance and increase of crime in our large cities is a sufficient answer. No, the plea that capital punishment acts as a deterrent to crime will not stand. The real reason why this barbarous practice persists in a so-called civilized world is that people still hold the primitive belief that the taking of one human life can be atoned for by taking another. It is the age-old obsession with punishment that keeps the official headsman busy plying his trade. 11

And it is precisely upon this point that I would build my case against capital punishment. Even if one grants that the idea of punishment is sound, crime 12 calls for something more—for careful study, for an understanding of causes, for proper remedies. To attempt to abolish crime by killing the criminal is the easy and foolish way out of a serious situation. Unless a remedy deals with the conditions which foster crime, criminals will breed faster than the hangman can spring his trap. Capital punishment ignores the causes of crime just as completely as the primitive witch doctor ignored the causes of disease; and, like the methods of the witch doctor, it is not only ineffective as a remedy, but is positively vicious in at least two ways. In the first place, the spectacle of state executions feeds the basest passions of the mob. And in the second place, so long as the state rests content to deal with crime in this barbaric and futile manner, society will be lulled by a false sense of security, and effective methods of dealing with crime will be discouraged.

It seems to be a general impression that there are fewer homicides in Great   13
Britain than in America because in England punishment is more certain, more prompt, and more severe. As a matter of fact, the reverse is true. In England the average term for burglary is eighteen months; with us it is probably four or five years. In England, imprisonment for life means twenty years. Prison sentences in the United States are harder than in any country in the world that could be classed as civilized. This is true largely because, with us, practically no official dares to act on his own judgment. The mob is all-powerful and demands blood for blood. That intangible body of people called "the public" vents its hatred upon the criminal and enjoys the sensation of having him put to death by the state—this without any definite idea that it is really necessary.

For the last five or six years, in England and Wales, the homicides reported   14
by the police range from sixty-five to seventy a year. Death sentences meted out by jurors have averaged about thirty-five, and hangings, fifteen. More than half of those convicted by juries were saved by appeals to the Home Office. But in America there is no such percentage of lives saved after conviction. Governors are afraid to grant clemency. If they did, the newspapers and the populace would refuse to re-elect them.

It is true that trials are somewhat prompter in England than America, but   15
there no newspaper dares publish the details of any case until after the trial. In America the accused is often convicted by the public within twenty-four hours of the time a homicide occurs. The courts sidetrack all other business so that a homicide that is widely discussed may receive prompt attention. The road to the gallows is not only opened but greased for the opportunity of killing another victim.

Thus, while capital punishment panders to the passions of the mob, no one   16
takes the pains to understand the meaning of crime. People speak of crime or criminals as if the world were divided into the good and the bad. This is not true. All of us have the same emotions, but since the balance of emotions is never the same, nor the inducing causes identical, human conduct presents a wide range of differences, shading by almost imperceptible degrees from that of the saint to that of the murderer. Of those kinds of conduct which are classed as dangerous, by no means all are made criminal offenses. Who can clearly define the difference between certain legal offenses and many kinds of

dangerous conduct not singled out by criminal statute? Why are many cases of cheating entirely omitted from the criminal code, such as false and misleading advertisements, selling watered stock, forestalling the market, and all the different ways in which great fortunes are accumulated to the envy and despair of those who would like to have money but do not know how to get it? Why do we kill people for the crime of homicide and administer a lesser penalty for burglary, robbery, and cheating? Can anyone tell which is the greater crime and which is the lesser?

Human conduct is by no means so simple as our moralists have led us to believe. There is no sharp line separating good actions from bad. The greed for money, the display of wealth, the despair of those who witness the display, the poverty, oppression, and hopelessness of the unfortunate—all these are factors which enter into human conduct and of which the world takes no account. Many people have learned no other profession but robbery and burglary. The processions moving steadily through our prisons to the gallows are in the main made up of these unfortunates. And how do we dare to consider ourselves civilized creatures when, ignoring the causes of crime, we rest content to mete out harsh punishments to the victims of conditions over which they have no control?   17

Even now, are not all imaginative and humane people shocked at the spectacle of a killing by the state? How many men and women would be willing to act as executioners? How many fathers and mothers would want their children to witness an official killing? What kind of people read the sensational reports of an execution? If all right-thinking men and women were not ashamed of it, why would it be needful that judges and lawyers and preachers apologize for the barbarity? How can the state censure the cruelty of the man who—moved by strong passions, or acting to save his freedom, or influenced by weakness or fear—takes human life, when everyone knows that the state itself, after long premeditation and settled hatred, not only kills, but first tortures and bedevils its victims for weeks with the impending doom?   18

For the last hundred years the world has shown a gradual tendency to mitigate punishment. We are slowly learning that this way of controlling human beings is both cruel and ineffective. In England the criminal code has consistently grown more humane, until now the offenses punishable by death are reduced to practically one. There is no doubt whatever that the world is growing more humane and more sensitive and more understanding. The time will come when all people will view with horror the light way in which society and its courts of law now take human life; and when that time comes, the way will be clear to devise some better method of dealing with poverty and ignorance and their frequent byproducts, which we call crime.   19

QUESTIONS FOR MEANING

1. In his opening paragraphs, Darrow claims that capital punishment is supported by "the self-righteous." What kind of people is he referring to? Do you agree with him?

2. Why does Darrow believe that capital punishment does not deter crime? Why does he believe it is still carried out?
3. Darrow argues that "Capital punishment ignores the causes of crime." At what points in his essay does he try to reveal what these causes are?
4. How would you describe Darrow's opinion of human nature?
5. Toward the end of his essay Darrow asks, "Why do we kill people for the crime of homicide and administer a lesser penalty for burglary, robbery, and cheating? Can anyone tell which is the greater crime and which is the lesser?" Can you?

QUESTIONS ABOUT STRATEGY

1. For what sort of audience do you think this essay was originally written? Is there any evidence in it that Darrow was not addressing "the great mass of people" or the "mob" to which he refers in paragraphs 5 and 13?
2. In paragraph 9, Darrow argues, "The old fashioned stories of men deliberately plotting and committing murder in cold blood have little foundation in real life." Consider whether you agree with him, but, consider also his purpose in making this claim.
3. How useful is the comparison between England and the United States?
4. Why does Darrow introduce "fathers," "mothers," and "children" into his second to last paragraph?
5. This essay was written more than fifty years ago. Do you think its argument is still valid, or does it seem out of date?

H.L. MENCKEN
The Penalty of Death

Henry Louis Mencken (1880–1956) was a journalist who enjoyed a national reputation throughout the first half of the twentieth century, especially during the 1920s. Although he worked for the Baltimore Sun *for over forty years, Mencken was no ordinary journalist. Fascinated by words, he wrote one of the best books ever written on the way we write and speak,* The American Language, *first published in 1919 and revised and enlarged in several subsequent editions. But it was as an essayist that Mencken won his largest audience. As co-editor of* The Smart Set *from 1914–1923, he was in a position to encourage writers such as James Joyce, D.H. Lawrence, and Sinclair Lewis. As founder and editor of* The American Mercury *in 1924, Mencken found a forum from which he could speak out on almost any subject that interested him. At a time in our history when many Americans were feeling complacent about life in a country that seemed the richest and strongest in the world, Mencken made a specialty of exposing fools and ridiculing popular notions. The following essay on capital punishment, from* Prejudices, Fifth Series *(1926), is characteristic of both his thought and style.*

Of the arguments against capital punishment that issue from uplifters, two 1
are commonly heard most often, to wit:

1. That hanging a man (or frying him or gassing him) is a dreadful business, degrading to those who have to do it and revolting to those who have to witness it.
2. That it is useless, for it does not deter others from the same crime.

The first of these arguments, it seems to me, is plainly too weak to need 2
serious refutation. All it says, in brief, is that the work of the hangman is unpleasant. Granted. But suppose it is? It may be quite necessary to society for all that. There are, indeed, many other jobs that are unpleasant, and yet no one thinks of abolishing them—that of the plumber, that of the soldier, that of the garbage-man, that of the priest hearing confessions, that of the sand-hog, and so on. Moreover, what evidence is there that any actual hangman complains of his work? I have heard none. On the contrary, I have known many who delighted in their ancient art, and practised it proudly.

In the second argument of the abolitionists there is rather more force, but 3
even here, I believe, the ground under them is shaky. Their fundamental error consists in assuming that the whole aim of punishing criminals is to deter other (potential) criminals—that we hang or electrocute A simply in order to so alarm B that he will not kill C. This, I believe, is an assumption which confuses a part with the whole. Deterrence, obviously, is *one* of the aims of punishment, but it is surely not the only one. On the contrary, there are at least half a dozen, and some are probably quite as important. At least one of them, practically considered, is *more* important. Commonly, it is described as revenge, but revenge is really not the word for it. I borrow a better term from the late Aristotle:

katharsis. Katharsis, so used, means a salubrious discharge of emotions, a healthy letting off of steam. A school-boy, disliking his teacher, deposits a tack upon the pedagogical chair; the teacher jumps and the boy laughs. This is *katharsis.* What I contend is that one of the prime objects of all judicial punishments is to afford the same grateful relief (*a*) to the immediate victims of the criminal punished, and (*b*) to the general body of moral and timorous men.

These persons, and particularly the first group, are concerned only indirectly   4
with deterring other criminals. The thing they crave primarily is the satisfaction of seeing the criminal actually before them suffer as he made them suffer. What they want is the peace of mind that goes with the feeling that accounts are squared. Until they get that satisfaction they are in a state of emotional tension, and hence unhappy. The instant they get it they are comfortable. I do not argue that this yearning is noble; I simply argue that it is almost universal among human beings. In the face of injuries that are unimportant and can be borne without damage it may yield to higher impulses; that is to say, it may yield to what is called Christian charity. But when the injury is serious Christianity is adjourned, and even saints reach for their sidearms. It is plainly asking too much of human nature to expect it to conquer so natural an impulse. A keeps a store and has a bookkeeper, B. B steals $700, employs it in playing at dice or bingo, and is cleaned out. What is A to do? Let B go? If he does he will be unable to sleep at night. The sense of injury, of injustice, of frustration will haunt him like pruritus. So he turns B over to the police, and they hustle B to prison. Thereafter A can sleep. More, he has pleasant dreams. He pictures B chained to the wall of a dungeon a hundred feet underground, devoured by rats and scorpions. It is so agreeable that it makes him forget his $700. He has got his *katharsis.*

The same thing precisely takes place on a larger scale when there is a crime   5
which destroys a whole community's sense of security. Every law-abiding citizen feels menaced and frustrated until the criminals have been struck down— until the communal capacity to get even with them, and more than even, has been dramatically demonstrated. Here, manifestly, the business of deterring others is no more than an afterthought. The main thing is to destroy the concrete scoundrels whose act has alarmed everyone, and thus made everyone unhappy. Until they are brought to book that unhappiness continues; when the law has been executed upon them there is a sigh of relief. In other words, there is *katharsis.*

I know of no public demand for the death penalty for ordinary crimes, even   6
for ordinary homicides. Its infliction would shock all men of normal decency of feeling. But for crimes involving the deliberate and inexcusable taking of human life, by men openly defiant of all civilized order—for such crimes it seems, to nine men out of ten, a just and proper punishment. Any lesser penalty leaves them feeling that the criminal has got the better of society—that he is free to add insult to injury by laughing. That feeling can be dissipated only by a recourse to *katharsis,* the invention of the aforesaid Aristotle. It is more effectively and economically achieved, as human nature now is, by wafting the criminal to realms of bliss.

The real objection to capital punishment doesn't lie against the actual exter-   7
mination of the condemned, but against our brutal American habit of putting it
off so long. After all, every one of us must die soon or late, and a murderer, it
must be assumed, is one who makes that sad fact the cornerstone of his meta-
physic. But it is one thing to die, and quite another thing to lie for long months
and even years under the shadow of death. No sane man would choose such a
finish. All of us, despite the Prayer Book, long for a swift and unexpected end.
Unhappily, a murderer, under the irrational American system, is tortured for
what, to him, must seem a whole series of eternities. For months on end he sits
in prison while his lawyers carry on their idiotic buffoonery with writs, injunc-
tions, mandamuses, and appeals. In order to get his money (or that of his
friends) they have to feed him with hope. Now and then, by the imbecility of a
judge or some trick of juridic science, they actually justify it. But let us say that,
his money all gone, they finally throw up their hands. Their client is now ready
for the rope or the chair. But he must still wait for months before it fetches him.

That wait, I believe, is horribly cruel. I have seen more than one man sitting   8
in the death-house, and I don't want to see any more. Worse, it is wholly useless.
Why should he wait at all? Why not hang him the day after the last court
dissipates his last hope? Why torture him as not even cannibals would torture
their victims? The common answer is that he must have time to make his peace
with God. But how long does that take? It may be accomplished, I believe, in
two hours quite as comfortably as in two years. There are, indeed, no temporal
limitations upon God. He could forgive a whole herd of murderers in a millionth
of a second. More, it has been done.

QUESTIONS FOR MEANING

1. Why does Mencken believe that capital punishment is justifiable?
2. Do you understand the meaning of *katharsis*? Can you think of examples
   from your own experience to illustrate this principle?
3. How absolute is Mencken's proposal? Does he want all murderers to be
   executed or does he recognize that circumstances make some murders
   worse than others?
4. What flaws does Mencken see in the American judicial system?
5. Vocabulary: refutation (2), salubrious (3), pedagogical (3), timorous (3),
   manifestly (5), dissipated (6), and buffoonery (7).

QUESTIONS ABOUT STRATEGY

1. How would you describe Mencken's style? Consider his diction in particular. What kind of effect does a word like "uplifters" have in paragraph 1?
   Why does Mencken write about *frying* a man rather than "electrocuting"
   him? Does language of this sort belong in an essay that moves on to discuss
   Aristotle? Is this shift strange and exciting—or is it a sign of sloppy writing?
2. Mencken begins his essay with a summary of what he believes to be the
   two principle arguments against capital punishment. Is this a fair summary?
   Are there any important arguments that he overlooks?

3. Do you think Mencken really knew many hangmen who "delighted in their ancient art?" If not, why do you think he says so?
4. Comment on Mencken's use of illustration, especially his example of the school boy with a tack in paragraph 3 and the storekeeper in paragraph 4. Are these examples useful in explaining *katharsis*? Are you persuaded that capital punishment is analogous to them?

MARGARET MEAD
A Life for a Life: What That Means Today

Margaret Mead (1901–1978) was one of the first women to earn an international reputation in anthropology, a field that had been previously dominated by men— with the notable exception of Ruth Benedict, under whom Mead studied at Columbia University. She was still in her twenties when she published her most famous book, Coming of Age in Samoa *(1928). Presenting an idyllic view of life in the South Pacific, Mead explored the relationship between child rearing and group cultures, arguing that Americans could learn much from cultures entirely different from our own. Although modern anthropologists now question the validity of Mead's early research, she is still respected as one of the most accomplished women of her generation.*

Mead's interests were not confined to anthropology but extended to psychology, economics, and a wide variety of social problems. She was opposed to capital punishment, and welcomed the 1972 Supreme Court decision that struck down all existing laws under which men and women could be sentenced to death. In this historic ruling, referred to as Furman v. Georgia *after the case which inspired it, the Court declared that the death penalty was unfair because it was applied haphazardly. However, the Court allowed states the opportunity to reestablish capital punishment by writing new laws that would be clear and nondiscriminatory. Many states began to do so, and the long national debate on capital punishment gathered new force. Mead contributed to that debate with the following essay, published in 1978 shortly before her death.*

As Americans we have declared ourselves to be champions of human rights in the world at large. But at home ...   1

At home the Congress and the majority of our state legislatures have been hurrying to pass new laws to ensure that persons convicted of various violent crimes (but not the same ones in all states) may be—or must be—executed.   2

In my view, it is a sorry spectacle to see a great nation publicly proclaiming efforts to modify violence and to protect human rights in distant parts of the world and at the same time devoting an inordinate amount of time and energy at every level of government to ensure that those men and women convicted of capital offenses will be condemned to death and executed. Decisions to carry out such vengeful, punitive measures against our own people would reverberate around the world, making a cold mockery of our very real concern for   3

human rights and our serious efforts to bring about peace and controlled disarmament among nations.

If we do in fact take seriously our chosen role as champions of human rights,   4
then certainly we must also reinterpret drastically the very ancient law of "a
life for a life" as it affects human beings in our own society today. I see this as a
major challenge, especially for modern women.

But first we must understand where we are now.   5

In the late 1960s we lived through a kind of twilight period when without   6
any changes in our laws, men and women were condemned to death but the
sentences were not carried out. Those who had been condemned were left to
sit and wait—often for years.

In 1972 there was a brief period when it seemed that capital punishment   7
had finally been abolished in the whole United States, as it has been in most of
the modern countries of western Europe and in many other countries. For then,
in the case of *Furman v. Georgia*, the Supreme Court of the United States
ruled that existing laws whereby certain convicted criminals were condemned
to death were haphazard and arbitrary in their application and constituted
cruel and unusual punishment, which is prohibited by the Eighth Amendment
to the Constitution. True, the Court was divided; even the five justices who
supported the ruling were quite sharply divided in their reasoning. Nevertheless, *Furman v. Georgia* saved the lives of 631 persons in prisons across the
country who were under sentence of death.

It seemed that we had passed a watershed.   8

But we were quickly disillusioned. The Supreme Court had not yet abolished   9
capital punishment; the justices merely had ruled out the discriminatory manner in which the current laws were applied. As Justice William O. Douglas
pointed out in his concurring opinion, the existing system allowed "the penalty
to be discriminatorily and disproportionately applied to the poor, the Blacks
and the members of unpopular groups."

In response, lawmakers in many states—often pushed by their constituents   10
and by law-enforcement agencies—tried to meet the objections by means of
new and contrasting laws. Some of these laws made the death penalty mandatory; no exceptions or mitigating circumstances were possible. Others made
the death penalty discretionary, that is, they provided very specific guidelines
for defining mitigating circumstances that should be taken into account. The
reason was that experts differed radically in their opinions as to what the
justices of the Supreme Court would find acceptable in revised laws.

In their haste, these lawmakers missed their chance to think in quite other   11
terms.

Meanwhile, of course, cases were tried and a few women and many men   12
were once more condemned. In July, 1976, the principles underlying the new
laws were tested as the Supreme Court of the United States announced rulings
in five of these cases, upholding three discretionary death-penalty statutes
and ruling against two that imposed mandatory capital punishment. As a result,
the death sentences of 389 persons in 19 states were later reduced to life
imprisonment.

But the lawmaking and the convictions have continued. At the end of 1977,   13
the number of condemned prisoners in the death rows of penitentiaries in the
33 states that then had capital punishment laws amounted to 407—five women
and 402 men—divided almost evenly between white Americans and Black or
Hispanic Americans. Two were Native Americans—Indians—and concerning
six, even this meager background information was lacking. Most were poor and
ill educated, too unimportant to be permitted to enter into plea bargaining and
too poor to hire the expensive legal talent that makes possible very different
treatment in the courts for more affluent and protected individuals.

In early 1977 one man, Gary Gilmore, whose two attempts at suicide were   14
given extravagant publicity, finally was executed in the midst of glaring national
publicity in the mass media. Looking back at this one sordidly exploited event,
can anyone picture how we would react if, without discussion, it were suddenly
decided to execute *all* the death row prisoners who were without resources to
prolong their lives?

What we are much more likely to do, I think, is to seesaw between the old,   15
old demand for drastic retribution for crimes against human beings that very
rightly rouse us to anger, fear and disgust and our rather special American
belief that almost everyone (except the suspected criminal we catch on the
run and kill forthwith) is entitled to a second chance. So we make harsh laws,
convict some of the people who break them—and then hesitate. What next?

Every month the number of those convicted, sentenced and waiting grows.   16
Violent criminals, they become the victims of our very ambiguous attitudes
toward violence and our unwillingness to face the true issues.

The struggle for and against the abolition of capital punishment has been   17
going on in our country and among enlightened peoples everywhere for well
over a century. In the years before the Civil War the fight to end the death
penalty was led in America by men like Horace Greeley, who also was fighting
strongly to abolish slavery, and by a tiny handful of active women like New
England's Dorothea Dix, who was fighting for prison reform. In those years
three states—Michigan in 1847, Rhode Island in 1852 and Wisconsin in 1853—
renounced the use of capital punishment, the first jurisdictions in the modern
world to do so.

Both sides claim a primary concern for human rights. Those who demand   18
that we keep—and carry out—the death penalty speak for the victims of
capital crimes, holding that it is only just that murderers, kidnapers, rapists,
hijackers and other violent criminals should suffer for the harm they have done
and so deter others from committing atrocious crimes.

In contrast, those who demand that we abolish capital punishment alto-   19
gether are convinced that violence breeds violence—that the death penalty
carried out by the State against its own citizens in effect legitimizes willful
killing. Over time, their concern has been part of a much more inclusive struggle
for human rights and human dignity. They were among those who fought
against slavery and they have been among those who have fought for the civil
rights of Black Americans, of immigrants and of ethnic minorities and Native
Americans, for the rights of prisoners of war as well as for the prisoners in

penitentiaries, for the rights of the poor, the unemployed and the unemploy-able, for women's rights and for the rights of the elderly and of children.

Now, I believe, we can—if we will—put this all together and realize that in   20
our kind of civilization "a life for a life" need not mean destructive retribution, but instead the development of new forms of community in which, because all lives are valuable, what is emphasized is the prevention of crime and the pro-tection of all those who are vulnerable.

The first step is to realize that in our society we have permitted the kinds of   21
vulunerability that characterize the victims of violent crime and have ignored, where we could, the hostility and alienation that enter into the making of violent criminals. No rational person condones violent crime, and I have no patience with sentimental attitudes toward violent criminals. But it is time that we open our eyes to the conditions that foster violence and that ensure the existence of easily recognizable victims.

Americans respond generously—if not always wisely—to the occurrence of   22
natural catastrophes. But except where we are brought face to face with an unhappy individual or a family in trouble, we are turned off by the humanly far more desperate social catastrophes of children who are trashed by the schools—and the local community—where they should be learning for them-selves what it means and how it feels to be a valued human being. We demean the men and women who are overwhelmed by their inability to meet their responsibilities to one another or even to go it alone, and we shut out awareness of the fate of the unskilled, the handicapped and the barely tolerated elderly. As our own lives have become so much more complex and our social ties extraordinarily fragile, we have lost any sense of community with others whose problems and difficulties and catastrophes are not our own.

We do know that human lives are being violated—and not only by criminals.   23
But at least we can punish criminals. That is a stopgap way. But it is not the way out of our dilemma.

We also know that in any society, however organized, security rests on   24
accepted participation—on what I have called here a sense of community in which everyone shares.

Up to the present, the responsibility for working out and maintaining the   25
principles on which any code of law must depend and for the practical admin-istration of justice has been primarily a male preoccupation. At best, women working within this framework have been able sometimes to modify and some-times to mitigate the working of the system of law.

Now, however, if the way out is for us to place the occurrence of crime and   26
the fate of the victim and of the criminal consciously within the context of our way of living and our view of human values, then I believe liberated women have a major part to play and a wholly new place to create for themselves in public life as professional women, as volunteers and as private citizens con-cerned with the quality of life in our nation. For it is women who have constantly had to visualize in personal, human terms the relationships between the inti-mate details of living and the setting in which living takes place. And it is this kind of experience that we shall need in creating new kinds of community.

Women working in new kinds of partnership with men should be able to   27
bring fresh thinking into law and the administration of justice with a greater
awareness of the needs of individuals at different stages of life and the poten-
tialities of social institutions in meeting those needs. What we shall be working
toward is a form of deterrence based not on fear of punishment—which we
know is ineffective, even when the punishment is the threat of death—but on
a shared way of living.

It will be a slow process at best to convince our fellow citizens that justice   28
and a decline in violence can be attained only by the development of communities in which the elderly and children, families and single persons, the gifted,
the slow and the handicapped can have a meaningful place and live with dignity
and in which rights and responsibilities are aspects of each other. And I believe
that we can make a start only if we have a long view, but know very well that
what we can do today and tomorrow and next year will not bring us to utopia.
We cannot establish instant security; we can only build for it step by step.

We must also face the reality that as far as we can forsee there will always   29
be a need for places of confinement—prisons of different kinds, to be frank—
where individuals will have to be segregated for short periods, for longer periods or even, for some, for a whole lifetime. The fear that the violent person
will be set free in our communities (as we all know happens all too often under
our present system of law) is an important component in the drive to
strengthen—certainly not to abolish—the death penalty. For their own protection as well as that of others, the few who cannot control their violent impulses
and, for the time being, the larger number who have become hopelessly violent
must be sequestered.

But we shall have to reconsider the whole question of what it means to be   30
confined under some form of restraint, whether for a short period or for a
lifetime. Clearly, prisons can no longer be set apart from the world. Prisoners
must have some real and enduring relationship to a wider community if they
are to have and exercise human rights. Whether as a way station or as a
permanent way of living for a few persons, prison life must in some way be
meaningful.

There is today a Prisoners Union, organized by former prisoners as well as a   31
variety of local unions within many prisons. We shall have to draw on the
knowledge and experience of groups of this kind. Here again I believe that
women, who have not been regularly and professionally involved in traditional
prison practices, may be freer to think and construct new practices than male
experts working alone.

The tasks are urgent and difficult. Realistically we know we cannot abolish   32
crime. But we can abolish crude and vengeful treatment of crime. We can
abolish—as a nation, not just state by state—capital punishment. We can accept the fact that prisoners, convicted criminals, are hostages to our own human failures to develop and support a decent way of living. And we can accept
the fact that we are responsible to them, as to all living beings, for the protection
of society, and especially responsible for those among us who need protection
for the sake of society.

QUESTIONS FOR MEANING

1. In paragraph 3, Mead refers to "human rights" and implies that capital punishment is a form of violence that violates these rights. What does she mean by this? Define "human rights" in your own words.
2. Why does Mead believe that women should be especially important in the movement to reform American justice?
3. Mead argues that "human lives are being violated—and not only by criminals." What does it mean to violate human life? Who does it besides criminals?
4. In her concluding paragraph, Mead argues that convicted criminals "are hostages to our own human failures to develop and support a decent way of living." Do you agree with this? If so, how would you define the "new forms of community" that Mead calls for?
5. Vocabulary: arbitrary (7), constituents (10), mitigating (10), discretionary (10), ambiguous (16), utopia (28), and sequestered (29).

QUESTIONS ABOUT STRATEGY

1. Is this essay addressed primarily to an audience of women? Does Mead's sense of audience limit the effectiveness of her argument?
2. Why does Mead devote paragraphs 6–17 to summarizing the history of capital punishment in America? Did you find this summary useful in understanding her argument?
3. In paragraphs 18 and 19, Mead contrasts people who favor capital punishment with people who oppose it. Does this comparison help or hurt her case?
4. Why does Mead link the rights of prisoners to "the rights of the poor, the unemployed and the unemployable?"
5. At what points in her essay does Mead claim to be writing objectively and realistically? Why did she feel it was necessary to reassure her audience in this way?

ERNEST VAN DEN HAAG

The Collapse of the Case Against Capital Punishment

Born in the Netherlands, Ernest van den Haag (b. 1914) came to the United States in 1940. A practicing psychoanalyst, he has taught sociology and criminal justice at Harvard, Yale, Columbia, and the New School for Social Research. Through numerous articles and many books, he has established himself as a conservative ideologue who is willing to take unpopular stands and argue articulately for them. His books include Passion and Social Restraint *(1963),* The Jewish Mystique *(1969),* Political Violence and Civil Disobedience *(1972), and* Punishing Criminals: Concerning a Very Old and Painful Question *(1975). The following essay originally appeared in the* National Review, *to which van den Haag is a regular contributor. As you read it, you should note the systematic way in which van den Haag tries to respond to all the arguments that have been made against capital punishment.*

Three questions about the death penalty so overlap that they must each be   1
answered. I shall ask seriatim: Is the death penalty constitutional? Is it useful?
Is it morally justifiable?*

I. The Constitutional Question

The Fifth Amendment states that no one shall be "deprived of life, liberty, or   2
property without due process of law," implying a "due process of law" to deprive persons of life. The Eighth Amendment prohibits "cruel and unusual
punishment." It is unlikely that this prohibition was meant to supersede the
Fifth Amendment, since the amendments were simultaneously enacted in
1791.[1]

The Fourth Amendment, enacted in 1868, reasserted and explicitly   3
extended to the states the implied authority to "deprive of life, liberty, or
property" by "due process of law." Thus, to regard the death penalty as unconstitutional one must believe that the standards which determine what is "cruel
and unusual" have so evolved since 1868 as to prohibit now what was authorized then, and that the Constitution authorizes the courts to overrule laws in
the light of *new* moral standards. What might these standards be? And what
shape must their evolution take to be constitutionally decisive?

---

*This is a greatly revised version of a paper first delivered at a symposium sponsored by the Graduate School of
Criminal Justice and the Criminal Justice Research Center of Albany, N.Y., in April 1977.

[1]Apparently the punishment must be both—else cruel *or* unusual would have done. Historically it appears that
punishments were prohibited if unusual in 1791 *and* cruel: the Framers did want to prohibit punishments, even
cruel ones, only if already unusual in 1791; they did prohibit new (unusual) punishments if cruel. The Eighth
Amendment was not meant to apply to the death penalty in 1791 since it was not unusual then; nor was the
Eighth Amendment intended to be used against capital punishment in the future, regardless of whether it may
have come to be considered cruel: it is neither a new penalty nor one unusual in 1791.

Consensus. A moral consensus, intellectual or popular, could have evolved   4
to find execution "cruel and unusual." It did not. Intellectual opinion is divided.
Polls suggest that most people would vote for the death penalty. Congress
recently has legislated the death penalty for skyjacking under certain conditions. The representative assemblies of two-thirds of the states did re-enact
capital punishment when previous laws were found constitutionally defective.[2]

If, however, there were a consensus against the death penalty, the Consti-   5
tution expects the political process, rather than judicial decisions, to reflect it.
Courts are meant to interpret the laws made by the political process and to set
constitutional limits to it—not to replace it by responding to a presumed moral
consensus. Surely the "cruel and unusual" phrase was not meant to authorize
the courts to become legislatures.[3] Thus, neither a consensus of moral opinion
nor a moral discovery by judges is meant to be disguised as a constitutional
interpretation. Even when revealed by a burning bush, new moral norms were
not meant to become constitutional norms by means of court decisions.[4] To be
sure, the courts in the past have occasionally done away with obsolete kinds of
punishment—but never in the face of legislative and popular opposition and
re-enactment. Abolitionists constantly press the courts now to create rather
than to confirm obsolescence. That courts are urged to do what so clearly is for
voters and lawmakers to decide suggests that the absence of consensus for
abolition is recognized by the opponents of capital punishment. What then can
the phrase "cruel and unusual punishment" mean today?

"Cruel" may be understood to mean excessive—punitive without, or be-   6
yond, a rational-utilitarian purpose. Since capital punishment excludes rehabil-
itation and is not needed for incapacitation, the remaining rational-utilitarian
purpose would be deterrence, the reduction of the rate at which the crime
punished is committed by others. I shall consider this reduction below. Here I
wish to note that, if the criterion for the constitutionality of any punishment
were an actual demonstration of its rational-utilitarian effectiveness, all legal
punishments would be in as much constitutional jeopardy as the death penalty.
Are fines for corporations deterrent? rehabilitative? incapacitative? Is a jail
term for marijuana possession? Has it ever been established that ten years in
prison are doubly as deterrent as five, or at least sufficiently more deterrent? (I
don't pretend to know what "sufficiently" might mean: whether 10 percent or
80 per cent added deterrence would warrant 100 per cent added severity.)

The Constitution certainly does not require a demonstration of rational-   7
utilitarian effects for any punishment. Such a demonstration so far has not been

---

[2]There may be a consensus against the death penalty among the college educated. If so, it demonstrates a) the
power of indoctrination wielded by sociologists; b) the fact that those who are least threatened by violence are
most inclined to do without the death penalty. College graduates are less often threatened by murder than the
uneducated.

[3]See Chief Justice Burger dissenting in *Furman:* "In a democratic society legislatures not courts are constituted
to respond to the will and consequently the moral values of the people."

[4]The First Amendment might be invoked against such sources of revelation. When specific laws do not suffice to
decide a case, courts, to be sure, make decisions based on general legal principles. But the death penalty (as
distinguished from applications) raises no serious legal problem.

available. To demand it for one penalty—however grave—and not for others, when it is known that no such demonstration is available, or has been required hitherto for any punishment, seems unjustified. Penalties have always been regarded as constitutional if they can be plausibly intended (rather than demonstrated) to be effective (useful), and if they are not grossly excessive, i.e., unjust.

Justice, a rational but non-utilitarian purpose of punishment, requires that   8
it be proportioned to the felt gravity of the crime. Thus, constitutional justice authorizes, even calls for, a higher penalty the graver the crime. One cannot demand that this constitutionally required escalation stop short of the death penalty unless one furnishes positive proof of its irrationality by showing injustice, i.e., disproportionality (to the felt gravity of the crime punished or to other punishments of similar crimes), as well as ineffectiveness, i.e., uselessness in reducing the crime rate. There is no proof of cruelty here in either sense.

"*Unusual*" is generally interpreted to mean either randomly capricious and   9
therefore unconstitutional, or capricious in a biased, discriminatory way, so as particularly to burden specifiable groups, and therefore unconstitutional. (Random arbitrariness might violate the Eighth, biased arbitrariness the Fourteenth Amendment, which promises "the equal protection of the laws.") Apart from the historical interpretation noted above (Footnote 1), "unusual" seems to mean "unequal" then. The dictionary equivalent—"rare"—seems to be regarded as relevant only inasmuch as it implies "unequal." Indeed it is hard to see why rarity should be objectionable otherwise.

For the sake of argument, let me grant that either or both forms of capri-   10
ciousness prevail[5] and that they are less tolerable with respect to the death penalty than with respect to milder penalties—which certainly are not meted out less capriciously. However prevalent, neither form of capriciousness would argue for abolishing the death penalty. Capriciousness is not inherent in that penalty, or in any penalty, but occurs in its distribution. Therefore, the remedy lies in changing the laws and procedures which distribute the penalty. It is the process of distribution which is capable of discriminating, not that which it distributes.

Unavoidable capriciousness. If capricious distribution places some   11
convicts, or groups of convicts, at an unwarranted disadvantage,[6] can it be remedied enough to satisfy the Eighth and Fourteenth Amendments? Some capriciousness is unavoidable because decisions of the criminal justice system necessarily rest on accidental factors at many points, such as the presence or absence of witnesses to an act; or the cleverness or clumsiness of police officers who exercise their discretion in arresting suspects and seizing evidence. All court decisions must rest on the available and admissible evidence for, rather

---

[5]Attention should be drawn to John Hagan's "Extralegal Attributes and Criminal Sentencing" (*Law and Society Review*, Spring 1974), which throws doubt on much of the discrimination which sociologists have found.

[6]I am referring throughout to discrimination among those already convicted of capital crimes. That discrimination can be tested. However, the fact that a higher proportion of blacks, or poor people, than of whites, or rich people, are found guilty of capital crimes does not *ipso facto* indicate discrimination, any more than does the fact that a comparatively high proportion of blacks or poor people become professional baseball players or boxers.

than the actuality of, guilt. Availability of evidence is necessarily accidental to the actuality of whatever it is that the evidence is needed for. Accident is the capriciousness of fate.

Now, if possible without loss of other desiderata, accident and human capri- 12
ciousness should be minimized. But, obviously, discretionary judgments cannot be avoided altogether. The Framers of the Constitution were certainly aware of the unavoidable elements of discretion which affect all human decisions, including those of police officers, of prosecutors, and of the courts. Because it always was unavoidable, discretion no more speaks against the constitutionality of the criminal justice system or of any of its penalties now than it did when the Constitution was written—unless something has evolved since, to make unavoidable discretion, tolerable before, intolerable now, at least for the death penalty. I know of no such evolution; and I would think it was up to the legislative branch of government to register it had it occurred.

The Constitution, though it enjoins us to minimize capriciousness, does not 13
enjoin a standard of unattainable perfection or exclude penalties because that standard has not been attained.[7] Actually, modern legislative trends hitherto have favored enlargement of discretion in the judicial process. I have always thought that enlargement to be excessive, immoral, irrational, and possibly unconstitutional—even when not abused for purposes of discrmination. Yet, though we should not enlarge it *praeter necessitatem*, some discretion is unavoidable and even desirable, and no reason for giving up any punishment.

Avoidable capriciousness. Capriciousness should be prevented by abolish- 14
ing penalties capriciously distributed only in one case: when it is so unavoidable and so excessive that penalties are randomly distributed between the guilty and the innocent. When that is not the case, the abuses of discretion which lead to discrimination against particular groups of defendants or convicts certainly require correction, but not abolition of the penalty abused by maldistribution.

II. Preliminary Moral Issues

Justice and equality. Regardless of constitutional interpretation, the mo- 15
rality and legitimacy of the abolitionist argument from capriciousness, or discretion, or discrimination, would be more persuasive if it were alleged that those selectively executed are not guilty. But the argument merely maintains that some other guilty but more favored persons, or groups, escape the death penalty. This is hardly sufficient for letting anyone else found guilty escape the penalty. On the contrary, that some guilty persons or groups elude it argues for extending the death penalty to them. Surely "due process of law" is meant to do justice; and "the equal protection of the law" is meant to extend justice equally to all. Nor do I read the Constitution to command us to prefer equality to justice. When we clamor for "equal justice for all" it is justice which is to be

---

[7]Although this is the burden of Charles Black's *Capital Punishment: The Inevitability of Caprice and Mistake* (Norton, 1974), *Codex ipsus loquitur.*

equalized and extended, and which therefore is the prior desideratum, not to be forsaken and replaced by equality but rather to be extended.

Justice requires punishing the guilty—as many of the guilty as possible, even if only some can be punished—and sparing the innocent—as many of the innocent as possible, even if not all are spared. Morally, justice must always be preferred to equality. It would surely be wrong to treat everybody with equal injustice in preference to meting out justice at least to some. Justice then cannot ever permit sparing some guilty persons, or punishing some innocent ones, for the sake of equality—because others have been unjustly spared or punished. In practice, penalties never could be applied if we insisted that they cannot be inflicted on any guilty person unless we can make sure that they are equally applied to all other guilty persons. Anyone familiar with law enforcement knows that punishments can be inflicted only on an unavoidably capricious, at best a random, selection of the guilty. I see no more merit in the attempt to persuade the courts to let all capital-crime defendants go free of capital punishment because some have wrongly escaped it than I see in an attempt to persuade the courts to let all burglars go because some have wrongly escaped imprisonment. 16

Although it hardly warrants serious discussion, the argument from capriciousness looms large in briefs and decisions because for the last seventy years courts have tried—unproductively—to prevent errors of procedure, or of evidence collection, or of decision-making, by the paradoxical method of letting defendants go free as a punishment, or warning, or deterrent, to errant law enforcers. The strategy admittedly never has prevented the errors it was designed to prevent—although it has released countless guilty persons. But however ineffective it be, the strategy had a rational purpose. The rationality, on the other hand, of arguing that a penalty must be abolished because of allegations that some guilty persons escape it, is hard to fathom—even though the argument was accepted by some Justices of the Supreme Court. 17

The essential moral question. Is the death penalty morally just and/or useful? This is the essential moral, as distinguished from constitutional, question. Discrimination is irrelevant to this moral question. If the death penalty were distributed quite equally and uncapriciously and with superhuman perfection to all the guilty, but was morally unjust, it would remain unjust in each case. Contrariwise, if the death penalty is morally just, however discriminatorily applied to only some of the guilty, it does remain just in each case in which it is applied. Thus, if it were applied exclusively to guilty males, and never to guilty females, the death penalty, though unequally applied, would remain just. For justice consists in punishing the guilty and sparing the innocent, and its equal extension, though desirable, is not part of it. It is part of equality, not of justice (or injustice), which is what equality equalizes. The same consideration would apply if some benefit were distributed only to males but not equally to deserving females. The inequality would not argue against the benefit, or against distribution to deserving males, but rather for distribution to equally deserving females. Analogously, the nondistribution of the death penalty to guilty females would argue for applying it to them as well, and not against applying it to guilty males. 18

The utilitarian (political) effects of unequal justice may well be detrimental   19
to the social fabric because they outrage our passion for equality, particularly
for equality before the law. Unequal justice is also morally repellent. Nonetheless unequal justice is justice still. What is repellent is the incompleteness, the
inequality, not the justice. The guilty do not become innocent or less deserving
of punishment because others escaped it. Nor does any innocent deserve punishment because others suffer it. Justice remains just, however unequal, while
injustice remains unjust, however equal. However much each is desired, justice
and equality are not identical. Equality before the law should be extended and
enforced, then—but not at the expense of justice.

Maldistribution among the guilty: a sham argument. Capriciousness, at   20
any rate, is used as a sham argument against capital punishment by all abolitionists I have ever known. They would oppose the death penalty if it could be
meted out without any discretion whatsoever. They would oppose the death
penalty in a homogeneous country without racial discrimination. And they
would oppose the death penalty if the incomes of these executed and of those
spared were the same. Abolitionists oppose the death penalty, not its possible
maldistribution. They should have the courage of their convictions.

Maldistribution between the guilty and the innocent: another sham ar-   21
gument. What about persons executed in error? The objection here is not that
some of the guilty get away, but that some of the innocent do not—a matter
far more serious than discrimination among the guilty. Yet, when urged by
abolitionists, this too is a sham argument, as are all distributional arguments.
For abolitionists are opposed to the death penalty for the guilty as much as for
the innocent. Hence, the question of guilt, if at all relevant to their position,
cannot be decisive for them. Guilt is decisive only to those who urge the death
penalty for the guilty. They must worry about distribution—part of the justice
they seek.

Miscarriages of justice. The execution of innocents believed guilty is a   22
miscarriage of justice which must be opposed whenever detected. But such
miscarriages of justice do not warrant abolition of the death penalty. Unless the
moral drawbacks of an activity or practice, which include the possible death of
innocent bystanders, outweigh the moral advantages, which include the innocent lives that might be saved by it, the activity is warranted. Most human
activities—construction, manufacturing, automobile and air traffic, sports, not
to speak of wars and revolutions—cause the death of some innocent bystanders. Nevertheless, if the advantages sufficiently outweigh the disadvantages,
human activities, including those of the penal system with all its punishments,
are morally justified. Consider now the advantages in question.

III. Deterrence

New evidence. Is there evidence for the usefulness of the death penalty in   23
securing the life of the citizens? Researchers in the past found no statistical
evidence for the effects sought: i.e., marginal deterrent effects, deterrent effects over and above those of alternative sanctions. However, in the last few

years new and more sophisticated research has led, for instance, Professor Isaac Ehrlich to conclude that over the period 1933–1969, "an additional execution per year...may have resulted on the average in seven or eight fewer murders."[8] Other investigators have confirmed Ehrlich's tentative results. Not surprisingly, refutations have been attempted, and Professor Ehrlich has answered them. He also published a new cross-sectional analysis of the data which confirms the conclusions of his original (time-series) study.[9] The matter will remain controversial for some time,[10] but two tentative conclusions can be drawn with some confidence by now. First, Ehrlich has shown that previous investigations, which did not find deterrent effects of the death penalty, suffer from fatal defects. Second, there is now some likelihood—much more than hitherto—of demonstrating marginal deterrent effects statistically.

The choice. Thus, with respect to deterrence, we must choose 1) to trade   24
the certain shortening of the life of a convicted murderer for the survival of between seven and eight innocent victims whose future murder by others may be less likely if the convicted murderer is executed. Or 2) to trade the certain lengthening of the life of a convicted murderer for the possible loss of the lives of between seven and eight innocent victims, who may be more likely to be murdered by others because of our failure to execute the convicted murderer.[11]

If we were certain that executions have a zero marginal effect, they could   25
not be justified in deterrent terms. But even the pre-Ehrlich investigations never did demonstrate this. They merely found that an above-zero effect cannot be demonstrated statistically. While we do not know at present the degree of confidence with which we can assign an above-zero marginal deterrent effect to executions, we can be more confident than in the past. It seems morally indefensible to let convicted murderers survive at the probable—even at the merely possible—expense of the lives of innocent victims who might have been spared had the murderers been executed.

Non-deterrence as a sham argument. Most of the studies purporting to   26
show that capital punishment produces no added deterrence, or that it cannot be shown to do so, were made by abolitionists, such as Professor Thorsten Sellin. They were used to show the futility of the death penalty. Relying on their

[8]"The Deterrent Effect of Capital Punishment: A Question of Life and Death." *American Economic Review,* June 1975. In the period studied capital punishment was already infrequent and uncertain. Its deterrent effect might be greater when more frequently imposed for capital crimes, so that a prospective offender would feel more certain of it.

[9]See *Journal of Legal Studies,* January 1977; *Journal of Political Economy,* June 1977; and (this is the cross-sectional analysis) *American Economic Review,* June 1977.

[10]*Per contra* see Brian Forst in *Minnesota Law Review,* May 1977, and *Deterrence and Incapacitation* (National Academy of Sciences, Washington, D.C., 1978). By now statistical analyses of the effects of the death penalty have become a veritable cottage industry. This has happened since Ehrlich found deterrent effects. No one much bothered when Thorsten Sellin found none. Still, it is too early for more than tentative conclusions. The two papers mentioned above are replied to, more than adequately in my view, in Isaac Ehrlich's "Fear of Deterrence," *Journal of Legal Studies,* June 1977.

[11]I thought that prudence as well as morality commanded us to choose the first alternative even when I believed that the degree of probability and the extent of deterrent effects might remain unknown. (See my "On Deterrence and the Death Penalty," *Journal of Criminal Law, Criminology, and Police Science,* June 1969.) That probability is more likely to become known now and to be greater than was apparent a few years ago.

intuition as well as on these studies, many abolitionists still are convinced that the death penalty is no more deterrent than life imprisonment. And they sincerely believe that the failure of capital punishment to produce additional deterrence argues for abolishing it. However, the more passionate and committed abolitionists use the asserted ineffectiveness of the death penalty as a deterrent as a sham argument—just as they use alleged capriciousness and maldistribution in application. They use the argument for debating purposes—but actually would abolish the death penalty even if it were an effective deterrent, just as they would abolish the death penalty if it were neither discriminatorily nor otherwise maldistributed.

Professors Charles Black (Yale Law School) and Hugo Adam Bedau (Tufts, Philosophy) are both well known for their public commitment to abolition of the death penalty, attested to by numerous writings. At a symposium held on October 15, 1977 at the Arizona State University at Tempe, Arizona, they were asked to entertain the hypothesis—whether or not contrary to fact—that the death penalty is strongly deterrent over and above alternative penalties: Would they favor abolition in the face of conclusive proof of a strong deterrent effect over and above that of alternative penalties? Both gentlemen answered affirmatively. They were asked whether they would still abolish the death penalty if they knew that abolition (and replacement by life imprisonment) would increase the homicide rate by 10 per cent, 20 per cent, 50 per cent, 100 per cent, or 1,000 per cent. Both gentlemen continued to answer affirmatively. 27

I am forced to conclude that Professors Black and Bedau think the lives of convicted murderers (however small their number) are more worth preserving than the lives of an indefinite number of innocent victims (however great their number). Or, the principle of abolition is more important to them than the lives of any number of innocent murder victims who would be spared if convicted murderers were executed. 28

I have had occasion subsequently to ask former Attorney General Ramsey Clark the same questions; he answered as Professors Black and Bedau did, stressing that nothing could persuade him to favor the death penalty—however deterrent it might be. (Mr. Clark has kindly permitted me to quote his view here.) 29

Now, Professors Black and Bedau and Mr. Clark do *not* believe that the death penalty adds deterrence. They do not believe therefore—regardless of the evidence—that abolition would cause an increase in the homicide rate. But the question they were asked, and which—after some dodging—they answered forthrightly, had nothing to do with the acceptance or rejection of the deterrent effect of the death penalty. It was a hypothetical question: If it were deterrent, would you still abolish the death penalty? Would you still abolish it if it were very deterrent, so that abolition would lead to a quantum jump in the murder rate? They answered affirmatively. 30

These totally committed abolitionists, then, are not interested in deterrence. They claim that the death penalty does not add to deterrence only as a sham argument. Actually, whether or not the death penalty deters is, to them, irrelevant. The intransigence of these committed humanitarians is puzzling as well as inhumane. Passionate ideological commitments have been known to have 31 such effects. These otherwise kind and occasionally reasonable persons do not want to see murderers executed ever—however many innocent lives can be saved thereby. *Fiat injustica, pereat humanitas.*

Experiments? In principle one could experiment to test the deterrent effect   32
of capital punishment. The most direct way would be to legislate the death penalty for certain kinds of murder if committed on weekdays, but never on Sunday. Or, on Monday, Wednesday, and Friday, and not on other days; on other days, life imprisonment would be the maximum sentence. (The days could be changed around every few years to avoid possible bias.) I am convinced there will be fewer murders on death-penalty than on life-imprisonment days. Unfortunately the experiment faces formidable obstacles.[12]

The burden of proof of usefulness. Let me add a common-sense remark.   33
Our penal system rests on the proposition that more severe penalties are more deterrent than less severe penalties. We assume, rightly, I believe, that a $5 fine deters rape less than a $500 fine, and that the threat of five years in prison will deter more than either fine.[13] This assumption of the penal system rests on the common experience that, once aware of them, people learn to avoid natural dangers the more likely these are to be injurious and the more severe the likely injuries. Else the survival of the human race would be hard to explain. People endowed with ordinary common sense (a class that includes a modest but significant number of sociologists) have found no reason why behavior with respect to legal dangers should differ from behavior with respect to natural dangers. Indeed, it doesn't. Hence, all legal systems proportion threatened penalties to the gravity of crimes, both to do justice and to achieve deterrence in proportion to that gravity.

But if, *ceteris paribus,* the more severe the penalty the greater the deter-   34
rent effect, then the most severe available penalty—the death penalty—would have the greatest deterrent effect. Arguments to the contrary assume either that capital crimes never are deterrable (sometimes merely because not all capital crimes have been deterred), or that, beyond life imprisonment, the deterrent effect of added severity is necessarily zero. Perhaps. But the burden of proof must be borne by those who presume to have located the point of zero marginal returns before the death penalty.

The threat of death needed in special circumstances. Another common-   35
sense observation. Without the death penalty, we necessarily confer immunity on just those persons most likely to be in need of deterrent threats: thus, prisoners serving life sentences can kill fellow prisoners or guards with impunity. Prison wardens are unlikely to be able to prevent violence in prisons as long

---

[12]Though it would isolate deterrent effects of the punishment from incapacitating effects, and also from the effect of Durkheimian "normative validation" when it does not depend on threats. Still, it is not acceptable to our sense of justice that people guilty of the same crime would deliberately get different punishments and that the difference would be made to depend deliberately on a factor irrelevant to the nature of the crime or of the criminal.

[13]As indicated before, demonstrations are not available for the exact addition to deterrence of each added degree of severity in various circumstances, and with respect to various acts. We have coasted so far on a sea of plausible assumptions. (It is not contended, of course, that the degree of severity alone determines deterrent effects. Other factors may reinforce or offset the effect of severity, be it on the motivational [incentive] side, or as added costs and risks.)

as they give humane treatment to inmates and have no serious threats of additional punishment available for the murderers among them who are already serving life sentences. I cannot see the moral or utilitarian reasons for giving permanant immunity to homicidal life prisoners, thereby endangering the other prisoners and the guards, in effect preferring the life prisoners to their victims who *could* be punished if they murdered.

Outside prison an offender who expects a life sentence for his offense may   36
murder his victim, or witnesses, or the arresting officer, to improve his chances of escaping. He could not be threatened with an additional penalty for his additional crime—an open invitation. Only the death penalty could deter in such cases.[14] If there is but a possibility that it will, we should retain it. But I believe there is a *probability* that the threat of the death penalty will deter.

Reserved for the worst crimes. However, effective deterrence requires that   37
the threat of the ultimate penalty be reserved for the worst crime from which the offender may be deterred by that threat. Hence, the extreme punishment should not be prescribed when the offender, because already threatened by it, might feel he can add further crimes with impunity. Thus, rape, or kidnapping, should not incur the death penalty, while killing the victim of either crime should.[15] (The death penalty for rape may actually function as an incentive to murder the victim/witness.) This may not stop an Eichmann after his first murder, but it will stop most people before. To be sure, an offender not deterred from murdering one victim by the threat of execution is unlikely to be deterred from additional murders by further threats. The range of effective punishments is not infinite; on the contrary, it is necessarily more restricted than the range of possible crimes. Some offenders cannot be deterred by any threat. But most people can be; and most people respond to the size of the threat addressed to them. Since death is the ultimate penalty—the greatest threat available— it must be reserved for the ultimate crime even though it cannot always prevent it.

IV. Some Popular Arguments

Consider now some popular arguments against capital punishment.   38

Barbarization. According to Beccaria, with the death penalty the "laws   39
which punish homicide . . . themselves commit it," thus giving "an example of barbarity." Those who speak of "legalized murder" use an oxymoronic phrase

---

[14]Particularly since he, unlike the person already in custody, may have much to gain from his additional crime (see Footnote 18).

[15]The Supreme Court has decided that capital punishment for rape (at least of adults) is "cruel and unusual" (*Coker* v. *Georgia,* 1977). For the reasons stated in the text, I welcome the decision—but not the justification given by the Supreme Court. The penalty may indeed be as excessive as the court feels it is, but not in the constitutional sense of being irrationally or extravagantly so, and thus contrary to the Eighth Amendment. The seriousness of the crime of rape and the appropriateness of the death penalty for it are matters for political rather than judicial institutions to decide. I should vote against the death penalty for rape—and not only for the reasons stated in the text above; but the Court should have left the matter to the vote of the citizens.

The charge of racially discriminatory application was most often justified when the penalty was inflicted for rape. Yet I doubt that the charge will be dropped, or that the agitation against the death penalty will stop, once it is no longer inflicted for rape. Discrimination never was more than a pretext used by abolitionists.

to echo this allegation. However, punishments—fines, incarcerations, or executions—although often physically identical to the crimes punished, are neither crimes, nor their moral equivalent. The difference between crimes and lawful acts, including punishments, is not physical, but legal: crimes differ from other acts by being unlawful. Driving a stolen car is a crime, though not physically distinguishable from driving a car lawfully owned. Unlawful imprisonment and kidnapping need not differ physically from the lawful arrest and incarceration used to punish unlawful imprisonment and kidnapping. Finally, whether a lawful punishment gives an "example of barbarity" depends on how the moral difference between crime and punishment is perceived. To suggest that its physical quality, *ipso facto,* morally disqualifies the punishment is to assume what is to be shown.

It is quite possible that all displays of violence, criminal or punitive, influence   40
people to engage in unlawful imitations. This seems one good reason not to have public executions. But it does not argue against executions. Objections to displaying on TV the process of violently subduing a resistant offender do not argue against actually subduing him.[16] Arguments against the public display of vivisections, or of the effects of painful medications, do not argue against either. Arguments against the public display of sexual activity do not argue against sexual activity. Arguments against public executions, then, do not argue against executions.[17] The deterrent effect of punishments depends on their being known. But it does not depend on punishments being carried out publicly. The threat of imprisonment deters, but incarcerated persons are not on public display.

Crimes of passion. Abolitionists often maintain that most capital crimes are   41
"acts of passion" which a) could not be restrained by the threat of the death penalty, and b) do not deserve it morally even if other crimes might. It is not clear to me why a crime motivated by, say, sexual passion is morally less deserving of punishment than one motivated by passion for money. Is the sexual passion morally more respectable than others? or more gripping? or just more popular? Generally, is violence in personal conflicts morally more excusable than violence among people who do not know each other? A precarious case might be made for such a view, but I shall not attempt to make it.

Perhaps it is true, however, that many murders are irrational "acts of pas-   42
sion" which cannot be deterred by the threat of the death penalty. Either for this reason or because "crimes of passion" are thought less blameworthy than other homicides, most "crimes of passion" are not punishable by death now.[18]

But if most murders are irrational acts, it would therefore seem that the   43

---

[16]There is a good argument here against unnecessary public displays of violence. (See my "What to Do about TV Violence," *The Alternative,* August/September 1976).

[17]It may be noted that in Beccaria's time executions were regarded as public entertainments. *Tempora mutantur et nos mutamur in illis.*

[18]I have reservations on both these counts, being convinced that many crimes among relatives, friends, and associates are as blameworthy and as deterrable as crimes among strangers. Thus, major heroin dealers in New York are threatened with life imprisonment. In the absence of the death penalty they find it advantageous to have witnesses killed. Such murders surely are not acts of passion in the classical sense, though they occur among associates. They are, in practice, encouraged by the present penal law in New York.

traditional threat of the death penalty has succeeded in deterring most rational people, or most people when rational, from committing murder, and that the fear of the penalty continues to deter all but those who are so irrational that they cannot be deterred by any threat. Hardly a reason for abolishing the death penalty. Indeed, that capital crimes are committed mostly by irrational persons and only by some rational ones would suggest that more rational persons might commit these crimes if the penalty were lower. This hardly argues against capital punishment. Else we would have to abolish penalties whenever they succeed in deterring people. Yet abolitionists urge that capital punishment be abolished because capital crimes are most often committed by the irrational—as though deterring the rational is not quite enough.

Samuel Johnson. Finally, some observations on an anecdote reported by   44
Boswell and repeated ever since *ad nauseam.* Dr. Johnson found pickpockets active in a crowd assembled to see one of their number hanged. He concluded that executions do not deter. His conclusion does not follow from his observation.

1. Since the penalty Johnson witnessed was what pickpockets had expected   45
all along, they had no reason to reduce their activities. Deterrence is expected to increase (i.e., crime is expected to decrease) only when penalties do. It is unreasonable to expect people who entered a criminal occupation—e.g., that of pickpocket—fully aware of the risks, to be subsequently deterred by those risks if they are not increased. They will not be deterred unless the penalty becomes more severe, or is inflicted more often.

2. At most, a public execution could have had the deterrent effect on pick-   46
pockets expected by Dr. Johnson because of its visibility. But visibility may also have had a contrary effect: the spectacle of execution was probably more fascinating to the crowd than other spectacles; it distracted attention from the activities of pickpockets and thereby increased their opportunities more than other spectacles would. Hence, an execution crowd might have been more inviting to pickpockets than other crowds. (As mentioned before, deterrence depends on knowledge, but does not require visibility.)

3. Even when the penalty is greatly increased, let alone when it is un-   47
changed, the deterrent effect of penalties is usually slight with respect to those already engaged in criminal activities.[19] Deterrence is effective in the main by restraining people not as yet committed to a criminal occupation from entering it. This point bears some expansion.

The risk of penalty is the cost of crime offenders expect. When this cost (the   48
penalty multiplied by the risk of suffering it) is high enough, relative to the benefit the crime is expected to yield, the cost will deter a considerable number of people who would have entered a criminal occupation had the cost been lower. When the net benefit is very low, only those who have no other opportunities at all, or are irrationally attracted to it, will want to engage in an illegal activity such as picking pockets. In this respect the effects of the cost of crime

---

[19]The high degree of uncertainty and arbitrariness of penalization in Johnson's time may also have weakened deterrent effects. Witnessing an execution cannot correct this defect.

are not different from the effects of the cost of automobiles or movie tickets, or from the effects of the cost (effort, risks, and other disadvantages) of any activity relative to its benefits. When (comparative) net benefits decrease because of cost increases, so does the flow of new entrants. But those already in the occupation usually continue. *Habits, law-abiding or criminal, are less influenced by costs than habit formation is.* That is as true for the risk of penalties as for any other cost.

Most deterrence studies disregard the fact that the major effect of the legal   49
threat system is on habit formation rather than on habits formed. It is a long-rather than a short-run effect. By measuring only the short-run effects (on habits already formed) rather than the far more important long-run (habit-forming) effects of the threat system, such studies underrate the effectiveness of the deterrence.

4. Finally, Dr. Johnson did not actually address the question of the deterrent   50
effect of execution in any respect whatever. To do so he would have had to compare the number of pocket-picking episodes in the crowd assembled to witness the execution with the number of such episodes in a similar crowd assembled for some other purpose. He did not do so, probably because he thought that a deterrent effect occurs only if the crime is altogether eliminated. That is a common misunderstanding. But crime can only be reduced, not eliminated. However harsh the penalties there are always non-deterrables. Many, perhaps most, people can be deterred, but never all.

V. Final Moral Considerations

The motive of revenge. One objection to capital punishment is that it grati-   51
fies the desire for revenge, regarded as morally unworthy. The Bible has the Lord declare: "Vengeance is mine" (Romans 12:19). He thus legitimized vengeance and reserved it to Himself, probably because it would otherwise be disruptive. But He did not deprecate the desire for vengeance.

Indeed Romans 12:19 barely precedes Romans 13:4, which tells us that the   52
ruler "beareth not the sword in vain; for he is the minister of God, a revenger to execute wrath upon him that doeth evil." It is not unreasonable to interpret Romans 12:19 to suggest that revenge is to be delegated by the injured to the ruler, "the minister of God" who is "to execute wrath." The Bible also enjoins, "the murderer shall surely be put to death" (Numbers 35:16–18), recognizing that the death penalty can be warranted—whatever the motive. Religious tradition certainly suggests no less. However, since religion expects justice and vengeance in the world to come, the faithful may dispense with either in this world, and with any particular penalties—though they seldom have. But a secular state must do justice here and now—it cannot assume that another power, elsewhere, will do justice where its courts did not.

The motives for the death penalty may indeed include vengeance. Ven-   53
geance is a compensatory and psychological reparatory satisfaction for an injured party, group, or society. I do not see wherein it is morally blameworthy.

When regulated and controlled by law, vengeance is also socially useful: legal vengeance solidifies social solidarity against lawbreakers and probably is the only alternative to the disruptive private revenge of those who feel harmed. Abolitionists want to promise murderers that what they did to their victims will never be done to them. That promise strikes most people as psychologically incongruous. It is.

At any rate, vengeance is irrelevant to the function of the death penalty. It   54
must be justified independently, by its purpose, whatever the motive. An action, a rule, or a penalty cannot be justified or discredited by the motive for it. No rule should be discarded or regarded as morally wrong (or right) because of the motive of those who support it. Actions, rules, or penalties are justified not by the motives of supporters but by their purpose and by their effectiveness in achieving it without excessively impairing other objectives.[20] Capital punishment is warranted if it achieves its purpose—doing justice and deterring crime—regardless of whether or not it is motivated by vengeful feelings.

Characteristics. Before turning to its purely moral aspects, we must exam-   55
ine some specific characteristics of capital punishment. It is feared above all punishments because 1) it is not merely irreversible, as most other penalties are, but also irrevocable; 2) it hastens an event which, unlike pain, deprivation, or injury, is unique in every life and never has been reported on by anyone. Death is an experience that cannot actually be experienced and that ends all experience. Actually, being dead is no different from not being born—a (non) experience we all had before being born. But death is not so perceived. The process of dying, a quite different matter, is confused with it. In turn, dying is feared mainly because death is anticipated—even though death is feared because confused with dying. At any rate, the fear of death is universal and is often attached to the penalty that hastens it—as though without that penalty death would not come. 3) However, the penalty is feared for another reason as well. When death is imposed as a deliberate punishment by one's fellow men, it signifies a complete severing of human solidarity. The convict is explicitly and dramatically rejected by his fellow humans, found unworthy of their society, of sharing life with them. The rejection exacerbates the natural separation anxiety of those who expect imminent death, the fear of final annihilation. Inchoate as these characteristics are in most minds, the specific deterrent effect of executions depends on them, and the moral justification of the death penalty, above and beyond the deterrent effect, does no less.

Methodological aside. Hitherto I have relied on logic and fact. Without   56
relinquishing either, I must appeal to plausibility as well, as I turn to questions of morality unalloyed by other issues. For, whatever ancillary service facts and logic can render, what one is persuaded to accept as morally right or wrong depends on what appears to be plausible in the end. Outside the realm of morals one relies on plausibility only in the beginning.

---

[20]Different motives (the reason why something is done) may generate the same action (what is done), purpose, or intent, just as the same motive may lead to different actions.

The value of life. If there is nothing for the sake of which one may be put to   57
death, can there ever be anything worth risking one's life for? If there is nothing
worth dying for, is there any moral value worth living for? Is a life that cannot
be transcended by—and given up, or taken, for—anything beyond itself more
valuable than one that can be transcended? Can it be that existence, life itself,
is the highest moral value, never to be given up, or taken, for the sake of
anything? And, psychologically, does a social value system in which life itself,
however it is lived, becomes the highest of goods enhance the value of human
life or cheapen it? I shall content myself here with raising these questions.[21]

Homo homini res sacra. "The life of each man should be sacred to each   58
other man," the ancients tell us. They unflinchingly executed murderers.[22] They
realized it is not enough to proclaim the sacredness and inviolability of human
life. It must be secured as well, by threatening with the loss of their own life
those who violate what has been proclaimed as inviolable—the right of innocents to live. Else the inviolability of human life is neither credibly proclaimed
nor actually protected. No society can profess that the lives of its members are
secure if those who did not allow innocent others to continue living are themselves allowed to continue living—at the expense of the community. To punish
a murderer by incarcerating him as one does a pickpocket cannot but cheapen
human life. Murder differs in quality from other crimes and deserves, therefore,
a punishment that differs in quality from other punishments. There is a discontinuity. It should be underlined, not blurred.

If it were shown that no punishment is more deterrent than a trivial fine,   59
capital punishment for murder would remain just, even if not useful. For murder is not a trifling offense. Punishment must be proportioned to the gravity of
the crime, if only to denounce it and to vindicate the importance of the norm
violated. Wherefore all penal systems proportion punishments to crimes. The
worse the crime the higher the penalty deserved. Why not then the highest
penalty—death—for the worst crime—wanton murder? Those rejecting the
death penalty have the burden of showing that no crime ever deserves capital
punishment.[23]—a burden which they have not so far been willing to bear.

Abolitionists insist that we all have an imprescriptible right to live to our   60
natural term: if the innocent victim had a right to live, so does the murderer.
That takes egalitarianism too far for my taste. The crime sets victim and murderer apart; if the victim did, the murderer does not deserve to live. If innocents
are to be secure in their lives murderers cannot be. The thought that murderers

[21]Insofar as these questions are psychological, empirical evidence would not be irrelevant. But it is likely to be
evaluated in terms depending on moral views.

[22]Not always. On the disastrous consequences of periodic failure to do so, Sir Henry Maine waxes eloquent with
sorrow in his *Ancient Law* (pp. 408–9).

[23]One may argue that some crimes deserve more than execution and that the above reasoning would justify
punitive torture as well. Perhaps. But torture, unlike death, is generally rejected. Therefore penalties have been
reduced to a few kinds—fines, confinement, and execution. The issue is academic because, unlike the death
penalty, torture has become repulsive to us. (Some reasons for this public revulsion are listed in Chapter 17 of
my *Punishing Criminals*, Basic Books, 1975.) As was noted above the range of punishments is bound to be
more limited than the range of crimes. We do not accept some punishments, however much deserved they may
be.

are to be given as much right to live as their victims oppresses me. So does the thought that a Stalin, a Hitler, an Idi Amin should have as much right to live as their victims did.

Failure of nerve. Never to execute a wrongdoer, regardless of how de-   61
praved his acts, is to proclaim that no act can be so irredeemably vicious as to deserve death—that no human being can be wicked enough to be deprived of life. Who actually can believe that? I find it easier to believe that those who affect such a view suffer from a failure of nerve. They do not think themselves— and therefore anyone else—competent to decide questions of life and death. Aware of human frailty, they shudder at the gravity of the decision and refuse to make it. The irrevocability of a verdict of death is contrary to the modern spirit that likes to pretend that nothing ever is definitive, that everything is open-ended, that doubts must always be entertained and revisions must always remain possible. Such an attitude may be helpful to the reflections of inquiring philosophers and scientists; but it is not proper for courts. They must make final judgments beyond a reasonable doubt. They must decide. They can evade decisions on life and death only by giving up their paramount duties: to do justice, to secure the lives of the citizens, and to vindicate the norms society holds inviolable.

One may object that the death penalty either cannot actually achieve the   62
vindication of violated norms, or is not needed for it. If so, failure to inflict death on the criminal does not belittle the crime, or imply that the life of the criminal is of greater importance than the moral value he violated or the harm he did to his victim. But it is not so. In all societies the degree of social disapproval of wicked acts is expressed in the degree of punishment threatened.[24] Thus, punishments both proclaim and enforce social values according to the importance given to them. There is no other way for society to affirm its values. There is no other effective way of denouncing socially disapproved acts. To refuse to punish any crime with death is to suggest that the negative value of a crime can never exceed the positive value of the life of the person who committed it. I find that proposition quite implausible.

QUESTIONS FOR MEANING

1. What is the "burning bush" van den Haag refers to in paragraph 5? Is he being sarcastic?
2. Does van den Haag give adequate definition of "cruel" and "unusual" in paragraphs 6–9? Paraphrase what he says about these words.
3. Explain the meaning of "sham argument" in paragraphs 20, 21, and 26.
4. Van den Haag argues that "if the advantages sufficiently outweigh the disadvantages, human activities, including those of the penal system with all its punishments, are morally justified." Is this common sense or over-simplification?

---

[24]Social approval is usually not unanimous, and the system of rewards reflects it less.

5. Is van den Haag correct in arguing that many opponents of capital punishment would oppose it under any circumstances? Would you?
6. Why does van den Haag believe that capital punishment is an inappropriate penalty for rape and kidnapping?
7. In discussing the question of deterrence, van den Haag claims, "Habits, law-abiding or criminal, are less influenced by costs than habit formation is." Explain what he means by this.
8. Why does van den Haag believe that vengeance is "socially useful"?
9. Do you agree with van den Haag that murder differs from all other crimes? If you do, is it logical to argue that it should have a different punishment?
10. Vocabulary: obsolescence (5), consensus (5), plausibly (7), capriciously (10), detrimental (19), homogeneous (20), hypothetical (30), intransigence (31), impunity (35), oxymoronic (39), exacerbates (55), and ancillary (56).

QUESTIONS ABOUT STRATEGY

1. Van den Haag assumes that his audience has a good vocabulary and at least some knowledge of Latin. Consider his diction and the effect it has on his ability to persuade you. When he uses phrases like "rational utilitarian" in paragraph 6, and "above-zero marginal deterrent effect" in paragraph 25, does he impress you with his intelligence or confuse you with his jargon?
2. Why does van den Haag break his argument into five separate subsections? Was this a wise decision?
3. Van den Haag tries to offer an argument that covers every point his opponents might raise. Does he go into too much detail? If so, what parts of the essay would you condense?
4. Does van den Haag persuade you that Prof. Ehrlich's research deserves to be taken seriously?
5. Many writers have claimed that the Bible supports their point of view. Is van den Haag's use of the Old Testament effective? Why does he limit himself to the Old Testament?
6. Toward the end of his essay, van den Haag claims that the first 55 paragraphs of his argument are based on "logic and fact." Is this true?

DAVID BRUCK
Decisions of Death

When the Supreme Court ruled against capital punishment in 1972, it did so because it believed that a penalty that is selectively applied amounts to "cruel and unusual punishment" which is prohibited by the Eighth Amendment. As Justice William O. Douglas wrote in his concurring opinion, "In a Nation committed to Equal Protection of the laws there is no permissible 'caste' aspect of law enforcement. Yet we know that the discretion of judges and juries in imposing the death penalty enables the penalty to be selectively applied, feeding prejudices against the accused if he is poor and despised, poor and lacking political clout, or if he is a member of a suspect or unpopular minority, and saving those who by social position may be in a more protected position." Although states that allow capital punishment have rewritten their laws since then, South Carolina attorney David Bruck has compiled evidence that suggests the death penalty is still unfair because it is still applied selectively. In his essay, which was first published in 1983, Bruck argues that capital punishment is a lottery rigged by race.

There are 1,150 men and 13 women awaiting execution in the United States.   1
It's not easy to imagine how many people 1,163 is. If death row were really a row, it would stretch for 1.3 miles, cell after six-foot-wide cell. In each cell, one person, sitting, pacing, watching TV, sleeping, writing letters. Locked in their cells nearly twenty-four hours a day, the condemned communicate with each other by shouts, notes, and hand-held mirrors, all with a casual dexterity that handicapped people acquire over time. Occasionally there is a break in the din of shouted conversations—a silent cell, its inhabitant withdrawn into a cocoon of madness. That's what death row would look like. That's what, divided up among the prisons of thirty-four states, it does look like.

This concentration of condemned people is unique among the democratic   2
countries of the world. It is also nearly double the number of prisoners who were on death row in 1972 when the Supreme Court, in *Furman* v. *Georgia,* averted a massive surge of executions by striking down all the nation's capital punishment laws.

But in another sense, death row is very small. If every one of these 1,163   3
inmates were to be taken out of his or her cell tomorrow and gassed, electro-cuted, hanged, shot, or injected, the total of convicted murderers imprisoned in this country would decline from some 33,526 (at last count) to 32,363—a reduction of a little over 3 percent. Huge as this country's death row population has become, it does not include—and has never included—more than a tiny fraction of those who are convicted of murder.

It falls to the judicial system of each of the thirty-eight states that retain   4
capital punishment to cull the few who are to die from the many who are convicted of murder. This selection begins with the crime itself, as the community and the press react with outrage or with indifference, depending on the

nature of the murder and the identity of the victim. With the arrest of a suspect, police and prosecutors must decide what charges to file, whether to seek the death penalty, and whether the defendant should be allowed to plea-bargain for his life. Most of these decisions can later be changed, so that at any point from arrest to trial the defendant's chances of slipping through the death penalty net depend on chance: the inclinations and ambitions of the local prosecutor, the legal and political pressures which impel him to one course of action or another, and the skill or incompetence of the court-appointed defense counsel.

In the courtroom, the defendant may be spared or condemned by the count- 5 less vagaries of the trial by jury. There are counties in each state where the juries almost always impose death, and counties where they almost never do. There are hanging judges and lenient judges, and judges who go one way or the other depending on who the victim's family happens to be, or the defendant's family, or who is prosecuting the case, or who is defending it.

Thus at each stage between arrest and sentence, more and more defendants 6 are winnowed out from the ranks of those facing possible execution: in 1979, a year which saw more than eighteen thousand arrests for intentional homicides and nearly four thousand murder convictions throughout the United States, only 159 defendants were added to death row. And even for those few who are condemned to die, there lies ahead a series of appeals which whittle down the number of condemned still further, sparing some and consigning others to death on the basis of appellate courts' judgments of the nuances of a trial judge's instructions to the jury, of whether the court-appointed defense lawyer had made the proper objections at the proper moments during the trial, and so on. By the time the appeals process has run its course, almost every murder defendant who faced the possibility of execution when he was first arrested has by luck, justice, or favor evaded execution, and a mere handful are left to die.

This process of selection is the least understood feature of capital punish- 7 ment. Because the media focus on the cases where death has been imposed and where the executions seem imminent, the public sees capital punishment not as the maze-like system that it is, but only in terms of this or that individual criminal, about to suffer just retribution for a particular crime. What we don't see in any of this now-familiar drama are hundreds of others whose crimes were as repugnant, but who are jailed for life or less instead of condemned to death. So the issues appear simple. The prisoner's guilt is certain. His crime is horrendous. Little knots of "supporters" light candles and hold vigils. His lawyers rush from court to court raising arcane new appeals.

The condemned man himself remembers the many points of his procession 8 through the judicial system at which he might have been spared, but was not. He knows, too, from his years of waiting in prison, that most of those who committed crimes like his have evaded the execution that awaits him. So do the prosecutors who have pursued him through the court system, and the judges who have upheld his sentence. And so do the defense lawyers, the ones glimpsed on the TV news in the last hours, exhausted and overwrought for reasons that, given their client's crimes, must be hard for most people to fathom.

I am one of those lawyers, and I know the sense of horror that propels those   9
last-minute appeals. It is closely related to the horror that violent crime awakens in all of us—the random kind of crime, the sniper in the tower or the gunman in the grocery store. The horror derives not from death, which comes to us all, but from death that is inflicted *at random*, for no reason, for being on the wrong subway platform or the wrong side of the street. Up close, that is what capital punishment is like. And that is what makes the state's inexorable, stalking pursuit of this or that particular person's life so chilling.

The lawyers who bring those eleventh-hour appeals know from their work   10
how many murderers are spared, how few are sentenced to die, and how chance and race decide which will be which. In South Carolina, where I practice law, murders committed during robberies may be punished by death. According to police reports, there were 286 defendants arrested for such murders from the time that South Carolina's death penalty law went into effect in 1977 until the end of 1981. (About a third of those arrests were of blacks charged with killing whites.) Out of all of those 286 defendants, the prosecution had sought the death penalty and obtained final convictions by the end of 1981 against 37. And of those 37 defendants, death sentences were imposed and affirmed on only 4; the rest received prison sentences. What distinguished those 4 defendants' cases was this: 3 were black, had killed white storeowners, and were tried by all-white juries; the fourth, a white, was represented at his trial by a lawyer who had never read the state's murder statute, had no case file and no office, and had refused to talk to his client for the last two months prior to the trial because he'd been insulted by the client's unsuccessful attempt to fire him.

If these four men are ultimately executed, the newspapers will report and   11
the law will record that they went to their deaths because they committed murder and robbery. But when so many others who committed the same crime were spared, it can truthfully be said only that these four men were *convicted* because they committed murder; they were *executed* because of race, or bad luck, or both.

If one believes, as many do, that murderers deserve whatever punishment   12
they get, then none of this should matter. But if the 1,163 now on death row throughout the United States had actually been selected by means of a lottery from the roughly 33,500 inmates now serving sentences for murder, most Americans, whatever their views on capital punishment as an abstract matter, would surely be appalled. This revulsion would be all the stronger if we limited the pool of those murderers facing execution by restricting it to blacks. Or if we sentenced people to die on the basis of the race of the *victim*, consigning to death only those—whatever their race—who have killed whites, and sparing all those who have killed blacks.

The reason why our sense of justice rebels at such ideas is not hard to   13
identify. Violent crime undermines the sense of order and shared moral values without which no society could exist. We punish people who commit such

crimes in order to reaffirm our standards of right and wrong, and our belief that life in society can be orderly and trusting rather than fearful and chaotic. But if the punishment itself is administered chaotically or arbitrarily, it fails in its purpose and becomes, like the crime which triggered it, just another spectacle of the random infliction of suffering—all the more terrifying and demoralizing because this time the random killer is organized society itself, the same society on which we depend for stability and security in our daily lives. No matter how much the individual criminal thus selected for death may "deserve" his punishment, the manner of its imposition robs it of any possible value, and leaves us ashamed instead of reassured.

It was on precisely this basis, just eleven years ago, that the Supreme Court   14
in *Furman* v. *Georgia* struck down every death penalty law in the United States, and set aside the death sentences of more than six hundred death row inmates. *Furman* was decided by a single vote (all four Nixon appointees voting to uphold the death penalty laws), and though the five majority justices varied in their rationales, the dominant theme of their opinions was that the Constitution did not permit the execution of a capriciously selected handful out of all those convicted of capital crimes. For Justice Byron White and the rest of the *Furman* majority, years of reading the petitions of the condemned had simply revealed "no meaningful basis for distinguishing the few cases in which [death] is imposed from the many in which it is not." Justice Potter Stewart compared the country's capital sentencing methods to being struck by lightning, adding that "if any basis can be discerned for the selection of these few to be sentenced to die, it is on the constitutionally impermissible basis of race." Justice William O. Douglas summarized the issue by observing that the Constitution would never permit any law which stated

> that anyone making more than $50,000 would be exempt from the death penalty ... [nor] a law that in terms said that blacks, those that never went beyond the fifth grade in school, those who made less than $3,000 a year, or those who were unpopular or unstable would be the only people executed. *A law which in the overall view reaches that result in practice has no more sanctity than a law which in terms provides the same.* [Emphasis added.]

On the basis of these views, the Supreme Court in *Furman* set aside every   15
death sentence before it, and effectively cleared off death row. Though *Furman* v. *Georgia* did not outlaw the death penalty as such, the Court's action came at a time when America appeared to have turned against capital punishment, and *Furman* seemed to climax a long and inexorable progression toward abolition. After *Furman*, Chief Justice Warren E. Burger, who had dissented from the Court's decision, predicted privately that there would never be another execution in the United States.

What happened instead was that the majority of state legislatures passed   16
new death sentencing laws designed to satisfy the Supreme Court. By this year, eleven years after *Furman*, there are roughly as many states with capital punishment laws on the books as there were in 1972.

In theory the capital sentencing statutes under which the 1,163 prisoners   17
now on death row were condemned are very different from the death penalty
laws in effect prior to 1972. Under the pre-*Furman* laws, the process of selection was simple: the jury decided whether the accused was guilty of murder,
and if so, whether he should live or die. In most states, no separate sentencing
hearing was held: jurors were supposed to determine both guilt and punishment at the same time, often without benefit of any information about the
background or circumstances of the defendant whose life was in their hands.
Jurors were also given no guidelines or standards with which to assess the
relative gravity of the case before them, but were free to base their life-or-death
decision on whatever attitudes or biases they happened to have carried with
them into the jury room. These statutes provided few grounds for appeal and
worked fast: as late as the 1950s, many prisoners were executed within a few
weeks of their trials, and delays of more than a year or two were rare.

In contrast, the current crop of capital statutes have created complex, multi-   18
tiered sentencing schemes based on lists of specified "aggravating" and "mitigating" factors which the jury is to consider in passing sentence. Sentencing
now occurs at a separate hearing after guilt has been determined. The new
statutes also provide for automatic appeal to the state supreme courts, usually
with a requirement that the court determine whether each death sentence is
excessive considering the defendant and the crime.

The first of these new statutes—from Georgia, Florida, and Texas—came   19
before the Supreme Court for review in 1976. The new laws were different from
one another in several respects—only Georgia's provided for case-by-case review of the appropriateness of each death sentence by the state supreme court;
Florida's permitted the judge to sentence a defendant to death even where the
jury had recommended a life sentence; and the Texas statute determined who
was to be executed on the basis of the jury's answer to the semantically per-
plexing question of whether the evidence established "beyond a reasonable
doubt" a "probability" that the defendant would commit acts of violence in the
future. What these statutes all had in common, however, was some sort of
criteria, however vague, to guide juries and judges in their life-or-death decisions, while permitting capital defendants a chance to present evidence to show
why they should be spared. Henceforth—or so went the theory behind these
new laws—death sentences could not be imposed randomly or on the basis of
the race or social status of the defendant and the victim, but only on the basis
of specific facts about the crime, such as whether the murder had been committed during a rape or a robbery, or whether it had been "especially heinous,
atrocious and cruel" (in Florida), or "outrageously or wantonly vile, horrible or
inhuman" (in Georgia).

After considering these statutes during the spring of 1976, the Supreme   20
Court announced in *Gregg* v. *Georgia* and two other cases that the new laws
satisfied its concern, expressed in *Furman,* about the randomness and unfair-
ness of the previous death sentencing systems. Of course, the Court had no
actual evidence that these new laws were being applied any more equally or
consistently than the ones struck down in *Furman.* But for that matter, the
Court had not relied on factual evidence in *Furman,* either. Although social

science research over the previous thirty years had consistently found the nation's use of capital punishment to be characterized by arbitrariness and racial discrimination, the decisive opinions of Justices White and Stewart in *Furman* cited none of this statistical evidence, but relied instead on the justices' own conclusions derived from years of experience with the appeals of the condemned. The *Furman* decision left the Court free to declare the problem solved later on. And four years later, in *Gregg* v. *Georgia,* that is what it did.

It may be, of course, that the Court's prediction in *Gregg* of a new era of   21 fairness in capital sentencing was a sham, window dressing for what was in reality nothing more than a capitulation to the mounting public clamor for a resumption of executions. But if the justices sincerely believed that new legal guidelines and jury instructions would really solve the problems of arbitrariness and racial discrimination in death penalty cases, they were wrong.

Before John Spenkelink—a white murderer of a white victim—was exe-   22 cuted by the state of Florida in May 1979, his lawyers tried to present to the state and federal courts a study which showed that the "new" Florida death penalty laws, much like the ones which they had replaced, were being applied far more frequently against persons who killed whites than against those who killed blacks. The appeals courts responded that the Supreme Court had settled all of these arguments in 1976 when it upheld the new sentencing statutes: the laws were fair because the Supreme Court had said they were fair; mere evidence to the contrary was irrelevant.

After Spenkelink was electrocuted, the evidence continued to mount. In   23 1980 two Northeastern University criminologists, William Bowers and Glenn Pierce, published a study of homicide sentencing in Georgia, Florida, and Texas, the three states whose new death penalty statutes were the first to be approved by the Supreme Court after *Furman.* Bowers and Pierce tested the Supreme Court's prediction that these new statutes would achieve consistent and even-handed sentencing by comparing the lists of which convicted murderers had been condemned and which spared with the facts of their crimes as reported by the police. What they found was that in cases where white victims had been killed, black defendants in all three states were from four to six times more likely to be sentenced to death than were white defendants. Both whites and blacks, moreover, faced a much greater danger of being executed where the murder victims were white than where the victims were black. A black defendant in Florida was thirty-seven times more likely to be sentenced to death if his victim was white than if his victim was black; in Georgia, black-on-white killings were punished by death thirty-three times more often than were black-on-black killings; and in Texas, the ratio climbed to an astounding 84 to 1. Even when Bowers and Pierce examined only those cases which the police had reported as "felony-circumstance" murders (i.e., cases involving kidnapping or rape, and thus excluding mere domestic and barroom homicides), they found that both the race of the defendant and the race of the victim appeared to produce enormous disparities in death sentences in each state.

A more detailed analysis of charging decisions in several Florida counties   24 even suggested that prosecutors tended to "upgrade" murders of white victims by alleging that they were more legally aggravated than had been apparent to the police who had written up the initial report, while "downgrading" murders of black victims in a corresponding manner, apparently to avoid the expensive and time-consuming process of trying such murders of blacks as capital cases. Their overall findings, Bowers and Pierce concluded,

> are consistent with a single underlying racist tenet: that white lives are worth more than black lives. From this tenet it follows that death as punishment is more appropriate for the killers of whites than for the killers of blacks and more appropriate for black than for white killers.

Such stark evidence of discrimination by race of offender and by race of victim, they wrote, is "a direct challenge to the constitutionality of the post-*Furman* capital statutes . . . [and] may represent a two-edged sword of racism in capital punishment which is beyond statutory control."

This new data was presented to the federal courts by attorneys for a Georgia death row inmate named John Eldon Smith in 1981. The court of appeals replied that the studies were too crude to have any legal significance, since they did not look at all the dozens of circumstances of each case, other than race, that might have accounted for the unequal sentencing patterns that Bowers and Pierce had detected.

The matter might have ended there, since the court's criticism implied that only a gargantuan (and extremely expensive) research project encompassing the most minute details of many hundreds of homicide cases would be worthy of its consideration. But as it happened, such a study was already under way, supported by a foundation grant and directed by University of Iowa law professor David Baldus. Using a staff of law students and relying primarily on official Georgia state records, Baldus gathered and coded more than 230 factual circumstances surrounding each of more than a thousand homicides, including 253 death penalty sentencing proceedings conducted under Georgia's current death penalty law. Baldus's results, presented in an Atlanta federal court hearing late last summer, confirmed that among defendants convicted of murdering whites, blacks are substantially more likely to go to death row than are whites. Although blacks account for some 60 percent of Georgia homicide victims, Baldus found that killers of black victims are punished by death less than one-tenth as often as are killers of white victims. With the scientific precision of an epidemiologist seeking to pinpoint the cause of a new disease, Baldus analyzed and reanalyzed his mountain of data on Georgia homicides, controlling for the hundreds of factual variables in each case, in search of any explanation other than race which might account for the stark inequalities in the operation of Georgia's capital sentencing system. He could find none. And when the state of Georgia's turn came to defend its capital sentencing record at the Atlanta federal court hearing, it soon emerged that the statisticians hired by the state to help it refute Baldus's research had had no better success in *their* search for an alternative explanation. (In a telephone interview after the Atlanta hearing, the attorney general of Georgia, Michael Bowers, assured me that "the bottom line is that Georgia does not discriminate on the basis of race," but referred all specific questions to his assistant, who declined to answer on the grounds that the court proceeding was pending.)

The findings of research efforts like Baldus's document what anyone who   27 has worked in the death-sentencing system will have sensed all along: the Supreme Court notwithstanding, there is no set of courtroom procedures set out in lawbooks which can change the prosecution practices of local district attorneys. Nor will even the most elaborate jury instructions ever ensure that an all-white jury will weigh a black life as heavily as a white life.

At bottom, the determination of whether or not a particular defendant   28 should die for his crime is simply not a rational decision. Requiring that the jury first determine whether his murder was "outrageously or wantonly vile, horrible, or inhuman," as Georgia juries are invited to do, provides little assurance that death will be imposed fairly and consistently. Indeed, Baldus's research revealed that Georgia juries are more likely to find that a given murder was "outrageously or wantonly vile, horrible, or inhuman" when the victim was white, and likelier still when the murderer is black—hardly a vindication of the Supreme Court's confidence in *Gregg* v. *Georgia* that such guidelines would serve to eliminate racial discrimination in sentencing.

At present, 51 percent of the inhabitants of death row across the country   29 are white, as were seven of the eight men executed since the Supreme Court's *Gregg* decision. Five percent of the condemned are Hispanic, and almost all of the remaining 44 percent are black. Since roughly half the people arrested and charged with intentional homicide each year in the United States are white, it would appear at first glance that the proportions of blacks and whites now on Death Row are about those that would be expected from a fair system of capital sentencing. But what studies like Baldus's now reveal is how such seemingly equitable racial distribution can actually be the product of racial discrimination, rather than proof that discrimination has been overcome.

The explanation for this seeming paradox is that the judicial system discrim-   30 inates on the basis of the race of the *victim* as well as the race of the defendant. Each year, according to the F.B.I.'s crime report, about the same numbers of blacks as whites are arrested for murder throughout the United States, and the totals of black and white murder victims are also roughly equal. But like many other aspects of American life, our murders are segregated: white murderers almost always kill whites, and the large majority of black killers kill blacks. While blacks who kill whites tend to be singled out for harsher treatment—and more death sentences—than other murderers, there are relatively few of them, and so the absolute effect on the numbers of blacks sent to death row is limited. On the other hand, the far more numerous black murderers whose victims were also black are treated relatively leniently in the courts, and are only rarely sent to death row. Because these dual systems of discrimination operate simultane- ously, they have the overall effect of keeping the numbers of blacks on death row roughly proportionate to the numbers of blacks convicted of murder— even while individual defendants are being condemned, and others spared, on the basis of race. In short, like the man who, with one foot in ice and the other in boiling water, describes his situation as "comfortable on average," the death sentencing system has created an illusion of fairness.

In theory, law being based on precedent, the Supreme Court might be ex-   31
pected to apply the principles of the *Furman* decision as it did in 1972 and strike down death penalty laws which have produced results as seemingly racist as these. But that's not going to happen. *Furman* was a product of its time: in 1972 public support for the death penalty had been dropping fairly steadily over several decades, and capital punishment appeared to be going the way of the stocks, the whipping post, and White and Colored drinking fountains. The resurgence of support for capital punishment in the country over the last decade has changed that, at least for now. Last summer the Supreme Court upheld every one of the four death sentences it had taken under consideration during its 1982–83 session, and in November the Court heard arguments by California in support of its claim that the states should not be required to compare murder sentences on a statewide basis in order to assure fairness in capital sentencing. The justices may have given an indication of their eventual decision on California's appeal when, just three hours before they heard that case, they lifted a stay of execution in a Louisiana case where a condemned prisoner named Robert Wayne Williams had been attempting to challenge the very limited method of comparison used by the Louisiana courts: as a result, Williams may well be dead by the time the California decision is handed down this spring. When in 1972 the Supreme Court was faced with a choice between fairness and the death penalty, it chose fairness. This time the odds are all with the death penalty.

Even with the Court's increasingly hard-line stance on capital appeals, there   32
will probably not be any sudden surge of executions in the next year or two. One of the unreckoned costs of the death penalty is the strain it places on the state and federal judicial systems. Any large number of imminent executions would overload those systems to the point of breakdown. A great deal is being said nowadays about the need to speed up capital appeals: Justice Lewis Powell even added his voice to the chorus last spring at the very moment that the Supreme Court had the question of stays of execution under consideration in a pending case. But this attitude tends to moderate the closer one gets to a specific case. No judge wants to discover after it's too late that he permitted someone to be executed on the basis of factual or legal error, and for that reason alone the backlog of death row prisoners can be expected to persist.

Still, the pace of executions is going to pick up to a more or less steady   33
trickle: possibly one a month, possibly two, maybe more. In September Missis-sippi's William Winter became the first governor since Ronald Reagan to permit an execution by lethal gas: Jimmy Lee Gray died banging his head against a steel pole in the gas chamber while the reporters counted his moans (eleven, according to the Associated Press). A month later, J. D. Autry came within minutes of dying by lethal injection in Texas, only to have Supreme Court Justice Byron White reverse his decision of the day before and stay the execu-tion. Now Autry is reprieved until the Supreme Court decides whether Califor-nia (and by implication Texas) must compare capital sentences to ensure some

measure of fairness: if the Court rules that they don't have to, Autry will in all likelihood be executed next year.

So far, the power of the death penalty as a social symbol has shielded from scrutiny the huge demands in money and resources which the death sentencing process makes on the criminal justice system as a whole. Whatever the abstract merits of capital punishment, there is no denying that a successful death penalty prosecution costs a fortune. A 1982 study in New York state concluded that just the trial and first stage of appeal in a death penalty case under that state's proposed death penalty bill would cost the taxpayers of New York over $1.8 million—more than twice as much as imprisoning the defendant for life. And even that estimate does not include the social costs of diverting an already overburdened criminal justice system from its job of handling large numbers of criminal cases to a preoccupation with the relative handful of capital ones. But the question of just how many laid-off police officers one execution is worth won't come up so long as the death penalty remains for most Americans a way of expressing feelings rather than a practical response to the problem of violent crime. 34

It is impossible to predict how long the executions will continue. The rise in violent crime in this country has already begun to abate somewhat, probably as a result of demographic changes as the baby boom generation matures beyond its crime-prone teenage and early adult years. But it may well turn out that even a marked reduction in the crime rate won't produce any sharp decrease in public pressure for capital punishment: the shift in public opinion on the death penalty seems to have far deeper roots than that. The death penalty has become a potent social symbol of national resolve, another way of saying that we're not going to be pushed around anymore, that we've got the willpower and self-confidence to stand up to anyone, whether muggers or Cubans or Islamic fanatics, that we're not the flaccid weaklings that "they" have been taking us for. The death penalty can only be understood as one of the so-called "social issues" of the Reagan era: it bears no more relationship to the problem of crime than school prayer bears to the improvement of public education. Over the past half-century, executions were at their peak during the Depression of the 1930s, and almost disappeared during the boom years of the 1950s and early 1960s. The re-emergence of the death penalty in the 1970s coincided with the advent of chronic inflation and recession, and with military defeat abroad and the decline of the civil rights movement at home. Given this historical record, it's a safe bet that whether the crime rates go up or down over the next several years, public support for executions will start to wane only as the country finds more substantial foundations for a renewal of confidence in its future. 35

In the meantime we will be the only country among all the Western industrial democracies which still executes its own citizens. Canada abolished capital punishment in 1976, as did France in 1981; England declined to bring back hanging just this summer. By contrast, our leading companions in the use of the death penalty as a judicial punishment for crime will be the governments of the Soviet Union, South Africa, Saudi Arabia, and Iran—a rogues' gallery of the most repressive and backward-looking regimes in the world. Just last week 36

Christopher Wren reported in *The New York Times* that the total number of executions in the People's Republic of China may reach five thousand or more this year alone.

It's no accident that democracies tend to abolish the death penalty while   37
autocracies and totalitarian regimes tend to retain it. In his new new book, *The Death Penalty: A Debate,* John Conrad credits Tocqueville with the explanation for this, quoting from *Democracy in America:*

> When all the ranks of a community are nearly equal, as all men think and feel in nearly the same manner, each of them may judge in a moment the sensations of all the others; he casts a rapid glance upon himself, and that is enough. There is no wretchedness into which he cannot readily enter, and a secret instinct reveals to him its extent . . . In democratic ages, men rarely sacrifice themselves for one another, but they display general compassion for the members of the human race. They inflict no useless ills, and they are happy to relieve the griefs of others when they can do so without much hurting themselves; they are not disinterested, but they are humane . . .

Tocqueville went on to explain that his identification of America's democratic political culture as the root of the "singular mildness" of American penal practices was susceptible of an ironic proof: the cruelty with which Americans treated their black slaves. Restraint in punishment, he wrote, extends as far as our sense of social equality, and no further: "the same man who is full of humanity toward his fellow creatures when they are at the same time his equals becomes insensible to their affliction as soon as that equality ceases."

In that passage, written 150 years ago, Tocqueville reveals to us why it is that   38
the death penalty—the practice of slowly bringing a fully conscious human face to face with the prospect of his own extinction and then killing him— should characterize the judicial systems of the least democratic and most repressive nations of the world. And it reveals too why the vestiges of this institution in America should be so inextricably entangled with the question of race. The gradual disappearance of the death penalty throughout most of the democratic world certainly suggests that Tocqueville was right. The day when Americans stop condemning people to death on the basis of race and inequality will be the day when we stop condemning anyone to death at all.

QUESTIONS FOR MEANING

1. Why does Bruck believe that capital punishment is like a lottery? In which paragraphs does he develop his argument that executions are determined by chance?
2. Explain the difference between capital punishment laws before and after 1972. Where does Bruck summarize the difference for you?
3. What does Bruck mean when he writes that capital punishment "has become a potent social symbol of national resolve"?

4. Bruck makes the unusual argument that the death penalty is expensive, a charge that is often raised against sentencing men and women to life imprisonment. What evidence does he offer to support his claim?
5. Vocabulary: vagaries (5), winnowed (6), imminent (7), repugnant (7), arcane (7), inexorable (9), disparities (23), gargantuan (26), epidemiologist (26), abate (35), flaccid (35), and inextricably (38).

QUESTIONS ABOUT STRATEGY

1. Bruck begins his essay with a description of "death row." Is this an effective opening? Why?
2. Why does Bruck pause to tell us that Jimmy Lee Gray was reported to have moaned eleven times before dying in a Mississippi gas chamber? Do details of this sort help us to understand the reality of capital punishment or is Bruck simply playing on our feelings? Consider his use of detail throughout the essay.
3. In paragraph 9, Bruck reveals that he is a lawyer. Why do you think he makes this revelation? Does it lead you to take what he says more seriously? If so, why?
4. Bruck uses many statistics in the course of his essay. How much do they add to his argument?
5. At the conclusion of paragraph 31, Bruck writes, "When in 1972 the Supreme Court was faced with a choice between fairness and the death penalty, it chose fairness." Is it fair to imply that capital punishment cannot be fair? Does Bruck succeed in persuading you of this?
6. How effective is the comparison Bruck draws between American penal laws and those of other countries?

WALTER BERNS
For Capital Punishment

Walter Berns (b. 1919) is a well-known political scientist. He did graduate work at Reed College and the London School of Economics before receiving his Ph.D. from the University of Chicago in 1953. He has been the recipient of Carnegie, Fulbright, and Guggenheim fellowships and taught at Yale, Cornell, Georgetown, and the University of Toronto. A contributor to numerous anthologies and scholarly journals, he is the author of several books, including Freedom, Virtue, and the First Amendment *(1957),* Constitutional Cases in American Government *(1963), and* The First Amendment and the Future of American Government *(1976). The following essay is drawn from his book* For Capital Punishment: Crime and the Morality of the Death Penalty *(1979).*

Until recently, my business did not require me to think about the punishment   1
of criminals in general or the legitimacy and efficacy of capital punishment in
particular. In a vague way, I was aware of the disagreement among professionals
concerning the purpose of punishment—whether it was intended to deter
others, to rehabilitate the criminal, or to pay him back—but like most laymen I
had no particular reason to decide which purpose was right or to what extent
they may all have been right. I did know that retribution was held in ill repute
among criminologists and jurists—to them, retribution was a fancy name for
revenge, and revenge was barbaric—and, of course, I knew that capital punishment had the support only of policemen, prison guards and some local politicians, the sort of people Arthur Koestler calls "hang hards" (Philadelphia's
Mayor Rizzo comes to mind). The intellectual community denounced it as both
unnecessary and immoral. It was the phenomenon of Simon Wiesenthal that
allowed me to understand why the intellectuals were wrong and why the police,
the politicians, and the majority of the voters were right: we punish criminals
principally in order to pay them back, and we execute the worst of them out of
moral necessity. Anyone who respects Wiesenthal's mission will be driven to
the same conclusion.

Of course, not everyone will respect that mission. It will strike the busy   2
man—I mean the sort of man who sees things only in the light cast by a concern
for his own interests—as somewhat bizarre. Why should anyone devote his
life—more than thirty years of it!—exclusively to the task of hunting down the
Nazi war criminals who survived World War II and escaped punishment?
Wiesenthal says his conscience forces him "to bring the guilty ones to trial."
But why punish them? What do we hope to accomplish now by punishing SS
Obersturmbannführer Adolf Eichmann or SS Obersturmführer Franz Stangl
or someday—who knows?—Reichsleiter Martin Bormann? We surely don't
expect to rehabilitate them, and it would be foolish to think that by punishing
them we might thereby deter others. The answer, I think, is clear: We want to
punish them in order *to pay them back*. We think they must be made to pay for

their crimes with their lives, and we think that we, the survivors of the world they violated, may legitimately exact that payment because we, too, are their victims. By punishing them, we demonstrate that there are laws that bind men across generations as well as across (and within) nations, that we are not simply isolated individuals, each pursuing his selfish interests and connected with others by a mere contract to live and let live. To state it simply, Wiesenthal allows us to see that it is right, morally right, to be angry with criminals and to express that anger publicly, officially, and in an appropriate manner, which may require the worst of them to be executed.

Modern civil-libertarian opponents of capital punishment do not understand this. They say that to execute a criminal is to deny his human dignity; they also say that the death penalty is not useful, that nothing useful is accomplished by executing anyone. Being utilitarians, they are essentially selfish men, distrustful of passion, who do not understand the connection between anger and justice, and between anger and human dignity.   3

Anger is expressed or manifested on those occasions when someone has acted in a manner that is thought to be unjust, and one of its origins is the opinion that men are responsible, and should be held responsible, for what they do. Thus, as Aristotle teaches us, anger is accompanied not only by the pain caused by the one who is the object of anger, but by the pleasure arising from the expectation of inflicting revenge on someone who is thought to deserve it. We can become angry with an inanimate object (the door we run into and then kick in return) only by foolishly attributing responsibility to it, and we cannot do that for long, which is why we do not think of returning later to revenge ourselves on the door. For the same reason, we cannot be more than momentarily angry with any one creature other than man; only a fool or worse would dream of taking revenge on a dog. And, finally, we tend to pity rather than to be angry with men who—because they are insane, for example—are not responsible for their acts. Anger, then, is a very human passion not only because only a human being can be angry, but also because anger acknowledges the humanity of its objects: it holds them accountable for what they do. And in holding particular men responsible, it pays them the respect that is due them as men. Anger recognizes that only men have the capacity to be moral beings and, in so doing, acknowledges the dignity of human beings. Anger is somehow connected with justice, and it is this that modern penology has not understood; it tends, on the whole, to regard anger as a selfish indulgence.   4

Anger can, of course, be that; and if someone does not become angry with an insult or an injury suffered unjustly, we tend to think he does not think much of himself. But it need not be selfish, not in the sense of being provoked only by an injury suffered by onself. There were many angry men in America when President Kennedy was killed; one of them—Jack Ruby—took it upon himself to exact the punishment that, if indeed deserved, ought to have been exacted by the law. There were perhaps even angrier men when Martin Luther King, Jr., was killed, for King, more than anyone else at the time, embodied a people's quest for justice; the anger—more, the "black rage"—expressed on that occasion was simply a manifestation of the great change that had occurred among   5 black men in America, a change wrought in large part by King and his associates in the civil-rights movement: the servility and fear of the past had been replaced by pride and anger, and the treatment that had formerly been accepted as a matter of course or as if it were deserved was now seen for what it was, unjust and unacceptable. King preached love, but the movement he led depended on anger as well as love, and that anger was not despicable, being neither selfish nor unjustified. On the contrary, it was a reflection of what was called solidarity and may more accurately be called a profound caring for others, black for other blacks, white for blacks, and, in the world King was trying to build, American for other Americans. If men are not saddened when someone else suffers, or angry when someone else suffers unjustly, the implication is that they do not care for anyone other than themselves or that they lack some quality that befits a man. When we criticize them for this, we acknowledge that they ought to care for others. If men are not angry when a neighbor suffers at the hands of a criminal, the implication is that their moral faculties have been corrupted, that they are not good citizens.

Criminals are properly the objects of anger, and the perpetrators of terrible crimes—for example, Lee Harvey Oswald and James Earl Ray—are properly the objects of great anger. They have done more than inflict an injury on an isolated individual; they have violated the foundations of trust and friendship, the necessary elements of a moral community, the only community worth living in. A moral community, unlike a hive of bees or a hill of ants, is one whose members are expected freely to obey the laws and, unlike those in a tyranny, are trusted to obey the laws. The criminal has violated that trust, and in so doing has injured not merely his immediate victim but the community as such. He has called into question the very possibility of that community by suggesting that men cannot be trusted to respect freely the property, the person, and the dignity of those with whom they are associated. If then, men are not angry when someone else is robbed, raped, or murdered, the implication is that no moral community exists, because those men do not care for anyone other than themselves. Anger is an expression of that caring, and society needs men who care for one another, who share their pleasures and their pains, and do so for the sake of the others. It is the passion that can cause us to act for reasons having nothing to do with selfish or mean calculation; indeed, when educated, it can become a generous passion, the passion that protects the community or country by demanding punishment for its enemies. It is the stuff from which heroes are made.

A moral community is not possible without anger and the moral indignation that accompanies it. Thus the most powerful attack on capital punishment was written by a man, Albert Camus, who denied the legitimacy of anger and moral indignation by denying the very possibility of a moral community in our time. The anger expressed in our world, he said, is nothing but hypocrisy. His novel *L'Etranger* (variously translated as *The Stranger* or *The Outsider*) is a brilliant portrayal of what Camus insisted is our world, a world deprived of God, as he put it. It is a world we would not choose to live in and one that Camus, the hero of the French Resistance, disdained. Nevertheless, the novel is a modern masterpiece, and Meursault, its antihero (for a world without anger can have no heroes), is a murderer.

He is a murderer whose crime is excused, even as his lack of hypocrisy is praised, because the universe, we are told, is "benignly indifferent" to how we live or what we do. Of course, the law is not indifferent; the law punished Meursault and it threatens to punish us if we do as he did. But Camus the novelist teaches us that the law is simply a collection of arbitrary conceits. The people around Meursault apparently were not indifferent; they expressed dismay at his lack of attachment to his mother and disapprobation of his crime. But Camus the novelist teaches us that other people are hypocrites. They pretend not to know what Camus the opponent of capital punishment tells us: namely, that "our civilization has lost the only values that, in a certain way, can justify that penalty . . . [the existence of] a truth or a principle that is superior to man." There is no basis for friendship and no moral law; therefore, no one, not even a murderer, can violate the terms of friendship or break that law; and there is no basis for the anger that we express when someone breaks that law. The only thing we share as men, the only thing that connects us one to another, is a "solidarity against death," and a judgment of capital punishment "upsets" that solidarity. The purpose of human life is to stay alive.   8

Like Meursault, Macbeth was a murderer, and like *L'Etranger,* Shakespeare's *Macbeth* is the story of a murder; but there the similarity ends. As Lincoln said, "Nothing equals Macbeth." He was comparing it with the other Shakespearean plays he knew, the plays he had "gone over perhaps as frequently as any unprofessional reader . . . *Lear, Richard Third, Henry Eighth, Hamlet*"; but I think he meant to say more than that none of these equals *Macbeth.* I think he meant that no other literary work equals it. "It is wonderful," he said. *Macbeth* is wonderful because, to say nothing more here, it teaches us the awesomeness of the commandment "Thou shalt not kill."   9

What can a dramatic poet tell us about murder? More, probably, than anyone else, if he is a poet worthy of consideration, and yet nothing that does not inhere in the act itself. In *Macbeth,* Shakespeare shows us murders committed in a political world by a man so driven by ambition to rule that world that he becomes a tyrant. He shows us also the consequences, which were terrible, worse even than Macbeth feared. The cosmos rebelled, turned into chaos by his deeds. He shows a world that was not "benignly indifferent" to what we call crimes and especially to murder, a world constituted by laws divine as well as human, and Macbeth violated the most awful of those laws. Because the world was so constituted, Macbeth suffered the torments of the great and the damned, torments far beyond the "practice" of any physician. He had known glory and had deserved the respect and affection of king, countrymen, army, friends, and wife; and he lost it all. At the end he was reduced to saying that life "is a tale told by an idiot, full of sound and fury, signifying nothing"; yet, in spite of the horrors provoked in us by his acts, he excites no anger in us. We pity him; even so, we understand the anger of his countrymen and the dramatic necessity of his death. *Macbeth* is a play about ambition, murder, tyranny; about horror, anger, vengeance, and, perhaps more than any other of Shakespeare's plays,   10 justice. Because of justice, Macbeth has to die, not by his own hand—he will not "play the Roman fool, and die on [his] own sword"—but at the hand of the avenging Macduff. The dramatic necessity of his death would appear to rest on its *moral* necessity. Is that right? Does this play conform to our sense of what a murder means? Lincoln thought it was "wonderful."

Surely Shakespeare's is a truer account of murder than the one provided by   11
Camus, and by truer I mean truer to our moral sense of what a murder is and what the consequences that attend it must be. Shakespeare shows us vengeful men because there is something in the souls of men—then and now—that requires such crimes to be revenged. Can we imagine a world that does not take its revenge on the man who kills Macduff's wife and children? (Can we imagine the play in which Macbeth does not die?) Can we imagine a people that does not hate murderers? (Can we imagine a world where Meursault is an outsider only because he does not *pretend* to be outraged by murder?) Shakespeare's poetry could not have been written out of the moral sense that the death penalty's opponents insist we ought to have. Indeed, the issue of capital punishment can be said to turn on whether Shakespeare's or Camus' is the more telling account of murder.

There is a sense in which punishment may be likened to dramatic poetry.   12
Dramatic poetry depicts men's actions because men are revealed in, or make themselves known through, their actions; and the essence of a human action, according to Aristotle, consists in its being virtuous or vicious. Only a ruler or a contender for rule can act with the freedom and on a scale that allows the virtuousness or viciousness of human deeds to be fully displayed. Macbeth was such a man, and in his fall, brought about by his own acts, and in the consequent suffering he endured, is revealed the meaning of morality. In *Macbeth* the majesty of the moral law is demonstrated to us; as I said, it teaches us the awesomeness of the commandment Thou shalt not kill. In a similar fashion, the punishments imposed by the legal order remind us of the reign of the moral order; not only do they remind us of it, but by enforcing its prescriptions, they enhance the dignity of the legal order in the eyes of moral men, in the eyes of those decent citizens who cry out "for gods who will avenge injustice." That is especially important in a self-governing community, a community that gives laws to itself.

If the laws were understood to be divinely inspired or, in the extreme case,   13
divinely given, they would enjoy all the dignity that the opinions of men can grant and all the dignity they require to ensure their being obeyed by most of the men living under them. Like Duncan in the opinion of Macduff, the laws would be "the Lord's anointed," and would be obeyed even as Macduff obeyed the laws of the Scottish kingdom. Only a Macbeth would challenge them, and only a Meursault would ignore them. But the laws of the United States are not of this description; in fact, among the proposed amendments that became the Bill of Rights was one declaring, not that all power comes from God, but rather "that all power is originally vested in, and consequently derives from the people"; and this proposal was dropped only because it was thought to be redundant: the Constitution's preamble said essentially the same thing, and what we know as the Tenth Amendment reiterated it. So Madison proposed to make the

Constitution venerable in the minds of the people, and Lincoln, in an early speech, went so far as to say that a "political religion" should be made of it. They did not doubt that the Constitution and the laws made pursuant to it would be supported by "enlightened reason," but fearing that enlightened reason would be in short supply, they sought to augment it. The laws of the United States would be obeyed by some men because they could hear and understand "the voice of enlightened reason," and by other men because they would regard the laws with that "veneration which time bestows on everything."

Supreme Court justices have occasionally complained of our habit of making "constitutionality synonymous with wisdom." But the extent to which the Constitution is venerated and its authority accepted depends on the compatibility of its rules with our moral sensibilities; despite its venerable character, the Constitution is not the only source of these moral sensibilities. There was even a period, before slavery was abolished by the Thirteenth Amendment, when the Constitution was regarded by some very moral men as an abomination: Garrison called it "a covenant with death and an agreement with Hell," and there were honorable men holding important political offices and judicial appointments who refused to enforce the Fugitive Slave Law even though its constitutionality had been affirmed. In time this opinion spread far beyond the ranks of the original abolitionists until those who held it composed a constitutional majority of the people, and slavery was abolished.   14

But Lincoln knew that more than amendments were required to make the Constitution once more worthy of the veneration of moral men. This is why, in the Gettysburg Address, he made the principle of the Constitution an inheritance from "our fathers." That it should be so esteemed is especially important in a self-governing nation that gives laws to itself, because it is only a short step from the principle that the laws are merely a product of one's own will to the opinion that the only consideration that informs the law is self-interest; and this opinion is only one remove from lawlessness. A nation of simply self-interested men will soon enough perish from the earth.   15

It was not an accident that Lincoln spoke as he did at Gettysburg or that he chose as the occasion for his words the dedication of a cemetery built on a portion of the most significant battlefield of the Civil War. Two-and-a-half years earlier, in his First Inaugural Address, he had said that Americans, north and south, were not and must not be enemies, but friends. Passion had strained but must not be allowed to break the bonds of affection that tied them one to another. He closed by saying this: "The mystic chords of memory, stretching from every battlefield, and patriot grave, to every living heart and hearthstone, all over this broad land, will yet swell the chorus of the Union, when again touched, as surely they will be, by the better angels of our nature." The chords of memory that would swell the chorus of the Union could be touched, even by a man of Lincoln's stature, only on the most solemn occasions, and in the life of a nation no occasion is more solemn than the burial of the patriots who have died defending it on the field of battle. War is surely an evil but as Hegel said, it is not an "absolute evil." It exacts the supreme sacrifice, but precisely because of that it can call forth such sublime rhetoric as Lincoln's. His words at Gettysburg serve to remind Americans in particular of what Hegel said people in   16 general needed to know, and could be made to know by means of war and the sacrifices demanded of them in wars: namely, that their country is something more than a "civil society" the purpose of which is simply the protection of individual and selfish interests.

Capital punishment, like Shakespeare's dramatic and Lincoln's political poetry (and it is surely that, and was understood by him to be that), serves to remind us of the majesty of the moral order that is embodied in our law, and of the terrible consequences of its breach. The law must not be understood to be merely a statute that we enact or repeal at our will, and obey or disobey at our convenience—especially not the criminal law. Wherever law is regarded as merely statutory, men will soon enough disobey it, and will learn how to do so without any inconvenience to themselves. The criminal law must possess a dignity far beyond that possessed by mere statutory enactment or utilitarian and self-interested calculations. The most powerful means we have to give it that dignity is to authorize it to impose the ultimate penalty. The criminal law must be made awful, by which I mean awe-inspiring, or commanding "profound respect or reverential fear." It must remind us of the moral order by which alone we can live as *human* beings, and in America, now that the Supreme Court has outlawed banishment, the only punishment that can do this is capital punishment.   17

The founder of modern criminology, the eighteenth century Italian, Cesare Beccaria, opposed both banishment and capital punishment because he understood that both were inconsistent with the principle of self-interest, and self-interest was the basis of the political order he favored. If a man's first or only duty is to himself, of course he will prefer his money to his country; he will also prefer his money to his brother. In fact, he will prefer his brother's money to his brother, and a people of this description, or a country that understands itself in this Beccarian manner, can put the mark of Cain on no one. For the same reason, such a country can have no legitimate reason to execute its criminals, or, indeed, to punish them in any manner. What would be accomplished by punishment in such a place? Punishment arises out of the demand for justice, and justice is demanded by angry, morally indignant men; its purpose is to satisfy that moral indignation and thereby promote the law-abidingness that, it is assumed, accompanies it. But the principle of self-interest denies the moral basis of that indignation.   18

Not only will a country based solely on self-interest have no legitimate reason to punish; it may have no need to punish. It may be able to solve what we call the crime problem by substituting a law of contracts for a law of crimes. According to Beccaria's social contract, men agree to yield their natural freedom to the "sovereign" in exchange for his promise to keep the peace. As it becomes more difficult for the sovereign to fulfill his part of the contract, there is a demand that he be made to pay for his nonperformance. From this comes compensation or insurance schemes embodied in statutes whereby the sovereign (or state), being unable to keep the peace by punishing criminals, agrees to compensate its contractual partners for injuries suffered at the hands of criminals, injuries the police are unable to prevent. The insurance policy takes the place of law enforcement and the *posse comitatus,* and John Wayne and   19

Gary Cooper, give way to Mutual of Omaha. There is no anger in this kind of law, and none (or no reason for any) in the society.

The principle can be carried further still. If we ignore the victim (and nothing   20 we do can restore his life anyway), there would appear to be no reason why— the worth of a man being his price, as Beccaria's teacher, Thomas Hobbes, put it—coverage should not be extended to the losses incurred in a murder. If we ignore the victim's sensibilities (and what are they but absurd vanities?), there would appear to be no reason why—the worth of a woman being *her* price— coverage should not be extended to the losses incurred in a rape. Other examples will no doubt suggest themselves.

This might appear to be an almost perfect solution to what we persist in   21 calling the crime problem, achieved without risking the terrible things sometimes done by an angry people. A people that is not angry with criminals will not be able to deter crime, but a people fully covered by insurance has no need to deter crime: they will be insured against all the losses they can, in principle, suffer. What is now called crime can be expected to increase in volume, of course, and this will cause an increase in the premiums paid, directly or in the form of taxes. But it will no longer be necessary to apprehend try, and punish criminals, which now costs Americans more than $1.5 billion a month (and is increasing at an annual rate of about 15 percent), and one can buy a lot of insurance for $1.5 billion. There is this difficulty, as Rousseau put it: To exclude anger from the human community is to concentrate all the passions in a "self-interest of the meanest sort," and such a place would not be fit for human habitation.

When, in 1976, the Supreme Court declared death to be a constitutional   22 penalty, it decided that the United States was not that sort of country; most of us, I think, can appreciate that judgment. We want to live among people who do not value their possessions more than their citizenship, who do not think exclusively or even primarily of their own rights, people whom we can depend on even as they exercise their rights, and whom we can trust, which is to say, people who, even in the absence of a policeman, will not assault our bodies or steal our possessions, and might even come to our assistance when we need it, and who stand ready, when the occasion demands it, to risk their lives in defense of their country. If we are of the opinion that the United States may rightly ask of its citizens this awful sacrifice, then we are also of the opinion that it may rightly impose the most awful penalty; if it may rightly honor its heroes, it may rightly execute the worst of its criminals. By doing so, it will remind its citizens that it is a country worthy of heroes.

QUESTIONS FOR MEANING

1. According to Berns, what causes anger? Is anger an honorable emotion? If so, why?
2. Berns defines "the busy man" as "the sort of man who sees things only in the light cast by a concern for his own interests." What other words might he have used besides "busy" to describe such men?

3. Why does Berns believe that the United States is in danger of becoming dominated by self-interest? Why does he believe the death penalty represents a commitment to the lives and needs of others?
4. What does Berns mean by "enlightened reason" in paragraph 13?
5. Do you understand Berns's summary of *The Stranger* and *Macbeth*? If you have read neither of these two works, which would you be most interested in reading as the result of the discussion in this essay?
6. Do you recognize the allusion with which paragraph 15 concludes?
7. Paraphrase what Berns says about the relationship between crime and insurance.
8. Why does Berns believe that "criminal law must be made awful"?
9. Berns concludes his argument by declaring that the United States is "a country worthy of heroes." What does this mean?

QUESTIONS ABOUT STRATEGY

1. What kind of audience do you think this essay was originally written for?
2. Why does Berns introduce the names of Simon Wiesenthal, President Kennedy, and Martin Luther King into his essay?
3. Where does Berns characterize his opponents? Does Berns make any attempt to appease them?
4. Berns presents himself as someone who is well-read in both literature and history. Does his analysis of Camus, Shakespeare, and the Civil War add force to his argument? Or is he just showing off how much he knows?
5. Berns begins his essay by acknowledging that he is a "layman" who had only recently begun to think seriously about capital punishment. Is this a good way to prepare an audience for a lengthy argument? Are there any risks to this approach?
6. Berns refers repeatedly to Lincoln throughout his essay. Did this strike you as strange in an argument on behalf of capital punishment? Does Berns succeed in convincing you that Lincoln would have agreed with him? Is this a type of argument or persuasion?

SUGGESTIONS FOR WRITING

1. Opponents of capital punishment traditionally argue that it does not deter crime. If you favor capital punishment, respond to this argument by drawing upon the work of Ernest van den Haag.
2. Both H.L. Mencken and Walter Berns defend capital punishment on the grounds that it psychologically satisfies the victims of violent crime. Summarize and compare their views. Then write an essay questioning whether the death penalty can be justified on these grounds.
3. If executions allow for a "healthy letting off of steam," as Mencken puts it, should they be made public? Write an essay for or against televising executions. Whatever your position, make sure you consider all of the consequences of letting people watch someone die.

4. Margaret Mead and Clarence Darrow both suggest that capital punishment does nothing to resolve the causes of violent crime. Identify a social problem which you believe to be a cause of violence and argue on behalf of a specific reform.

5. Write an argument in defense of capital punishment that will respond to David Bruck's charge that the administration of the death penalty is haphazard and unjust.

6. Van den Haag argues that some opponents of capital punishment would oppose the death penalty under any circumstances. If you yourself oppose capital punishment, do you take an absolute position or are there any crimes for which you would make an exception? If you would allow capital punishment for special cases, write an essay explaining why the death penalty would be appropriate for the special case or cases you have in mind.

7. If you are absolutely opposed to capital punishment, what penalty would you impose upon someone who has committed premeditated murder? Be specific in working out the details of how your alternative punishment would be carried out.

8. According to H.L. Mencken, "The real objection to capital punishment doesn't lie against the actual extermination of the condemned, but against our brutal American habit of putting it off so long." Do you agree? Write an essay for or against capital punishment that will focus on the advantages or disadvantages of lengthy appeals. Can our system of extended appeals be defended as a necessary safeguard against executing the innocent? Or is it a subtle form of torture—both for the criminal and his victims?

9. If you believe that capital punishment is a "cruel and unusual punishment" and as such unconstitutional, write a counterargument to what van den Haag says on this point.

10. What is the history of capital punishment in your state? If there is no death penalty, do a research paper on how and when it came to be abolished. If your state has reintroduced capital punishment since 1972, explain the new law and either defend it or attack it.

11. Research the case of someone executed within the last ten years, and then argue whether or not the death penalty was appropriate in this case.

12. Darrow and Bruck both compare American justice to laws in other countries. Do a research paper on a country that has abolished capital punishment, revealing what the consequences have been.

Section 3
Censorship: Who Decides What's Acceptable?

NAT HENTOFF
When Nice People Burn Books

A staff writer for The New Yorker *and* The Village Voice, *Nat Hentoff (b. 1925) is the author of over twenty books, on subjects ranging from the history of jazz to the need for educational reform. Much of his work is devoted to chronicling political and social problems, and this has led Hentoff to describe himself as an "advocacy writer." As a member of the board of the American Civil Liberties Union and the steering committee of the Reporters Committee for Freedom of the Press, he has been especially concerned with the problem of censorship. In 1980 he published a book on this subject,* The First Freedom: The Tumultuous History of Free Speech in America. *"When Nice People Burn Books" is one of several essays he has recently written in order to show that censorship can take many forms.*

It happened one splendid Sunday morning in a church. Not Jerry Falwell's 1
Baptist sanctuary in Lynchburg, Virginia, but rather the First Unitarian Church
in Baltimore. On October 4, 1981, midway through the 11 A.M. service, pernicious ideas were burned at the altar.

As reported by Frank P. L. Somerville, religion editor of the *Baltimore Sun,* 2
"Centuries of Jewish, Christian, Islamic, and Hindu writings were 'expurgated'—because of sections described as 'sexist.'"

"Touched off by a candle and consumed in a pot on a table in front of the 3
altar were slips of paper containing 'patriarchal' excerpts from Martin Luther,
Thomas Aquinas, the Koran, St. Augustine, St. Ambrose, St. John Chrysostom,
the Hindu Code of Manu V, an anonymous Chinese author, and the Old Testament." Also hurled into the purifying fire were works by Kierkegaard and Karl
Barth.

The congregation was much exalted: "As the last flame died in the pot, and 4
the organ pealed, there was applause," Somerville wrote.

I reported this news of the singed holy spirit to a group of American Civil 5
Liberties Union members in California, and one woman was furious. At me.

"We did the same thing at our church two Sundays ago," she said. "And long 6
past time, too. Don't you understand it's just *symbolic*?"

112

I told this ACLU member that when the school board in Drake, North Dakota, 7
threw thirty-four copies of Kurt Vonnegut's *Slaughterhouse Five* into the
furnace in 1973, it wasn't because the school was low on fuel. That burning was
symbolic, too. Indeed, the two pyres—in North Dakota and in Balitmore—were
witnessing to the same lack of faith in the free exchange of ideas. *qd pt.*

What an inspiring homily for the children attending services at a liberated 8
church: They now know that the way to handle ideas they don't like is to set
them on fire.

The stirring ceremony in Baltimore is just one more illustration that the 9
spirit of the First Amendment is not being savaged only by malign forces of the
Right, whether private or governmental. Campaigns to purge school libraries,
for example, have been conducted by feminists as well as by Phyllis Schlafly.
Yet, most liberal watchdogs of our freedom remain fixed on the Right as *the*
enemy of free expression.

For a salubrious change, therefore, let us look at what is happening to free- 10
dom of speech and press in certain enclaves—some colleges, for instance—
where the New Right has no clout at all. Does the pulse of the First Amendment
beat more vigorously in these places than where the Yahoos are? *Gulliver's Travels*

Well, consider what happened when Eldridge Cleaver came to Madison, 11
Wisconsin, last October to savor the exhilarating openness of dialogue at the
University of Wisconsin. Cleaver's soul is no longer on ice; it's throbbing instead
with a religious conviction that is currently connected financially, and presum-
ably theologically, to the Reverend Sun Myung Moon's Unification Church. In
Madison, Cleaver never got to talk about his pilgrim's progress from the Black
Panthers to the wondrously ecumenical Moonies. In the Humanities Building—
Humanities—several hundred students and others outraged by Cleaver's
apostasy shouted, stamped their feet, chanted "Sieg Heil," and otherwise prevented him from being heard.

After ninety minutes of the din, Cleaver wrote on the blackboard, "I regret 12
that the totalitarians have deprived us of our constitutional rights to free assembly and free speech. Down with communism. Long live democracy."

And, raising a clenched fist while blowing kisses with his free hand, Cleaver 13
left. Cleaver says he'll try to speak again, but he doesn't know when.

The University of Wisconsin administration, through Dean of Students Paul 14
Ginsberg, deplored the behavior of the campus totalitarians of the Left, and
there was a fiercely denunciatory editorial in the Madison *Capital Times:*
"These people lack even the most primitive appreciation of the Bill of Rights."

It did occur to me, however, that if Eldridge Cleaver had not abandoned his 15
secularist rage at the American Leviathan *sea monster* and had come to Madison as the still
burning spear of black radicalism, the result might have been quite different if
he had been shouted down that night by young apostles of the New Right. That
would have made news around the country, and there would have been collectively signed letters to the *New York Review of Books* and *The Nation* warning
of the prowling dangers to free speech in the land. But since Cleaver has long
since taken up with bad companions, there is not much concern among those
who used to raise bail for him as to whether he gets to speak freely or not.

A few years ago, William F. Buckley Jr., invited to be commencement speaker 16

wholesome/healthful

Yahoos- brutish creatures subject to the Houyhnhnms- rational or man.

at Vassar, was told by student groups that he not only would be shouted down if he came but might also suffer some contusions. All too few liberal members of the Vassar faculty tried to educate their students about the purpose of a university, and indeed a good many faculty members joined in the protests against Buckley's coming. He finally decided not to appear because, he told me, he didn't want to spoil the day for the parents. I saw no letters on behalf of Buckley's free-speech rights in any of the usual liberal forums for such concerns. After all, he had not only taken up with bad companions; he was an original bad companion.

get example

※ During the current academic year, there were dismaying developments concerning freedom for bad ideas in the college press. The managing editor of *The Daily Lobo*, the University of New Mexico's student newspaper, claimed in an editorial that Scholastic Aptitude Test scores show minority students to be academically inferior. Rather than rebut his facile misinterpretation of what those scores actually show—that class, not race, affects the results—black students and their sympathizers invaded the newspaper's office.   17

The managing editor prudently resigned, but the protesters were not satisfied. They wanted the head of the editor. The brave Student Publications Board temporarily suspended her, although the chairman of the journalism department had claimed the suspension was a violation of her First Amendment rights. She was finally given her job back, pending a formal hearing, but she decided to quit. The uproar had not abated, and who knew what would happen at her formal hearing before the Student Publications Board?   18

When it was all over, the chairman of the journalism department observed that the confrontation had actually reinforced respect for First Amendment rights on the University of New Mexico campus because infuriated students now knew they couldn't successfully insist on the firing of an editor because of what had been published.   19

What about the resignations? Oh, they were free-will offerings.   20

I subscribe to most of the journalism reviews around the country, but I saw no offer of support to those two beleaguered student editors in New Mexico from professional journalists who invoke the First Amendment at almost any public opportunity.   21

Then there was a free-speech war at Kent State University, as summarized in the November 12, 1982, issue of *National On-Campus Report.* Five student groups at Kent State are vigorously attempting to get the editor of the student newspaper fired. They are: "gay students, black students, the undergraduate and graduate student governments, and a progressive student alliance."   22

Not a reactionary among them. Most are probably deeply concerned with the savaging of the free press in Chile, Uruguay, Guatemala, South Africa, and other such places.   *hostility; antagonism*

What had this editor at Kent State done to win the enmity of so humanistic a grand alliance? He had written an editorial that said that a gay student group should not have access to student-fee money to sponsor a Hallowe'en dance. Ah, but how had he gone about making his point?   24

"In opening statements," says the *National On-Campus Report,* "he employed words like 'queer' and 'nigger' to show that prejudice against any group   25 is undesirable." Just like Lenny Bruce. Lenny, walking on stage in a club, peering into the audience, and asking, "Any spics here tonight? Any kikes? Any niggers?"

Do you think Lenny Bruce could get many college bookings today? Or write a column for a college newspaper?   26

In any case, the rest of the editorial went on to claim that the proper use of student fees was for educational, not social, activities. The editor was not singling out the Kent Gay/Lesbian Foundation. He was opposed to *any* student organization using those fees for dances.   27

Never mind. He had used impermissible words. Queer. Nigger. And those five influential cadres of students are after his head. The editor says that university officials have assured him, however, that he is protected at Kent State by the First Amendment. If that proves to be the case, those five student groups will surely move to terminate, if not defenestrate, those university officials.   28

It is difficult to be a disciple of James Madison on campus these days. Take the case of Phyllis Schlafly and Wabash College. The college is a small, well-regarded liberal arts institution in Crawfordsville, Indiana. In the spring of 1981, the college was riven with discord. Some fifty members of the ninety-odd faculty and staff wrote a stiff letter to the Wabash Lecture Series Committee, which had displayed the exceedingly poor taste to invite Schlafly to speak on campus the next year.   29

The faculty protesters complained that having the Sweetheart of the Right near the Wabash River would be "unfortunate and inappropriate." The dread Schlafly is "an ERA opponent . . . a far-right attorney who travels the country, being highly paid to tell women to stay at home fulfilling traditional roles while sending their sons off to war."   30

Furthermore, the authors wrote, "The point of view she represents is that of an ever-decreasing minority of American women and men, and is based in sexist mythology which promulgates beliefs inconsistent with those held by liberally educated persons, and this does not merit a forum at Wabash College under the sponsorship of our Lecture Series."   31

This is an intriguing document by people steeped in the traditions of academic freedom. One of the ways of deciding who gets invited to a campus is the speaker's popularity. If the speaker appeals only to a "decreasing minority of American women and men," she's not worth the fee. So much for Dorothy Day, were she still with us.   32

And heaven forfend that anyone be invited whose beliefs are "inconsistent with those held by liberally educated persons." Mirror, mirror on the wall. . . .   33

But do not get the wrong idea about these protesting faculty members: "We subscribe," they emphasized, "to the principles of free speech and free association, of course."   34

All the same, "it does not enhance our image as an all-male college to endorse a well-known sexist by inviting her to speak on our campus." If Phyllis Schlafly is invited nonetheless, "we intend not to participate in any of the activities surrounding Ms. Schlafly's visit and will urge others to do the same."   35

The moral of the story: If you don't like certain ideas, boycott them.   36

The lecture committee responded to the fifty deeply offended faculty mem-   37 bers in a most unkind way. The committee told the signers that "William Buckley would endorse your petition. No institution of higher learning, he told us on a visit here, should allow to be heard on its campus any position that it regards as detrimental or 'untrue.'

"Apparently," the committee went on, "error is to be refuted not by rational persuasion, but by censorship."   38

Phyllis Schlafly did come to Wabash and she generated a great deal of discussion—most of it against her views—among members of the all-male student body. However, some of the wounded faculty took a long time to recover. One of them, a tenured professor, took aside at a social gathering the wife of a member of the lecture committee that had invited Schlafly. Both were in the same feminist group on campus.   39

The professor cleared her throat, and said to the other woman, "You are going to leave him, aren't you?"   40

"My husband? Why should I leave him?"   41

"Really, how can you stay married to someone who invited Phyllis Schlafly to this campus?"   42

And really, should such a man even be allowed visitation rights with the children?   43

Then there is the Ku Klux Klan. As Klan members have learned in recent months, both in Boston and in Washington, their First Amendment right peaceably to assemble—let alone actually to speak their minds—can only be exercised if they are prepared to be punched in the mouth. Klan members get the same reception that Martin Luther King Jr. and his associates used to receive in Bull Conner's Birmingham.   44

As all right-thinking people know, however, the First Amendment isn't just for anybody. That presumably is why the administration of the University of Cincinnati has refused this year to allow the KKK to appear on campus. Bill Wilkerson, the Imperial Wizard of the particular Klan faction that has been barred from the University of Cincinnati, says he's going to sue on First Amendment grounds.   45

Aside from the ACLU's, how many *amicus* briefs do you think the Imperial Wizard is likely to get from liberal organizations devoted to academic freedom?   46

The Klan also figures in a dismaying case from Vancouver, Washington. There, an all-white jury awarded $1,000 to a black high school student after he had charged the Battle Ground School District (including Prairie High School) with discrimination. One of the claims was that the school had discriminated against this young man by permitting white students to wear Ku Klux Klan costumes to a Hallowe'en assembly.   47

Symbolic speech, however, is like spoken or written speech. It is protected under the First Amendment. If the high school administration had originally forbidden the wearing of the Klan costumes to the Hallowe'en assembly, it would have spared itself that part of the black student's lawsuit, but it would have set a precedent for censoring symbolic speech which would have shrunken First Amendment protections at Prairie High School.   48

What should the criteria be for permissible costumes at a Hallowe'en assem-   49 bly? None that injure the feelings of another student? So a Palestinian kid couldn't wear a PLO outfit. Or a Jewish kid couldn't come as Ariel Sharon, festooned with maps. And watch out for the wise guy who comes dressed as that all-around pain-in-the-ass, Tom Paine.

School administrators might say the best approach is to have no costumes   50 at all. That way, there'll be no danger of disruption. But if there were real danger of physical confrontation in the school when a student wears a Klan costume, is the school so powerless that it can't prevent a fight? And indeed, what a compelling opportunity the costumes present to teach about the Klan, to ask those white kids who wore Klan costumes what they know of the history of the Klan. To get black and white kids *talking* about what the Klan represents, in history—and right now.

Such teaching is too late for Prairie High School. After that $1,000 award to   51 the black student, the white kids who have been infected by Klan demonology will circulate their poison only among themselves, intensifying their sickness of spirit. There will be no more Klan costumes in that school, and so no more Klan costumes to stimulate class discussion.

By the way, in the trial, one offer of proof that the school district had been   52 guilty of discrimination was a photograph of four white boys wearing Klan costumes to that Hallowe'en assembly. It's a rare picture. It was originally printed in the school yearbook but, with the lawsuit and all, the picture was cut out of each yearbook before it was distributed.

That's the thing about censorship, whether good liberals or bad companions   53 engage in it. Censorship is like a greased pig. Hard to confine. You start trying to deal with offensive costumes and you wind up with a blank space in the yearbook. Isn't that just like the Klan? Causing decent people to do dumb things.

QUESTIONS FOR MEANING

1. How many of the names in the third paragraph can you identify? What do they have in common?
2. Hentoff writes that book burners sometimes defend themselves by arguing that their actions are only symbolic. Later in his essay he writes of the importance of "symbolic speech." What does he mean by "symbolic," and why does he believe that symbols are important?
3. Do you recognize the allusion to "Yahoos"? In what great work of literature did these creatures originally appear? How would you define them in your own words?
4. Is Hentoff being ironic when he writes of "bad companions" in paragraph 15? Do you detect irony anywhere else in the essay? How can you tell?
5. Do you understand the unexplained references to Lenny Bruce, William F. Buckley, Dorothy Day, Ariel Sharon, and Tom Paine? What do these allusions reveal about the audience for whom Hentoff originally wrote?
6. Vocabulary: pernicious (1), expurgated (2), homily (8), apostasy (11), ecumenical (11), cadres (28), and promulgates (31).

QUESTIONS ABOUT STRATEGY

1. Does Hentoff advance his argument principally through the use of induction or deduction?
2. What is the function of paragraph 14?
3. What sort of people does Hentoff seem most anxious to persuade?
4. Why does Hentoff single out James Madison among the Founding Fathers? Would a reference to Jefferson or Monroe have served just as well?
5. Consider the paragraphing of this essay. Most of the paragraphs are fairly short and a few are very short. Is the result emphatic or choppy?

SUSAN BROWNMILLER
Pornography Hurts Women

Susan Brownmiller (b. 1935) has worked as an actress, a researcher for Newsweek, *and a network newswriter for the American Broadcasting Company. She is best known for her contributions to the Woman's movement. She was a cofounder of Radical Feminists and helped to organize Women Against Pornography, an organization that has actively campaigned against the publication and sale of works which degrade women. Her most recent book is* Feminity *(1984). But the following essay is an excerpt from the book that made her reputation,* Against Our Will: Men, Women, and Rape *(1975). The thesis of this book is that rape is a political act through which men repress women by keeping them in a constant state of fear. The controversy that this book provoked helped make it one of the most widely read of all feminist works.*

Pornography has been so thickly glossed over with the patina of chic these   1
days in the name of verbal freedom and sophistication that important distinctions between freedom of political expression (a democratic necessity), honest sex education for children (a societal good) and ugly smut (the deliberate devaluation of the role of women through obscene, distorted depictions) have been hopelessly confused. Part of the problem is that those who traditionally have been the most vigorous opponents of porn are often those same people who shudder at the explicit mention of any sexual subject. Under their watchful, vigilante eyes, frank and free dissemination of educational materials relating to abortion, contraception, the act of birth, and female biology in general is also dangerous, subversive and dirty. (I am not unmindful that a frank and free discussion of rape, "the unspeakable crime," might well give these righteous vigilantes further cause to shudder.) Because the battle lines were falsely drawn a long time ago, before there was a vocal women's movement, the anti-pornography forces appear to be, for the most part, religious, Southern, conservative and right-wing, while the pro-porn forces are identified as Eastern, atheistic and liberal.

But a woman's perspective demands a totally new alignment, or at least a   2
fresh appraisal. The majority report of the President's Commission on Obscenity and Pornography (1970), a report that argued strongly for the removal of
all legal restrictions on pornography, soft and hard, made plain that 90 percent
of all pornographic material is geared to the male heterosexual market (the
other 10 percent is geared to the male homosexual taste), that buyers of porn
are "predominantly white, middle-class, middle-aged married males" and that
the graphic depictions, the meat and potatoes of porn, are of the naked female
body and of the multiplicity of acts done to that body.

Discussing the content of stag films, "a familiar and firmly established part   3
of the American scene," the commission report dutifully, if foggily, explained,
"Because pornography historically has been thought to be primarily a masculine interest, the emphasis in stag films seems to represent the preferences of
the middle-class American male. Thus male homosexuality and bestiality are
relatively rare, while lesbianism is rather common."

The commissioners in this instance had merely verified what purveyors of   4
porn have always known: hard-core pornography is not a celebration of sexual
freedom; it is a cynical exploitation of female sexual activity through the device
of making all such activity, and consequently all females, "dirty." Heterosexual
male consumers of pornography are frankly turned on by watching lesbians in
action (although never in the final scenes, but always as a curtain raiser); they
are turned off with the sudden swiftness of a water faucet by watching naked
men act upon each other. One study quoted in the commission report came to
the unastounding conclusion that "seeing a stag film in the presence of male
peers bolsters masculine esteem." Indeed. The men in groups who watch the
films, it is important to note, are *not* naked.

When male response to pornography is compared to female response, a   5
pronounced difference in attitude emerges. According to the commission,
"Males report being more highly aroused by depictions of nude females, and
show more interest in depictions of nude females than [do] females." Quoting
the figures of Alfred Kinsey, the commission noted that a majority of males (77
percent) were "aroused" by visual depictions of explicit sex while a majority of
females (68 percent) were not aroused. Further, "females more often than
males reported 'disgust' and 'offense.'"

From whence comes this female disgust and offense? Are females sexually   6
backward or more conservative by nature? The gut distaste that a majority of
women feel when we look at pornography, a distaste that, incredibly, it is no
longer fashionable to admit, comes, I think, from the gut knowledge that we
and our bodies are being stripped, exposed and contorted for the purpose of
ridicule to bolster that "masculine esteem" which gets its kick and sense of
power from viewing females as anonymous, panting playthings, adult toys,
dehumanized objects to be used, abused, broken and discarded.

This, of course, is also the philosophy of rape. It is no accident (for what else   7
could be its purpose?) that females in the pornographic genre are depicted in
two cleanly delineated roles: as virgins who are caught and "banged" or as
nymphomaniacs who are never sated. The most popular and prevalent porno-

graphic fantasy combines the two: an innocent, untutored female is raped and "subjected to unnatural practices" that turn her into a raving, slobbering nymphomaniac, a dependent sexual slave who can never get enough of the big, male cock.

There can be no "equality" in porn, no female equivalent, no turning of the tables in the name of bawdy fun. Pornography, like rape, is a male invention, designed to dehumanize women, to reduce the female to an object of sexual access, not to free sensuality from moralistic or parental inhibition. The staple of porn will always be the naked female body, breasts and genitals exposed, because as man devised it, her naked body is the female's "shame," her private parts the private property of man, while his are the ancient, holy, universal, patriarchal instrument of his power, his rule by force over *her*.

Pornography is the undiluted essence of anti-female propaganda. Yet the very same liberals who were so quick to understand the method and purpose behind the mighty propaganda machine of Hitler's Third Reich, the consciously spewed-out anti-Semitic caricatures and obscenities that gave an ideological base to the Holocaust and the Final Solution, the very same liberals who, enlightened by blacks, searched their own conscience and came to understand that their tolerance of "nigger" jokes and portrayals of shuffling, rolling-eyed servants in movies perpetuated the degrading myths of black inferiority and gave an ideological base to the continuation of black oppression—these very same liberals now fervidly maintain that the hatred and contempt for women that find expression in four-letter words used as expletives and in what are quaintly called "adult" or "erotic" books and movies are a valid extension of freedom of speech that must be preserved as a Constitutional right.

To defend the right of a lone, crazed American Nazi to grind out propaganda calling for the extermination of all Jews, as the ACLU has done in the name of free speech, is, after all, a self-righteous and not particularly courageous stand, for American Jewry is not currently threatened by storm troopers, concentration camps and imminent extermination, but I wonder if the ACLU's position might change if, come tomorrow morning, the bookstores and movie theaters lining Forty-second Street in New York City were devoted not to the humiliation of women by rape and torture, as they currently are, but to a systematized, commercially successful propaganda machine depicting the sadistic pleasures of gassing Jews or lynching blacks?

Is this analogy extreme? Not if you are a woman who is conscious of the ever-present threat of rape and the proliferation of a cultural ideology that makes it sound like "liberated" fun. The majority report of the President's Commission on Obscenity and Pornography tried to pooh-pooh the opinion of law enforcement agencies around the country that claimed their own concrete experience with offenders who were caught with the stuff led them to conclude that pornographic material is a causative factor in crimes of sexual violence. The commission maintained that it was not possible at this time to scientifically prove or disprove such a connection.

But does one need scientific methodology in order to conclude that the anti-female propaganda that permeates our nation's cultural output promotes a climate in which acts of sexual hostility directed against women are not only tolerated but ideologically encouraged? A similar debate has raged for many years over whether or not the extensive glorification of violence (the gangster as hero; the loving treatment accorded bloody shoot-'em-ups in movies, books and on TV) has a causal effect, a direct relationship to the rising rate of crime, particularly among youth. Interestingly enough, in this area—nonsexual and not specifically related to abuses against women—public opinion seems to be swinging to the position that explicit violence in the entertainment media does have a deleterious effect; it makes violence commonplace, numbingly routine and no longer morally shocking.

More to the point, those who call for a curtailment of scenes of violence in movies and on television in the name of sensitivity, good taste and what's best for our children are not accused of being pro-censorship or against freedom of speech. Similarly, minority group organizations, black, Hispanic, Japanese, Italian, Jewish, or American Indian, that campaign against ethnic slurs and demeaning portrayals in movies, on television shows and in commercials are perceived as waging a just political fight, for if a minority group claims to be offended by a specific portrayal, be it Little Black Sambo or the Frito Bandido, and relates it to a history of ridicule and oppression, few liberals would dare to trot out a Constitutional argument in theoretical opposition, not if they wish to maintain their liberal credentials. Yet when it comes to the treatment of women, the liberal consciousness remains fiercely obdurate, refusing to be budged, for the sin of appearing square or prissy in the age of the so-called sexual revolution has become the worst offense of all.   13

QUESTIONS FOR MEANING

1. Does Brownmiller believe that pornography should be censored? Where does she state her position most clearly?
2. According to Brownmiller, what is the relationship between pornography and rape? Do you agree with her that women live in the "ever-present threat of rape"?
3. What is "foggy" about the quotation cited in paragraph 3?
4. Why does Brownmiller believe that there can be "no female equivalent" of male heterosexual pornography, "no turning of the tables in the name of bawdy fun"? Do you agree with her?
5. Vocabulary: patina (1), chic (1), vigilante (1), nymphomaniac (7), patriarchal (8), caricatures (9), permeates (12), and obdurate (13).

QUESTIONS ABOUT STRATEGY

1. Why does Brownmiller use a word like "cock" in the middle of an argument against pornography?
2. Brownmiller asks if her analogy between pornography and Nazi propaganda is extreme. What do you think? How would you respond to the rhetorical question with which paragraph 12 begins?

3. Writing in the mid-seventies, Brownmiller complained that it was not fashionable to oppose pornography—that "appearing square or prissy in the age of the so-called sexual revolution had become the worst offense of all." What advantage is there in claiming that one's argument is unfashionable? Would Brownmiller be able to make this claim today?
4. Is Brownmiller writing primarily for men, women, or both? Would her argument convince someone who did not agree with her already?

WENDY KAMINER

Pornography and the First Amendment: Prior Restraints and Private Action

Wendy Kaminer (b. 1949) graduated from Smith College in 1971 and the Boston University Law School in 1975. An active feminist, she is the author of Women Volunteering: The Pleasure, Pain, & Politics of Unpaid Work from 1830 to the Present *(1984). In 1980, she contributed the following essay to* Take Back the Night, *an anthology of feminist perspectives on pornography. Although Kaminer believes that pornography reinforces sexist stereotypes that demean and endanger women, she opposes efforts to censor it. Her essay explains the procedural safeguards, mandated by the First Amendment, that protect the basic right to free expression and make it impossible, in her view, to prohibit pornography without prohibiting other forms of speech as well. She encourages women to speak out against pornography without asking the government to take any action against it.*

Feminist protests against pornography often seem to posit a choice between   1
the First Amendment rights of a few pornographers and the safety, dignity, and independence of all women. Pornography is speech that legitimizes and fosters the physical abuse and sexual repression of women, and censorship appeals to some as a simple matter of self-preservation. A battle line has been drawn between "feminists" and "First Amendment absolutists," and the Women's Liberation Movement, which has been a struggle for civil rights and freedom of choice, has suddenly become tainted, in the popular view, with a streak of antilibertarianism.

None of this has been necessary. The bitter debate over pornography and   2
free speech derives from misconceptions on both sides about the methods and goals of the anti-pornography movement and the practical meaning of First Amendment guarantees of free speech. Feminists need not and should not advocate censorship, but we have every right to organize politically and to protest material that is degrading and dangerous to women.

There are two basic constitutional principles that must be understood in   3
formulating a position against pornography:

1. Public v. private action. The First Amendment guarantees freedom of speech against government interference and repression. It does not restrict or even apply to private actions.
2. Prior restraint. The government cannot impose restraints on the publication of speech that has not first been proven illegal. It can only act after the fact to punish someone for saying something illegal; it cannot stop her from saying it.

The First Amendment is a restriction of the power of the government to   4
restrain or repress speech; it establishes a right to free speech in the individual in relation with her government. It does not affect or apply to private relationships; it does not restrict private actions.

Women can protest pornography with impunity under the First Amendment   5
as long as they do not invoke or advocate the exercise of government authority. Only the government, by definition, can violate a First Amendment right. A woman who goes as far as "trashing" a porn shop could be convicted of a variety of offenses under the state criminal law and would probably be liable to the target business in a civil-damage action, but she would not have violated any rights to free speech.

We have our own First Amendment right to protest pornography, to engage   6
in consciousness-raising and political organizing. The First Amendment is designed to maintain an open "marketplace of ideas," an arena in which competing private-interest groups can assert their views free of government repression. Women speaking out against pornography are fulfilling a classic First Amendment role.

The First Amendment applies to government action at the state or federal   7
level. Generally the control of obscenity or pornography in practice is a matter of state law, although there are federal statutes prohibiting interstate, international, or postal traffic in obscene materials. But official regulation of speech at any level is governed by constitutionally mandated rules of legal procedure designed to protect the basic right *to* speak.

The heart of the First Amendment is its procedural safeguards against the   8
imposition of prior restraints on any form of speech. It protects the act of expression, although it may not always protect the substance of what is said. Obscenity may, in principle, be prohibited under state law and is generally treated as a criminal offense. But the government may not restrain or prohibit any material before a judicial determination that it is, in fact, obscene. The government may not, in practice, take any general action, either civil or criminal, against a class of speech; it may only act against an individual utterance *after* it has been proven to fall within an unprotected class or to present an immediate threat to the national security.

Freedom of speech is largely a matter of procedure; the First Amendment   9
works by narrowly proscribing the power of the government to enforce speech-related prohibitions. Its enforcement process is borrowed from criminal law. All

speech is presumed protected until proven otherwise, just as all defendants in criminal cases are presumed innocent until proven guilty. In each case the government bears a heavy burden of proof, and a conviction of guilt or a finding of obscenity depends on the weight of the evidence. Every instance of speech must be judged individually on its own merits before it may be prohibited, just as every criminal defendant must be tried before he may be sentenced.

Obscenity is not, in theory, protected by the First Amendment. In 1957 in 10 *Roth* v. *United States*, 354 U.S. 476, the Supreme Court held that obscenity (like libel) was simply not speech and could be prohibited. But the practical problems of defining obscenity and separating it from protected speech are overwhelming. The current definition of obscenity was enunciated by the Supreme Court in 1973, in *Miller* v. *California*, 413 U.S. 15. It is material "that the average person, applying community standards, would find . . . as a whole, appeals to the prurient interest," material that "depicts or describes, in a patently offensive way, sexual conduct specifically defined by the applicable state law," and material that "taken as a whole, lacks serious artistic, political, or scientific value."

Most hard-core pornography would probably be found legally obscene under 11 *Miller* and could therefore be prohibited. But effective, generalized enforcement of obscenity laws is not possible without violating the very basic prohibition of prior restraints.

Every single book, magazine, or film must be proven to be obscene in an 12 individualized judicial proceeding before it may be enjoined. This makes it almost impossible for the government to take any generalized action against businesses that regularly deal in pornography. A bookstore selling allegedly obscene material cannot be closed by the state until every book in it has been found obscene—in court. A store with an inventory of 1,000 books cannot be closed because of 50 or 100 or even 500 obscenity convictions. The state cannot restrain the sale of remaining or future stock that has not been proven obscene and must all be presumed to be protected speech. Broad civil-injunctive relief against pornography-related businesses is barred by the prohibition of prior restraints, regardless of the number of underlying obscenity convictions.

Even individual convictions for obscenity are difficult to obtain, and the 13 process in each case is complicated by First Amendment procedures. The seizure of any allegedly obscene material for use in a pending trial must be based on a narrowly drawn judicial warrant and cannot completely cut off access to the material. Thus, a district attorney may seize one copy of a book as evidence in a given case, but he cannot prohibit its sale or distribution before a hearing or judicial determination of obscenity. Seizures of material for evidence in obscenity cases must comport with due-process requirements under the First Amendment as well as with Fourth Amendment standards for search and seizure. Obscenity prosecutions are long, costly, and unpredictable and are, necessarily, a piecemeal approach to the problem of pornography.

The attempt to define and control obscenity simply hasn't worked for feminists or First Amendment lawyers. The Court has been struggling with a legal definition for the past twenty years since the current obscenity doctrine was formulated in *Roth.* The definition has undergone relatively minor changes since then, the most important being the shift to local standards of "prurience." In addition, the courts changed the requirement that the work in question be "entirely without redeeming value" to an evaluation of the work "as a whole." These changes have apparently not increased the general number of obscenity prosecutions or the rate of convictions.

Moreover, the current definition of obscenity is conceptually unsound, for it 15 does not set forth a predictable, objective test even for hard-core, sexually explicit material. Instead, it involves a balancing of the social and cultural utility of the material at issue with community standards of prurience. This belies the principle on which it is based: that obscenity can be identified and prohibited.

There is, of course, a good deal of frustration among feminists about ineffec- 16 tive obscenity laws, and a natural concern for developing feasible legal alter- natives. It has been suggested that pornography could be readily prohibited because it is dangerous and incites violence against women, based on the "clear and present danger" standard of review traditionally invoked by the Court in free-speech cases. The perception that pornography is dangerous is basic and must be impressed upon the public consciousness, but it does not translate so simply into First Amendment law.

The clear and present danger standard would actually afford greater legal 17 protection to pornography than current obscenity laws. It is a strict standard of review, governing the regulation or prohibition of *protected* speech. It is, arguably, sounder constitutional law than the formulation of obscenity as "non- speech," and it more accurately reflects a feminist view of pornography as dangerous propaganda, but it would substantially restrict government control over obscene material. The clear and present danger standard is more logically invoked in *defense* of pornography. It was, in fact, unsuccessfully advocated by the defendant in *Roth* v. *United States,* 354 U.S. 476, in which the Court, instead, carved out an obscenity exception to the First Amendment. Feminists who urge the adoption of this standard should understand its legal and political implications. Otherwise they may find themselves unwittingly on the side of the pornographers and First Amendment absolutists.

The clear and present danger standard describes a very narrow exception 18 to the general restriction of government power over protected First Amend- ment activity. It was formulated to review instances of official repression of political speech: Clear and present danger essentially means an immediate threat to the national security. The standard was first enunciated by the Su- preme Court in 1919 after the First World War, to allow for prosecutions for antidraft pamphleteering under the Espionage Act; it was used in the early 1950's to uphold convictions for allegedly "subversive" speech under the Smith Act; it has recently been invoked unsuccessfully by the government in an attempt to restrain the publication of the Pentagon Papers. It is applied in cases in which the government appears as the "aggrieved party," i.e., in its role as guardian of the national security. Its use in a pornography case would raise an initial problem of identifying a plaintiff; pornography may be a crime against women, but it is not necessarily a crime against the state.

Adoption of a clear and present danger standard to prohibit pornography   19
would be an implicit recognition that it is protected political speech, which
would considerably heighten practical problems of proof and enforcement. It is
probably easier to prove that a given instance of speech is "obscene" than to
prove that it presents "an immediate danger," and the clear and present danger
standard imposes a particularly heavy burden of proof on the government. It
must demonstrate in every case, with direct factual evidence, a compelling,
even overwhelming threat to the national security. This does not mean that the
speech at issue might be or could be dangerous, and it does not refer to the
cumulative effect of a certain kind of speech. It means a tangible, immediate,
and individualized danger that can only be avoided by suppressing publication.

Sociological studies and expert testimony pointing to a connection between   20
pornography generally and violence against women would not establish a clear
and present danger in an individual case, as a matter of law. It might not even
be properly admissible as evidence. Use of this sort of generalized evidence to
demonstrate that a given instance of speech is dangerous would be like trying
a defendant in a criminal case with evidence of "similar" crimes committed by
"similar" people. Every instance of speech must always be tried on its own
merits; restraints could still only be imposed on specific utterances actually
found to present an immediate danger. Moreover, a retreat to a clear and
present danger standard and the acceptance of pornography as protected
speech would actually strengthen these prohibitions against prior restraints.

The final irony is that in politicizing pornography, feminists are unintention-   21
ally signaling a need for a return to a more "permissive," clear and present
danger standard in obscenity cases. Pornography is being redefined by women
in terms of power instead of sex and "prurience"; it is being characterized as
dangerous political speech. The courts are being asked to weigh the argued
connection of pornography with violence against the underlying right of
speech. This is the kind of balancing involved in a clear and present danger
case, but again this is the standard applied to protected speech and the strongest restriction of government authority under the First Amendment. By framing
pornography as political speech, feminists are, in some respects, legitimizing it
in ways that First Amendment absolutists never could.

This does not mean that pornography protests are necessarily counterpro-   22
ductive, but it underscores the need fully to understand the legal process while
shaping an effective anti-pornography movement. It makes little sense for feminists to focus on a legal "war" against pornography or to direct much energy
to reformulating obscenity prohibitions.

The primary obstacles to effective legal control of pornography are proce-   23
dural not definitional; it's not so much a matter of the standard that is used to
identify unprotected speech in each case (which may change) but the procedures by which they are applied, which must remain constant. We cannot point
to a dearth of women judges, prosecutors, or jurors to explain the failure of the
system to enforce obscenity laws, because the problem is not in the way in
which pornography is perceived but in the ways in which laws must be enforced. We must understand that procedural safeguards cannot be suspended
simply to deal with pornography or any other single class of speech. These

procedures are meaningless if not applied in every instance, because they are specifically designed to insure a consistent legal process; in First Amendment cases they provide additionally for the narrow enforcement of speech-related regulations, so as not to infringe upon or deter protected activities. The underlying principle of the First Amendment is that the power of the government to regulate speech and political dissent that would derive from a system of prior restraints would be more dangerous than any given instance of unprotected speech.

We simply cannot look to the government to rid us of pornography; legally there are no "final solutions." The feminist movement against pornography must remain an anti-defamation movement, involved in education, consciousness-raising, and the development of private strategies against the industry. We have a crucial role of our own to play in a marketplace in which pornography is flourishing.   24

But it is essential for us to maintain a larger political perspective and a sense of ourselves as one of many competing private-interest groups. We can and should speak out, and take action against pornographers because they comprise a hostile group with interests antithetical to our own, that threatens our independence and well-being; but we cannot ask the government to speak for us. The Women's Movement is a civil rights movement, and we should appreciate the importance of individual freedom of choice and the danger of turning popular sentiment into law in areas affecting individual privacy.   25

Legislative or judicial control of pornography is simply not possible without breaking down the legal principles and procedures that are essential to our own right to speak and, ultimately, our freedom to control our own lives. We must continue to organize against pornography and the degradation and abuse of women, but we must not ask the government to take up our struggle for us. The power it will assume to do so will be far more dangerous to us all than the "power" of pornography.   26

QUESTIONS FOR MEANING

1. Why does Kaminer argue that the present legal definition of obscenity is inadequate? And why does she believe that the "primary obstacles to effective legal control of pornography are procedural not definitional"? Explain this distinction in your own words.
2. What is meant by the important legal principle known as "prior restraint"?
3. Explain the "clear and present danger" standard first invoked by the government in 1919. Can you give an example of a "clear and present danger" that would be forceful enough to justify an exception to the First Amendment guarantee of free speech? According to Kaminer, why would this be a dangerous clause to invoke against pornography?
4. What is the constitutional difference between private and public action? Within this context, can you explain what "private" and "public" mean?
5. Vocabulary: posit (1), tainted (1), antilibertarianism (1), prurient (10), enjoined (12), comport (13), and dearth (23).

QUESTIONS ABOUT STRATEGY

1. At what points in her essay does Kaminer remind us that she is personally opposed to pornography even though she is arguing against attempts to censor it?
2. To what extent does Kaminer succeed in advancing a middle view between "feminists" and "First Amendment absolutists"?
3. Comment on Kaminer's choice of the third person pronoun in paragraph 3. Does it exclude men?
4. Why does Kaminer put quotation marks around the phrase "final solutions" in paragraph 24?
5. Does Kaminer help you to understand the complexity of the law or does she bewilder you with legal jargon. Identify any parts of this argument that you found difficult to understand. Would it be possible to rewrite them more simply?

IRVING KRISTOL

Pornography, Obscenity, and the Case for Censorship

Irving Kristol (b. 1920) is one of the most prominent of the political writers and thinkers who define themselves as "neoconservatives," or new conservatives, in order to suggest that they view national affairs from a fresh perspective. He was managing editor of Commentary *1947–1952, cofounder and coeditor of* Encounter *1953–1958, and has also worked as an editor for Basic Books. He has taught at New York University since 1969, and his essays appear regularly in numerous magazines and newspapers including the* Wall Street Journal, *where he is a member of the board of contributors. A fellow of the American Academy of Arts and Sciences, Kristol wrote the following essay in 1971 when liberal values seemed to be ascendant. As its title suggests, Kristol believes that censorship can be desirable. You will find that his argument is both thoughtful and provocative.*

Being frustrated is disagreeable, but the real disasters in life begin when you get what you want. For almost a century now, a great many intelligent, well-meaning, and articulate people—of a kind generally called liberal or intellectual, or both—have argued eloquently against any kind of censorship of art and/or entertainment. And within the past ten years, the courts and the legislatures of most Western nations have found these arguments persuasive—so persuasive that hardly a man is now alive who clearly remembers what the answers to these arguments were. Today, in the United States and other democracies, censorship has to all intents and purposes ceased to exist.

Is there a sense of triumphant exhilaration in the land? Hardly. There is, on   2
the contrary, a rapidly growing unease and disquiet. Somehow, things have not
worked out as they were supposed to, and many notable civil libertarians have
gone on record as saying this was not what they meant at all. They wanted a
world in which *Desire under the Elms* could be produced, or *Ulysses* published, without interference by philistine busybodies holding public office. They
have got that, of course; but they have also got a world in which homosexual
rape takes place on the stage, in which the public flocks during lunch hours to
witness varieties of professional fornication, in which Times Square has become
little more than a hideous market for the sale and distribution of printed filth
that panders to all known (and some fanciful) sexual perversions.

But disagreeable as this may be, does it really matter? Might not our unease   3
and disquiet be merely a cultural hangover—a "hang-up," as they say? What
reason is there to think that anyone was ever corrupted by a book?

This last question, oddly enough, is asked by the very same people who seem   4
convinced that advertisements in magazines or displays of violence on television do indeed have the power to corrupt. It is also asked, incredibly enough
and in all sincerity, by people—for example, university professors and school-
teachers—whose very lives provide all the answers one could want. After all, if
you believe that no one was ever corrupted by a book, you have also to believe
that no one was ever improved by a book (or a play or a movie). You have to
believe, in other words, that all art is morally trivial and that, consequently, all
education is morally irrelevant. No one, not even a university professor, really
believes that.

To be sure, it is extremely difficult, as social scientists tell us, to trace the   5
effects of any single book (or play or movie) on an individual reader or any
class of readers. But we all know, and social scientists know it too, that the ways
in which we use our minds and imaginations do shape our characters and help
define us as persons. That those who certainly know this are nevertheless
moved to deny it merely indicates how a dogmatic resistance to the idea of
censorship can—like most dogmatism—result in a mindless insistence on the
absurd.

I have used these harsh terms—"dogmatism" and "mindless"—advisedly. I   6
might also have added "hypocritical." For the plain fact is that none of us is a
complete civil libertarian. We all believe that there is some point at which the
public authorities ought to step in to limit the "self-expression" of an individual
or a group, even where this might be seriously intended as a form of artistic
expression, and even where the artistic transaction is between consenting
adults. A playwright or theatrical director might, in this crazy world of ours,
find someone willing to commit suicide on the stage, as called for by the script.
We would not allow that—any more than we would permit scenes of real
physical torture on the stage, even if the victim were a willing masochist. And I
know of no one, no matter how free in spirit, who argues that we ought to
permit gladiatorial contests in Yankee Stadium, similar to those once performed
in the Colosseum at Rome—even if only consenting adults were involved.

The basic point that emerges is one that Walter Berns has powerfully argued: 7

No society can be utterly indifferent to the ways its citizens publicly entertain themselves.* Bearbaiting and cockfighting are prohibited only in part out of compassion for the suffering animals; the main reason they were abolished was because it was felt that they debased and brutalized the citizenry who flocked to witness such spectacles. And the question we face with regard to pornography and obscenity is whether, now that they have such strong legal protection from the Supreme Court, they can or will brutalize and debase our citizenry. We are, after all, not dealing with one passing incident—one book, or one play, or one movie. We are dealing with a general tendency that is suffusing our entire culture.

I say pornography *and* obscenity because, though they have different dictionary definitions and are frequently distinguishable as "artistic" genres, they are nevertheless in the end identical in effect. Pornography is not objectionable simply because it arouses sexual desire or lust or prurience in the mind of the reader or spectator; this is a silly Victorian notion. A great many nonpornographic works—including some parts of the Bible—excite sexual desire very successfully. What is distinctive about pornography is that, in the words of D. H. Lawrence, it attempts "to do dirt on [sex] . . . [It is an] insult to a vital human relationship." 8

In other words, pornography differs from erotic art in that its whole purpose is to treat human beings obscenely, to deprive human beings of their specifically human dimension. That is what obscenity is all about. It is light years removed from any kind of carefree sensuality—there is no continuum between Fielding's *Tom Jones* and the Marquis de Sade's *Justine*. These works have quite opposite intentions. To quote Susan Sontag: "What pornographic literature does is precisely to drive a wedge between one's existence as a full human being and one's existence as a sexual being—while in ordinary life a healthy person is one who prevents such a gap from opening up." This definition occurs in an essay *defending* pornography—Miss Sontag is a candid as well as gifted critic—so the definition, which I accept, is neither tendentious nor censorious. 9

Along these same lines, one can point out—as C. S. Lewis pointed out some years back—that it is no accident that in the history of all literatures obscene words, the so-called four-letter words, have always been the vocabulary of farce or vituperation. The reason is clear; they reduce men and women to some of their mere bodily functions—they reduce man to his animal component, and such a reduction is an essential purpose of farce or vituperation. 10

Similarly, Lewis also suggested that it is not an accident that we have no offhand, colloquial, neutral terms—not in any Western European language at any rate—for our most private parts. The words we do use are either (1) nursery terms, (2) archaisms, (3) scientific terms, or (4) a term from the gutter (i.e., a demeaning term). Here I think the genius of language is telling us something important about man. It is telling us that man is an animal with a difference: He has a unique sense of privacy, and a unique capacity for shame 11

*This is as good a place as any to express my profound indebtedness to Walter Berns's superb essay "Pornography vs. Democracy," in the Winter 1971 issue of *The Public Interest*.

when this privacy is violated. Our "private parts" are indeed private, and not merely because convention prescribes it. This particular convention is indigenous to the human race. In practically all primitive tribes, men and women cover their private parts; and in practically all primitive tribes, men and women do not copulate in public.

It may well be that Western society, in the latter half of the twentieth century,   12
is experiencing a drastic change in sexual mores and sexual relationships. We have had many such "sexual revolutions" in the past—the bourgeois family and bourgeois ideas of sexual propriety were themselves established in the course of a revolution against eighteenth-century "licentiousness"—and we shall doubtless have others in the future. It is, however, highly improbable (to put it mildly) that what we are witnessing is the Final Revolution which will make sexual relations utterly unproblematic, permit us to dispense with any kind of ordered relationships between the sexes, and allow us freely to redefine the human condition. And so long as humanity has not reached that utopia, obscenity will remain a problem.

One of the reasons it will remain a problem is that obscenity is not merely   13
about sex, any more than science fiction is about science. Science fiction, as every student of the genre knows, is a peculiar vision of power: What it is really about is politics. And obscenity is a peculiar vision of humanity: What it is really about is ethics and metaphysics.

Imagine a man—a well-known man, much in the public eye—in a hospital   14
ward, dying an agonizing death. He is not in control of his bodily functions, so that his bladder and his bowels empty themselves of their own accord. His consciousness is overwhelmed and extinguished by pain, so that he cannot communicate with us, nor we with him. Now, it would be, technically, the easiest thing in the world to put a television camera in his hospital room and let the whole world witness this spectacle. We do not do it—at least we do not do it as yet—because we regard this as an *obscene* invasion of privacy. And what would make the spectacle obscene is that we would be witnessing the extinguishing of humanity in a human animal.

Incidentally, in the past our humanitarian crusaders against capital punish-   15
ment understood this point very well. The abolitionist literature goes into great physical detail about what happens to a man when he is hanged or electrocuted or gassed. And their argument was—and is—that what happens is shockingly obscene, and that no civilized society should be responsible for perpetrating such obscenities, particularly since in the nature of the case there must be spectators to ascertain that this horror was indeed being perpetrated in fulfillment of the law.

Sex—like death—is an activity that is both animal and human. There are   16
human sentiments and human ideals involved in this animal activity. But when sex is public, the viewer does not see—cannot see—the sentiments and the ideals. He can only see the animal coupling. And that is why, when men and women make love, as we say, they prefer to be alone—because it is only when you are alone that you can make love, as distinct from merely copulating in an animal and casual way. And that, too, is why those who are voyeurs, if they are

not irredeemably sick, also feel ashamed at what they are witnessing. When sex is a public spectacle, a human relationship has been debased into a mere animal connection.

It is also worth noting that this making of sex into an obscenity is not a mutual and equal transaction but rather an act of exploitation by one of the partners—the male partner. I do not wish to get into the complicated question as to what, if any, are the essential differences—as distinct from conventional and cultural differences—between male and female. I do not claim to know the answer to that. But I do know—and I take it as a sign that has meaning—that pornography is, and always has been, a man's work; that women rarely write pornography; and that women tend to be indifferent consumers of pornography.* My own guess, by way of explanation, is that a woman's sexual experience is ordinarily more suffused with human emotion than is man's, that men are more easily satisfied with autoerotic activities, and that men can therefore more easily take a more "technocratic" view of sex and its pleasures. Perhaps this is not correct. But whatever the explanation, there can be no question that pornography is a form of "sexism," as the women's liberation movement calls it, and that the instinct of women's liberation has been unerring in perceiving that when pornography is perpetrated, it is perpetrated against them, as part of a conspiracy to deprive them of their full humanity.

But even if all this is granted, it might be said—and doubtless will be said— that I really ought not to be unduly concerned. Free competition in the cultural marketplace—it is argued by people who have never otherwise had a kind word to say for laissez-faire—will automatically dispose of the problem. The present fad for pornography and obscenity, it will be asserted, is just that, a fad. It will spend itself in the course of time; people will get bored with it, will be able to take it or leave it alone in a casual way, in a "mature way," and, in sum, I am being unnecessarily distressed about the whole business. The *New York Times,* in an editorial, concludes hopefully in this vein.

> In the end . . . the insensate pursuit of the urge to shock, carried from one excess to a more abysmal one, is bound to achieve its own antidote in total boredom. When there is no lower depth to descend to, ennui will erase the problem.

I would like to be able to go along with this line of reasoning, but I cannot. I think it is false, and for two reasons, the first psychological, the second political.

The basic psychological fact about pornography and obscenity is that it appeals to and provokes a kind of sexual regression. The sexual pleasure one gets from pornography and obscenity is autoerotic and infantile; put bluntly, it is a masturbatory exercise of the imagination, when it is not masturbation pure

17

18

19

20

---

*There are, of course, a few exceptions. *L'Histoire d'O,* for instance, was written by a woman. It is unquestionably the most *melancholy* work of pornography ever written. And its theme is precisely the dehumanization accomplished by obscenity.

and simple. Now, people who masturbate do not get bored with masturbation, just as sadists do not get bored with sadism, and voyeurs do not get bored with voyeurism.

In other words, infantile sexuality is not only a permanent temptation for   21
the adolescent or even the adult—it can quite easily become a permanent, self-reinforcing neurosis. It is because of an awareness of this possibility of regression toward the infantile condition, a regression which is always open to us, that all the codes of sexual conduct ever devised by the human race take such a dim view of autoerotic activities and try to discourage autoerotic fantasies. Masturbation is indeed a perfectly natural autoerotic activity, as so many sexologists blandly assure us today. And it is precisely because it is so perfectly natural that it can be so dangerous to the mature or maturing person, if it is not controlled or sublimated in some way. That is the true meaning of Portnoy's complaint. Portnoy, you will recall, grows up to be a man who is incapable of having an adult sexual relationship with a woman; his sexuality remains fixed in an infantile mode, the prisoner of his autoerotic fantasies. Inevitably, Portnoy comes to think, in a perfectly *infantile* way, that it was all his mother's fault.

It is true that, in our time, some quite brilliant minds have come to the   22
conclusion that a reversion to infantile sexuality is the ultimate mission and secret destiny of the human race. I am thinking in particular of Norman O. Brown, for whose writings I have the deepest respect. One of the reasons I respect them so deeply is that Mr. Brown is a serious thinker who is unafraid to face up to the radical consequences of his radical theories. Thus, Mr. Brown knows and says that for his kind of salvation to be achieved, humanity must annul the civilization it has created—not merely the civilization we have today, but all civilization—so as to be able to make the long descent backward into animal innocence.

And that is the point. What is at stake is civilization and humanity, nothing   23
less. The idea that "everything is permitted," as Nietzsche put it, rests on the premise of nihilism and has nihilistic implications. I will not pretend that the case against nihilism and for civilization is an easy one to make. We are here confronting the most fundamental of philosophical questions, on the deepest levels. In short, the matter of pornography and obscenity is not a trivial one, and only superficial minds can take a bland and untroubled view of it.

In this connection, I must also point out, those who are primarily against   24
censorship on liberal grounds tell us not to take pornography or obscenity seriously, while those who are for pornography and obscenity on radical grounds take it very seriously indeed. I believe the radicals—writers like Susan Sontag, Herbert Marcuse, Norman O. Brown, and even Jerry Rubin—are right, and the liberals are wrong. I also believe that those young radicals at Berkeley, some seven years ago, who provoked a major confrontation over the public use of obscene words, showed a brilliant political instinct. And once Mark Rudd could publicly ascribe to the president of Columbia a notoriously obscene relationship to his mother, without provoking any kind of reaction, the SDS [Students for a Democratic Society] had already won the day. The occupation

of Columbia's buildings merely ratified their victory. Men who show themselves unwilling to defend civilization against nihilism are not going to be either reso- lute or effective in defending the university against anything.

I am already touching upon a political aspect of pornography when I suggest   25 that it is inherently and purposefully subversive of civilization and its institu- tions. But there is another and more specifically political aspect, which has to do with the relationship of pornography and/or obscenity to democracy, and especially to the quality of public life on which democratic government ulti- mately rests.

Though the phrase "the quality of life" trips easily from so many lips these   26 days, it tends to be one of those clichés with many trivial meanings and no large, serious one. Sometimes it merely refers to such externals as the enjoy- ment of cleaner air, cleaner water, cleaner streets. At other times it refers to the merely private enjoyment of music, painting, or literature. Rarely does it have anything to do with the way the citizen in a democracy views himself— his obligations, his intentions, his ultimate self-definition.

Instead, what I would call the "managerial" conception of democracy is the   27 predominant opinion among political scientists, sociologists, and economists, and has, through the untiring efforts of these scholars, become the conventional journalistic opinion as well. The root idea behind this managerial conception is that democracy is a "political system" (as they say) which can be adequately defined in terms of—can be fully reduced to—its mechanical arrangements. Democracy is then seen as a set of rules and procedures, and *nothing but* a set of rules and procedures, whereby majority rule and minority rights are recon- ciled into a state of equilibrium. If everyone follows these rules and procedures, then a democracy is in working order. I think this is a fair description of the democratic idea that currently prevails in academia. One can also fairly say that it is now the liberal idea of democracy par excellence.

I cannot help but feel that there is something ridiculous about being this   28 kind of a democrat, and I must further confess to having a sneaking sympathy for those of our young radicals who also find it ridiculous. The absurdity is the absurdity of idolatry—of taking the symbolic for the real, the means for the end. The purpose of democracy cannot possibly be the endless functioning of its own political machinery. The purpose of any political regime is to achieve some version of the good life and the good society. It is not at all difficult to imagine a perfectly functioning democracy which answers all questions except one—namely, why should anyone of intelligence and spirit care a fig for it?

There is, however, an older idea of democracy—one which was fairly com-   29 mon until about the beginning of this century—for which the conception of the quality of public life is absolutely crucial. This idea starts from the proposition that democracy is a form of self-government, and that if you want it to be a meritorious polity, you have to care about what kind of people govern it. Indeed, it puts the matter more strongly and declares that if you want self-government, you are only entitled to it if that "self" is worthy of governing. There is no inherent right to self-government if it means that such government is vicious, mean, squalid, and debased. Only a dogmatist and a fanatic, an idolater of democratic machinery, could approve of self-government under such conditions.

And because the desirability of self-government depends on the character 30 of the people who govern, the older idea of democracy was very solicitous of the condition of this character. It was solicitous of the individual self, and felt an obligation to educate it into what used to be called "republican virtue." And it was solicitous of that collective self which we call public opinion and which, in a democracy, governs us collectively. Perhaps in some respects it was nervously oversolicitous—that would not be surprising. But the main thing is that it cared, cared not merely about the machinery of democracy but about the quality of life that this machinery might generate.

And because it cared, this older idea of democracy had no problem in prin- 31 ciple with pornography and/or obscenity. It censored them—and it did so with a perfect clarity of mind and a perfectly clear conscience. It was not about to permit people capriciously to corrupt themselves. Or, to put it more precisely: In this version of democracy, the people took some care not to let themselves be governed by the more infantile and irrational parts of themselves.

I have, it may be noticed, uttered that dreadful word censorship. And I am 32 not about to back away from it. If you think pornography and/or obscenity is a serious problem, you have to be for censorship. I will go even further and say that if you want to prevent pornography and/or obscenity from becoming a problem, you have to be for censorship. And lest there be any misunderstanding as to what I am saying, I will put it as bluntly as possible: If you care for the quality of life in our American democracy, then you have to be for censorship.

But can a liberal be for censorship? Unless one assumes that being a liberal 33 *must* mean being indifferent to the quality of American life, then the answer has to be yes, a liberal can be for censorship—but he ought to favor a liberal form of censorship.

Is that a contradiction in terms? I do not think so. We have no problem in 34 contrasting *repressive* laws governing alcohol and drugs and tobacco with laws *regulating* (i.e., discouraging the sale of) alcohol and drugs and tobacco. Laws encouraging temperance are not the same thing as laws that have as their goal prohibition or abolition. We have not made the smoking of cigarettes a criminal offense. We have, however, and with good liberal conscience, prohibited cigarette advertising on television, and may yet, again with good liberal conscience, prohibit it in newspapers and magazines. The idea of restricting individual freedom, in a liberal way, is not at all unfamiliar to us.

I therefore see no reason why we should not be able to distinguish repressive 35 censorship from liberal censorship of the written and spoken word. In Britain, until a few years ago, you could perform almost any play you wished, but certain plays, judged to be obscene, had to be performed in private theatrical clubs, which were deemed to have a "serious" interest in theater. In the United States, all of us who grew up using public libraries are familiar with the circumstances under which certain books could be circulated only to adults, while still other books had to be read in the library reading room, under the librarian's skeptical eye. In both cases, a small minority that was willing to make a serious effort to see an obscene play or read an obscene book could do so. But the impact of obscenity was circumscribed and the quality of public life was only marginally affected.*

I am not saying it is easy in practice to sustain a distinction between liberal and repressive censorship, especially in the public realm of a democracy, where popular opinion is so vulnerable to demagoguery. Moreover, an acceptable system of liberal censorship is likely to be exceedingly difficult to devise in the United States today, because our educated classes, upon whose judgment a liberal censorship must rest, are so convinced that there is no such thing as a problem of obscenity, or even that there is no such thing as obscenity at all. But, to counterbalance this, there is the further, fortunate truth that the tolerable margin for error is quite large, and single mistakes or single injustices are not all that important.   36

This possibility of error, of course, occasions much distress among artists and academics. It is a fact, one that cannot and should not be denied, that any system of censorship is bound, upon occasion, to treat unjustly a particular work of art—to find pornography where there is only gentle eroticism, to find obscenity where none really exists, or to find both where its existence ought to be tolerated because it serves a larger moral purpose. Though most works of art are not obscene, and though most obscenity has nothing to do with art, there are some few works of art that are, at least in part, pornographic and/or obscene. There are also some few works of art that are in the special category of the comic-ironic "bawdy" (Boccaccio, Rabelais). It is such works of art that are likely to suffer at the hands of the censor. That is the price one has to be prepared to pay for censorship—even liberal censorship.   37

But just how high is this price? If you believe, as so many artists seem to believe today, that art is the only sacrosanct activity in our profane and vulgar world—that any man who designates himself an artist thereby acquires a sacred office—then obviously censorship is an intolerable form of sacrilege. But for those of us who do not subscribe to this religion of art, the costs of censorship do not seem so high at all.   38

If you look at the history of American or English literature, there is precious little damage you can point to as a consequence of the censorship that prevailed throughout most of that history. Very few works of literature—of real literary merit, I mean—ever were suppressed; and those that were, were not suppressed for long. Nor have I noticed, now that censorship of the written word has to all intents and purposes ceased in this country, that hitherto suppressed or repressed masterpieces are flooding the market. Yes, we can now read   39

---

*It is fairly predictable that someone is going to object that this point of view is "elitist"—that, under a system of liberal censorship, the rich will have privileged access to pornography and obscenity. Yes, of course, they will—just as, at present, the rich have privileged access to heroin if they want it. But one would have to be an egalitarian maniac to object to this state of affairs on the grounds of equality.

Fanny Hill and the Marquis de Sade. Or, to be more exact, we can now openly purchase them, since many people were able to read them even though they were publicly banned, which is as it should be under a liberal censorship. So how much have literature and the arts gained from the fact that we can all now buy them over the counter, that indeed, we are all now encouraged to buy them over the counter? They have not gained much that I can see.

And one might also ask a question that is almost never raised: How much   40
has literature lost from the fact that everything is now permitted? It has lost quite a bit, I should say. In a free market, Gresham's Law can work for books or theater as efficiently as it does for coinage—driving out the good, establishing the debased. The cultural market in the United States today is being preempted by dirty books, dirty movies, dirty theater. A pornographic novel has a far better chance of being published today than a nonpornographic one, and quite a few pretty good novels are not being published at all simply because they are not pornographic, and are therefore less likely to sell. Our cultural condition has not improved as a result of the new freedom. American cultural life was not much to brag about twenty years ago; today one feels ashamed for it.

Just one last point, which I dare not leave untouched. If we start censoring   41
pornography or obscenity, shall we not inevitably end up censoring political opinion? A lot of people seem to think this would be the case—which only shows the power of doctrinaire thinking over reality. We had censorship of pornography and obscenity for 150 years, until almost yesterday, and I am not aware that freedom of opinion in this country was in any way diminished as a consequence of this fact. Fortunately for those of us who are liberal, freedom is not indivisible. If it were, the case for liberalism would be indistinguishable from the case for anarchy; and they are two very different things.

But I must repeat and emphasize: What kinds of laws we pass governing   42
pornography and obscenity, what kind of censorship—or, since we are still a federal nation, what kinds of censorship—we institute in our various localities may indeed be difficult matters to cope with; nevertheless the real issue is one of principle. I myself subscribe to a liberal view of the enforcement problem: I think that pornography should be illegal *and* available to anyone who wants it so badly as to make a pretty strenuous effort to get it. We have lived with under-the-counter pornography for centuries now, in a fairly comfortable way. But the issue of principle, of whether it should be over or under the counter, has to be settled before we can reflect on the advantages and disadvantages of alternative modes of censorship. I think the settlement we are living under now, in which obscenity and democracy are regarded as equals, is wrong; I believe it is inherently unstable; I think it will, in the long run, be incompatible with any authentic concern for the quality of life in our democracy.

QUESTIONS FOR MEANING

1. Do you understand the first sentence of this essay? Is it an exaggeration? Can you think of examples from your own experience in which getting

what you want has failed to give you the satisfaction you expected? If you have a serious goal in life, why might it be a "disaster" to actually reach it?

2. Why does Kristol believe that books can be corrupting? Why does he argue that teachers should agree with him?

3. What does Kristol think of the current state of art, theatre, and literature? Censorship is usually perceived as a threat to the arts, but Kristol argues that the real threat is pornography not censorship. Where and how does he support this claim?

4. Can you identify D.H. Lawrence, Sinclair Lewis, C.S. Lewis, and the Marquis de Sade?

5. Should censors be concerned exclusively with sex or are there other types of obscenity beyond what's called "pornography"? Would it be obscene for a television reporter to thrust a microphone at a woman who has just climbed out of the burning car wreck in which her children died? Should an interview of this sort be allowed on the air? Is it possible to protect privacy without the exercise of censorship?

6. Kristol writes that a student radical named Mark Rudd once invoked against the president of Columbia University "a notoriously obscene relationship with his mother." Because he is opposed to obscenity, Kristol has been careful not to quote what the student said. He assumes, however, that you can figure it out for yourself. What words did the student use?

7. How does Kristol define "democracy"?

8. What is Gresham's Law?

9. Vocabulary: philistine (2), vituperation (10), propriety (12), licentiousness (12), voyeurs (16), ennui (18), and nihilism (23).

QUESTIONS ABOUT STRATEGY

1. At the time Kristol wrote this essay, Susan Sontag was a well recognized feminist critic sympathetic to radical causes. Why did Kristol, a conservative, find it to his advantage to quote her in support of his own argument?

2. What is the function of paragraph 15? Capital punishment and censorship are not usually seen as related topics. Is Kristol losing his focus and going off on a tangent? Or is he advancing his argument by an analogy that would appeal to the part of his audience he most needs to convince? Is it reasonable to assume that people who oppose capital punishment are often the same people who oppose censorship?

3. Kristol includes two disclaimers in paragraph 17. Identify them and explain what they are doing there.

4. Why does Kristol argue that pornography "appeals to and provokes a kind of sexual regression"? In making this argument what type of criticism do you think he may have been anticipating?

5. Although the title of this essay reveals that Kristol is in favor of censorship, he does not use "that dreadful word" until paragraph 32. Why does he wait so long? How important are paragraphs 32 and 33 within the essay as a whole?

6. How effective is the analogy in paragraph 34 between regulating words and regulating alcohol, drugs, and tobacco?
7. In recognizing that censors sometimes act oppressively, Kristol argues that "the tolerable margin for error is quite large, and single injustices are not all that important." Is this a persuasive counterargument?
8. At the end of his essay, Kristol turns to the commonly made argument that censoring pornography will eventually lead to censoring political ideas and speech. He dismisses this argument within a single paragraph, as if it is not worthy of prolonged consideration. Is his rebuttal persuasive or should he have said more?

JOHN STUART MILL
Of the Liberty of Thought and Discussion

John Stuart Mill (1806–1873) was an economist, a philosopher, and a political reformer of remarkable intelligence. He began to study Greek when he was three years old, and Latin when he was seven. By the time he was twelve, he had mastered the best literature in both languages and moved on to study logic, mathematics, and political economy. Although Mill had one of the best minds in the nineteenth century, his rigorous education led to a nervous breakdown when he was twenty. He recovered his health only after he discovered the importance of poetry, music, and art—a process which he describes in his Autobiography *(1873). His most important works include* A System of Logic *(1843),* The Principles of Political Economy *(1848),* Utilitarianism *(1863) and* On the Subjection of Women *(1869). The following essay is drawn from* On Liberty *(1859), a work that is widely recognized as one of the most carefully argued defenses of political and intellectual freedom ever written.*

The time, it is to be hoped, is gone by when any defense would be necessary   1
of the "liberty of the press" as one of the securities against corrupt or tyrannical government. No argument, we may suppose, can now be needed against permitting a legislature or an executive, not identified in interest with the people, to prescribe opinions to them and determine what doctrines or what arguments they shall be allowed to hear. This aspect of the question, besides, has been so often and so triumphantly enforced by preceding writers that it needs not be specially insisted on in this place. Though the law of England, on the subject of the press, is as servile to this day as it was in the time of the Tudors, there is little danger of its being actually put in force against political discussion except during some temporary panic when fear of insurrection drives ministers and

judges from their propriety;[1] and, speaking generally, it is not, in constitutional countries, to be apprehended that the government, whether completely responsible to the people or not, will often attempt to control the expression of opinion, except when in doing so it makes itself the organ of the general intolerance of the public. Let us suppose, therefore, that the government is entirely at one with the people, and never thinks of exerting any power of coercion unless in agreement with what it conceives to be their voice. But I deny the right of the people to exercise such coercion, either by themselves or by their government. The power itself is illegitimate. The best government has no more title to it than the worst. It is as noxious, or more noxious, when exerted in accordance with public opinion than when in opposition to it. If all mankind minus one were of one opinion, mankind would be no more justified in silencing that one person than he, if he had the power, would be justified in silencing mankind. Were an opinion a personal possession of no value except to the owner, if to be obstructed in the employment of it were simply a private injury, it would make some difference whether the injury was inflicted only on a few persons or on many. But the peculiar evil of silencing the expression of an opinion is that it is robbing the human race, posterity as well as the existing generation—those who dissent from the opinion, still more than those who hold it. If the opinion is right, they are deprived of the opportunity of exchanging error for truth; if wrong, they lose, what is almost as great a benefit, the clearer perception and livelier impression of truth produced by its collision with error.

It is necessary to consider separately these two hypotheses, each of which has a distinct branch of the argument corresponding to it. We can never be sure that the opinion we are endeavoring to stifle is a false opinion; and if we were sure, stifling it would be an evil still.   2

First, the opinion which it is attempted to suppress by authority may possibly be true. Those who desire to suppress it, of course, deny its truth; but they are not infallible. They have no authority to decide the question for all mankind and exclude every other person from the means of judging. To refuse a hearing   3

---

[1]These words had scarcely been written when, as if to give them an emphatic contradiction, occurred the Government Press Prosecutions of 1858. That ill-judged interference with the liberty of public discussion has not, however, induced me to alter a single word in the text, nor has it at all weakened my conviction that, moments of panic excepted, the era of pains and penalties for political discussion has, in our own country, passed away. For, in the first place, the prosecutions were not persisted in; and, in the second, they were never, properly speaking, political prosecutions. The offense charged was not that of criticizing institutions or the acts or persons of rulers, but of circulating what was deemed an immoral doctrine, the lawfulness of tyrannicide.

If the arguments of the present chapter are of any validity, there ought to exist the fullest liberty of professing and discussing, as a matter of ethical conviction, any doctrine, however immoral it may be considered. It would, therefore, be irrelevant and out of place to examine here whether the doctrine of tyrannicide deserves that title. I shall content myself with saying that the subject has been at all times one of the open questions of morals; that the act of a private citizen in striking down a criminal who, by raising himself above the law, has placed himself beyond the reach of legal punishment or control has been accounted by whole nations, and by some of the best and wisest of men, not a crime but an act of exalted virtue; and that, right or wrong, it is not of the nature of assassination, but of civil war. As such, I hold that the instigation to it, in a specific case, may be a proper subject of punishment, but only if an overt act has followed, and at least a probable connection can be established between the act and the instigation. Even then it is not a foreign government but the very government assailed which alone, in the exercise of self-defense, can legitimately punish attacks directed against its own existence.

to an opinion because they are sure that it is false is to assume that *their* certainty is the same thing as *absolute* certainty. All silencing of discussion is an assumption of infallibility. Its condemnation may be allowed to rest on this common argument, not the worse for being common.

Unfortunately for the good sense of mankind, the fact of their fallibility is far   4 from carrying the weight in their practical judgment which is always allowed to it in theory; for while everyone well knows himself to be fallible, few think it necessary to take any precautions against their own fallibility, or admit the supposition that any opinion of which they feel very certain may be one of the examples of the error to which they acknowledge themselves to be liable. Absolute princes, or others who are accustomed to unlimited deference, usually feel this complete confidence in their own opinions on nearly all subjects. People more happily situated, who sometimes hear their opinions disputed and are not wholly unused to be set right when they are wrong, place the same unbounded reliance only on such of their opinions as are shared by all who surround them, or to whom they habitually defer; for in proportion to a man's want of confidence in his own solitary judgment does he usually repose, with implicit trust, on the infallibility of "the world" in general. And the world, to each individual, means the part of it with which he comes in contact: his party, his sect, his church, his class of society; the man may be called, by comparison, almost liberal and large-minded to whom it means anything so comprehensive as his own country or his own age. Nor is his faith in this collective authority at all shaken by his being aware that other ages, countries, sects, churches, classes, and parties have thought, and even now think, the exact reverse. He devolves upon his own world the responsibility of being in the right against the dissentient worlds of other people; and it never troubles him that mere accident has decided which of these numerous worlds is the object of his reliance, and that the same causes which make him a churchman in London would have made him a Buddhist or a Confucian in Peking. Yet it is as evident in itself, as any amount of argument can make it, that ages are no more infallible than individuals—every age having held many opinions which subsequent ages have deemed not only false but absurd; and it is as certain that many opinions, now general, will be rejected by future ages, as it is that many, once general, are rejected by the present.

The objection likely to be made to this argument would probably take some   5 such form as the following. There is no greater assumption of infallibility in forbidding the propagation of error than in any other thing which is done by public authority on its own judgment and responsibility. Judgment is given to men that they may use it. Because it may be used erroneously, are men to be told that they ought not to use it all? To prohibit what they think pernicious is not claiming exemption from error, but fulfilling the duty incumbent on them, although fallible, of acting on their conscientious conviction. If we were never to act on our opinions, because those opinions may be wrong, we should leave all our interests uncared for, and all our duties unperformed. An objection which applies to all conduct can be no valid objection to any conduct in partic- ular. It is the duty of governments, and of individuals, to form the truest opinions they can; to form them carefully, and never impose them upon others unless they are quite sure of being right. But when they are sure (such reasoners may say), it is not conscientiousness but cowardice to shrink from acting on their opinions and allow doctrines which they honestly think dangerous to the welfare of mankind, either in this life or in another, to be scattered abroad without restraint, because other people, in less enlighted times, have persecuted opinions now believed to be true. Let us take care, it may be said, not to make the same mistake; but governments and nations have made mistakes in other things which are not denied to be fit subjects for the exercise of authority: they have laid on bad taxes, made unjust wars. Ought we therefore to lay on no taxes and, under whatever provocation, make no wars? Men and governments must act to the best of their ability. There is no such thing as absolute certainty, but there is assurance sufficient for the purposes of human life. We may, and must, assume our opinion to be true for the guidance of our own conduct; and it is assuming no more when we forbid bad men to pervert society by the propagation of opinions which we regard as false and pernicious.

I answer, that it is assuming very much more. There is the greatest difference   6
between presuming an opinion to be true because, with every opportunity for contesting it, it has not been refuted, and assuming its truth for the purpose of not permitting its refutation. Complete liberty of contradicting and disproving our opinion is the very condition which justifies us in assuming its truth for purposes of action; and on no other terms can a being with human faculties have any rational assurance of being right.

When we consider either the history of opinion or the ordinary conduct of   7
human life, to what is it to be ascribed that the one and the other are no worse than they are? Not certainly to the inherent force of the human understanding, for on any matter not self-evident there are ninety-nine persons totally incapable of judging of it for one who is capable; and the capacity of the hundredth person is only comparative, for the majority of the eminent men of every past generation held many opinions now known to be erroneous, and did or approved numerous things which no one will now justify. Why is it, then, that there is on the whole a preponderance among mankind of rational opinions and rational conduct? If there really is this preponderance—which there must be unless human affairs are, and have always been, in an almost desperate state— it is owing to a quality of the human mind, the source of everything respectable in man either as an intellectual or as a moral being, namely, that his errors are corrigible. He is capable of rectifying his mistakes by discussion and experience. Not by experience alone. There must be discussion to show how experience is to be interpreted. Wrong opinions and practices gradually yield to fact and argument; but facts and arguments, to produce any effect on the mind, must be brought before it. Very few facts are able to tell their own story, without comments to bring out their meaning. The whole strength and value, then, of human judgment depending on the one property, that it can be set right when it is wrong, reliance can be placed on it only when the means of setting it right are kept constantly at hand. In the case of any person whose judgment is really deserving of confidence, how has it become so? Because he has kept his mind open to criticism of his opinions and conduct. Because it has been his practice

to listen to all that could be said against him; to profit by as much of it as was just, and to expound to himself, and upon occasion to others, the fallacy of what was fallacious. Because he has felt that the only way in which a human being can make some approach to knowing the whole of a subject is by hearing what can be said about it by persons of every variety of opinion, and studying all modes in which it can be looked at by every character of mind. No wise man ever acquired his wisdom in any mode but this; nor is it in the nature of human intellect to become wise in any other manner. The steady habit of correcting and completing his own opinion by collating it with those of others, so far from causing doubt and hesitation in carrying it into practice, is the only stable foundation for a just reliance on it; for, being cognizant of all that can, at least obviously, be said against him, and having taken up his position against all gainsayers—knowing that he has sought for objections and difficulties instead of avoiding them, and has shut out no light which can be thrown upon the subject from any quarter—he has a right to think his judgment better than that of any person, or any multitude, who have not gone through a similar process.

It is not too much to require that what the wisest of mankind, those who are 8 best entitled to trust their own judgment, find necessary to warrant their relying on it, should be submitted to by that miscellaneous collection of a few wise and many foolish individuals called the public. The most intolerant of churches, the Roman Catholic Church, even at the canonization of a saint admits, and listens patiently to, a "devil's advocate." The holiest of men, it appears, cannot be admitted to posthumous honors until all that the devil could say against him is known and weighed. If even the Newtonian philosophy were not permitted to be questioned, mankind could not feel as complete assurance of its truth as they now do. The beliefs which we have most warrant for have no safeguard to rest on but a standing invitation to the whole world to prove them unfounded. If the challenge is not accepted, or is accepted and the attempt fails, we are far enough from certainty still, but we have done the best that the existing state of human reason admits of: we have neglected nothing that could give the truth a chance of reaching us; if the lists are kept open, we may hope that, if there be a better truth, it will be found when the human mind is capable of receiving it; and in the meantime we may rely on having attained such approach to truth as is possible in our own day. This is the amount of certainty attainable by a fallible being, and this the sole way of attaining it.

Strange it is that men should admit the validity of the arguments for free 9 discussion, but object to their being "pushed to an extreme," not seeing that unless the reasons are good for an extreme case, they are not good for any case. Strange that they should imagine that they are not assuming infallibility when they acknowledge that there should be free discussion on all subjects which can possibly be *doubtful*, but think that some particular principle or doctrine should be forbidden to be questioned because it is so *certain*, that is, because *they are certain* that it is certain. To call any proposition certain, while there is anyone who would deny its certainty if permitted, but who is not permitted, is to assume that we ourselves, and those who agree with us, are the judges of certainty, and judges without hearing the other side.

In the present age—which has been described as "destitute of faith, but 10 terrified at skepticism"—in which people feel sure, not so much that their opinions are true as that they should not know what to do without them—the claims of an opinion to be protected from public attack are rested not so much on its truth as on its importance to society. There are, it is alleged, certain beliefs so useful, not to say indispensable, to well-being that it is as much the duty of governments to uphold those beliefs as to protect any other of the interests of society. In a case of such necessity, and so directly in the line of their duty, something less than infallibility may, it is maintained, warrant, and even bind, governments to act on their own opinion confirmed by the general opinion of mankind. It is also often argued, and still oftener thought, that none but bad men would desire to weaken these salutary beliefs; and there can be nothing wrong, it is thought, in restraining bad men and prohibiting what only such men would wish to practice. This mode of thinking makes the justification of restraints on discussion not a question of the truth of doctrines but of their usefulness, and flatters itself by that means to escape the responsibility of claiming to be an infallible judge of opinions. But those who thus satisfy themselves do not perceive that the assumption of infallibility is merely shifted from one point to another. The usefulness of an opinion is itself matter of opinion— as disputable, as open to discussion, and requiring discussion as much as the opinion itself. There is the same need of an infallible judge of opinions to decide an opinion to be noxious as to decide it to be false, unless the opinion condemned has full opportunity of defending itself. And it will not do to say that the heretic may be allowed to maintain the utility or harmlessness of his opinion, though forbidden to maintain its truth. The truth of an opinion is part of its utility. If we would know whether or not it is desirable that a proposition should be believed, is it possible to exclude the consideration of whether or not it is true? In the opinion, not of bad men, but of the best men, no belief which is contrary to truth can be really useful; and can you prevent such men from urging that plea when they are charged with culpability for denying some doctrine which they are told is useful, but which they believe to be false? Those who are on the side of received opinions never fail to take all possible advantage of this plea; you do not find *them* handling the question of ability as if it could be completely abstracted from that of truth; on the contrary, it is, above all, because their doctrine is "the truth" that the knowledge or the belief of it is held to be so indispensable. There can be no fair discussion of the question of usefulness when an argument so vital may be employed on one side, but not on the other. And in point of fact, when law or public feeling do not permit the truth of an opinion to be disputed, they are just as little tolerant of a denial of its usefulness. The utmost they allow is an extenuation of its absolute necessity, or of the positive guilt of rejecting it.

In order more fully to illustrate the mischief of denying a hearing to opinions 11 because we, in our own judgment, have condemned them, it will be desirable to fix down the discussion to a concrete case; and I choose, by preference, the cases which are least favorable to me—in which the argument against freedom of opinion, both on the score of truth and on that of utility, is considered the strongest. Let the opinions impugned be the belief in a God and in a future state, or any of the commonly received doctrines of morality. To fight the battle on such ground gives a great advantage to an unfair antagonist, since he will be sure to say (and many who have no desire to be unfair will say it internally), Are these the doctrines which you do not deem sufficiently certain to be taken under the protection of law? Is the belief in a God one of the opinions to feel sure of which you hold to be assuming infallibility? But I must be permitted to observe that it is not the feeling sure of a doctrine (be it what it may) which I call an assumption of infallibility. It is the undertaking to decide that question *for others*, without allowing them to hear what can be said on the contrary side. And I denounce and reprobate this pretension not the less if put forth on the side of my most solemn convictions. However positive anyone's persuasion may be, not only of the falsity but of the pernicious consequences—not only of the pernicious consequences, but (to adopt expressions which I altogether condemn) the immorality and impiety of an opinion—yet if, in pursuance of that private judgment, though backed by the public judgment of his country or his contemporaries, he prevents the opinion from being heard in its defense, he assumes infallibility. And so far from the assumption being less objectionable or less dangerous because the opinion is called immoral or impious, this is the case of all others in which it is most fatal. These are exactly the occasions on which the men of one generation commit those dreadful mistakes which excite the astonishment and horror of posterity. It is among such that we find the instances memorable in history, when the arm of the law has been employed to root out the best men and the noblest doctrines; with deplorable success as to the men, though some of the doctrines have survived to be (as if in mockery) invoked in defense of similar conduct toward those who dissent from *them*, or from their received interpretation.

Mankind can hardly be too often reminded that there was once a man called [12] Socrates, between whom and the legal authorities and public opinion of his time there took place a memorable collision. Born in an age and country abounding in individual greatness, this man has been handed down to us by those who best knew both him and the age as the most virtuous man in it; while *we* know him as the head and prototype of all subsequent teachers of virtue, the source equally of the lofty inspiration of Plato and the judicious utilitarianism of Aristotle, "*i maestri di color che sanno*," the two headsprings of ethical as of all other philosophy. This acknowledged master of all the eminent thinkers who have since lived—whose fame, still growing after more than two thousand years, all but outweighs the whole remainder of the names which make his native city illustrious—was put to death by his countrymen, after a judicial conviction, for impiety and immorality. Impiety, in denying the gods recognized by the State; indeed, his accuser asserted (see the *Apologia*) that he believed in no gods at all. Immorality, in being, by his doctrines and instructions, a "corruptor of youth." Of these charges the tribunal, there is every ground for believing, honestly found him guilty, and condemned the man who probably of all then born had deserved best of mankind to be put to death as a criminal.

To pass from this to the only other instance of judicial iniquity, the mention [13] of which, after the condemnation of Socrates, would not be an anticlimax: the event which took place on Calvary rather more than eighteen hundred years ago. The man who left on the memory of those who witnessed his life and conversation such an impression of his moral grandeur that eighteen subsequent centuries have done homage to him as the Almighty in person, was ignominiously put to death, as what? As a blasphemer. Men did not merely mistake their benefactor, they mistook him for the exact contrary of what he was and treated him as that prodigy of impiety which they themselves are now held to be for their treatment of him. The feelings with which mankind now regard these lamentable transactions, especially the later of the two, render them extremely unjust in their judgment of the unhappy actors. These were, to all appearance, not bad men—not worse than men commonly are, but rather the contrary; men who possessed in a full, or somewhat more than a full measure, the religious, moral, and patriotic feelings of their time and people: the very kind of men who, in all times, our own included, have every chance of passing through life blameless and respected. The high priest who rent his garments when the words were pronounced, which, according to all the ideas of his country, constituted the blackest guilt, was in all probability quite as sincere in his horror and indignation as the generality of respectable and pious men now are in the religious and moral sentiments they profess; and most of those who now shudder at his conduct, if they had lived in his time, and been born Jews, would have acted precisely as he did. Orthodox Christians who are tempted to think that those who stoned to death the first martyrs must have been worse men than they themselves are ought to remember that one of those persecutors was Saint Paul....

Let us now pass to the second division of the argument, and dismissing the   14
supposition that any of the received opinions may be false, let us assume them to be true and examine into the worth of the manner in which they are likely to be held when their truth is not freely and openly canvassed. However unwillingly a person who has a strong opinion may admit the possibility that his opinion may be false, he ought to be moved by the consideration that, however true it may be, if it is not fully, frequently, and fearlessly discussed, it will be held as a dead dogma, not a living truth....

To what an extent doctrines intrinsically fitted to make the deepest impres-   15
sion upon the mind may remain in it as dead beliefs, without being ever realized in the imagination, the feelings, or the understanding, is exemplified by the manner in which the majority of believers hold the doctrines of Christianity. By Christianity, I here mean what is accounted such by all churches and sects— the maxims and precepts contained in the New Testament. These are considered sacred, and accepted as laws, by all professing Christians. Yet it is scarcely too much to say that not one Christian in a thousand guides or tests his individual conduct by reference to those laws. The standard to which he does refer it is the custom of his nation, his class, or his religious profession. He has thus, on the one hand, a collection of ethical maxims which he believes to have been vouchsafed to him by infallible wisdom as rules for his government; and, on the other, a set of everyday judgments and practices which go a certain length with

some of those maxims, not so great a length with others, stand in direct opposition to some, and are, on the whole, a compromise between the Christian creed and the interests and suggestions of worldly life. To the first of these standards he gives his homage; to the other his real allegiance. All Christians believe that the blessed are the poor and humble, and those who are ill-used by the world; that it is easier for a camel to pass through the eye of a needle than for a rich man to enter the kingdom of heaven; that they should judge not, lest they be judged; that they should swear not at all; that they should love their neighbor as themselves; that if one take their cloak, they should give him their coat also; that they should take no thought for the morrow; that if they would be perfect they should sell all that they have and give it to the poor. They are not insincere when they say that they believe these things. They do believe them, as people believe what they have always heard lauded and never discussed. But in the sense of that living belief which regulates conduct, they believe these doctrines just up to the point to which it is usual to act upon them. The doctrines in their integrity are serviceable to pelt adversaries with; and it is understood that they are to be put forward (when possible) as the reasons for whatever people do that they think laudable. But anyone who reminded them that the maxims require an infinity of things which they never even think of doing would gain nothing but to be classed among those very unpopular characters who affect to be better than other people. The doctrines have no hold on ordinary believers—are not a power in their minds. They have an habitual respect for the sound of them, but no feeling which spreads from the words to the things signified and forces the mind to take *them* in and make them conform to the formula. Whenever conduct is concerned, they look round for Mr. A and B to direct them how far to go in obeying Christ.

Now we may be well assured that the case was not thus, but far otherwise, with the early Christians. Had it been thus, Christianity never would have expanded from an obscure sect of the despised Hebrews into the religion of the Roman empire. When their enemies said, "See how these Christians love one another" (a remark not likely to be made by anybody now), they assuredly had a much livelier feeling of the meaning of their creed than they have ever had since. And to this cause, probably, it is chiefly owing that Christianity now makes so little progress in extending its domain, and after eighteen centuries is still nearly confined to Europeans and the descendants of Europeans. Even with the strictly religious, who are much in earnest about their doctrines and attach a greater amount of meaning to many of them than people in general, it commonly happens that the part which is thus comparatively active in their minds is that which was made by Calvin, or Knox, or some such person much nearer in character to themselves. The sayings of Christ coexist passively in their minds, producing hardly any effect beyond what is caused by mere listening to words so amiable and bland. There are many reasons, doubtless, why doctrines which are the badge of a sect retain more of their vitality than those common to all recognized sects, and why more pains are taken by teachers to keep their meaning alive; but one reason certainly is that the peculiar doctrines

16

are more questioned and have to be oftener defended against open gainsayers. Both teachers and learners go to sleep at their post as soon as there is no enemy in the field.

The same thing holds true, generally speaking, of all traditional doctrines— those of prudence and knowledge of life as well as of morals or religion. All languages and literatures are full of general observations on life, both as to what it is and how to conduct oneself in it—observations which everybody knows, which everybody repeats or hears with acquiescence, which are received as truisms, yet of which most people first truly learn the meaning when experience, generally of a painful kind, has made it a reality to them. How often, when smarting under some unforeseen misfortune or disappointment, does a person call to mind some proverb or common saying, familiar to him all his life, the meaning of which, if he had ever before felt it as he does now, would have saved him from the calamity. There are indeed reasons for this, other than the absence of discussion; there are many truths of which the full meaning *cannot* be realized until personal experience has brought it home. But much more of the meaning even of these would have been understood, and what was understood would have been far more deeply impressed on the mind, if the man had been accustomed to hear it argued *pro* and *con* by people who did understand it. The fatal tendency of mankind to leave off thinking about a thing when it is no longer doubtful is the cause of half their errors. A contemporary author has well spoken of "the deep slumber of a decided opinion."   17

But what! (it may be asked), Is the absence of unanimity an indispensable condition of true knowledge? Is it necessary that some part of mankind should persist in error to enable any to realize the truth? Does a belief cease to be real and vital as soon as it is generally received—and is a proposition never thoroughly understood and felt unless some doubt of it remains? As soon as mankind have unanimously accepted a truth, does the truth perish within them? The highest aim and best result of improved intelligence, it has hitherto been thought, is to unite mankind more and more in the acknowledgment of all important truths; and does the intelligence only last as long as it has not achieved its object? Do the fruits of conquest perish by the very completeness of the victory?   18

I affirm no such thing. As mankind improve, the number of doctrines which are no longer disputed or doubted will be constantly on the increase; and the well-being of mankind may almost be measured by the number and gravity of the truths which have reached the point of being uncontested. The cessation, on one question after another, of serious controversy is one of the necessary incidents of the consolidation of opinion—a consolidation as salutary in the case of true opinions as it is dangerous and noxious when the opinions are erroneous. But though this gradual narrowing of the bounds of diversity of opinion is necessary in both senses of the term, being at once inevitable and indispensable, we are not therefore obliged to conclude that all its consequences must be beneficial. The loss of so important an aid to the intelligent and living apprehension of a truth as is afforded by the necessity of explaining it to, or defending it against, opponents, though not sufficient to outweigh, is no   19 trifling drawback from the benefit of its universal recognition. Where this advantage can no longer be had, I confess I should like to see the teachers of mankind endeavoring to provide a substitute for it—some contrivance for making the difficulties of the question as present to the learner's consciousness as if they were pressed upon him by a dissentient champion, eager for his conversion.

But instead of seeking contrivances for this purpose, they have lost those they formerly had. The Socratic dialectics, so magnificently exemplified in the dialogues of Plato, were a contrivance of this description. They were essentially a negative discussion of the great questions of philosophy and life, directed with consummate skill to the purpose of convincing anyone who had merely adopted the commonplaces of received opinion that he did not understand the subject—that he as yet attached no definite meaning to the doctrines he professed; in order that, becoming aware of his ignorance, he might be put in the way to obtain a stable belief, resting on a clear apprehension both of the meaning of doctrines and of their evidence. The school disputations of the Middle Ages had a somewhat similar object. They were intended to make sure that the pupil understood his own opinion, and (by necessary correlation) the opinion opposed to it, and could enforce the grounds of the one and confute those of the other. These last-mentioned contests had indeed the incurable defect that the premises appealed to were taken from authority, not from reason; and, as a discipline to the mind, they were in every respect inferior to the powerful dialectics which formed the intellects of the *"Socratici viri"*; but the modern mind owes far more to both than it is generally willing to admit, and the present modes of education contain nothing which in the smallest degree supplies the place either of the one or of the other. A person who derives all his instruction from teachers or books, even if he escape the besetting temptation of contenting himself with cram, is under no compulsion to hear both sides; accordingly it is far from a frequent accomplishment, even among thinkers, to know both sides; and the weakest part of what everybody says in defense of his opinion is what he intends as a reply to antagonists. It is the fashion of the present time to disparage negative logic—that which points out weaknesses in theory or errors in practice without establishing positive truths. Such negative criticism would indeed be poor enough as an ultimate result, but as a means to attaining any positive knowledge or conviction worthy the name it cannot be valued too highly; and until people are again systematically trained to it, there will be few great thinkers and a low general average of intellect in any but the mathematical and physical departments of speculation. On any other subject no one's opinions deserve the name of knowledge, except so far as he has either had forced upon him by others or gone through of himself the same mental process which would have been required of him in carrying on an active controversy with opponents. That, therefore, which, when absent, it is so indispensable, but so difficult, to create, how worse than absurd it is to forego when spontaneously offering itself! If there are any persons who contest a received opinion, or who will do so if law or opinion will let them, let us thank them for it, open our minds to listen to them, and rejoice that there is someone

20

to do for us what we otherwise ought, if we have any regard for either the certainty or the vitality of our convictions, to do with much greater labor for ourselves.

It still remains to speak of one of the principal causes which make diversity of opinion advantageous, and will continue to do so until mankind shall have entered a stage of intellectual advancement which at present seems at an incalculable distance. We have hitherto considered only two possibilities: that the received opinion may be false, and some other opinion, consequently, true; or that, the received opinion being true, a conflict with the opposite error is essential to a clear apprehension and deep feeling of its truth. But there is a commoner case than either of these: when the conflicting doctrines, instead of being one true and the other false, share the truth between them, and the nonconforming opinion is needed to supply the remainder of the truth of which the received doctrine embodies only a part. Popular opinions, on subjects not palpable to sense, are often true, but seldom or never the whole truth. They are a part of the truth, sometimes a greater, sometimes a smaller part, but exaggerated, distorted, and disjointed from the truths by which they ought to be accompanied and limited. Heretical opinions, on the other hand, are generally some of these suppressed and neglected truths, bursting the bonds which kept them down, and either seeking reconciliation with the truth contained in the common opinion, or fronting it as enemies, and setting themselves up, with similar exclusiveness, as the whole truth. The latter case is hitherto the most frequent, as, in the human mind, one-sidedness has always been the rule, and many-sidedness the exception. Hence, even in revolutions of opinion, one part of the truth usually sets while another rises. Even progress, which ought to superadd, for the most part only substitutes one partial and incomplete truth for another; improvement consisting chiefly in this, that the new fragment of truth is more wanted, more adapted to the needs of the time than that which it displaces. Such being the partial character of prevailing opinions, even when resting on a true foundation, every opinion which embodies somewhat of the portion of truth which the common opinion omits ought to be considered precious, with whatever amount of error and confusion that truth may be blended. No sober judge of human affairs will feel bound to be indignant because those who force on our notice truths which we should otherwise have overlooked, overlook some of those which we see. Rather, he will think that so long as popular truth is one-sided, it is more desirable than otherwise that unpopular truth should have one-sided assertors, too, such being usually the most energetic and the most likely to compel reluctant attention to the fragment of wisdom which they proclaim as if it were the whole.

Thus, in the eighteenth century, when nearly all the instructed, and all those of the uninstructed who were led by them, were lost in admiration of what is called civilization, and of the marvels of modern science, literature, and philosophy, and while greatly overrating the amount of unlikeness between the men of modern and those of ancient times, indulged the belief that the whole of the difference was in their own favor: with what a salutary shock did the paradoxes of Rousseau explode like bombshells in the midst, dislocating the compact mass of one-sided opinion and forcing its elements to recombine in a better form and with additional ingredients. Not that the current opinions were on the whole farther from the truth than Rousseau's were; on the contrary, they were nearer to it; they contained more of positive truth, and very much less of error. Nevertheless there lay in Rousseau's doctrine, and has floated down the stream of opinion along with it, a considerable amount of exactly those truths which the popular opinion wanted; and these are the deposit which was left behind them when the flood subsided. The superior worth of simplicity of life, the enervating and demoralizing effect of the trammels and hypocrisies of artificial society are ideas which have never been entirely absent from cultivated minds since Rousseau wrote; and they will in time produce their due effect, though at present needing to be asserted as much as ever, and to be asserted by deeds; for words, on this subject, have nearly exhausted their power.

In politics, again, it is almost a commonplace that a party of order or stability   23
and a party of progress or reform are both necessary elements of a healthy state of political life, until the one or the other shall have so enlarged its mental grasp as to be a party equally of order and of progress, knowing and distinguishing what is fit to be preserved from what ought to be swept away. Each of these modes of thinking derives its utility from the deficiencies of the other; but it is in a great measure the opposition of the other that keeps each within the limits of reason and sanity. Unless opinions favorable to democracy and to aristocracy, to property and to equality, to cooperation and to competition, to luxury and to abstinence, to sociality and individuality, to liberty and discipline, and all the other standing antagonisms of practical life, are expressed with equal freedom and enforced and defended with equal talent and energy, there is no chance of both elements obtaining their due; one scale is sure to go up, and the other down. Truth, in the great practical concerns of life, is so much a question of the reconciling and combining of opposites that very few have minds sufficiently capacious and impartial to make the adjustment with an approach to correctness, and it has to be made by the tough process of a struggle between combatants fighting under hostile banners. On any of the great open questions just enumerated, if either of the two opinions has a better claim than the other, not merely to be tolerated, but to be encouraged and countenanced, it is the one which happens at the particular time and place to be in a minority. That is the opinion which, for the time being, represents the neglected interests, the side of human well-being which is in danger of obtaining less than its share. I am aware that there is not, in this country, any intolerance of differences of opinion on most of these topics. They are adduced to show, by admitted and multiplied examples, the universality of the fact that only through diversity of opinion is there, in the existing state of human intellect, a chance of fair play to all sides of the truth. When there are persons to be found who form an exception to the apparent unanimity of the world on any subject, even if the world is in the right, it is always probable that dissentients have something worth hearing to say for themselves, and that truth would lose something by their silence....

I do not pretend that the most unlimited use of the freedom of enunciating   24
all possible opinions would put an end to the evils of religious or philosophical

sectarianism. Every truth which men of narrow capacity are in earnest about is sure to be asserted, inculcated, and in many ways even acted on, as if no other truth existed in the world, or at all events none that could limit or qualify the first. I acknowledge that the tendency of all opinions to become sectarian is not cured by the freest discussion, but is often heightened and exacerbated thereby; the truth which ought to have been, but was not, seen, being rejected all the more violently because proclaimed by persons regarded as opponents. But it is not on the impassioned partisan, it is on the calmer and more disinterested bystander, that this collision of opinions works its salutary effect. Not the violent conflict between parts of the truth, but the quiet suppression of half of it, is the formidable evil; there is always hope when people are forced to listen to both sides: it is when they attend only to one that errors harden into prejudices, and truth itself ceases to have the effect of truth by being exaggerated into falsehood. And since there are few mental attributes more rare than that judicial faculty which can sit in intelligent judgment between two sides of a question, of which only one is represented by an advocate before it, truth has no chance but in proportion as every side of it, every opinion which embodies any fraction of the truth, not only finds advocates, but is so advocated as to be listened to.

We have now recognized the necessity to the mental well-being of mankind 25 (on which all their other well-being depends) of freedom of opinion, and freedom of the expression of opinion, on four distinct grounds, which we will now briefly recapitulate:

First, if any opinion is compelled to silence, that opinion may, for aught we 26 can certainly know, be true. To deny this is to assume our own infallibility.

Secondly, though the silenced opinion be an error, it may, and very commonly 27 does, contain a portion of truth; and since the general or prevailing opinion on any subject is rarely or never the whole truth, it is only by the collision of adverse opinions that the remainder of the truth has any chance of being supplied.

Thirdly, even if the received opinion be not only true, but the whole truth; 28 unless it is suffered to be, and actually is, vigorously and earnestly contested, it will, by most of those who receive it, be held in the manner of a prejudice, with little comprehension or feeling of its rational grounds. And not only this, but, fourthly, the meaning of the doctrine itself will be in danger of being lost or enfeebled, and deprived of its vital effect on the character and conduct: the dogma becoming a mere formal profession, inefficacious for good, but cumbering the ground and preventing the growth of any real and heartfelt conviction from reason or personal experience.

Before quitting the subject of freedom of opinion, it is fit to take some notice 29 of those who say that the free expression of all opinions should be permitted on condition that the manner be temperate, and do not pass the bounds of fair discussion. Much might be said on the impossibility of fixing where these supposed bounds are to be placed; for if the test be offense to those whose opinions are attacked, I think experience testifies that this offense is given whenever the attack is telling and powerful, and that every opponent who pushes them hard, and whom they find it difficult to answer, appears to them, if he shows any strong feeling on the subject, an intemperate opponent. But this, though an important consideration in a practical point of view, merges in a more fundamental objection. Undoubtedly, the manner of asserting an opinion, even though it be a true one, may be very objectionable and may justly incur severe censure. But the principal offenses of the kind are such as it is mostly impossible, unless by accidental self-betrayal, to bring home to conviction. The gravest of them is, to argue sophistically, to suppress facts or arguments, to misstate the elements of the case, or misrepresent the opposite opinion. But all this, even to the most aggravated degree, is so continually done in perfect good faith by persons who are not considered, and in many other respects may not deserve to be considered, ignorant or incompetent, that it is rarely possible, on adequate grounds, conscientiously to stamp the misrepresentation as morally culpable, and still less could law presume to interfere with this kind of controversial misconduct. With regard to what is commonly meant by intemperate discussion, namely invective, sarcasm, personality, and the like, the denunciation of these weapons would deserve more sympathy if it were ever proposed to interdict them equally to both sides; but it is only desired to restrain the employment of them against the prevailing opinion; against the unprevailing they may not only be used without general disapproval, but will be likely to obtain for him who uses them the praise of honest zeal and righteous indignation. Yet whatever mischief arises from their use is greatest when they are employed against the comparatively defenseless; and whatever unfair advantage can be derived by any opinion from this mode of asserting it accrues almost exclusively to received opinions. The worst offense of this kind which can be committed by a polemic is to stigmatize those who hold the contrary opinion as bad and immoral men. To calumny of this sort, those who hold any unpopular opinion are peculiarly exposed, because they are in general few and uninfluential, and nobody but themselves feels much interested in seeing justice done them; but this weapon is, from the nature of the case, denied to those who attack a prevailing opinion: they can neither use it with safety to themselves, nor, if they could, would it do anything but recoil on their own cause. In general, opinions contrary to those commonly received can only obtain a hearing by studied moderation of language and the most cautious avoidance of unneccessary offense, from which they hardly ever deviate even in a slight degree without losing ground, while unmeasured vituperation employed on the side of the prevailing opinion really does deter people from professing contrary opinions and from listening to those who profess them. For the interest, therefore, of truth and justice it is far more important to restrain this employment of vituperative language than the other; and, for example, if it were necessary to choose, there would be much more need to discourage offensive attacks on infidelity than on religion. It is, however, obvious that law and authority have no business with restraining either, while opinion ought, in every instance, to determine its verdict by the circumstances of the individual case—condemning everyone, on whichever side of the argument he places himself, in whose mode of advocacy either want of candor, or malignity, bigotry, or intolerance of feeling manifest themselves; but not inferring these vices from the side which a person takes, though it be the contrary side of the question to our own; and giving merited honor to everyone, whatever opinion he may hold, who has calmness to see and honesty to state what his opponents and their opinions really are, exaggerating nothing to their discredit, keeping nothing back which tells, or can be supposed to tell, in their favor. This is the real morality of public discussion; and if often violated, I am happy to think that there are many controversialists who to a great extent observe it, and a still greater number who conscientiously strive toward it.

QUESTIONS FOR MEANING

1. Why does Mill believe that controversy is important? Who is it that is most likely to benefit from public debate? Is anyone apt to be hurt?
2. How does Mill define "infallibility"? What help does he offer us in deciding whose judgment we can afford to trust?
3. Why does Mill describe the Catholic Church as the "most intolerant of Churches"? Do you know anything about English history that might help account for Mill's hostility to Catholicism?
4. How fair is Mill's appraisal of the average Christian? Does he himself believe in Christ? Why is he sympathetic to the people who were responsible for putting Christ to death?
5. What does Mill mean when he writes, "Both teachers and learners go to sleep at their post as soon as there is no enemy in the field"?
6. Do you know anything about the work of Rousseau cited in paragraph 22? If you've never heard of Rousseau, what could you infer about his work from Mill's references to it?
7. In addition to being a famous defense of freedom of thought and discussion, Mill's essay is also an argument about how men and women should argue. Define what he means by "the real morality of public discussion" in paragraph 29. According to Mill, what determines if an argument is "moral" or "immoral"?
8. How would John Stuart Mill feel about the classes you are taking this semester?
9. Would Mill tolerate the publication of pornography?

QUESTIONS ABOUT STRATEGY

1. Mill illustrates the danger of persecution by citing the examples of Socrates and Christ. Why does he discuss them in this order?
2. Mill tends to favor long ponderous paragraphs. What effect does his paragraphing have on your reading? Do you see any specific points at which a paragraph could be broken up?
3. What is the function of paragraph 5?
4. In paragraph 19 Mill writes, "The cessation, on one question after another, of serious controversy is one of the necessary incidents of the consolidation

of opinion—a consolidation as salutary in the case of true opinions as it is dangerous and noxious when the opinions are erroneous." In making this concession, is Mill contradicting himself?

5. Why does Mill summarize his argument in paragraphs 25–28? And why does he alter the order in which he originally discussed his four basic points?

6. Judging from Mill's prose, what kind of man does he seem to have been? Specifically, to what extent does he sound like someone who tried to live according to the principles set forth in this argument?

FRANK TRIPPETT

The Growing Battle of the Books

Born in Mississippi, Frank Trippett (b. 1926) attended Duke University and the University of Mississippi before becoming a reporter and editor. From 1955–1961, he was state capital bureau chief for the St. Petersburg Times, *an experience which led to his first book,* The States: United they Fall *(1967), a study of American state legislatures. His political writing about state and local governments earned Trippett a special citation from the American Political Science Association. An associate editor at* Newsweek *from 1961–1968, and a senior editor at* Look *from 1968–1971, Trippett is now a senior writer for* Time *magazine, which published the following essay in 1981.*

Written words running loose have always presented a challenge to people 1
bent on ruling others. In times past, religious zealots burned heretical ideas and heretics with impartiality. Modern tyrannies promote the contentment and obedience of their subjects by ruthlessly keeping troubling ideas out of their books and minds. Censorship can place people in bondage more efficiently than chains.

Thanks to the First Amendment, the U.S. has been remarkably, if not entirely, 2
free of such official monitoring. Still, the nation has always had more than it needs of voluntary censors, vigilantes eager to protect everybody from hazards like ugly words, sedition, blasphemy, unwelcome ideas and, perhaps worst of all, reality. Lately, however, it has been easy to assume that when the everything-goes New Permissiveness gusted forth in the 1960s, it blew the old book-banning spirit out of action for good.

Quite the contrary. In fact, censorship has been on the rise in the U.S. for the 3
past ten years. Every region of the country and almost every state has felt the flaring of the censorial spirit. Efforts to ban or squelch books in public libraries and schools doubled in number, to 116 a year, in the first five years of the 1970s over the last five of the 1960s—as Author L. B. Woods documents in *A Decade of Censorship in America—The Threat to Classrooms and Libraries, 1966–*

1975. The upsurge in book banning has not since let up, one reason being that some 200 local, state and national organizations now take part in skirmishes over the contents of books circulating under public auspices. The American Library Association, which has been reporting an almost yearly increase in censorial pressures on public libraries, has just totted up the score for 1980. It found, without surprise, yet another upsurge: from three to five episodes a week to just as many in a day. Says Judith Krug, director of the A.L.A.'s Office for Intellectual Freedom: "This sort of thing has a chilling effect."

That, of course, is precisely the effect that censorship always intends. And   4 the chill, whether intellectual, political, moral or artistic, is invariably hazardous to the open traffic in ideas that not only nourishes a free society but defines its essence. The resurgence of a populist censorial spirit has, in a sense, sneaked up on the nation. National attention has focused on a few notorious censorship cases, such as the book-banning crusade that exploded into life-threatening violence in Kanawha County, W. Va., in 1974. But most kindred episodes that have been cropping up all over have remained localized and obscure. The Idaho Falls, Idaho, school book review committee did not make a big splash when it voted, 21 to 1, to ban *One Flew Over the Cuckoo's Nest*—in response to one parent's objection to some of the language. It was not much bigger news when Anaheim, Calif., school officials authorized a list of *approved* books that effectively banned many previously studied books, including Richard Wright's classic *Black Boy.* And who recalls the Kanawha, Iowa, school board's banning *The Grapes of Wrath* because some scenes involved prostitutes?

Such cases, numbering in the hundreds, have now been thoroughly tracked   5 down and sorted out by English Education Professor Edward B. Jenkinson of Indiana University in a study, *Censors in the Classroom—The Mind Benders.* He began digging into the subject after he became chairman of the Committee Against Censorship of the National Council of Teachers of English. His 184-page report reviews hundreds of cases (notorious and obscure), suggests the scope of censorship activity (it is ubiquitous), discusses the main censorial tactics (usually pure power politics) and points to some of the subtler ill effects. Popular censorship, for one thing, induces fearful teachers and librarians to practice what Jenkinson calls "closet censorship." The targets of the book banners? Jenkinson answers the question tersely: "Nothing is safe."

Case histories make that easy to believe. The books that are most often   6 attacked would make a nice library for anybody with broad-gauged taste. Among them: *Catcher in the Rye, Brave New World, Grapes of Wrath, Of Mice and Men, Catch-22, Soul on Ice,* and *To Kill a Mockingbird. Little Black Sambo* and *Merchant of Venice* run into recurring protests based on suspicions that the former is anti-black, the latter anti-Semitic. One school board banned *Making It with Mademoiselle,* but reversed the decision after finding out it was a how-to pattern book for youngsters hoping to learn dressmaking. Authorities in several school districts have banned the *American Heritage Dictionary* not only because it contains unacceptable words but because some organizations, the Texas Daughters of the American Revolution among them, have objected to the sexual intimations of the definition of the word *bed* as a transitive verb.

Censorship can, and often does, lead into absurdity, though not often slap- 7
stick absurdity like the New Jersey legislature achieved in the 1960s when it
enacted a subsequently vetoed antiobscenity bill so explicit that it was deemed
too dirty to be read in the legislative chambers without clearing out the public
first. The mother in Whiteville, N.C., who demanded that the Columbus County
library keep adult books out of the hands of children later discovered that her
own daughter had thereby been made ineligible to check out the Bible. One
group, a Florida organization called Save Our Children, has simplified its censorship goals by proposing to purge from libraries all books by such reputed
homosexuals as Emily Dickinson, Willa Cather, Virginia Woolf, Tennessee
Williams, Walt Whitman and John Milton.

Most often, censors wind up at the ridiculous only by going a very dangerous 8
route. The board of the Island Trees Union Free School District on Long Island,
N.Y., in a case still being contested by former students in court, banned eleven
books as "anti-American, anti-Christian, anti-Semitic and just plain filthy." Later
they discovered that the banished included two Pulitzer prizewinners: Bernard
Malamud's *The Fixer* and Oliver La Farge's *Laughing Boy.* For censors to ban
books they have never read is commonplace. For them to deny that they are
censoring is even more so. Said Attorney George W. Lipp Jr., announcing plans
to continue the legal fight for the Island Trees board: "This is not book burning
or book banning but a rational effort to transmit community values."

Few censors, if any, tend to see that censorship itself runs counter to certain 9
basic American values. But why have so many people with such an outlook
begun lurching forth so aggressively in recent years? They quite likely have
always suffered the censorial impulse. But they have been recently emboldened
by the same resurgent moralistic mood that has enspirited evangelical fundamentalists and given form to the increasingly outspoken constituency of the
Moral Majority. At another level, they probably hunger for some power over
something, just as everybody supposedly does these days. Thus they are
moved, as American Library Association President Peggy Sullivan says, "by a
desperation to feel some control over what is close to their lives."

Americans are in no danger of being pushed back to the prudery of the 19th 10
century. The typical U.S. newsstand, with its sappy pornutopian reek, is proof
enough of that, without even considering prime-time TV. But the latter-day
inflamed censor is no laughing matter. One unsettling feature of the current
censorial vigilantism is its signs of ugly inflammation. There is, for instance, the
cheerily incendiary attitude expressed by the Rev. George A. Zarris, chairman
of the Moral Majority in Illinois. Says Zarris: "I would think moral-minded people
might object to books that are philosophically alien to what they believe. If they
have the books and feel like burning them, fine." The notion of book burning is
unthinkable to many and appalling to others, if only because it brings to mind
the rise of Adolf Hitler's Germany—an event marked by widespread bonfires
fed by the works of scores of writers including Marcel Proust, Thomas Mann,
H.G. Wells and Jack London.

Unthinkable? In fact, the current wave of censorship has precipitated two of 11
the most outrageous episodes of book burning in the U.S. since 1927, when
Chicago Mayor William ("Big Bill") Thompson, an anglophobe miffed by a view

sympathetic to the British, had a flunky put the torch on the city hall steps to one of Historian Arthur Schlesinger Sr.'s books. In Drake, N. Dak., the five-member school board in 1973 ordered the confiscation and burning of three books that, according to Professor Jenkinson, none of the members had read: Kurt Vonnegut's *Slaughterhouse Five*, James Dickey's *Deliverance* and an anthology of short stories by writers like Joseph Conrad, John Steinbeck and William Faulkner. Said the school superintendent later: "I don't regret it one bit, and we'd do it again. I'm just sorry about all the publicity that we got." In Warsaw, Ind., a gaggle of citizens in 1977 publicly burned 40 copies of *Values Clarifications*, a textbook, as a show of support for a school board that decided to ban both written matter and independent-minded teachers from its system. Said William I. Chapel, a member of that board: "The bottom line is: Who will control the minds of the students?"

An interesting question. It baldly reveals the ultimate purpose of all censorship—mind control—just as surely as the burning of books dramatizes a yearning latent in every consecrated censor. The time could not be better for recalling something Henry Seidel Canby wrote after Big Bill Thompson put Arthur Schlesinger to the flame. Said Canby: "There will always be a mob with a torch ready when someone cries, 'Burn those books!'" The real bottom line is: How many more times is he going to be proved right?   12

QUESTIONS FOR MEANING

1. Can you define "the chilling effect" that censorship has according to this essay?
2. How many of the banned books referred to in this essay have you yourself read? Knowing that they have been censored, would you be more or less inclined to read them?
3. In paragraph 6, Trippett mentions that there are "sexual intimations" in the *American Heritage Dictionary*'s "definition of the word *bed* as a transitive verb." Show that you understand what he means by using the word in this sense in a sentence.
4. What causes people to feel "a desperation to feel some control over what is close to their lives"? Why might parents be especially anxious to censor books in the 1980s? What do they fear? Are their fears legitimate?
5. A schoolboard member quoted by Trippett argues that censorship amounts to a question of who will control the minds of students. Should anyone control the minds of students? If so, who?

QUESTIONS ABOUT STRATEGY

1. Do you detect any bias in Trippett's essay? How fair is he to his opponents?
2. Trippett argues that censorship is dangerous, and yet in paragraph 7 he cites several comic examples. Why does he do this?
3. How impressed are you by the individual cases of censorship that Trippett describes? Does he persuade you that censorship is a growing problem?

4. Comment on Trippett's use of the verb "lurching" in paragraph 9. What are the connotations of this word. What makes it an interesting word choice?
5. In a lively piece of phrasing, Trippett associates a "typical U.S. newsstand" with "sappy pornutopian reek." What kind of magazines is he referring to? How would you define "pornutopian reek," and why is it "sappy"?

FLANNERY O'CONNOR
Total Effect and the Eighth Grade

Flannery O'Connor (1925–1964) ranks as one of the best American writers in this century. During her relatively short life she published only two novels, Wise Blood *(1952) and* The Violent Bear it Away *(1960), and a collection of short stories,* A Good Man is Hard to Find *(1955). A second collection of stories,* Everything That Rises Must Converge *(1965) was published posthumously. In the years since her death, increasing numbers of readers have come to discover the strangely wonderful combination of grotesque humor and religious mystery that characterizes the best of O'Connor's fiction. She has been the subject of many critical studies, and her* Complete Stories *won the National Book Award when published in 1972. "Total Effect and the Eighth Grade" was written in 1963; it is drawn from* Mystery and Manners, *a collection of O'Connor's essays and occasional prose edited by Sally and Robert Fitzgerald.*

In two recent instances in Georgia, parents have objected to their eighth- and ninth-grade children's reading assignments in modern fiction. This seems to happen with some regularity in cases throughout the country. The unwitting parent picks up his child's book, glances through it, comes upon passages of erotic detail or profanity, and takes off at once to complain to the school board. Sometimes, as in one of the Georgia cases, the teacher is dismissed and hackles rise in liberal circles everywhere.

The two cases in Georgia, which involved Steinbeck's *East of Eden* and John Hersey's *A Bell for Adano*, provoked considerable newspaper comment. One columnist, in commending the enterprise of the teachers, announced that students do not like to read the fusty works of the nineteenth century, that their attention can best be held by novels dealing with the realities of our own time, and that the Bible, too, is full of racy stories.

Mr. Hersey himself addressed a letter to the State School Superintendent in behalf of the teacher who had been dismissed. He pointed out that his book is not scandalous, that it attempts to convey an earnest message about the nature of democracy, and that it falls well within the limits of the principle of "total effect," that principle followed in legal cases by which a book is judged not for isolated parts but by the final effect of the whole book upon the general reader.

I do not want to comment on the merits of these particular cases. What concerns me is what novels ought to be assigned in the eighth and ninth grades as a matter of course, for if these cases indicate anything, they indicate the haphazard way in which fiction is approached in our high schools. Presumably there is a state reading list which contains "safe" books for teachers to assign; after that it is up to the teacher.

English teachers come in Good, Bad, and Indifferent, but too frequently in   5
high schools anyone who can speak English is allowed to teach it. Since several novels can't easily be gathered into one textbook, the fiction that students are assigned depends upon their teacher's knowledge, ability, and taste: variable factors at best. More often than not, the teacher assigns what he thinks will hold the attention and interest of the students. Modern fiction will certainly hold it.

Ours is the first age in history which has asked the child what he would   6
tolerate learning, but that is a part of the problem with which I am not equipped to deal. The devil of Educationism that possesses us is the kind that can be "cast out only by prayer and fasting." No one has yet come along strong enough to do it. In other ages the attention of children was held by Homer and Virgil, among others, but, by the reverse evolutionary process, that is no longer possible; our children are too stupid now to enter the past imaginatively. No one asks the student if algebra pleases him or if he finds it satisfactory that some French verbs are irregular, but if he prefers Hersey to Hawthorne, his taste must prevail.

I would like to put forward the proposition, repugnant to most English   7
teachers, that fiction, if it is going to be taught in the high schools, should be taught as a subject and as a subject with a history. The total effect of a novel depends not only on its innate impact, but upon the experience, literary and otherwise, with which it is approached. No child needs to be assigned Hersey or Steinbeck until he is familiar with a certain amount of the best work of Cooper, Hawthorne, Melville, the early James, and Crane, and he does not need to be assigned these until he has been introduced to some of the better English novelists of the eighteenth and nineteenth centuries.

The fact that these works do not present him with the realities of his own   8
time is all to the good. He is surrounded by the realities of his own time, and he has no perspective whatever from which to view them. Like the college student who wrote in her paper on Lincoln that he went to the movies and got shot, many students go to college unaware that the world was not made yesterday; their studies began with the present and dipped backward occasionally when it seemed necessary or unavoidable.

There is much to be enjoyed in the great British novels of the nineteenth   9
century, much that a good teacher can open up in them for the young student. There is no reason why these novels should be either too simple or too difficult for the eighth grade. For the simple, they offer simple pleasures; for the more precocious, they can be made to yield subtler ones if the teacher is up to it. Let the student discover, after reading the nineteenth-century British novel, that the nineteenth-century American novel is quite different as to its literary characteristics, and he will thereby learn something not only about these individual

works but about the sea-change which a new historical situation can effect in a literary form. Let him come to modern fiction with this experience behind him, and he will be better able to see and to deal with the more complicated demands of the best twentieth-century fiction.

Modern fiction often looks simpler than the fiction that preceded it, but in   10
reality it is more complex. A natural evolution has taken place. The author has for the most part absented himself from direct participation in the work and has left the reader to make his own way amid experiences dramatically rendered and symbolically ordered. The modern novelist merges the reader in the experience; he tends to raise the passions he touches upon. If he is a good novelist, he raises them to effect by their order and clarity a new experience— the total effect—which is not in itself sensuous or simply of the moment. Unless the child has had some literary experience before, he is not going to be able to resolve the immediate passions the book arouses into any true, total picture.

It is here the moral problem will arise. It is one thing for a child to read about   11
adultery in the Bible or in *Anna Karenina*, and quite another for him to read about it in most modern fiction. This is not only because in both the former instances adultery is considered a sin, and in the latter, at most, an inconvenience, but because modern writing involves the reader in the action with a new degree of intensity, and literary mores now permit him to be involved in any action a human being can perform.

In our fractured culture, we cannot agree on morals; we cannot even agree   12
that moral matters should come before literary ones when there is a conflict between them. All this is another reason why the high schools would do well to return to their proper business of preparing foundations. Whether in the senior year students should be assigned modern novelists should depend both on their parents' consent and on what they have already read and understood.

The high-school English teacher will be fulfilling his responsibility if he   13
furnishes the student a guided opportunity, through the best writing of the past, to come, in time, to an understanding of the best writing of the present. He will teach literature, not social studies or little lessons in democracy or the customs of many lands.

And if the student finds that this is not to his taste? Well, that is regrettable.   14
Most regrettable. His taste should not be consulted; it is being formed.

QUESTIONS FOR MEANING

1. Where does the title of this essay come from? Explain what "total effect" means.
2. What does O'Connor think of high school English teachers? Do you agree with her?
3. According to O'Connor, what is the proper function of a high school education, and how much say should students have in defining their own needs?
4. Does O'Connor really believe that "our children are too stupid now to enter the past imaginatively"? If she doesn't mean it, why did she write it?

5. What does O'Connor mean by the "devil of Educationalism"?
6. Why does O'Connor believe that modern fiction is often more difficult than it looks?
7. Does O'Connor believe that teachers should be restricted to a list of approved books? If so, does she indicate who should do the approving? Should this responsibility rest primarily upon teachers or parents?

QUESTIONS ABOUT STRATEGY

1. A good summary should be clear and objective. How would you describe the tone of paragraphs 2–3, where O'Connor summarizes two censorship cases that were in the news when she wrote? Does she give any indication what her own thesis will be? Or is she perfectly neutral?
2. Can you detect the use of irony anywhere in this essay? If so, where? What function does it serve?
3. In paragraph 6, O'Connor compares the teaching of English to the teaching of Algebra. Is this a valid comparison? Or is she confusing the issue by comparing subjects that are fundamentally different?
4. Is a college student really capable of thinking Lincoln could have gone to the movies, or is this an exaggeration that weakens O'Connor's case?
5. To what extent is O'Connor's argument likely to displease both parents and teachers? Is this a thoughtful argument balanced between those who favor censorship and those who oppose it? Does O'Connor go beneath the surface of controversy and reveal an underlying problem of serious importance? Or does she miss the point about what this controversy is all about?

FRANCES FITZGERALD
Rewriting History

*Frances FitzGerald (b. 1940) comes from a family with a strong interest in politics
and international affairs. Her father was a deputy director of the CIA, and her
mother is a former American ambassador to the United Nations. A magna cum
laude graduate of Radcliffe, FitzGerald went to Vietnam as a free-lance writer in
1966. She stayed for over a year gathering the material for* Fire in the Lake *(1972).
One of the first serious books on the American involvement in Vietnam, it won the
1973 Pulitzer Prize for writing about contemporary affairs. "Rewriting History" is
an editor's title for an excerpt from FitzGerald's much respected second book,*
America Revised *(1979), a study of the ways in which American history books have
changed over the years, presenting significantly different views of the past in
response to various types of pressure.*

To the uninitiated, the very thought of what goes on in a textbook house   1
must inspire a good deal of vertigo. Way up in some office building sit people—
ordinary mortals with red and blue pencils—deciding all the issues of American
history, not to mention those of literature and biology. What shall we think of
the Vietnam War? Of the American Revolution? What is the nature of American
society and what are its values? The responsibility of these people seems awesome, for, as is not true of trade publishers, the audiences for their products
are huge, impressionable, and captive. Children have to read textbooks; they
usually have to read all of each textbook and are rarely asked to criticize it for
style or point of view. A textbook is there, much like Mt. Everest awaiting
George Mallory, and it leaves no alternative. The textbook editors, therefore,
must appear to be the arbiters of American values, and the publishing companies the Ministries of Truth for children. With such power over the past and the
future, textbook people—or so the uninitiated assume—should all be philosophers. Oddly, however, few people in the textbook business seem to reflect on
their role as truth givers. And most of them are reluctant to discuss the content
of their books. Occasionally, a young editor full of injured idealism will "leak" a
piece of information about house policy. In one publishing house, a young
woman pulled me inside her office conspiratorially to show me a newspaper
article attacking a literary anthology that her company had published a few
years before. The article expressed outrage about the profanity in the book,
pointing to the use of the word "damn" in one short story. "Don't tell anyone I
showed you this, or I'll lose my job," the young woman whispered. She went on
to say that she had had to revise the anthology—a task that consisted of
removing the offending selection and finding stories by two American women
and a Puerto Rican man to replace three short stories by Anglo-Saxon men.

"Isn't that a bit arbitrary?" I asked.   2
"Oh, yes," she said. "But, you see, we're under such great pressure. We'd   3
never sell the book without a Hispanic-American."

The reticence of the textbook people derives, one soon discovers, from the   4

George Orwell 1984

essential ambiguity of their position. On one hand, they are running what amount to Ministries of Truth for children, and, on the other, they are simply trying to make money in one of the freest of free enterprises in the United States, where companies often go under. The market sets limits to the publishers' truth-giving powers. These limits are invisible to outsiders, and they shift like sandbars over time, but the textbook people have a fairly good sense of where they are likely to run aground—and for the rest they feel their way along. Under the circumstances, there is no point in discussing final, or even intermediate, principles, since these would merely upset the navigation. It takes someone used to operating under the norms of trade publishing to demonstrate where principles conflict with market realities.

Robert Bernstein, the president of Random House, runs a large book-publishing complex. In 1974, the head of Pantheon, a Random House division, showed Bernstein the manuscript of what Bernstein thought was an excellent new ninth-grade history of Mississippi. The product of a collaboration between students and faculty of Tougaloo and Millsaps Colleges, the book, unlike the old textbook in use in Mississippi schools, discussed racial conflict frankly and pointed out the contributions that black people had made to the state. The manuscript had been turned down by several textbook houses, but Bernstein—against the advice of some of his own textbook people—backed its publication as a textbook. Pantheon published it as both a trade book and a textbook, under the title *Mississippi: Conflict and Change.* Most of the books never left the warehouse, because the one customer for them, the Mississippi State Textbook Purchasing Board, refused to approve the text for use in state schools at state expense, even though the one textbook in use had gone largely unchanged for ten years and the board was authorized to approve as many as five state histories. As an activist in civil-rights and civil-liberties causes, Bernstein was outraged. So were the authors of the book, and so were some parents, students, and local school officials in Mississippi, and they retained the N.A.A.C.P. Legal Defense and Educational Fund to file suit against the Mississippi State Textbook Purchasing Board on the ground that its one approved history deprecated black Mississippians and championed white supremacy. "This business is shockingly political," Bernstein told me. "Especially in the South it's shocking."

Shocking as it might be, though, Random House did not join the Legal Defense Fund in bringing suit. Historically, textbook houses do not bring such actions, and rarely, if ever, do they protest when their books are banned by school authorities or burned by outraged citizens. Unlike many trade publishers in similar circumstances (and unlike Pantheon in this case), they acquiesce, give way to pressure, and often cut out the offending passages. In the fall of 1974, a group of parents and other citizens in Kanawha County, West Virginia, demonstrated and finally shut down schools throughout the county in protest against some books newly acquired for classroom use or for the school libraries. Among the objects of their wrath were a number of stories by black writers (the protesters claimed that these were critical of whites), an anti-war poem, and a Mark Twain satire on the Book of Genesis. The incident made national news for weeks and created a good deal of consternation among publishers,

5

6

teachers, and civil-liberties groups. The Teacher Rights Division of the National Education Association studied the controversy and concluded, not surprisingly, that it was basically a cultural conflict between liberal values and the fundamentalists beliefs of the community. No national organization found anything objectionable in the books, and yet at least one publishing house revised its literary anthology to meet Kanawha County standards.

Trade-book publishers tend to look upon such incidents as First Amendment   7
issues, and to see the acquiescence of textbook publishers as pure cowardice— as a betrayal of civil-liberties principles for commercial ends. But there is a sense in which they are wrong. For it is one thing to defend the right to publish a book and quite another to insist that schools must use the book. Why should the editors of Random House, Rand McNally, or Ginn & Company act as the arbiters of the classroom? Who are they to insist that children read Langston Hughes instead of Henry Wadsworth Longfellow, or works by three Anglo-Saxon men instead of works by two American women and one Hispanic-American man? A group like the National Education Association or the Legal Defense Fund can bring a case against a school board for censorship. But textbook publishers are only the servants of the schools, the providers of what they require. And yet textbook publishers rarely make this argument, since, taken to its logical conclusion, it implies that they have—and should have—no standards; that truth is a market commodity, determined by what will sell. Naturally, the publishers do not want to make this admission; hence the swampiness of their public statements, and their strangely unfocussed anxiety when they're asked about their editorial decisions.

To look further into the question of textbook selection and rejection is to   8
see that there is some matter of principle involved. In most countries, national authorities—academies or Ministries of Education—more or less dictate educational policy and the content of textbooks. But the American educational system has always been highly decentralized, and resistant to national authority of any sort. From the publishers' point of view, the educational system is a market, but from the point of view of the schools it is a rough kind of democracy. If a state or a school district wants a certain kind of textbook—a certain kind of truth—should it not have it? The truth is everywhere political, and this system is in principle no less reasonable and no more oppressive of the individual than the alternative of a national authority. In fact, it might be argued that it is less oppressive—that, given the size of the United States, the texts reflect the values and attitudes of society at large much more accurately than they would without decentralization. At least to some degree, they reflect the society itself.

The texts represent the society imperfectly, because the democracy of the   9
educational system is not perfect. In the first place, texts are chosen by adults, and not by the children who must read them. An alternative system is difficult to conceive, but the fact remains that the texts do not represent children. In the second place, not all adults, or even all teachers, have a voice in the selection of schoolbooks. The system of selection is far from uniform across the country, and depends upon a variety of institutions analogous to the Electoral

College or to the Senate as it was conceived by the Founding Fathers. About half of the states, for instance, have some form of state-level control over the selection of elementary-school textbooks; slightly fewer states have that control over the choice of secondary-school textbooks. In most of these states, a board of education, a superintendent of schools, or a special textbook committee reviews all texts submitted by the publishers and lists or adopts a certain number of them in each category for use in the public schools. The practices of these review boards vary widely, as does their membership. Some boards, for instance, can by law adopt only a few books in each category, and in practice they may, as the one in Mississippi did, adopt only one. Others simply weed out a few books they judge substandard and leave the real power of decision to the schools. In the so-called non-adoption states, the school districts usually have committees to examine the texts, and the practices of the committees differ more than those of the state boards. The system is, in fact, so complicated nationwide that publishers employ people to spend most of their time figuring out how it works.

The theory behind the practice of state- or districtwide adoptions is that   10
some educational authority should stand between the world of commerce and the hard-pressed teachers to insure that the books meet certain educational standards. The standards are not, however, entirely academic. The guidelines for most state boards include dicta on the subject matter of the books and on the attitudes they display. The 1976 guidelines of the State Instructional Materials Councils for Florida, for instance, note, "Instructional materials should accurately portray man's place in ecological systems, including the necessity for the protection of our environment and conservation of our natural resources. [They] should encourage thrift and humane treatment of people and should not contain any material reflecting unfairly upon persons because of their race, color, creed, national origin, ancestry, sex, or occupation." The State of Oregon has traditionally prohibited its schools from using texts that speak slightingly of the Founding Fathers. In some cases, the unwritten criteria of state boards are more specific and more important to the selection of books; in certain instances, they contradict the written guidelines.

Then, too, the whole system is less than democratic, because it is biassed   11
toward the large adoption units—the large adoption states and the big-city school districts—and particularly biassed toward the ones that make a narrow selection of books. For example, the recommendation of a social-studies book by the Texas State Textbook Committee can make a difference of hundreds of thousands of dollars to a publisher. Consequently, that committee has traditionally had a strong influence on the content of texts. In certain periods, the committee has made it worthwhile for publishers to print a special Lone Star edition of American history, for use in Texas alone. Much more important, it has from time to time exercised veto power over the content of texts used nationwide. For example, in 1961 a right-wing fringe group called Texans for America intimidated the committee, and it pressed several publishers to make substantial changes in their American-history and geography texts. Macmillan, for one, deleted a passage saying that the Second World War might have been

averted if the United States had joined the League of Nations. The Silver Burdett Company took out two passages concerning the need for the United States to maintain friendly relations with other countries and the possibility that some countries would occasionally disagree with us and substituted passages saying that some countries were less free than the United States. Various publishers deleted references to Pete Seeger, Langston Hughes, and several other offenders against the sensibilities of Texans for America. Not only the largest states but combinations of smaller ones have often exerted an influence disproportionate to the size of their school populations. The fact that most of the former Confederate states have state-level adoptions has meant that until recently conservative white school boards have imposed their racial prejudices not only on the children in their states but on children throughout the nation.

In sum, the system of adoptions has a significant impact on the way Americans are taught their own history. Because of the Texas State Textbook Committee, New England children, whose ancestors heartily disapproved of the Mexican War, have grown up with heroic tales of Davy Crockett and Sam Houston. Because of actions taken by the Detroit school board and the Newark Textbook Council in the early sixties, textbooks began for the first time to treat the United States as a multiracial society.   12

The school establishment is not the only group that shapes American history in the textbooks. It is often private-interest groups or citizens' organizations that bring about the most important political changes in the texts. The voices of these outside pressure groups have risen and fallen almost rhythmically in the course of the past fifty years. Sometimes there seems to be a great deal of public interest in textbooks, sometimes very little. What is noteworthy is that until 1960 the voices were pretty much alike; after that, they became much more varied, and the public debate over texts altered dramatically.   13

The history of public protests against textbooks goes back at least to the middle of the nineteenth century, but these protests grew in size and intensity with the establishment of universal secondary education, in the twentieth. The first important outbreak of them occurred in the years following the First World War. In that period, the mayor of Chicago and the Hearst newspapers, using adjectives such as "unpatriotic" and "un-American," created an uproar over what they said was the pro-British bias of certain texts. (According to Henry Steele Commager, one of the objects of their rage was an account of the battle of Bunker Hill in a text by Andrew C. McLaughlin. That being a simpler era in the history of textbook publishing, McLaughlin himself answered the charges. According to Commager, he volunteered to change a sentence that read, "Three times the British returned courageously to the attack" to one reading, "Three times the cowardly British returned to the attack.") Simultaneously, the Daughters of the American Revolution attacked some of the texts for not putting enough stress on American military history. The Ku Klux Klan got into the act by complaining of pro-Jewish and pro-Catholic sentiments. Then a number of fundamentalist groups protested against the teaching of evolutionary theory, and eventually succeeded in purging some biology texts of references to evolution. Finally, and with no publicity at all, several utilities associations, includ-   14 ing the National Electric Light Association, the American Gas Association, and the American Railway Association, put pressure on the publishers and school officials to doctor the texts in their favor. They got results until their efforts were discovered by the Federal Trade Commission. This wave of right-wing indignation receded as the Depression hit, and for the next ten years such groups remained silent. During the thirties, the peace was broken only by the Women's Christian Temperance Union and the liquor interests, whose debate seems to have ended in a draw.

Then, in 1939, there erupted the most furious of all textbook controversies   15
to date, the subject of which was a series on American civilization by Dr. Harold Rugg. A professor at Columbia University Teachers College, Dr. Rugg had written his series (intended for pupils in elementary and junior high school) in the twenties and had begun publishing it in 1930. His aim in writing it had been to bring some realism into the schoolbook description of American society, and to a great extent he succeeded. In one volume, *An Introduction to Problems of American Culture,* he discussed unemployment, the problems faced by new immigrants, class structure, consumerism, and the speedup of life in an industrial society. These questions had never before been dealt with extensively in any school text, and the frankness of his approach remains startling even today. Rugg is probably still the only text writer who has advocated national economic planning and who has used the word "Socialist" on the first page of a book. His series does not, however, advocate Socialism. The books are full of pieties about the need for American children to become "tolerant, understanding and cooperating citizens." The series sold very well in the thirties. It was used in school systems containing nearly half of all American children, and for almost a decade there were no complaints about it. In 1939, a chorus of protests suddenly broke out. The first was from the Advertising Federation of America, which was offended by Rugg's disparaging remarks about advertising; then the National Association of Manufacturers, the American Legion, and a columnist for the Hearst press joined in, calling the series Socialist or Communist propaganda. The charges caught on and spread to community groups across the country. Dr. Rugg went on an extensive lecture tour to defend the series, during which he announced publicly that he was neither a Communist nor a Socialist. But in vain. A number of school boards banned the books, and others simply took them out of circulation. In 1938, the Rugg books sold 289,000 copies; in 1944, they sold only 21,000 copies; not long afterward, they disappeared from the market altogether.

During the forties, business associations and right-wing citizens' groups at-   16
tacked a number of other liberal textbooks and maintained a high level of pressure on the publishers. By 1950 or so, the merely conservative groups had been so successful that they had nothing more to complain about: the texts had become reflections of the National Association of Manufacturers viewpoint. This surrender by the publishers did not, however, end the war; it merely moved the battle lines farther to the right. In the mid-fifties, the anti-fluoridation lobby went on the offensive, followed a few years later by the John Birch Society, which—quite imaginatively—blamed the textbooks for the North Koreans'

success in "brainwashing" a handful of American prisoners of war. The textbook publishers took this seriously, for by that time they were so sensitive to right-wing pressure that they were checking their books before publication with a member of the Indiana State Textbook Commission named Ada White. Mrs. White believed, among other things, that Robin Hood was a Communist, and she urged that books that told the Robin Hood story be banned from Indiana schools. The publishers were no less mindful of the Texas State House of Representatives, which—in a state that already required a loyalty oath from all textbook writers—approved a resolution urging that "the American history courses in the public schools emphasize in the textbooks our glowing and throbbing history of hearts and souls inspired by wonderful American principles and traditions."

The mid-sixties must have been a bewildering period for the textbook companies. In the space of a year or two, the political wind veered a hundred and eighty degrees. For the first time in publishing history, large-scale protests came from the left and from non-white people, and for the first time such protests were listened to. The turnaround began with a decision made by the Detroit Board of Education. In 1962, the local branch of the N.A.A.C.P. charged that one history text, published by Laidlaw Brothers, depicted slavery in a favorable light, and called on the Detroit board to withdraw it from the city school system. The N.A.A.C.P. and other civil-rights organizations had denounced racial prejudice in the textbooks a number of times in prior years with no real effect. This time, however, the Detroit board withdrew the text, and subsequently began to examine for racial bias all the history texts used in the school system. The Newark Textbook Council soon followed suit. The movement then spread to other big-city school systems and was taken up by organizations representing other racial and ethnic minority groups—Mexican-Americans, Puerto Ricans, American Indians, Asian-Americans, Armenian-Americans, and so on—all of whom claimed, with justice, to have been ignored or abused by the textbooks. Within a few years, a dozen organizations, from the B'nai B'rith's Anti-Defamation League to a new Council on Interracial Books, were studying texts for racial, ethnic, and religious bias and making recommendations for a new generation of texts. What began as a series of discreet protests against individual books became a general proposition: all texts had treated the United States as a white, middle-class society when it was in fact multiracial and multicultural. And this proposition, never so much as suggested before 1962, had by the late sixties come to be a truism for the educational establishment.

The causes of this sudden upsurge of protest and the equally sudden change of perspective among educators are easy to understand in retrospect. As a result of the migrations from South to North during and after the Second World War, black Americans had become by the sixties a strong minority of the population in many Northern cities. In Detroit and Newark, they had become a majority. At the same time, the civil-rights movement had begun to focus national attention on the ugly facts of racial discrimination and prejudice in all areas of American life. A need for a change in the depiction of blacks and other minorities in textbooks, on television, and in advertising was merely one of the themes of the civil-rights movement, but it was the one that was the easiest to deal with. White Americans could resist racial integration in employment, in housing, and in the schools, but no one could deny the minorities at least a token place in the picture of American society. There was no principle to support a counter-argument, and, more important, no reason to make one. An alteration in the symbols could be made without any change in the reality.

The abrupt reversal of perspective in the schools created some panic in the   19
textbook houses. Three or four years—the time it usually takes to produce a new basic text—seemed like an aeon relative to the change in consciousness. A single year was enough to outdate any given picture of America, and nobody could know what the next change would be. (On the evidence of one elementary-school social-studies text, the panic must have reached an all-time high at Noble & Noble. As late as 1964, *New York: Past and Present* made only fleeting reference to blacks. Two years later, another Noble & Noble book, *The New York Story*, included five chapters on blacks.) No sooner had the editors begun to paste in pictures of Ralph Bunche and write reports on the civil-rights movement than along came the women's movement, sending them quite literally back to the drawing board—this time to change their representation of half the human species.

Only in the mid-seventies did the rate of change slow and the positions   20
harden enough for the publishers to write guidelines for authors and editors on the treatment of racial and other minorities in the textbooks. These guidelines—which have since been published and thus set fast, at least for a while—give instructions on such things as the percentage of illustrations to be devoted to the various groups, and ways to avoid stereotyping in text or pictures. The most interesting thing about them is the rather substantial modifications they make in the English language. The Holt, Rinehart & Winston guidelines on gender, for instance, include such strictures as "Avoid 'the founding fathers,' use 'the founders.'" (Holt also says, "Men are to be shown participating in a variety of domestic chores, such as cooking, sewing, housework, child-rearing, etc. Care should be taken to avoid implying that they are inept at these activities.") Houghton Mifflin advises its editors to make sparing use of quoted material with male references, such as "These are the times that try men's souls"; it has discouraged the use of "the fatherland" and female pronouns referring to boats. To avoid ethnic stereotyping, its guidelines warn against the overuse of names like "Mary" and "John" and the use of only one ethnic name in lists of arbitrarily chosen names. Macmillan, for its part, urges its editors not to transform ordinary words into negative concepts by adding "black" to them, as in "black market," and it gives "native Americans" as an alternative term for American Indians. There is, as the editors recognize, a certain arbitrariness about these decisions on usage. Allyn & Bacon, for instance, subscribes to "native Americans" but not to "Hispanic-Americans." "We won't use the term Hispanic-Americans," one editor told me, "unless, of course, that becomes the way to go."

As the sixties ended, the publishers may have thought they had found some   21 peace. But it was not to be. Just as soon as their guidelines were issued and pictures of female mechanics and native-American chairpersons began to appear in the books, the reaction set in. The demonstrations in Kanawha County were followed by a spate of smaller-scale protests in communities across the country. Then the John Birch Society emerged from a decade of near-silence to direct or help along (it was difficult to tell which) demonstrations in Washington against one of the new federally funded social-studies programs. Some of the protesters were merely registering conservative objections to what they saw as the excesses of the sixties; others went further, and attacked the whole drive for racial equality and women's rights.

More than automobile manufacturers or toothpaste executives, textbook   22
publishers see themselves as beleaguered, even persecuted, people. And there is some justice in this view, for textbooks have become the lightning rods of American society. In the past, public protest over textbooks occurred only in times of rapid political or social change. Now a great number of organizations and informal groups take an interest in the content of texts. In addition to the racial and ethnic organizations, many of which disagree on what constitutes a "fair and accurate representation" of any given group, a multitude of educational and civil-rights groups have research departments devoted exclusively to the analysis of textbooks. Many of these departments—on the right and on the left—have with experience become sophisticated both in their analyses of text materials and in their methods of approaching publishers, school boards, and the federal bureaucracy. The public battle over texts is thus more intense and more complicated than it has ever been before. At the same time, the publishers have become much more sensitive to the market. Having availed themselves of many of the new market-research techniques, they can now register not just the great upheavals in society but also the slight tremors. They find this a mixed blessing. On the one hand, there are fewer surprises; on the other hand, they have had to become horrendously self-conscious. Does this math text have enough Polish-sounding people buying oranges? Does that third-grade reader show a woman fireperson? What will play in New York that will not offend the sensibilities of Peoria? As the publishers well know, it is impossible to satisfy everyone—or anyone for a long period.

There is perhaps only one group left in the country which does not bother   23
the publishers—or anyway not very often—and that is the academic community. True, scholars do help "develop" textbooks, and occasionally they are permitted to have a significant role in determining their content. In the nineteen-sixties, the federal government was spending large sums for the development of new teaching materials, and groups of scholars selected by the learned societies developed a new generation of textbooks in the natural and social sciences. (The history texts, however, were not affected, for the American Historical Association did not take part.) But most scholars do not take secondary-school (or even college) textbooks seriously—not even when they have a hand in writing them. They do not make a practice of reading textbooks in their field, and no academic journal reviews textbooks on a regular basis. One consequence is that new scholarship trickles down extremely slowly into the

school texts; as it proceeds, usually by way of the college texts, the elapsed time between the moment an idea or an approach gains currency in the academic community and the moment it reaches the school texts may be fifteen years or more. Another consequence is that there is no real check on the intellectual quality—or even the factual accuracy—of school textbooks. The result is that on the scale of publishing priorities the pursuit of truth appears somewhere near the bottom.

In a perfectly democratic, or custom-designed, world, every teacher would   24
be allowed to choose his or her own history textbook—which is to say that the publishing houses would publish books in a variety large enough to suit all tastes. But this has somehow never happened, in spite of all the structural changes the textbook business has undergone in the United States over the past hundred years. The late nineteenth century ought to have been the period for a great diversity of books, because scores of publishers were competing then in a burgeoning school market. At the time, however, the content of texts was the least of a publisher's worries, for—particularly in the West, where the competition was the most intense—the sale of books depended largely on which company could most successfully bribe or otherwise corrupt the whiskey dealers, preachers, and political-party hacks who sat on the school boards. This degree of free enterprise proved uneconomical in the long run. In the eighteen-nineties, three of the major companies banded together to form the American Book Company, which acquired a seventy-five- to eighty-per-cent monopoly of the textbook market. Yet this streamlining of the industry did not make for a wider selection of books. Indeed, when the American Book Company acquired a total monopoly in geography publishing, it produced no new books in that field for many years. Competition was eventually reëstablished, and there was some greater variety in the texts until the ideological freeze of the Cold War. In recent years, the industry has been a model of American free enterprise: four hundred companies (forty of them major ones) have competed fiercely, but with a fairly high degree of probity, to sell more or less the same product to the same people.

In the mid-sixties, there were high hopes in the publishing industry that this   25
situation would change. Sitting at the feet of Marshall McLuhan, the publishers decided that the era of mass production was over—along with the era of literacy and linear reasoning—and that they should at once prepare to deliver instant all-around audiovisual programming with individualized feedback for every child. The era of software had come—the era of total communication and perfect customization. Not only—or even principally—the textbook publishers but a lot of high-rolling communications-industry executives dreamed of equipping every classroom in America with television sets, video cameras, holography sets, and computer terminals. As a first step toward this post-industrial future, the executives built conglomerates designed to put all kinds of software components and communications capability under one roof. Xerox acquired Ginn & Company; RCA bought Random House; C.B.S. acquired Holt, Rinehart & Winston; Raytheon bought D.C. Heath; and Time Inc. acquired Little, Brown and Company and Silver Burdett and, with General Electric, formed the General Learning Corporation.

The problem was that all the new theories about education, information, and   26
business in the future rested on the availability of large-scale government
funding, a growing student population, and a ballooning economy. And none of
these conditions held for very long. As soon as the costs of the Vietnam War
came home, the schools drastically curtailed their multimedia programs, the
government cut back funding of research projects to develop new teaching
methods and materials, and the conglomerates began to look like no more than
the sum of their parts. And then, with great speed, fashions changed, and
educational theory turned conservative. Parents and school boards complained
that children couldn't read or write anymore—that what they needed was
textbook drill. Publishers, up to their ears in machinery, began to look on
textbooks as the basic winter coat. While they continued to produce some of
the cheapest of the new materials—such things as magazines and filmstrips—
they put their money back into books: both the hardbacks and a new generation
of paperbacks, which allowed teachers a choice of supplementary material. "It
began to dawn on them," one trade-book editor says, "that the book is finally
the most efficient retrieval system we possess."

The big basic history textbook thus seems here to stay, at least for a bit, and   27
to stay just about what it has always been in this century—a kind of lowest
common denominator of American tastes. The books of the seventies are somewhat more diverse than those of the fifties, but still they differ from one another
not much more than one year's crop of Detroit sedans. This is hardly surprising,
since, like cars, textbooks are expensive to design and relatively cheap to
duplicate. The development of a new eleventh-grade history text can cost five
hundred thousand dollars (more this year, perhaps), with an additional
hundred thousand in marketing costs. Since the public schools across the
country now spend less than one per cent of their budgets on buying books
(textbook publishing is only a seven-hundred-million-dollar-a-year business),
publishers cannot afford to have more than one or two basic histories on the
market at the same time. Consequently, all of them try to compete for the
center of the market, designing their books not to please anyone in particular
but to be acceptable to as many people as possible. The word "controversial" is
as deeply feared by textbook publishers as it is coveted by trade-book publishers. What a textbook reflects is thus a compromise, an America sculpted and
sanded down by the pressures of diverse constituents and interest groups.

QUESTIONS FOR MEANING

1. Why does FitzGerald believe that publishers have "power over the past and
   the future?" Is this an exaggeration? Can you think of anything besides
   textbooks that shapes our understanding of past and future?
2. If you have never heard of George Mallory, can you figure out who he was
   from the way he's mentioned in paragraph 1?
3. When FitzGerald writes about "Ministries of Truth," she is alluding to what
   famous twentieth century novel?
4. Who chooses textbooks? What sort of guidelines do they follow in choosing
   books for adoption? Who gets left out of the selection process?

5. Why has the state of Texas been able to have so much influence with publishers?
6. Why did the 1960s bring a great change in the demands that publishers try to satisfy? Why did a reaction eventually set in during the 1970s?
7. What does FitzGerald mean by "scholars," and why do they have little interest in textbooks?
8. Why don't textbook publishers protest censorship? Why do they respond to public criticism by cutting offending passages from their books?
9. Does FitzGerald justify her claim that "on the scale of publishing priorities the pursuit of truth appears somewhere near the bottom"?
10. Vocabulary: vertigo (1), reticence (4), acquiesce (6), consternation (6), arbiters (7), disparaging (15), truism (17), horrendously (22), and ideological (24).

QUESTIONS ABOUT STRATEGY

1. What sort of tone does FitzGerald adopt towards the publishing industry? Is she critical, ironic, or sympathetic? Is her tone consistent throughout her argument?
2. Good writers know that changing a word or two can entirely change an idea. Consider the words of Andrew C. McLaughlin quoted in paragraph 14. Is this a good example of the type of censorship that concerns FitzGerald? This was sixty years ago. Do you think any writer or publisher would be this crude today?
3. What does the story of Dr. Harold Rugg illustrate?
4. Consider FitzGerald's diction in paragraphs 25 and 26 where she writes about "all-around audiovisual programming with individualized feedback" and quotes an editor describing books as "the most efficient retrieval system we possess." Is this use of jargon deliberate or accidental? How does it compare with FitzGerald's prevailing style?
5. This argument is only a selection from the introductory chapter of a book FitzGerald has written on the subject of American history textbooks. If you were to read the rest of the book, what points would you most want FitzGerald to pursue in more detail?

WARREN BURGER
Board of Education, Island Trees v. Pico

Warren Burger (b. 1907) is the fifteenth chief justice of the United States. He studied at the University of Minnesota and practiced law in St. Paul until 1953 when Dwight Eisenhower appointed him an assistant attorney general in charge of the civil division of the Justice Department. Burger was named to the U.S. Court of Appeals for the District of Columbia in 1956 and acquired a reputation as a strict constructionist in criminal law. Conservatives were pleased when Richard Nixon appointed Burger chief justice in May 1969, but Burger has shown himself to be independent minded. An advocate of judicial reform, Burger has called for streamlining court procedures and requiring better training for judges and lawyers. But he is reluctant to expand the power of the courts, as the following opinion reveals. It is an unabridged transcript of Burger's dissenting opinion from a recent Court decision on censorship in public schools. Following the custom of the Court, Burger uses ante *(Latin for "before") in order to direct readers to specific pages in the majority opinion from which he is dissenting.*

SUPREME COURT OF THE UNITED STATES

No. 80-2043

BOARD OF EDUCATION, ISLAND TREES UNION FREE SCHOOL DISTRICT NO. 26 ET AL., PETITIONERS *v.* STEVEN A. PICO, BY HIS NEXT FRIEND, FRANCES PICO ET AL.

ON WRIT OF CERTIORARI TO THE UNITED STATES COURT OF APPEALS
FOR THE SECOND CIRCUIT

[June 25, 1982]

CHIEF JUSTICE BURGER, with whom JUSTICE POWELL, JUSTICE REHNQUIST, and   1
JUSTICE O'CONNOR join, dissenting.

The First Amendment, as with other parts of the Constitution, must deal   2
with new problems in a changing world. In an attempt to deal with a problem
in an area traditionally left to the states, a plurality of the Court, in a lavish
expansion going beyond any prior holding under the First Amendment, ex-

presses its view that a school board's decision concerning what books are to be in the school library is subject to federal court review.[1] Were this to become the law, this Court would come perilously close to becoming a "super censor" of school board library decisions. Stripped to its essentials, the issue comes down to two important propositions: *first*, whether local schools are to be administered by elected school boards, or by federal judges and teenage pupils; and *second*, whether the values of morality, good taste, and relevance to education are valid reasons for school board decisions concerning the contents of a school library. In an attempt to place this case within the protection of the First Amendment, the plurality suggests a new "right" that, when shorn of the plurality's rhetoric, allows this Court to impose its own views about what books must be made available to students.[2]

I

A

I agree with the fundamental proposition that "students do not 'shed their rights to freedom of speech or expression at the schoolhouse gate.'" *Ante*, at 11. For example, the Court has held that a school board cannot compel a student to participate in a flag salute ceremony, *West Virginia Bd. of Education* v. *Barnette*, 319 U.S. 624 (1943), or *prohibit* a student from expressing certain views, so long as that expression does not disrupt the educational process. *Tinker* v. *Des Moines School Dist.*, 393 U.S. 503 (1969). Here, however, no restraints of any kind are placed on the students. They are free to read the books in question, which are available at public libraries and bookstores; they are free to discuss them in the classroom or elsewhere. Despite this

3

---

[1]At the outset, the plurality notes that certain school board members found the books in question "objectionable" and "improper" for junior and senior high school students. What the plurality apparently finds objectionable is that the inquiry as to the challenged books was initially stimulated by what is characterized as "a politically conservative organization of parents concerned about education," which had concluded that the books in question were "improper fare for school students." *Ante*, at 2. As noted by the District Court, however, and in the plurality opinion, *ante*, at 5, both parties substantially agreed about the motivation of the school board in removing the books:

"[T]he board acted not on religious principles but on its conservative educational philosophy, and on its belief that the nine books removed from the school library and curriculum were irrelevant, vulgar, immoral, and in bad taste, making them educationally unsuitable for the district's junior and senior high school students." 474 F. Supp. 387, 392 (1979).

[2]In oral argument counsel advised the Court that of the original plaintiffs, only "[o]ne of them is still in school ... until this June, and will assumedly graduate in June. *There is a potential question of mootness.*" Transcript of Oral Argument 4-5 (Emphasis added.) The sole surviving plaintiff has therefore either recently been graduated from high school or is within days or even hours of graduation. Yet the plurality expresses views on a very important constitutional issue. Fortunately, there is no binding holding of the Court on the critical constitutional issue presented.

We do well to remember the admonition of Justice Frankfurter that "the most fundamental principle of constitutional adjudication is not to face constitutional questions but to avoid them, if at all possible." *United States* v. *Lovett*, 328 U.S. 303, 320 (1946) (Frankfurter, J., concurring.) In the same vein, Justice Stone warned that "the only check upon our own exercise of power is our own sense of self-restraint." *United States* v. *Butler*, 297 U.S. 1, 79 (1936) (Stone, J., dissenting.)

absence of any direct external control on the students' ability to express themselves, the plurality suggests that there is a new First Amendment "entitlement" to have access to particular books in a school library.

The plurality cites *Meyer* v. *Nebraska*, 262 U.S. 390 (1923), which struck   4
down a state law that restricted the teaching of modern foreign languages in public and private schools, and *Epperson* v. *Arkansas*, 393 U.S. 97 (1968), which declared unconstitutional under the Establishment Clause a law banning the teaching of Darwinian evolution, to establish the validity of federal court interference with the functioning of schools. The plurality finds it unnecessary "to re-enter this difficult terrain," *ante*, at 7, yet in the next breath relies on these very cases and others to establish the previously unheard of "right" of access to particular books in the public school library.[3] The apparent underlying basis of the plurality's view seems to be that students have an enforceable "right" to receive the information and ideas that are contained in junior and senior high school library books. *Ante*, at 12. This "right" purportedly follows "ineluctably" from the sender's First Amendment right to freedom of speech and as a "necessary predicate" to the recipient's meaningful exercise of his own rights of speech, press, and political freedom. *Ante*, at 12-13. No such right, however, has previously been recognized.

It is true that where there is a willing distributor of materials, the govern-   5
ment may not impose unreasonable obstacles to dissemination by the third party. *Virginia State Board of Pharmacy* v. *Virginia Citizens Consumer Council, Inc.*, 425 U.S. 748 (1976). And where the speaker desires to express certain ideas, the government may not impose unreasonable restraints. *Tinker* v. *Des Moines School Dist., supra*. It does not follow, however, that a school board must affirmatively aid the speaker in its communication with the recipient. In short the plurality suggests today that if a writer has something to say, the government through its schools must be the courier. None of the cases cited by the plurality establish this broad-based proposition.

First, the plurality argues that the right to receive ideas is derived in part   6
from the sender's first amendment rights to send them. Yet we have previously held that a sender's rights are not absolute. *Rowan* v. *Post Office Dept.*, 397 U.S. 728 (1970).[4] Never before today has the Court indicated that the government has an *obligation* to aid a speaker or author in reaching an audience.

Second, the plurality concludes that "the right to receive ideas is a necessary   7
predicate to the *recipient's* meaningful exercise of his own rights of speech, press, and political freedom." *Ante*, at 13 (emphasis in original). However, the "right to receive information and ideas," *Stanley* v. *Georgia*, 394 U.S. 557, 564 (1969), cited *ante*, at 12, does not carry with it the concomitant right to have those ideas affirmatively provided at a particular place by the government. The plurality cites James Madison to emphasize the importance of having an in-

---

[3]Of course, it is perfectly clear that, unwise as it would be, the board could wholly dispense with the school library, so far as the First Amendment is concerned.

[4]In *Rowan* a unanimous Court upheld the right of a homeowner to direct the local post office to stop delivery of unwanted materials that the householder viewed as "erotically arousing or sexually provocative."

formed citizenry. *Ante*, at 13. We all agree with Madison of course, that knowledge is necessary for effective government. Madison's view, however, does not establish a *right* to have particular books retained on the school library shelves if the school board decides that they are inappropriate or irrelevant to the school's mission. Indeed, if the need to have an informed citizenry creates a "right," why is the government not also required to provide ready access to a variety of information? This same need would support a constitutional "right" of the people to have public libraries as part of a new constitutional "right" to continuing adult education.

The plurality also cites *Tinker, supra*, to establish that the recipient's right   8
to free speech encompasses a right to have particular books retained in the school library shelf. *Ante*, at 14. But the cited passage of *Tinker* notes only that school officials may not *prohibit* a student from expressing his or her view on a subject unless that expression interferes with the legitimate operations of the school. The government does not "contract the spectrum of available knowledge." *Griswold* v. *Connecticut*, 381 U.S. 479, 482 (1965), cited *ante*, at 12, by choosing not to retain certain books on the school library shelf; it simply chooses not to be the conduit for that particular information. In short, even assuming the desirability of the policy expressed by the plurality, there is not a hint in the First Amendment, or in any holding of this Court, of a "right" to have the government provide continuing access to certain books.

B

Whatever role the government might play as a conduit of information,   9
schools in particular ought not be made a slavish courier of the material of third parties. The plurality pays homage to the ancient verity that in the administration of the public schools "'there is a legitimate and substantial community interest in promoting respect for authority and traditional values be they social, moral, or political.'" *Ante*, at 10. If, as we have held, schools may legitimately be used as vehicles for "inculcating fundamental values necessary to the maintenance of a democratic political system," *Ambach* v. *Norwick*, 441 U.S. 68, 77 (1979), school authorities must have broad discretion to fulfill that obligation. Presumably all activity within a primary or secondary school involves the conveyance of information and at least an implied approval of the worth of that information. How are "fundamental values" to be inculcated except by having school boards make content-based decisions about the appropriateness of retaining materials in the school library and curriculum? In order to fulfill its function, an elected school board *must* express its views on the subjects which are taught to its students. In doing so those elected officials express the views of their community; they may err, of course, and the voters may remove them. It is a startling erosion of the very idea of democratic government to have this Court arrogate to itself the power the plurality asserts today.

The plurality concludes that under the Constitution school boards cannot   10
choose to retain or dispense with books if their discretion is exercised in a "narrowly partisan or political manner." *Ante*, at 16. The plurality concedes

that permissible factors are whether the books are "pervasively vulgar," *ante*, at 17, or educationally unsuitable. *Ibid.* "Educational suitability," however, is a standardless phrase. This conclusion will undoubtedly be drawn in many—if not most—instances because of the decisionmaker's content-based judgment that the ideas contained in the book or the idea expressed from the author's method of communication are inappropriate for teenage pupils.

The plurality also tells us that a book may be removed from a school library 11 if it is "pervasively vulgar." But why must the vulgarity be "pervasive" to be offensive? Vulgarity might be concentrated in a single poem or a single chapter or a single page, yet still be inappropriate. Or a school board might reasonably conclude that even "random" vulgarity is inappropriate for teenage school students. A school board might also reasonably conclude that the school board's retention of such books gives those volumes an implicit endorsement. Cf. *FCC* v. *Pacifica Foundation*, 438 U.S. 726 (1978).

Further, there is no guidance whatsoever as to what constitutes "political" 12 factors. This Court has previously recognized that public education involves an area of broad public policy and "'go[es] to the heart of representative government.'" *Ambach* v. *Norwick*, 441 U.S. 68, 74 (1979). As such, virtually all educational decisions necessarily involve "political" determinations.

What the plurality views as valid reasons for removing a book at their core 13 involve partisan judgments. Ultimately the federal courts will be the judge of whether the motivation for book removal was "valid" or "reasonable." Undoubtedly the validity of many book removals will ultimately turn on a judge's evaluation of the books. Discretion must be used, and the appropriate body to exercise that discretion is the local elected school board, not judges.[5]

We can all agree that as a matter of *educational policy* students should 14 have wide access to information and ideas. But the people elect school boards, who in turn select administrators, who select the teachers, and these are the individuals best able to determine the substance of that policy. The plurality fails to recognize the fact that local control of education involves democracy in a microcosm. In most public schools in the United States the *parents* have a large voice in running the school.[6] Through participation in the election of school board members, the parents influence, if not control, the direction of their childrens' education. A school board is not a giant bureaucracy far removed from accountability for its actions; it is truly "of the people and by the

[5]Indeed, this case is illustrative of how essentially all decisions concerning the retention of school library books will become the responsibility of federal courts. As noted above, *supra*, n. 1, the parties agreed that the school board in this case acted not on religious principles but "on its belief that the nine books removed from the school library and curriculum were irrelevant, vulgar, immoral, and in bad taste, making them educationally unsuitable for the district's junior and senior high school students."

Despite this agreement as to motivation, the case is to be remanded for a determination of whether removal was in violation of the standard adopted by the plurality. The school board's error appears to be that they made their own determination rather than relying on experts. *Ante*, at 20.

[6]*Epperson* v. *Arkansas, supra*, at 104. There are approximately 15,000 school districts in the country. U.S. Bureau of the Census, Statistical Abstract of the United States (102 ed. 1981) (Table 495: Number of Local Governments, by Taxing Power and Type, and Public School Systems—States: 1971 and 1977). See also Diamond, The First Amendment and Public Schools: The Case Against Judicial Intervention, 59 TX L. Rev. 477, 506–507, n. 130 (1981).

people." A school board reflects its constituency in a very real sense and thus could not long exercise unchecked discretion in its choice to acquire or remove books. If the parents disagree with the educational decisions of the school board, they can take steps to remove the board members from office. Finally, even if parents and students cannot convince the school board that book removal is inappropriate, they have alternative sources to the same end. Books may be acquired from book stores, public libraries, or other alternative sources unconnected with the unique environment of the local public schools.[7]

II

No amount of "limiting" language could rein in the sweeping "right" the plurality would create. The plurality distinguishes library books from textbooks because library books "by their nature are optional rather than required reading." *Ante*, at 8. It is not clear, however, why this distinction requires *greater* scrutiny before "optional" reading materials may be removed. It would appear that required reading and textbooks have a greater likelihood of imposing a "'pall of orthodoxy'" over the educational process than do optional reading. *Ante*, at 16. In essence, the plurality's view transforms the availability of this "optional" reading into a "right" to have this "optional" reading maintained at the demand of teenagers.   15

The plurality also limits the new right by finding it applicable only to the *removal* of books once acquired. Yet if the First Amendment commands that certain books cannot be *removed*, does it not equally require that the same books be *acquired*? Why does the coincidence of timing become the basis of a constitutional holding? According to the plurality, the evil to be avoided is the "official suppression of ideas." *Ante*, at 17. It does not follow that the decision to *remove* a book is less "official suppression" than the decision not to acquire a book desired by someone.[8] Similarly, a decision to eliminate certain material from the curriculum, history for example, would carry an equal—probably greater—prospect of "official suppression." Would the decision be subject to our review?   16

III

Through use of bits and pieces of prior opinions unrelated to the issue of this case, the plurality demeans our function of constitutional adjudication. Today the plurality suggests that the *Constitution* distinguishes between   17

[7]Other provisions of the Constitution, such as the Establishment Clause, *Epperson* v. *Arkansas, supra*, and the Equal Protection Clause, also limit the discretion of the school board.

[8]The formless nature of the "right" found by the plurality in this case is exemplified by this purported distinction. Presumably a school district could, for any reason, choose not to purchase a book for its library. Once it purchases that book, however, it is "locked in" to retaining it on the school shelf until it can justify a reason for its removal. This anomalous result of "book tenure" was pointed out by the District Court in this case. 474 F. Supp. 387, 395–396. See also *Presidents Council* v. *Community School Board*, 457 F. 2d 289, 293 (CA2 1972). Under the plurality view, if a school board wants to be assured that it maintains control over the education of its students, every page of every book sought to be acquired must be read before a purchase decision is made.

school libraries and school classrooms, between *removing* unwanted books and *acquiring* books. Even more extreme, the plurality concludes that the Constitution *requires* school boards to justify to its teenage pupils the decision to remove a particular book from a school library. I categorically reject this notion that the Constitution dictates that judges, rather than parents, teachers, and local school boards, must determine how the standards of morality and vulgarity are to be treated in the classroom.

QUESTIONS FOR MEANING

1. Why does Burger believe that federal courts should not be involved in choosing books for school libraries? What flaws does he perceive in the reasoning of colleagues on the Supreme Court who disagreed with him?
2. What basic principles does Burger share with his opponents on the Court? What concessions does he make to them?
3. To what extent does this argument amount to an interpretation of how to read the Constitution? What worries Burger beyond the question of what books should be in school libraries?
4. Burger argues that a local school board is a "democracy in a microcosm." What does this mean? Does Burger support this claim? What do you know about school boards and how they are elected? How representative are they? What sort of people are usually elected? Are there any people who are not represented on school boards?
5. Why does Burger see a difference between school libraries and public libraries? How do their functions differ?
6. Vocabulary: plurality (2), lavish (2), ineluctably (4), concomitant (7), conduit (9), verity (9), inculcated (9), arrogate (9), implicit (11), and adjudication (17).

QUESTIONS ABOUT STRATEGY

1. Does Burger advance his argument inductively or deductively?
2. Is Burger's argument inhibited in any way by legal jargon? How would you characterize his style as a writer?
3. Why does Burger repeatedly put quotation marks around "right"?
4. Much of Burger's argument depends upon the analysis of language. He questions a number of words and phrases used by other justices: "pervasively vulgar," "educational suitability," and "necessary predicate." He also explores the relationship between the right to *send* ideas and the right to *receive* them, as well as censorship by *removal* and censorship by *non-acquisition*. Are you persuaded that his concern with language is valid, or do you think he perceives difficulties where none exist? What is the relationship between language and the law? Why is it important for judges and lawyers to write well?
5. Is there any point where Burger weakens his case by pushing his argument further than it had to go? Does he ever go out on a legal limb and seem to take an unnecessarily extreme position?

GEORGE WILL

Et Tu, Topeka?

George Will (b. 1941) graduated from Trinity College in 1962 and received his Ph.D. from Princeton in 1967. He has taught political science at Michigan State University and the University of Toronto, served as Washington editor for National Review, and been a contributing editor to Newsweek since 1975. His syndicated column won a Pulitzer Prize for distinguished commentary in 1977. "Et Tu, Topeka" is reprinted from The Pursuit of Virtue and Other Tory Notions (1982), a collection of Will's editorials. With characteristic wit, Will argues that individual boycotts should not be confused with officially imposed censorship.

Ah, serendipity. Beneath *The Washington Post's* report of the press confer-   1
ence at which the Coalition for Better Television (CBTV) announced plans to organize boycotts of products produced by sponsors of the sleaziest television shows, there appeared a report by the *Post's* Tom Shales about a new show:

> A better title for "That's My Line" might be, maybe, "Sick Society." The CBS entry in the amazingly incredible, real-people, variety freak-show genre ... lurches imp-ishly from a feature about a man who teaches other men "how to pick up girls" for quick sex to a fey hunk of sleazery about a Topeka, Kansas, clothing store where men strip down to their underpants while women ogle and shriek at them ... Basically it's another monomaniacal titillation derby.

Et tu, Topeka?   2

Shales suggests that perhaps the pollution of the prairie by such vulgarity   3
might be television's fault: any entrepreneur knows that if he is sufficiently vulgar, network camera crews will beat a path to his door. I have a less cheerful view of mankind: Topeka or Timbuktu can produce ninnies without the tele-vision incentive. Wordsworth, who lived a long way from Kansas and a long time before television, noted mankind's "degrading thirst for outrageous stimulation."

But the pure commercial logic of oligopolistic competition impels three   4
profit-maximizing (which means, basically: audience-maximizing) networks to pander to society's lowest common denominator. And in doing so, they drive it steadily lower. CBTV's aim is to temper that logic by adding a new variable to the economic calculations that control television.

Networks live lives of cheerful, not to say brazen, contradiction. They trum-   5
pet their prowess at causing people to buy material goods: Hey, we can modify behavior in thirty seconds. Yet they deny, or disclaim responsibility for, the coarsening consequences of hour after hour of base programs. You can al-most—almost, I stress—admire the brass of the tiny coterie of network pro-grammers who complain that CBTV's "narrow" portion of the public—perhaps only a few million citizens—may influence programming.

But more unlovely than the aggressive vulgarity of many programs is the   6
ravening hypocrisy of the programmers as they criticize their critics. It is hard
(and hardly obligatory) to credit the sincerity of people who shout "Censorship!"—with that word's connotations of coercive state action—when people
are simply planning to practice selective buying of beer and panty hose. A
network spokesman decreed that boycotts are "censorship" and are "a totally
unacceptable method of trying to influence programming." I called to ask what
he considered acceptable. He said—are you ready for this?—"Oh, writing a
letter."

Plumbing the shallows of such minds will not dredge up serious arguments   7
against boycotts. Another network theorist called to deploy for me all the stock
phrases of First Amendment law. He accused CBTV of planning to "conspire"
to create a "clear and present danger" of a "chilling effect" on the "expression
of ideas."

Leave aside the inherent disingenuousness of a defense of programs like   8
Soap or *Dynasty* or *Three's Company* as vehicles of "ideas." People who
argue that way are beyond, or beneath, embarrassment, so they do not blush
when quoting Milton, Mill, Jefferson and Holmes to defend their rapacity. It is
bad enough that the networks are turning the airwaves into Love Canals of the
mind. But a chemical company that recklessly dumps toxic wastes at least
spares us the effrontery of claiming to serve civilization's spiritual well-being.

By invoking the noble language of the literature of liberty—"the free expres-   9
sion of ideas," and all that—the networks try to beguile the public into forget-
ting what networks never forget: commercial television's purpose is to sell
rivers of beer and mountains of pantyhose ("Hey, America—show us your
Underalls!"). What CBTV proposes, far from being a "conspiracy," is as public
as a calliope and as American as Martin Luther King's boycott of Montgomery,
Alabama, buses.

The hysterical network response is heartening. The networks' criterion of   10
an "acceptable" protest is clear: acceptable means impotent. It is acceptable
for an individual to write a letter, but unacceptable for individuals to "conspire"—meaning organize—because organizing might work. An advertiser
says, "It takes only a percentage-point-or-two shift in the retail sales of washing
machines or K-cars to make a tremendous difference in profits." Profits? Quit
talking about those, dummy, and start quoting Milton.

Let's all get started. Dial soap helps sponsor the execrable *Flamingo Road*.   11
Aren't you glad you don't use Dial? Don't you wish nobody did?

QUESTIONS FOR MEANING

1. Do you recognize the allusion in the title of this essay? What does it imply?
   Why do you think Will chose to focus on an episode from Topeka—rather
   than Miami, New York, or San Francisco?
2. Will reminds his audience that Wordsworth "lived a long way from Kansas
   and a long time before television." When and where did Wordsworth live,
   and why is he remembered?

3. Will complains about "the coarsening consequences of hour after hour of base programs." What does he mean by "base programs," and what are the effects of watching such shows?
4. According to Will, what is the primary purpose of commercial television? Is he right about this?
5. Why does Will believe that boycotts are not a form of censorship?
6. Vocabulary: serendipity (1), fey (1), oligopolistic (4), ravening (6), coercive (6), disingenuousness (8), effrontery (8), beguile (9), criterion (10), and execrable (11).

QUESTIONS ABOUT STRATEGY

1. Will is a lively stylist who moves easily among subjects as diverse as poetry and panty hose. Identify all the allusions that Will makes in this essay, and consider the effect that their range has upon you as a reader.
2. Why does Will compare CBTV to Martin Luther King? What does this reveal about his sense of audience?
3. Will frequently uses alliteration as a way of making his prose "scan," or move smoothly and gracefully. If you examine this essay carefully, you will find examples of this technique in almost every paragraph. Read these examples out loud and listen to how they sound. Is the effect pleasing to the ear—or does it seem mechanical and contrived?

SUGGESTIONS FOR WRITING

1. What is pornography? Is it anything that contains sex or four letter words, or is it something much more specific? Write an essay of definition making clear the meaning of this much used word.
2. Both Brownmiller and Kaminer argue that pornography hurts women. Write an argument about how pornography hurts men.
3. Few people like to admit to reading pornography, and yet there seems to be a large market for it. Why do people read pornography? Can you defend it on any grounds besides the First Amendment?
4. Have you ever been upset by a book you were required to read in school? If so, write an essay explaining what bothered you about this book. Would you prevent your teacher from using this book with other students? Try to base your case upon some fundamental principle, and not just your personal taste in what you like or don't like to read.
5. What are the rights of parents in determining what their children are taught? When teachers and parents differ about the desirability of a particular book, who should have the final word—and why? Write an essay arguing on behalf of either parents or teachers.
6. Flannery O'Connor and Warren Burger both address the issue of censorship in public schools. What about college? Should a college teacher have absolute authority in choosing what books to teach? Or should he or she be subject to some restraint? Write an essay defining the responsibilities of

college teachers and the extent to which the college classroom should be free of censorship.

7. According to the National Council of Teachers of English, the most frequently censored books in American schools include: *Catcher in the Rye, The Grapes of Wrath, Nineteen Eighty-Four, Lord of the Flies, The Adventures of Huckleberry Finn, Brave New World, The Scarlet Letter, A Farewell to Arms, One Flew Over the Cuckoo's Nest*, and *One Day in the Life of Ivan Denisovich*. Choose any one of these books that you have not previously read. Read it. And then argue for or against its use in a senior high school English class.

8. Go to a public library and interview the librarian in charge of circulation. Ask if the library has ever been pressured into withdrawing a book from circulation. Ask also if the library keeps a record of complaints made against the books in its collection. If so, ask if you can see this record and use it for evidence in determining the extent to which censorship is an issue in your own community.

9. Many people are opposed to the amount of sex and violence on television, and, as George Will points out, it's possible to organize and pressure the various networks. Should television networks and book publishers be subject to the same standards? If you think different standards are called for, explain why you think so and define what those standards should be.

10. All of the material in this unit concerns the limits of censorship in a democracy. Do a research paper on the nature of censorship elsewhere in the world, focusing in particular on the penalties that writers can suffer in totalitarian states.

Section 4
Animal Experimentation: Do Rats Have Rights?

ROBERT J. WHITE and CATHERINE ROBERTS
American Scholars Debate

In 1971, The American Scholar *published the following debate between Robert J. White and Catherine Roberts.*

Robert J. White (b. 1926) has both a M.D. from Harvard and a Ph.D. from the University of Minnesota. Since 1961, he has been a member of the medical faculty at Case Western University and director of neurosurgery and brain research at Cleveland Metropolitan General Hospital. White has won many awards for pioneering brain transplants in animals.

Catherine Roberts (b. 1917) earned both her B.A. and her Ph.D. from the University of California at Berkeley. From 1946 to 1961, she was a microbiologist at the Carlsberg Labatorium in Copenhagen, where she won the Emil Christian Hansen Silver Medal for her work on yeast microbiology. Her books include the Scientific Conscience *(1967) and* The Three Faces of Humanism *(1975).*

ROBERT J. WHITE
Antivivisection: The Reluctant Hydra

> The humanity which would prevent human suffering is a deeper and truer humanity than the humanity which would save pain or death in the animal.
>
> —Charles W. Eliot

The quotation above from that distinguished intellectual and former Harvard University president, written decades ago, continues to crystallize clearly the basic position of medical science toward the employment of animals in research and teaching. I would state it more simply: the alleviation of human suffering justifies the sacrifice of lower animals. Because this statement is as valid today as it was then, and yet has so little impact on the public conscience, I am almost reluctant to shed the mantle of clinical and professional detachment and take up the cudgels against that ill-defined, elusive Hydra—the antivivisection

1

movement. To a degree, my inertia is also derived from my conviction that medical science has always seemed to assume a low-profile posture in justifying the utilization of lower animals for research and education (as it has so often done with other public health issues); it has invariably waited until one of those vigorous cyclic antivivisection campaigns, using the most advanced techniques in news management, has reached its apogee before attempting to combat the pernicious effects on public and congressional opinion. And then, unfortunately, it has employed almost exclusively its own scientific journals as the instruments for presenting its position to an already prejudiced audience. While the scientific community has lobbied successfully in congressional committees against restrictive legislation directed at medical research, it has neglected to present to the American public its case for the continuation of animal experimentation with sufficient force and clarity to eliminate the ever-present danger of government control of biological research through the limitation of animal availability and experimental design. The intelligent citizenry of this country must be educated not only regarding the already multiple advantages of medical research but, what is more important, the absolute necessity of continued proliferation of biological research.

Man, in a sense, has unwittingly painted himself into an ecological corner, 2 and without the opportunity of biological testing in lower animals he may be unable to extract himself from his polluted environment. Acknowledging man's equally wanton disregard of animal life, as he has slowly but inevitably poisoned this planet (to say nothing of our careless attrition of individual species to the point of extinction), I do not intend that this essay should be, by any stretch of the imagination, construed as an indictment of the broad humanitarian movement; quite the contrary, for many of its objectives, particularly in the ecological field, are not only most laudable but fully subscribed to by many within the scientific community. Rather, my proprietary interest here is to emphasize need for animal experimentation in neurological research. As a consequence, my confrontation is exclusively with those societies, collectively known as the antivivisection movement, whose single unifying principle is the almost religiously held tenet that it is morally wrong to use lower animals in medical research and teaching. Professor Saul Bevolson, in tracing the historical development of the antivivisection movement in this country, demonstrates that the movement, while spawned and nurtured by the humanitarian establishment, is, in reality, separate in organizational structure. Dr. Maurice Visscher has felt the necessity of characterizing the antivivisection movement as a spectrum with certain gradations of moral and ethical absoluteness with regard to man's right to sacrifice lower animal life for scientific knowledge and medical advancement. Thus, this philosophical spectrum is anchored at one end by the abolitionist who sees no justification under any circumstances for the employment of the nonhuman animal for scientific study, and at the other extreme by the regulatory antivivisectionists who would place external controls (obviously governmental) on medical research by limiting the type and number of animals utilized, and demanding review of the experimental methods with particular reference to purpose and duplication. Make no mistake, in spite of their highly publicized concern for the housing and veterinary care of research animals, the true thrust of these organizations is directed toward the eventual elimination from medical investigation and research of all nonhuman subjects.

As a concerned scientist and as a practicing neurosurgeon, I am simply   3
unable to plumb the depths of a philosophy that places such a premium on animal life even at the expense of human existence and improvement. It would appear that this preoccupation with the alleged pain and suffering of the animals used in medical research may well represent, at the very least, social prejudice against medicine or, more seriously, true psychiatric aberrations. Regardless of the social or psychiatric shortcomings of the antivivisectionists, it has always amazed me that the biological profession is forced into a position of periodically preparing defense briefs on animal experimentation (unfortunately appearing only in scientific journals) as a result of the Herculean efforts of these societies, while the meat-packing industry, which slaughters millions of animals annually, seldom if ever finds it necessary today to defend its activities.

As I write this article, I relive my vivid experiences of yesterday when I   4
removed at operation a large tumor from the cerebellum and brain stem of a small child. This was a surgical undertaking that would have been impossible a few decades ago, highly dangerous a few years ago, but is today, thanks to extensive experimentation on the brains of lower animals, routinely accomplished with a high degree of safety.

The human brain is the most complex, the most superbly designed structure   5
known. Before it, all human scientific and engineering accomplishment pales. Our understanding of its intimate functions, such as intelligence and memory, is extremely limited. Even the more easily characterized capabilities of sensory reception and motor activity are only now being elucidated. Without the use of the experimental animal, particularly a species whose central nervous system is similar to that of man, we simply cannot decipher the mysteries of cerebral performance. Without this knowledge of brain function, we will never be able to develop new and improved methods for the treatment of neurological diseases, so many of which now must be placed in an incurable category. Even today the surgery of the brain is in its infancy, and on many occasions the critical tolerance between success and failure in human cerebral operations is narrow. Yet this gap can be significantly increased through properly oriented research. These serious considerations moved Dr. Harvey Cushing, the eminent brain surgeon, to remark, "Those who oppose the employment of animals for such purposes . . . leave us the only alternative of subjecting our fellow man, as a lesser creature, to our first crude manipulations."

In a more personal sense, I have a score of my own to settle with these   6
misguided societies that for decades have been attempting to confuse the public about the true purpose of animal experimentation by depicting the medical and veterinary scientist as the most cruel of men, seeking every opportunity to visit pain and suffering on defenseless laboratory creatures. The more aggressive of these organizations, which are committed to the total abolition of animal research, have recently installed me as their *célèbre terrible*, monster-

scientist, perpetrator of abominable crimes. And thus I join the distinguished company of such legendary scientists as Claude Bernard, Louis Pasteur, Lord Lister, Victor Horsley and Alfred Blalock! Dr. Catherine Roberts herself has already prejudged my work and me by earnestly stating, "The details of his experiments are so horrifying that they seem to reach the limits of scientific depravity." Fortunately, my researches do not stand alone in her sweeping condemnation of medical science, for in the same article she described organ transplantation and profound hypothermia as "life degrading scientific achievements." I am sure that she, as well as other staunch antivivisectionists, would be willing to include in this list: open-heart surgery, control of infection, surgical metabolism and shock studies since literally thousands of animals were sacrificed in the development of these lifesaving techniques. In a sense, condemnation of these achievements amounts to condemnation of the most meaningful advances in medicine and surgery in the last thirty years.

What of our own experiments, which have evoked such vituperative treatment at the hands of the antivivisection press? Here are the "shocking" details.   7

In 1964, we were successful for the first time in medical history in totally   8 isolating the subhuman primate brain outside of its body and sustaining it in a viable state by connecting it with the vascular system of another monkey or with a mechanical perfusion circuit that incorporated engineering units designed to perform the functions of the heart, lungs and kidneys while simultaneously circulating blood to and from the brain. We were overjoyed since scientists had attempted to construct such a model surgically for the last one hundred years without success. As late as the 1930s Dr. Alexis Carrel, the Nobel laureate, with the collaboration of Colonel Charles Lindberg, had been able to support the viability of almost all body organs in an isolated state with simple perfusion equipment that forcefully propelled nonsanguineous nutrient fluid through the blood vessels of the separated tissue. Only the nervous system, because of its complexity and delicacy, escaped their magnificent scientific capabilities. Parenthetically, it should be mentioned that Dr. Carrel had his problems with the antivivisectionists of his time.

With further refinements in operative technique, perfusion/structural design   9 and blood processing, we were able to demonstrate normalization of intrinsic electrical activity and metabolic performance of the isolated monkey brain for extended periods of time. We now had the methodology to unlock many of the subtle mysteries surrounding cerebral function that heretofore had resisted all attempts at solution because of the difficulties of neurogenically and vascularly isolating the entire brain *in situ*. What is perhaps of greater importance in terms of understanding and treating neurological disease, we could now easily impose on our brain models abnormal clinical states such as infarction, circulatory arrest, infection and malignancy with absolute control of environmental circumstances and with a real hope of elucidating their effects on brain tissue alone. Once the characteristics of these states were defined, these same models would be of inestimable value in developing new and meaningful therapeutic regimens aimed at eliminating these clinical disease states.

As we set about exploring and documenting the capabilities of the isolated   10 brain in an atmosphere not unlike the conditions described for the fifth level in Michael Crichton's book, *The Andromeda Strain*, we gradually became aware of a growing public interest in the preparation, an interest that intensified after our success in transplanting the brain in the experimental animal in 1966. A succession of competent medical journalists visited our laboratories and subsequently prepared a number of highly informative and reasoned articles dealing with our investigative efforts. I personally have always approved of this kind of interchange. In spite of our best efforts to assist in the preparation of the textual material, however, an unreviewed and unauthorized article written by Orianna Fallachi appeared in *Look* (November 28, 1967), in which this well-known interviewer attempted to humanize the monkey by depicting it as a small child. This single article (or lengthy excerpts from it) has now enjoyed world-wide publication and translation. Besides her treatment of the monkey as a small patient, Miss Fallachi's detailed description of the preoperative preparation (including the induction of anesthesia) and her vivid portrayal of the isolated brain model apparently struck a sympathetic and responsive chord among the membership of the antivivisection societies in this country as well as throughout the world. Like Mary Shelley, Miss Fallachi had created a Doctor Frankenstein and an up-to-date monster, at least as far as the antivivisectionsts are concerned. True, this tale has its amusing—if not outlandish—elements, but its overall effect is tragic, since Miss Fallachi's creations are not only as factitious as Mary Shelley's, but in reality the direct antithesis of the Frankenstein legend.

Admittedly, the nervous system is the most difficult body organ system to   11
investigate, not only because of its intrinsic complexity but also because, somewhere within its billions of cells and fibers, pain and suffering are represented. For this reason, the neurophysiologist is, on occasion, unable to avoid producing some discomfort in his animal when he is specifically studying pain in any or all of its complicated ramifications within the neural system. Actually, the isolated brain model is completely denervated by virtue of the fact that all pain pathways have been surgically severed; consequently, this brain model enjoys a completely painless existence by all known physiological criteria.

Since the isolated brain is incapable of perceiving these modalities, one can   12
only wonder at the creditability and objectivity of the antivivisection prose, which has been so uncomplimentary in its descriptions of this subhuman research model.

The nervous system—the repository, so to speak, of pain and suffering, but,   13
more important, of the qualities and capabilities that uniquely distinguish an organism—is most critical to this discussion since direct surgical or electronic manipulation or chemical modification of this system in the experimental animal offers to the antivivisectionist the most logical area for condemnation of biological research. At issue here would not be the indiscriminate infliction of pain and suffering (these experiments are basically free of pain), but rather purposeful alteration of the innate behavior of the organism in order to advance our knowledge of emotion, memory and intelligence, with the final phase again being the interpretive extrapolation of this information to the human and to

human mental functioning. As yet we have heard little from the antivivisection-ists regarding the inappropriateness of these experiments with reference to animal welfare. It may be, however, that their historical fixation on the "twin sins" of pain and suffering in neurological investigation has blinded them to the realities of modern experimental research. Just as I must vigorously dissent from the antivivisection philosophy (and the belief of certain physiologists) that the production of some pain, no matter how minimal, is never justified, so too I cannot conceive of the development of a valid argument opposing behavioral research, if only for the simple reason that mental illness cannot successfully be treated until mental performance is understood.

To circumvent the employment of nonhuman animals in medical research,   14 the antivivisection movement has recently turned for assistance to science itself. It has been suggested that many of the physiological and biochemical studies conducted on animals could be programmed for computer analysis and thereby reduce and eventually eliminate the need for the living experimental preparations. Actually, computers, since their inception, have been used in biological research and, with their growing complexity, have markedly extended the frontiers of investigation. If anything, computer availability has contributed to the increasing demand for animals for research.

An equally unrealistic approach to the elimination of animal experimenta-   15 tion has been based on the cell culture work of Professor Sureyat Aygun, Director of the Bacteriological Institute of the University of Ankara, and a leading antivivisection proponent. The theory here is that, with proper culture techniques, cells or embryos could eventualy be developed into entire organ systems. The technological advances and expense necessary to accomplish such a program to replace present-day animal research facilities are unachievable. There is no more need to seek alternatives to the use of lower animals for medical research than to search for nonflesh substitutions for meat in our diets. While it may well be true that ecological "facts of life" could eventually require the elimination of certain endangered species from both the laboratory and commercial market, there is nothing to suggest that some suitable species cannot be substituted. Even Dr. Albert Schweitzer recognized in his own unique philosophical scheme of things that scientific experiments with animals were necessary for the alleviation of human ills.

The American public demonstrates its overwhelming support of medical   16 research by annually contributing millions of dollars through direct federal financing and private subscription; yet this same public is tragically unaware that progress in medical science is continually threatened by the antivivisection movement. At the urging of a small but determined group of antivivisectionists, the United States Congress is constantly considering legislation that, if enacted into law, will seriously restrict the freedom of individual scientists participating in medical research, in the same way that laws have so seriously hampered similar research in Britain. Since, through research grants to qualified individuals and institutions, the federal government provides the major financial support for medical investigation in this country, all laws affecting the conduct of such research are of paramount importance to the health of the entire citizenry.

Unless American medicine and its allied biological professions cast off their mantles of detachment and undertake the responsibility of educating through established lines of communication our citizens to the necessities of medical research, the antivivisection movement may eventually win the day.

In the final analysis, there is no way that I can personally resolve or even 17 arbitrate the impasse that exists between the theology of the antivivisection movement and the immutable stance of practicality maintained by biological research, since like R.D. Guthrie, I believe that the inclusion of lower animals in our ethical system is philosophically meaningless and operationally impossible and that, consequently, antivivisection theory and practice have no moral or ethical basis.

CATHERINE ROBERTS
Animal Experimentation and Evolution

I should like to thank Dr. White for accepting my proposal to debate the 1 problem of animal experimentation in contemporary biomedicine. His accept-ance is particularly gracious in view of my recent critique of the methods and goals of his current neurosurgical research. Since the value of any confrontation between two minds in radical opposition is proportional to the breadth and clarity of their respective visions, we have agreed to speak from the widest evolutionary, social, ethical and religious perspectives of which we are capable.

It would be a delusion to maintain that, since animal experimentation is 2 apparently here to stay as an aid in saving human life and reducing human suffering, the problem under debate is really no problem at all. That one of the most distinguished neurosurgeons of our time has set aside a portion of his heavily committed schedule to justify a decade of research on animals is clear evidence to the contrary. Experimental biomedicine, already feeling the impact of an intensified attack upon its methodology, is quite aware that the problem is real and hopes to silence its adversaries by defending its actions to the intellectual and ethical satisfaction of all concerned. I am convinced that this hope is futile.

Meanwhile, the use of sentient animals in laboratory experiments continues 3 to spread all over the civilized world. This growing practice represents inevita-ble human progress, so we are told, because it is carried out for the good of man and because the human, by any standard, is more important than the animal. It is undeniably true that Homo sapiens comes first. There are, however, compelling intellectual and ethical grounds for believing that the experimental use of highly developed forms of life is actually impeding human progress and that for the sake of men, as much as for animals, the practice must be ended. The final answer to the question of whether to retain or abolish the sentient laboratory animal may require one of the most decisive choices yet made by evolving life.

Human behavior is an elective response to alternatives. Throughout man's 4
long evolutionary history, he has been continually confronted with choices.
Prehistoric man, living with lower animals in a harsh and hostile environment,
was forced to make vital decisions upon which his physical survival depended.
Whether, in contrast to the animals, he made moral choices between good and
evil because of his religious instinct and experience, we do not know.

Some six thousand years ago, when civilizations began to emerge, the human 5
species had long since become a fixed and recognizable physical type and was
well into its psychosocial phase of evolution. Unlike the long period of slow
development of body and mind that preceded it, this new evolutionary stage
brought a sudden expansion of human consciousness through accelerated communication and transmission of acquired knowledge, wisdom and experience,
as well as of the religious norms of human behavior. The growth and dispersion
of the three great monotheistic religions laid particular stress upon ethical
conduct. Men were exhorted to make choices in conformity with moral standards of good and evil that were held to be absolute and eternal divine revelations. To a large extent the expansion of the civilized consciousness has
depended upon the recognition that the conscience, guided by its traditional
religious heritage, was able to distinguish between good and evil and was thus
obliged to make moral choices. Civilized man, as the historical record shows,
has exhibited the extremes of conformity and nonconformity to this obligation.
Yet, however great his range of ethical conduct, he has, until recently, been fully
aware that he had a functional conscience.

Man in the twentieth century is still very much in the psychosocial stage of 6
human evolution, which differs, however, from all preceding stages in the nature of its interplay between consciousness and conscience. The organized
acquisition of new biological knowledge and its rapid communication and application are expanding human consciousness at a breathtaking rate. The faster
the pace, the greater the number of ethical choices to be made. But in a
predominantly godless world where most civilizations no longer take seriously
religion or the human-divine relation, the sacred criteria for choosing between
good and evil are largely neglected. Although standards of decent human behavior and recognition of what are called Christian virtues have never been
uprooted, the contemporary ideal is, in fact, a free conscience, where any
ethical standard and conduct is as good as the next. Democracy, equality, and
freedom from traditional authority at all costs! The modern conscience, breaking with the past and denying the existence of absolute and eternal criteria to
guide its choices, often considers itself autonomous and infallible but is in truth
pitifully immature and undernourished. Conforming mainly to the authority of
expanding scientific knowledge about the reality of nature, it has increasing
difficulty in function and operation. Scientists themselves are beginning to
experience these difficulties. Aware of their social responsibility and not knowing how to meet it, some are working to keep society better informed of the
implications of their results and, in turn, to obtain outside aid in guiding the
further advance of biology and medicine. At the same time, an increasing number of men and women, bewildered by contemporary progress, are experienc-

ing failure of conscience: they no longer dare to choose. The result is a morally chaotic world that is becoming an almost unbearable place in which to live and die.

What seems to be most lacking is a unified sense of rectitude about what we are doing and where we are going. Most of us have experienced periods of acute helplessness and frustration in the face of a seemingly uncontrollable scientific advance that is sweeping life toward an unknown goal. Our great mistake is to suppose that this biological and technological progress is synonymous with the main path of human evolution. It is not. It is only a sidepath—but one that life may have had to experience in order better to distinguish good from evil. Ever since Homo sapiens left the main road for the attractions of scientific knowledge and power, he has been increasingly unable to find the happiness he seeks. Nor can he ever find on a sidepath leading away from the stream of evolution to which he belongs the inner joy and peace that are his birthright.   7

The main path for evolving human life leads toward ultimate reality: true human evolution, regardless of what secular and scientific humanists think, is a spiritual ascent toward the Good* and is based upon the interplay between consciousness and conscience. But with so much human energy being spent on expanding the consciousness alone, we obstinately maintain that this *must* be life's predestined path because there is no other. At the same time we are uneasy in the presentiment that it may be leading us to our final doom. Having lived for years with the theoretical possibility of nuclear suicide or the transformation of Homo sapiens into a dehumanized scientific robot, and being quite unable to prevent the horrors of unnecessary war and starvation, we cannot rid ourselves of the fear of extinction known to our primitive forefathers. Far more knowledgeable and sophisticated than they, but far less able to sense the evolutionary rhythm of life and death and to accept the natural corruption of living matter and the incorruptibility of the spirit, we have become frantically preoccupied with ensuring the physical survival of both the species and the individual. Our consternation is intensified because we are still guided by a sick scientific conscience that lacks sufficient strength and resolution to make moral choices.   8

Life, now faced with decisive evolutionary alternatives, has need of all its resources of mind, spirit and intuition to make the required choices. No longer can it allow its further development to be guided by a conscience that bases its decisions solely on scientific knowledge.   9

Most biomedical scientists appear to be students of life who have not yet seen it whole. This implies no wholesale condemnation of their perspective.   10

*Plato himself never made more than veiled allusions to the nature of his concept of the Good, although it was both the summit of his hierarchy of ideas and the spiritual reality to which he was irresistibly drawn throughout his life. He, and later Plotinus, who expounded the concept at great length, saw that the Good, this divine center of perfection and transcendent source of all else, is fully knowable only to itself and thus beyond man's power of rational understanding. Yet they also saw that knowledge of the good is attainable through becoming good, and that this progressive approach to perfection through participation is man's inevitable destiny. They saw the Good as a divine center leading the human race upward; and as spiritual aspirants with mystical experience and intuition, they knew that the human soul must strive toward goodness, righteousness, beauty and truth, and that this act toward the Good is the highest form of human love.

Their time-honored goals of understanding, aiding and saving life remain noble ones, and their motives certainly include love for their fellowmen and sympathy and compassion for their sufferings. Opponents of vivisection, blinded by its horrors, tend to ignore this fact, but it is unfair to scientists to do so. Modern vivisectors are not criminals for whom new restrictive laws are needed, but human beings whose conscience needs to be awakened from its moral apathy. For with their increasing power over life and death and their belief that science must do all it can, they are allowing many of their expanding goals to become as ethically shoddy as their means.

Let us first ask the biomedical scientists who depend upon laboratory ani-   11
mals why they consider human life so precious that it must be saved at all costs. They would better serve mankind by giving more thought to the criterion of life and less to that of death. They must tell us what all their feverish biological activity is really for. They must make it absolutely clear and unambiguous why they are compelled to penetrate the secrets of life down to the minutest scientific detail and to apply their knowledge before its full implications are understood. So far their only answer seems to be that human progress demands that life's intellectual potentials be realized so that we can all live longer and suffer less. *But the realization of life's spiritual potentials, whereby the operation of a healthy conscience could place human behavior in harmonious accord with the mainstream of evolution, is ignored by these modern life specialists.* In proclaiming that the "best" state is the longest possible life of a healthy body and mind, they intensify man's unnatural fear of the struggle, suffering, and preparation for death that is necessary for the spiritual maturation of the species.

The failure of modern biomedicine to see life whole has resulted in confused   12
goals and paradoxical behavior. We reduce life's rate of propagation by mechanical and chemical means and destroy with little compunction unwanted human embryos so that we may give better care to the fewer individuals remaining. But modern medicine is not satisfied with ensuring a minimum of medical aid to all. Medical care now embraces resuscitation by drugs and machines to delay the natural termination of aged lives, together with various kinds of euthanasia to put abrupt ends to lives of suffering. Medical care prolongs the life of a patient by replacing a defective organ with a fresh one snatched from a dying patient regarded mainly as a donor. Medical care embraces such vast possibilities for the treatment of human ills and the permanent alteration of the human body that we already have plans for the surgical, pharmacological and genetic regulation of human behavior. No longer content with treating the sick and, in fact, often morally at sea as to how far treatment should go, some biomedical scientists are issuing scientific directives for the ethical improvement of the healthy.

That many of the goals of contemporary science are highly questionable is   13
already obvious to those scientists who are feeling the conscience crisis within biology and medicine, but so far they have remained singularly passive with respect to scientific methodology. There has been no organized protest from within biomedicine against the dogma that the advance of science justifies all

conceivable means, even to the infliction of agony upon lower forms of sentient life. In contrast, antivivisectionists, who are rightly intensifying their attack upon biomedical methodology, remain uncritical of scientific goals. In their desire to rescue the laboratory animal, they are now advocating more efficient alternative methods of research and are thus indiscriminately encouraging research regardless of its ultimate purpose. The problem of animal experimentation cannot be satisfactorily solved by supporting means or ends of dubious morality. Evolving life needs to be seen from a still higher perspective. Its conscience is at stake.

Animals, lacking, so far as we know, conscience and knowledge of the Good, 14 strive to realize their limited potentials by choosing what is best for their survival and a life in harmony with their environment. Men, aware of the spiritual realm, have quite different strivings. Moral choice between good and evil is a uniquely human responsibility that spiritually elevates man above the rest of creation. His relation to the lower sentient life at his mercy then becomes vital for his further ascent. So far his enormous intellectual, emotional and spiritual superiority has not eradicated his anthropocentric view that human evolution must progress by the unrestrained exploitation of subhuman life.

Despite the wishful thinking of many antivivisectionists, the silent suffering 15 and the anguished screams of laboratory animals *have* saved human lives, reduced human suffering, and prevented and cured diseases. But this welcome boon to mankind is not the essence of human progress or evolution. It is simply care and maintenance of physical life. That human ills can be effectively ameliorated through prior cruelty to animals is true from a self-centered point of view. From the evolutionary perspective, where the interrelation of all forms of sentient life comes into view, progressive well-being depends upon the highest form protecting and caring for the lower with compassion, mercy and understanding. Innocent life has rights that we, who are not innocent, have not yet understood. But, one might say, if the spiritual potential of physical life is to be realized, surely it is only common sense to use all possible means to maintain individual life as long as possible. Granted, insofar as such means are conducive to spiritual enlightenment. The continued acceptance, however, of immoral means by doctors and patients disfigures their goals, increases their ethical apathy and insensivity, and becomes at last a gross deflection from the Good toward which all human life is evolving.

Our present knowledge of anatomy, physiology, genetics and pathology can- 16 not, of course, be unlearned. But regardless of the true benefits accruing from its application in medicine, we have no justification whatever for continuing to wrest still more knowledge out of lower sentient life by torture, multilation and death.

All the biomedical knowledge we now possess has not in any way made man 17 more moral. And since much of it was acquired through the agony of countless millions of innocent lives, and since Homo sapiens would have survived without it, its acquisition has no doubt done more evolutionary harm than good. For man comes first—and he has degraded his potential and retarded its realization by more than five hundred years of scientific atrocities against animals. The scientific age still sees no valid reason for abolishing this practice. But abolish it we must, because evolving human life puts increasing demands upon the self-restraint and self-sacrifice of its members. Man evolves through the suffering and death of individuals. To choose to oppose these inevitabilities through the continued infliction of cruelty upon animals is evolutionary stagnation, if not regression.

In Denmark the first chair of behavioral physiology was recently established 18 for Dr. A. Mosfeldt Laursen, whose experimental investigations of mental diseases and insight into the handling of laboratory animals have gained wide recognition. Although there is no general agreement about the therapeutic value of violent mutilation and injury of the brains of the mentally ill, Dr. Laursen's animal experiments have convinced him that surgically induced brain lesions can be effective in eliminating some of the fear and terror so often associated with mental diseases. Through the widely used method of implanting electrodes into specific areas of the brains of anesthetized animals, he has studied the conscious responses of cats to doses of electric current varying from weakly stimulating to permanently injurious. At the same time, he has developed special methods for keeping his laboratory animals relaxed and trusting in order to attain the best experimental results. I would say that any "expert in behavioral problems" who chooses to gain the confidence and trust of healthy animals so that he can mutilate and torment them shows a deplorable lack of understanding of human behavior. As one of Dr. Laursen's own countrymen, P. Agersted, so well put it in challenging the motivation of animal experimenters: "Animal suffering benefits mankind. What is done is done for the sake of humanity. Apparently none of these scientists realize that they could just as well use this motive for stopping painful animal experimentation. ... For many, many more people than is generally supposed suffer at the thought of what goes on in laboratories, and still more would become extremely agitated and uneasy in their minds if they knew of the atrocities of the extreme forms of animal experimentation." Surely this thought, centering attention upon the increasingly intolerable *mésalliance* between contemporary scientists and sentient animals, deserves serious consideration by all those who are engaged in the prevention and cure of mental diseases.

Dr. White's contributions to neurological research have added the mammal- 19 ian brain to the other organs that have been successfully isolated and transplanted. Although he does not claim the feasibility of transplanting the human brain, he hopes someday to maintain it in an isolated state, and he expects this scientific feat, together with his animal experiments, will lead to a more effective treatment of diseases of the brain and to a greater understanding of its nature and function. Despite some opposition to his work, he enthusiastically carries on in the conviction that his studies represent inevitable biological achievements. With equal conviction, I believe that they are not biological achievements at all, because any true study of life, being a part of the spiritual ascent of evolution, must be moral in both means and ends. I further believe that no human achievement in the vast region of mind, soul, consciousness and subconsciousness can be expected except through the directives of a spiritually enlightened conscience.

Lacking these directives, Dr. White's compassion for human mental suffering 20

and his pursuit of scientific knowledge of mental phenomena have led to flagrant interference with the consciousness of animal life and a lamentable increase in the total suffering of creation. He has produced living chimeras—
disembodied canine brains transplanted within the carotid-jugular circulation
of recipient dogs, and disembodied monkey brains kept alive and functioning
in an isolated state. In establishing primitive communication with the isolated
brain, he has stated that it "displays a remarkable retention of inherent electric
rhythmicity that strongly suggests it may retain some semblance of 'consciousness.'" The scores of remnants of mutilated creatures that he has kept alive in
the laboratory have made the world a worse place for all of us to live in. In
choosing his goals and his means, he has denied his evolutionary responsibility
to distinguish good from evil and has ignored his faith. For whatever his final
authority for his choices, it cannot have been Christianity.

Dr. White has forgotten that the purest form of Christianity and all other   21
higher religions preach mercy, love, nonviolence and gentleness and that these
qualities have been the hallmarks of mankind's spiritual leaders in their relations with sentient life. He is apparently unaware of the growing number of
Catholics who are confidently working to end the Church's silence on animal
experimentation. They know that she cannot be expected "to sanction everything she has not yet formally condemned." Despite such efforts, the perspectives and possibilities of our scientific age continue to blind many Christians to
the incongruities between the moral core of their religion and the decisions of
science. By cutting ourselves off from the superior knowledge of our spiritual
heritage, we fail to see life whole and continue to flounder in ethical confusion
and decadence. A theocentric reaction is bound to set in. The intellectual revolt
of the young may already presage a spiritual renaissance in which the summit
of evolving life will no longer tolerate scientific atrocities against its lower
forms. Man is an evolutionary as well as a social animal, and evolution is not a
matter of chance. Man needs "to think with the whole of his past." He must at
last see, with Plotinus, that as creation aspires toward the Good, it needs
increasing unity and harmony in its relationships.

Transplantation biology is concerned with what science considers to be   22
inevitable evolutionary relationships of creatures and their parts. It has partially
surmounted the formidable natural obstacles of immunological intolerance and
rejection through the suffering of untold numbers of animals. While experimental fusions of their living parts to intact animals have received publicity, it is not
generally known outside professional circles that much of the practical success
of transplantation biology stems from studies of the mutual physiological effects of the surgical fusion of whole animals in pairs. This procedure, parabiosis
(life alongside life), is now a routine laboratory technique and is sometimes
even extended "to unite several animals in enforced togetherness." Accepted
as a biological necessity, laboratory parabiosis is, in fact, a biological outrage
and a violation of the natural relationships of living creatures. In the name of
evolutionary sanity, let us leave these things and center our attention upon
those relations that can be meaningful for creation.

For the continued existence of mammalian species, biological evolution re-   23 quires the sexual association of individuals in pairs. The further Homo sapiens advances into his psychosocial phase of evolution, the greater his need for relationships other than those based upon animal sexuality. As it has been wisely said, "centuries of carnal embracement, yet man is no nearer to understanding man." Our crying need at the moment is for a relationship that will give all men, regardless of birth, education or faith, a unified sense of rectitude in their endeavors. We need to come together to communicate more perfectly and to understand that, however many imperfections, sins, and egoistic motives and desires we possess in common, we remain most firmly related by the highest that is within us—by those sparks of love, compassion, goodness and righteousness that come from the spiritual realm. If these divine sparks were to coalesce, we would be able to make right choices, and the interrelations of man with man, and man with animal, would be in accord with the Good to which we are being drawn. Psychosocial evolution is now demanding the emergence of spiritual parabiosis—life alongside life, with the highest caring for the lower with the same mercy, tenderness and understanding it bestows upon itself.

Evolving life can therefore no longer tolerate the biological injustice of inflicting agony upon animals to ameliorate and prolong the physical existence of human lives. Brief respites from suffering and death made possible by the ruthlessness of scientists against lower life contribute nothing whatever to the spiritual ascent of mankind. Evolving life has need instead of gentle souls like Saint Francis and Gandhi to show us how to come together to live lives of nonviolence, in joy and peace with the whole of sentient creation. For the meek, strengthened and made wise in their decisions by divine sanction and their spiritual heritage, *shall* inherit the earth.   24

The choice to abolish the sentient laboratory animal is an evolutionary inevitability and a moral imperative. Were Dr. White to join the forces that are already striving to bring it about, true biological achievement would be his.   25

Dr. White Replies:

I was fascinated by Dr. Roberts' paper, finding it a revelation of a sensitive scientist's inner self and her personally evolved theological and philosophical matrix of belief rather than merely the expected sterile recitation of the well-known "sins" of vivisection. True, her employment of the Platonic concept of *Summum Bonum* (The Good) seems to be overly simplistic and clearly self-defeating in her attempt to construct a theological edifice with which to blunt and smother the onslaught of biological science and technology; still, her recognition of the need for scientists to come to grips with the far-reaching effects of their researches, particularly on human life, must be complimented. I must also admit, however, to a certain sense of *déjà vu* in reading this presentation since the substance has been similarly developed in her previous publications.   26

To assist myself in arriving at a reasoned judgment of this particular Roberts manuscript, I took the liberty of forwarding a copy to the Jesuit theologian, Father Nicholas A. Predovich, of John Carroll University in Cleveland, for a   27 learned opinion regarding the religious implications of Dr. Roberts' thesis, since my expertise in theology extends only to the theology of ancient Egypt. In addition, I permitted myself the luxury of taking the document with me to the Soviet Union last fall in hopes that my commentary might at least be distinguished by having been composed at twenty-five thousand feet in Soviet airspace and under a certain psychological and physiological stress, since I do not enjoy flying in Russian aircraft during adverse weather conditions.

Before attempting to review the paper, I must state that the evidence at   28
hand strongly argues that Dr. Roberts' true purpose in seeking this "exchange of opinions" was not with a view toward settling the issue of vivisection but was rather of a grander design, to provide herself with another distinguished forum from which to amplify her personal religious philosophy and again offer it as a solution to the problems developing for mankind from the ever-increasing number of scientific discoveries. But these are problems of human existence and survival, not of animal survival. Consequently, her entire thesis seems hardly germane to the subject of vivisection, and one is hard pressed to uncover the link between her pseudoplatonic theology and animal experimentation. Perhaps both Dr. Roberts and I owe the readers of this journal an apology for having consumed so many pages in discussing a topic of such little relevance today.

To clarify the "ground rules" of our individual literary efforts, I must take   29
issue with her in regard to an alleged agreement between us to address ourselves to animal experimentation in the "widest evolutionary, social, ethical and religious perspectives," since it is obvious from my presentation that I was and am unable to conceive of animal experimentation in terms of human values. There simply is no historical, evolutionary, biological, philosophical, social or theological justification for applying principles of human morality and ethics to nonhuman creatures. Admittedly, the entire scientific community does not universally ascribe to my opinion. Nevertheless, R.D. Guthrie has recently demonstrated the impossibility of including animals in our human ethical system.

Since Dr. Roberts' thesis rests so heavily on her personally derived Platonic   30
theology, I have taken the liberty of quoting directly from Father Predovich's critique of her religious and philosophical theories as set forth in his communication to me.

In reviewing Dr. Roberts' manuscript, Father Predovich is disturbed by the   31
lack of a clear definition of what she means by the word *life* since it obviously forms such an integral part of her argument. Indicating the importance of distinguishing between an *univocal* and *analogous* concept of life, he writes:

If Dr. Roberts has a *univocal* concept of life, then all forms of life such as vegetative, sentient and rational should be preserved and fostered as much as man can make them. If life is only one thing, then what makes the vegetable and the animal different from man? If we must conclude that life is an *analogous* concept, that is, somewhat the same, yet totally different in the plant and in the animal and in man, then shouldn't we, as rational beings, see that different principles will apply differently for each of the forms of life?

Surely one recognizes the *univocal* concept of life as peculiarly Schweitz-   32
erian, and yet even Dr. Schweitzer admitted to the necessity of animal experimentation for the betterment of mankind.

I was disturbed by Dr. Roberts' concept of conscience and her denial of   33
man's personalistic character, and so was Father Predovich. He continues:

> To speak in terms of conscience and the human being using his conscience,
> confuses the issue and makes conscience purely a mechanical process based on
> one's own insight into the reality that is labeled evolution. Rather, conscience
> looks to the whole of reality, to history, to the insights of other human beings, and
> is formed from all of this. Conscience is a process that results from integrating
> many things. It does not appear that C. Roberts would agree with this notion of
> human conscience.
>
> In spite of appearances, this paper by Dr. Roberts lacks insight into the human
> condition as *personalistic*. Homo sapiens seems to be treated like a scientific
> phenomenon rather than an existential "I-Thou" reality, which he is. If, as Martin
> Buber proves so well, man is destined to deep, free, open, interpersonal relation-
> ships with other men, then obviously, even in the evolutionary process, man's
> greatest effort will be to effect, to help grow, to urge into becoming such interper-
> sonal relationships. The preservation of biological species, though worthwhile per
> se, is itself subordinated to the highest form of evolution of man, that is, evolution
> into interpersonal relationships with all men, and finally into the total human
> community with God. This is the Omega Point that I think Teilhard de Chardin
> was talking about rather than a mere evolutionary process of a human species.

Eventually Dr. Roberts' theological balloon returns to earth with a predict-   34
able thud, since she immediately undertakes to overwhelm us with her
prejudicial descriptions of various animal experiments, notably in the fields of
behavioral psychology and parabiosis. Those tried and trite words, cruelty,
screams, torture, pain, suffering, mutilation, *et cetera*, that form the litany of
the antivivisection language begin to appear with increasing monotony. I can
only assure the readers of the SCHOLAR that I have participated for over two
decades in animal research in all the areas she so selectively portrays (behavioral, neurophysiological, parabiosis and organ transplantation), that I have
visited institutes for experimentation all over the world, including the Soviet
Union and other Iron Curtain countries, and have not witnessed the cruelty or
dehumanization that she insists characterizes biomedical animal research.
True, some discomfort may be experienced by animals during specific studies,
for example, in pain research, but almost invariably the investigator goes out of
his way to eliminate all vestiges of suffering, not only because they may affect
his scientific results but, more important, because of his innate sympathy for
his experimental subjects. Dr. Roberts repeats with relish the often-used
phrase of antivivisection literature, "dehumanization" (of the scientist participating in animal research). This should obviously be classified as a psychiatric
syndrome. Fortunately, psychiatric literature and I are ignorant of this spectacular clinical diagnosis—since it does not exist.

I share Dr. Roberts' worry regarding the serious impact on human existence   35
of recently acquired biological knowledge, and, fortunately, she is correct in
emphasizing the growing concern within the scientific community itself over
the implications of its own research. The awesome capability of biomedical
science to modify and qualify human life in the immediate future will be a
reality if the same momentum, so characteristic of its present state, continues.
The recent works of Albert Rosenfeld *(The Second Genesis: The Coming
Control of Life)*, Alvin Toffler *(Future Shock)* and Gordon R. Taylor *(Biological Time Bomb)* are devoted to this topic, and while the authors' judgments
are somewhat visionary, nevertheless they collectively emphasize that life as
we know it today will be radically altered in the very near future. Unfortunately,
this truly crucial question has nothing to do with the subject under discussion
here—vivisection.

I must remind Dr. Roberts that our advanced technological society and   36
increasing population have produced additional serious health hazards through
industrial and human pollution of our air, water and land, and that the use of
animals to establish acceptable levels of biological contamination and to design
methods of control and decontamination for humans represents a new dimension of biomedical research that may prove to be utterly crucial to human
survival.

In her final paragraph Dr. Roberts kindly invites me "to join the forces that   37
are already striving to bring it [abolishment of laboratory experiments with
animals] about," stressing that if I did: "true biological achievement would be
[mine]."

Dr. Roberts cannot be serious in arguing that the elimination of animal   38
experimentation carries a priority equal to or surpassing the need for meaningful solutions of the major problems developing or already existent at the
sociological-biomedical interface! I am afraid that I cannot join her "moral"
crusade since I cannot even grant vivisection a position of relevancy; but, what
is more important, I consider the employment of animals in biological and
medical research so critical to continued human existence and survival as to be
beyond logical challenge.

Dr. Roberts Replies:

My thanks to Dr. White for his contribution to this debate. Since our rebuttals   39
must be held within definite limits, I shall first point out a few misconceptions
and errors of fact in his paper that are not fully covered in mine and then pass
on to a more general refutation of his arguments.

1. He says that antivivisectionists are preoccupied with the "alleged" pain   40
and suffering of laboratory animals. This statement is misleading. To allege is
to assert without proof; yet biomedical journals abound in observations of
experimentally inflicted pain and suffering in animals upon which antivisection-
ists can base their claims.

2. He writes that behavioral research involving electrical, chemical or sur-   41
gical interference with the nervous system to acquire knowledge of animal

emotion, memory and intelligence for extrapolation to human mental functioning is "basically free of pain." This statement is incorrect. Experimental alterations of animal behavior, whether for medical, pharmacological or psychological purposes, are frequently associated with what scientists choose to call "discomfort." A. Mosfeldt Laursen's experiments on feline behavior referred to in my paper can hardly have been painless. Electrical stimulation elicited salivation, lip-smacking, head and shoulder twitching, mewing, sniffing, hissing and gagging; intensifying the current to produce brain lesions led to apathy and diminished fright. To take another example, E.D. Weitzman and G.S. Ross, also working on the electrical manipulation of the nervous system, described with masterly objectivity the screams of tortured animals as "high-pitched vocalization" in a paper with the revealing title, "A behavioral method for the study of pain perception in the monkey."

3. Erroneously concluding that pain and suffering tend to be absent from behaviorial research, Dr. White is led into the further error that antivivisectionists are of the same opinion and are therefore loath to condemn it. This is a misconception based on ignorance of the facts. In 1967 H.F. Harlow's psychological research on anthropoid emotion based on protracted solitary confinement of Rhesus monkeys was criticized for both the suffering involved and the irrelevancy of applying the results to man. Today, in this time of ecological crisis, there is a growing awareness that the suffering man inflicts upon animals comprises many forms; religious circles, in particular, are discussing the rights of animals to participate in activities natural to their kind—rights that, even with adequate food and shelter and freedom from disease and physical pain, are denied them under the artificial conditions of the laboratory. Even some biologists have protested against the cruelly frustrating confinement of livestock in factory farming but so far have characteristically failed to condemn the similar plight of the confined laboratory animal.   42

4. It is only surmise that antivivisectionists are generally unconcerned about the slaughter of animals for meat production. Many antivivisectionists, subsisting on a salutary fleshless diet, are actively demonstrating how unnecessary the carnivorous state is for man.   43

5. Although Dr. White correctly points out that antivivisectionists may differ over means and goals, he is not correct in implying that they are fully agreed that the biologist's freedom should be curtailed by legislation restricting the use of laboratory animals. Opposition to this view was raised some years ago: "... further restrictive legislation would only prevent many scientists from doing what they now earnestly desire to do"; "... the medical scientist who employs experimental animals will one day have acquired sufficient subjective humaneness to realize that the most desirable world, now and forever, is built upon spiritual insight—and it will then be his own sense of moral responsibility, rather than external restriction, which will reveal to him when it is time to stop." These thoughts fell upon barren ground at the time, but the intellectual upheavals of the past five years have produced a radically new mental environment more favorable to the growth and dispersal of ideas centered upon the problem of good and evil. And here we come to the basic issue under debate: the present state of the scientific conscience. With respect to biomedicine, Dr.   44

White holds that it is in a healthy, flourishing state, in no need of improvement. I hold that it is in crying need of profound renewal and reform. His refusal to include either sentient animals or antivivisection arguments in his ethical system echoes the supposedly immutable claim of established biology that its further advance depends upon the continued exploitation of subhuman life. Based upon ignorance of the evolutionary forces now at work, this claim reflects a state of conscience out of step with the new biology already in the process of creation.

Open discontent with established biology as an adequate science of life is mounting—a development closely related to our present ecological interests in the reality and potential of life in all its associated forms. The frustratingly inadequate reality of contemporary human life, pointing directly to man's unrealized potential, is leading to ever greater ethical dissatisfaction with human endeavors that seem to impede our approach toward the ultimate reality of the Good. Scientific endeavor in an ailing scientific age is naturally wide open to criticism. Recognizing that modern science is now on the defensive and sympathizing in varying degrees with the attacks upon its irrelevancy, amorality and immorality, experimental biologists are coming together to question the automatic expansion of science, to plan worldwide moratoria on research, to weigh the threats of science against its promises, to define the scientist's moral responsibility, and to discuss scientific methods as well as goals. Some, in moral protest, are dropping out of the scientific establishment altogether. For the first time in the history of science, biologists are earnestly examining their consciences and questioning the kind of biology that Dr. White is defending. As yet, their number is small, their aims uncertain, their methods hesitant. They are nevertheless creators destined to succeed. For the creation of a new biology that sees life in terms of human values and the choice between good and evil is a part of the evolutionary ascent. 45

The new biologists, no longer satisfied with the supreme authority of established science, are striving for a higher ethical vision and a purer conscience than their predecessors had. They will hardly find it in the dogma that the ends justify the means, whether it be held by revolutionary colleagues intent on changing the established order by force and violence or by scientific colleagues intent on acquiring new knowledge by any effective methodology. The new biologists will be unable to approach life as did Claude Bernard, Alexis Carrel, or other scientists who chose to profane mercilessly the innate potentials of sentient beings in the belief that all biological ends and means deserve evolutionary sanction. Condemnation and rejection of such scientific ethics may not suffice for biology's complete change of mind and heart; some sort of associated regret or remorse—what the Greeks called *metanoia*—for biological violations already committed may also be required. So far animal experimenters have shown little inclination to admit that their vision and conscience have been at fault. Whether Carrel's growing religious insight finally caused him to repent his experimental research, I do not know; his mature views on the future evolution of man show no more understanding of the true man-animal relation than do his very revealing early letters to Guthrie, and thus express a lack of perception at variance with the new biology. 46

For the new biology, perceiving that the realization of man's potentials is   47
forcing him into a new relation with subhuman life, is seeking spiritual counsel.
Much of what it seeks lies in our neglected heritage of theocentric humanism
where enlightened men of the past strove to know themselves and to become
real through moral aspiration. The new biologists will also find spiritual truths
about evolving life in unexpected contemporary places. As the theologian, G.F.
Woods, has written, "The quest for moral perfection is far more than a quest
for private excellence. It involves the attainment of right relationships with God
and with our fellow-men. And it includes a right relation of recreated humanity
to the natural world." To secure this right relation the new biology must re-
nounce both the Carrelian and the Teilhardian evolutionary visions of unlimited
quantitative expansion of science by all conceivable means. The new biology
must have a higher and purer theocentric vision: in gentleness, mercy, humility
and self-restraint it must limit its advance to qualitative expansion.

Nothing can stop its further emergence as the human race approaches real-   48
ity by bettering itself and its relations with the rest of sentient creation. The
new biology is part of the conscience of evolving life reorientating itself toward
the Good and turning ignorance into self-knowledge so that man can spiritually
surpass himself in accordance with the divine will. The ethical system of established biology is a gross deflection from the Good and is destined to be replaced
by biological righteousness. Sentient animals in the laboratory are not there
to stay.

QUESTIONS FOR MEANING

1. What was the nature of the research White did on the brain, and why did it
   upset people when reported in *Look* magazine? Explain why White considers his work significant.
2. On what basic principle does White rest his case in defense of animal
   experimentation? Why does Roberts reject this premise? What principle
   underlies her counterargument?
3. Why does White object to the various alternatives to animal experimentation that have been proposed by antivivisectionists?
4. Both White and Roberts introduce environmental concerns into their arguments. How does White use pollution in the environment to justify medical research involving animals? How does Roberts draw upon the same
   problem and turn it to her own purposes?
5. Why does Roberts limit her concern to sentient animals? Does she believe
   that some forms of life have more value than others?
6. What does Roberts mean by "psychosocial"?
7. Why does Roberts believe that we live in a "morally chaotic world"? Explain
   what she means by "evolution." What is the purpose of evolution? Why is
   biological and technological progress only a "sidepath"?
8. What explanation does Roberts give for the modern obsession with extending human life?
9. Writing in 1971, Roberts refers to the "intellectual revolt of the young"
   which she hopes may "presage a spiritual renaissance." What inspired this

hope? What sort of things were young people doing in the early 70s that
seemed, at the time, idealistic and progressive?

10. Roberts argues that men and women need "relationships other than those
based upon animal sexuality." What sort of relationships does she envision?
Would such relationships fill any need in your own life?

QUESTIONS ABOUT STRATEGY

1. What difficulties does a neurosurgeon have in explaining his views to a
nonmedical audience? Does the complexity of White's research work to his
advantage or disadvantage when soliciting public approval? Can we approve what we don't understand? Are there any points in White's argument
where you got lost? If so, is that his fault?

2. Roberts claims that many Christians are blind to "the incongruities between the moral core of their religion and the decisions of science." Is her
argument basically religious or philosophical? How much of its force depends upon appealing to the Christian conscience? How persuasive would
a non-Christian find her argument?

3. Who treats the other the most respectfully, White or Roberts? Identify any
recognition that either writer extends to the other. Does either White or
Roberts ever resort to ad hominem arguments? Were you bothered by any
personal attacks in the course of this debate?

4. Why does White tell us that his rebuttal was "distinguished by having been
composed at twenty-five thousand feet in Soviet airspace and under a
certain psychological and physiological stress." How does this line affect
you? Is it an apology or a boast? Does it make White seem human while
reminding us of his importance? Or does it imply that he did not take this
assignment as seriously as he might have? Should a writer ever introduce
his or her work with an apology?

5. Who won this debate? Evaluate separately both the original arguments and
the subsequent rebuttals.

C.R. GALLISTEL

Bell, Magendie, and the Proposals to Restrict the Use of Animals in Neurobehavioral Research

Charles Ransom Gallistel (b. 1941) was born in Indianapolis. He received his B.A. from Stanford University in 1963 and his Ph.D. from Yale in 1966. He is a professor of psychology at the University of Pennsylvania, where he is also chairperson of the psychology department. Since 1972, he has been a consulting editor of the Journal of Comparative and Physiological Psychology. *Gallistel is the coauthor of* The Child's Understanding of Number *(1978) and a contributor to numerous scholarly journals. His unequivocal defense of animal experimentation in "Bell, Magendie, and the Proposals to Restrict the Use of Animals in Neurobehavorial Research" provoked considerable discussion upon its 1981 publication in the* American Psychologist.

ABSTRACT: The discovery by Magendie of the sensory and motor functions of the dorsal and ventral roots of the spinal nerves provides an illuminating case study of the scientific and ethical considerations that arise when one contemplates restricting neurobehavioral research on animals because of the suffering it causes them. Such restrictions reduce the number of worthless experiments only at the cost of reducing the number of worthwhile experiments—experiments that shed new light on the sources of behavior and provide the knowledge that enables us to alleviate human suffering. Therefore, one should urge the abandonment of animal research in part or in toto only if one believes that the moral value attached to the avoidance of animal suffering is greater than the moral value attached to the enrichment of human understanding and the alleviation of human suffering.

A bill called the "Research Modernization Act" is now before Congress, where it is picking up influential support. The bill would ban most surgical experiments using live animals, on the theory that the same knowledge may usually be gained by computer simulations, experiments on bacteria, and so on (see Broad, 1980). The bill would establish a review committee that would allow *at most* one experiment of a given type to be done on live animals. The proponents of this legislation claim that the law is a moral imperative and that it would not cause serious harm to research in the life sciences. I wish to argue that this bill would devastate behavorial neurobiology and that it is an affront to moral sensibility.

Behavioral neurobiology tries to establish the manner in which the nervous system mediates behavioral phenomena. It does so by studying the behavioral consequences of one or more of the following procedures: (a) destruction of a part of the nervous system, (b) stimulation of a part, and (c) administration of drugs that alter neural functioning. These three techniques are as old as the discipline. A recent addition is (d) the recording of electrical activity. All four procedures cause the animal at least some temporary distress. In the past they have frequently caused intense pain, and they occasionally do so now. Also, they often impair the animal's proper functioning, sometimes transiently, sometimes permanently.

From the beginning, this enterprise has provoked moral censure, to which   3
the experimentalists have often reacted defensively. The terms of this debate have changed hardly at all in 200 years. Consider the following passage, written shortly after 1800 (Le Gallois, 1813, pp. 19-21):

> Before I close this introduction, I wish in some degree to exculpate the physiologists who make experiments upon living animals, from the reproaches of cruelty, so frequently uttered against them. I do not pretend wholly to justify them. I would only remark, that the most part of those who utter these reproaches may be deserving of the same. For example, do they not go, or have they never gone a hunting? How can the sportsman, who for his own pleasure mutilates so many animals, and often in so cruel a manner, be more humane than the physiologist who is forced to make them perish for his instruction? Whether the rights we assume over those animals be lawful or not, it is certain that few people scruple to destroy, in a variety of ways, such of those animals as cause them the least inconvenience, though ever so trifling; and that we only feed the most part of those that surround us, to sacrifice them to our wants. I can scarcely comprehend that we should be wrong in killing them for our instruction, when we think we are right in destroying them for our food.
>
> I own that it would be barbarous to make animals suffer in vain, if the object of the experiment could be obtained without it. But it is impossible. Experiments upon living animals are one of the greatest lights of physiology. The difference between the dead and the living animal is infinite. If the ablest mechanician is unable to discover all the effect of a machine after having seen it work, how could the most learned anatomist devise, by the study only of the organs, the effect of a machine as prodigiously complicated as the body of an animal. To find out its secrets, it is not enough to observe the simultaneous exercise of all the functions in the animal, while in health; it is above all important to study the effect of the derangement, or the cessation of such or such a function. It is in determining by this analysis what the function of such or such an organ is, as well as its relation with the other functions, that the art of experiments upon living animals consists. But to be able to do it with some degree of precision, it is indispensably necessary to multiply the victims, on account of the variety of circumstances and accidents which may render their result uncertain or inconclusive. I should be tempted to say of physiological experiments, what has been said of charities: *perdenda sunt multa; ut semel ponas bene.* SENECA. [Translation: Many are a waste, that one may come out well.]

The passage just quoted seems to me to contain most of the basic facts and   4
positions in the debate between behavioral neurobiologists and antivivisectionists. Let me first summarize what I take to be matters of fact:

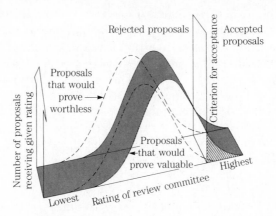

FIGURE 1.   Rating of Review Committee
The dilemma faced by review committees that are determined to eliminate worthless experiments. The shaded area represents the proposals that are allowed to be carried out. Even though the criterion for acceptance has been set so high as to eliminate most of the research that if carried out would have proved valuable, some research projects that in fact prove worthless are still done. Before the fact, many worthless experiments (e.g., Bell, 1811) look as good as or better than many very valuable experiments (e.g., Magendie, 1822). The number of worthless experiments permitted becomes negligible only when the criterion is so high that nearly all the valuable experiments are rejected.

1. Experimental surgery causes pain and distress to animals.   5
2. Researchers are well aware of this pain. Since the discovery of ether   6
   in 1847, they have used anesthetics to reduce or prevent the pain,
   wherever such reduction or prevention does not affect the conclusions that can be drawn from the experiment.
3. There is no way to establish the relation between the nervous system   7
   and behavior without some experimental surgery.
4. Most experiments conducted by behavioral neurobiologists, *like sci-*   8
   entific experiments in general, may be seen in retrospect to have
   been a waste of time, in the sense that they did not prove anything or
   yield any new insight.
5. There is no way of discriminating in advance the waste-of-time ex-   9
   periments from the illuminating ones with anything approaching certainty. Such judgments are necessarily made under conditions of high
   uncertainty. As shown by the theory of signal detection, a necessary
   consequence of this uncertainty is that any attempt to reduce the
   number of neurobehavioral experiments by prior evaluation of their
   possible significance will necessarily give rise to many "false negatives," without eliminating "false positives." That is, prior restraints
   on neurobehavioral experiments will lead to rejection of experiments
   whose results would in fact have been important and allowance of
   experiments whose results will prove unimportant. This will be true
   no matter how stringent and cumbersome the a priori evaluation (see
   Figure 1).

These five statements must be taken as facts. Any attempt to advance a pro-   10
or antivivisectionist position by denying one or another of these statements
evades the ethical question by denying the very circumstances that give it
force. The force of these circumstances can best be appreciated by the study
of specific historical cases. One case that should be analyzed at length by
anyone contemplating restricting neurobehavioral experiments is the discovery that the dorsal and ventral roots of the spinal cord are sensory and motor,
respectively.

In 1822 François Magendie discovered that in young puppies the dorsal and   11
ventral roots of the peripheral nerves come together outside the spinal column,
so that they can be separately severed with relative ease. Magendie had been
wondering for some time what would be the effect of cutting one or another
root on the behavior of the limb or body segment served by the nerve. In the
other animals he was familiar with, the roots fused before exiting from the
spine. They could only be cut individually after breaking open the spine, which,
in the days before anesthesia, was all but impossible to do without damaging the spinal cord. Soon after discovering the favorable anatomical disposition of the roots in young puppies, Magendie began exposing the spines of
6–8-week-old puppies and cutting either the dorsal or the ventral roots of one
or more nerves. After several such experiments he was able to publish his
famous three-page communication in which he concluded that the dorsal roots
carried sensory signals while the ventral roots carried motor signals (Magendie,
1822).

Magendie's experiments place the ethical problems posed by neurobehav-   12
ioral research in sharp relief for the following reasons: (a) The results were of
the utmost importance. (b) The animals used were puppies and the pain of the
necessary surgical procedure was both intense and unalleviated by anesthetics,
whose discovery lay 25 years in the future. (c) Other very similar experiments
had been conducted by some of the leading neuroscientists of the day—most
notably the English anatomist Charles Bell—without yielding the decisive,
all-important insight. (d) The experiments, because they rapidly became well-
known and because they were sometimes performed in public, incurred widespread moral censure and helped fuel the antivivisection movement in 19th
century England.

Let me elaborate on these points. First, as regards the significance of the   13
results, I can do no better than quote from the introduction to a recent book by
Cranefield (1974, p. xiii) on the history of the Bell-Magendie precedence dispute:

> The discovery that the dorsal and ventral roots are the sensory and motor roots
> is one of the most important in the history of biology. The importance of the
> discovery has never been doubted; as E.H. Ackerknecht has recently written to
> me, "it is, after Harvey, probably the most momentous *single* discovery in physi-
> ology, and it had a more immediate influence on practical medicine than Harvey's
> discovery. Romberg's book on neurology, the first of its kind, is unthinkable with-
> out it."

A comparison with Harvey is by no means idle, since just as no rational physiology of the cardiovascular system was possible before Harvey's discovery, so no rational physiology of the nervous system was possible before the discovery of the separate functions of the roots of the spinal nerves. It was the first unequivocal localization of function in the nervous system and it made possible and led directly to the study of the spinal reflex. The study of the spinal reflex culminated in the work of Sherrington, work that led to our modern concepts of the physiology of the entire central nervous system.

As regards the pain caused the animals—the other horn of the dilemma, so   14
to speak—little elaboration is necessary, except to note that the pain was hideous, that there was no way known to the science of the day of mitigating it, and last, for the reasons already explained, that the animal of choice was the one most likely to arouse human sympathy—the puppy.

The third point, the similar but inconclusive experiments conducted by   15
other leading neuroscientists of that time, requires considerable elaboration. The elaboration is rich both in its irony and in its implications for the question of whether antivivisectionist sentiment may be appeased without doing serious damage to the progress of neuroscience. In 1811, in a privately circulated pamphlet, Charles Bell reported the results of experiments on rabbits involving the sectioning of dorsal and/or ventral roots. The report of these experiments is sketchy, and the wording of the conclusions is diffuse and obscure; but, in essence, Bell concluded erroneously that the ventral roots subserved voluntary behavior while the dorsal roots subserved involuntary behavior. Bell's conclusions were steered in the direction of error by a theory of nervous system function that he had derived from his anatomical studies. In subsequent publications Bell made brief allusions to these results and to related results from experiments involving the sectioning of cranial nerves in donkeys; but he did not give any clear statement of their implications, nor did he attach much importance to them *until* Magendie published his paper in 1822. Immediately thereafter Bell and his students began a clamorous, unprincipled, but largely successful campaign to claim priority for what was properly Magendie's discovery.

In the course of this campaign, Bell advanced more or less self-contradictory   16
claims. He repeatedly reproached Magendie for the cruelty of the experiments, claiming that the experiments were unnecessary and counterproductive and that the correct conclusion could be reached by anatomical observation alone. On the other hand, he argued that he, himself, had performed the crucial experiment first in 1811 and that Magendie had been inspired to "replicate" it by one of Bell's pupils, who demonstrated the related cranial nerve experiment to Magendie in late 1821. Bell even reissued "improved" versions of his earlier publications, in which crucial passages were reworded so as to appear to anticipate Magendie's conclusions.

Bell's reproaches and his claims that experiments were unnecessary were   17
picked up by antivivisectionists and helped to get passed the laws that to this

day make neurobehavioral work more difficult in England than in America or on the Continent. The claim that experiments on living animals are unnecessary finds its echo today in the claim made by antivivisectionists that it is possible to do neurobehavioral research by computer simulation, without ever cutting into a living animal.

These claims are absurd and nothing illustrates their absurdity better than the case at hand. There is nothing in anatomical observation per se that can do more than faintly suggest the functions of the roots. Bell himself knew that the results from the experiments on living animals were central to his claim of priority. Without them he had no claim, which is why—after 1822—he repeatedly emphasized his experiments on rabbits and donkeys. The irony is that Bell's erroneous inferences from anatomical observation played no small role in misleading his interpretation of his vivisection experiments. If anatomical observations are of little use, computer simulation is of still less use. What is there to simulate? You can make a computer whose input and output wires are segregated; you can make one in which they are intertwined; you can even make one in which the same wires are used for both functions. None of this modeling will tell you what the case is with the dorsal and ventral roots of mammalian nerves.   18

The sorry story of Bell's attempt to claim priority also illustrates the undesirability of setting up committees to pass in advance on whether the results to be obtained from a given experiment performed by a given experimenter are sufficiently important to outweigh the pain to be inflicted. Bell was one of the most important neuroscientists of his day. Furthermore, his vivisection experiments were inspired by a very general if vague and murky (in retrospect!) theory. Magendie was also a scientist of great stature, but he had no theory; indeed, he mistrusted and eschewed the system building that Bell was addicted to. Magendie just wanted to see what would happen. In Bell's hands, the crucial experiment led only to vague conclusions, to which Bell himself attributed little importance. In Magendie's hands, the experiment led to a clear conclusion whose importance was immediately obvious to all of the leading neuroscientists of his time.   19

Had Bell and Magendie simultaneously submitted proposals for the experiment to a Humane-Vivisection Committee for its permission, it is hard not to believe that they would have given the nod to Bell rather than to Magendie, assuming they gave either permission. If Magendie in 1822 had asked permission of a committee that happened to be aware of Bell's 1811 work—which is to assume an unusually well-informed committee—they would no doubt have refused permission on the grounds that the experiment had already been done by a first-rate researcher with meaningless results.   20

In summary, the debate over the ethics of surgical experiments on animals in behavioral neurobiology must come to grips with the following two dilemmas:

1. While it is true that these experiments cause pain and/or distress to the animals, it is equally true that the science cannot progress without them.   22

2. While it is true that most of the animals which suffer in the course of   23
   neurobehavioral research suffer in vain, it is equally true that there is
   no way to restrict experimentation only to those experiments that
   will yield meaningful data.

A consideration of the Bell-Magendie case makes it clear why restricting   24
research on living animals is certain to restrict the progress in our understanding of the relation between the nervous system and behavior. Therefore, one
should advocate such restrictions only if one believes that the moral value of
this scientific knowledge and of the many human and humane benefits that
flow from it cannot outweigh the suffering of a rat.

It is an affront to my own ethical sensibility to hear arguments that the   25
suffering of animals is of greater moral weight than are the advancement of
human understanding and the consequent alleviation of human suffering. Like
Le Gallois, I can scarcely comprehend how it can be right to use animals to
provide food for our bodies but wrong to use them to provide food for thought.
But, of course, I place a very high moral value on the advancement of human
understanding. Those for whom science has no moral value will find my argument without force, assuming that they are also unmoved by the prospect that
such understanding will alleviate human suffering.

REFERENCES*

Bell, C. (1811). *Idea of a new anatomy of the brain*. London: Strahan.

Broad, W.J. (1980). Legislating an end to animals in the lab. *Science, 208*,
575–576.

Cranefield, P.F. (1974). *The way in and the way out: François Magendie,
Charles Bell and the roots of the spinal nerves*. Mount Kisco: Futura.

Le Gallois, M. (1813). *Experiments on the principle of life* (N.C. Nancrede &
J.C. Nancrede, Trans.). Philadelphia: Thomas.

Magendie, F. (1822). Expériences sur les fonctions des racines des nerfs rach-
idien. *Journal de Physiologie Expérimentale et Pathologique, 2*, 276–
279.

* This essay uses the APA author/year style of documentation. The following essay by Deborah Mayo uses the
same system. For a discussion of this system see Part Three (pp. 563–65, 570–72).

QUESTIONS FOR MEANING

1. What is behavioral neurobiology and what does it do to animals?
2. Who was François Magendie and what did he discover? Describe his experiments and explain why they were significant.
3. Why are many scientific experiments a waste of time? How does Gallistel
   justify this?
4. Because he could assume that his audience understood the difference
   between "sensory signals" and "motor signals," Gallistel does not explain

the distinction. Do you understand these functions? If you know nothing about biology or psychology, where could you go to learn basic scientific vocabulary?

5. Why is Gallistel critical of Charles Bell? What does the Bell/Magendie conflict illustrate?

6. Vocabulary: simulations (1), imperative (1), affront (1), transiently (2), censure (3), exculpate (3), prodigiously (3), and erroneously (15).

QUESTIONS ABOUT STRATEGY

1. Gallistel makes no attempt to hide the fact that animal experimentation involves animal suffering. Was he wise to admit this? Does this admission strengthen or weaken his argument?

2. The quotation included in paragraph 3 is unusually long. Was it worth including? What is it meant to illustrate? Could Gallistel have paraphrased it in fewer words without losing anything important?

3. Consider the tone of this essay—and the last paragraph in particular. Is Gallistel unnecessarily combative? Should he show more tolerance for his opponents? Or is his attitude understandable when seen within the context of what has been written on the other side?

4. What does the graph (Figure 1) add to this essay? Could it have been left out?

DEBORAH G. MAYO
Against a Scientific Justification of Animal Experiments

A magna cum laude graduate of Clark University, where she had a double major in philosophy and mathematics, Deborah Mayo (b. 1952) has done extensive research on the use of statistics in science, economics, and philosophy. She received her Ph.D. from the University of Pennsylvania in 1979 and currently teaches philosophy at Virginia Polytechnic Institute and State University. She has received several fellowships from the National Endowment for the Humanities and published essays in numerous scholarly journals. "Against a Scientific Justification of Animal Experiments" was first published in 1983. Drawing upon her training in logic and statistical testing, Mayo questions the scientific validity of experiments involving laboratory animals—thus moving the debate over animal experimentation beyond the questions of ethics and morality most often focused upon by other writers. As you read her essay, you will find that she has amassed an impressive amount of evidence to support her point of view.

Introduction

Discussions of the treatment of animals typically focus on their use as food 1
and clothing, omitting the widespread use of animals in laboratory research.
Animals serve as experimental subjects in teaching surgical operations; in testing the efficiency and safety of drugs, food, cars, household cleaners, and
makeup; in psychological studies of pain, stress, and depression; and in satisfying the curiosity and desire of humans to learn more about biological processes.
In so doing they are subjected to shocks, burns, lesions, crashes, stresses,
diseases, mutilations, and the general array of slings and arrows of the laboratory environment.

If it is agreed that killing and torturing animals is prima facie wrong, then 2
additional justification is necessary in order to defend the sacrifice of millions
of animals each year to research. The justification most frequently offered is
that animal research provides increases both in scientific knowledge and in the
health, safety, and comfort of humans. As Lowrance (1976) remarks:

> For most people, any qualms over jeopardizing the animals are more than offset
> by the desire to gain knowledge useful in alleviating human suffering (p. 52) ....
> Few people would engage in such work were it not so essential (p. 54).

So closely is scientific experimentation associated with animal experimentation
that those who oppose or criticize animal experiments are often taken to be
opposing or criticizing science. One finds advocates of humane experimental
methods labeled as anti-science and referred to as "those whose love of animals
leads them into a hatred of science and even humanity ..." (Lane-Petter, 1963,

p. 472). The classic volume, *Experimental Surgery* (Markowitz et al., 1959) introduces the student to the Antivivisection Movement with the following remarks (emphasis added):

> It must be apparent ... that ordinary antivivisectionists are immune to the usual methods of exposition by reasoned argument. *They strain at a dog and swallow a baby* .... They are an unfortunate evil in our midst, and we must accustom ourselves to their presence as we do to bad weather, and to disease.

The error in depicting critics of animal experiments as anti-science becomes clear when one begins to question the extent to which the purported scientific aims of these experiments are actually accomplished. For then it turns out that the experiments and not their critics are unscientific. However, humanists concerned with the treatment of animals too rarely question the scientific basis of animal experiments and fail to uncover dissent within the scientific community itself. To the philosopher's arguments that animal experimentation is morally indefensible, the animal researcher responds that they benefit humanity. But if the most common uses of animals in research can be shown to be neither significantly beneficial to humans nor scientifically sound, then any appeal to such benefits in justifying these uses is undermined. It is the purpose of this paper to undermine the justification of common types of animal experiments by questioning their practical and scientific relevance and validity. Those experiments that cannot be justified on scientific grounds can be no more justified than the frivolous killing and torturing of animals. In fact they are even less capable of justification, since such experiments block more fruitful uses of scientific resources.

Irrelevant Experiments

I shall first consider the relevance of animal experiments and then discuss various problems leading to their invalidity. In an important sense, invalidity is not separate from irrelevance, since invalid experiments are surely irrelevant ones. However, in this section I shall focus on experiments that are irrelevant because of the triviality or obviousness of the question they ask. Indeed, many experiments do not even have a specific question in mind at the outset. They are often carried out simply to see what will happen and after the results are in some sort of hypothesis is formulated. Whether the hypothesis has been formulated before or after the experiment is not reported in the description of the experiment. Yet, formulating the hypothesis on the basis of the experiment can be shown to lead researchers to conclude, wrongly, that something of relevance has been observed (see Mayo, 1981).

I must emphasize that the examples I here consider are not at all exceptional or unusual. On the contrary, each represents a basic type of experiment that is performed with minor variations on millions of animals each year. An examination of the *Psychopharmaceutical Abstracts*, in which summaries of published experimental results are reported, will attest to the triviality and repetitiveness of the great majority of inquiries. What is particularly disturbing about the irrelevant experiments mentioned here is the amount of pain and suffering they involve. That such irrelevant painful experiments are not rare even at present is made plain in Jeff Diner's (1979) *Physical and Mental Suffering of Experimental Animals*, in which research from 1975–1978 is reviewed. It must also be kept in mind that these experiments are examples of ones considered important enough to publish. It is fair to assume that, in reality, many more experiments with even less relevance are performed. I limit myself to considering only recent experiments, to make it clear that these are not atrocities of the past.

(i) Infant monkeys were blinded at the University of Chicago in order to   5
assess whether blindness inhibited social interactions as measured by facial expressions. The result: blind monkeys showed all normal facial expressions, except threat (Berkson & Becker, 1975).

(ii) Pigeons were starved to 70% of their weight in the City University of   6
New York. It was concluded that following starvation pigeons ate more than usual *(Journal of Comparative and Physiological Psychology*, Sept., 1971).

(iii) The Department of Psychology at the University of Iowa studied the   7
effects of brain lesions on the grooming behavior of cats. Cats underwent surgery to produce various types of brain lesions and films were taken of their subsequent grooming behavior. It was reported that:

> Statistical analyses of the grooming behavior shown on the films indicated that cats with pontile lesions and cats with tectal lesions spent less time grooming . . . . Other studies revealed that cats with pontile or tectal lesions were deficient in removing tapes stuck on their fur (Swenson & Randall, 1977).

(iv) At the Downstate Medical Center rats were surgically brain damaged   8
and then stimulated by pinching their tails. They were then offered substances to drink. It was reported that (Mufson et al., 1976):

> Brain-damaged animals during tail pinch-induced drinking trials are responsive to the sensory properties of the test liquid. Chocolate milk is consumed, but tap water is actively rejected. Tail pinch to sham-operated control rats failed to induce such behavior; instead, it induced rage behavior towards the hand that pinched the tail.

(Is it to be concluded from this that brain damage decreases rage at painful stimuli and increases the desire for chocolate milk?)

(v) The following experiment carried out at the George Washington Univer-   9
sity Medical Center is a typical example of radiation research. Non-anesthetized rabbits had their heads irradiated while being restrained in "a Lucite restraining

device." It is reported that "The developing skin, mucosal and eye lesions were recorded and often photographed, but no treatment was offered" (Bradley et al., 1977). The report continues to describe in detail the monstrous radiation-induced damage without drawing any conclusions.

(vi) An extremely widespread sort of experiment involves assessing the   10
effects of various drugs on "punished responding." Punished responding typi-cally involves first teaching an animal to perform some task such as pressing a key by rewarding it with food, and later changing these rewards to punish-ments, such as electric shocks. A number of such experiments have been car-ried out by Dr. J.E. Barrett using pigeons. Here, the "punishments" consist of electric shocks administered through electrodes implanted around the pubis bone. The results are rather inconclusive. It is reported that (Barrett & Witkin, 1976):

> The broad range of effects obtained in the present experiment make it difficult to readily characterize the effects of drug interactions on behavior.

(vii) At Emory University cats were used to study how two different kinds   11
of painful stimuli, foot shock and tooth shock, influence behavior. To administer tooth shock, electrodes were implanted in the upper canine teeth of the cats. Foot shock was administered by means of stainless steel rods that formed the grid floor of the shuttle box in which the cats were placed. The cats were trained to escape the shocks by jumping across a barrier. However, when the cats were also subjected to the tooth shock, they were unable to escape the foot shock. It was concluded that tooth shock exerted a stronger influence than foot shock on behavior. The report regrets that (Anderson et al., 1976):

> Since 14 mA was the maximum amount of current that could be generated by our apparatus, it was not possible to determine if foot shock levels greater than that would have led to escape responding.

(viii) The *British Journal of Ophthalmology* published the experiments of   12
Dr. Zauberman, which measured the number of grams of force needed to strip the retinas from the eyes of cats. There was nothing said about how this or similar experiments that were carried out could be relevant to the problem of detached retinas in humans.

(ix) A good deal of research has as its goal the determination of the effects   13
of various operations on the sexual behavior of animals. For example, for a number of years the American Museum of Natural History in New York has conducted research on the effect of surgical mutilation on the sexual behavior of cats. In 1969 cats raised in isolation had penis nerves severed. The results of years of sex testing on these cats were overwhelmingly unsurprising: genital desensitization together with sexual inexperience inhibits the normal sexual behavior in cats (cited in Pratt, 1976, p. 72).

Numerous other experiments by the same researchers were conducted to   14
determine the effect of surgically destroying the olfactory area on the brain on
sexual behavior in cats, monkeys, hamsters, rats, and mice. The conclusions
from all of these experiments were reported to be "contradictory."

(x) Some experiments are rendered trivial or useless because they do no   15
more than repeat an experiment already performed numerous times. Even
worse is the continuous repetition of experiments whose relevance is dubious
in the first place. For example, there is the experiment that has been carried
out since the time of Claude Bernard, one of the founders of modern vivisection
methods. This experiment involves sewing up the ends of the intestines of dogs
rendering them unable to defecate. Death has been observed to follow in some
cases between 5 and 11 days, in other cases between 8 and 34 days. To what
use is such information to be put?

One of the reasons for continually repeating an experiment that has already   16
produced a result is that by using enough animals a result that is of a sufficient
degree of statistical significance can be obtained. It is thought that the more
observations the greater the evidence. However, this is based upon a statistical
fallacy. The more experiments needed in order to observe an effect that is
statistically significant, the smaller and more trivial the effect is. With enough
experiments, even a chance occurrence is rendered overwhelmingly significant,
statistically speaking.

Invalidity of Experiments

Experimental investigations are multi-staged affairs involving a host of back-   17
ground variables, the gathering, modeling, and analyses of data and inferences
based upon the data. At each stage a variety of flaws can arise to render the
experiment and inferences based upon it invalid. I shall consider some of the
most pronounced flaws that arise in carrying out animal experiments and making inferences from them in medical and pharmacological research. These flaws
stem from the disparity between experimentally induced conditions and conditions in humans, from within- and between-species differences, and from
confounding variables before, during, and after experimental treatment. I consider each of these in turn.

Artificial Induction of Disease

One type of medical research involves ascertaining whether certain patho-   18
logical conditions in humans can be alleviated or cured by certain drugs. Animals are used as "models" upon which to test these treatments. To do this it is
necessary for the animal subject to have the condition in question, and in order
to bring this about healthy animals are made sick. To this end they surgically
have organs removed or damaged; they are injected with pathogenic organisms
and cancer cells; they have irritants applied to their eyes and shaved skins; are
forced to inhale various substances, and consume deficient diets. To produce

such conditions as fear, anxiety, ulcers, heart diseases, and shock, animals are stressed by electric shocks or subjected to specially made pain devices, such as the Blalock Press and the Noble-Collip Drum.

It turns out, however, that the conditions artificially induced have little in common with the naturally occurring diseases in animals (when these exist) and much less in common with the diseases in man. This renders any conclusions drawn on the basis of treating these induced conditions of little relevance for treating humans (or even animals in cases where the condition naturally occurs). Extrapolating results from animal research to humans also frequently fails because of an absence of comparative examples of diseases in animals (particularly with hereditary diseases). For example, ulcers do not occur naturally in animals, and cancer in animals is quite different from cancer in man. 19

It is for this reason that the usefulness of animals in cancer research has been questioned. Most of the anticancer agents in use today have been tested in animals, most commonly rodents who have had tumors transplanted into them. This method, however, is of questionable validity. As noted in a review of testing anticancer drugs (*The Lancet*, April 15, 1972): 20

> Since no animal tumor is closely related to a cancer in human beings, an agent which is active in the laboratory may well prove to be useless clinically.

The situation would not be so serious if these agents were merely useless. In fact they are quite harmful, often causing side effects that may themselves precipitate further ills or even death. When researchers announce that a substance has been found to be effective in treating animal cancers, it is not revealed that the cell kinetics in animal cancers are vastly different than in humans. As the review above states:

> Animal tumours favored as test models have short doubling-times and a large proportion of cells in cycle with short generation-times. Probably, in many human cancers, intermitotic times are much longer and many cells are out of cycle . . . .

Since all anticancer agents in use have had their effectiveness assessed by animal tests, virtually all of them act only on rapidly dividing cells. This is one reason that treating human cancers (which typically do not divide rapidly) with these agents fails. The possibility of transplanting actual human cancers to animals is a suggestion which has been tried, but with poor results. As *The Lancet* review remarks, "This is hardly surprising, in view of the vastly different biochemical make-up of the animal model and of the human tumour which responds."

Hence, people are given drug after drug in the hope of arresting cancer when in fact these drugs have been evaluated upon cancers and organisms "vastly different" from their own. It may be argued that no better method is available 21 for treating cancer, and so for the time being it is the best that can be done. Such, however, is not the case. In the last 30 years or so new techniques have been developed which hold much promise. These new techniques involve testing anticancer agents on cultures of human cancer cells. This has the advantage of permitting the sensitivity of individual cancers to chemotherapy to be estimated, providing each patient with treatment custom-tailored to the type of cancer involved. This would prevent individuals from having to suffer the agonies of numerous trial agents that may be entirely ill-suited for treating their particular strain of cancer. If these newer techniques are to be developed sufficiently, some of the attention presently given to animal testing will have to be channeled into these alternatives. Unfortunately, researchers have been reluctant to do so.

The need to induce pathological conditions in animals in order to test some treatment upon them gives rise to an additional area of medical research. This area involves experiments that have as their sole aim the determination of how various pathological conditions can best be brought about in animals. Although such research has provided means for inducing a number of conditions, cures for these conditions have not been forthcoming.   22

For instance, research has repeatedly been carried out in order to find ways of inducing peritonitis in dogs. Peritonitis is the painful condition suffered by humans after rupturing their appendices. Even after a standard method for producing this disease in dogs was available (i.e., surgically tying off the appendix and feeding the dog castor oil), further experiments to find improved methods were made. One such experiment is reported by Hans Ruesch in *Slaughter of the Innocent* (Ruesch, 1978, pp. 105–106):   23

> With each dog strapped down and his belly laid open, the 'surgeons'—subsidized by the American taxpayers who of course had never been asked for their consent—tied off and crushed the appendix, then cut out part of the intestinal tract and the spleen. With the intestinal system thus multilated and unable to function normally, the dog was made to swallow a large dose of castor oil. The authors stated that thus 'a fatal, fulminating, diffuse peritonitis of appendical origin may be uniformly produced in dogs.'

There was no attempt to cure peritonitis, the aim having been merely to cause it. It was reported that the average survival time of the agonized dogs in this experiment was 39 hours.

Arguments to the effect that it is wrong to cause pain and suffering to animals are often rejected by claiming that animals simply do not suffer. Descartes, for example, asserted that the cries of an animal are no more significant than the creaking of a wheel. Ironically, it is precisely upon the assumption that animals *do* suffer from stress, fear, and pain in a manner similar to humans that the validity of much of animal experimentation rests. Few, if any, conditions are studied as widely in animals as are pain, stress, ulcers, fear, and   24 anxiety. An enormous amount of data has been compiled about how to produce such conditions, a good deal of which arose from the research of Hans Selye (1956). To obtain this data, millions of animals, primarily rats, mice, rabbits, and cats were and continue to be subjected to burns, poisons, shocks, frustrations, muscle and bone crushing, exposure, and gland removal. However, as is generally the case with artificially induced conditions in animals, laboratory-induced stress and stress-related conditions have little in common with stress and stress-related diseases in humans. To support this claim, it is necessary to consider something about how these conditions are induced in the laboratory animal.

One of the tools developed in 1942 to aid Selye in his research on stress, is   25
the stress producing Noble-Collip Drum, named after its inventors, R.L. Noble and J.B. Collip. The animals, locked and strapped (paws taped) inside the revolving metal drum, are tossed about and in so doing are thrust against iron projections in the drum. This treatment (often involving thousands of tosses at a rate of 40 tosses a minute) crushes bones, tissues, and teeth, and ruptures and scrambles organs. In assessing the considerable work of Selye, the *British Medical Journal* (May 22, 1954, p. 1195) concluded that experimentally induced stress had little in common with conditions that humans develop. Ulcers brought about in animals subjected to a rotating drum differ from ulcers in humans, not only because of a difference in species, but because ulcers in humans stem from rather different origins (e.g., long-term psychological stresses) than do those created in the laboratory through physical torture. Unsurprisingly, treatments developed from Selye's stress research (e.g., administering a hormone excreted by tortured animals, ACTH) are of very dubious value. As one surgeon points out (Ogilvie, 1935):

> They [gastric and duodenal ulcers] never occur naturally in animals, and they are hard to reproduce experimentally. They have been so produced, but usually by methods of gross damage that have no relation to any possible causative factor in man; moreover, these experimental ulcers are superficial and heal rapidly, and bear little resemblance to the indurated chronic ulcers we see in our patients.

The Noble-Collip drum has been criticized not only as being inhumane, but as being too crude to be scientifically useful. In what is considered a definitive review of experimentally produced shock, H.B. Stoner made this remark about it. "It is impossible to describe the effect of the injury and study the injured tissue quantitatively .... The method seems altogether too crude for modern purposes" (Stoner, 1961). Despite this, the Noble-Collip Drum is still used in experiments on stress and shock. Typically, these experiments attempt to test the effect of various drugs on the ability of unanesthetized animals to withstand the trauma of the drum.

The most widely used means for bringing about stress, terror, anxiety, and   26
shock is administering electric shocks. A number of researchers are fond of

experiments in which animals are trained to avoid electric shocks by performing some task, such as pressing a lever, and thousands of such experiments are performed yearly. After the animal has learned this "shock avoidance," frequently the experimental condition will be changed so that what previously permitted the animal to avoid shock now delivers shock. When such an experiment was performed on rhesus monkeys, it was found to produce "conflict" followed by gastroduodenal lesions. Countless experiments of this sort are repeatedly performed simply to bring about stressful conditions—without any attempt to treat these. When there is an attempt to treat the induced stress-related condition, the results are often useless or meaningless because of the disparity between natural and artificially induced conditions.

Electric shocks are also commonly used to induce aggression in animals, mainly rats. When the restrained animals are given a sufficient number of shocks, they will bite, box, or strike each other. Then the effects of a number of drugs on shock-induced aggression are assessed. In one case, which is typical of such research, the effect of mescaline on rats in a shock-induced aggression situation was tested (Sbordone & Garcia, 1977). Although in some cases the drug appeared to increase aggression, it was also found that the same aggression was shown by some nontreated rats. Hence, attributing the increased aggression to the drug is of questionable validity. Pratt (1976) describes the work of a prominent researcher in aggression studies, Dr. Roger Ulrich: 27

> Ulrich's work since 1962 ... has consisted largely in causing pain to rats and observing the resulting aggressive behavior. This investigator would give painful foot-shocks to the rats through an electrified grid floor ... (p. 61). Ulrich then introduced other distressing stimuli .... Bursts of intense noise (135 db, sustained for more than 1 min.) were introduced. The effects of castration were tried; ... and, finally one pair had their whiskers cut off and were blinded by removal of their eyes (pp. 61–62).

All of this aggression research has done little to control human aggression, which is rather different from the shock-induced aggression in rats. Ulrich himself has very recently come to question the usefulness of his past research. In a letter appearing in the *Monitor* he confesses (Ulrich, 1978):

> Initially my research was prompted by the desire to understand and help solve the problem of human aggression but I later discovered that the results of my work did not seem to justify its continuance. Instead I began to wonder if perhaps financial rewards, professional prestige, the opportunity to travel, etc. were the maintaining factors.

Another condition that electric shocks are employed to induce is epilepsy. Monkeys are given electric shocks that produce convulsions similar to those caused by epilepsy and eventually drive them insane. The insane monkey is then given a variety of drugs with the hope of curing or controlling epilepsy. However, while the monkeys display behavior that appears similar to epilepsy in man, their shock-induced fits have little bearing on human epilepsy, which has rather different origins. Hence, inferences from such experiments to treating human epilepsy are of very questionable validity. Unsurprisingly, the animal-tested drugs have failed to cure or control epilepsy.

The development of drugs to prevent brain hemorrhages proceeds in a   28
similar manner. To evaluate the efficacy of drugs on animals, it is first required to create blood clots in the brains of test animals. To this end, their skulls are cracked by hammer blows, causing the brain to form blood clots. Drugs are then given to the animals to determine which seem to improve their wretched state. But blood clots from hammer blows are rather different from those arising in humans, which are a gradual result of circulation problems or from long-term unhealthy eating and living habits.

In the interest of studying the effects of certain drugs on overeating (hyper-   29
phagia) researchers tested the drugs on rats that had overeaten (Wallach et al., 1977). However, in order to induce overeating in these rats they were forced to eat by painfully pinching their tails. The procedure was described as follows: "Tail pinch was applied for 10 minutes. Pressure was gradually increased until the animal either ate or became frantic." However, humans do not overeat because they are under pain of torture to do so. As such, the effects of drugs on the overeating of animals forced to overeat are irrelevant for assessing their effect on humans who overeat.

Underlying all these cases of induction of diseases is the assumption that by   30
artificially produced disease in animals and its natural occurrence (if it exists) ical state in man, one can make inferences about the latter on the basis of treating the former. This assumption is often false because of the disparity between experimentally induced conditions in animals and the corresponding conditions in humans. Indeed, there is also likely to be a disparity between artifically produced disease in animals and its natural occurrence (if it exists) in that animal. An example of this is seen in the case of inducing a deficiency of vitamin E in mice. Because this deficiency brought about a syndrome similar to muscular dystrophy, it was theorized that vitamin E would be effective in treating muscular dystrophy in man. In 1961, researchers showed (Loosli, 1967) that hereditary muscular dystrophy in mice and the dystrophy brought about by a vitamin E deficiency in mice were fundamentally different. Hence, the inference that vitamin E is useful in treating muscular dystrophy (as opposed to vitamin E deficiency) is invalid not only for humans, but for mice as well. The researchers concluded that it is never certain that experimentally induced disease sufficiently copies an inborn error.

In addition to producing misleading inferences, the techniques of animal   31
research are seen to be detrimental in that they take attention away from more fruitful methods, such as clinical observation of humans. In a 1978 address, Dr. Alice Heim, chairperson of the psychological section of the British Association for the Advancement of Science, remarked (*The Times*, September, 1978):

Surely it is more valuable to work with disturbed human beings who seek help than to render cats and other animals 'experimentally neurotic'; then try to 'cure' them; and then try to draw an analogy between these animals and the immensely more complex *homo sapiens*.

Differences Between and Within Species

In addition to using animals as "models" for disease, animals are widely used 32
to test the efficiency and safety of drugs and environmental substances by toxicologists and pharmacologists. The problem of differences between species is perhaps greatest in toxicological research. This problem often prevents the valid extrapolation of the results of animal tests to humans.

In experiments carried out to determine how poisonous various chemicals 33
are, the classic measure of toxicity used is called the *median lethal dose*, abbreviated as LD_{50}. It is defined as the dose of a substance needed to kill 50% of a given species of animals. Each year, millions of animals, usually mice, are force-fed drugs, insecticides, floor polishes, food additives, lipsticks, and other chemical substances, and the dosage required to kill about half of them (within 14 days) is calculated. But the significance of the LD_{50} measure is far from clear.

The purpose of the LD_{50} test is to determine the degree to which substances 34
are poisonous to humans. However, for a number of reasons it fails to provide such a determination. For one thing, many of the test substances are relatively innocuous and hence enormous quantities must be forced down the animals' throats to cause them to die. In such cases, the death is often caused simply by the damage done by the massive quantities and not the test substance itself. The calculated LD_{50}s for these substances have no bearing on the manner in which the substance is to be used by humans.

Having found the LD_{50}, experiments with increasingly lower dosages are 35
made to ascertain the supposedly safe dosage of the drug (the LD_0). The next step is to extrapolate this safe dosage to humans. This extrapolation is made simply by multiplying the weight of the animal proportionately to the weight of humans. However, this safe level applies only to the test animal and it may differ radically for humans. This is particularly true when, as is often the case, the animal's death is attributable to the sheer volume of the substance. Extrapolating in this manner is also based on the assumption that the drug acts in a linear fashion—that twice the dosage means twice the effect. In fact, there is typically a threshold below which substances may have no real effect.

It might be thought that despite the differences between test animals and 36
humans, that the LD_{50} may still provide a rank order of the degree of toxicity of substances. Such is not the case. One problem is that a substance with a low LD_{50} may be extremely poisonous over a long period of time, such as lead and asbestos. Hence, the LD_{50} is not useful for ascertaining the result of chronic exposure. In addition, it has been found that in different laboratories not only do the LD_{50} values differ, but the orderings differ as well. This arises from interspecies differences and a number of environmental factors that I shall take up later.

Scientists themselves have come to see the LD_{50} tests as clumsy and crude   37
and lacking in reliability. In one study on four widely used household chemicals,
it was found that the LD_{50}s in six laboratories differed both absolutely and
relatively. It was concluded that "neither a particular method nor a single value
may be regarded as a correct one" (Loosli, 1967, p. 120). Still, in the US, as in
most countries, health agencies require that the LD_{50} be calculated for each of
the thousands of new substances introduced each year.

Another test promoted by the FDA involves the use of rabbits' eyes to   38
determine how dangerous various substances are to human eyes. In addition to
cosmetics, detergents and pesticides are also tested in this way. In 1973, Revlon
alone used 1500 rabbits for eye and skin irritancy tests. As is usual for toxicity
tests, no anesthesia is used since it is claimed to interfere with the results of
the tests. The rabbits are immobilized in restraining devices for weeks, their
eyes (which lack tear glands) being held open with clamps. In assessing the
severity of eye irritants, the measure is not numerical, as with the LD_{50}. Rather,
the eyes of the restrained rabbits are observed after several hours of having
the irritant applied, and are described in terms of such categories as ulcerated
cornea, inflamed iris, and gross destruction. Such crude determinations yield
results that are unreliable and unmeaningful. In 1971, 25 of the best known
laboratories jointly conducted a comprehensive evaluation of irritancy tests on
rabbits. It was noted that "extreme variation" existed in the way the laboratories assessed the effects of irritants on rabbits.

The study (Weil & Scala, 1971) concluded that: 39

> The rabbit eye and skin procedure currently recommended by the Federal agen-
> cies ... should not be recommended as standard procedures in any new regula-
> tions. Without careful reeducation these tests result in unreliable results.

As this was reported by the very laboratories that carry out such tests, it may
be regarded as an understatement. Despite the acknowledged crudity and
unreliability of these toxicity tests and measures, they are still routinely carried
out, primarily as a means by which manufacturers can protect themselves and
obtain the right to market new substances.

Underlying the use of animal models for pharmacological tests is the pre-   40
sumption that it will be possible to extrapolate to humans. However, the vast
differences that exist between species make the results from one species an
unreliable indicator for another. There are a number of ways that substances
can produce different effects in different animals. Chemicals act upon living
things in five main stages: absorption, distribution, excretion, metabolism, and
mechanism of action, and interspecies differences may arise during any of
these. Even if the difference is quite small at each stage, they may accumulate
to yield a large total interspecies discrepancy. These interspecies differences
make inferences from animal experiments very much dependent upon which
animal is used as the research model.

Richard Ryder (1975, p. 150) illustrates the gross differences between species in the effectiveness of drugs by citing the following results. The effect of a 'Product X' was found to vary as follows: 41

Species	Body weight, mg/kg
Man	1
Sheep	10
Rabbit	200
Monkey	15.2

From these results it is clear that testing the substance on rabbits will be a poor indicator of its effectiveness in humans. Still, rabbits are a popular animal for this sort of testing.

Interspecies differences may lead to concluding that substances that are innocuous or beneficial in humans are harmful, and that substances that have insidious effects on humans are harmless. For example, penicillin is extremely poisonous to guinea pigs. Had penicillin been subjected to the routine animal tests, as new drugs presently are, it would never have been tried on humans. On the other hand, what is a deadly poison to humans, strychnine, may be safely consumed by guinea pigs. Similarly, a dose of belladonna that is fatal to humans is harmless for a rabbit, the often used laboratory animal. Morphine, while sedating most species, incites frantic excitement in cats, dogs, and mice. Arsenic, deadly for humans, can be safely consumed in enormous quantities by sheep. Still, foxes and chickens die from almonds, and parrots are poisoned by parsley. Tuberculin, which, because it cured TB in guinea pigs, was thought to also be a cure in humans, turned out to cause TB in humans. Digitalis, which because it was seen to produce severely high blood pressure in dogs was thought to be dangerous for humans, turned out to be a major treatment for humans with heart disease.   42

In certain species, aspirin is highly toxic and it has been seen to produce malformations in the fetuses of rats (*Newsweek*, Nov. 20, 1972). Other substances that are not teratogenic for humans, but are known to cause malformations in the offspring of laboratory animals, are adrenaline, insulin, and certain antibiotics. The converse is the case with drugs such as thalidomide, which was tested extensively in animals (e.g., the popular laboratory Wistar rat) without any adverse effects to the fetus, but which turned out to produce monstrous human babies. The thalidomide tragedy drove people to conclude that more animal testing was needed to protect the safety of humans, when, ironically, the tragedy was a product of animal testing. More specifically, it resulted from the invalidating factor of interspecies differences. After thalidomide was found to produce deformed humans, researchers tried repeatedly to produce similar effects on animals. One hundred fifty different strains and   43 substrains of rabbits were tested, but with no malformations. Finally, it was found that such malformations could be produced in New Zealand white rabbits. One might ask what the point was in carrying out these experiments after thalidomide was already seen to produce malformed human fetuses. The teratogenic effects of a number of other drugs have also been shown not only to vary with species, but also with different strains of the same species.

It is interesting to note that the German drug company that marketed tha-   44
lidomide, was, after being tried for two and a half years, acquitted on charges of having marketed a dangerous drug. The acquittal was based on the testimonies of numerous medical authorities who claimed that animal tests are never conclusive for making inferences about humans. Despite the failure of animal tests to reveal the danger of thalidomide, Turkish professor S.T. Aygun was able to discover its teratogenic properties through the use of chick embryos, and prevented its being marketed in Turkey. Thalidomide's dangers have also been revealed by testing it on sea-urchin eggs (Krieg, 1964). Much more on alternatives to animal testing may be found in Ruesch, 1978. Unfortunately, even those medical authorities who have come to see animal testing as scientifically unsound are reluctant to voice their views. The following remarks made by two doctors in 1976 express this point (Stiller & Stiller, 1976):

> In praxis all animal experiments are scientifically indefensible, as they lack any scientific validity and reliability in regard to humans. They only serve as an alibi for the drug manufacturers, who hope to protect themselves thereby.... But who dares to express doubts of our much-vaunted technological medicine, or even just to ask questions, without meeting the solid opposition from the vested interests of science, business, and also of politics and news media?

Confusion of Background Variables

Invalid inferences arise when what is attributed to the experimental treat-   45
ment actually arises from the influences of nontreatment variables. Animals even of the same species react differently under the same treatment as a result of nontreatment variables, both of the genetic and environmental kind. Different responses result from differences in the health of the animal, its age, sex, litter, and strain, its living conditions, stressful or painful stimuli, and even odors and the time of day. These variables arise before, during, and after the experimental treatment. I will now consider some ways in which these nontreatment variables may be confused with treatment variables and hence give rise to faulty inferences.

Animals that ultimately become subjects for research may start out with   46
very different characteristics. An experimental response may be the effect not of the experimental treatment in question, but of some former condition of the animal quite unrelated to the treatment. Hence, the background of experimental animals is of major relevance to the reliability of conclusions based upon

them—a fact that is often ignored. How are research animals obtained, and how does their background influence the reliability of experiments made upon them?

Animals that find themselves in research laboratories may be of the "specially bred" variety, or they may have arisen from a "random source," that is, from dealers or pounds. In the case of dogs and cats, the great majority come from random sources and are typically stray, unwanted, or stolen pets. For example, of the over 300,000 dogs used in biomedical research in the US in 1969, only about 40,000 were bred specially for the laboratory. By the time a random-source animal reaches the laboratory, an average of one month has been spent either in pounds, with dealers, in transport, or in the wild. Within this period the animal is subjected to poor diet and shelter, and a variety of stressful, unhygienic conditions. In an article in *Life* (February 4, 1966), the outrageous conditions maintained by dog dealers were exposed. The article reports: 47

> Unscrupulous dog 'dealers' taking advantage of the growing demand for dogs for vital medical research, are running a lucrative and unsavory business. Laboratories now need almost two million dogs a year . . . Some dealers keep big inventories of dogs in unspeakably filthy compounds that seem scarcely less appalling than the concentration camps of World War II. Many do not sell directly to labs but simply dispose of their packs at auction where the going rate is 30¢ a pound. Puppies, often drenched in their own vomit, sell for 10¢ apiece.

Unsurprisingly, as one researcher testified, 40% of the dogs obtained this way die before they can even be used for research.

Hence, when such animals get sick or die upon receiving some treatment there is little reason to suppose the treatment was to blame. One researcher, testifying at a congressional hearing following the exposition in *Life*, told of the following case. A drug had been condemned on the basis of an experiment in which all the dogs receiving it died, but it turned out to be distemper and not the drug that was responsible for the deaths (U.S. House, 1966). Nor have conditions improved much since the passage of the Laboratory Animals Welfare Act of 1966, which requires licensing and inspections. The rate of animal deaths prior to experimentation is still high. A more detailed discussion of the humane animal laws may be found in Pratt, 1976 and Ruesch, 1978.   48

Animals that arrive at the laboratory with infections often render results equivocal. Experiments that are particularly vulnerable to the existence of intercurrent infections are immunology, radiation, and carcinogenesis studies. Carcinogenesis, for example, is affected by the efficiency of immunological responses and rate of cell turnover, and both of these are affected by indigenous pathogens.   49

To avoid the problem that the variability of the health of research animals presents, means by which animals are bred uniformly free of disease have been   50 developed. Strains of bacteriologically sterile animals, most often rodents, are bred especially for use in the laboratory. These germ-free animals are born by cesarean section, raised in sterile surroundings, and fed sterile foods. The germ-free condition of specially bred animals is advertised as a major selling point in advertisements by suppliers of research animals. One recent ad (*Laboratory Animal Science*, February, 1977) boasts "*New* Cesarean derived, Barrier reared CAMM RATS-Certified Pathogen Free."

However, the resulting "uniform biological material" as these animals are   51 often called, differs radically from normal animals. Animals raised in totally sterile conditions fail to develop immunologies that provide a natural defense mechanism against disease. Hence, they are likely to be far more susceptible to disease than their naturally bred counterparts.

By using specially bred animals that are biologically uniform there is less   52 variability in response, and as such, the results are claimed to be more reliable. It is true that there will be more reliability in the sense of more agreement among successive experiments with uniform as opposed to non-uniform animals. However, there will not be more reliability in the sense of accurately representing natural, random-bred, heterogeneous animal and human populations. For this, uniformly bred animals provide extremely unreliable models. It is true that uniform research animals yield less variability in response, and hence an effect may be detected with fewer animals. However, the effect detected is not a reliable indicator of the effect that would arise in animals found in nature, much less in humans.

The demand for uniformity in research animals, is, according to a prominent   53 researcher, M.W. Fox, often a "pseudo-sophistication." According to Fox, "Few investigators inquire or are aware of how the prior life history and environmental experiences of the animal may influence his experiment" (Fox, 1974, pp. 96–97). However, a knowledge of how the background of the animal influences the experimental results is necessary to ensure the validity of the experiment. Even when not bred to be germ-free, the laboratory animal may fail to develop the resistance to various stresses that it would in its natural habitat where it would normally be faced with a number of stresses. An example of such a natural stress is brought about when baby animals are left alone while their mothers go in search of food. Hence, the laboratory animal is apt to be less hearty than its natural counterpart.

For the most part, research animals are chosen not on the basis of how   54 appropriate they are for a given experiment—even when such information is available. Rather, they are selected for possessing such characteristics as taking up little space, being inexpensive, being nocturnal, being docile and adaptable to laboratory environments. An advertisement for Marshall beagles (*Laboratory Animal Science*, February, 1977) boasts of having designed their research animal as one might design a car model. The ad reads:

TRY OUR 1977 MODELS. Large selection of COMPACTS, MID SIZE & FULL SIZE MODELS. The Marshall Beagle is built with you in mind. All models feature sturdy unitized body construction and Easy Handling.

As a result, inappropriate animals are often used for detecting the effect of an experimental treatment. One way in which an animal may be inappropriate is if it tends to spontaneously generate the effect in question even when the experimental treatment is absent (i.e., in control animals).

Rats and mice, for example, tend spontaneously to develop a high incidence   55
of tumors. This renders them unsuitable for detecting tumors. Still, no animals are used as often as rats and mice for assessing the effect of numerous experimental treatments upon the production of tumors. The reason is that they are inexpensive and take up little room. Examples of recent experimental treatments tested this way are saccharin and oral contraceptives. The *British Medical Journal* (October 28, 1972, p. 190) made the following remark concerning the report of the Council on Safety of Medicines on tests of oral contraceptives:

> The tables in the report show incidences of 25% of lung tumours and 17% of liver tumours in *control mice* and 26% adrenal tumours, 30% pituitary tumours, and 99% mammary tumours in *control rats*. It is difficult to see how experiments on strains of animals so exceedingly liable to develop tumours of these various kinds can throw useful light on the carcinogenicity of any compound for man.

In this experiment, rats exposed to high dosages (up to 400 times the human   56
use) of contraceptives were found to have more tumors than those not exposed. But this does not mean that the additional tumors were caused by the contraceptives, particularly given the high rate of tumors in untreated controls. The question of how many more tumors must be observed to conclude that treated rats differ significantly from untreated rats poses an important statistical problem. Given the high rate of tumors in controls, a rather high rate of tumors in a large sample of treated rats should be required. The report, however, does not indicate how many more tumors were observed. The Committee's report itself (Committee on Safety of Medicines, 1972) concludes that:

> ...although a carcinogenic effect can be produced when some of the preparations are used in high doses throughout the life-span in certain strains of rat and mouse, this evidence cannot be interpreted as constituting a carcinogenic hazard to women when these preparations are used as oral contraceptives.

The report also notes that many animals died from the high dosage of the compound given.

The conclusion of this committee contrasts with the conclusions of the FDA   57
with respect to the banning of DDT and the recently proposed banning of saccharin. In both cases the evidence consists of an increase of tumors observed in rats given extremely high doses of the substance in question. Without additional evidence, conclusions about the danger of these substances are ill-grounded, both because of the high doses and the high spontaneous rate of tumors in rats.

Even if the experimental effect observed does not result from a condition   58 already present in the animal before entering the lab, it may arise from non-treatment factors introduced after entering the lab. Claude Bernard, the founder of modern animal experimentation, himself admitted that "The experimental animal is never in a normal state. The normal state is merely a supposition, an assumption." The animal is placed in an abnormal state because of the host of stressors it is confronted with.

Animals in the lab are deprived of their natural habitat, and often are terror-   59
ized by what they see even before they themselves are experimented upon. It is not uncommon for animals, particularly dogs, to be subject to devocalization prior to experimentation (sometimes referred to as "the anesthesia of the public"), which is itself a trauma. Also common is for an animal to be used for additional research after it has already undergone one or more experiments. (This practice, illegal in Britain, is legal in the US.)

When an animal is in fear or pain, all its organs and biochemical systems are   60
affected. Measurement parameters such as blood pressure, temperature, metabolic rate, and enzyme reactions have been found to vary up to three times their normal value as a result of pain and stress (Hillman, 1970). Hence the value of any of these parameters measured following an experimental treatment may result not from the treatment, but from unrelated pain and stress to which the experimental animal has been subjected. As such, any experiment attempting to detect variations smaller than those already known to be attributable to experimental stress is invalidated. As one physiologist studying the effects of fear and pain notes, "It [experimental stress] is almost certainly the main reason for the wide variation reported among animals upon whom painful experiments have been done" (Hillman, 1970).

Animals may be stressed simply by being handled by the experimenter,   61
or by the order in which they are taken to the experimental room from the cage. When animals are taken one by one from a cage or pen, the last animals taken differ markedly from the first few taken because of the stress brought about from the changing composition of the cage or pen. As one researcher (Magalhaes, 1974, p. 103) states:

> Even apparently minor procedures such as successively removing rats from their colony cage for decapitation and subsequent biochemical analysis can have a marked influence on the results. One experimenter found that the corticosteroid measures obtained from the first few rats taken out of their cage were very much lower compared to those from the last few to be taken.

To avoid this problem, animals are sometimes experimented upon in their usual animal facility instead of removing them to the laboratory. But this gives rise to a number of other variables that tend to bias the experimental result, as the following notes (Magalhaes, 1974. p. 104):

> ...the distress vocalizations, struggling and release of alarm odors during restraint (while taking blood samples, for example) may affect other animals that are to be

sampled later, and from such animals 'later down the line' the samples might be qualitatively very different.

Experimental effects are also influenced by the manner in which the exper-   62
imental treatment is administered. For example, different results are likely to be obtained if a substance is force-fed to an animal by a stomach tube as opposed to having it be eaten naturally. As we have already noted, the response may arise not from the substance administered, but from the large quantity the animal is forced to consume. As the toxicologist Dr. Leo Friedman points out: "We know that administration of *enough* of any substance in high enough dosage will produce some adverse effect" (Friedman, 1970). For example, massive amounts of common table salt cause birth defects in pregnant rats. However, there is no evidence that low doses of salt cause birth defects in humans.

There are a number of less obvious background variables that can arise to   63
confuse the effect of the experimental treatment, and hence lead to invalid inferences. Such variables include the time of day, the temperature of the room, and even the color of the clothing worn by the experimenter. Drug toxicity, for example, has been found to vary with the time of day at which animals are given the drug. Other time-dependent reactions are susceptibility to seizures and irradiation. Animals apparently have certain 24-hour rhythms, including periods of maximum activity and periods of minimum activity (Ader, 1974). Animals react differently to test treatments according to whether they occur during their period of maximum or minimum activity.

For example, it is known that restraining rats causes them to suffer gastric   64
lesions. However, when restraint occurs during the rats' periods of maximum activity, the rats are significantly more susceptible to the development of gastric lesions than those restrained during periods of minimum activity (Ader, 1974, p. 111). Presumably, being restrained during a period of maximum activity is perceived by the rat as being more stressful than being restrained during a period of minimum activity. It would seem likely, then, that rats restrained (as they are) for the introduction of some experimental treatment may show disturbances that are largely the result not of the treatment, but of the time of day. The influence of time also serves to explain some of the variation found between labs. After observing the significant effects of time, one researcher (Ader, 1974, p. 120, emphasis added) was led to conclude:

> ... it does not seem facetious to ask how many discrepancies in the literature are attributable not to who is right and who is wrong, but to *when* the behavior was sampled.

Conclusion

The considerations I have discussed provide a strong argument against a   65
scientific justification of a great deal of animal experimentation; for they have identified numerous sources that often prevent such experiments from being

scientifically relevant or valid. Often, an animal experiment is rendered irrelevant because the question it seeks to answer is trivial or obvious, or has already been answered countless times. Invalid experiments frequently arise from the disparity between artificially induced conditions in the laboratory and natural ones, from differences within and among species, and from a number of background variables whose effects are confused with experimental variables.

A few of these problems can be avoided to some extent, for example, by   66
being careful to control a large number of backgound variables. For the most part, however, these problems exist as limitations in principle to the beneficial use of animals in research. For instance, animals will never be able to produce tumors, ulcers, or a number of other pathological conditions in a manner that is similar to humans. The complex psychological problems humans face are not the sorts of things that can be induced in laboratory animals. The differences in drug toxicity in animals cannot be overcome, and accounting for the vast number of background variables is practically impossible.

Admittedly, it is possible to claim that animal experimentation is justifiable   67
despite the fact that it is of no practical value. Ruesch (1978, p. 144) cites one such attempt made by Professor Leon Asher. According to Asher:

> ... one might ask oneself whether it isn't a sacred case of conscience to follow the call toward the solution of the mysteries of life, and whether man shouldn't consider it a *religious duty* to satisfy the desire for exploration that Providence has placed in our hearts, without asking whether our research on life has any value for medical science or any other practical value.

However, not all actions that satisfy a "desire for exploration" may be considered permissible (much less a religious duty). Experimenting on humans may also satisfy such a desire, and one is likely to learn much more from humans than from animals. Surely, pointless inquisitiveness does not justify the infliction of pain and suffering, and both humans and animals have the capacity to suffer.

Increasing emphasis on research has also done harm to patient care. As   68
Ryder notes (1975, p. 75):

> A doctor's merit is no longer rated on how many patients he cures but on how many papers he publishes in learned journals. This has encouraged a great deal of trivial research and often there has been a decline in the standards of clinical care.

The employment of human data (which is available in great abundance) is one way to replace a good deal of medical, psychological, and toxicological research on animals with a more scientifically sound alternative.

Other promising alternatives to animal experiments are the use of tissue   69
cultures and mathematical models. Tissue culture involves cultivating living

cells outside the organism, and has the advantage of permitting the growth of human as opposed to animal cells. Mathematical models, derived from theory or from past experiments, may be used to predict responses or effects from a variety of experimental conditions that are formulated mathematically. The strongest argument in favor of developing these alternatives is that much of animal experimentation is scientifically, and hence morally, indefensible.

REFERENCES

Ader, R. (1974). Environmental variables in animal experimentation: the relevance of 24-hour rhythms in the study of animal behavior. In H. Magalhaes (Ed.), *Environmental variables in animal experimentation.* Lewisburg, Pennsylvania: Bucknell University Press.

Anderson, K.V., Pear, G.S., & Honeycutt, C. (1976). Behavioral evidence showing the predominance of diffuse pain stimuli over discrete stimuli in influencing perception. *Journal of Neuroscience Research, 2,* 283–289.

Barrett, J.E. & Witkin, J.M. (1976). Interaction of D-Amphetamine with Pentobarbital and Chlordiazeopoxide: effects on punished and unpunished behavior of pigeons. *Pharmacology, Biochemistry, and Behavior, 5,* 285–292.

Berkson, G. & Becker, J.D. (1975). Facial expressions and social responsiveness of blind monkeys. *Journal of Abnormal Psychology, 84,* 519–523.

Bradley, E.W., Zook, B.C., Casarett, G.W., Bondelid, R.O., Maier, J.G. & Rogers, C.C. Effects of fast neutrons on rabbits. *International Journal of Radiation, Oncology, Biology and Physics, 2,* 1133–1139.

Committee on Safety of Medicines. (1972). *Carcinogenicity tests of oral contraceptives.* London: H.M.S.O.

Diner, J. (1979). Physical and mental suffering of experimental animals: a review of scientific literature 1975–1978. Washington: Animal Welfare Institute.

Fox, M.W. (1974). Space and social distance in the ecology of laboratory animals. In H. Magalhaes (Ed.), *Environmental variables in animal experimentation* (pp. 96–105). Lewisburg, Pennsylvania: Bucknell University Press.

Friedman, L. (1970). Symposium on the evaluation of the safety of food additives and chemical residues: II the role of the laboratory animal study of intermediate duration for evaluation of safety. *Toxicology and Applied Pharmacology, 16,* 498–506.

Hillman, H. (1970). *Scientific undesirability of painful experiments.* Zurich: WFPA.

Krieg, M.B. (1964). *Green Medicine.* Chicago: Rand McNally.

Lane-Petter, E. (1963). Humane Vivisection. *Laboratory Animal Care, 13*, 469–473.

Loosli, R. (1967). Duplicate testing and reproducibility. In R.H. Regamey et. al. (Eds.), *International Symposium on laboratory animals* (pp. 117–123). Basel: Karger.

Lowrance, M. (1976). *Of Acceptable Risk*. Los Altos, California: Kaufmann.

Magalhaes, H. (Ed.). (1974). *Environmental variables in animal experimentation*. Lewisburg, Pennsylvania: Bucknell University Press.

Markowitz, J., Archibald, J. & Downie, H.G. (1959). *Experimental surgery* (4th ed.). Baltimore: Williams & Wilkins.

Mayo, D. (1981). Testing statistical testing. In J.C. Pitt (Ed.), *Philosophy in economics* (pp. 175–203). Dordrecht: Reidel.

Mufson, E.J., Balagura, S., & Riss, W. (1976). Tail pinch-induced arousal and stimulus-bound behavior in rats with lateral hypothalamic lesions. *Brain, Behavior and Evolution, 13*, 154–164.

Ogilvie, W.H. (1935, February 23). [Letter to the Editor]. *Lancet*, p. 419.

Pratt, D. (1976). *Painful experiments on animals*. New York: Argus.

Regamey, R.H., Hennessen, W., Ikic, D., & Ungar, J. (Eds.). (1967). *International symposium on laboratory animals*. Basel: Karger.

Ruesch, H. (1978). *Slaughter of the Innocent*. New York: Bantam.

Ryder, R. (1975). *Victims of science*. London: Davis-Poynter.

Sbordone, R.J. & Garcia, J. (1977). Untreated rats develop 'pathological' aggression when paired with a mescaline-treated rat in shock-elicited aggression situation. *Behavioral Biology, 21*, 451–461.

Selye, H. (1956). *The stress of life*. New York: McGraw.

Stiller, H. & Stiller, M. (1976). *Tierversuch und Tierexperimentator*. Munich: Hirthammer.

Stoner, H.B. (1961). Critical analysis of traumatic shock models. *Federation Proceedings, 20*, Supplement 9, pp. 38–48.

Swenson, R.M. & Randall, W. (1977). Grooming behavior in cats with pontile lesions and cats with tectal lesions. *Journal of Comparative and Physiological Psychology, 91*, 313–326.

Ulrich, R.E. (1978, March). [Letter to the Editor]. *American Psychological Association Monitor*, p. 16.

Wallach, M.B., Dawber, M., McMahon, M., & Rogers, C. (1977). A new anorexigen assay: stress-induced hyperphagia in rats. *Pharmacology, Biochemistry and Behavior, 6*, 529–531.

Weil, M. & Scala, R. (1971). Study of intra-and inter-laboratory variability in the results of rabbit eye and skin irritations tests. *Toxicology and Applied Pharmacology, 19,* 276–360.

QUESTIONS FOR MEANING

1. Is Deborah Mayo entirely opposed to animal experimentation? Would she ban all tests on animals?
2. What is Mayo's principle objection to the peritonitis experiment described in paragraph 23?
3. What's wrong with the eye tests described in paragraph 38?
4. Explain what LD_{50} means.
5. Does Mayo offer any explanation why scientists may be tempted to do trivial and even useless research?
6. Why is it important to know the background of any animal being experimented upon? What's wrong with using animals that have been specially bred for use in laboratories? What other variables can affect the results of an experiment?
7. What alternatives are there to animal experimentation? Does Mayo offer any specific evidence to suggest that such alternatives are feasible?
8. Vocabulary: purported (2), disparity (17), confounding (17), ascertaining (18), pathological (18), extrapolating (19), precipitate (20), kinetics (20), induce (22), toxicological (32), innocuous (34), linear (35), insidious (42), teratogenic (43), carcinogenesis (49), and indigenous (49).

QUESTIONS ABOUT STRATEGY

1. Mayo argues that animal experimentation is bad science. Does she convince you that this is so? How "scientific" is her own argument? Does she sound as if she knows what she's talking about?
2. Does this essay ever seem emotional? In presenting detailed descriptions of experiments in which the suffering of animals is vividly portrayed, does Mayo ever advance her argument by playing upon the feelings of her audience?
3. Does Mayo ever repeat herself? If so, where? Is repetition justifiable in an essay of this length?
4. Why does Mayo break her essay into individually titled subsections?
5. Where in her essay does Mayo recognize the premise which supports arguments on behalf of animal experimentation? Are there any other points in the essay where Mayo represents her opponents' point of view?

ANDREW N. ROWAN
Animals in Education

*Most of the debate on animal experimentation focuses on the way animals are used
in research laboratories. It is easy to overlook the extent to which animals are used,
and possibly abused, in education. In the following essay, Andrew N. Rowan
(b. 1946) summarizes the concerns of educators who have addressed the question of
how animals should be used in teaching biology. Formerly associated with the
Institute for the Study of Animal Problems in Washington, D.C., Rowan is currently
Assistant Dean for New Programs at Tufts School of Veterinary Medicine. He has
written numerous articles on the nature of animal experimentation, coedited* The
Use of Alternatives in Drug Research *(1980), and recently published* Of Mice,
Models & Men: A Critical Evaluation of Animal Research *(1984).*

A number of different views of the moral status of animals exist in today's   1
society; some have been entrenched for many years. Two of the most widely
held views are the humanitarian—humans should treat animals kindly and with
consideration and should not be cruel; and the dominionistic—humans have
been given dominion over other animals and we may do what we want with
them provided that the consequences are not unfavorable to human beings
(Kellert 1980). However, these attitudes are being called into question with
increasing frequency.

The current resurgence of interest in animal "rights" (Singer 1975; Regan   2
and Singer 1976; Clark 1977; Frey 1980) has resulted in much greater attention
being paid to the distinction between warranted and unwarranted exploitation
of animals as opposed to the simpler and more emotive concepts of kindness
and cruelty (Fox and Rowan 1980). While it is important to foster behavior
favoring kindness and discouraging cruelty, these concepts are not particularly
useful in helping to resolve conflicts between human and animal interests, such
as the use of animals in biomedical research and education. For example, we
are not being kind to a frog when we pith it for a classroom demonstration, but
are we being cruel? For a small but vocal minority, the answer in an unequivocal
"yes." For the majority, the answer is not so clear-cut, and this is where the
concept of justified and unjustified exploitation is more useful in making social
cost-benefit decisions. Education plays an important role in developing social
consensus on such value-laden issues (Hoskins 1979; Kieffer 1979); but, to
date, most educational efforts present very limited concepts of human/animal
interactions. Animals are illustrated in their role in nature, or as anthropomor-
phized beings that behave and act very much like humans, or as useful didactic
tools, especially in interactive situations between student and animal. Live
animal studies are popular with teachers and students because the animal's
immediate reaction to a stimulus provides positive reinforcement of learning
and serves to stimulate interest and hold attention. However, maintenance of
the animals in the classroom is not so welcome a past-time and neglect, particularly over holiday periods, can be a problem.

There is a difference between the study of animals in humane education   3
curricula in elementary grades and the use of animals in biology classes. In
humane education classes, the animals are used to develop positive feelings
and a humanitarian ethic (be kind, do not be cruel) towards our fellow creatures. In the biology classroom, the animal is perceived as a model of living
processes and the prevailing attitude is that one should maintain a distance
from the object of study so that emotions and sentiment do not interfere with
accurate observation and the collection of data. Unfortunately, it is all too easy
for the student to confuse scientific and humane purposes. Some students
perceive the mere manipulation of an animal as "scientific" and the presence
of an ethical concern for the animal's fate as emotional, unscientific, and, hence,
undesirable.

Because many students become preoccupied with the mechanical elements   4
of animal experimentation—rather than developing the self-critical and intui-
tive skills that are the basis of top-flight research—animal welfare advocates
have raised questions about the use of vertebrates in school projects that do
(or could) involve pain and/or distress. In contrast, the supporters of animal
research point to the need to motivate, encourage, and nurture students who
show an interest in animal research so that they will pursue biomedical careers.
Unfortunately, many of the arguments for or against the use of vertebrates in
such projects are anecdotal and scattered. Well-designed studies to determine
the truth or falsity of these assertions are few and far between. In an attempt
to clarify the issues and, perhaps elucidate a few answers, a conference was
organized on the use of vertebrates in secondary school and science fairs by
the Institute for the Study of Animal Problems in connection with the Myrin
Institute (McGiffin and Brownley 1980).

There were approximately forty invited participants, representing all view-   5
points and including teachers, education researchers, biomedical scientists,
science education administrators, and animal welfare advocates. In spite of the
range of viewpoints and professions, the conference reached a relatively broad
consensus when all present agreed that the study of live animals is an essential
feature of biology education. This was perhaps best expressed by Mayer (1980)
when he stated that he believed "in using animals to inculcate the kind of
affective objectives that will stand the students in good stead, not only in the
classroom, but what is more important outside the classroom as well. Only then
will they come to develop that respect for all living things we must have if our
current environment is to remain unscathed for future generations to possess
and enjoy."

Another speaker stressed that animal studies involving hands-on experience   6
provided a quality of perception that could not be obtained by other teaching
methods but stressed that little evidence exists to demonstrate that this qualitative experience is necessary to develop biological literacy (Kelly 1980). Because few high school students will go on to further biological studies, the
school biology curriculum should aim more at providing the general populace
with an understanding of and respect for living things than the development of
such inert knowledge as techniques for dissecting rats or frogs. In fact, it is

important that students are taught not only biological concepts, but also the place animals play in human psychological and cultural experiences. For example, the cultivation of empathy for animals does not simply mean describing what an animal does, one must also be able to predict what it might do in given circumstances (Kelly 1980). This requires a perspective on the animal that combines realism with respect and that is neither cold-bloodedly scientific nor overly emotional.

The participants seemed to agree in general terms with much of the argu- 7 ment relating to the objectives of biology education and the place of live animals within those objectives, though pleas were made for in-service training in animal care for biology teachers. The major disagreements came in the last part of the conference in the discussion on science fairs and extra-curricular biology projects. Those involved in the organization and operation of the International Science and Engineering Fair (ISEF) program strongly supported the right of accomplished students to explore more sophisticated techniques in animal research. On the other side, many of the participants argued that high school students too rarely understood what they were doing to be allowed to conduct unsupervised research projects on animals. In fact, it was the question of supervision that was central to the whole debate because the ISEF program relies so heavily on adult supervisors. Unfortunately, several of the participants with extensive experience in biology education and science fairs disagreed strongly with the ISEF organizers that the quality of adult supervision was adequate or that supervision safeguards against abuse (Mayer 1980; Rowsell 1980). For example, Mayer commented that a good deal of "animal experimentation is not only beyond the skill of the student but frequently beyond the skill of the teacher. It ends up teaching no lesson except that animals suffer and die in inexperienced hands."

Several attempts were made to reach a compromise position regarding proj- 8 ects for science fairs that involved significant manipulation of the animal or its environment. However, the suggestion that such research projects should only be conducted in registered research facilities under the direct supervision of a trained biomedical research scientist did not find favor with the ISEF organizers. They believed this would discriminate against students who were not close to, and hence unable to use, such facilities. However, recent developments in the National Association of Biology Teachers may well render such debate academic. The Executive Board of the NABT adopted a policy that included an admonition that students doing projects with vertebrate animals should not undertake experimental procedures that would subject animals to pain or discomfort or interfere with their health in any way (NABT 1980). The National Science Teachers Association has also adopted a new code of practice on live animals that includes similar wording. If these codes are widely publicized and strictly enforced, the Dr. Kildare syndrome should disappear from the biology classroom.

However, a number of pressing problems remain that the conference could 9 not address. For example, there is a need for research on the development of student attitudes and the extent to which, and manner in which, animal studies affect such attitudes. Perhaps the most pressing need at this point, is for teachers and educational organizations to recognize that animals are sentient beings and that we have a duty to portray them as something other than disposable biological tools, especially when they are being used in the biology classroom.

REFERENCES*

Clark, S.R.L. 1977. *The moral status of animals*. Oxford: Oxford University Press.

Fox, M.W., and Rowan, A.N. 1980. A background to the journal and delineation of its scope and goals. *International Journal for the Study of Animal Problems* 1(1):2.

Frey, R.G. 1980. *Interests and rights: The case against animals*. Oxford: Clarendon Press.

Hoskins, B.B. 1979. Sensitizing introductory biology students to bioethics issues. *American Biology Teacher* 41(3):151.

Kelly, P.J. 1980. Understanding and attitudes derived from the use of animals in schools. In McGiffin, H.L., and Brownley, N.L., *Animals in education*.

Kieffer, G.H. 1979. Can bioethics be taught. *American Biology Teacher* 41(3):176.

McGiffin, H.L. and Brownley, N.L. 1980. *Animals in education: The use of animals in high school biology classes and science fairs*. Washington, D.C.: Institute for the Study of Animal Problems.

Mayer, W.V. 1980. Objectives of animal use in biology classes. In McGiffin, H.L., and Brownley, N.L. *Animals in education*.

National Association of Biology Teachers. 1980. NABT guidelines for the use of live animals at the pre-university level. *American Biology Teacher* 41(7):426.

Regan, T. and Singer, P. (eds.) 1976. *Animal rights and human obligations*. Englewood Cliffs, New Jersey: Prentice-Hall.

Rowsell, H.C. 1980. High school science fairs: Evaluation of live animal experimentation—the Canadian experience. In McGiffin. H.L., and Brownley, N.L., *Animals in education*.

Singer, P. 1975. *Animal liberation*. New York: New York Review.

* This essay uses the author/date system for documentation recommended by the University of Chicago. It is very similar to the APA author/year system. The differences are that Chicago-style parenthetical references do not have a comma between the author and the date. For works with more than one author, "and" takes the place of the ampersand. In the reference list, Chicago does not require parentheses around the date of publication. Also, the volume and issue number are separated from the page reference by a colon rather than a comma [editor's note].

QUESTIONS FOR MEANING

1. What are the benefits of using animals in the classroom? What problems regarding their use need to be resolved?
2. Why are the concepts of "kindness" and "cruelty" inadequate for determining the use that is made of animals in education?
3. How should animals be used in the elementary and secondary school classroom? Why are guidelines for using animals in science fairs and other extracurricular projects difficult to determine?
4. *Dr. Kildare* was a popular television show in the 1960s, starring Richard Chamberlain as an idealistic young doctor. What do you think Andrew Rowan means by the "Dr. Kildare syndrome"?
5. Vocabulary: entrenched (1), consensus (2), didactic (2), unscathed (5), empathy (6), admonition (8), and sentient (9).

QUESTIONS ABOUT STRATEGY

1. Is this an argument or simply a report? What is Rowan's conclusion? Could this conclusion become the premise for another essay?
2. Rowan wants us to consider types of animal experimentation that occur within our schools. After reading this essay, is there anything else that you wish you'd been told? How were animals used in your high school? How are they being used in the school you are attending now?

PETER SINGER
All Animals Are Equal[1]

Born in Melbourne, Peter Singer (b. 1946) taught philosophy at University College, Oxford, and at New York University before returning to Australia, where he is now Professor of Philosophy and Director of the Centre of Human Bioethics at Monash University. His books include Democracy and Disobedience *(1974),* Practical Ethics *(1979),* Marx *(1980),* The Expanding Circle *(1981), and* The Reproduction Revolution: New Ways of Making Babies *(1982). He is best known for his work on behalf of animal rights. If the rise of the animal liberation movement can be traced to any single work it would be Singer's 1973 essay "All Animals Are Equal." Singer subsequently expanded his essay into a book,* Animal Liberation: A New Ethic for Our Treatment of Animals *(1975), and coedited an anthology of essays on this subject,* Animal Rights and Human Obligations *(1975). As you read the original essay and consider its careful reasoning, you should be able to recognize that Singer's argument deserves to be taken seriously.*

In recent years a number of oppressed groups have campaigned vigorously for equality. The classic instance is the Black Liberation movement, which demands an end to the prejudice and discrimination that has made blacks second-class citizens. The immediate appeal of the black liberation movement and its initial, if limited success made it a model for other oppressed groups to follow. We became familiar with liberation movements for Spanish-Americans, gay people, and a variety of other minorities. When a majority group—women—began their campaign, some thought we had come to the end of the road. Discrimination on the basis of sex, it has been said, is the last universally accepted form of discrimination, practiced without secrecy or pretense even in those liberal circles that have long prided themselves on their freedom from prejudice against racial minorities.

One should always be wary of talking of "the last remaining form of discrimination." If we have learnt anything from the liberation movements, we should have learnt how difficult it is to be aware of latent prejudice in our attitudes to particular groups until this prejudice is forcefully pointed out.

A liberation movement demands an expansion of our moral horizons and an extension or reinterpretation of the basic moral principle of equality. Practices that were previously regarded as natural and inevitable come to be seen as the result of an unjustifiable prejudice. Who can say with confidence that all his or her attitudes and practices are beyond criticism? If we wish to avoid being numbered amongst the oppressors, we must be prepared to re-think even our most fundamental attitudes. We need to consider them from the point of view of those most disadvantaged by our attitudes, and the practices that follow from these attitudes. If we can make this unaccustomed mental switch we may discover a pattern in our attitudes and practices that consistently operates so as to benefit one group—usually the one to which we ourselves belong—at the expense of another. In this way we may come to see that there is a case for a new liberation movement. My aim is to advocate that we make this mental switch in respect of our attitudes and practices towards a very large group of beings: members of species other than our own—or, as we popularly though misleadingly call them, animals. In other words, I am urging that we extend to other species the basic principle of equality that most of us recognise should be extended to all members of our own species.

All this may sound a little far-fetched, more like a parody of other liberation   4 movements than a serious objective. In fact, in the past the idea of "The Rights of Animals" really has been used to parody the case for women's rights. When Mary Wollstonecroft, a forerunner of later feminists, published her *Vindication of the Rights of Women* in 1792, her ideas were widely regarded as absurd, and they were satirized in an anonymous publication entitled *A Vindication of the Rights of Brutes*. The author of this satire (actually Thomas Taylor, a distinguished Cambridge philosopher) tried to refute Wollstonecroft's reasonings by showing that they could be carried one stage further. If sound when applied to women, why should the arguments not be applied to dogs, cats and horses? They seemed to hold equally well for these "brutes"; yet to hold that brutes had rights was manifestly absurd; therefore the reasoning by which this conclusion had been reached must be unsound, and if unsound when applied to brutes, it must also be unsound when applied to women, since the very same arguments had been used in each case.

One way in which we might reply to this argument is by saying that the case   5 for equality between men and women cannot validly be extended to non-human animals. Women have a right to vote, for instance, because they are just as capable of making rational decisions as men are; dogs, on the other hand, are incapable of understanding the significance of voting, so they cannot have the right to vote. There are many other obvious ways in which men and women resemble each other closely, while humans and other animals differ greatly. So, it might be said, men and women are similar beings, and should have equal rights, while humans and non-humans are different and should not have equal rights.

The thought behind this reply to Taylor's analogy is correct up to a point,   6 but it does not go far enough. There *are* important differences between humans and other animals, and these differences must give rise to *some* differences in the rights that each have. Recognizing this obvious fact, however, is no barrier to the case for extending the basic principle of equality to non-human animals. The differences that exist between men and women are equally undeniable, and the supporters of Women's Liberation are aware that these differences may give rise to different rights. Many feminists hold that women have the right to an abortion on request. It does not follow that since these same people are campaigning for equality between men and women they must support the right of men to have abortions too. Since a man cannot have an abortion, it is meaningless to talk of his right to have one. Since a pig can't vote, it is meaningless to talk of its right to vote. There is no reason why either Women's Liberation or Animal Liberation should get involved in such nonsense. The extension of the basic principle of equality from one group to another does not imply that we must treat both groups in exactly the same way, or grant exactly the same rights to both groups. Whether we should do so will depend on the nature of the members of the two groups. The basic principle of equality, I shall argue, is equality of consideration; and equal consideration for different beings may lead to different treatment and different rights.

So there is a different way of replying to Taylor's attempt to parody   7
Wollstonecroft's arguments, a way which does not deny the differences be-tween humans and non-humans, but goes more deeply into the question of equality, and concludes by finding nothing absurd in the idea that the basic principle of equality applies to so-called "brutes". I believe that we reach this conclusion if we examine the basis on which our opposition to discrimination on grounds of race or sex ultimately rests. We will then see that we would be on shaky ground if we were to demand equality for blacks, women, and other groups of oppressed humans while denying equal consideration to non-humans.

When we say that all human beings, whatever their race, creed or sex, are   8
equal, what is it that we are asserting? Those who wish to defend a hierarchical, inegalitarian society have often pointed out that by whatever test we choose, it simply is not true that all humans are equal. Like it or not, we must face the fact that humans come in different shapes and sizes; they come with differing moral capacities, differing intellectual abilities, differing amounts of benevolent feeling and sensitivity to the needs of others, differing abilities to communicate effectively, and differing capacities to experience pleasure and pain. In short, if the demand for equality were based on the actual equality of all human beings, we would have to stop demanding equality. It would be an unjustifiable demand.

Still, one might cling to the view that the demand for equality among human   9
beings is based on the actual equality of the different races and sexes. Although humans differ as individuals in various ways, there are no differences between the races and sexes *as such*. From the mere fact that a person is black, or a woman, we cannot infer anything else about that person. This, it may be said, is what is wrong with racism and sexism. The white racist claims that whites are superior to blacks, but this is false—although there are differences between individuals, some blacks are superior to some whites in all of the capacities and abilities that could conceivably be relevant. The opponent of sexism would say the same: a person's sex is no guide to his or her abilities, and this is why it is unjustifiable to discriminate on the basis of sex.

This is a possible line of objection to racial and sexual discrimination. It is   10
not, however, the way that someone really concerned about equality would choose, because taking this line could, in some circumstances, force one to accept a most inegalitarian society. The fact that humans differ as individuals, rather than as races or sexes, is a valid reply to someone who defends a hier-archical society like, say, South Africa, in which all whites are superior in status to all blacks. The existence of individual variations that cut across the lines of race or sex, however, provides us with no defence at all against a more sophis-ticated opponent of equality, one who proposes that, say, the interests of those with I.Q. ratings above 100 be preferred to the interests of those I.Q.s below 100. Would a hierarchical society of this sort really be so much better than one

based on race or sex? I think not. But if we tie the moral principle of equality to the factual equality of the different races or sexes, taken as a whole, our opposition to racism and sexism does not provide us with any basis for objecting to this kind of inegalitarianism.

There is a second important reason why we ought not to base our opposition to racism and sexism on any kind of factual equality, even the limited kind asserts that variations in capacities and abilities are spread evenly between the different races and sexes: we can have no absolute guarantee that these abilities and capacities really are distributed evenly, without regard to race or sex, among human beings. So far as actual abilities are concerned, there do seem to be certain measurable differences between both races and sexes. These differences do not, of course, appear in each case, but only when averages are taken. More important still, we do not yet know how much of these differences is really due to the different genetic endowments of the various races and sexes, and how much is due to environmental differences that are the result of past and continuing discrimination. Perhaps all of the important differences will eventually prove to be environmental rather than genetic. Anyone opposed to racism and sexism will certainly hope that this will be so, for it will make the task of ending discrimination a lot easier; nevertheless it would be dangerous to rest the case against racism and sexism on the belief that all significant differences are environmental in origin. The opponent of, say, racism who takes this line will be unable to avoid conceding that if differences in ability did after all prove to have some genetic connection with race, racism would in some way be defensible. 11

It would be folly for the opponent of racism to stake his whole case on a dogmatic commitment to one particular outcome of a difficult scientific issue which is still a long way from being settled. While attempts to prove that differences in certain selected abilities between races and sexes are primarily genetic in origin have certainly not been conclusive, the same must be said of attempts to prove that these differences are largely the result of environment. At this stage of the investigation we cannot be certain which view is correct, however much we may hope it is the latter. 12

Fortunately, there is no need to pin the case for equality to one particular outcome of this scientific investigation. The appropriate response to those who claim to have found evidence of genetically-based differences in ability between the races or sexes is not to stick to the belief that the genetic explanation must be wrong, whatever evidence to the contrary may turn up: instead we should make it quite clear that the claim to equality does not depend on intelligence, moral capacity, physical strength, or similar matters of fact. Equality is a moral ideal, not a simple assertion of fact. There is no logically compelling reason for assuming that a factual difference in ability between two people justifies any difference in the amount of consideration we give to satisfying their needs and interests. The principle of the equality of human beings is not a description of an alleged actual equality among humans: it is a prescription of how we should treat humans. 13

Jeremy Bentham incorporated the essential basis of moral equality into his 14 utilitarian system of ethics in the formula: "Each to count for one and none for more than one." In other words, the interests of every being affected by an action are to be taken into account and given the same weight as the like interests of any other being. A later utilitarian, Henry Sidgwick, put the point in this way: "The good of any one individual is of no more importance, from the point of view (if I may say so) of the Universe, than the good of any other."[2] More recently, the leading figures in contemporary moral philosophy have shown a great deal of agreement in specifying as a fundamental presupposition of their moral theories some similar requirement which operates so as to give everyone's interests equal consideration—although they cannot agree on how this requirement is best formulated.[3]

It is an implication of this principle of equality that our concern for others   15
ought not to depend on what they are like, or what abilities they possess—although precisely what this concern requires us to do may vary according to the characteristics of those affected by what we do. It is on this basis that the case against racism and the case against sexism must both ultimately rest; and it is in accordance with this principle that speciesism is also to be condemned. If possessing a higher degree of intelligence does not entitle one human to use another for his own ends, how can it entitle humans to exploit non-humans?

Many philosophers have proposed the principle of equal consideration of   16
interests, in some form or other, as a basic moral principle; but, as we shall see in more detail shortly, not many of them have recognised that this principle applies to members of other species as well as to our own. Bentham was one of the few who did realize this. In a forward-looking passage, written at a time when black slaves in the British dominions were still being treated much as we now treat non-human animals, Bentham wrote:

> The day *may* come when the rest of the animal creation may acquire those rights which never could have been witholden from them but by the hand of tyranny. The French have already discovered that the blackness of the skin is no reason why a human being should be abandoned without redress to the caprice of a tormentor. It may one day come to be recognised that the number of the legs, the villosity of the skin, or the termination of the *os sacrum*, are reasons equally insufficient for abandoning a sensitive being to the same fate. What else is it that should trace the insuperable line? Is it the faculty of reason, or perhaps the faculty of discourse? But a full-grown horse or dog is beyond comparison a more rational, as well as a more conversable animal, than an infant of a day, or a week, or even a month, old. But suppose they were otherwise, what would it avail? The question is not, Can they reason? nor Can they *talk*? but, *Can they suffer*?[4]

In this passage Bentham points to the capacity for suffering as the vital   17
characteristic that gives a being the right to equal consideration. The capacity for suffering—or more strictly, for suffering and/or enjoyment or happiness—is not just another characteristic like the capacity for language, or for higher mathematics. Bentham is not saying that those who try to mark "the insuperable line" that determines whether the interests of a being should be considered happen to have selected the wrong characteristic. The capacity for suffering

and enjoying things is a pre-requisite for having interests at all, a condition that must be satisfied before we can speak of interests in any meaningful way. It would be nonsense to say that it was not in the interests of a stone to be kicked along the road by a schoolboy. A stone does not have interests because it cannot suffer. Nothing that we can do to it could possibly make any difference to its welfare. A mouse, on the other hand, does have an interest in not being tormented, because it will suffer if it is.

If a being suffers, there can be no moral justification for refusing to take that   18
suffering into consideration. No matter what the nature of the being, the principle of equality requires that its suffering be counted equally with the like suffering—in so far as rough comparisons can be made—of any other being. If a being is not capable of suffering, or of experiencing enjoyment or happiness, there is nothing to be taken into account. This is why the limit of sentience (using the term as a convenient, if not strictly accurate, shorthand for the capacity to suffer or experience enjoyment or happiness) is the only defensible boundary of concern for the interests of others. To mark this boundary by some characteristic like intelligence or rationality would be to mark it in an arbitrary way. Why not choose some other characteristic, like skin color?

The racist violates the principle of equality by giving greater weight to the   19
interests of members of his own race, when there is a clash between their interests and the interests of those of another race. Similarly the speciesist allows the interests of his own species to override the greater interests of members of other species.[5] The pattern is the same in each case. Most human beings are speciesists. I shall now very briefly describe some of the practices that show this.

For the great majority of human beings, especially in urban, industrialized   20
societies, the most direct form of contact with members of other species is at meal-times: we eat them. In doing so we treat them purely as means to our ends. We regard their life and well-being as subordinate to our taste for a particular kind of dish. I say "taste" deliberately—this is purely a matter of pleasing our palate. There can be no defense of eating flesh in terms of satisfying nutritional needs, since it has been established beyond doubt that we could satisfy our need for protein and other essential nutrients far more efficiently with a diet that replaced animal flesh by soy beans, or products derived from soy beans, and other high-protein vegetable products.[6]

It is not merely the act of killing that indicates what we are ready to do to   21
other species in order to gratify our tastes. The suffering we inflict on the animals while they are alive is perhaps an even clearer indication of our speciesism than the fact that we are prepared to kill them.[7] In order to have meat on the table at a price that people can afford, our society tolerates methods of meat production that confine sentient animals in cramped, unsuitable conditions for the entire durations of their lives. Animals are treated like machines that convert fodder into flesh, and any innovation that results in a higher "conversion ratio" is liable to be adopted. As one authority on the subject has said, "cruelty is acknowledged only when profitability ceases".[8] So hens are crowded four or five to a cage with a floor area of twenty inches by eighteen

inches, or around the size of a single page of the *New York Times*. The cages have wire floors, since this reduces cleaning costs, though wire is unsuitable for the hens' feet; the floors slope, since this makes the eggs roll down for easy collection, although this makes it difficult for the hens to rest comfortably. In these conditions all the birds' natural instincts are thwarted: they cannot stretch their wings fully, walk freely, dust-bathe, scratch the ground, or build a nest. Although they have never known other conditions, observers have noticed that the birds vainly try to perform these actions. Frustrated at their inability to do so, they often develop what farmers call "vices," and peck each other to death. To prevent this, the beaks of young birds are often cut off.

22 This kind of treatment is not limited to poultry. Pigs are now also being reared in cages inside sheds. These animals are comparable to dogs in intelligence, and need a varied, stimulating environment if they are not to suffer from stress and boredom. Anyone who kept a dog in the way in which pigs are frequently kept would be liable to prosecution, in England at least, but because our interest in exploiting pigs is greater than our interest in exploiting dogs, we object to cruelty to dogs while consuming the produce of cruelty to pigs. Of the other animals, the condition of veal calves is perhaps worst of all, since these animals are so closely confined that they cannot even turn around or get up and lie down freely. In this way they do not develop unpalatable muscle. They are also made anaemic and kept short of roughage, to keep their flesh pale, since white veal fetches a higher price; as a result they develop a craving for iron and roughage, and have been observed to gnaw wood off the sides of their stalls, and lick greedily at any rusty hinge that is within reach.

23 Since, as I have said, none of these practices cater for anything more than our pleasures of taste, our practice of rearing and killing other animals in order to eat them is a clear instance of the sacrifice of the most important interests of other beings in order to satisfy trivial interests of our own. To avoid species-ism we must stop this practice, and each of us has a moral obligation to cease supporting the practice. Our custom is all the support that the meat-industry needs. The decision to cease giving it that support may be difficult, but it is no more difficult than it would have been for a white Southerner to go against the traditions of his society and free his slaves; if we do not change our dietary habits, how can we censure those slaveholders who would not change their own way of living?

24 The same form of discrimination may be observed in the widespread practice of experimenting on other species in order to see if certain substances are safe for human beings, or to test some psychological theory about the effect of severe punishment on learning, or to try out various new compounds just in case something turns up. People sometimes think that all this experimentation is for vital medical purposes, and so will reduce suffering overall. This comfortable belief is very wide of the mark. Drug companies test new shampoos and cosmetics that they are intending to put on the market by dropping them into the eyes of rabbits, held open by metal clips, in order to observe what damage results. Food additives, like artificial colorings and preservatives, are tested by what is known as the "LD_{50}"—a test designed to find the level of consumption

at which 50% of a group of animals will die. In the process, nearly all of the animals are made very sick before some finally die, and others pull through. If the substance is relatively harmless, as it often is, huge doses have to be force-fed to the animals, until in some cases sheer volume or concentration of the substance causes death.

Much of this pointless cruelty goes on in the universities. In many areas of   25
science, non-human animals are regarded as an item of laboratory equipment, to be used and expended as desired. In psychology laboratories experimenters devise endless variations and repetitions of experiments that were of little value in the first place. To quote just one example, from the experimenter's own account in a psychology journal: at the University of Pennsylvania, Perrin S. Cohen hung six dogs in hammocks with electrodes taped to their hind feet. Electric shock of varying intensity was then administered through the electrodes. If the dog learnt to press its head against a panel on the left, the shock was turned off, but otherwise it remained on indefinitely. Three of the dogs, however, were required to wait periods varying from 2 to 7 seconds while being shocked before making the response that turned off the current. If they failed to wait, they received further shocks. Each dog was given from 26 to 46 "sessions" in the hammock, each session consisting of 80 "trials" or shocks, administered at intervals of one minute. The experimenter reported that the dogs, who were unable to move in the hammock, barked or bobbed their heads when the current was applied. The reported findings of the experiment were that there was a delay in the dogs' responses that increased proportionately to the time the dogs were required to endure the shock, but a gradual increase in the intensity of the shock had no systematic effect in the timing of the response. The experiment was funded by the National Institutes of Health, and the United States Public Health Service.[9]

In this example, and countless cases like it, the possible benefits to man-   26
kind are either non-existent or fantastically remote; while the certain losses to members of other species are very real. This is, again, a clear indication of speciesism.

In the past, argument about vivisection has often missed this point, because   27
it has been put in absolutist terms: would the abolitionist be prepared to let thousands die if they could be saved by experimenting on a single animal? The way to reply to this purely hypothetical question is to pose another: would the experimenter be prepared to perform his experiment on an orphaned human infant, if that were the only way to save many lives? (I say "orphan" to avoid the complication of parental feelings, although in doing so I am being overfair to the experimenter, since the nonhuman subjects of experiments are not orphans.) If the experimenter is not prepared to use an orphaned human infant, then his readiness to use nonhumans is simple discrimination, since adult apes, cats, mice and other mammals are more aware of what is happening to them, more self-directing and, so far as we can tell, at least as sensitive to pain, as any human infant. There seems to be no relevant characteristic that human infants possess that adult mammals do not have to the same or a higher degree. (Someone might try to argue that what makes it wrong to experiment on a

human infant is that the infant will, in time and if left alone, develop into more than the nonhuman, but one would then, to be consistent, have to oppose abortion, since the fetus has the same potential as the infant—indeed, even contraception and abstinence might be wrong on this ground, since the egg and sperm, considered jointly, also have the same potential. In any case, this argument still gives us no reason for selecting a nonhuman, rather than a human with severe and irreversible brain damage, as the subject for our experiments.)

The experimenter, then, shows a bias in favor of his own species whenever he carries out an experiment on a nonhuman for a purpose that he would not think justified him in using a human being at an equal or lower level of sentience, awareness, ability to be self-directing, etc. No one familiar with the kind of results yielded by most experiments on animals can have the slightest doubt that if this bias were eliminated the number of experiments performed would be a minute fraction of the number performed today. 28

Experimenting on animals, and eating their flesh, are perhaps the two major forms of speciesism in our society. By comparison, the third and last form of speciesism is so minor as to be insignificant, but it is perhaps of some special interest to those for whom this paper was written. I am referring to speciesism in contemporary philosophy. 29

Philosophy ought to question the basic assumptions of the age. Thinking through, critically and carefully, what most people take for granted is, I believe, the chief task of philosophy, and it is this task that makes philosophy a worthwhile activity. Regrettably, philosophy does not always live up to its historic role. Philosophers are human beings and they are subject to all the preconceptions of the society to which they belong. Sometimes they succeed in breaking free of the prevailing ideology: more often they become its most sophisticated defenders. So, in this case, philosophy as practiced in the universities today does not challenge anyone's preconceptions about our relations with other species. By their writings, those philosophers who tackle problems that touch upon the issue reveal that they make the same unquestioned assumptions as most other humans, and what they say tends to confirm the reader in his or her comfortable speciesist habits. 30

I could illustrate this claim by referring to the writings of philosophers in various fields—for instance, the attempts that have been made by those interested in rights to draw the boundary of the sphere of rights so that it runs parallel to the biological boundaries of the species *homo sapiens*, including infants and even mental defectives, but excluding those other beings of equal or greater capacity who are so useful to us at mealtimes and in our laboratories. I think it would be a more appropriate conclusion to this paper, however, if I concentrated on the problem with which we have been centrally concerned, the problem of equality. 31

It is significant that the problem of equality, in moral and political philosophy, is invariably formulated in terms of human equality. The effect of this is that the question of the equality of other animals does not confront the philosopher, or student, as an issue in itself—and this is already an indication of the failure of philosophy to challenge accepted beliefs. Still, philosophers have found it 32 difficult to discuss the issue of human equality without raising, in a paragraph or two, the question of the status of other animals. The reason for this, which should be apparent from what I have said already, is that if humans are to be regarded as equal to one another, we need some sense of "equal" that does not require any actual, descriptive equality of capacities, talents or other qualities. If equality is to be related to any actual characteristics of humans, these characteristics must be some lowest common denominator, pitched so low that no human lacks them—but then the philosopher comes up against the catch that any such set of characteristics which covers *all* humans will not be possessed *only by humans*. In other words, it turns out that in the only sense in which we can truly say, as an assertion of fact, that all humans are equal, at least some members of other species are also equal—equal, that is, to each other and to humans. If, on the other hand, we regard the statement "All humans are equal" in some non-factual way, perhaps as a prescription, then, as I have already argued, it is even more difficult to exclude non-humans from the sphere of equality.

This result is not what the egalitarian philosopher originally intended to assert. Instead of accepting the radical outcome to which their own reasonings naturally point, however, most philosophers try to reconcile their beliefs in human equality and animal inequality by arguments that can only be described as devious. 33

As a first example, I take William Frankena's well-known article "The Concept of Social Justice."[10] Frankena opposes the idea of basing justice on merit, because he sees that this could lead to highly inegalitarian results. Instead he proposes the principle that: 34

> ... all men are to be treated as equals, not because they are equal, in any respect but simply because they are human. They are human because they have emotions and desires, and are able to think, and hence are capable of enjoying a good life in a sense in which other animals are not.

But what is this capacity to enjoy the good life which all humans have, but no other animals? Other animals have emotions and desires, and appear to be capable of enjoying a good life. We may doubt that they can think—although the behavior of some apes, dolphins and even dogs suggest that some of them can—but what is the relevance of thinking? Frankena goes on to admit that by "the good life" he means "not so much the morally good life as the happy or satisfactory life," so thought would appear to be unnecessary for enjoying the good life; in fact to emphasise the need for thought would make difficulties for the egalitarian since only some people are capable of leading intellectually satisfying lives, or morally good lives. This makes it difficult to see what Frankena's principle of equality has to do with simply being *human*. Surely every sentient being is capable of leading a life that is happier or less miserable than some alternative life, and hence has a claim to be taken into account. In this respect the distinction between humans and non-humans is not a sharp 35 division, but rather a continuum along which we move gradually, and with overlaps between the species, from simple capacities for enjoyment and satisfaction, or pain and suffering, to more complex ones.

Faced with a situation in which they see a need for some basis for the moral gulf that is commonly thought to separate humans and animals, but can find no concrete difference that will do the job without undermining the equality of humans, philosophers tend to waffle. They resort to high-sounding phrases like "the intrinsic dignity of the human individual;"[11] They talk of the "intrinsic worth of all men" as if men (humans?) had some worth that other beings did not,[12] or they say that humans, and only humans, are "ends in themselves" while "everything other than a person can only have value for a person."[13]

This idea of a distinctive human dignity and worth has a long history; it can be traced back directly to the Renaissance humanists, for instance to Pico della Mirandola's *Oration on the Dignity of Man*. Pico and other humanists based their estimate of human dignity on the idea that man possessed the central, pivotal position in the "Great Chain of Being" that led from the lowliest forms of matter to God himself; this view of the universe, in turn, goes back to both classical and Judeo-Christian doctrines. Contemporary philosophers have cast off these metaphysical and religious shackles and freely invoke the dignity of mankind without needing to justify the idea at all. Why should we not attribute "intrinsic dignity" or "intrinsic worth" to ourselves? Fellow-humans are unlikely to reject the accolades we so generously bestow on them, and those to whom we deny the honor are unable to object. Indeed, when one thinks only of humans, it can be very liberal, very progressive, to talk of the dignity of all human beings. In so doing, we implicitly condemn slavery, racism, and other violations of human rights. We admit that we ourselves are in some fundamental sense on a par with the poorest, most ignorant members of our own species. It is only when we think of humans as no more than a small sub-group of all the beings that inhabit our planet that we may realize that in elevating our own species we are at the same time lowering the relative status of all other species.

The truth is that the appeal to the intrinsic dignity of human beings appears to solve the egalitarian's problems only as long as it goes unchallenged. Once we ask *why* it should be that all humans—including infants, mental defectives, psychopaths, Hitler, Stalin and the rest—have some kind of dignity or worth that no elephant, pig or chimpanzee can ever achieve, we see that this question is as difficult to answer as our original request for some relevant fact that justifies the inequality of humans and other animals. In fact, these two questions are really one: talk of intrinsic dignity or moral worth only takes the problem back one step, because any satisfactory defence of the claim that all and only humans have intrinsic dignity would need to refer to some relevant capacities or characteristics that all and only humans possess. Philosophers frequently introduce ideas of dignity, respect and worth at the point at which other reasons appear to be lacking, but this is hardly good enough. Fine phrases are the last resource of those who have run out of arguments.

In case there are those who still think it may be possible to find some relevant characteristic that distinguishes all humans from all members of other species,

I shall refer again, before I conclude, to the existence of some humans who quite clearly are below the level of awareness, self-consciousness, intelligence, and sentience, of many non-humans. I am thinking of humans with severe and irreparable brain damage, and also of infant humans. To avoid the complication of the relevance of a being's potential, however, I shall henceforth concentrate on permanently retarded humans.

Philosophers who set out to find a characteristic that will distinguish humans from other animals rarely take the course of abandoning these groups of humans by lumping them in with the other animals. It is easy to see why they do not. To take this line without re-thinking our attitudes to other animals would entail that we have the right to perform painful experiments on retarded humans for trivial reasons; similarly it would follow that we had the right to rear and kill these humans for food. To most philosophers these consequences are as unacceptable as the view that we should stop treating non-humans in this way.   40

Of course, when discussing the problem of equality it is possible to ignore the problem of mental defectives, or brush it aside as if somehow insignificant.[14] This is the easiest way out. What else remains? My final example of speciesism in contemporary philosophy has been selected to show what happens when a writer is prepared to face the question of human equality and animal inequality without ignoring the existence of mental defectives, and without resorting to obscurantist mumbo-jumbo. Stanley Benn's clear and honest article "Egalitarianism and Equal Consideration of Interests"[15] fits this description.   41

Benn, after noting the usual "evident human inequalities" argues, correctly I think, for equality of consideration as the only possible basis for egalitarianism. Yet Benn, like other writers, is thinking only of "equal consideration of human interests." Benn is quite open in his defence of this restriction of equal consideration: 42

> ... not to possess human shape *is* a disqualifying condition. However faithful or intelligent a dog may be, it would be a monstrous sentimentality to attribute to him interests that could be weighed in an equal balance with those of human beings ... if, for instance, one had to decide between feeding a hungry baby or a hungry dog, anyone who chose the dog would generally be reckoned morally defective, unable to recognize a fundamental inequality of claims.
>
> This is what distinguishes our attitude to animals from our attitude to imbeciles. It would be odd to say that we ought to respect equally the dignity or personality of the imbecile and of the rational man ... but there is nothing odd about saying that we should respect their interests equally, that is, that we should give to the interests of each the same serious consideration as claims to considerations necessary for some standard of well-being that we can recognize and endorse.

Benn's statement of the basis of the consideration we should have for imbeciles seems to me correct, but why should there be any fundamental inequality of claims between a dog and a human imbecile? Benn sees that if equal consid-   43 eration depended on rationality, no reason could be given against using imbeciles for research purposes, as we now use dogs and guinea pigs. This will not do: "But of course we do distinguish imbeciles from animals in this regard," he says. That the common distinction is justifiable is something Benn does not question; his problem is how it is to be justified. The answer he gives is this:

> ... we respect the interests of men and give them priority over dogs not *insofar* as they are rational, but because rationality is the human norm. We say it is *unfair* to exploit the deficiencies of the imbecile who falls short of the norm, just as it would be unfair, and not just ordinarily dishonest, to steal from a blind man. If we do not think in this way about dogs, it is because we do not see the irrationality of the dog as a deficiency or a handicap, but as normal for the species. The characteristics, therefore, that distinguish the normal man from the normal dog make it intelligible for us to talk of other men having interests and capacities, and therefore claims, of precisely the same kind as we make on our own behalf. But although these characteristics may provide the point of the distinction between men and other species, they are not in fact the qualifying conditions for membership, or the distinguishing criteria of the class of morally considerable persons; and this is precisely because a man does not become a member of a different species, with its own standards of normality, by reason of not possessing these characteristics.

The final sentence of this passage gives the argument away. An imbecile, Benn concedes, may have no characteristics superior to those of a dog; nevertheless this does not make the imbecile a member of "a different species" as the dog is. *Therefore* it would be "unfair" to use the imbecile for medical research as we use the dog. But why? That the imbecile is not rational is just the way things have worked out, and the same is true of the dog—neither is any more responsible for their mental level. If it is unfair to take advantage of an isolated defect, why is it fair to take advantage of a more general limitation? I find it hard to see anything in this argument except a defence of preferring the interests of members of our own species because they are members of our own species. To those who think there might be more to it, I suggest the following mental exercise. Assume that it has been proven that there is a difference in the average, or normal, intelligence quotient for two different races, say whites and blacks. Then substitute the term "white" for every occurrence of "men" and "black" for every occurrence of "dog" in the passage quoted; and substitute "high I.Q." for "rationality" and when Benn talks of "imbeciles" replace this term by "dumb whites"—that is, whites who fall well below the normal white I.Q. score. Finally, change "species" to "race". Now re-read the passage. It has become a defence of a rigid, no-exceptions division between whites and blacks, based on I.Q. scores, *not withstanding an admitted overlap* between whites and blacks in this respect. The revised passage is, of course, outrageous, and this is not only because we have made fictitious assumptions in our substitutions. The point is that in the original passage Benn was defending a rigid division in the amount of consideration due to members of different species, despite admitted cases of overlap. If the original did not, at first reading strike us as being as outrageous as the revised version does, this is largely because although we are not racists ourselves, most of us are speciesists. Like the other articles, Benn's stands as a warning of the ease with which the best minds can fall victim to a prevailing ideology.

NOTES

1. Passages of this article appeared in a review of *Animals, Men and Morals*, edited by S. and R. Godlovitch and J. Harris (Gollancz and Taplinger, London 1972) in *The New York Review of Books*, April 5, 1973. The whole direction of my thinking on this subject I owe to talks with a number of friends in Oxford in 1970-71, especially Richard Keshen, Stanley Godlovitch, and, above all, Roslind Godlovitch.

2. *The Methods of Ethics* (7th Ed.) p. 382.

3. For example, R.M. Hare, *Freedom and Reason* (Oxford, 1963) and J. Rawls. *A Theory of Justice* (Harvard, 1972); for a brief account of the essential agreement on this issue between these and other positions, see R.M. Hare, "Rules of War and Moral Reasoning," *Philosophy and Public Affairs*, vol. I, no. 2 (1972).

4. *Introduction to the Principles of Morals and Legislation*, ch. XVII.

5. I owe the term "speciesism" to Dr. Richard Ryder.

6. In order to produce 1 lb. of protein in the form of beef or veal, we must feed 21 lbs. of protein to the animal. Other forms of livestock are slightly less inefficient, but the average ratio in the U.S. is still 1:8. It has been estimated that the amount of protein lost to humans in this way is equivalent to 90% of the annual world protein deficit. For a brief account, see Frances Moore Lappe, *Diet for a Small Planet* (Friends of The Earth/Ballantine, New York 1971) pp. 4-11.

7. Although one might think that killing a being is obviously the ultimate wrong one can do to it, I think that the infliction of suffering is a clearer indication of speciesism because it might be argued that at least part of what is wrong with killing a human is that most humans are conscious of their existence over time, and have desires and purposes that extend into the future—see, for instance, M. Tooley, "Abortion and Infanticide," *Philosophy and Public Affairs*, vol. 2, no. 1 (1972). Of course, if one took this view one would have to hold—as Tooley does—that killing a human infant or mental defective is not in itself wrong, and is less serious than killing certain higher mammals that probably do have a sense of their own existence over time.

8. Ruth Harrison, *Animal Machines* (Stuart, London, 1964). This book provides an eye-opening account of intensive farming methods for those unfamiliar with the subject.

9. *Journal of the Experimental Analysis of Behavior*, vol. 13, no. 1 (1970).

Any recent volume of this journal, or of other journals in the field, like the *Journal of Comparative and Physiological Psychology*, will contain reports of equally cruel and trivial experiments. For a fuller account, see Richard Ryder, "Experiments on Animals" in *Animals, Men and Morals*.

10. In R. Brandt (ed.) *Social Justice* (Prentice Hall, Englewood Cliffs, 1962); the passage quoted appears on p. 19.

11. Frankena, *op. cit.* p. 23.

12. H.A. Bedau, "Egalitarianism and the Idea of Equality" in *Nomos IX: Equality*, ed. J.R. Pennock and J.W. Chapman, New York 1967.

13. G. Vlastos, "Justice and Equality" in Brandt, *Social Justice*, p. 48.

14. E. G. Bernard Williams, "The Idea of Equality," in *Philosophy, Politics and Society* (second series) ed. P. Laslett and W. Runciman (Blackwell, Oxford, 1962) p. 118; J. Rawls, *A Theory of Justice*, pp. 509-10.

15. *Nomos IX: Equality*; the passages quoted are on pp. 62ff.

QUESTIONS FOR MEANING

1. What is Singer's premise in arguing that animals deserve equal consideration with humans? Why can animals be said to have "interests"? Explain what Singer means by "equality."

2. What is "speciesism," and what two forms does it most commonly take?

3. Why have philosophers traditionally argued on behalf of "human dignity"? If you reject Singer's argument that "all animals are equal," explain why human beings have more "dignity" or "worth" than nonhuman animals. Try to answer the question that Singer poses in paragraph 38: Why can "infants, mental defectives, psychopaths, Hitler, Stalin, and the rest—have some kind of dignity or worth that no elephant, pig, or chimpanzee can ever achieve"?

4. Singer challenges the argument (represented by William Frankena in paragraph 34) that the ability to think distinguishes humans from other animals. Have you ever had experience with an animal that seemed to think?

5. Singer asks, "What is the relevance of thinking?" Is this a strange question for a philosopher to ask? How important is thinking to Singer himself? Is he contradicting himself?

6. What is the role of philosophy in the modern world? What are the responsibilities of philosophers, and how should they write? What is Singer's opinion of philosophy as practiced in most universities? Do you agree? If you have ever taken a course in philosophy, what did you learn from it? Would Singer have respected your teacher?

7. Judging from this essay, what philosopher seems to have had an especially strong influence on Singer in shaping his position regarding the rights of animals?

8. Vocabulary: latent (2), advocate (3), refute (4), parody (4), hierarchical (8), folly (12), insuperable (16), waffle (36), and intrinsic (37).

QUESTIONS ABOUT STRATEGY

1. What is the function of paragraphs 1 and 2? Why does Singer wait until the end of the third paragraph before introducing the subject of "members of species other than our own—or, as we popularly though misleadingly call them, animals"? Explain why it can be misleading to call animals "animals." Why does Singer want us to reconsider our use of this term?
2. Explain the analogy that Thomas Taylor made between the rights of women and the rights of "brutes." Why does Singer go to the trouble of describing a work in which the idea of equality for women was ridiculed?
3. Singer was very much aware that he was arguing a point of view with which many people would disagree. At what points in his essay does he anticipate and respond to opposition?
4. What is the basic strategy of this argument? Where does Singer place the responsibility for assuming the burden of proof? To what extent does Singer's argument depend upon exposing the shortcomings of his opponents? If his opponents can be shown to reason badly, would it necessarily follow that Singer argues well? Distinguish between those paragraphs in which Singer analyzes the work of other philosophers and those in which he advances his own case.
5. What does this essay tell you about the type of audience Singer was writing for? What sort of political principles does Singer assume his audience shares with him? Is the logic of this argument strong enough to convince someone who did not share Singer's politics?
6. If you were to take Singer's argument and put it into the form of a syllogism, how would it read?

EDWARD C. MELBY

A Statement from the Association for Biomedical Research

Edward C. Melby, Jr. (b. 1929) is a veterinarian who received his D.V.M. from Cornell University in 1954. He was in private practice for several years before devoting himself to teaching and research. He taught laboratory animal medicine at the Johns Hopkins School of Medicine from 1962 to 1974, when he returned to Cornell as Professor of Medicine and Dean of the College of Veterinary Medicine. He is the author of the Handbook of Laboratory Animal Science, *Volumes 1–3 (1974–1976). As President of the Association for Biomedical Research, he offered the following testimony before a congressional committee in 1981, when several laws that would restrict animal-based research were under serious consideration.*

Mr. Chairman, Members of the Subcommittee, I am Edward C. Melby, Jr., 1
President of the Association for Biomedical Research. I am also Dean of the Faculty and Professor of Medicine of the College of Veterinary Medicine at Cornell University. Prior to accepting that appointment in 1974, I served 12 years as a Professor and Director of the Division of Comparative Medicine of the Johns Hopkins University School of Medicine.

The Association for Biomedical Research (ABR), established in 1979, rep- 2
resents nearly 200 universities, hospitals, medical schools, veterinary schools, research institutes, animal producers and suppliers, pharmaceutical, chemical, petroleum and contract testing companies. ABR's primary objective is to help assure the continuation of responsible biomedical research.

It is our understanding that we are here today to discuss the use of live 3
animals in medical research and laboratory testing. Perhaps one of the most significant steps taken in the past few years was the passage of the Laboratory Animal Welfare Act, Public Law 89-544, in 1966, for it marked a new era in research regulation. Amendments in 1970 as well as subsequently have broadened the Act to its present form known as the "Animal Welfare Act" and it now protects show horses, zoo and aquarium species, and other categories of animals as well as those used in laboratories. Ironically, the two largest categories of animals in the United States—largest by far—are not covered by the present Act; pet dogs and cats, and farm animals. It is important to understand this dichotomy perhaps best expressed through citing the numbers of animals involved. In FY 1980, 188,700 dogs were studied in research in the United States according to official U.S. Department of Agriculture figures. This can be compared to the over three billion—that is three billion—chickens raised for food each year in the United States or the thirteen million—that is thirteen million— dogs killed each year by public pounds, municipal animal shelters, and "humane" societies, according to reliable estimates. There are believed to be about 35 million pet dogs in the United States at any moment, yet the Animal Welfare Act does not cover them. We will return to this point in a moment. But think about those numbers because it is important to put these data into proper

perspective; 188,700 dogs studied in medicine and science compared to over thirteen million killed as unclaimed, unwanted dogs each year by towns and cities across America.

ABR was established precisely because no private, non-profit, non-governmental organization seemed to exist which would interact in *a positive way* with scientists, animal welfare organizations, science-based industries in medicine and health, universities and research institutions, and government regulators. ABR has, therefore, in its mere two years of existence, established lines of communication among these varied organizations and, in a more formal way, met with USDA officials to hold serious discussions on improving the Animal Welfare Act. These efforts are ongoing and have been very useful, we believe.

ABR here wishes to emphasize that it welcomes proposals, questions, and discussions with representatives of any interest in the field of animal use in biomedical research. Surprisingly, no animal welfare organization or "humane" society has presented any written proposal to us, nor has any legislator sought the views of the constituency ABR represents through contacting ABR. We hope such representations will be made in the future and assure the Subcommittee that ABR will respond thoughtfully and reliably to any consultation requested. We offer our services as a sounding board to all concerned with biomedical research.

The Subcommittee has expressed an interest in whether laboratory animals are studied unnecessarily or inappropriately. ABR has no reason to believe that in science as in politics or law, there is perfection. The difficulty with words like "unnecessary" or "inappropriate" is that what seems unnecessary to one person from one vantage point, may seem absolutely necessary to another from a different vantage point. Had a Pasteur or a Madam Curie in France, or a Fleming or a Lister in England, or a Salk or a DeBakey in the United States been prevented from following their studies on vaccines, X-rays, penicillin, antiseptics, polio or heart surgery because they were judged "unnecessary," these advances and concepts so taken for granted would not have been developed as they were. Verification of their results by a certain amount of replication was and is an essential part of the scientific process.

Having said that, it is clear to us that endless repetition and duplication without purpose is to be avoided. It is our opinion that the peer review system of the major granting agencies, such as the National Institutes of Health, the editorial review process for originality of thought by scientific journals, and the cost effectiveness of private industry, prevent most so-called "unnecessary" animal experiments. Those persons and organizations opposed to *all* studies of animals will, of course, consider all such studies as "unnecessary"—a view far from that of mainstream America, we believe. Nevertheless, any improvements which would prevent unnecessary experiments without preventing those which turn out, sometimes unexpectedly, to have been very necessary, would be welcome. The Association for Biomedical Research believes that none of the legislative proposals now in the Congress succeed in making this distinction, but ABR is anxious to work toward this goal.

The use of techniques labelled by some as "alternatives" to animals is as old
as chemistry, physics, astronomy and modern science itself. Recent NIH studies
have shown that roughly one third of its current budget is spent on research
using mammals and about one fourth on research using humans themselves,
the remainder being in research which studies neither people nor mammals
directly. In other words, NIH's average yearly support over the last three fiscal
years for projects which do not involve laboratory mammals constitutes 55% of
total research dollars expended. Further in FY 1980, approximately 28% of NIH
funds were committed to projects using neither humans or mammals. In dollars
this translates into $704.8 million. This, combined with the finding that animal
use declined by 40% in the decade 1968 through 1978 in the United States by
a National Research Council–Institute of Laboratory Animal Resources survey
published in 1980, must be taken by any reasonable person as strong evidence
of science incorporating non-animal techniques as soon as they become scientifically reliable. So-called "alternatives" are consistently incorporated into
research, education and testing requirements as the particular medical or scientific field warrants. In addition, the significant pressures of inflation on
scientific endeavors have made acquisition and use of animals increasingly
expensive. As a result, universities and private industry have experienced considerable motivation to replace animals with less expensive, non-animal techniques wherever possible. A significant percentage of industry's research and
development budget is dedicated to the search for in vitro techniques as standard procedures. It must be emphasized, however, that the criterion of scientific
excellence must remain the principal determinant of any research method.
Where appropriate alternatives to the use of living animals have and will continue to be developed; the benefits obtained through their precision and reproducibility certainly make alternatives a most attractive choice. Several of
the present legislative proposals before the Congress in respect to these so-
called "alternatives" are therefore redundant and, in our view, dangerous to the
conduct of science by the time-tested, scientific peer review process in this
country. The Soviet Union, it should be recalled, has still not recovered in
medicine and biology from the period of "Lysenkoism" when the government
dictated false biological information as a mandated approach to science.

The appropriate care, acquisition and maintenance of laboratory animals is
of continuing interest and concern to all responsible scientists. ABR therefore
supports efforts to amend those components of the Animal Welfare Act in need
of improvement, to which I referred earlier. Indeed, ABR would recommend
expansion of the present Act's coverage to pet dogs and cats, and those in
municipal pounds or animal shelters, whose municipalities or owning organizations receive federal funds. ABR would be pleased to interact with Congressional sponsors of bills related to animal welfare to insure participation of the
larger biomedical community, including the major research and teaching organizations and research-based industries of America.

We would be pleased to respond to any questions or comments you may
have, and hope that members of the Congress or their staff will contact our
office at any time information from the biomedical perspective is required.

As part of these hearings, we wish to offer specific comment on four bills   11
(HR 556, HR 4406, HR 930 and HR 220) now under consideration by the
Subcommittee on Science, Research and Technology. For purposes of clarity I
list these according to the specific points identified by the Committee for
review:

1. Excessive, unnecessary, uneconomic or inappropriate use of animals   12
   in current practice:

   Biomedical research institutions in this country operate under a   13
   peer review system comprised of before-the-fact reviews of applications and subsequent reviews of data and results in scientific meetings as well as by reviewers and editors of scientific journals. In 1966
   the Animal Welfare Act (Public Law 89-547) was enacted. At about
   the same time, the scientific community sponsored an independent,
   peer review accreditation program under the auspices of the American Association for Accreditation of Laboratory Animal Care which
   now accredits some 440 institutions. Institutions now follow guidelines prescribed by the NIH Office of Protection of Research Risks,
   and a signed statement by each investigator is prepared in making
   application for research funds that principles for the proper use of
   animals are being followed.

   According to studies carried out under the auspices of the National   14
   Academy of Sciences–National Research Council, reported in 1980,
   there was a 40% decrease in total animal use in the decade 1968
   through 1978. Although the reasons are varied, there is good evidence
   to indicate that the supply and use of healthier animals has reduced
   loss as well as variation in results and hence, reduced the need for
   confirmation through repetitive studies. Additionally, there has been
   the ongoing process of incorporating "new technologies" including
   tissue culture, computer modeling, in vitro diagnostic and assay in-
   strumentation and, most recently, the advent of recombinant DNA
   techniques. This has been an ongoing process. For example, records
   of the College I head indicate that tissue culture techniques were
   introduced on this campus in the mid-1940's. The very nature of
   science requires that such new technologies be implemented as soon
   as they are demonstrated to be the equal or superior to existing
   techniques. Furthermore, economic pressures require that more effective substitutions be introduced wherever possible.

2. Ways to promote more humane and appropriate use of animals, in-   15
   cluding alternatives to animal use:

   Concurrent with the enormous expansion of biomedical research   16
   following World War II, the scientific community has made a major
   commitment to the improvement of laboratory animal science.
   Indeed, an entirely new area of scientific specialization and the infrastructure to support it, has evolved to meet that need. Training programs have evolved in both the two and four year colleges to train

animal technicians and technologists; a new specialty board recognized by the American Veterinary Medical Association, the American College of Laboratory Animal Medicine, certifies veterinarians with advanced training and experience in that specialty; and most institutions provide in-house training programs for animal technicians and graduate students, many following the programs fostered by the American Association for Laboratory Animal Science. Through these and related efforts the personnel directly involved in the care and use of laboratory animals have gained significant understanding of the humane care and specialized requirements of the various animal species used.

I believe it is important to repeat observations made earlier in this testimony. So-called "alternatives" are consistently incorporated into research, education and testing requirements as the particular medical or scientific field warrants. In recent years, the significant pressures of inflation on scientific endeavors have made acquisition and use of animals increasingly expensive. As a result, universities and private industry have experienced considerable motivation to replace animals with less expensive, non-animal techniques wherever possible. It must be emphasized, however, that the criterion of scientific excellence must remain the principle determinant of any research method. Where appropriate alternatives to the use of living animals have been developed; the benefits obtained through their precision and reproducibility certainly make alternatives a most attractive choice. Both HR 930 and HR 220 have been written in such a manner as to be a constructive force and we generally support that approach. 17

3. Incentives for development of more and improved alternatives to animal use: 18

The object of all research must be that of uncovering facts and truths, regardless of the approach. In science there are enumerable "incentives for excellence and accuracy," including various awards, recognition by learned societies, research grant support, authorship of books and scientific papers and perhaps most importantly, the acceptance and recognition of one's peers. As mentioned previously, alternatives to animal use have continually been developed, accepted and implemented based upon scientific validity, improvement of effectiveness, cost reduction and efficiency. It is questionable whether or not additional "incentives" can really be granted to stimulate the development of meaningful alternatives to animal use, especially if this is carried out without reference to whether or not such methods are scientifically useful in the understanding of human or animal disease or for predicting safety of drugs. If the approach necessitates the use of animals, the scientist must be sensitive to the animal's requirements. It is our belief that the continuing progress of scientific knowledge will continue, as it has in the past, to recognize, develop and implement such alternatives without artificial stimulants. 19

4. Responses from academic, private and public research institutions to　20
problems raised by pending legislative proposals:

In reviewing the several bills now before the Congress, two are　21
particularly worthy of comment. HR 556 is, in our opinion, an intru-
sion into the scientist's ability to use a wide variety of approaches
based upon experience, experimental design and intended objectives.
To artificially require deviation from accepted scientific principles
would create a situation not unlike the Lysenko era in the Soviet
Union. As presented, the bill would mandate a wholesale diversion of
30% to 50% of *all* federal research funds from existing, peer reviewed
projects, thus jeopardizing the entire scientific research program of
the nation. As objectionable as that mandate might be, the fundamental issue with the approach taken by the bill is that it fails to recognize
innovative and creative scientific inquiry, mandating restrictions on
what have proven to be the most fruitful approaches to biological and
medical research since the advancement of the germ theory of
disease.

HR 4406 proposes to amend the existing animal welfare act in a　22
number of ways. Perhaps of greatest concern is the attempt to modify
section 3(a) which would attempt to define "pain" in animals. It has
been clearly demonstrated that the concept and interpretation of
pain is exceptionally complex and clarification is not amenable by the
sort of definition proposed. In section 10, we object strongly to the
recommendation that inspectors be given authority to "confiscate or
destroy" animals which, in the sole judgment of the inspector are
"suffering as a result of failure to comply with any provision—" unless
the institution's animal care committee is convened. In the day to day
working situation of a complex institution such as the University I
serve, such a provision for the convening of a committee for immediate action is clearly fraught with impossible problems. Furthermore,
the scientific qualifications of individual "inspectors" is and will probably always remain a questionable aspect.

5. Areas in which animal-based research or testing remains crucial to　23
protection or enhancement of human health:

This topic must be addressed in a variety of ways and to adequately　24
respond to the question would require a voluminous amount of data.
I will, therefore, limit my observations but would be pleased to provide members of the Committee with additional information should
that be helpful.

In the area of infectious disease, prior to advances in chemother-　25
apy and vaccines, such diseases were the cause of most deaths in the
industrialized world. Today, many have been reduced to the point
where infectious disease ranks among the lowest causes of death.
Biologic production and testing has always been dependent on animal
use since only the complex, biologically interrelated systems of the

whole animal can respond in a fashion indicative to that of man. Certain aspects of testing have been delegated to "alternatives" and where proven efficacious, these practices will continue and expand. Similarly, the toxic effects of many antibiotics and other chemotherapeutic agents have first been recognized through their application in animals. This method of testing is the only one endorsed by the FDA for human use and the USDA for animal use, for no acceptable alternatives currently exist which embody the total host response provided by animals. Relatively recent examples of the importance of such testings and the use of a variety of systems are found in the development of polio vaccine and the identification of thalidomide as a teratogen.

In the underdeveloped countries, many infectious diseases still   26 account for tremendous morbidity and mortality. According to the 1980 World Health Organization Summary Reports, 200,000,000 people are affected by schistosomiasis; 100,000,000 by leishumaniasis with 400,000 new cases developing annually; 300–400,000,000 cases of malaria which kills in excess of 1,000,000 children each year, and, 100,000,000 humans are affected by trypanosomiasis. It is estimated that the morbidity from these four diseases alone is four times the entire population of the United States. At the present time, there are no alternatives to the use of animals in demonstrating the host response to these infectious agents. Any severe reduction in the use of animals to continue important studies on these diseases, aimed at treatment and prevention, would severely impede the progress being made by many U.S. research institutions, including Cornell, thus prolonging the suffering and death of millions of humans throughout the world.

In the United States, hepatitis B infection remains an important   27 cause of death and illness. Recent evidence indicates that infected individuals demonstrate a very high rate of developing cancer of the liver in later life. Outside of the United States, hepatitis is a major contributor to human suffering. At the present time, Cornell University, under contract from NIH, is developing an important animal model for hepatitis B virus research and vaccine testing using the feral woodchuck, *Marmota monax*. Should attempts be made to eliminate the use of this or other valuable animal models for hepatitis B research, it will severely impact the ability to develop a protective vaccine for man.

In spite of significant progress in treatment and control, leprosy   28 remains a major world-wide disease with many cases occurring here in the United States. To date, the only method for studying the growth and establishment of infection of the causative agent is through the use of the armadillo. Continued research in this disease will be dependent on the use of this animal model.

The above examples are directed to human disease, yet it is important to   29
recognize that millions of domestic animals are saved in the United States each
year through the use of prophylactic vaccination. Recent United States Department of Argiculture figures show that in 1970, for every 10,000 poultry sent to
slaughter, 158 poultry had Marek's Disease. In 1979, as the result of the development of a new vaccine, the incidence of Marek's Disease was reduced to 11
cases per 10,000 poultry. As an example of other control measures, in 1950,
there were 1.4 cases of hog cholera per 10,000 animals. In 1979, this figure was
reduced to zero. Hog cholera has been virtually eliminated. In 1950, there were
.86 cases of cattle tuberculosis per 10,000 animals slaughtered. This disease is
transmissible to man. In 1979, cattle tuberculosis was reduced to .008 cases per
10,000, thus decreasing the prevalence of this disease by 1000-fold. A significant number of vaccines used in control of diseases of animals were developed
and tested at Cornell University, the most recent being the canine parvovirus
vaccine to protect against a new disease which simultaneously occurred in
several parts of the world in 1978. Recognizing the tremendous number of dogs
lost to this disease since 1978, and the significant distress this brought to animal
owners, we question the wisdom of mandating discontinuing the use of living
animals in such research.

In the area of non-infectious disease, the major cause of mortality in the   30
United States is that of diseases associated with the cardiovascular system.
During the past three decades, animals have played an instrumental role in the
development of new surgical, therapeutic and electronic devices which have
played an enormous role in decreasing both mortality and morbidity. As an
example, it is estimated that 50,000 coronary bypass operations take place
annually in this country, thus relieving thousands suffering from pain and for
many, prolonging their lives.

Cancer ranks second, after cardiovascular disease, as a cause of death in   31
America. Tremendous advances have been made in cancer chemotherapy and
the public is just recognizing that permanent cures are now possible for many
forms of cancer. Granted, much remains to be done in solving the ravages of
this disease, but I must point out that all chemotherapeutic agents have first
been tested in animals for signs of toxicity. Indeed, animals remain the key for
further progress in our conquest of cancer.

Other diseases of significance in the United States have likewise benefited   32
from animal experimentation. Animal "models," or those animals in which similar if not identical disease syndromes exist, obviously represent a fertile source
of investigation. In many instances, the information gained can be of direct
benefit to the animal populations involved, thus preventing death or improving
the quality of their lives. As examples, one can cite spontaneous systemic lupus
erythematosus, rheumatoid arthritis, and hemolytic anemia. In the field of en-
docrinology we have benefited immensely from the use of animals to delineate
the growth changes and bodily responses altered through disorders of the
endocrine system. Such studies have shed new light on diseases such as thy-
roiditis, pituitary giantism, Cushing's syndrome, Addison's disease, and many

others. The isolation, purification, testing and synthesis of a number of hormones have significantly influenced the lives of millions. Again, because of the complexities of the systems involved, only living animals manifest the full range of physiologic changes needed to develop, test and produce such compounds.

In diseases of the central nervous system, significant advances have been 33 made in products such as lithium for patients with manic depression. At the present time, investigators at Cornell are testing several new synthetic lithium compounds in animals which promise to bring beneficial therapeutic effects without the severe toxicity currently encountered with the parent compound.

Chronic debilitating diseases, such as rheumatoid and osteoarthritis, have 34 benefited greatly from animal research. During the past two decades, surgical procedures developed in animals have led to the production and implantation of total hip joint prosthetic devices, knees, and other bone replacements in man. Such devices have provided pain-free locomotion in thousands of Americans who were previously immobile.

The examples cited above are chosen merely to illustrate the importance of 35 animal experimentation to relieve pain, suffering and death in both man and animals. The listing is representative of only a small portion of those diseases and disorders in which animals have made useful contributions to human medicine; most were selected because they are currently used or are under study at Cornell University; thus, I have personal knowledge concerning this work.

The Subcommittee should also be aware of the fact that, since World War II, 36 there have been 52 Nobel Prize winners in medicine and physiology. Thirty-seven of these awards were achieved with NIH grant awards. We have had 21 Nobel Prize winners in chemistry; twelve of these received NIH support. Within the past few days, this year's Nobel Prize recipients were announced. Their scientific observations and discoveries were made by utilizing animal models—non-human primates. The science being conducted in this country is perhaps the finest in the world. Congress must strive to preserve the right of scientific freedom to insure continued creativity and excellence.

In this correspondence I have intended to be informative, yet to construc- 37 tively criticize the various bills currently before the Subcommittee on Science, Research and Technology. We are aware that under certain conditions our research animals are subjected to painful procedures, yet we do everything possible to minimize the number of such procedures and to use drugs to abrogate pain. Rest assured that we agree that alternatives to living animals should be employed whenever appropriate and that science will continue, as it has in the past, the development of new alternative methods. It is our opinion that enactment of HR 930 or HR 220 would promote such alternatives without disrupting biomedical research. We wish to emphasize to the Committee the significant past achievements in biomedical science, many of which have been accomplished through the use of living animals, and stress the importance of their use in ongoing and future studies. Attempts to reduce the use of animals through restrictive legislation or through the imposition of unnecessary bureaucratic authority which extends beyond the time-tested, peer review system, would seriously impede efforts to improve the lives of both man and animals.

On behalf of the Association for Biomedical Research, thank you for permitting me to comment on these issues.   38

QUESTIONS FOR MEANING

1. Why does Melby believe that animal experimentation is already subject to sufficient control? Explain what he means by "peer review."
2. What pressures outside the research community affect the number of animals used in testing? How, in particular, does the economy affect animal experimentation?
3. What is the Association for Biomedical Research? What is its purpose, and what exactly does it do? Does it seem like a reputable organization?
4. What specific accomplishments is Melby able to cite in support of animal experiments? How seriously do you take these achievements? Does Melby persuade you that American science is worthy of respect?
5. Vocabulary: dichotomy (3), verification (6), redundant (8), auspices (13), implemented (14), infrastructure (16), innovative (21), amenable (22), and delineate (32).

QUESTIONS ABOUT STRATEGY

1. Why does Melby begin by explaining who he is? Was this an appropriate way to begin? Under what circumstances might you begin an essay this way?
2. How does Melby present himself to the Committee? At what points in his testimony does he try to emphasize that he is a reasonable man?
3. How does Melby go about appealing to the animal-lovers in his audience? Does he make any argument that would appeal to people who have pets? Why does he do this?
4. Does Melby present any information that caused you to reconsider your own position on this subject? If so, what was it? Try to explain why you found this point or points effective.

SUGGESTIONS FOR WRITING

1. Drawing upon White, Gallistel, and Melby, write an essay defending the use of animals in medical research.
2. Is all research equally valid? Can some experiments on animals be justified even if others cannot, or must one take an absolute position on this issue? If you think that some types of research are acceptable, write an essay that will define what is and what isn't permissible.
3. Is an elephant equal to a pig? Write an essay with the thesis that all animals are *not* equal. Make sure that you take the views of Peter Singer into account and respond directly to them.

4. Interview someone who uses animals in either teaching or research, and then write a paper defending or attacking the way animals are used in your own school or community.

5. Can you oppose the use of animals in scientific research and still eat meat? Or is this a contradiction in your own values? Write an essay on the relationship between eating animals and experimenting upon them. Is there a difference between these two activities that makes one defensible and the other not? Are you opposed to both? Or do you see nothing wrong with the way humans make use of animals? What is your position?

6. Thousands of cats and dogs are abandoned each year by owners who no longer wish to care for them. Some die slow deaths from starvation and disease. Others are rescued by humane societies which house and feed them and try to find new homes for them. If a new home cannot be found, the abandoned animal is either destroyed or sold to a research facility. Should unwanted pets be used for animal experiments? Are former pets entitled to special protection?

7. Catherine Roberts argues that animal experimentation violates basic Christian principles. Can you write an argument defending animal experimentation from a Christian point of view?

8. Research the position of other religions regarding animals. Write a paper defending or attacking animal experimentation according to Buddhist, Hindu, Moslem, or Jewish beliefs.

9. Gallistel and Mayo both observe that animal experimentation in Great Britain is more restricted than it is in the United States. Do a research paper on the nature of the laws that protect animals in Britain and argue whether or not such laws would be desirable in our own country. Your argument is likely to be especially convincing if you are able to determine what effect British laws have had upon the practice of science. Is major research still being done in Great Britain, or has British law crippled the practice of science there?

10. Write an argument against animal experimentation, drawing your support from the research of Deborah Mayo.

Section 5
Abortion: Whose Life Is It?

SHIRLEY CHISHOLM
Outlawing Compulsory Pregnancy Laws

A graduate of Brooklyn College and Columbia University, Shirley Chisholm
(b. 1924) was a member of the New York State Assembly from 1964 to 1968, when
she became the first black woman ever elected to Congress. In the House of
Representatives, Chisholm has worked for legislation to provide equal opportunities
for women, minorities, and the poor. She is a member of the advisory council of the
National Organization of Women and the national board of directors of Americans
for Democratic Action. She has written about her political experiences in two books,
Unbought and Unbossed *(1970) and* The Good Fight, *an account of her 1972*
campaign for the Democratic presidential nomination. "Outlawing Compulsory
Pregnancy Laws" is an editor's title for the introduction Chisholm provided to
Abortion Rap, *a feminist anthology that was published in 1971, when the movement*
to legalize abortion was at its height.

There are many political, legal, social, moral and economic issues involved in 1
government-sponsored birth control programs and policies. I will address myself to some of those issues that surround the most widely used method of birth
control in the world today—abortion.

Alice S. Rossi, in an excellent article in the July–August 1969 issue of *Dis-* 2
sent, made this most cogent comment about the word *abortion*:

"Free association to the word *abortion* would probably yield a fantastic 3
array of emotional responses: pain, relief, murder, crime, fear, freedom, genocide, guilt, sin. Which of these associations people have no doubt reflects their
age, marital status, religion or nationality. To a forty-four-year-old Japanese or
Hungarian woman, the primary response might be 'freedom' and 'relief'; to an
unmarried American college girl, 'fear' and 'pain'; to a Catholic priest, 'murder'
and 'sin'; to some black militants, 'genocide.'"

There are many ways to avoid the negative associations and connotations 4
that surround the word. We could, for example, borrow the term advanced by
the British when they recently rewrote their laws—"pregnancy termination."

I believe that that would get us closer to the heart of the issue but it would 5
still not be close enough.

Not close enough because the basic issue—and the only real choice of alter- 6

natives for the pregnant woman who does not want the child—is abortion or
compulsory pregnancy. If we view the issue in this perspective we are at what
one might call "ground zero."

Does our government or any other government have the right by which to   7
force a woman to have a child that she does not want? In Hungary, Gyorgy
Peters, the chief government statistician, has answered (presumably with back-
ing from high officials) with an emphatic "No!" He reportedly has said, "The
introduction of regulations with which the state would interfere with the freedom of the parents contradicts our political and moral concepts." What then
must we, as representatives of a democracy, answer to the question?

The majority of family-planning advocates would be aghast if our govern-   8
ment were to suggest laws *requiring* the use of any contraceptive, or, as in a
recent case in California, legal sterilization.

Yet it has been government policy in this country that compels pregnant   9
women to carry a full-term pregnancy, often against the wishes of both parents.

Dr. Garrett Hardin has, perhaps rightly, equated this situation with compul-   10
sory servitude and has said, "When we recognize that these (abortion or compulsory pregnancy) are the real operational alternatives (for the pregnant
woman), the false problems created by the pseudo-alternatives disappear."

What has been the situation in Washington, that showplace of the nation,   11
under the compulsory pregnancy law?

Dr. Milan Vuitch, who was the central figure in Judge Gessel's recent ruling   12
on the District's compulsory pregnancy law, estimates that more than 20,000
abortions a year are performed in the greater Washington area. He further estimates that only 25 percent of them are performed in hospitals. That
means that there are more than 15,000 illegal abortions performed in or near
Washington.

The municipal hospitals in the District have the same anti-black, anti-poor   13
policies in effect that I find in the New York City hospitals. D.C. General, for
instance, reports 80 therapeutic abortions for 1968. That is roughly .016 percent for the legal abortions in the greater Washington area. That figure has even
more impact, I believe, when one realizes that it is only .004 percent of the total
abortions performed, both legally and illegally, in this area.

The impact multiplies dramatically when we consider that D.C. General also   14
reports between 800 and 1,000 incomplete abortions. Incomplete means that
the abortion was induced, either by drugs, instrument or naturally, but that it
did not complete naturally . . . therefore it must be completed by a physician.

In short, they expended 10 to 12 times more effort on repairing botched,   15
non-professional surgery than they did on performing medically safe, professional surgery. That is nothing short of complete absurdity. Botched abortions
are the single largest cause of maternal deaths in the United States, and it is
evidently going to be government policy to keep it that way.

There are no clear statistics on exactly how many illegal abortions there are   16
each year in this country. Estimates range from as low as 200,000 to 1.5 million.
One thing that is clear, however, is that if we repealed our compulsory pregnancy laws the incidents would be reduced.

There are many statistics from other countries that support my contention.   17

But let me quote from an article about the new British law that appeared in the *Washington Post* in June of 1969.

"Some doctors contend the only value of the bill is to prevent the harm done 18 by secret abortionists. They say Hungary allows abortions for anyone who wants one, and illegal operations have reportedly faded away. Czechoslovakia has a 'social clause' similar to Britain's, and clandestine abortions have dropped to 4,000 a year instead of 100,000."

If there are now 1,500,000 illegal abortions in this country, a drop of the 19 same percentage would reduce the number of illegal operations performed to about 30,000; that is only about twice as many as are now performed in the District of Columbia alone.

Let us look briefly at some of the countries where the compulsory pregnancy 20 laws have been weakened or, if you prefer, where abortion laws have been liberalized:

Experience in Sweden and Denmark has shown that as legal abortions in- 21 creased the death rate associated with it decreased.

In 1967 in Hungary there were 187,000 legal abortions as against 148,000 22 live births. Similarly Czechoslovakia's birthrate has been reduced but not as drastically as Hungary's.

Rumania, after substituting a more restrictive law in 1966, discovered that 23 its birth rate almost tripled in one year, the previous rate being 13.7 per 1,000.

It would seem that the absence of compulsory pregnancy laws alone can 24 contribute a great deal to the control of the population growth, especially when one considers that at least the Eastern bloc countries mentioned do not widely practice the more modern methods of contraception.

Of course no discussion of abortion would be complete without discussing 25 the politically volatile issue of religious and moral concepts.

Since we are already outside of the country, let's stay there momentarily to 26 inspect the abortion rates of a few countries with large Catholic populations:

The illegal abortion rate in Uruguay is almost two and one half times the 27 number of annual live births.

In Roman Catholic Chile, 27 percent of the women reported that they had 28 had abortions at one time or another.

In Roman Catholic France, the annual number of abortions equals the annual 29 number of live births.

Coming back to this country, we find that in a poll conducted in 1967, no less 30 than 72 percent of the Catholics polled favored abortion reform, as did 83 percent of the Protestants and 98 percent of the Jewish.

No lesser a Catholic luminary than Cardinal Cushing of Boston was quoted 31 as having said, "It does not seem reasonable to me to forbid in civil law a practice that can be considered a matter of private morality."

Outlawing compulsory pregnancy laws, which some might still prefer to call 32 legalizing abortion, would not be forcing doctors or hospitals to perform abortions against their beliefs. By outlawing these laws we would instead be honoring the basic and individual right of a woman to terminate an unwanted pregnancy.

The basic underlying question in any discussion of compulsory pregnancy   33
laws (which I choose to use rather than the term *abortion laws*) is what should
a woman who is pregnant against *her* will do, and what should the professional
and public response toward her be if she chooses to terminate the pregnancy?

If the underlying thesis of family planning is to reduce even the number of   34
wanted pregnancies, is it not illogical then to continue to force women with
unwanted pregnancies to have the child? I think that it is!

QUESTIONS FOR MEANING

1. Why might black militants associate abortion with "genocide"?
2. Why does Chisholm believe "compulsory pregnancy laws" are "anti-black,
   anti-poor"?
3. Chisholm argues that "the basic issues—and the only real choice of alternatives for the pregnant woman who does not want the child—is abortion
   or compulsory pregnancy." What are the "pseudo-alternatives" dismissed
   in paragraph 10?
4. Why does Chisholm believe that women have a "basic and individual right
   ...to terminate an unwanted pregnancy"? What does "right" mean, and
   where do rights come from?
5. In paragraph 32, Chisholm argues that liberalized abortion laws would not
   force "doctors or hospitals to perform abortion against their beliefs." Under
   what circumstances might a doctor refuse to perform an abortion? What
   type of hospital might refuse to allow its facilities to be used for abortions,
   and what would be the consequences of such a policy?

QUESTIONS ABOUT STRATEGY

1. In her opening paragraph, Chisholm defines abortion as "the most widely
   used method of birth control in the world today." Later in her essay, she
   offers statistics from Hungary and Rumania to demonstrate the relationship between population growth and liberal abortion laws. How effective is
   this comparison with Eastern European countries? For what reasons might
   Eastern European countries wish to reduce the size of their populations?
   Does Chisholm persuade you that the rate of population growth is too high
   in the United States?
2. Recognizing the importance of language, Chisholm argues that the negative
   connotations of the word *abortion* could be avoided by substituting the
   phrase "pregnancy termination." Does this suggestion help or hurt her
   argument?
3. Comment on Chisholm's use of citations. Would you welcome more information about the various men and women she cites as authorities? Does
   she reveal the source of the statistics that she relies upon? Would this
   essay be more convincing if it provided more documentation? Or can
   Chisholm be excused from this responsibility because her essay was intended only as an introduction to a collection of essays by other writers?

4. Because the Catholic Church has been adamant in its opposition to abortion, Chisholm discusses Catholics in paragraphs 25–31. How would these paragraphs impress someone who opposed abortion on religious or moral grounds?
5. Is there anything about the style and organization of this essay that suggests its author, as a member of Congress, is used to public speaking?

HAVEN BRADFORD GOW
Abortion and the Abuse of the English Language

In January 1973, the Supreme Court made one of the most controversial decisions in its history. In this decision, known as Roe vs. Wade, the Court ruled that most state laws that restricted abortion were unconstitutional. The effect of this ruling was to legalize abortion throughout the first half of a woman's pregnancy. (At the point where the life of the unborn child could be considered "viable"—or towards the end of the second trimester—the states were still allowed the power to regulate abortion if they wished to do so.) Although there had been an active campaign to legalize abortion for several years, many Americans were shocked by the Court's decision and protests began almost immediately.

During the next ten years, the debate over abortion law would become increasingly bitter—and often full of loaded terms, as the following essay by Haven Bradford Gow (b. 1950) reveals. An English major from Southeastern Massachusetts University, Gow received an M.A. in American Studies from Boston College in 1975. He is currently an associate editor for Police Times, *a columnist for* Chinatown News, *a Wilbur Foundation literary fellow, and a commentator for television stations in Chicago.*

Orwell warned us. The eminent British novelist and social critic warned us three decades ago about the abuse and decline of the English language, and the degenerative effects such a decline would have on public discussion of important issues, and on the moral and political climate of a nation. The abuse and decline of the English language, he knew, is a symptom of our inability to think clearly; but he knew, too, that it is easy to have foolish, inaccurate and imprecise thoughts, because of the sad general decline of English. 1

Like Orwell, Edwin Newman, the well-known newsman for The National Broadcasting Company, is disturbed about the pernicious decline of the English language and, in an admirable and much needed attempt to help correct this unhappy situation, Mr. Newman has written two fine books, *Speaking Freely: Will America Be the Death of English?* and *A Civil Tongue.* 2

Newman discerns an intimate connection between the poor state of lan- 3 guage in a nation and the problems it faces. In *Speaking Freely*, he argues that "It is at least conceivable that our politics would be improved if our English were, and so would other parts of our national life." He declares: "If we were more careful about what we say, and how, we might be more critical and less gullible." When words lose their value, we find that ideas lose value, too.

Although Newman never examines in his two books the abuse and misuse of   4
English language by those involved in the explosive and emotional public debate on abortion, it seems both wise and fruitful to consider how language has indeed been misused by both the opponents and proponents of abortion.

I happen to agree with those who defend and affirm the sanctity of human   5
life, born and unborn. I think abortion is the killing of an unborn baby. But a serious problem arises when opponents of abortion refer to abortion as "murder." The difficulty is that our legal system has always made a distinction between abortion and murder, even prior to the U.S. Supreme Court's legalization of abortion-on-demand in January, 1973. True enough, prior to the Court's 1973 ruling, doctors could be and were prosecuted for performing abortions, but they were never prosecuted for the crime of "murder." Consequently, I think it regrettable that opponents of abortion have failed to make clear that when they refer to abortion as "murder," they are using the word "murder" in a moral rather than a legal sense.

But certainly the pro-abortionists are especially guilty of the most blatant   6
abuses and misuses of language to cover-up the immorality of abortion. In the October 29, 1978 issue of *The National Catholic Register*, Monsignor R.G. Peters makes some particularly trenchant observations about this matter. For example, he discusses last spring's California trial of William Waddill, the physician who was tried on murder charges for allegedly strangling to death a newborn baby girl who had survived a saline abortion attempt.

Monsignor Peters points out that William Waddill's attorney, Charles Weed-   7
man, in an all-too-rare moment of the honest use of language, conceded that abortion is "killing a baby." But today, Mr. Weedman went on to say, this— "killing a baby"—is permitted by law.

Monsignor Peters then proceeds to ask the tough questions that need to be   8
asked. He asks, "What do you think would happen to the abortion clinic business if the ads read, 'Have your baby killed quickly and cheaply' or 'The newest baby-killing clinic in town?' The pro-life people could stop crusading and go fishing. The abortionists would be out of business. Words are that important."

One thing that feminist writer-editor-spokeswoman Gloria Steinem knows is   9
that words indeed are important. That is why she is always careful to say that she does not necessarily favor abortion, but rather advocates "reproductive freedom" and the "right" of women to "control their own bodies." When asked if she is pro-abortion, she smoothly responds that she rather is "pro-choice." In other words, Gloria Steinem and other feminists who support the U.S. Supreme Court's ruling of January, 1973, do not necessarily favor the killing of unborn babies; rather they simply are "pro-choice," that is, they merely believe that women should be "free to choose" to kill their unborn children.

Another example of the dishonest use of language by pro-abortionists is the   10
use of the phrase "legislating morality." Many opponents of abortion become
defensive when an advocate of abortion (or of "pro-choice") accuses them of
attempting to "legislate morality." Were many of the proponents and opponents
of abortion to examine carefully the phrase "legislating morality," they would
conclude that there simply is nothing wrong or harmful about "legislating morality." The fact is that laws against murder, incest, rape, child prostitution,
stealing and extortion demonstrate that this nation has always legislated morality—and rightly so. The proper question, then, is not "Should we legislate
morality?" but, rather, "When is it appropriate to legislate morality?" For it is
indeed true that fighting abortion is an attempt to "legislate morality," but only
in the same sense that we "legislate morality" when we outlaw incest, rape and
murder. When we make incest, rape and murder illegal, we "impose moral,
ethical and religious views" on those who find nothing wrong with incest, rape
and murder.

The pro-abortionists also use language dishonestly when they use such eu-   11
phemisms as "termination of pregnancy" and "emptying the uterus" to describe
what occurs in abortion. Were the pro-abortionists to candidly and openly
confess what actually occurs in an abortion—that is, the killing of an unborn
child—perhaps many persons would think twice about advocating or undergo-
ing abortions. Monsignor R.G. Peters says it very well: "If everybody said what
they really meant, the argument would go a lot differently, and many pro-
abortionists would be surprised to find out what they are really defending."

QUESTIONS FOR MEANING

1. Why does Gow believe that it is important to use clear and honest language? Why does he believe it is especially important to do so when discussing what happens during an abortion? Explain why Gow objects to
   phrases such as "pro-choice" and "emptying the uterus."
2. Although Gow believes that "abortion is the killing of an unborn baby," he
   objects to equating "killing" with "murder." Explain the difference between
   these two terms.
3. Vocabulary: gullible (3), discerns (3), trenchant (6), euphemisms (11),
   and candidly (11)

QUESTIONS ABOUT STRATEGY

1. Is Gow himself ever guilty of abusing language? How would a feminist
   respond to someone who describes himself as "pro-life"?
2. Consider the opening line of this essay. What advantage is there to beginning an essay with a sentence that is so short and cryptic?
3. In paragraph 5, Gow admits that he is opposed to abortion. Does this
   admission help his argument by inspiring confidence in the author's honesty? Or does it weaken the argument by revealing a bias that is already
   implicit in the argument itself?

4. Does Gow rely too much on any one of his sources?

5. One of the principal arguments on behalf of legalized abortion is that the government should not "legislate morality." Gow responds to this argument in paragraph 10 by reminding his audience that we outlaw incest, rape, and murder. Is abortion analogous to these crimes as Gow seems to imply? Or is there a fundamental difference that Gow fails to acknowledge?

SISSELA BOK

Who Shall Count as a Human Being?
A Treacherous Question in the
Abortion Discussion

Sissela Bok (b. 1934) is the daughter of Nobel Prize-winning social scientist Gunnar Myrdal. She was born in Stockholm, attended the Sorbonne between 1953 and 1955, and became a U.S. citizen in 1959. A philosopher and educator with a Ph.D. from Harvard, Bok has concentrated most of her work on questions of ethics. She has been a fellow in the Interfaculty Program in Medical Ethics at Harvard, a lecturer on medical ethics in the Harvard–MIT Division of Health Sciences and Technology, and, since 1975, has served on the Medical Committee of Amnesty International. As a writer, Bok has won much praise for writing clearly on abstract subjects. Her first book, Lying: Moral Choice in Public and Private Life *(1978), received the George Orwell Award from the National Council of Teachers of English. Her most recent book is* Secrets: On the Ethics of Concealment and Revelation *(1983). In the following essay, Bok tries to answer one of the most difficult questions posed by the debate on abortion: "Who shall count as a human being?"*

"The temptation to introduce premature ultimates—Beauty in Aesthetics, the Mind and its faculties in Psychology, Life in Physiology, are representative examples—is especially great for believers in Abstract Entities. The objection to such Ultimates is that they bring an investigation to a dead end too suddenly."
—I.A. Richards, *Principles of Literary Criticism*, p. 40.

In discussions of abortion policy, the premature ultimate is 'humanity.' Does   1
the fetus possess 'humanity'? How does one go about deciding whether a living being possesses it? And what rights go with such possession? These and similar questions have arisen beginning with the earliest speculations about human origins and characteristics. They are still thought central to the abortion debate. I propose to show in this paper that they cannot help us come to grips with the problem of abortion; indeed that they obfuscate all discussion in this domain and lend themselves to dangerous interpretations precisely because of their obscurity.

The concept of 'humanity' is indispensable to two main arguments against   2
abortion. The first defines the fetus as a human being and then concludes that
abortion must be murder since it is generally considered murder to take the
life of a human being. The second argument is designed to speak to those who
do not believe that fetuses are human and cannot share, therefore, the conclusion that abortion is murder. It stresses, not the inherent wrong in individual
acts of abortion, but rather the fearful consequences flowing from a *social
acceptance* of abortion. According to this argument, it is impossible to draw a
line in the period of prenatal development when humanity can be said to begin.
There will therefore be no way to stop at early abortions, since they cannot be
distinguished from later and yet later abortions; eventually society may even
come to permit infanticide and the taking of lives generally. We are all at risk,
according to such an argument, once we allow abortions to take place.

An analysis of these two arguments will show the ways in which the concept   3
of 'humanity' operates as a premature ultimate.[1] I propose to substitute for this
vague concept an inquiry into the commonly shared principles concerning the
protection of life. These principles help to define workable rules for abortions
and make it possible to draw a clear line between abortion, on the one hand,
and the taking of life in infanticide, euthanasia, and genocide, on the other.

A. Humanity.

A long tradition of religious and philosophical and legal thought has ap-   4
proached the problem of abortion by trying to determine whether there is
human life before birth, and, if so, when it *becomes* human. If human life is
present from conception on, according to this tradition, it must be protected as
such from that moment. And if the embryo becomes human at some point
during the pregnancy, then that is the point at which the protection should
set in.

John Noonan[2] generalizes the predominant Catholic view as follows: 5

> "Once conceived, the being was recognized as a man because he had man's
> potential. The criterion for humanity, then, was simple and all-embracing: If you
> are conceived by human parents, you are human."

Similarly, no less than ten resolutions had been introduced in Congress in   6
the three months following the U.S. Supreme Court's decisions on abortion.[3]
These resolutions call for a constitutional amendment providing that

> "neither the United States, nor any state shall deprive any human being, *from the
> moment of conception*, of life without the due process of law ..."

Others have held that the moment when *implantation* of the fertilized egg   7
occurs, 6–7 days after conception, is more significant from the point of view of

individual humanity than conception itself. This view permits them to allow the intrauterine device and the 'morning after pill' as not taking human life, merely interfering with implantation. Whether or not one considers such distinctions to be theoretically possible, however, modern contraceptive developments are making them increasingly difficult to draw in practice.

Another widely shared approach to establishing humanity is that of stressing the time when the embryo first begins to *look human*. A photo of the first cell having divided in half clearly does not depict what most people mean when they use the expression 'human being.' Even the four-week embryo does not look human in this sense, whereas the six-week-old one begins to do so. Recent techniques of depicting the embryo and the fetus have remarkably increased our awareness of this early stage; this new 'seeing' of life before birth may come to increase the psychological recoil from aborting those who already look human—thus adding a psychological factor to the medical and other factors already influencing the trend to earlier and earlier abortions.

8

Another dividing line, once more having to do with perceiving the fetus, is held to occur when the mother can feel the fetus moving. *Quickening*—when these moments are first felt—has traditionally represented an important distinction; in some legal traditions, such as that of the common law, abortion was permitted before quickening, but considered a misdemeanor afterwards, until the more restrictive 19th century legislation was established. It is certain that the first-felt movements of the fetus represent an awe-inspiring change for the mother, comparable perhaps, in some primitive sense, to a 'coming to life' of the being she carries.

9

Yet another distinction occurs when the fetus is considered *viable*. According to this view, once the fetus is capable of living independently of its mother, it must be regarded as a human being and protected as such. The U.S. Supreme Court decisions on abortion established viability as the "compelling" point for the state's "important and legitimate interest in potential life," while eschewing the question of when 'life' or 'human life' begins.[4]

10

A set of later distinctions cluster around the process of birth itself. This is the moment when life begins, according to certain religious traditions, and the point at which 'persons' are fully recognized in the law, according to the Supreme Court.[5] The first breaths taken by newborn babies have been invested with symbolic meaning since the earliest gropings toward understanding what it means to be alive and human. And the rituals of acceptance of babies or children have often defined humanity to the point where the baby could be killed if it were not named or declared accepted by the elders of the community or by the head of the household.

11

In the positions here examined, and in the abortion debate generally, a number of concepts are at times used as if they were interchangeable. 'Humanity,' 'human life,' 'life,' are such concepts, as are 'man,' 'person,' 'human being,' or 'human individual.' In particular, those who hold that humanity begins at conception or at implantation often have the tendency to say that at that time a human being or a person or a man exists as well, whereas others find it impossible to equate them.

12

Each of these terms can, in addition, be used in different senses which   13
overlap but are not interchangeable. For instance, humanity and human life, in
one sense, are possessed by every cell in our bodies. Many cells have the full
genetic makeup required for asexual reproduction—so called cloning—of a
human being. Yet clearly this is not the sense of those words intended when the
protection of humanity or human life is advocated. Such protection would press
the reverence for human life to the mad extreme of ruling out haircuts and
considering mosquito bites murder.

It may be argued, however, that for most cells which have the potential of   14
cloning to form a human being, extraordinarily complex measures would be
required which are not as yet perfected beyond the animal stage. Is there, then,
a difference, from the point of view of human potential, between these cells
and egg cells or sperm cells? And is there still another difference in potential
between the egg cell before and after conception? While there is a statistical
difference in the *likelihood* of their developing into a human being, it does not
seem possible to draw a clear line where humanity definitely begins.

The different views as to when humanity begins are little dependent upon   15
factual information. Rather, these views are representative of different world-
views, often of a religious nature involving deeply held commitments with moral
consequences. There is no disagreement as to what we now know about life
and its development before and after conception; differences arise only about
the names and moral consequences we attach to the changes in this development and the distinctions we consider important. Just as there is no point at
which Achilles can be pinpointed as catching up with the tortoise, though
everyone knows he does, so everyone is aware of the distance traveled, in terms
of humanity, from before conception to birth, though there is no one point at
which humanity can be agreed upon as setting in. Our efforts to pinpoint and
to define reflect the urgency with which we reach for abstract labels and
absolute certainty in facts and in nature; and the resulting confusion and puz-
zlement are close to what Wittgenstein described, in *Philosophical Investigations*, as the "bewitchment of our intelligence by means of language."

Even if some see the fertilized egg as possessing humanity and as being "a   16
man" in the words used by Noonan, however, it would be quite unthinkable to
act upon all the consequences of such a view. It would be necessary to undertake a monumental struggle against all spontaneous abortions—known as miscarriages—often of severely malformed embryos expelled by the mother's
body. This struggle would appear increasingly misguided as we learn more
about how to preserve early prenatal life. Those who could not be saved would
have to buried in the same way as dead infants. Those who engaged in abortion
would have to be prosecuted for murder. Extraordinary practical complexities
would arise with respect to detection of early abortion, and to the question of
whether the use of abortifacients in the first few days after conception should
also count as murder. In view of these inconsistencies, it seems likely that this
view of humanity, like so many others, has been adopted for limited purposes
having to do with the prohibition of induced abortion, rather than from a real
belief in the full human rights of the first few cells after conception.

A related reason why there are so many views and definitions is that they   17
have been sought for such different *purposes*. I indicated above that many of
the views about humanity developed in the abortion dispute seem to have been
worked out for one such purpose: that of defending a preconceived position on
abortion, with little concern for the other consequences flowing from that
particular view. But there have been so many other efforts to define humanity
and to arrive at the essence of what it means to be human—to distinguish men
from angels and demons, plants and animals, witches and robots. The most
powerful one has been the urge to know about the human species and to trace
the biological or divine origins and the essential characteristics of mankind. It
is magnificently set forth beginning with the very earliest writings in philosophy
and poetry; in fact, this consciousness of oneself and wonder at one's condition
has often been thought one of the essential distinctions between men and
animals.

A separate purpose, both giving strength to and flowing from these efforts   18
to describe and to understand humanity, has been that of seeking to define
what a *good* human being is—to delineate human aspirations. What ought fully
human beings to be like, and how should they differ from and grow beyond
their immature, less perfect, sick or criminal fellow men? Who can teach such
growth—St. Francis or Nietzsche, Buddha or Erasmus? And what kind of families and societies give support and provide models for growth?

Finally, definitions of humanity have been sought in order to try to set limits   19
to the protection of life. At what level of developing humanity can and ought
lives to receive protection? And who, among those many labelled less than
human at different times in history—slaves, enemies in war, women, children,
the retarded—should be denied such protection?

Of these three purposes for defining 'humanity,' the first is classificatory and   20
descriptive in the first hand (though it gives rise to normative considerations).
It has roots in religious and metaphysical thought, and has branched out into
biological and archeological and anthropological research. But the latter two,
so often confused with the first, are primarily *normative* or prescriptive. They
seek to set norms or guidelines for who is fully human and who is at least
minimally human—so human as to be entitled to the protection of life. For the
sake of these normative purposes, definitions of 'humanity' established elsewhere have been sought in order to determine action—and all too often the
action has been devastating for those excluded.

It is crucial to ask at this point why the descriptive and the normative   21
definitions have been thought to coincide; why it has been taken for granted
that the line between human and non-human or not yet-human is identical with
that distinguishing those who may be killed from those who are to be protected.

One or both of two fundamental assumptions are made by those who base   22
the protection of life upon the possession of 'humanity.' The first is that human
beings are not only different from, but *superior to* all other living matter. This
is the assumption which changes the definition of humanity into an evaluative
one. It lies at the root of Western religious and social thought, from the Bible
and the Aristotelian concept of the "ladder of nature" all the way to Teilhard

de Chardin's view of mankind as close to the intended summit and consumma-
tion of the development of living beings.

The second assumption holds that the superiority of human beings somehow   23
justifies their using what is non-human as they see fit, dominating it, even killing
it when they wish to. St. Augustine, in *The City of God*,[6] expresses both of
these anthropocentric assumptions when he holds that the injunction "Thou
shalt not kill" does not apply to killing animals and plants, since, having no
faculty of reason,

> "therefore by the altogether righteous ordinance of the Creator both their life and
> death are a matter subordinate to our needs."

Neither of these assumptions is self-evident. And the results of acting upon   24
them, upon the bidding to subdue the earth, to subordinate living matter to
human needs, are no longer seen by all to be beneficial. The ancient certainties
about man's preordained place in the universe are faltering. The supposition
that only human beings have rights is no longer regarded as beyond question.[7]

Not only, therefore, can the line between human and non-human not be   25
drawn empirically so as to permit normative conclusions: the very enterprise
of *basing* normative conclusions on such distinctions can no longer be taken
for granted. Despite these difficulties, many still try to employ definitions of
'humanity' to do just that. And herein lies by far the most important reason for
abandoning such efforts: the monumental misuse of the concept of 'humanity'
in so many practices of discrimination and atrocity throughout history. Slavery,
witch-hunts, and wars have all been justified by their perpetrators on the
ground that they thought their victims to be less than fully human. The insane
and the criminal have for long periods been deprived of the most basic necessities for similar reasons, and excluded from society. A theologian, Dr. Joseph
Fletcher, has even suggested as recently as last year that someone who has an
I.Q. below 40 is "questionably a person" and that those below the 20-mark are
not persons at all.[8] He adds that:

> "This has bearing, obviously, on decision-making in gynecology, obstetrics, and
> pediatrics, as well as in general surgery and medicine."

Here, a criterion for 'personhood' is taken as a guideline for action which   26
could have sinister and far-reaching effects. Even when entered upon with the
best of intentions, and in the most guarded manner, the enterprise of basing
the protection of human life upon such criteria and definitions is dangerous.
To question someone's humanity or personhood is a first step to mistreatment
and killing.

We must abandon, therefore, this quest for a definition of humanity capable   27
of showing us who has a right to live. We must seek, instead, common principles
for the protection of life that reflect a clear understanding of the harm that

comes from the taking of life. Why do we hold life to be sacred? Why does it require protection beyond that given to anything else? The question seems unneccessary at first glance—surely most people share what has been called "the elemental sensation of vitality and the elemental fear of its extinction," and what Hume called "our horrors at annihilation."[9] Many think of this elemental sensation as incapable of further analysis. They view any attempt to say *why* we hold life sacred as an instrumentalist, utilitarian rocking of the boat which may loosen this fundamental respect for life. Yet a failure to scrutinize this respect, to ask what it protects and what it ought to protect, lies at the root not only of the confusion about abortion, but of the persistent vagueness and consequent abuse of the notion of the respect for life. The result is that everyone, including those who authorize or perform the most brutal killings in war, can protest their belief in life's sacredness. I shall therefore list the most important reasons which underlie the elemental sense of the sacredness of life. Having done so, these reasons can be considered as they apply or do not apply to the embryo and the fetus.

B. Reasons for Protecting Life.

1. Killing is viewed as the greatest of all dangers *for the victim.*
   —The knowledge that there is a threat to life causes intense anguish and apprehension.
   —The actual taking of life can cause great suffering.
   —The continued experience of life, once begun, is considered so valuable, so unique, so absorbing, that no one who has this experience should be unjustly deprived of it. And depriving someone of this experience means that all else of value to him will be lost.
2. Killing is brutalizing and criminalizing *for the killer.* It is a threat to others and destructive to the person engaging therein.
3. Killing often causes *the family of the victim and others* to experience grief and loss. They may have been tied to the dead person by affection or economic dependence; they may have given of themselves in the relationship, so that its severance causes deep suffering.
4. All of society, as a result, has a stake in the protection of life. Permitting killing to take place sets patterns for victims, killers, and survivors that are threatening and ultimately harmful to all.

These are neutral principles governing the protection of life. They are shared by most human beings reflecting upon the possibility of dying at the hands of others. It is clear that these principles, if applied in the absence of the confusing terminology of 'humanity,' would rule out the kinds of killing perpetrated by conquerors, witch-hunters, slave-holders, and Nazis. Their victims feared death and suffered; they grieved for their dead; and the societies permitting such killing were brutalized and degraded.

Turning now to abortion once more, how do these principles apply to the taking of the lives of embryos and fetuses?

C. Reasons to Protect Life in the Prenatal Period.

Consider the very earliest cell formations soon after conception. Clearly the   30
reasons for protecting human life fail to apply here:

This group of cells cannot feel the anguish or pain connected with death,   31
nor can it fear death. Its experiencing of life has not yet begun; it is not yet
conscious of the interruption of life nor of the loss of anything it has come to
value in life, nor is it tied by bonds of affection to others. If the abortion is
desired by both parents, it will cause no grief such as that which accompanies
the death of a child. Almost no human care and emotion and resources have
been invested in it. Nor is such an early abortion brutalizing for the person
voluntarily performing it, or a threat to other members of the society where it
takes place.

Some may argue that one can conceive of other deaths with those factors   32
absent, which nevertheless would be murder. Take the killing of a hermit in his
sleep by someone who instantly commits suicide. Here there is no anxiety or
fear of the killing on the part of the victim, no pain in dying, no mourning by
family or friends (to whom the hermit has, in leaving them forever, already in
a sense 'died'), no awareness by others that a wrong has been done; and the
possible brutalization of the murderer has been made harmless to others
through his suicide. Speculate further that the bodies are never found. Yet we
would still call the act one of murder. The reason we would do so is inherent in
the act itself and depends on the fact that his life was taken and that he was
denied the chance to continue to experience it.

How does this deprivation differ from abortion in the first few days of preg-   33
nancy? I find that I cannot use words like 'deprive,' 'deny,' 'take away,' and
'harm' when it comes to the group of cells, whereas I have no difficulty in using
them for the hermit. These words require, if not a person conscious of his loss,
at least someone who at a prior time has developed enough to be or have been
conscious thereof. Because there is no semblance of human form, no conscious
life or capability to live independently, no knowledge of death, no sense of pain,
one cannot use such words meaningfully to describe early abortion.

In addition, whereas it is possible to frame a rule permitting abortion which   34
will cause no anxiety on the part of others covered by the rule—other embryos
or fetuses—it is not possible to frame such a rule permitting the killing of
hermits without threatening other *hermits*. All hermits would have to fear for
their lives if there were a rule saying that hermits can be killed if they are alone
and asleep and if the agent commits suicide.

The reasons, then, for the protection of lives are minimal in very early   35
abortions. At the same time, many of these reasons are clearly present with
respect to *infanticide*, most important among them the brutalization of those
participating in the act and the resultant danger for all who are felt to be
undesirable by their families or by others. This is not to say that acts of infanticide have not taken place in our society; indeed, as late as the 19th century,
newborns were frequently killed, either directly or by giving them into the care
of institutions such as foundling hospitals, where the death rate could be as

high as 90% in the first year of life.[10] A few primitive societies, at the edge of extinction, without other means to limit families, still practice infanticide. But I believe that the *public acceptance* of infanticide in all other societies is unthinkable, given the advent of modern methods of contraception and early abortion and of institutions to which parents can give their children, assured of their survival and of the high likelihood that they will be adopted and cared for by a family.

D. Dividing Lines.

If, therefore, very early abortion does not violate these principles of protection for life, but infanticide does, we are confronted with a new kind of continuum in the place of that between less human and more human: that of the growth in strength, as the fetus develops during the prenatal period, of these principles, these reasons for protecting life. In this second continuum, it would be as difficult as in the first to draw a line based upon objective factors. Since most abortions can be performed earlier or later during pregnancy, it would be preferable to encourage early abortions rather than late ones and to draw a line before the second half of the pregnancy, permitting later abortions only on a clear showing of need. For this purpose, the two concepts of *quickening* and *viability*—so unsatisfactory in determining when humanity begins—can provide such limits.

Before quickening, the reasons to protect life are, as has been shown, negligible, perhaps absent altogether. During this period, therefore, abortion could be permitted upon request. Alternatively, the end of the first trimester could be employed as such a limit, as is the case in a number of countries.   36

Between quickening and viability, when the operation is a more difficult one medically and more traumatic for parents and medical personnel, it would not seem unreasonable to hold that special reasons justifying the abortion should be required in order to counterbalance this resistance: reasons not known earlier, such as the severe malformation of the fetus. After viability, finally, all abortions save the rare ones required to save the life of the mother,[11] should be prohibited, because the reasons to *protect* life may now be thought to be partially present; even though the viable fetus cannot fear death or suffer consciously therefrom, the effects on those participating in the event, and thus on society indirectly, could be serious. This is especially so because of the need, mentioned above, for a protection against infanticide. In the unlikely event, however, that the mother should wish to be separated from the fetus at such a late stage,[12] the procedure ought to be delayed until it can be one of premature birth, not one of harming the fetus in an abortive process.   37

Medically, however, the definition of 'viability' is difficult. It varies from one fetus to another. At one stage in pregnancy, a certain number of babies, if born, will be viable. At a later stage, the percentage will be greater. Viability also depends greatly on the state of our knowledge concerning the support of life after birth and on the nature of the support itself. Support can be given much earlier in a modern hospital than in a rural village, or in a clinic geared to doing   38 abortions only. It may some day even be the case that almost any human life will be considered viable before birth, once artificial wombs are perfected.

As technological progress pushes back the time when the fetus can be   39
helped to survive independently of the mother, a question will arise as to whether the cut-off point marked by viability ought also to be pushed back. Should abortion then be prohibited much earlier than is now the case, because the medical meaning of 'viability' will have changed, or should we continue to rely on the conventional meaning of the word for the distinction between lawful and unlawful abortion?

In order to answer this question it is necessary to look once more at the   40
reasons for which 'viability' was thought to be a good dividing line in the first place. Is viability important because the baby can survive outside of the mother? Or because this chance of survival comes at a time in fetal development when the *reasons* to protect life have grown strong enough to prohibit abortion? At present, the two coincide, but in the future, they may come to diverge increasingly.

If the time comes when an embryo *could* be kept alive without its mother   41
and thus be 'viable' in one sense of the word, the *reasons* for protecting life from the point of view of victims, agents, relatives and society would still be absent; it seems right, therefore, to tie the obligatory protection of life to the present conventional definition of 'viability' and to set a socially agreed upon time in pregnancy after which abortion should be prohibited.

To sum up, the justifications a mother has for not wishing to give birth can   42
operate up to a certain point in pregnancy; after that point, the reasons society has for protecting life become sufficiently weighty so as to prohibit late abortions and infanticide.

E. The Slippery Slope.

Some argue, however, that such views of abortion could lead, if widely fol-   43
lowed, to great dangers for society. This second major argument against abortion appears to set aside the question of when the fetus becomes human. It focuses, rather, on the risks for society—for the newborn, the handicapped, and the aged—which may stem from allowing abortions; it evokes the age-old fear of the slippery slope.[13] Because there are no sharp transitions in the period of fetal development, this argument holds, it would be unreasonable to permit abortion at one time in pregnancy and prohibit it shortly thereafter; in addition, it would be impossible to enforce such prohibitions. Later and later abortions may therefore be allowed, and there will be risks of slipping towards infanticide, euthanasia, even genocide.

The assumption made here is that once we admit reasons for justifying early   44
abortions—reasons such as rape, incest, or maternal illness—nothing will prevent people from acting upon these very same reasons later in pregnancy or even after birth. If abortion is permissible at four weeks of pregnancy, then why not at four weeks and one day, four weeks and two days, and so on until birth and beyond? The reason that this argument possesses superficial plausibility has to do, once more with the concept of 'humanity'. Since all agree that

the newborn infant is a human being, and since there are no ways of drawing clear lines before birth in the development of this human being, there appears to be no clear way of saying that the fetus is *not* human. On the assumption that humanity is the *only* criterion, there can then be a slippage from abortion to infanticide, with no clear dividing line between the two. Once more, then, 'humanity' turns out to be at stake. It is the concept providing the "slipperiness" to the slope—the dimension along which no distinctions can be made which make sense and are enforceable.

Once again, here, 'humanity' operates as a premature ultimate, bringing   45
discussion to a dead end too soon. For the discontinuity which is not found in fetal development can be established by society, and indeed has been so established in modern societies permitting abortion. The argument that the reasons *for* aborting may still be declared to exist at childbirth completely ignores the reasons advanced *against* killing. These reasons grow in strength during pregnancy. Sympathy for the victim, grief on the part of those aware of the loss, recoil on the part of those who would do the killing, and a sense of social catastrophe would accompany the acceptance of infanticide by a contemporary democracy.

But, it may be asked, how can one know that these reasons would pre-   46
vail? How can one be sure that the discontinuity will be respected by most, and that there will not be pressure to move closer and closer to an acceptance of infanticide?

The best way to answer such a question is to see whether that kind of   47
development has actually taken place in one or more of the societies which permit abortion. To the best of my knowledge, the societies which have permitted abortion for considerable lengths of time have not experienced any tendency to infanticide. The infant mortality statistics of Sweden and Denmark, for example, are extremely low, and the protection and care given to all living children, including those born with special handicaps, is exemplary.[14] It is true that facts cannot satisfy those who want a *logical* demonstration that dangerous developments cannot under any circumstances come about. But the burden of proof rests upon them to show *some* evidence of such developments taking place before opposing a policy which will mean so much to women and their families, and also to show why it would not be possible to stop any such development *after* it begins to take place.

The fear of slipping from abortion towards infanticide, therefore, while su-   48
perficially plausible, does not seem to be supported by the available evidence, so long as a cut-off time in pregnancy is established, either by law or in medical practice, after which all fetuses are protected against killing.[15]

I have sketched an approach to seeking community norms for abortion and   49
tried to show the difficulties and dangers in using considerations of 'humanity' to set such norms. Needless to say, *individual* choices for or against abortion will have to be more complex and influenced by religious and moral considerations.[16] Every effort must be made to show that abortion is a last resort. It presents difficulties not present in contraception, yet it is sometimes the only way out of great dilemma.

NOTES*

1. The focus of this paper is on abortion as a problem of social policy. Decisions made by individuals must take other factors into consideration. See S. Bok, "Ethical Problems of Abortion," *Hastings Studies* 4 (April 1974): 8–9; first prepared for the Harvard Interfaculty Seminar on Children, chaired by Nathan B. Talbot. The results and findings of this seminar will be published by Little, Brown and Company (Boston) and entitled *Raising Children in Modern Urban America: Problems and Prospective Solutions.*

2. John Noonan Jr., "An Almost Absolute Value in History," in *The Morality of Abortion*, ed. John Noonan, Jr. (Cambridge: Harvard University Press, 1970), 51. For a thorough discussion of this and other views concerning the beginnings of human life, see Daniel Callahan, *Abortion: Law, Choice and Morality* (New York: Macmillian, 1970).

3. "How the Constitution is Amended," *Family Planning/Population Reporter* 2, no. 3 (June 1973): 56.

4. Roe v. Wade, *The United States Law Week*, 23 January 1973, 4227, 4229.

5. *Ibid.*, 4227. For a discussion of this and other positions taken in the 1973 Supreme Court abortion decisions see L. Tribe, Foreword, *Harvard Law Review* 87 (November 1973): 1–54.

6. Augustine, *The City of God Against the Pagans*, trans. Marcus Dods (Cambridge: Harvard University Press, 1957), Book I, Ch. XX.

7. Christopher D. Stone, "Should Trees Have Standing? Toward Legal Rights for Natural Objects," *Southern California Law Review* 45 (Spring 1972): 450–451 provides an interesting analysis of the extension of rights to those not previously considered persons, such as children, and a discussion of possible future extensions to natural objects.

8. Joseph Fletcher, "Indicators of Humanhood: A Tentative Profile of Man," *The Hastings Center Report* 2, no. 5 (November 1972): 1–4.

9. Edward Shils, "The Sanctity of Life," in *Life or Death: Ethics and Options*, ed. D.H. Labby (Seattle: University of Washington Press, 1968), 12.

10. William Langer, "Checks on Population Growth: 1750–1850," *Scientific American*, February 1972, 92.

11. Every effort must be made by physicians to construe the Supreme Court's statement (*supra*) "If the State is interested in protecting fetal life after viability, it may go so far as to proscribe abortion during that period except when it is necessary to preserve the life or health of the mother" to concern, in effect, only the life or threat to life of the mother. See Alan Stone, "Abortion and the Supreme Court: What Now?" *Modern Medicine*, 30 April 1973, 33–37 for a discussion of this question and what it means for physicians.

*This essay uses notes for documentation, following the form established by *The Chicago Manual of Style* [editor's note].

12. For an insightful discussion of this dilemma, see Judith Thomson, "A Defense of Abortion," *Philosophy and Public Policy* 1, no. 1 (Fall 1971): 47–66. My conclusions are set forth in detail in "Ethical Problems of Abortion," (footnote 1).

13. See S. Bok, "The Leading Edge of the Wedge," *The Hastings Center Report* 1, no. 3 (December 1971): 9–11.

14. Moreover, Nazi Germany, which is frequently cited as a warning of what is to come once abortion becomes lawful, had very strict laws prohibiting abortion. In 1943, Hitler's regime made the existing penalties for women having abortions and for those performing them even more severe by removing the limit on imprisonment and by including the possibility of hard labor for "especially serious cases." See *Reichsgezetzblatt*, 1926, Teil I, Nr. 28, par. 218, and 1943, Teil I, Art. I, "Angriffe auf Ehe, Familie, und Mutterschaft."

15. Another type of line-drawing and slippery slope problem is that which would exist if abortions, once permissible, came to be coercively obtained in the case of mothers thought unable to bring up children, or in cases where deformed children were expected. To outlaw abortions out of a fear that involuntary abortions would take place, however, would be the wrong response to such a danger, just as outlawing voluntary divorces, operations, and adoptions on the grounds that they might lead to involuntary divorces, operations, and adoptions, would be. The battle against coercion must be fought at all times, with respect to many social options, but this is no reason to prohibit the options themselves.

16. See "Ethical Problems of Abortion" (footnote 1).

QUESTIONS FOR MEANING

1. According to Bok, what are the two main arguments against abortion? To what extent does her essay succeed in responding to these arguments?
2. What are the various points at which human life can be said to begin? And what is it that determines which of these views prevails within different social groups?
3. In paragraphs 17–19, Bok summarizes three purposes for defining "humanity." Why does she believe that attempting such a definition is dangerous?
4. Why does Bok emphasize the difference between early and late abortions? Why does she oppose the latter except in special cases? What makes a special case a special case?
5. What is the difference between abortion and infanticide? Why does Bok believe that one does not lead to another? Is there any reason to believe that she may be wrong about this? Has medicine changed in the decade since Bok wrote this essay, making this subject more problematic?
6. Bok lists four reasons for protecting human life and claims that these are "neutral principles." What does she mean by this? Can you give an example of a *non*neutral principle for protecting human life?

7. What does Bok mean by "discontinuity" in paragraphs 45 and 46?
8. Vocabulary: obfuscate (1), eschewing (10), cloning (13), aspirations (18), normative (20), anthropocentric (23), scrutinize (27), continuum (35), and exemplary (47).

QUESTIONS ABOUT STRATEGY

1. As a trained philosopher, what special skills does Bok bring to an argumentative essay on abortion?
2. Does the language of philosophical discourse limit the audience that can understand this essay? Is difficult language inevitable in a serious analysis of a difficult question, or could parts of this essay be written more simply without any loss of meaning?
3. What is the advantage of dividing the essay into parts A, B, C, D, and E? Is there any disadvantage to this type of organization?
4. Where in her essay does Bok acknowledge that there are aspects to the abortion question that her argument does not cover?
5. How would you characterize the tone of this essay?

CLIFFORD GROBSTEIN
When Does Human Life Begin?

Clifford Grobstein (b. 1916) was born in New York City. He attended City College and received his Ph.D. from UCLA in 1940. A highly respected biologist, Grobstein has been a research fellow at the National Cancer Institute and the United States Public Health Service. A fellow of the American Academy of Arts and Sciences, he has taught at Oregon State and Stanford. He is currently Professor of Biological Sciences and Public Policy at the University of California at San Diego. In the following essay, Grobstein responds to essentially the same question that Sissela Bok addressed from a philosophical point of view. But Grobstein writes as a biologist, determined to draw his conclusions from scientifically verifiable fact.

In the debate over abortion, several scientists and prestigious scientific organizations have suggested that science has no contribution to make to the contentious issue of when a human life begins. I respectfully dissent from this view and will briefly describe my rationale. 1

The following six statements appear to me—and I believe to most development biologists—to be scientifically valid. First, all contemporary forms of life are continuous through generations; none arises *de novo*. Life is transmitted, not initiated in each new generation. 2

Second, human life is no exception. Both egg and sperm are living and are human cells. Therefore, fertilization is not when human life begins but is a highly significant step in its continuity. 3

Third, what fertilization initiates is a new generation. The initiation has two aspects: activation of the dormant egg to continue development, and formation of a new hereditary constitution through the combination of genes from the two parents. 4

Fourth, though the product of egg-sperm fusion, the one-celled zygote, is new in its heredity, it is not yet a new individual in the sense of being a person by either scientific or common standards. By common standards, it does not have any of the characteristics we ordinarily associate with people. For example, it lacks even the rudiment of a nervous system and is incapable of even the simplest behavioral responses to stimuli. By scientific standards, the zygote is not yet a single multicellular individual because, depending on circumstances, it may split to produce twins or it may produce less than one individual. In mice, two early embryos can be experimentally fused to become one individual. 5

Fifth, up to at least the eight-cell stage, cells may be deleted from or added to a mouse embryo, and it may still develop into a single, normal individual. This means that early cell divisions simply produce more *individual cells* and not integrated *parts* of a multicellular individual. This non-integrated state persists for at least several days. 6

Sixth, only several days still later are the cells distinguishable as two groups—those that will become the embryo proper and those that will become 7 the supportive tissues such as the placenta. As late as two weeks after fertilization the embryonic precursor can still split to cause twinning. This indicates that singleness has not yet been achieved.

These six statements clearly say that human life *at the level of cells* exists   8
prior to, during, and after fertilization. Human multicellular life is transmitted between generations by a cellular bridge. In the process a new genetic constitution is established, but it may be expressed in more, or less, than one multicellular individual. The establishment of a new, stable multicellular individual, with a new genetic makeup, occurs at about two weeks after fertilization.

Individuality in this biological sense is an essential characteristic of a human   9
being or person. Biological individuality also is a characteristic of most complex animals, certainly of all mammals. To distinguish *human* individuality requires additional characteristics, including bodily and, particularly, facial features, special behaviors, inner awareness, and the capacity to evoke recognition and empathy. Such characteristics gradually come into being as development proceeds. Thus, there is no recognizable human body form two weeks after fertilization, but there is by about eight weeks.

Self-awareness and an active "inner" life are also crucial in evaluating the   10
status of the developing fetus. The genesis of these human features is not fully understood scientifically. Nonetheless, science can provide certain boundaries. For example, there is a close association between all subjective experience, such as feeling, and the activities of the central nervous system, particularly of the brain. Objective indicators of nervous function include the presence of nerve cells, electrical activity, synaptic connections, and particular enzymes and transmitter substances. Without these, the nervous system cannot function, and it would seem reasonable to assume that subjective experience is not yet present.

There is not even a structural rudiment of a nervous system in human   11
embryos until about four weeks after fertilization. Not until eight weeks after fertilization are there recognizable nerve cells, synaptic connections, electrical activity, and neurotransmitter chemicals. Only at this stage do therapeutically aborted embryos begin to show primitive response movements. Another four weeks later comparable maturational indicators appear in the lower brain, and still later they appear in higher brain regions. This suggests that the fetus during the first trimester lacks an adequate neural foundation for minimal subjective experience, let alone self-awareness.

This suggests a direction in which science can play a useful role in clarifying   12
the genesis of persons. Science is not the arbiter, but it can be an advisor to clashing traditions and value systems. Having defined our purposes, we can use objective knowledge to fashion reasonable approaches. Arbitrary definitions may serve one purpose but do violence to others. Indicators of brain function offer an approach to knotty issues of both the beginning and the end of human life. Greater knowledge of the brain can narrow and defuse the sterile debate that is based only on conflicting fixed values.

QUESTIONS FOR MEANING

1. Why is a fertilized egg not an individual human being from a biological point of view?
2. What are the most important stages in the development of a fetus, and when do they occur?
3. Why does Grobstein believe that debate on the nature of human life is often "sterile"? And how can science help overcome this sterility?
4. Vocabulary: contentious (1), *de novo* (2), dormant (4), fusion (5), zygote (5), rudiment (5), synaptic (11), neural (11).

QUESTIONS ABOUT STRATEGY

1. What is the premise of Grobstein's argument, and where does he state it?
2. How would you describe the language of this essay? Is it appropriate to the subject? Does it inspire confidence or repugnance? Is it objective or cold-blooded?
3. How does the organization of this essay help make its content more easily understandable?
4. Does Grobstein recognize that science has its limitations? Why does he claim that science can be an "advisor" but not an "arbiter"?
5. Does Grobstein's essay imply an argument that he himself stops short of making? If asked to advise someone considering an abortion, what sort of advice might he be likely to give? Why does he limit himself to providing information about the fetus and not take a specific stand on the morality of abortion? Would his essay be stronger or weaker if it included a clear statement for or against abortion?

JOHN D. ROCKEFELLER III
No Retreat on Abortion

John D. Rockefeller III (1906–1978) was the eldest of the children born to John D. Rockefeller, Jr., and Abby Aldrich Rockefeller. He graduated from Princeton in 1929 and devoted his life to the interests of his famous family. In addition to being a director of Rockefeller Center and the Rockefeller Brothers Fund, he was chairman of the board of the Rockefeller Foundation. With assets of between 700 and 800 million dollars, the Rockefeller Foundation funds worldwide programs to combat hunger and improve health care in developing nations. Rockefeller's interest in abortion springs from the foundation's concern with population control. "No Retreat on Abortion" was first published by Newsweek *in 1976, when groups opposed to abortion were beginning to mobilize against the Supreme Court ruling that had legalized abortion three years earlier.*

It is ironic that in this Bicentennial year there is a strong effort across the   1
nation to turn the clock back on an important social issue. Ever since the Supreme Court legalized abortion in January 1973, anti-abortion forces have been organizing to overturn the decision. They have injected the issue into the campaigns of 1976, including the appearance of a Presidential candidate who ran on the single issue of opposition to abortion.

There have been efforts within the Congress to initiate a constitutional   2
amendment prohibiting abortion. There is litigation being pressed in state courts and appeals to the Supreme Court. Last November the National Conference of Catholic Bishops issued a "Pastoral Plan for Pro-Life Activities" calling for a wide-ranging anti-abortion effort in every Congressional district including working to defeat any congressman who supports the Supreme Court decision.

Those who oppose abortion have won the battle of the slogans by adopting   3
"Right to Life" as theirs. And, by concentrating on the single issue of the fetus, they have found abortion an easy issue to sensationalize. Thus, they have tended to win the publicity battle, too.

In contrast, those who support legalized abortion—and opinion polls dem-   4
onstrate them to be a majority—have been comparatively quiet. After all, they won their case in the Supreme Court decision. Legalized abortion is the law of the land. It is also in the mainstream of world opinion. The number of countries where abortion has been broadly legalized has increased steadily, today covering 60 percent of the world population.

In this situation, there is a natural tendency to relax, to assume that the   5
matter is settled and that the anti-abortion clamor will eventually die down. But it is conceivable that the United States could become the first democratic nation to turn the clock back by yielding to the pressure and reversing the Supreme Court decision. In my judgment, that would be a tragic mistake.

The least that those who support legalized abortion should do is try to clarify   6
the issue and put it in perspective. The most powerful arguments about abor-

tion are in the field of religious and moral principles—and this is where the opposing views clash head-on. Abortion is against the moral principles defended by the Roman Catholic Church, and some non-Catholics share this viewpoint. But abortion is *not* against the principles of most other religious groups. Those opposed to abortion seek to ban it for everyone in society. Their position is thus coercive in that it would restrict the religious freedom of others and their right to make a free moral choice. In contrast, the legalized abortion viewpoint is non-coercive. No one would think of forcing anyone to undergo an abortion or forcing doctors to perform the procedure when it violates their consciences. Where abortion is legal, everyone is free to live by her or his religious and moral principles.

There are also strong social reasons why abortion should remain legalized. 7 In a woman's decision to have an abortion, there are three key considerations— the fetus, the woman herself, and the future of the unwanted child. Abortion opponents make an emotional appeal based on the first consideration alone. But there is steadily growing understanding and acceptance of a woman's fundamental right to control what happens to her body and to her future. In the privacy of her own mind, and with whatever counseling she seeks, she has the right to make her decision, and no one is better qualified. If she is denied that right, the result may well be an unwanted child, with all the attendant possibilities of abuse and neglect.

Finally, as a practical matter, legalization of abortion is a much more sound 8 and humane social policy than prohibition. Banning abortions does not eliminate them; it never has and it never will. It merely forces women to go the dangerous route of illegal or self-induced abortions. Even worse, it makes abortion a "rich-poor" issue. At a high price, a well-to-do woman can always find a safe abortion. But, unable to pay the price, the poor woman all too often finds herself in incompetent hands.

Experience in three Catholic countries of Latin America that I visited provides dramatic evidence of a high incidence of abortion even when it is against 9 the law. Estimates are that there is one abortion for every two live births in Colombia, and that more than half a million illegal abortions are performed every year in Mexico. In Chile, hospital admissions caused by illegal abortions gone wrong exceed 50,000 per year.

In contrast, the access to safe procedures in the United States has resulted 10 in a drastic decline in deaths associated with abortion. In the period 1969–74, such deaths have fallen by two-thirds. Statistics also strongly suggest that about 70 percent of the legal abortions that have been performed would still have occurred had abortion been against the law. The only difference is that they would have been dangerous operations instead of safe ones.

When you combine the religious, moral and social issues raised above with 11 the fact that women need and will seek abortions even if they are illegal, the case for legalized abortion is overwhelming. We dare not turn the clock back to the time when the religious strictures of one group were mandatory for everyone—not in a democracy.

We must uphold freedom of choice. Moreover, we must work to make free   12
choice a reality by extending safe abortion services throughout the United
States. Only one-fourth of the non-Catholic general hospitals and one-fifth of
the public hospitals in the country now provide such services. It is still extremely difficult to have a legal and safe abortion if you are young or poor or
live in a smaller city or rural area.

On a broader front, we must continue the effort to make contraceptive   13
methods better, safer and more readily available to everyone. Freedom of
choice is crucial, but the decision to have an abortion is always a serious matter.
It is a choice one would wish to avoid. The best way to do that is to avoid
unwanted pregnancy in the first place.

QUESTIONS FOR MEANING

1. Writing in 1976, Rockefeller found it "ironic" that 200 years after the Declaration of Independence many Americans were strongly opposed to abortion. Why does he believe this is "ironic," and how does this observation
   serve to introduce his thesis?
2. What are the consequences that Rockefeller fears if access to legal abortions is once again restricted?
3. Rockefeller recognizes that the Catholic Church opposes abortion but
   claims that "abortion is *not* against the principles of most other religious
   groups." Can you identify a religion that accepts abortion? Are there any
   religions that Rockefeller overlooks which are opposed to abortion?

QUESTIONS ABOUT STRATEGY

1. What was Rockefeller trying to accomplish through this essay? Is his argument designed for any one audience in particular?
2. How would you characterize Rockefeller's point of view? His name is almost
   automatically associated with big business and great wealth. Is there anything especially "business-like" about the tone or substance of this essay?
3. What is the function of paragraph 12? What advantage is there in demanding that a particular policy be advanced even further as opposed to simply
   asking that it not be abandoned?
4. Does Rockefeller make any concessions to the men and women who oppose
   abortion?

WALKER PERCY

A View of Abortion, With Something to Offend Everybody

Walker Percy (b. 1916) graduated from the University of North Carolina in 1937, and received his M.D. from Columbia University in 1941. His novel, The Moviegoer *(1961), won a National Book Award in 1962. Other works by Percy include* The Last Gentleman *(1966),* Love in the Ruins *(1971),* The Message in the Bottle *(1975),* Lancelot *(1976),* The Second Coming *(1980), and* Lost in the Cosmos *(1983). A fellow of the American Academy of Arts and Sciences and a member of the National Institute of Arts and Letters, Percy is widely recognized as an important contemporary novelist. He published the following essay in the* New York Times *when Congress was debating legislation that sought to define when human life begins.*

I feel like saying something about this abortion issue. My credentials as an   1
expert on the subject: none. I am an M.D. and a novelist. I will speak only as a
novelist. If I give an opinion as an M.D., it wouldn't interest anybody since, for
one thing, any number of doctors have given opinions and who cares about
another.

The only obvious credential of a novelist has to do with his trade. He traffics   2
in words and meanings. So the chronic misuse of words, especially the fobbing
off of rhetoric for information, gets on his nerves. Another possible credential
of a novelist peculiar to these times is that he is perhaps more sensitive to the
atrocities of the age than most. People get desensitized. Who wants to go about
his business being reminded of the six million dead in the holocaust, the 15
million in the Ukraine? Atrocities become banal. But a 20th century novelist
should be a nag, an advertiser, a collector, a proclaimer of banal atrocities.

True legalized abortion—a million and a half fetuses flushed down the Dis-   3
posall every year in this country—is yet another banal atrocity in a century
where atrocities have become commonplace. This statement will probably offend one side in this already superheated debate, so I hasten in the interests of
fairness and truth to offend the other side. What else can you do when some of
your allies give you as big a pain as your opponents? I notice this about many
so-called pro-lifers. They seem pro-life only on this one perfervid and politi-
cized issue. The Reagan Administration, for example, professes to be anti-
abortion but has just recently decided, in the interests of business, that it is
proper for infant formula manufacturers to continue their hard-sell in the third
world despite thousands of deaths from bottle feeding. And Senator Jesse
Helms and the Moral Majority, who profess a reverence for unborn life, don't
seem to care much about born life: poor women who don't get abortions, have
their babies, and can't feed them.

Nothing new here of course. What I am writing this for is to call attention to   4 a particularly egregious example of doublespeak that the abortionists—"pro-choicers," that is—seem to have hit on in the current rhetorical war.

Now I don't know whether the human-life bill is good legislation or not. But   5
as a novelist I can recognize meretricious use of language, disingenuousness, and a con job when I hear it.

The current con, perpetrated by some jurists, some editorial writers, and   6
some doctors is that since there is no agreement about the beginning of human life, it is therefore a private religious or philosophical decision and therefore the state and the courts can do nothing about it. This is a con. I will not presume to speculate who is conning whom and for what purpose. But I do submit that religion, philosophy, and private opinion have nothing to do with this issue. I further submit that it is a commonplace of modern biology, known to every high school student and no doubt to you the reader as well, that the life of every individual organism, human or not, begins when the chromosomes of the sperm fuse with the chromosomes of the ovum to form a new DNA complex that thenceforth directs the ontogenesis of the organism.

Such vexed subjects as the soul, God, and the nature of man are not at issue.   7
What we are talking about and what nobody I know would deny is the clear continuum that exists in the life of every individual from the moment of fertilization of a single cell.

There is a wonderful irony here. It is this: The onset of individual life is not a   8
dogma of the church but a fact of science. How much more convenient if we lived in the 13th century, when no one knew anything about microbiology and arguments about the onset of life were legitimate. Compared to a modern textbook of embryology, Thomas Aquinas sounds like an American Civil Liberties Union member. Nowadays it is not some misguided ecclesiastics who are trying to suppress an embarrassing scientific fact. It is the secular juridical–journalistic establishment.

Please indulge the novelist if he thinks in novelistic terms. Picture the scene.   9
A Galileo trial in reverse. The Supreme Court is cross-examining a high school biology teacher and admonishing him that, of course, it is only his personal opinion that the fertilized human ovum is an individual human life. He is enjoined not to teach his private beliefs at a public school. Like Galileo he caves in, submits, but in turning away is heard to murmer, *"But it's still alive!"*

To pro-abortionists: According to the opinion polls, it looks as if you may get   10
your way. But you're not going to have it both ways. You're going to be told what you're doing.

QUESTIONS FOR MEANING

1. What does Percy believe that a novelist can contribute to the debate on abortion? How does he define the responsibilities of a novelist?
2. Explain what Percy means in paragraph 2 when he protests against "the fobbing off of rhetoric for information."

3. What does Percy say that would offend people who favor legalized abortion? What does he say that would offend people who share his own view that abortion is wrong?
4. Why does Percy believe that "religion, philosophy, and private opinion" have nothing to do with the question of when human life begins?
5. Identify Thomas Acquinas. Who was Galileo, and for what "crime" was he tried?
6. Vocabulary: trafficks (2), perfervid (3), egregious (4), meretricious (5), disingenuousness (5), ontogenesis (6), dogma (8), ecclesiastics (8), and secular (8).

QUESTIONS ABOUT STRATEGY

1. Why does Percy begin his essay by disclaiming any credentials as an "expert"? Why does he reveal that he has an M.D. and then declare that he wants to write from the point of view of a novelist rather than a physician?
2. What use does Percy make of history in paragraph 2?
3. Consider the tone of paragraph 3. Is it forceful or unnecessarily offensive?
4. What is the function of paragraph 7? Why does Percy repeat what he had already claimed in paragraph 6?
5. Do you understand the imaginary scene that Percy sketches in paragraph 9? Explain this scene and the point it is meant to illustrate.

SHIRLEY K. BELL

Is Abortion Morally Justifiable?

When debating the ethics of abortion, it is easy to lose sight of the dilemma of many nurses and physicians. Many physicians devote themselves to specialties in which they would never be called upon to perform an abortion; others may choose to refer a patient elsewhere. But what is the position of a nurse who is called upon to assist in an abortion? Can a nurse refuse to do so because she is personally opposed to abortion, or would such a refusal be a violation of the nurse's responsibility to provide medical care wherever such care is necessary? This is the question that Shirley K. Bell (b. 1941) attempts to answer in "Is Abortion Morally Justifiable?" A registered nurse who received her Ed.D. in 1984, Bell is an assistant professor in the College of Nursing at Ohio State University. For her writing about nursing she was the 1977 recipient of the Excellence in Writing Award from the American Journal of Nursing.

"It is one of the ironies of history that the issues most in need of cool and dispassionate thinking for their resolution emerge during the course of human events at just those times of crisis, when emotions are running high and the fires of irrationalism are most likely to have been kindled" (1, p. 103).

Abortion. Just the word can raise some people's emotions to the highest   1
level. Most of us have an opinion: we are either for abortion or against it. The pro-abortion forces quote individual rights of the mother, right to privacy, right to autonomy, and claim that this is a choice for the mother alone. On the other side are the anti-abortion or "right to life" forces who defend the fetus's right to live, and don't want mothers involved in the killing of their unborn babies.

Is abortion legally, morally, and religiously justifiable? Prior to 1973, most   2
states had restrictive abortion laws, in that it was a criminal offense for anyone to perform an abortion. The development of these laws was a reflection of the changing views on abortion, for at the time our Constitution was adopted and throughout the major portion of the 19th century, abortion was viewed with less disfavor than under most American statutes in effect before the United States Supreme Court's decision in *Roe vs. Wade* declared these laws were unconstitutional. Undoubtedly, criminal abortion laws were a product of Victorian social concern and were designed to discourage illicit sex. But they were also designed to save women's lives, as the procedure was considered hazardous, particularly, before the discovery of antibiotics. In addition, the states, on the assumption that a new human life was present at the moment of conception, arrogated as their duty the protection of prenatal life.

In the majority decision of the Supreme Court in *Roe vs. Wade*, the Court   3
recognized the right of personal privacy of a pregnant woman. The decision was that for the period of pregnancy to the period of viability, the attending physician, in consultation with his patient is free to determine without regula-

tion by the state, that, in his medical judgment, the patient's pregnancy should be terminated. After the period of viability, the state may regulate abortions (2). This ruling has been interpreted to mean that during the first and most of the second trimester, the decision regarding an abortion is between the patient and her physician. After that time, especially during the third trimester, the state may regulate abortions.

This legal decision, however, has not answered the moral or religious questions that surround abortion. The religious objections to abortion are based on the belief that the fetus is a fully independent human being and, therefore, abortion is tantamount to murder of a human being and, therefore, is wrong. However, this line of thought is not specifically stated in *The Holy Bible* or other religious books. In reality, it is an idea that has evolved slowly over the years in certain religious traditions. So even though the abortion question is an ethical issue that involves a conflict between moral values, it doesn't seem to have a basis in religious objection (3).

The main component of the religious argument is that the fetus is a human being, which seems to be a concern that needs further examination. As the time of conception is yet to be pinpointed to a specific point in time, when does the fetus become a human being? Is the zygote a human being? Is the embryo a human being? Are we really talking about the *potential* to become a human being?

A fertilized human ovum has the potential to become a child and then an adult, but is the fertilized ovum a human being? The analogy may be drawn between this and a fertilized chicken egg. The potential is there for the egg to be hatched into a chicken, but does the egg have the characteristics we apply to a live chicken? Can it eat food, lay eggs, and so on? No. So isn't it really the potential that is there? Isn't this similar to the fetus up to the point of viability? Isn't it at the point of viability that the fetus has an ability to breathe, eat, digest food, and carry on the biological functions without life support? The question then may be directed toward what is it that makes one a unique human being.

The characteristics of a unique human being may be referred to by some as the characteristics of a person. Ruf (4, p. 156) asks the following question to help bring this issue into focus: "Should all the rights and protections morally due to clear cases of persons be granted to all human embryos and fetuses?" In searching for those general characteristics of personhood, one needs to look at other possible beings who might be classified as persons.

Warren (5, p. 45) states that the traits most central to the concept of personhood are: consciousness, reasoning, self-motivated activity, capacity to communicate, and the presence of self-concepts and self-awareness. Consciousness is described as being conscious of objects and events external and/or internal to the being, and in particular the capacity to feel pain. Reasoning is described as the developed capacity to solve new and relatively complex problems, and self-motivated activity is activity relatively independent of either genetic or direct external control. The capacity to communicate is clarified to include, by whatever means, messages of an indefinite variety of types and on indefinitely many possible topics. The presence of self-concepts and self-awareness include either individual or racial characteristics or both. Discussion could go on as to whether all or part of these traits are essential for someone to be considered a person. Questions could be raised as to which traits are more important than others. But all that needs to be demonstrated to state that a fetus is not a person is that a fetus satisfies none of the concepts of the conditions of person-hood. And, if this is so, a fetus should not be granted all the rights and protections due persons.

If the fetus is not a person and, therefore, should not be afforded rights and obligations of a person, what then is the pregnant woman's rights? The Supreme Court has legally defined the woman's right to privacy under the *14th Amendment*. But, are there other rights of women that may have priority over even their legal rights? An exploration of various components of the pregnant woman's ethical decision may help to clarify this.   9

The conditions surrounding the pregnancy will need to be considered. Exceptions to the abortion situation have often been made in cases of rape. In this, the mother is pregnant by force. But, she is also pregnant against her wishes. This is one condition that may diminish the woman's responsibility to the fetus. Another condition may be a situation in which the woman feels she is protected against pregnancy but a failure in contraception results in a pregnancy. This situation may also result in a diminished responsibility of the woman toward the fetus. An exception to the rule may be a woman who intentionally plans to become pregnant and then, after the fact, desires an abortion (6). But even in this situation does the woman have a stronger right to self-determination than her duty to the fetus?   10

Thomson (7, pp. 4–5) has developed an interesting analogy to help us discuss the pregnant woman's most imminent right.   11

> But now let me ask you to imagine this. You wake up in the morning and find yourself back to back in bed with an unconscious violinist. He has been found to have a fatal kidney ailment, and the Society of Music Lovers has canvassed all the available medical records and found that you alone have the right blood type to help. They have therefore kidnapped you, and last night the violinist's circulatory system was plugged into yours, so that your kidneys can be used to extract poisons from his blood as well as your own. The director of the hospital now tells you, "Look, we're sorry the Society of Music Lovers did this to you—we would never have permitted it if we had known." But still, they did it, and the violinist now is plugged into you. To unplug you would be to kill him. But never mind, it's only for nine months. By then he will have recovered from his ailment, and can safely be unplugged from you.

Of course the argument is made that this act was done against your will. You were kidnapped, but isn't this a matter of degree? Can't a pregnant woman also be viewed as being kidnapped and held hostage for nine months to support another potential person's life? In this instance, doesn't the right of a woman to control her own body and control her own fertility take precedence? Isn't an individual's rights to personal autonomy of utmost importance here? Does the fetus's right to a potential life require the use of another's body against her will? While many people would be outraged at being connected to the violinist, they are not able to see the analogy to that of a woman with an unwanted pregnancy.

Bok (6) offers two more arguments which may be used against abortion. 12 One, that if abortion is accepted as a standard practice, it will lead to actions against other groups, such as defective newborns, and could lead to a Nazi-like state. (Ironically, Nazi Germany had very strict criminal abortion laws.) The other argument is that physicians and nurses would lose their protective attitude toward life if they were involved in abortion procedures.

The advance of modern medical technology has also led to some additional 13 knowledge of methods of abortion, life and living, grief and grieving, that may have an effect on the abortion decision. The ability to diagnose genetic diseases in utero has facilitated the physician's ability to determine if the abortion of a fetus will prevent the suffering or grieving that may accompany the birth and subsequent death of a severely defective child.

With people living longer through the benefits of modern medicine, the 14 question of overpopulation also must be taken into consideration. Advocates of abortion will also argue that abortion may be used as a method of birth control, even if it is the last resort, to prevent overpopulation and the undesired effects which may occur if this option is not available. These effects may include child abuse of unwanted children, maternal deaths as a result of illegal abortions, added poverty, and added illness. This particular argument was advanced as early as 1920 by the Soviet Union. According to Villard (8, pp. 395–396) the Soviets thought "it is immoral for parents to have more children than they can provide adequate food for. Measures taken by the State against such an unfortunate contingency are therefore thoroughly justified and would make for the progress of the human race."

Even the types of abortions have been analyzed to differentiate between 15 those that withdraw life support and those that may actually kill the fetus, leading to a spontaneous abortion. Abortions that fit into the first category include the morning after pill, the vacuum abortion, and the little used hysterotomy. The saline abortion, which is commonly used in the second trimester to induce abortion, may be classified in the second category. If a pregnant woman is having trouble making her decision, she may want to consider the ethics of each of these methods.

As can be seen, opposing views on abortion constitute a moral dilemma—a 16 dilemma that often finds the nurse in the middle. On the one hand is her own personal belief, and on the other, may be a conflicting belief of the patient. To provide nursing care to patients who may be in opposition to the nurse's stand, it is important that the nurse have a philosophical basis with which to view this dilemma, not just her emotional beliefs.

Once the emotionalism surrounding the question of abortion is lessened, and 17 abortion is examined in a rational manner, it would seem apparent that abortion can be morally justified. Prior to the time of viability, the mother's right to autonomy and self-determination about her own body supersedes the rights of an unborn, potential human being.

Keeping these arguments in mind, isn't the real question of abortion one of   18
mandated pregnancy—the right of self-determination and control over the use
of one's body versus the rights of an unborn potential human being?

REFERENCES*

(1) Holmes RL. Violence and nonviolence. In: Shaffer J, ed. Violence. New
York: David McKay, 1971: 101–135.

(2) Blackman H. Roe vs. Wade, decision on abortion by the United States
Supreme Court. In: Reiser SJ et al, eds. Ethics in medicine. Cambridge: MIT
Press, 1977: 401–415.

(3) Newton L. The irrelevance of religion in the abortion debate. HCR 1978
Aug: 16–17.

(4) Ruf HL. Moral investigations: an introduction to the study of current moral
problems. Washington: University Press of America, 1977.

(5) Warren MA. On the moral and legal status of abortion. In: Wasserstrom
RA, ed. Today's moral problems. New York: Macmillan, 1979: 35–51.

(6) Bok S. Ethical problems of abortion. In: Reiser SJ et al, eds. Ethics in
medicine. Cambridge: MIT Press, 1977: 432–443.

(7) Thomson JJ. A defense of abortion. In: Cohen M et al, eds. The rights and
wrongs of abortion. Princeton: Princeton University Press, 1974: 3–22.

(8) Villard HG. Legalized elimination of the unborn in Soviet Russia. In: Reiser
SJ et al, eds. Ethics in medicine. Cambridge: MIT Press, 1977: 394–396.

QUESTIONS FOR MEANING

1. Why did abortion laws become more restrictive in the late nineteenth
   century?
2. During what part of a woman's pregnancy does the state retain the power
   to regulate abortions? What is the reason for this?
3. Why does Bell conclude that a fetus is not a person? What authorities does
   she cite in arriving at this conclusion?
4. What are the different types of abortion, and why might someone argue
   that there are ethical differences among them?

---

* This essay uses a numbered system for documentation. This is a type of documentation used frequently in
medical and scientific writing. (See Part Three, pp. 565–66) When using a numbered system, you do not usually
need to give page references within the parenthetical reference, but you can do so when you want to direct your
audience to a specific page. Bell's essay demonstrates how this can be done.

The form of the reference list varies from one field to another. This particular reference list follows the form
established by the International Committee of Medical Journal Editors. Do not use it as a model unless you are
writing for a medical journal. Use the format recommended by a handbook for your chosen field [editor's note].

5. Bell argues that nurses need a "philosophical basis" from which to view abortion and that "emotional beliefs" are inadequate for determining the type of care nurses provide their patients. Explain what she means by this. What's wrong with basing health care decisions on "emotional beliefs"?

QUESTIONS ABOUT STRATEGY

1. How does Bell view people who oppose abortion? Does she ever say anything that would cause such people to feel offended?
2. In paragraph 4, Bell draws a distinction between religious and ethical objections to abortion, arguing that the Bible and "other religious books" do not specifically forbid abortion. Should she have said more about this, or does the reference to Newton satisfy you that this claim is well supported?
3. Bell's argument is based upon a series of summaries from her reading. Are these summaries clearly written? Without necessarily being familiar with the material being summarized, are you persuaded that the summaries are fair and accurate? What is there about them that leads you to view them as you do?
4. Do you understand the analogy cited in paragraph 11? Bell recognizes that many people do not see the connection between unwanted pregnancy and kidnapping. Explain the analogy in your own words.

RONALD REAGAN
Abortion and the Conscience of the Nation

Ronald Reagan (b. 1911) is the fortieth president of the United States. He grew up in Dixon, Illinois, and after graduating from Eureka College became a sports announcer for radio stations in Davenport and Des Moines, Iowa. He signed a contract with Warner Brothers in 1937 and went on to appear in more than fifty films, the last of which was released in 1964. Reagan's first political involvement came in 1947, when he began a five-year term as president of the Screen Actors Guild. He became a Republican in 1962 and was elected governor of California in 1966, a position to which he was reelected four years later. After unsuccessful attempts to secure his party's nomination in 1968 and 1976, Reagan became president in 1980. He was reelected in 1984, carrying every state except Minnesota and the District of Columbia. Widely associated with traditional family values, Reagan published the following essay in 1983, the tenth anniversary of the Supreme Court decision that had legalized abortion.

The 10th Anniversary of the Supreme Court decision in *Roe v. Wade* is a   1
good time for us to pause and reflect. Our nationwide policy of abortion-on-demand through all nine months of pregnancy was neither voted for by our people nor enacted by our legislators—not a single State had such unrestricted abortion before the Supreme Court decreed it to be national policy in 1973. But the consequences of this judicial decision are now obvious: since 1973, more than 15 million unborn children have had their lives snuffed out by legalized abortions. That is over ten times the number of Americans lost in all our nation's wars.

Make no mistake, abortion-on-demand is not a right granted by the Consti-   2
tution. No serious scholar, including one disposed to agree with the Court's result, has argued that the framers of the Constitution intended to create such a right. Shortly after the *Roe v. Wade* decision, Professor John Hart Ely, now Dean of Stanford Law School, wrote that the opinion "is not constitutional law and gives almost no sense of an obligation to try to be." Nowhere do the plain words of the Constitution even hint at a "right" so sweeping as to permit abortion up to the time the child is ready to be born. Yet that is what the Court ruled.

As an act of "raw judicial power" (to use Justice White's biting phrase), the   3
decision by the seven-man majority in *Roe v. Wade* has so far been made to stick. But the Court's decision has by no means settled the debate. Instead, *Roe v. Wade* has become a continuing prod to the conscience of the nation.

Abortion concerns not just the unborn child, it concerns every one of us.   4
The English poet, John Donne, wrote: "... any man's death diminishes me, because I am involved in mankind; and therefore never send to know for whom the bell tolls; it tolls for thee."

We cannot diminish the value of one category of human life—the unborn—   5
without diminishing the value of all human life. We saw tragic proof of this

truism last year when the Indiana courts allowed the starvation death of "Baby Doe" in Bloomington because the child had Down's Syndrome.

Many of our fellow citizens grieve over the loss of life that has followed *Roe* 6 *v. Wade.* Margaret Heckler, soon after being nominated to head the largest department of our government, Health and Human Services, told an audience that she believed abortion to be the greatest moral crisis facing our country today. And the revered Mother Teresa, who works in the streets of Calcutta ministering to dying people in her world-famous mission of mercy, has said that "the greatest misery of our time is the generalized abortion of children."

Over the first two years of my Administration I have closely followed and 7 assisted efforts in Congress to reverse the tide of abortion—efforts of Congressmen, Senators and citizens responding to an urgent moral crisis. Regrettably, I have also seen the massive efforts of those who, under the banner of "freedom of choice," have so far blocked every effort to reverse nationwide abortion-on-demand.

Despite the formidable obstacles before us, we must not lose heart. This is 8 not the first time our country has been divided by a Supreme Court decision that denied the value of certain human lives. The *Dred Scott* decision of 1857 was not overturned in a day, or a year, or even a decade. At first, only a minority of Americans recognized and deplored the moral crisis brought about by denying the full humanity of our black brothers and sisters; but that minority persisted in their vision and finally prevailed. They did it by appealing to the hearts and minds of their countrymen, to the truth of human dignity under God. From their example, we know that respect for the sacred value of human life is too deeply engrained in the hearts of our people to remain forever suppressed. But the great majority of the American people have not yet made their voices heard, and we cannot expect them to—any more than the public voice arose against slavery—*until* the issue is clearly framed and presented.

What, then, is the real issue? I have often said that when we talk about 9 abortion, we are talking about two lives—the life of the mother and the life of the unborn child. Why else do we call a pregnant woman a mother? I have also said that anyone who doesn't feel sure whether we are talking about a second human life should clearly give life the benefit of the doubt. If you don't know whether a body is alive or dead, you would never bury it. I think this consideration itself should be enough for all of us to insist on protecting the unborn.

The case against abortion does not rest here, however, for medical practice 10 confirms at every step the correctness of these moral sensibilities. Modern medicine treats the unborn child as a patient. Medical pioneers have made great breakthroughs in treating the unborn—for genetic problems, vitamin deficiencies, irregular heart rhythms, and other medical conditions. Who can forget George Will's moving account of the little boy who underwent brain surgery six times during the nine weeks before he was born? Who is the *patient* if not that tiny unborn human being who can feel pain when he or she is approached by doctors who come to kill rather than to cure?

The real question today is not when human life begins, but, *What is the* 11 *value of human life?* The abortionist who reassembles the arms and legs of a tiny baby to make sure all its parts have been torn from its mother's body can hardly doubt whether it is a human being. The real question for him and for all of us is whether that tiny human life has a God-given right to be protected by the law—the same right we have.

What more dramatic confirmation could we have of the real issue than the   12
Baby Doe case in Bloomington, Indiana? The death of that tiny infant tore at the hearts of all Americans because the child was undeniably a live human being—one lying helpless before the eyes of the doctors and the eyes of the nation. The real issue for the courts was *not* whether Baby Doe was a human being. The real issue was whether to protect the life of a human being who had Down's Syndrome, who would probably be mentally handicapped, but who needed a routine surgical procedure to unblock his esophagus and allow him to eat. A doctor testified to the presiding judge that, even with his physical problem corrected, Baby Doe would have a "non-existent" possibility for "a minimally adequate quality of life"—in other words, that retardation was the equivalent of a crime deserving the death penalty. The judge let Baby Doe starve and die, and the Indiana Supreme Court sanctioned his decision.

Federal law does not allow Federally-assisted hospitals to decide that   13
Down's Syndrome infants are not worth treating, much less to decide to starve them to death. Accordingly, I have directed the Departments of Justice and HHS to apply civil rights regulations to protect handicapped newborns. All hospitals receiving Federal funds must post notices which will clearly state that failure to feed handicapped babies is prohibited by Federal law. The basic issue is whether to value and protect the lives of the handicapped, whether to recognize the sanctity of human life. This is the same basic issue that underlies the question of abortion.

The 1981 Senate hearings on the beginning of human life brought out the   14
basic issue more clearly than ever before. The many medical and scientific witnesses who testified disagreed on many things, but not on the *scientific* evidence that the unborn child is alive, is a distinct individual, or is a member of the human species. They did disagree over the *value* question, whether to give value to a human life at its early and most vulnerable stages of existence.

Regrettably, we live at a time when some persons do *not* value all human   15
life. They want to pick and choose which individuals have value. Some have said that only those individuals with "consciousness of self" are human beings. One such writer has followed this deadly logic and concluded that "shocking as it may seem, a newly born infant is not a human being."

A Nobel Prize winning scientist has suggested that if a handicapped child   16
"were not declared fully human until three days after birth, then all parents could be allowed the choice." In other words, "quality control" to see if newly born human beings are up to snuff.

Obviously, some influential people want to deny that every human life has   17
intrinsic, sacred worth. They insist that a member of the human race must have certain qualities before they accord him or her status as a "human being."

Events have borne out the editorial in a California medical journal which   18
explained three years before *Roe v. Wade* that the social acceptance of abortion

is a "defiance of the long-held Western ethic of intrinsic and equal value for every human life regardless of its stage, condition, or status."

Every legislator, every doctor, and every citizen needs to recognize that the 19 real issue is whether to affirm and protect the sanctity of all human life, or to embrace a social ethic where some human lives are valued and others are not. As a nation, we must choose between the sanctity of life ethic and the quality of life ethic.

I have no trouble identifying the answer our nation has always given to this 20 basic question, and the answer that I hope and pray it will give in the future. America was founded by men and women who shared a vision of the value of each and every individual. They stated this vision clearly from the very start in the Declaration of Independence, using words that every schoolboy and schoolgirl can recite:

> We hold these truths to be self-evident, that all men are created equal, that they are endowed by their Creator with certain unalienable rights, that among these are life, liberty, and the pursuit of happiness.

We fought a terrible war to guarantee that one category of mankind—black 21 people in America—could not be denied the inalienable rights with which their Creator endowed them. The great champion of the sanctity of all human life in that day, Abraham Lincoln, gave us his assessment of the Declaration's purpose. Speaking of the framers of that noble document, he said:

> This was their majestic interpretation of the economy of the Universe. This was their lofty, and wise, and noble understanding of the justice of the Creator to His creatures. Yes, gentlemen, to all His creatures, to the whole great family of man. In their enlightened belief, nothing stamped with the divine image and likeness was sent into the world to be trodden on ... They grasped not only the whole race of man then living, but they reached forward and seized upon the farthest posterity. They erected a beacon to guide their children and their children's children, and the countless myriads who should inhabit the earth in other ages.

He warned also of the danger we would face if we closed our eyes to the 22 value of life in any category of human beings:

> I should like to know if taking this old Declaration of Independence, which declares that all men are equal upon principle and making exceptions to it where will it stop. If one man says it does not mean a Negro, why not another say it does not mean some other man?

When Congressman John A. Bingham of Ohio drafted the Fourteenth 23 Amendment to guarantee the rights of life, liberty, and property to all human beings, he explained that *all* are "entitled to the protection of American law, because its divine spirit of equality declares that all men are created equal." He said the rights guaranteed by the amendment would therefore apply to "any human being." Justice William Brennan, writing in another case decided only the year before *Roe v. Wade*, referred to our society as one that "strongly affirms the sanctity of life."

Another William Brennan—not the Justice—has reminded us of the terrible   24
consequences that can follow when a nation rejects the sanctity of life ethic:

> The cultural environment for a human holocaust is present whenever any society can be misled into defining individuals as less than human and therefore devoid of value and respect.

As a nation today, we have *not* rejected the sanctity of human life. The   25
American people have not had an opportunity to express their view on the sanctity of human life in the unborn. I am convinced that Americans do not want to play God with the value of human life. It is not for us to decide who is worthy to live and who is not. Even the Supreme Court's opinion in *Roe v. Wade* did not explicitly reject the traditional American idea of intrinsic worth and value in all human life; it simply dodged this issue.

The Congress has before it several measures that would enable our people   26
to reaffirm the sanctity of human life, even the smallest and the youngest and the most defenseless. The Human Life Bill expressly recognizes the unborn as human beings and accordingly protects them as persons under our Constitution. This bill, first introduced by Senator Jesse Helms, provided the vehicle for the Senate hearings in 1981 which contributed so much to our understanding of the real issue of abortion.

The Respect Human Life Act, just introduced in the 98th Congress, states in   27
its first section that the policy of the United States is "to protect innocent life, both before and after birth." This bill, sponsored by Congressman Henry Hyde and Senator Roger Jepsen, prohibits the Federal government from performing abortions or assisting those who do so, except to save the life of the mother. It also addresses the pressing issue of infanticide which, as we have seen, flows inevitably from permissive abortion as another step in the denial of the inviolability of innocent human life.

I have endorsed each of these measures, as well as the more difficult route   28
of constitutional amendment, and I will give these initiatives my full support. Each of them, in different ways, attempts to reverse the tragic policy of abortion-on-demand imposed by the Supreme Court ten years ago. Each of them is a decisive way to affirm the sanctity of human life.

We must all educate ourselves to the reality of the horrors taking place.   29
Doctors today know that unborn children can feel a touch within the womb and that they respond to pain. But how many Americans are aware that abortion techniques are allowed today, in all 50 states, that burn the skin of a baby with a salt solution, in an agonizing death that can last for hours?

Another example: two years ago, the *Philadelphia Inquirer* ran a Sunday   30 special supplement on "The Dreaded Complication." The "dreaded complication" referred to in the article—the complication feared by doctors who perform abortions—is the *survival* of the child despite all the painful attacks during the abortion procedure. Some unborn children *do survive the late-term abortions* the Supreme Court has made legal. Is there any question that these victims of abortion deserve our attention and protection? Is there any question that those who *don't* survive were living human beings before they were killed?

Late-term abortions, especially when the baby survives, but is then killed by   31
starvation, neglect, or suffocation, show once again the link between abortion and infanticide. The time to stop both is now. As my Administration acts to stop infanticide, we will be fully aware of the real issue that underlies the death of babies before and soon after birth.

Our society has, fortunately, become sensitive to the rights and special needs   32
of the handicapped, but I am shocked that physical or mental handicaps of newborns are still used to justify their extinction. This Administration has a Surgeon General, Dr. C. Everett Koop, who has done perhaps more than any other American for handicapped children, by pioneering surgical techniques to help them, by speaking out on the value of their lives, and by working with them in the context of loving families. You will not find his former patients advocating the so-called quality of life ethic.

I know that when the true issue of infanticide is placed before the American   33
people, with all the facts openly aired, we will have no trouble deciding that a mentally or physically handicapped baby has the same intrinsic worth and right to life as the rest of us. As the New Jersey Supreme Court said two decades ago, in a decision upholding the sanctity of human life, "a child need not be perfect to have a worthwhile life."

Whether we are talking about pain suffered by unborn children, or about   34
late-term abortions, or about infanticide, we inevitably focus on the humanity of the unborn child. Each of these issues is a potential rallying point for the sanctity of life ethic. Once we as a nation rally around any one of these issues to affirm the sanctity of life, we will see the importance of affirming this principle across the board.

Malcolm Muggeridge, the English writer, goes right to the heart of the matter: 35
"Either life is always and in all circumstances sacred, or intrinsically of no account; it is inconceivable that it should be in some cases the one, and in some the other." The sanctity of innocent human life is a principle that Congress should proclaim at every opportunity.

It is possible that the Supreme Court itself may overturn its abortion rulings.   36
We need only recall that in *Brown v. Board of Education* the Court reversed its own earlier "separate-but-equal" decision. I believe if the Supreme Court took another look at *Roe v. Wade,* and considered the real issue between the sanctity of life ethic and the quality of life ethic, it would change its mind once again.

As we continue to work to overturn *Roe v. Wade,* we must also continue to   37
lay the groundwork for a society in which abortion is not the accepted answer

to unwanted pregnancy. Pro-life people have already taken heroic steps, often at great personal sacrifice, to provide for unwed mothers. I recently spoke about a young pregnant woman named Victoria, who said, "In this society we save whales, we save timber wolves and bald eagles and Coke bottles. Yet, everyone wanted me to throw away my baby." She has been helped by Sav-a-Life, a group in Dallas, which provides a way for unwed mothers to preserve the human life within them when they might otherwise be tempted to resort to abortion. I think also of House of His Creation in Coatesville, Pennsylvania, where a loving couple has taken in almost 200 young women in the past ten years. They have seen, as a fact of life, that the girls are *not* better off having abortions than saving their babies. I am also reminded of the remarkable Rossow family of Ellington, Connecticut, who have opened their hearts and their home to nine handicapped adopted and foster children.

The Adolescent Family Life Program, adopted by Congress at the request of   38
Senator Jeremiah Denton, has opened new opportunities for unwed mothers to give their children life. We should not rest until our entire society echoes the tone of John Powell in the dedication of his book, *Abortion: The Silent Holocaust*, a dedication to every woman carrying an unwanted child: "Please believe that you are not alone. There are many of us that truly love you, who want to stand at your side, and help in any way we can." And we can echo the always-practical woman of faith, Mother Teresa, when she says, "If you don't want the little child, that unborn child, give him to me." We have so many families in America seeking to adopt children that the slogan "every child a wanted child" is now the emptiest of all reasons to tolerate abortion.

I have often said we need to join in prayer to bring protection to the unborn.   39
Prayer and action are needed to uphold the sanctity of human life. I believe it will not be possible to accomplish our work, the work of saving lives, "without being a soul of prayer." The famous British Member of Parliament, William Wilberforce, prayed with his small group of influential friends, the "Clapham Sect," for *decades* to see an end to slavery in the British empire. Wilberforce led that struggle in Parliament, unflaggingly, because he believed in the sanctity of human life. He saw the fulfillment of his impossible dream when Parliament outlawed slavery just before his death.

Let his faith and perseverance be our guide. We will never recognize the true   40
value of our own lives until we affirm the value in the life of others, a value of which Malcolm Muggeridge says: "... however low it flickers or fiercely burns, it is still a Divine flame which no man dare presume to put out, be his motives ever so humane and enlightened."

Abraham Lincoln recognized that we could not survive as a free land when   41
some men could decide that others were not fit to be free and should therefore be slaves. Likewise, we cannot survive as a free nation when some men decide that others are not fit to live and should be abandoned to abortion or infanticide. My Administration is dedicated to the preservation of America as a free land, and there is no cause more important for preserving that freedom than affirming the transcendent right to life of all human beings, the right without which no other rights have any meaning.

QUESTIONS FOR MEANING

1. Who was Dred Scott, and what was the Supreme Court decision that bears his name?
2. What is Down's Syndrome, and how serious a handicap is it? Can children with Down's Syndrome ever lead meaningful lives?
3. What type of abortion is Reagan describing in paragraph 29? Is this description accurate?
4. Why does Reagan believe that abortion cannot be distinguished from infanticide?
5. Vocabulary: genetic (10), esophagus (12), sanctity (13), vulnerable (14), inviolability (27), and transcendent (41).

QUESTIONS ABOUT STRATEGY

1. What is the premise of Reagan's argument, and where does he first state it?
2. Consider the way Reagan uses the phrase "unborn children" in his opening paragraph. Is this an effective use of language? Is this an honest use of language?
3. Are there any parts of this argument which strike you as especially political? Does Reagan ever lose sight of his subject and introduce themes that seem likely to appeal only to the emotions of a sympathetic crowd?
4. Reagan introduces black rights into paragraphs 8, 21, and 41. Why does he do this? Is there an analogy between a fetus and a slave? Why is it useful for Reagan to have Lincoln on his side? Whom is Reagan trying to attract by making these historical references?
5. Is this argument strong enough to convince someone who favors abortion? If so, what points are the strongest? If not, where does Reagan fail?
6. What advantage is there in introducing specific names and families into paragraph 37?
7. It is not unusual for politicians to have others do their writing for them. Can you detect any signs, either in style or substance, that this argument had multiple authors? Are there any references that seem uncharacteristic of Reagan's public image—or does the essay sound recognizably in his own voice?

LINDA BIRD FRANCKE
The Ambivalence of Abortion

Linda Bird Francke (b. 1939) worked as an advertising copywriter before becoming a contributing editor to Newsweek *and* New York *magazines in 1968. The following essay provoked enormous response when Francke published it anonymously in the* New York Times. *She subsequently became a regular columnist for the* Times *and interviewed other women who had undergone abortions.* The Ambivalence of Abortion *is the title of the book that resulted from these interviews in 1978. Francke's work has appeared in numerous anthologies, and she is co-chairperson of the Writer's Resource Center in Southhampton, New York. She is also the author of* Fathers and Daughters *(1980) and* Growing Up Divorced *(1983).*

We were sitting in a bar on Lexington Avenue when I told my husband I was   1
pregnant. It is not a memory I like to dwell on. Instead of the champagne and
hope which had heralded the impending births of the first, second and third
child, the news of this one was greeted with shocked silence and Scotch.
"Jesus," my husband kept saying to himself, stirring the ice cubes around and
around. "Oh, Jesus."

Oh, how we tried to rationalize it that night as the starting time for the movie   2
came and went. My husband talked about his plans for a career change in the
next year, to stem the staleness that fourteen years with the same investment-
banking firm had brought him. A new baby would preclude that option.

The timing wasn't right for me either. Having juggled pregnancies and child   3
care with what freelance jobs I could fit in between feedings, I had just taken
on a full-time job. A new baby would put me right back in the nursery just when
our youngest child was finally school age. It was time for *us*, we tried to rationalize. There just wasn't room in our lives now for another baby. We both agreed.
And agreed. And agreed.

How very considerate they are at the Women's Services, known formally as   4
the Center for Reproductive and Sexual Health. Yes, indeed, I could have an
abortion that very Saturday morning and be out in time to drive to the country
that afternoon. Bring a first morning urine specimen, a sanitary belt and nap-
kins, a money order or $125 cash—and a friend.

My friend turned out to be my husband, standing awkwardly and ill at ease   5
as men always do in places that are exclusively for women, as I checked in at
nine A.M. Other men hovered around just as anxiously, knowing they had to be
there, wishing they weren't. No one spoke to each other. When I would be
cycled out of there four hours later, the same men would be slumped in their
same seats, locked downcast in their cells of embarrassment.

The Saturday morning women's group was more dispirited than the men in   6
the waiting room. There were around fifteen of us, a mixture of races, ages and
backgrounds. Three didn't speak English at all and a fourth, a pregnant Puerto
Rican girl around eighteen, translated for them.

There were six black women and a hodgepodge of whites, among them a T-   7 shirted teenager who kept leaving the room to throw up and a puzzled middle-aged woman from Queens with three grown children.

"What form of birth control were you using?" the volunteer asked each one   8
of us. The answer was inevitably "none." She then went on to describe the various forms of birth control available at the clinic, and offered them to each of us.

The youngest Puerto Rican girl was asked through the interpreter which   9
she'd like to use: the loop, diaphragm, or pill. She shook her head "no" three times. "You don't want to come back here again, do you?" the volunteer pressed. The girl's head was so low her chin rested on her breastbone. "Sí," she whispered.

We had been there two hours by that time, filling out endless forms, giving   10
blood and urine, receiving lectures. But unlike any other group of women I've been in, we didn't talk. Our common denominator, the one which usually floods across language and economic barriers into familiarity, today was one of shame. We were losing life that day, not giving it.

The group kept getting cut back to smaller, more workable units, and finally   11
I was put in a small waiting room with just two other women. We changed into paper bathrobes and paper slippers, and we rustled whenever we moved. One of the women in my room was shivering and an aide brought her a blanket.

"What's the matter?" the aide asked her. "I'm scared," the woman said. "How   12
much will it hurt?" The aide smiled. "Oh, nothing worse than a couple of bad cramps," she said. "This afternoon you'll be dancing a jig."

I began to panic. Suddenly the rhetoric, the abortion marches I'd walked in,   13
the telegrams sent to Albany to counteract the Friends of the Fetus, the Zero Population Growth buttons I'd worn, peeled away, and I was all alone with my microscopic baby. There were just the two of us there, and soon, because it was more convenient for me and my husband, there would be one again.

How could it be that I, who am so neurotic about life that I step over bugs   14
rather than on them, who spend hours planting flowers and vegetables in the spring even though we rent out the house and never see them, who make sure the children are vaccinated and inoculated and filled with vitamin C, could so arbitrarily decide that this life shouldn't be?

"It's not a life," my husband had argued, more to convince himself than me.   15
"It's a bunch of cells smaller than my fingernail."

But any woman who has had children knows that certain feeling in her taut,   16
swollen breasts, and the slight but constant ache in her uterus that signals the arrival of a life. Though I would march myself into blisters for a woman's right to exercise the option of motherhood, I discovered there in the waiting room that I was not the modern woman I thought I was.

When my name was called, my body felt so heavy the nurse had to help me   17
into the examining room. I waited for my husband to burst through the door and yell "stop," but of course he didn't. I concentrated on three black spots in the acoustic ceiling until they grew in size to the shape of saucers, while the doctor swabbed my insides with antiseptic.

"You're going to feel a burning sensation now," he said, injecting Novocain   18
into the neck of the womb. The pain was swift and severe, and I twisted to get

away from him. He was hurting my baby, I reasoned, and the black saucers quivered in the air. "Stop," I cried. "Please stop." He shook his head, busy with his equipment. "It's too late to stop now," he said. "It'll just take a few more seconds."

What good sports we women are. And how obedient. Physically the pain   19
passed even before the hum of the machine signaled that the vacuuming of my uterus was completed, my baby sucked up like ashes after a cocktail party. Ten minutes start to finish. And I was back on the arm of the nurse.

There were twelve beds in the recovery room. Each one had a gaily flowered   20
draw sheet and a soft green or blue thermal blanket. It was all very feminine. Lying on these beds for an hour or more were the shocked victims of their sex, their full wombs now stripped clean, their futures less encumbered.

It was very quiet in that room. The only voice was that of the nurse, locating   21
the new women who had just come in so she could monitor their blood pressure, and checking out the recovered women who were free to leave.

Juice was being passed about, and I found myself sipping a Dixie cup of   22
Hawaiian Punch. An older woman with tightly curled bleached hair was just getting up from the next bed. "That was no goddamn snap," she said, resting before putting on her miniskirt and high white boots. Other women came and went, some walking out as dazed as they had entered, others with a bounce that signaled they were going right back to Bloomingdale's.

Finally then, it was time for me to leave. I checked out, making an appoint-   23
ment to return in two weeks for an IUD insertion. My husband was slumped in the waiting room, clutching a single yellow rose wrapped in a wet paper towel and stuffed into a Baggie.

We didn't talk the whole way home, but just held hands very tightly. At home   24
there were more yellow roses and a tray in bed for me and the children's curiosity to divert.

It had certainly been a successful operation. I didn't bleed at all for two days   25
just as they had predicted, and then I bled only moderately for another four days. Within a week my breasts had subsided and the tenderness vanished, and my body felt mine again instead of the eggshell it becomes when it's protecting someone else.

My husband and I are back to planning our summer vacation and his career   26
switch.

And it certainly does make more sense not to be having a baby right now—   27
we say that to each other all the time. But I have this ghost now. A very little ghost that only appears when I'm seeing something beautiful, like the full moon on the ocean last weekend. And the baby waves at me. And I wave at the baby. "Of course, we have room," I cry to the ghost. "Of course, we do."

QUESTIONS FOR MEANING

1. How does Francke present herself in this essay? What sort of marriage does she seem to have? How would you describe her attitude towards the other women at the clinic?

2. Francke discovers that marching for abortion rights is very different from actually having one. Why did she and her husband choose not to have another child? How does she feel now that her abortion is over? Does she regret her decision? Why is it that she sees the baby's ghost only when she's seeing something beautiful?
3. Why is it important to divert the children's curiosity after Francke returns home from having an abortion?

QUESTIONS ABOUT STRATEGY

1. Why does Francke bother reporting that she told her husband that she was pregnant in a bar—and that the bar was on Lexington Avenue? Or that the beds in the recovery room had flowered sheets? Or that her husband held "a single yellow rose wrapped in a wet paper towel and stuffed into a Baggie"? What effect do details of this sort have upon you when you read this essay?
2. Do you detect any irony in this essay? If so, where?
3. Why does Francke repeat herself at the end of the paragraph 3?
4. What is the function of paragraph 9? What is Francke trying to illustrate?
5. Why is paragraph 26 so short?
6. Does Francke exploit any techniques usually associated with fiction? Is this an argumentative essay? If so, what is its thesis, and how is it advanced?
7. This is a very personal essay. What risks does a writer face when choosing to write about a painful personal experience? Does Francke avoid these risks or is her essay flawed in some way because she is writing about herself?

RACHEL RICHARDSON SMITH
Abortion, Right and Wrong

Although large numbers of people adhere to fervently held beliefs on abortion, many others are unsure about where they stand on this issue. The continuing debate on this often-painful subject has led many people to realize that the issue is more complex than they had at first perceived. Political and medical developments within the last ten years have also led many people to reassess their initial beliefs and to question whether they can be for or against abortion in absolute terms. The dilemma of people who see themselves as unable to be either "pro-choice" or "pro-life" is the subject of the following essay by Rachel Richardson Smith—a mother, writer, and student of theology.

I cannot bring myself to say I am in favor of abortion. I don't want anyone to   1
have one. I want people to use contraceptives and for those contraceptives to be foolproof. I want people to be responsible for their actions; mature in their decisions. I want children to be loved, wanted, well cared for.

I cannot bring myself to say I am against choice. I want women who are   2
young, poor, single or all three to be able to direct the course of their lives. I want women who have had all the children they want or can afford or their bodies can withstand to be able to decide their future. I want women who are in bad marriages or destructive relationships to avoid being trapped by pregnancy.

So in these days when thousands rally in opposition to legalized abortion,   3
when facilities providing abortions are bombed, when the president speaks glowingly of the growing momentum behind the anti-abortion movement, I find myself increasingly alienated from the pro-life groups.

At the same time, I am overwhelmed with mail from pro-choice groups. They,   4
too, are mobilizing their forces, growing articulate in support of their cause, and they want my support. I am not sure I can give it.

I find myself in the awkward position of being both anti-abortion and pro-   5
choice. Neither group seems to be completely right—or wrong. It is not that I think abortion is wrong for me but acceptable for someone else. The question is far more complex than that.

Part of my problem is that what I think and how I feel about this issue are   6
two entirely different matters. I know that unwanted children are often ne-glected, even abandoned. I know that many of those seeking abortions are children themselves. I know that making abortion illegal will not stop all women from having them.

I also know from experience the crisis an unplanned pregnancy can cause.   7
Yet I have felt the joy of giving birth, the delight that comes from feeling a baby's skin against my own. I know how hard it is to parent a child and how deeply satisfying it can be. My children sometimes provoke me and cause me endless frustration, but I can still look at them with tenderness and wonder at the

miracle of it all. The lessons of my own experience produce conflicting emotions. Theory collides with reality.

It concerns me that both groups present themselves in absolutes. They are 8 committed and they want me to commit. They do not recognize the gray area where I seem to be languishing. Each group has the right answer—the only answer.

Yet I am uncomfortable in either camp. I have nothing in common with the 9 pro-lifers. I am horrified by their scare tactics, their pictures of well-formed fetuses tossed in a metal pan, their cruel slogans. I cannot condone their flagrant misuse of Scripture and unforgiving spirit. There is a meanness about their position that causes them to pass judgment on the lives of women in a way I could never do.

The pro-life groups, with their fundamentalist religious attitudes, have a fear 10 and an abhorrence of sex, especially premarital sex. In their view abortion only compounds the sexual sin. What I find incomprehensible is that even as they are opposed to abortion they are also opposed to alternative solutions. They are squeamish about sex education in the schools. They don't want teens to have contraceptives without parental consent. They offer little aid or sympathy to unwed mothers. They are the vigilant guardians of a narrow morality.

I wonder how abortion got to be the greatest of all sins? What about poverty, 11 ignorance, hunger, weaponry?

The only thing the anti-abortion groups seem to have right is that abortion 12 is indeed the taking of human life. I simply cannot escape this one glaring fact. Call it what you will—fertilized egg, embryo, fetus. What we have here is human life. If it were just a mass of tissue there would be no debate. So I agree that abortion ends a life. But the anti-abortionists are wrong to call it murder.

The sad truth is that homicide is not always against the law. Our society does 13 not categorically recognize the sanctity of human life. There are a number of legal and apparently socially acceptable ways to take human life. "Justifiable" homicide includes the death penalty, war, killing in self-defense. It seems to me that as a society we need to come to grips with our own ambiguity concerning the value of human life. If we are to value and protect unborn life so stringently, why do we not also value and protect life already born?

Why can't we see abortion for the human tragedy it is? No woman plans for 14 her life to turn out that way. Even the most effective contraceptives are no guarantee against pregnancy. Loneliness, ignorance, immaturity can lead to decisions (or lack of decisions) that may result in untimely pregnancy. People make mistakes.

What many people seem to misunderstand is that no woman wants to have 15 an abortion. Circumstances demand it; women do it. No woman reacts to abortion with joy. Relief, yes. But also ambivalence, grief, despair, guilt.

The pro-choice groups do not seem to acknowledge that abortion is not a 16 perfect answer. What goes unsaid is that when a woman has an abortion she loses more than an unwanted pregnancy. Often she loses her self-respect. No woman can forget a pregnancy no matter how it ends.

Why can we not view abortion as one of those anguished decisions in which 17 human beings struggle to do the best they can in trying circumstances? Why is abortion viewed so coldly and factually on the one hand and so judgmentally on the other? Why is it not akin to the same painful experience families must sometimes make to allow a loved one to die?

I wonder how we can begin to change the context in which we think about 18 abortion. How can we begin to think about it redemptively? What is it in the trauma of loss of life—be it loved or unloved, born or unborn—from which we can learn? There is much I have yet to resolve. Even as I refuse to pass judgment on other women's lives, I weep for the children who might have been. I suspect I am not alone.

QUESTIONS FOR MEANING

1. Explain why Smith objects to both "pro-life" and "pro-choice" groups.
2. What basic premise does Smith share with the men and women who actively oppose abortion?
3. What does Smith mean in paragraph 7 when she writes, "Theory collides with reality"?
4. Why does Smith believe that abortion is a "human tragedy"?
5. Vocabulary: alienated (3), languishing (8), flagrant (9), abhorrence (10), compounds (10), incomprehensible (10), squeamish (10), categorically (13), and akin (17).

QUESTIONS ABOUT STRATEGY

1. What is the thesis of this essay? Where is it clearly stated?
2. What kind of person does Smith seem to be? Is she fair-minded or simply confused?
3. Why does Smith introduce her own experience into paragraph 7? What is this paragraph meant to establish?
4. In paragraph 13, Smith compares abortion to "socially acceptable ways to take human life." Are her analogies valid?
5. Compare the opening and closing statements of this essay. Which is stronger?

SUGGESTIONS FOR WRITING

1. There are few issues which are as difficult to discuss as abortion. As Haven Gow pointed out, the language with which we discuss abortion is often heavy with loaded terms. Writing as objectively as you can, summarize the principle arguments for and against abortion.

2. Drawing upon the essays by Sissela Bok, Clifford Grobstein, and Walker Percy write an essay arguing when human life begins.

3. Writing before abortion was legalized, Shirley Chisholm argued that the law discriminated against the poor. Is this still true? Specifically, should medicaid pay for abortions?

4. Advocates of abortion frequently argue that a woman has a right to control her own body. Establish this right by making a logical argument on its behalf.

5. Do fathers have rights? Write a deductive argument determining whether a woman should be allowed to have an abortion if the father of her child opposes abortion and is willing to raise the child on his own.

6. Should an adolescent be allowed to have an abortion without her parents' consent? Is your position absolute, or would it depend upon the circumstances? Write an essay defining the rights of a pregnant minor.

7. Does a college health service have a responsibility to help a pregnant student get an abortion if she wants one? If so, why? If not, why not?

8. Linda Bird Francke wrote about the psychological cost of abortion. Do a research paper investigating the long-term effects of abortion on women who have had one.

9. During recent years, several abortion clinics have been bombed. Is this a form of terrorism? Can violence of this sort be justified by men and women who claim to oppose abortion on moral grounds? Write an essay defining the extent to which one can make a legitimate protest when deeply held beliefs are at stake.

10. Men and women who describe themselves as "pro-choice" often argue that the government should not "legislate morality." Write an argument determining the relationship between personal beliefs and public policy. Are there any circumstances under which government can make laws designed to distinguish between moral and immoral acts?

Nuclear Power: Will It Blow Over?

BARRY COMMONER
Nuclear Power

*A biologist, educator, and environmental activist, Barry Commoner (b. 1917)
attended Columbia University and received his Ph.D. from Harvard in 1941. The
author of more than two hundred articles, Commoner won the Phi Beta Kappa
Award and the International Prize for Safeguarding the Environment for his book*
The Closing Circle: Nature, Man and Technology *(1971). In 1980, he ran for
president as the nominee of the Citizens Party in a campaign that emphasized his
concern about the many ways we risk permanently harming the world in which we
live. He is currently Professor of Earth and Environmental Sciences at Queens
College, where he directs the Center for the Biology of Natural Systems. "Nuclear
Power" is an excerpt from one of Commoner's books on energy,* The Poverty of
Power *(1976).*

A nuclear power station produces electricity from energy released by the 1
splitting, or fission, of certain types of very heavy atoms—in typical U.S. reactors, chiefly Uranium-235. Like any other atom, Uranium-235 consists of a heavy
central core—the nucleus—surrounded by a cloud of much lighter electrons.
In Uranium-235 there are 92 electrons in the cloud that surrounds the nucleus.
They are held there by attractive forces between their own negative electric
charges and the nucleus' 92 positive charges. The nucleus is made up of 92
positively charged protons and 143 neutrons (a neutron has the same mass as
a proton, but carries no charge); the atomic weight, 235, is the sum of the
protons' and neutrons' weights.

Most atomic nuclei contain neutrons, which can be ejected from them by the 2
impact of sufficiently energetic radiation. The earth receives such radiation
from space—cosmic rays, which, on striking an atom, produce secondary showers of neutrons; in turn, these can collide with the nuclei of other atoms. The
response of Uranium-235 is rare among natural atoms: When a neutron—
moving sufficiently slowly—collides with it, there is a good possibility that the
Uranium-235 nucleus will split. The fission products are two atomic fragments,
each roughly one-half of the original atom, plus some free but fast-moving
neutrons. All of these fission products, in their sum, are slightly lighter than the

Uranium-235 nucleus from which they were formed. This slight difference in mass is converted to energy, in accordance with the famous Einstein equation which states that the amount of energy (E) is equivalent to the mass (m) multiplied by the square of the speed of light (c). Since the speed of light is a very large number, its square is enormous, so that a truly tremendous amount of energy is given off when the very small mass "disappears" (that is, is converted into energy) as a uranium atom is split.

A neutron does not split a uranium nucleus with the sureness of William   3
Tell's arrow cleaving an apple. Atomic nuclei are so far apart compared to the size of the neutron that a hit is very rare. As the physicist Hans Thirring has put it:

> The chance of hitting a nucleus with an uncharged particle traversing the space of an atom is less than that of hitting a single fly in a large theatre with a pistol-shot without aiming. Many millions of atoms must therefore be traversed by a neutron before it happens to hit a nucleus and to cause a fission.

If some of the free, fast neutrons produced when the Uranium-235 atoms   4
split are slowed down and then collide with and split fresh Uranium-235 atoms, a chain reaction is set off which can quickly spread through a lump of uranium, releasing huge amounts of energy in a very short time. (In a nuclear bomb, matters are arranged to maximize this effect and the intense, sudden release of energy causes a huge explosion.) Although Uranium-235 is present in many ores, and although showers of neutrons regularly occur on the earth, nevertheless such explosions do not happen naturally because the chain reaction is blocked by another uranium isotope, Uranium-238. The Uranium-238 nucleus contains three more neutrons than the Uranium-235 nucleus, but both exhibit the same chemical behavior because that is governed by the atoms' electron shells, which are identical. Uranium ore contains 0.7 percent Uranium-235, almost 99.3 percent Uranium-238, and a trace of Uranium-234. Unlike Uranium-235, the more common Uranium-238 atoms are not split by neutrons, but rather capture them and, as a result, after some intervening steps, are transformed into Plutonium-239 (about which more later). Thus, in the natural situation, because Uranium-238 is the more prevalent isotope, it preferentially absorbs the neutrons and a Uranium-235 fission reaction cannot start.

In order to establish a chain reaction—without which no nuclear energy   5
could be released—two features are built into the design of a nuclear reactor. The fuel is made from material in which the Uranium-235 has been enriched, its concentration increased from 0.7 percent to about 3 percent. This cuts down the chance of a chain-stopping neutron/ Uranium-238 collision. (Enrichment is carried out in one of three huge government plants, where a gaseous uranium compound diffuses through numerous delicately designed porous membranes which gradually hold back the slightly heavier gas molecules that contain Uranium-238.) In addition, in the reactor the uranium fuel is embedded in material—the moderator—which slows down the high-velocity neutrons that

are emitted from the split uranium atoms. One of the pecularities of the Uranium-235/neutron collision is that, unlike the collision with Uranium-238, it is favored if the neutrons are slow. In a typical reactor the uranium is formed into long, thin rods that are submerged in water (the moderator), the entire assemblage making up the reactor core. When Uranium-235 atoms split, the fast neutrons they emit pass quickly through the thin rods into the water, where, following a series of collisions with the water molecules, the neutrons slow down to about a thousandth of their original speed. These slow neutrons find their way back into a fuel rod, where they are likely to collide with a Uranium-235 atom and split it.

Once suitably enriched, the uranium is made into fuel rods. When these are installed in the reactor moderator bath, a self-sustaining fission chain reaction becomes possible. Like every self-propagating chain reaction, such as an ordinary fire, the process must be controlled or it will get out of hand. In a nuclear reactor, control is a rather delicate problem. One reason is that the nuclear reactions are so fast that the chain reaction can propagate itself very quickly; to avoid a runaway reaction, an excessive rate must be corrected within a tenth of a second. In the reactor the chain reaction is controlled by inserting rods of a metal such as boron into the core. Boron is a good neutron absorber and can therefore cut down the number of free neutrons in the core, and reduce the overall rate of the chain reaction. The speed of the chain reaction and the reactor's rate of energy production are regulated by varying the length of control rod that is inserted into the core.

As the fragments of the split uranium atoms fly apart, their kinetic energy is converted to heat. In present U.S. reactors, water is used both to slow down (moderate) the neutrons and to absorb the heat generated by the fission process. In one type of reactor the fuel rods are bathed in water which is under pressure, so that it becomes quite hot (600° F.) without boiling. The hot water is circulated through pipes which go through a secondary boiler, where they produce steam that is used to drive a conventional turbine electric generator. In another type of reactor (the "boiling water" reactor) the water that bathes the fuel rods itself boils and produces steam which is fed into the turbines. The steam is then condensed to water and returned to the reactor vessel. In both cases the water that bathes the fuel rods becomes highly radioactive and must be kept away from people and the environment.

After the reactor has operated for a time, the fuel becomes "spent": The accumulated fission products take up enough neutrons to block the fission chain reaction, which gradually slows down. At this point the fuel rods must be replaced, a task which is extraordinarily difficult because they have now become highly radioactive. (The various nuclear reactions that occur in the fuel rods produce a mixture of radioactive elements of different kinds.) In practice the spent rods are stored temporarily in a well-shielded container, usually under a deep layer of water. Sooner or later the spent fuel must be "reprocessed"—a step in which, by various chemical means, different atomic species are separated from the radioactive mélange. One product of the reprocessing is leftover Uranium-235 itself, which can then be re-used in new fuel rods. Another valuable product is Plutonium-239 (formed when a Uranium-238 atom captures a neutron), which is also a fissionable fuel. The rest of the material is useless waste that must be scrupulously contained for many thousands of years as its intense radioactivity slowly decays.

The various operations which constitute the nuclear-power system in the   9 United States are scattered across the entire country. The uranium mines and refinery operations are in various Western states. From there the uranium is shipped to one of two plants in Illinois and Oklahoma, where it is converted into the gaseous form, uranium hexafluoride, that is used in the enrichment process. The enrichment plants are in Oak Ridge, Tennessee, Paducah, Kentucky, and Portsmouth, Ohio. Once enriched, the uranium is shipped to about a dozen fuel-rod fabrication plants that are spread across the country, as are the fifty-odd reactors themselves. The only plant for reprocessing reactor waste that has operated thus far is in upstate New York. The plant is now closed; if and when it reopens, the uranium and plutonium recovered at the plant will be shipped back to the fuel-rod fabrication plants and so re-enter the cycle. Permanent waste-storage facilities do not exist as yet. Thus, the materials involved in the nuclear-power system—uranium in its natural and enriched states and highly radioactive spent fuel and waste—are moved about a great deal, in trucks, railroad cars, and aircraft (until the latter practice was recently forbidden).

The economic structure of the nuclear-power system is equally complex.   10 Most of the ore lies on Federal lands and is publicly owned until the mining rights are leased to private firms. Mining, milling, and conversion of the ore to uranium hexafluoride are now in private hands; but the next step, enrichment, is carried out at government-owned plants. Fabrication of fuel rods is done by private firms, although until recently, by law, the uranium remained the property of the government. Most of the reactors are owned and operated by private power companies. Reprocessing facilities for spent reactor fuel are privately owned, but all of the proposed schemes for permanent waste disposal, if and when they operate, are to be publicly owned. It should be added that the large and expensive research program that lies behind the entire nuclear-power system has been operated almost entirely at public expense, as is the regulatory part of the system.

Although most nuclear power plants are privately owned, government deci-   11 sions strongly influence their economic feasibility. The cost of the electricity that the system produces depends on the cost of reactor fuel, which in turn is determined largely by the government's charge for enrichment. Since most of the cost of enrichment is the huge capital investment of government funds in the enrichment plants—several billion dollars—the price of this service can be quite arbitrarily determined by choosing a particular rate of capital amortization. The price of nuclear fuel, and therefore the cost of electricity produced from it, has been kept down by such government decisions. In addition, the government has made large amounts of technical information—the results of its vast research program—freely available to industry. This saves industry major development costs.

As it exists today, the U.S. nuclear-power system is a one-way process: Uranium ore goes in and electricity, highly radioactive waste, and the waste heat inevitably emitted by any power plant come out. Nuclear power plants produce more waste heat than most conventional plants of equal size and therefore cause more serious thermal-pollution problems. 12

The problem of permanently "disposing" of the radioactive waste—somehow keeping the damaging radiation away from people and environmental situations—has been studied for a number of years, but the problem has not yet been solved. The difficulties involved in finding some final resting place for this hideously dangerous material can be judged from the following: The waste produced by a billion-watt nuclear power plant (the typical size of recent ones) is equivalent in radioactivity to about 2500 tons of radium. In contrast, the total amount of radium used thus far in the world for medical and scientific purposes—all of it handled in very small amounts and elaborately contained and shielded—probably amounts to a few pounds. Another sobering comparison is that the radiation from the wastes produced by a city's nuclear power plant— if it were released into the environment—would be sufficient to kill 100 times the city's population. 13

In bulk, this radioactive waste does not amount to much—a fact that can readily lead to a highly deceiving conclusion. Thus, the head of the Federal Energy Administration, Frank G. Zarb, in a recent speech in support of his conviction, relative to the nuclear-waste problem, that "the facts are reassuring," offered the following evidence: 14

> A single aspirin tablet has the same volume as the waste produced in generating 7,000 kilowatt-hours, which is about one person's share of the country's electric output for an entire year. Compared to large quantities of other harmful materials, the volume of nuclear waste is minuscule . . . .

What Mr. Zarb fails to mention is that, unlike a real aspirin tablet, his radioactive one is sufficiently toxic to kill 100 people.

Nuclear wastes are persistent. Their radioactivity will remain at a very harmful level, and will need to be meticulously isolated from people and the environment for about 200,000 years. This fact provokes a melancholy question: Who is to stand watch over this radioactive legacy? What social institution can promise to last that long? One reply, from perhaps the most thoughtful proponent of nuclear power, A.M. Weinberg, is that the task must be assumed by a kind of nuclear priesthood: 15

> We nuclear people have made a Faustian bargain with society. On the one hand we offer—in the catalytic nuclear burner [the breeder]—an inexhaustible source of energy . . . . But the price that we demand of society for this magical energy

source is both a vigilance and longevity of our social institutions that we are quite unaccustomed to .... In a sense we have established a military priesthood which guards against inadvertent use of nuclear weapons ... peaceful nuclear energy probably will make demands of the same sort on our society.

This concept—which cloaks the devil in a laboratory coat and the soldier in a cassock—is almost as forbidding as the fact to which it seeks to respond.

The current status of the waste-disposal problem is described in the latest government report on the nuclear-power industry. A diagram in the report depicts the movement of uranium from the mines through the successive phases of the nuclear-power system. A final arrow marked "high-level solid waste" points to an impressive building labeled "Federal Repository." The possible contents of such a repository are described in three accompanying diagrams, but their effect is rather spoiled by the notation that they are an "artist's concept." In fact there is no Federal repository for the permanent storage of highly radioactive waste. The final disposition of this enormously dangerous material remains, indeed, an "artist's concept."   16

Proposals abound, none of them satisfactory. One idea is to improve the present reprocessing method. This now leaves in the waste 0.5 percent of the long-lived radioactive isotopes originally present in the spent fuel; the proposed new method would reduce this residue to .0001 percent of the original material. That would shorten the time during which the waste is too dangerous for human contact from about 200,000 years to perhaps 1000 years. Depending on one's outlook, this might perhaps bring the storage problem within what one nuclear expert has called the "time horizon of present rational planning." Since the present reprocessing system is already so difficult that none of the three plants that are supposed to handle commercial-reactor wastes is now in operation, this approach does not seem to be a very practical one.   17

Another idea—to store the radioactive waste in the Antarctic ice—would violate a specific prohibition in the Antarctic Treaty of 1959. At one time the AEC proposed to store the waste in deep salt mines in Kansas. The people of Kansas rejected the idea, since no one was able to assure them that the radioactivity would not eventually leak into underground water supplies. The most elaborate and redundantly fearsome idea has been proposed by experts at the Lawrence Livermore Laboratory, one of the nation's leading nuclear-research institutions. They would set off an underground nuclear bomb beneath the waste-reprocessing plant, creating a large hole, into which the radioactive waste would be poured, to be contained—it is hoped—within the glassy walls created by the intense heat of the nuclear explosion.   18

The entire waste-disposal situation has been summed up by two experts who, as it happens, are optimistic about solving it, with the comment that AEC efforts "... have yet to produce, after a decade and a half, one operational long-term storage facility—a sign of both commendable caution and inadequate work."   19

With no acceptable outlet for its radioactive waste, the nuclear-power sys-   20 tem's temporary storage facilities have become heavily overloaded. Temporary storage is provided next to each reactor, so that the spent fuel can be safely stored while its initially intense radioactivity decays somewhat. Without an operational waste-disposal system, these temporary facilities have been used routinely to hold spent fuel. There are enough such storage facilities for about 930 metric tons of spent fuel. A recent survey shows that storage space for all but 50 metric tons of fuel is now occupied; many reactors have been deprived of their temporary spent-fuel storage site. Our nuclear cup runneth over.

QUESTIONS FOR MEANING

1. Explain what is meant by "fission" and "atomic weight."
2. Why don't nuclear reactions occur naturally? What is the importance of Uranium-238?
3. What two features are built into the design of nuclear reactors in order to produce the chain reaction which produces nuclear energy?
4. How is the speed of nuclear chain reactions controlled within a reactor?
5. What role has the government played in determining whether the development of nuclear power plants is economically feasible for private companies? Could private companies produce nuclear power without federal assistance?
6. Why does Commoner believe that nuclear power plants cause more serious pollution problems than conventional power plants of similar size?
7. Vocabulary: cleaving (3), propagate (6), kinetic (7), mélange (8), scrupulously (8), amortization (11), and legacy (15).

QUESTIONS ABOUT STRATEGY

1. How clear is Commoner's explanation of the process of producing nuclear energy? Does he provide enough information so that a nonscientific audience can understand this process? Does he ever confuse you by assuming you know more than you do? If so, identify the points you do not understand, and make sure that you have not overlooked an explanation of these points within the essay itself.
2. At what point does this essay become an argument against nuclear power?
3. What is the function of paragraph 9? Why does Commoner emphasize that the nuclear power system is spread out across the entire country?
4. Where does Commoner anticipate the opposition, considering what proponents of nuclear power have to say in its defense? How does Commoner respond to these counterarguments?
5. The fifth verse of the Twenty-Third Psalm reads, "Thou preparest a table before me in the presence of mine enemies: thou anointest my head with oil; my cup runneth over." Consider the last sentence in Commoner's essay and the source of its allusion. Is Commoner being ironic?

EDWARD TELLER
Reactor Safety and the Antinuclear Movement

Edward Teller (b. 1908) was born in Budapest and studied in Germany, receiving his Ph.D. from the University of Leipzig in 1930. He came to the United States in 1935 and became an American citizen in 1941. An early researcher in thermonuclear reactions, Teller ranks as one of the most important physicists in the twentieth century. Between 1942 and 1945 he worked closely with Enrico Fermi and Robert Oppenheimer in developing the atomic bomb. It was principally Teller's research that led to the creation of the hydrogen bomb in 1952. He has taught at Columbia, Chicago, and the University of California. Since 1975 he has been a senior research fellow at the Hoover Institute at Stanford University. A leading proponent of nuclear energy, Teller responded to its critics with the following argument in his book, Energy From Heaven and Earth *(1977).*

1   Anything that is new and strange is frightening. A new technology, developed in strictest secrecy, was first known to the world when a hundred thousand Japanese were killed and a great war was suddenly ended. Fear was unavoidable.

2   Fear was delayed, however. In the first years after World War II, the irrational aspects of fear did not show up. Relief at having the war over was enormous. Hope for a permanently peaceful world seemed real to many people. The need to reconstruct a world left in shambles was immediate.

3   Soon there were signals of danger: trouble in China, the division of Europe, failure of the Baruch plan for internationalization of atomic control. Work on atomic energy continued in a relatively inconspicuous fashion, and the public generally seemed to accept control of the atomic nucleus as one more strange fact in an increasingly strange world where peace seemed to supplant the immediacy of dangers.

4   But complacency was unrealistic. The explosion of the first Russian atomic bomb in 1949, and development of the hydrogen bomb in 1952, could not be ignored. President Eisenhower decided that a new encouragement, a renewed impetus toward international cooperation could come from the peaceful atom. He proposed that controlled fission, for producing energy from atomic sources, be used to strengthen the fabric of peace. The idea for this development actually came from the president's friend Lewis Strauss, head of the American Atomic Energy Commission, who urged an "Atoms for Peace" conference.

5   Proposed by the United States, the first International Atoms for Peace Conference was held in Geneva in 1955. The Kremlin answered its initial invitation with a resounding "*nyet.*" But when it became clear that there was going to be a party, with them or without, the Russians came. Happily, their scientists made genuine contributions and enjoyed the conference. They were not the persons who had refused the first invitation.

That conference substituted euphoria for anxiety. The age of the peaceful   6
atom had arrived.

The good life depends upon ample energy if that good life is to be achieved   7
by the means realized through the Industrial Revolution. Toil was reduced by
control of the forces of nature. The elimination of suffering from poverty by
reasoned use of technology came closer to reality in the United States than in
any other society. If a similar result could be achieved for a world recovering
from a terrible war, if the age-old hardships in the underdeveloped portion of
the world could be brought to an end, then perhaps the exploitation of man by
man could come to an end. The American Dream could become a reality
throughout the world. But ample energy was one condition for achieving all
of this.

Today more people realize that curing the world's ills is not so simple. Energy   8
alone will not do it; neither will any straightforward change in social order.
Whenever we have been too optimistic we have stumbled. Nonetheless, there
was a point to that optimism. An immediate benefit seemed within reach in the
1950s. When trouble on the Suez Canal threatened the flow of oil in 1956, many
anticipated a ready solution. They believed that nuclear reactors would deliver
energy soon and in great quantities.

Their hopes were disappointed. Nuclear reactors proved to be impractical   9
at that time because of their cost. It was cheaper to ship oil in big tankers even
though they could not navigate through Suez. The cost of the long voyage
around the Cape of Good Hope was more than compensated by savings realized
from the great capacity of the vessels.

America's national laboratories, particularly at Argonne near Chicago and at   10
Oak Ridge in Tennessee, worked in secrecy. Scientists there had developed the
principles of the great nuclear reactors but had not yet progressed to effective,
economical engineering application.[1]

After 1955, when schools of nuclear engineering were established, private   11
enterprise took over. Costs were gradually reduced, and reactors became practical. By 1967, twelve years after the first Atoms for Peace Conference, they
appeared to be competitive in price.

And none too soon! The supply of petroleum, which had all but monopolized   12
the energy market, no longer seemed inexhaustible for the future. In the United
States a movement for protecting and improving the environment had made a
belated but necessary start. A new supply of energy, plentiful, clean, and economical though not cheap, would have been enthusiastically welcomed. Yet this
time also marked the beginning of serious difficulties for development of that
very energy supply.

Fuel for nuclear reactors, including separation of the active isotope uranium   13
235, was inexpensive. The greatest cost was—and still is—in capital invest-

---

[1]Admiral Hyman Rickover adapted this work to nuclear submarines—well-engineered, extremely safe, but
expensive instruments of warfare. (The first, the *Nautilus*, was commissioned in September 1954.) In the course
of time nuclear submarines may become cheap enough to haul oil under the Arctic ice cover to consumers all
over the world.

ment.[2] In the late 1960s and early 1970s, a sharp rise in interest rates worked to the disadvantage of nuclear industries, which needed long-range capital investment for an energy yield that would be realized only after the elapse of several years.

The oil embargo of 1973, with a fourfold increase in oil price, highlighted the   14
desirability of nuclear reactors. But after widespread planning for reactors there arose a chorus of objections to these plans. Objections proliferated.

These objections were not an outgrowth of nuclear accidents, although some   15
accidents had occurred. Anyone who imagines he has found a foolproof system is apt to learn that the fool is bigger than the proof. Industrial reactor accidents resulted in the loss of many millions of dollars. But not a single person was killed, nor did the health of a single individual suffer because the reactors were nuclear. As stated in Chapter 9, no one has been injured as a result of the operation of industrial nuclear reactors. To prevent misunderstanding I reiterate: the accidents referred to in that preceding chapter occurred in experimental reactors or weapons laboratories; they have no parallel in the nuclear industry. The ambitious aim for achieving operation of big nuclear plants without human suffering has been attained. The protests were not based on actual lack of safety.

There is a rhythm in industrial development and in public criticism of that   16
development that may result in an unfortunate countermarch. During the expensive initial phases of planning, research, and development, there is little criticism. When plans have matured, much effort and investment have been expended, and the potential product is clearly perceived, then public protest can become clamorous and obstructive. It may develop into an insurmountable obstacle.

The cause is lack of foresight, and responsibility for that should be shared.   17
In the case of reactor development, part of the responsibility must be attributed to excessive concentration of authority. Originally the same office was responsible both for new development and for licensing, that is, giving the "go-ahead" signal. Thus, the same person was given authority for creating, and for pronouncing the creation as good. (The Bible reserves this dual role to God.)

This arrangement has been modified in a realignment of authority for development and licensing. The Energy Research and Development Administration   18
(ERDA) was made responsible for new development,[3] while the Nuclear Regulatory Commission (NRC) makes decisions on licensing. The NRC was first headed by Bill Anders, an engineer astronaut who staked his life on the faultless functioning of more than 100,000 parts in the rockets that carried him around the moon and back. Unquestionably, he knows about safety.

More responsibility should perhaps be laid to the critics who voiced their   19

[2]This point should be remembered by advocates of novel energy sources including abundant solar energy. At present a solar electricity generating plant would require investment at least five times greater than the capital investment for a nuclear reactor of comparable average generating potential.

[3]Now replaced, further, by the Department of Energy (DOE). If in doubt, reorganize!

criticism belatedly, and then pursued it in many cases with broad and unsubstantiated arguments rather than specific reasons related to engineering.

The antinuclear movement has become widespread and powerful. The only   20
way to meet and understand it is to discuss in detail each argument that is raised against reactors. This may not convince professional objectors, but it is necessary for the general public, whose vital interest is at stake.

The first question is: What is the possibility of a major reactor accident? The   21
industrial reactor health record so far is perfect. But can reactors remain as safe in the future? Might the law of probabilities turn against us? Can we continue to guard against human error?

Reactor safety results from multiple safeguards. Every possibility of mal-   22
function is prevented by three or four or even five independent measures.[4] An impairment of any of these safety measures is considered an "accident" and the deficiency is repaired, regardless of cost.

The actual probability of an accident, particularly a major one, has been   23
evaluated in a careful engineering study by Professor Norman C. Rasmussen and his associates at Massachusetts Institute of Technology. Their conclusion is that the probability of a big accident is less than one in a million. To put it in more familiar terms, a person is not likely to be killed by lightning, but it does happen. Nuclear accidents in industrial reactors are far less probable. A remarkable, and more quantitative comparison was made in the Rasmussen report: The probability of a single person being killed by a meteorite is similar to that of his being killed by a reactor; that ten persons should be killed by a meteorite or a reactor is far less likely but the probability for each is similar; that one hundred should be killed by either is again equally improbable; that one thousand people should be wiped out is so unlikely as to defy imagination, but the probabilities are essentially the same for meteorite or reactor.

Rasmussen's report was prepared meticulously. Each type of possible mal-   24
function was evaluated on the basis of detailed engineering experience. Yet the report has been criticized and the criticism is to some extent justified. One may argue that the Rasmussen report is too optimistic; one may also argue that it is not optimistic enough.

It is extraordinarily difficult to estimate the probability of excessively im-   25
probable events. The greatest danger remains: something may have been forgotten. It is impossible to estimate the limits of our own imaginations.

On the other hand, the multiple reactor safeguards give us a special benefit   26
that is not calculated and is virtually impossible to calculate. It is extemely unlikely that all the safeguards would fail at the same time, and the safety from this circumstance is taken into account. But the failure of a single safeguard leads to long-term improvements in safety. Any such failure results in substantial monetary loss, since the reactor is not permitted to operate unless all safeguards are in good condition. To avoid financial damage, the safeguard is

[4]One popular example of a pessimist is a man who wears both a belt and suspenders. In case of nuclear reactors we added even more safeguards. Thus one may say we are superpessimistic. It pays.

improved. Thus, year after year, reactors become more safe. There is a dent in the pocketbooks, but not in the people. Rasmussen could not take such future improvements into account.

One example of improvement through accident occurred at the famous   27
Browns Ferry reactor in Alabama in the spring of 1975. A candle was used in testing for leaks in a supposedly airtight part of the reactor. The flame was sucked into an inaccessible part which contained complex wiring. An electrical fire started. The reactor was shut down, but because of mistakes the fire was not put out for several hours and a number of safety devices were knocked out. The financial loss exceeded $120 million, but damage to health was zero. A danger point for health damage was not even approached.

Of course no hundred-million-dollar candle will ever be similarly used again.   28
Furthermore, we have learned that wiring which serves independent safe-guards must be better separated. The accident was a demonstration of the health safety inherent in reactors. At the same time the accident led to improve-ments in reactor construction. And that is most important.

A specific imaginary accident has played a great role in the reactor debate.   29
William D. Kendall, a physicist not previously concerned with reactors, rediscovered the possibility of an "emergency core cooling accident." The com-plicated name describes a complicated situation. It is characteristic of the discussion in its present state that Kendall's objection is concerned with a double failure: a rapid loss of cooling water due to complete rupture of piping, and a subsequent failure of the standby system for delivering the coolant water held in readiness for such an emergency.

Despite the complexity of the hypothetical problem, it is worthwhile for the   30
public to understand the merits of this debate. It can illustrate the way reactor safety is discussed today.

First, it should be emphasized that the functioning of the emergency system   31
would be important only in a very peculiar situation: If the proper primary coolant is lost rapidly, the nuclear fuel may become so hot that the emergency coolant cannot enter; it may vaporize on its way in. If that should happen, the nuclear fuel may melt and radioactive products may be released in great quan-tity. But they would not be released to the ouside. The whole reactor is sur-rounded by a strong container. Even in the worst case envisioned, no one would be hurt.

Two improvements were introduced after the possibility of failure of both   32
the primary and secondary cooling systems had been emphasized. One was to decrease the diameter of the rods containing the fuel. This reduces the heat that the coolant must carry away after the reactor is shut down, because the temperature near the center of a big rod must be quite high in order to create the necessary heat flow from the rod's axis to its surface. Heat energy within the nuclear fuels can be reduced considerably by using smaller rods. It must be realized that use of these small rods will not of itself suffice; after a reactor has been shut down, the nuclear fuel is strongly radioactive and continues to gen-erate more energy—a small amount compared with the energy generated dur-

ing operation, but still enough to cause melting. With smaller rods, it will take a longer time to reach the melting point.

Of course, the radioactive "afterheat" will not go on forever. The longer we   33
wait, the less the danger. A second after shutdown considerable energy is produced, requiring much coolant in a short time. An hour after shutdown the rate of delayed heat production is reduced ten thousandfold. Afterheat continues to diminish with the passage of time.

The second and perhaps more important improvement in the emergency   34
core cooling system is that in an emergency situation water is injected at higher pressure. Thus it can overcome the pressure of the vapor that may result when the coolant hits the hot rods.

It is indeed fortunate that decades ago in Idaho we established the system   35
that permits simulation of practically any accident, including the failure of the emergency core cooling system. Such simulations have been carried out, but we can hardly expect a simulation to reproduce an actual accident with complete accuracy. Furthermore, it is impossible to reproduce all the various conditions under which accidents can be imagined. To ask for a complete safety test in the emergency core cooling system is similar to demanding that automobile accidents be simulated, evaluated, and then avoided under all conditions that can occur in actual driving.

One argument made by opponents of nuclear reactors is that, while car   36
accidents are terrible, nuclear accidents are catastrophic. The answer to that is that, while car accidents occur often, catastrophic nuclear accidents have not occurred. Moreover, because an accident might conceivably become catastrophic, we have multiple safeguards. In addition to studying the emergency core cooling system, we prevent the situation in which the emergency system would have to go into action. Even if radioactivity should actually escape from the reactor, we confine it within the housing that surrounds the reactor. Study of the emergency core cooling system has the limited purpose of increasing the reliability of one among several safety devices. If any one of the several safety devices works, trouble will be avoided.

We have mentioned that a few years ago there was appropriate criticism   37
that nuclear development and nuclear safety were ultimately the responsibility of a single individual. In January 1975, however, safety and licensing were entrusted to an independent entity, the Nuclear Regulatory Commission (NRC). Within the first few months of this agency's separate existence, a leak was discovered in the water cooling system of one of the boiling-water reactors. Because such a leak might eventually develop into a rupture, requiring that the emergency core cooling system should take over, the small leak was taken very seriously. Not only was the reactor shut down, but also orders were given that within the next month all similar boiling-water reactors, numbering approximately two dozen, should be shut down and inspected. Within weeks this order had been carried out, at considerable cost. None of the other boiling-water reactors had any leaks.

Such vigilance should reassure the public. Paradoxically, in some cases it   38 had the opposite effect. The simple circumstance that a great number of reactors were ordered shut down was used by some people to "prove" that reactors are unsafe.

One very real hazard, especially in California, is from earthquakes. To the original suggestion of the Advisory Committee on Reactor Safeguards, that reactors shut down automatically at the first sign of a tremor, more precautions have been added over the years. Under present regulations no reactor can be built near an "active" earthquake fault. The definition of an active earthquake fault is remarkable. To deem it otherwise proof is required that the fault has not been active in the past twenty thousand years. Such proof can, of course, never be given with complete confidence, yet it is useful to make the attempt.   39

We should also realize that reactors have a much greater inherent resistance to earthquakes than most man-made structures. Human habitations, of course, are hollow. They are apt to collapse in a severe earthquake. A reactor, by contrast, has essentially no cavities. An earthquake will shake the reactor as a whole, and is not apt to damage it. Probably the only big man-made structures that are safer than nuclear reactors are Egypt's great pyramids, which have stood for six thousand years.   40

A particularly vulnerable structure in an earthquake is a dam, including dams constructed for hydroelectric purposes. Water from collapsed dams has killed thousands of people. A catastrophe of this kind was narrowly avoided on February 9, 1971, in the San Fernando, California, earthquake. The two dams in the San Fernando Valley were so badly damaged that they had to be dismantled. While the water was drained, eighty thousand people in a twenty-square-mile area were evacuated for two days because no one knew whether the dams would hold. It is believed that the dams did not promptly collapse because at the time of the earthquake the water level was relatively low.   41

The recently built earth-filled Teton Dam collapsed in Idaho on June 5, 1976, just three days before the decisive vote on California's antinuclear Proposition 15. Property damage exceeded a billion dollars, while only sixty million dollars had been spent on the dam's construction. Fortunately the dam broke in the daytime and there was ample warning; only ten persons were killed. At night the consequences would have been far more tragic.[5]   42

We have had lots of experience with dams, but relatively little scientific evaluation. In the case of nuclear reactors the opposite is true: we have had limited, though still substantial, experience, but extremely careful scientific evaluation. It is likely that reactors are among the few structures that would withstand a severe earthquake and would be promptly available for further service.   43

This argument should not, of course, be used to indiscriminately forbid dam construction. Besides producing electricity, dams prevent natural floods. Here, as in all cases, dangers and benefits should be balanced, and safety measures improved.   44

---

[5]The Toccoa, Georgia, dam disaster in November 1977 claimed thirty-eight lives.

There is hope for even greater safety in the future. Indicators of impending   45
earthquakes are being studied and developed.[6] In early February 1975, the
Chinese used such indicators to take precautionary measures in a populous
major industrial area of southern Manchuria.[7] The earthquake there registered
7.3 on the Richter scale, which measures tremors and quakes on a scale where
each additional unit means a factor ten in energy; Richter 7 has ten times the
energy of Richter 6. Yet extensive casualties were prevented because the populace had been prepared or evacuated in advance. Before a predicted earthquake, a reactor would be shut down in advance of the time that the earthquake
is expected. After the passage of several hours in such a shut-down condition,
a reactor would be completely safe. Loss of electrical energy production from
reactors during the dangerous period should be gladly accepted.

Accidents constitute the only real danger from reactors, and by use of care-   46
ful and well-thought-out procedures this danger has been reduced to an im-
measurably small probability.

In public discussions, however, a threat of danger from "nuclear ashes"   47
figures almost as importantly as the danger of a nuclear accident. It is claimed,
for instance, that radioactivity from one element, plutonium, will continue to
be a hazard to our descendants for more than one thousand human generations.
Human institutions change, and some believe that within thousands of years a
situation might develop whereby the plutonium could poison a vast number of
human beings.

The lifetime of plutonium is indeed 24,000 years. This element is more   48
valuable than gold, however, because it can serve as a nuclear fuel. Instead of
constituting a menace for a thousand human generations, it should be burned
up in a nuclear reactor in not more than one generation. But we need to
understand what actually is going to happen to spent fuel elements, the so-
called "nuclear ashes." Because of their residual radioactivity, spent fuel elements continue to produce heat as they leave a reactor. They are kept under
water, which serves as a coolant and also prevents the escape of radiation.This
step in itself would appear to be a satisfactory solution, except that spent fuel
elements accumulate year after year, and will, in time, become too numerous
to contain in temporary storage. In a couple of decades, if not earlier, we should
have permanent storage for radioactive wastes.

There is a popular misconception about the existence of adequate means of   49
disposing of spent fuel elements. In reality the reason for continued anxiety is
that no definitive method has as yet been *adopted* for the treatment of these
materials. To achieve permanent disposal, a lot of time and care must be spent.
For this reason, and probably for reasons of bureaucratic delay and confusion

[6]One indicator depends on a decrease in sound velocity for compressional waves in the earth's crust due to the
opening of cracks. Later the sound velocity increases as water fills these cracks. Then the earthquake is apt to
follow in a day or two. An indication used in China is the rapid lowering of water levels in wells, which occurs
when water enters the cracks.

[7]A more recent earthquake in China unfortunately was *not* predicted. Many people perished. Earthquake prediction is not yet an exact science.

as well, details of the disposal procedure have not yet been completed. Some observers, therefore, have the impression that no satisfactory methods of final disposal exist. The fact is that several inexpensive methods are under careful consideration. Their cost is not likely to add more than one percent to the expense of generating electricity. The only difficulty remaining is to make a choice and work out details.[8]

I want to describe the proposed storage method which to me sounds best. 50 After spent fuel rods have cooled for a year or two they produce considerably less heat. Then they can be dissolved and the heavy, valuable, relatively long-lived elements can be separated from the light ones. The heavy elements consist of remnants of the original nuclear fuel and other elements obtained by the capture of one or more neutrons in the original fuel. To this must be added their radioactive decay products, among which plutonium 239 is by far the most important.[9]

Plutonium can hardly be called nuclear ash. It is "flammable," and even in 51 the reactor some of the plutonium is burned up before the fuel is removed. Many of the heavy elements are highly useful. Most of them have long lifetimes, and in the course of time all of them are likely to find important employment. They will be carefully guarded, not only because they are dangerous, but also because they are valuable.

Usable fission products will also have to be separated. These fission prod- 52 ucts, the fragments into which the uranium has split, are the real nuclear ashes. While many of these fragments are usable, they are produced in such abundance that some of them, possibly the major portion, will have to be stored. Because of their radioactivity they still produce some energy, but this energy output is so small that it is not worth utilizing. (Uses of fission products will be discussed shortly.) After separation of the heavy elements and usable fission products, the remainder can be incorporated into a practically insoluble borosilicate glass.[10] This process has been developed and we know that such glass

---

[8]The difficulties of making a choice were discussed in approximately A.D. 1200, by the French philosopher Buridan. His teachings are best remembered in the story of Buridan's ass. The poor beast starved to death between two equidistant and equally desirable stacks of hay. In the case of spent nuclear fuel elements we have more than two choices. We also have four asses, popularly known as DOE, NRC, EPA, and CEQ, which furthermore, are yoked together and must act in unison. A further complication is that the present administration is taking a position against the "reprocessing" necessary to separate the plutonium. The reason is fear that plutonium could be used to make nuclear explosives. Actually, nuclear explosives could be produced in many other ways, while lack of reprocessing causes difficulties in the nuclear fuel supply and will perpetuate the fear of nuclear ashes.

[9]Uranium 238, the main portion of uranium, captures a neutron and gives uranium 239. Two beta decays follow, giving plutonium 239...

[10]Glass would not be insoluble in the "hydrothermal" solutions that could arise from the combination of radioactive decay heat and water encroachment into a closed repository. See G.J. McCarthy et al., "Interactions Between Nuclear Waste and Surrounding Rock," Nature, Vol. 273, No. 5659 (1978).

The heat output of the glass can be lowered, of course, by dilution. Also, advanced mineral-like waste forms that can survive under even these severe conditions are being developed at Pennsylvania State University by McCarthy and his associates. Gregory J. McCarthy, William B. White, and Diane E. Pfoertsch, "Synthesis of Nuclear Waste Monazites, Ideal Actinide Hosts for Geologic Disposal," Materials Research Bulletin (University Park, Pa.), Vol. 13 (1978).

can be made to consist of approximately 30 percent fission products and 70 percent glassy substance, mostly silicon, boron, and oxygen. As to volume, the material can be handled without much difficulty. Assuming a full nuclear economy in the United States, it has been estimated that the amount of this glass that would be produced in the last quarter of the twentieth century would cover a football field to a depth of ten meters.

I think it would be best to place this material a mile underground in a dry and stable—that is, earthquake-free—geological layer. It could be placed in cavities within salt deposits, for instance. It is quite easy to wash out such cavities. Salt has the added advantage of affording protection from water. If, in spite of the original geological evaluation, an earthquake should occur, any rift in the salt is apt to heal. Thus, we would achieve triple protection. Water cannot get in through the salt, but if water should, somehow, reach the material, the radioactivity would be in an insoluble form and, most importantly, the material would be a mile underground. Water, the most plausible means of transporting radioactivity, would not be available to the radioactive substance.

After approximately three hundred years in this deep burial place the radioactivity would have become less than that of the original uranium ore from which it was derived. It would continue to decay through passing time. The crust of the earth would actually be depleted of radioactivity. Thus, we would have permanently freed the biosphere, the region of the living, from the radioactive products.

Uses of fission products, the real nuclear ashes, are many, both actual and potential. As tracers they follow the complicated paths of similar atoms in a variety of processes, including biological processes. They can be used in the preservation of foodstuffs, without radioactivity being transferred to them. Numerous industrial uses have been developed, as in measuring and controlling the thickness of some mass-produced foils, or in observing the erosion of bearings in machinery. In many of these applications, the essential property of the fission products is that they are observable in extraordinarily small amounts. Safe handling of radioactivity, in fact, is possible because one-millionth of what is harmful can be readily observed. Peculiarly enough, what should serve as reassurance manages to scare people. Few objects seem to be as frightening as a clicking Geiger counter, even though an older type luminous-dial watch would set it to clicking with great vigor.

Let us consider some other industrial uses of fission products. There are varied examples illustrating the wide scope of possible applications. Fission products are now used in hundreds of ways. In the future, thousands of applications are to be expected.

We can illustrate the use of radioactive fission products as tracers in an improbable sounding case. When your clothes go to the cleaner, spots are not actually removed, at least not completely. They are more evenly distributed over the garment or perhaps shared by the clothes of other customers. This happens not because the people at the laundry are malevolent or negligent, but because chemistry is an imperfect art. A good detergent will minimize the spot distribution, and should retain the dirt in the cleaning solution. But how do detergent manufacturers find out how well they accomplish this purpose?

What can be done is to add a small amount of radioactive substance to the   58 material that makes the spot, so it will share the fate of the spot. It can then be determined in a quick, quantitative manner what fraction of the spot and the radioactivity remains attached to the clothes, and what fraction is washed away. Do not be nervous about this; no radioactivity will be attached to your spot. This procedure is used only in tests.

For Appalachia, a very different use of fission products has been proposed.   59 The forests in that region produce soft wood that is all but valueless. Radioactivity can be used to change this soft wood into hard wood suitable for floors or furniture making. The soft wood is soaked in an organic solution that penetrates between its easily separated fibers. Before the soaking a short-lived radioactive substance is added in moderate amounts to the solution. The effect of radioactivity on the organic solution is to "polymerize" the molecules, to join them into long chains. The polymerized substance will tie wood fibers together. These wood fibers can no longer be separated easily; soft wood will have been effectively turned into hard wood. Meanwhile the radioactivity will have decayed to the vanishing point. If the half-life of the radioactivity used is one day, for instance, in a month only one-billionth of it will remain. We should note that the use of short-lived fission products, while very interesting and important, will not contribute to the disposal problem. Whether a short-lived radioactive substance is employed to cure thyroid cancer or used on wood in Appalachia, it will have to be produced for that special purpose. Extracting it from spent fuel elements would be impractical because it would vanish before it could be utilized.

An extremely important use is to tie radioactive substances to chemicals   60 that seek cancerous cells in the human body even after metastasis has occurred, that is, after cancer has spread from its first location to some other part of the body. This has been done successfully with iodine in the treatment of cancer of the thyroid.

My friend Lowell Wood suggested exploring a similar possibility. Though   61 only a little work has been done on it, it could be extremely important. There is some evidence that the widely used antibiotic tetracycline tends to attach itself to cancerous cells. This seems to be the case in different kinds of cancer. Radioactive tetracycline has actually been used in experiments with rats. Lawrence Livermore Laboratory in California has a good supply of ultraheavy hydrogen, tritium. It also has good methods of handling the radioactive tritium. In experiments on rats with spontaneous breast tumors, untreated animals died, while 70 percent of the treated animals recovered. The experiments were discontinued, which I regret. Some time they should be resumed. I am not sure that tetracycline is "it." But it would be astounding if some more or less complicated molecule is not found that tends to attach itself to cancer cells and thus serve as an effective carrier of radioactivity.

As a final example I should mention caesium, an abundant radioactive fission   62 product with the rather long average lifetime of a little over forty years. Caesium emits penetrating gamma rays. An important and extensive proposed use is to irradiate sludge, particularly sludge with a high organic content.

Sludge as a rule is not only useless, it is also dangerous because of the many   63
bacteria and other microorganisms existing and breeding in it. Irradiation by the gamma rays from caesium will kill all the microorganisms without essentially altering the sludge and, of course, without rendering it radioactive. The radioactive caesium is not mixed in with the sludge; it is in solid containers, probably in the form of needles. Gamma rays not only manage to escape from the needles, but penetrate deeply into the sludge. As a result, the sludge is sterilized and thus not only becomes harmless, but may in some cases be used as animal fodder.

In spite of the many uses of radioactivity, it is virtually certain that a consid-   64
erable amount will remain that must have safe disposal. Recovery of this radioactivity is not particularly desirable because the nuclear industry is apt to produce enough fission products for new uses as they are discovered.

If nuclear accidents can be prevented and radioactive ashes buried, what   65
more is there to worry about? Opponents of nuclear reactors are never at a loss; they will tell you that low-level radiation could kill thousands, maybe millions of people.

That statement sounds, and is, extravagent, yet millions believe it. What are   66
the facts? The most significant fact is that we know more about radiation hazard than about any other contemporary hazard.[11] Chemical poisons are specific. But a small alteration in the structure of a molecule can change it from a food or curative drug into a poison or a carcinogen whose effect may be delayed, and consequently hard to verify. Chemicals act on biological systems the way a key acts on a lock. A small variation in the key might destroy the desired effect or may cause it to stick in the lock, thereby blocking the desired function, which in our case is a needed chain of biological events. Our knowledge of biology does not suffice for predicting how a molecule will affect the human body.[12]

The effects of radiation are much simpler. Radiation acts like a hammer; it   67
breaks molecules. And different kinds of radiation—gamma rays, beta rays, or alpha particles—act quite similarly. The energy deposited by radiation in a given volume of specific tissue is a good measure of the damage to be expected. Furthermore, it is relatively easy to find out what amounts of radiation will get to any tissue, carried by a specific radioactive substance. Gamma rays are the most important among external sources, since they penetrate deep into the body.[13]

If the exposure were substantial, death or radiation sickness would result.   68

[11]We continue to seek comparable knowledge about food additives, medications, and pollution from coal or petroleum, for example.

[12]The situation is even more complicated in the case of allergens that act differently on different people. Biological hazards appear to be quite unpredictable.

[13]Neutrons are equally important, but exposure to neutrons is not expected as a consequence of the operation of nuclear reactors.

The consequences are well understood, and high radiation doses must of course be avoided. When radiation doses fall to a low level they can still cause mutations, thereby damaging offspring. They may also contribute to cancer after some delay, which, as a rule, is a number of years. Even though these effects are small, and therefore difficult to observe, we know a lot about them. The reason for that is simple: experience. All of us are exposed to background radiation from natural sources, including cosmic rays, radioactive potassium in our blood, or radioactive traces in natural food that are derived from uranium in the soil. Most of us get additional slight radiation from diagnostic x-rays.

Radiation is commonly measured in *roentgens* or *r-units* (sometimes called   69 "rems"). The radiation that an American receives from nonnuclear sources amounts to 0.17 r-units per year. If one thousand r-units were received over the whole body, death would surely result. Half that dose would give a 50 percent mortality rate. Below that dose the danger of death decreases rapidly but radiation sickness—the symptoms of which are changes in blood composition and damage to the intestinal walls, accompanied by vomiting and a loss of hair—is observed at a dose as low as one hundred r-units. Below that amount no immediate biological effects are observed, but genetic changes and delayed development of cancer will be present down to an undetermined lower level.

The average dose of 0.17 r-units per year to which we all are exposed from   70 natural background and diagnostic x-rays does not produce any noticeable effects. Beyond a slight increase in mutations and a possible contribution to "natural" cancer incidence, there may actually be no effects. Experiments on rats and mice have shown beneficial effects at levels much higher than the natural background; these beneficial effects are not understood and may not be applicable to humans. They show, however, that we know next to nothing about these exceedingly low-level radiations except the obvious and important point that their effect is very small.

Here is the relevant point concerning nuclear reactors: a bystander is not   71 apt to receive radiation from a reactor amounting to more than 1 percent of natural background radiation, that is, 1 percent of 0.17, or 0.0017 r-units. On the average he will get less than that amount. The effects of natural backgrounds are so small that they remain unknown, unverified by explicit experiments in spite of diligent efforts to determine them. It is this unknown source of possible trouble that is played up as an important effect. The unknown seems to be frightening even when we know that it is much less dangerous than what nature itself provides. This is a remarkable feat of scare propaganda....

The discussion here on weak radiation may seem too long. Its length corre-   72 sponds to the public emphasis upon this topic. Objectively we could have dismissed it in two short sentences: "There is no reason to worry about weak radiation from nuclear reactors. That radiation is negligible compared to the natural background radiation that has acted on living things as long as they have existed."

Having tried every possible argument to show that nuclear reactors are   73 dangerous, opponents also want to prove that nuclear reactors are useless. In particular, they ask if there will be enough nuclear fuel to run them. At present, reactors utilize essentially only one rare isotope, uranium 235, amounting to less than 1 percent of uranium. We have learned economical ways to mine ores containing 0.16 percent uranium. What burns up in the reactors is about one part in one hundred thousand of what is mined. If we fail to improve these procedures, our nuclear fuel may not last very much longer than our petroleum reserves. The price of uranium ore has already risen. In oil equivalents, it was 25¢ per barrel of oil not many years ago. Now it is between $1.50 and $2.00 per barrel. Does this indicate an unavoidable trend?

Opposition to nuclear reactors by a vocal minority has something to do with the developing shortage. Uranium exploration pays off only after the passage of years. If there is a possibility that nuclear reactors may be banned, then why continue to search for more uranium?   74

In 1945 ore had to contain 2 percent uranium to be exploited. Today, after technical improvements in mining procedures, 0.16 percent suffices. We have learned a lot about utilizing relatively poor ores. And there is lots more poor ore than rich ore, so that the total uranium in poor ores amounts to a huge reserve. If we could utilize ore with even lower uranium content there would be enough uranium. But this means more research, and why invest in research when opponents of nuclear power may win?   75

These same opponents use their prediction of a uranium shortage as an argument against nuclear power. It is an excellent example of a prophecy that may become self-fulfilling. . . .   76

Two serious questions remain. Both concern the misuse of nuclear energy.   77

In December 1973, in a provocative series of articles in *The New Yorker*, John McPhee discussed possible acts of nuclear sabotage, and the possibility that plutonium produced by nuclear reactors might be stolen and used to construct a homemade nuclear explosive. With the continuing prevalence of terrorism, these dangers should not be disregarded.[14]   78

Terrorists do not necessarily want to kill the maximum number of people that they can. They seek to accomplish their aims through acts of terror. Nuclear weapons or even homemade nuclear explosives may not be as dangerous as means more available to terrorists. But people have been conditioned to fear the nuclear menace more than any other single danger.   79

McPhee's *New Yorker* articles were, in fact, justified. At the time they were written nuclear reactors and their products, which could be used in bombs, were guarded in a manner less than completely satisfactory. Considerable change has occurred since. Those articles shook up the authorities. Vigilance was redoubled and refined. Today the danger has decreased; it is no longer significant.   80

It has been argued that reactors and nuclear materials cannot be guarded adequately without turning our country into a police state. But compare this   81

[14]Such possibilities were discussed during the first meeting of our Reactor Safeguard Committee in England. John Wheeler remarked, "Maybe a saboteur is present right in this room." Klaus Fuchs, a member of the British delegation, was present and listening to this remark. A few weeks later he was arrested. He turned out to be Russia's most important spy.

worry with the problem of airplane hijacking. Skyjacking is incomparably easier to perform than acts of nuclear terrorism would be. Defense against skyjacking is made particularly difficult by the need to screen many millions of passengers. With respect to security, as the number of essential persons decreases, safeguards become easier to introduce, more feasible, and more effective. There is no question that reactor products can be guarded. This difficult task, which a few years ago was performed somewhat perfunctorily, is now carried out in a satisfactory manner.

I wish I could be as optimistic and positive about the remaining objection: as 82 nuclear reactors spread among nations their production will enable almost every country to acquire nuclear weapons. This statement, most unfortunately, is true. I believe that eventually nuclear proliferation is unavoidable unless we find far better solutions to international problems than are now on the horizon. This is the main worry influencing our present administration.

Should the United States therefore abandon this dangerous business? It is 83 my firm belief that if we dropped out of nuclear energy development it would have only a minor effect on slowing down the proliferation of nuclear reactors. Today only one-third of the nuclear power reactors are to be found in the United States, which has about seventy in operation; and rapid expansion continues in other countries. If we ceased participating we would no longer have the influence we now use to stabilize the world situation.

Preventing war is of the utmost importance. Most particularly we want to 84 avoid nuclear war. United States policy for at least two decades has been to decrease the danger of nuclear conflict by encouraging various arms limitations. This policy has been unsuccessful. Its chief result has been that we have lost our leadership in the military field to the Russians. This can hardly be called an advantage. Peace may well depend on the power held by those who desire peace.

There is another way in which peace can be reinforced. That is to diminish 85 the reasons for conflict. This goal has been pursued by the United States through foreign aid and other means. It cannot be argued that this path is easy. The great advantage of this course, however, is that practically all of its effects are positive.

Shortage of energy is a painful problem that now affects the great majority 86 of mankind. The United States suffers from it, Western Europe is affected seriously; in Japan the shortage is even greater. But those most terribly hit are the underdeveloped nations. For them, energy shortage translates into shortage of food. Effective agriculture is impossible without fertilizers, without water, and without mechanized equipment. All of these require energy.

We are deeply conscious today of the dangers of pollution. Of all pollution, 87 of all defilement, the most widespread and the worst is pollution by poverty. Three-fourths of mankind is suffering from it. If the energy shortage continues there will be no cure; if nuclear reactors are abandoned, the energy shortage will increase.

There is in fact no prospect that nuclear reactors will be abandoned throughout the world. If the United States continues to participate in development of 88

nuclear reactors, in production of nuclear fuels, and in reasonable use of nuclear "wastes," there is greater hope that the worldwide problem of possible
misuse of nuclear energy will be solved.

In all other respects opponents of nuclear power in the United States have   89
no valid argument. In the case of nuclear proliferation the argument is real and
frightening, but the answer proposed by antinuclear propagandists is the answer of the ostrich: "Let's hide our heads in the sand."

Antinuclear forces selected California for a first major test. They tried to ban   90
nuclear reactors under the guise of making them safe. Their Proposition 15 on
the California ballot amounted to a prohibition of future nuclear reactors, and
would have reduced the power of existing reactors to a level that would hardly
have been more safe but certainly would have been less economical.

Why was California selected? In that state's economy nuclear reactors cer-   91
tainly play a significant role. There were also statements (not completely free
of malice) that California's climate is favorable to the growing of fruits and nuts,
but especially nuts.

Nearly five hundred thousand signatures were needed to put the proposition   92
on the ballot. They were easily obtained. By the time of the vote in June 1976,
only one and a half million people voted against nuclear reactors: three million
voters supported nuclear reactors by voting against the antinuclear proposition. It seems that even in California the nuts are in a minority.

At the time of the 1976 presidential elections, six more states had antinu-   93
clear propositions: Oregon, Washington, Colorado, Arizona, Montana, and Idaho.
All were defeated by an average margin of two to one.

Even these voter mandates did not end the controversy. Scare propaganda   94
continues unabated. It seems that developing good and safe technology in order
to produce more energy is not all that is needed. In a democracy it is also
necessary that citizens should understand what is going on.

Achieving understanding on the part of the people may be the most difficult   95
problem of all. The work of an educator is not unlike the task of Sysiphus. If
you have answered a number of questions your next job is to answer them all
over again.

QUESTIONS FOR MEANING

1. According to Teller, what was the initial rationale for developing nuclear
   power? Who made this decision, and what historical events influenced him
   in making it?
2. Why does Teller believe that reactors are becoming safer? What specific
   improvements does he cite in order to support his claim?
3. Explain what Teller means by "fission products."
4. Teller acknowledges that the Rasmussen report on nuclear reactor safety
   was very controversial. What does his discussion of this report in paragraph
   23 reveal about his own attitude toward it? What is your appraisal of the
   comparison Rasmussen made between being hit by a meteorite and being
   injured in a nuclear accident?

5. How does Teller account for the continuing problem of nuclear waste disposal? What assurances does he offer in order to support his claim that there are several possible solutions, and all we have to do is "to make a choice and work out details"? What method of waste disposal does Teller himself favor?
6. Where does Teller put the blame for the developing shortage of uranium?
7. Why does Teller believe that there is little reason to worry about nuclear sabotage or the theft of nuclear materials by terrorists?
8. What fear does Teller share with opponents of nuclear power? Why does he believe this problem should not cause the United States to abandon nuclear power development?
9. Vocabulary: euphoria (6), clamorous (16), meticulously (24), vigilance (38), quantitative (58), fodder (63), explicit (71), diligent (71), perfunctorily (81), and guise (90).

QUESTIONS ABOUT STRATEGY

1. What is the tone of this essay? How seriously does Teller take his subject and his audience?
2. Why does Teller devote the first part of his essay to summarizing the history of the development of nuclear power? What does this summary contribute to his argument on behalf of nuclear power?
3. Where in his argument does Teller acknowledge that there are unresolved problems in nuclear engineering? To what extent does his argument depend upon his ability to persuade us that science will solve these problems "in the course of time"?
4. In paragraph 18 Teller writes, "The NRC was first headed by Bill Anders, an engineer astronaut who staked his life on the faultless functioning of more than 100,000 parts in the rockets that carried him around the moon and back. Unquestionably, he knows about safety." Is this an example of logical or fallacious reasoning? Why?
5. After describing the nuclear accident at Browns Ferry, Alabama, in which a candle caused a fire that resulted in more than $120 million worth of damage, Teller concludes: "Of course no hundred-million-dollar candle will ever be similarly used again." How seriously do you take this assurance? What assumption lies behind Teller's claim?
6. In paragraphs 41–43, Teller compares nuclear power plants with dams and concludes that nuclear power plants are much more likely to withstand a severe earthquake. Does this persuade you that nuclear power plants are safe—or only that many dams are unsafe?
7. Does Teller ever resort to ad hominem arguments?

HELEN CALDICOTT

What You Must Know About Radiation

*Helen Caldicott (b. 1938) is an Australian pediatrician who specialized in cystic
fibrosis and taught at Harvard Medical School before giving up the practice of
medicine in order to campaign against nuclear weapons. She is the founder of
Women's Action for Nuclear Disarmament and cofounder and president emeritus
of Physicians for Social Responsibility. She was the focus of the Academy Award-
winning film,* If You Love This Planet *and is the author of two books on the arms
race,* Nuclear Madness *(1981) and* Missile Envy: The Arms Race and Nuclear War
*(1984). She is also a leading opponent of nuclear energy, a subject on which she has
lectured throughout the United States. "What You Must Know About Radiation" was
first published in* Redbook *shortly after the nuclear accident at Three Mile Island,
Pennsylvania.*

All radiation is dangerous. No radiation is safe, and we live with a certain   1
amount of background radiation all the time. It comes from the sun, and from
cosmic rays that originate in outer space. Now, eons of time ago, when we were
just amoebae and paramecia and other small organisms and when the ozone
layer in the atmosphere was very thin, a lot of radiation came through, and the
radiation changed our genes—and genes, I remind you, are the very essence of
life; they control everything about us. So as radiation poured in from the sun
eons of time ago, the structure and functions of the genes in the amoebae and
the paramecia and other small organisms were changed and a process of evolution began, eventually producing fish, birds, plants and living animals, including human beings.

Now, a change in a gene is called a "mutation." And there were some muta-   2
tions that were good. They allowed fish to develop lungs and birds to develop
wings—that sort of thing. But there also were mutations that created disease
and deformities, that made many organisms unfit to survive in their environment. Those organisms died off. The others lived. Many people call this process
of separation of the fit creatures from the unfit ones an illustration of the
Darwinian theory of the "survival of the fittest." In any case, that's how we think
human beings evolved. But radiation continues to produce mutations in cells.
Some of these mutations cause changes—"cancer."

Today the background radiation from the sun is much less than it was in the   3
beginning, millions of years ago. That's because the ozone layer is thicker—
it tends to strain out a lot of the radiation—and we live more or less in equilibrium with background radiation, though we do get a certain amount of cancer
from it.

Although we get radiation from natural sources—from air, rocks and our   4
own body cells—we also, in modern times, get it from man-made sources.
X-rays, administered in doctors' offices and hospitals, are the commonest
source today.

It has been estimated that 40 to 50 percent of all medical x-rays are unnec- 5
essary, and since the effect of all radiation is cumulative—that is, each
exposure increases the risk of getting cancer—you must never have an x-ray
without knowing absolutely why and without being assured that it is truly
necessary. If you are a heavy smoker, obviously you will need more chest
x-rays than a nonsmoker. Or if you cough up blood or have pneumonia or break
your arm, you really need an x-ray. The risk from one x-ray is minimal, and the
benefit can be great if it is truly necessary. But keep in mind that doctors often
order x-rays without thinking much about it. X-rays have become routine.
Instead of putting his hand on a patient's belly, palpating it and working out a
clinical diagnosis, a doctor may order an x-ray. And some doctors may simply
want to have an x-ray for their files as part of your record.

Then there are dental x-rays. You don't need a dental x-ray every six months; 6
you don't even need one every year. When I was a child my dentist didn't have
an x-ray machine, and I've got well-filled teeth. Very occasionally, if you have
severe pain or you have a root abscess or something like that, you need a tooth
x-rayed. But you see, like doctors, some dentists do not think of the dangers.
And some buy x-ray machines and pay for them by taking a lot of x-rays and
charging the patients for them.

When a doctor or dentist suggests an x-ray, ask, "Why? What are you going 7
to find out from this x-ray?" Get the doctor to draw a picture and explain the
pathology so that you understand; *you* make the decision. But don't ever have
an unnecessary x-ray.

The reason for care is that human beings are more sensitive to the effects of 8
radiation than any other animal. We get cancer more readily. We don't know
why. And children and fetuses are about 10 to 20 times more sensitive than
adults because their cells are rapidly dividing and growing. It is during the time
when a child is growing and the cells are multiplying that radiation damage to
the genes can have its most devastating effect.

The British epidemiologist Dr. Alice Stewart has shown that one x-ray of a 9
pregnant abdomen increases the risk of eventual leukemia in the baby by 40
percent above the normal incidence. Fortunately, we don't often x-ray pregnant
abdomens nowadays. We use ultrasound to determine where the fetal head is.
But if you *have* had an x-ray while pregnant, let me reassure you: The increased
incidence of 40 percent isn't much, because normally only about 1 in 40,000
children will develop leukemia.

I have been talking about natural radiation and x-ray radiation. Now let us 10
talk about nuclear radiation. This is the kind that comes from atomic bombs
and is developed in nuclear energy plants.

In order to run the atomic reactors that produce energy and make nuclear 11
bombs, we need uranium. Uranium is a natural ore that is found in the ground,
and it's safe enough if it's left in the ground. But when it is mined, it emits
radioactive byproducts—radium and a radioactive gas called "radon." Unfortunately, uranium is worth a lot of money; both the Government and private
utilities pay a very good price for it.

Large-scale uranium mining in the United States started in the '40s, during   12
World War II, in connection with the Manhattan Project, which was created to
produce the first atomic bombs. Many of the miners who were doing this work
inhaled the radon gas, which attaches itself to tiny dust particles and lodges in
the terminal air passages in the lungs. Nothing happened to these men at the
time, but 15, 25, 30 years later some of these men found themselves coughing
up blood or having other symptoms of chest disease. This time x-rays were
definitely in order. So they got x-rays, and on each x-ray plate there was a big
mass—a big white mass. It was cancer.

Now, what happened? Well, here are the cells in the lung and here is the   13
radon, which has been continuously emitting its radioactive alpha particles.
Inside each cell is a nucleus, which is the "brain" of the cell. In the nucleus are
chromosomes, and on the chromosomes are the genes. Now, in every cell in the
body there's a gene that controls the rate of cell division, and that is called
the "regulatory gene." And what happened to the men who got cancer from the
radon gas was that one of the alpha particles in the gas by chance hit the
regulatory gene in one of the cells and damaged it. And the cell sat very quietly
for all those years until one day, instead of dividing to produce just two daughter cells as it should, it went berserk and produced millions and trillions of
daughter cells—a clone of abnormal cells—and that is cancer. In other words,
it may actually take only one alpha particle emitted from one atom, to hit one
cell and one gene, to initiate the cancer cycle. And this is very serious, because
in this country right now, a lot of the men who mined uranium in the past are
dying of lung cancer.

It is a terrible thing that when uranium mining first began in this country   14
none of the big companies paid any attention to the need for safety precautions,
in spite of the fact that it was known that men in Europe who had mined other
ores that contained some uranium died of cancer. So now there is an epidemic
of lung cancer among former American uranium miners. The same kind of
indifference to human welfare exists in industries that produce dangerous non-
radioactive chemicals.

Regulations of the Environmental Protection Agency are being watered   15
down because of the tremendous pressure that is exerted on government by
industry. Industry makes hundreds of new chemicals every year. Very few are
tested for their potential as causes of cancer. They are just dumped into the
environment, as they were in Love Canal, Niagara Falls, New York, and in many
other places around the country, where they become concentrated in the food
chains, in our air, in our water, in our soil. Our whole world is rapidly becoming
polluted with substances we haven't even looked at from the medical point of
view. All to make money, to produce useless objects like plastic bottles that we
throw away.

After uranium is mined it is taken to a milling plant. There it is crushed and   16
chemically treated. The uranium is then removed and the stuff produced as a
byproduct, called "uranium tailings," is discarded. These tailings, a sandy material, contain the radioactive products of radium and thorium, which continue

to emit radon gas for hundreds of thousands of years. If you live next to a uranium tailings dump, you have double the risk of getting cancer, compared to a nonexposed population.

There are millions of tons of tailings lying around in this country. There's a   17
huge pile of uranium tailings right next to Grants, New Mexico. Just last spring the Navaho Indians, many of whom were uranium miners in the early 1950s and are dying of lung cancer, staged an antinuclear demonstration a few miles from Grants. At the same time the people of Grants, which bills itself as "the Uranium Capital of the United States," staged a different demonstration. It was a huge pronuclear parade and rally, which included more than 15 floats, many of them provided by milling and mining companies in the area. One of the floats bore the following statement: "This community lives from uranium—it's our bread and butter." And all the time, tailings were being blown over Grants from that lethal pile, and the people in that area have a double risk of getting lung cancer. But they don't know; they really don't understand the dangers.

They didn't understand the dangers in other places either. In some places   18
tailings were used as landfill, and homes, stores and other structures were built on top of them. In other places tailings were simply dumped. Salt Lake City has a uranium tailings dump of 1.7 million tons. It is called the "Vitro Dump," after the city's Vitro Chemical Company mill. In New Jersey there are two churches that stand on or next to areas where tailings were dumped. In addition, because tailings are like sand and were free for the taking, contractors and builders used them in concrete mix; and in Grand Junction, Colorado, there are thousands of structures in which tailings were used—among them two schools, three shopping malls, an airport and many, many houses.

Obviously the people were never told that the tailings might be dangerous,   19
and all the time they were emanating radiation. Then, about 1971, a pediatrician, Dr. Robert M. Ross, Jr., sounded an alarm: He was finding too many birth defects and too much cancer among his young patients. A committee composed of doctors and researchers was appointed to investigate, and some months later they compared statistics from Mesa County, where Grand Junction is located, with those of the whole state. They found that the death rate from birth defects in Mesa County was more than 50 percent higher than in all of Colorado from 1965 to 1968. Cleft lip and cleft palate were nearly twice as common in Mesa County as in all of Colorado, and death from cancer was significantly higher in the Grand Junction area than in the rest of the state. Though there was controversy about those figures, and there still is, another statistic was recently added by Dr. Stanley W. Ferguson, of the Colorado State Health Department: Between 1970 and 1976, the incidence of leukemia in Grand Junction more than doubled. Efforts to remedy this situation began in 1972 and are still going on, but it's a patchwork affair predicated on "permissible levels of radiation." Of course, I'm convinced that no level of radiation is safe, and since its effects are cumulative, we'll probably be hearing of case after case of cancer in that area in the years to come.

It was only about a year ago that the United States Congress passed a bill   20 making it mandatory that all the millions of tons of tailings in this country be disposed of properly—a practically hopeless task because so much of the stuff has accumulated. In the meantime a great deal of harm has been done.

The next step in the nuclear cycle is enrichment. It takes a full ton of 21 uranium ore to make four pounds of pure uranium, and about 99 percent of this pure uranium is unfissionable—not usable for making energy. This is called Isotope Uranium-238. About a half ounce out of the four pounds is fissionable; this is called Uranium-235. Uranium-235 is what is used for nuclear power, but the 0.7 percent that is got from the natural ore must be enriched to 3.0 percent to be used in a reactor. If it is enriched to 20 percent or more, it is suitable for making atomic bombs. The bomb used on Hiroshima was a uranium bomb and it was called "Little Boy." They have nice names for their bombs.

After enrichment comes fabrication. If you've seen the film *The China Syn-* 22 *drome*, you know that the enriched uranium is made into little pellets like aspirin tablets and packed into hollow rods that are about three quarters of an inch thick and about 12 feet long. When this has been done the rods are taken to the nuclear plant, where they are packed into the core of the nuclear reactor. When they have finished there are 100 tons of uranium in the reactor core, at which point they submerge it all in water. Now, when you pack uranium so densely and in such a way, it reaches "critical mass." That means that the atoms spontaneously start breaking apart, and this action produces about 200 new radioactive elements called "fission products," which are the broken-down products of the original uranium atoms. These fission products are the same materials that are formed when an atom bomb explodes.

An atom bomb explodes as the uranium fissions because it is an uncontrolled 23 reaction. But in a nuclear power plant this process is controlled and the fission-ing uranium doesn't explode. Instead, the heat produced by the fission process boils the water in which the uranium-bearing rods have been submerged, and the steam that is formed turns a turbine that makes electricity.

So in fact, all a nuclear reactor does is boil water. It's a very sophisticated 24 way to boil water. Because inside of each 1,000-megawatt reactor is as much radioactive material as would be released by the explosion of 1,000 bombs of the size of the one that was dropped on Hiroshima.

The reason we are discussing all this is that something happened at Three 25 Mile Island, near Harrisburg, Pennsylvania, last spring. What happened? Well, accident, certainly human error and possibly mechanical failure caused large quantities of water to escape from the container holding the immensely hot uranium rods. Apparently the operators of the plant were unaware of the escaping water. Because the water wasn't immediately replaced, the rods be-came uncovered and remained uncovered for at least 50 minutes. Looking back at it now, most nuclear engineers can't understand what kept the uranium fuel in the uncovered rods from melting down.

What would have happened if there had been a meltdown? The low water 26 level and subsequent inefficient cooling of the rods would have allowed the intrinsic heat of the fission products in the uranium to melt the 100 tons of uranium into a globular mass. It then would have continued to melt right through the bottom of the container and—nuclear experts say—hundreds of feet into the earth "toward China"! That's what is called the "China syndrome" by the nuclear industry.

If a meltdown had occurred at Three Mile Island, a massive steam explosion would have ruptured the reactor container and released all the radiation—as much as in 1,000 Hiroshima-sized bombs—into the air. It would not have been an atomic explosion, but it would have contaminated an area the size of Pennsylvania for thousands of years. Nobody could have lived there any more for thousands of years! And depending on the direction of the wind, other huge areas could have been contaminated. 27

Such an accident would cost about $17 billion in property damage. And what about human damage? Let's say that as many as 10 million people would have been exposed—that would be entirely possible. Well, some statisticians report that almost immediately about 3,300 people would die of lethal radiation exposure. Two or three weeks later about 10,000 to 100,000 more could die of what is called acute radiation illness. First they'd go bald. Their hair would drop out; we saw this for the first time after the bomb was dropped on Hiroshima. Then they would begin to hemorrhage under the skin. They would develop skin ulcers, awful ulcers in their mouths, vomiting and diarrhea, and they'd die of bleeding or infection. 28

That would happen in a relatively short time, but there are long-term effects too. Hundreds of thousands of men would be rendered sterile from the radiation damage to their testicles. Hundreds of thousands of women would stop menstruating, many permanently. Thousands of people would develop hypothyroidism. With their thyroid glands damaged, their metabolic rate would slow down, they would become constipated, they would be unable to think properly, they'd lose their appetites and at the same time become fat. 29

Thousands more would have acute respiratory impairment, the radiation having damaged their lungs. Thousands of babies affected by radiation while still in their mothers' wombs would be born with microcephaly, or with very small heads—"pinheads," they called them in Hiroshima, where this happened after the bomb fell. Thousands more would be born cretins, with ablated thyroids and neurological damage. 30

And five, ten, 20, 30 years later, hundreds of thousands of cases of cancer would occur, to say nothing of the varieties of genetic defects—dwarfism, mental retardation, hemophilia, and others—that would develop and be passed on and on through future generations. 31

My list of sick, dying and dead comes to just less than half a million people. Possibly the estimate could be for a few less, since Three Mile Island had been in operation for only three months before the accident and had only 80 percent of the inventory of radioactive products that a normal, long-term operating, 1,000-megawatt reactor would contain. But it would have been a catastrophe such as the world has never seen, because only 200,000 people died in Hiroshima and Nagasaki, though the incidence of cancer is still increasing among the bomb survivors there. 32

Now, what I want to know is, why doesn't our Government tell us of the 33 dangers to which we are being exposed? Why hasn't it told us what a meltdown would mean? What can we expect as a result of the careless dumping of nuclear wastes, which, if not as swiftly devastating as a meltdown or a bomb, can be just as deadly over a period of time? Where does the allegiance of our elected representatives belong—to the utility companies or to us? Did Dwight Eisenhower, when he was President and they were testing hydrogen bombs in Nevada in 1953, set a permanent policy when he told the Atomic Energy Commission to "keep the public confused" about radioactive fallout? (The AEC certainly was receptive to Eisenhower's advice. Recently declassified commission records show that it repeatedly brushed aside questions about health hazards; and in February, 1955, Willard F. Libby, a member of the commission, said: "People have got to learn to live with facts of life, and part of the facts of life is fallout.")

The accident at Three Mile Island in Pennsylvania revealed still other alarm-   34
ing things. People operating the nuclear plant for Metropolitan Edison didn't know what they were doing. In the first 48 hours after the accident, primary coolant (water that surrounds the rods) was vented into the atmosphere as steam. Rule number one in the nuclear energy business is, Never vent primary coolant! It's like, if you are a surgeon, you never cut off a head—you just don't do that! But the primary coolant was vented after the cladding of many of the rods had melted and released highly radioactive fission products into the water. They weren't measuring anything in the first 48 hours, either, so they don't know exactly what they let out—plutonium? strontium? cesium? radioactive iodine? That's the first thing. The second thing is that a whole lot of radioactive water from the primary coolant spilled onto the reactor floor. An attempt was made to transfer some of this to a tank in an auxiliary building that stands beside the reactor, but the tank already contained radioactive water—perhaps not so radioactive as the primary coolant, but radioactive just the same. To make room for the primary coolant, 4,000 gallons of radioactive water from the tank was emptied into the Susquehanna River.

Now, water from that tank is routinely emptied into the Susquehanna, but   35
first, as Government spokesmen would say, it has to be tested and diluted to a "permissible level of radioactivity." As I see it, no level of radioactivity is permissible, so that's bad enough. But during those first critical 48 hours, the 4,000 gallons of radioactive water they emptied into the river weren't even tested. They also released a lot of radioactive gases into the air, many of which are precursors of products such as Strontium-90, Cesium-137 and Radioactive Iodine-131.

More proof that the people operating that plant didn't know what they were   36
doing: Not only did they make "a series of errors"—I quote the *New York Times*—"in the operation of the plant," but when the accident occurred they continued to make errors. A very serious problem. And because Metropolitan Edison doesn't know how much radioactive stuff was emptied into the environment, there is no hard data on which to make predictions about what will happen to people in the Harrisburg area in the future. And yet Joseph A. Califano, Jr., then Secretary of the Department of Health, Education and Wel-

fare, said that only one person—at worst, ten people—would die of cancer as a result of the accident. He had no primary data on which to base the announcement. It's very worrying.

Let me tell you about Strontium-90. Strontium-90 stays poisonous for 600   37
years. Released into the atmosphere, it settles on the grass from the air, the rain and the dew, and its potency gets compounded many times over the concentration that is in the air. When this happens in dairying areas, cattle eat the grass and the Strontium-90 is concentrated in cow's milk, which both calves and babies drink. It concentrates most highly in human breast milk, and it gets there when pregnant women and nursing mothers eat dairy products that are contaminated by Strontium-90. Now, anybody who ingests a radioactive substance can be affected, but it's very important to know that babies are inordinately sensitive to the effects of radiation. You can't taste the radiation. It's odorless, invisible and tasteless, and when a baby drinks milk containing Strontium-90 the body treats it as if it were calcium; it's deposited in the growing bones. It causes bone cancer. It also causes leukemia—many of those children die.

Between January, 1951, and October, 1958, when a large number of atomic   38
and hydrogen bombs were tested in the Nevada desert, the winds carried the fallout to agricultural as well as populated areas in Utah and Strontium-90 was found in milk. At that time the Nobel Prize-winning scientist Linus Pauling said if babies drank milk containing Strontium-90, they might get leukemia later. And the Government said Pauling was wrong. Then early this year the New England Journal of Medicine published a paper saying that the incidence of leukemia in Utah children in the "high fallout" counties who were under 14 at the time of the testing had increased nearly two and a half times above normal level.

Radioactive Iodine-131 also concentrates in milk, and if there are bodies of   39
water nearby, it concentrates in fish. Although it is active for only a few weeks, once it gets into milk or fish its potency is compounded thousands of times. And its effect, when ingested by humans, is vicious and lasting. Taken up by the thyroid, it can cause thyroid cancer. Keep in mind that I have named only three or four dangerous elements. Actually almost 200 of those dangerous elements that are made in nuclear reactors are contained in nuclear waste.

Nuclear waste. Garbage. Nobody needs it. Nobody wants it. And nobody   40
knows what to do with it. And it has to be disposed of, isolated from the environment, because many of those elements remain potent for one million years. If those materials leak, they get into our air, they get into our water, they get into our food chain and get recycled through human bodies for hundreds and thousands of years, causing cancers after cancers after cancers, to say nothing of birth deformities and genetic disease.

Now, by present methods of technology, nuclear waste, which is active for   41
up to one million years, can be safely stored for only ten to 20 years. But even before that the containers begin to corrode; there are leaks; it gets into all parts of our environment. Even if the most brilliant scientist we have should think he's found the answer for storing nuclear wastes, he'll be dead long before

his hypothesis can be verified. This is the heritage we are leaving to our descendents.

You can imagine our descendents, like the people at Love Canal, Niagara   42
Falls, New York, where nonnuclear but dangerous chemicals were dumped, waking up one morning with their food already contaminated, their kids already being born deformed and dying of leukemia and cancer, and with adults too dying of cancer. It will be too late. But we're risking millions of lives so we can turn our lights on. And to keep the economy running. And because government and big business have invested a lot of money.

In the nuclear industries they say, "Don't worry, we're scientists; we'll find   43
the answer." That's like my saying to a patient, "You have cancer; you have about six months to live; but don't worry, I'm a good doctor and by 1995 I might find a cure."

Now let's talk about plutonium, out of which both atomic and hydrogen   44
bombs are made. That's one of the most dangerous elements known. It is man-made in a nuclear reactor; it didn't exist until we fissioned uranium. And it's named, appropriately, after Pluto, the god of the underworld. It is so incredibly toxic that a millionth of a gram—and a gram is about the size of a grape—can cause cancer. When plutonium is exposed to the air it produces particles as fine as talcum powder that are totally invisible. And if you inhale any of those particles, they will almost certainly give you lung cancer.

If you took just ten pounds of plutonium and put a speck of it in every human   45
lung, that would be enough to kill every single person on earth. Ten pounds! And each nuclear reactor makes 500 pounds of it every year. Five hundred pounds! What's worse, plutonium remains toxic for half a million years. It is not biodegradable, that is, it doesn't decompose; so the plutonium-contaminated waste remains toxic all that time.

There are areas around Denver, Colorado, that are contaminated by pluto-   46
nium radiation, and the testicular cancer rate in a suburb next to Rock Flats, about 13 miles from the center of Denver, is 140 percent higher than the normal incidence. You see, plutonium lodges in the testicles and it's in the testicles that the sperm are, where the genes for the future generations are! Plutonium also crosses the placental barrier, where it can damage the developing fetus. It can kill a cell that's going to form the left side of a baby's brain, or, say, the left arm, or whatever. Do you remember what thalidomide did? Plutonium is thalidomide forever! It will damage fetus after fetus after fetus, down the generations, virtually for the rest of time. And, of course, its effects are not limited to the unborn. It causes lung cancer. It causes bone cancer. It causes liver cancer, and more.

The nuclear reactor was first designed as part of the Manhattan Project to   47
make plutonium, the plutonium to be used in making nuclear weapons. And in making bombs and other atomic weapons they have produced 74 million gallons of high-level radioactive waste, and scientists and engineers and environmental specialists all have studied the problem—and nobody seems to know what to do with it.

Nobody has devised a foolproof, leakproof, fail-safe place to sequester those   48
wastes over the thousands and thousands of years they remain dangerous. At

the present time, wastes, contained in large carbon-steel tanks, are being stored on the site of the Government's Hanford Reservation, a nuclear energy complex near Richland, Washington. They are also being stored on the site of the Savannah River Plant, another Government facility that produces nuclear weapons materials, near Aiken, South Carolina. At Hanford the tanks have already leaked 450,000 gallons of poisonous radioactive waste into the soil near the Columbia River. Eventually these radioactive elements will probably enter the Columbia River, where they will become concentrated in the fish we eat, in the water we drink and, if the water is used for irrigation, in plants and animals.

The dangers of nuclear power are not only accidental meltdowns, escaping   49
radiation and all the radioactive wastes we don't know how to dispose of. The dangers are even greater because it is a small step from nuclear power to nuclear weaponry.

When Robert Strange McNamara was U.S. Secretary of Defense he figured   50
out that if the United States had 400 nuclear weapons, we could wipe out one third of the Soviet population and destroy two thirds of her industry—and that would be a deterrent. The United States now has at least 30,000 nuclear warheads and can kill every human being on earth 12 times over. *Overkill*—that's the Pentagon term. The Russians can overkill Americans 20 times.

Do you know that probably every town and city in this country with a   51
population of 25,000 or more is targeted at this instant with a nuclear weapon? The same is true for towns and cities in the U.S.S.R., China, Europe and England. From the moment that a button is pressed in one country and buttons in other countries are pressed in retaliation, it would take about one-half hour to two hours to complete the war. And that would be the end of civilization as we know it. Shelters would be useless. People in shelters would be asphyxiated. That's because a 20-megaton bomb produces a fire storm of 3,000 square miles that uses up all the oxygen, including that in the shelter.

It is known that the man who had his finger on the button in this country   52
five and a half years ago was not what any psychiatrist would term psychiatrically stable at the end of his term in office. Leonid Brezhnev has been a sick man and, people say, has been treated with cortisone. A good drug. But occasionally it can induce acute psychosis. Not long ago, while still in power, the dictator Idi Amin, of Uganda, who is not exactly given to good judgment, let alone respect for human life, bragged that he would have an atomic bomb in a few years. Granted that some leaders seem more stable than others, but ask yourself: Who is there that any of us would entrust with the safety of the world?

There are now 35 countries that have nuclear weapons capability because   53
they have been sold nuclear reactors—some small, some large—by this country and by others. And since each 1,000-megawatt reactor produces about 500 pounds of plutonium every year, so, theoretically, many of those 35 countries could make 50 atomic bombs every year from each 1,000-megawatt reactor.

Albert Einstein said, "The splitting of the atom has changed everything save   54
man's mode of thinking; thus we drift toward unparalleled catastrophe."

What would happen if all the weapons were used? One, the synergistic   55
effects could be so great, with the ozone destroyed, icecaps melting, radiation everywhere, and so on, that probably not an organism would survive. Maybe

the cockroaches would survive because they're 400,000 times more radiation-resistant than humans. Or if you did survive—if there had been no fire storm to eat up all the oxygen in your shelter—and you stayed in your shelter for at least two weeks (otherwise you would die from the intense radiation) what would you find when you came out? There would be countless dead and dying—Guyana, where the earth was covered with the dead, would have nothing on us. There would be no doctors, drugs or hospital beds in big cities, because those are targeted. You might find some doctors in small communities, but what could they do? Disease would be rampant. And you can imagine the earth inhabited by bands of roving mutant humanoids generations hence. This would be like no science fiction story ever invented.

Look at the changing seasons—the spring and the flowers and the trees   56
coming into leaf. Look at the fall of the year and the leaves turning gold. Look at our growing children. One child. One baby. We're a fantastic species. We're capable of such creativity, love and friendship.

I've got three children. And I am a doctor who treats children, a great many   57
of them having the commonest genetic disease of childhood—cystic fibrosis. I live with dying children. I live with grieving parents. I understand the value of every single human life.

The ultimate in preventive medicine is to eliminate nuclear power and nu-   58
clear weapons. I look on this as a religious issue too. Because what is our responsibility to God but to continue creation?

Someone said, "Evil flourishes only when good men and women do nothing."   59
And there are many of us—good men and women—and we can do a lot.

We have only a short time to turn the destructive powers around. A short   60
time. I appeal especially to women to do this work because we understand the genesis of life. Our bodies are built to nurture life. We have wombs; we have breasts; we have periods to remind us that we can produce life! We also have won a voice in the affairs of the world and are becoming more influential every day. I beg you—do what you can today.

QUESTIONS FOR MEANING

1. In her opening sentence Caldicott claims, "All radiation is dangerous." What support does she offer to substantiate this claim?
2. Caldicott criticizes physicians for ordering unnecessary x-rays, observing that "some doctors may simply want to have an x-ray for their files, as part of your record," and arguing that a doctor might act more responsibly by "putting his hand on a patient's belly, palpating it and working out a clinical diagnosis." What might explain a doctor's decision to order x-rays, and other tests that may prove unnecessary?
3. Why are children especially susceptible to radiation?
4. What does paragraph 9 teach you about reading statistics? Consider this lesson and use it to analyze paragraph 16. Is there anything more that you wish you were told about the risk of getting cancer if you live near a trailings dump?

5. Explain "critical mass," "China syndrome," Strontium-90, Cesium-137, and Radioactive Iodine-131.
6. What evidence does Caldicott provide of human error during the nuclear accident at Three Mile Island?
7. Why does Caldicott believe that "it is a small step from nuclear power to nuclear weaponry"?
8. Vocabulary: eons (1), equilibrium (3), predicated (19), ablated (30), and synergistic (55).

QUESTIONS ABOUT STRATEGY

1. What role does fear play in this argument? What does Caldicott urge us to fear? Are you persuaded that these fears are legitimate, or is Caldicott making an ad populum argument?
2. In addition to discussing nuclear power, Caldicott also writes about x-rays, nonnuclear chemical dumps, and nuclear weapons. How successful is she in relating these different subjects to one another? Would her argument be stronger or weaker if she limited herself to the question of nuclear power?
3. In paragraph 57 Caldicott writes, "I live with dying children. I live with grieving parents. I understand the value of every single human life." How do these words affect you? After reading this essay, how do you picture Helen Caldicott? What sort of person does she seem to be?
4. In her concluding paragraph, Caldicott makes an appeal to women reminiscent of the appeals made by Jeanne Shields on gun control and Margaret Mead on capital punishment. Would you ever end an essay this way? What advantage is there to it? What are the risks?

ROBERT L. DU PONT
The Nuclear Power Phobia

Robert L. Du Pont (b. 1936) graduated from Emory University in 1958 and received his M.D. from Harvard Medical School in 1963. Since 1968, he has been a psychiatrist much involved in public service. From 1968 to 1970, he was a research psychiatrist for the District of Columbia Department of Corrections, and, in 1970, he became the administrator of the Narcotics Treatment Administration, a division of the U.S. Department of Human Resources. From 1973 to 1978, he was director of the National Institute on Drug Abuse and U.S. delegate to the United Nations Commission on Narcotic Drugs. A fellow of the American Psychiatric Association, he has taught psychiatry at George Washington University since 1972, and, since 1978, he has been president of the Institute for Behavior and Health. A contributor to numerous journals, Du Pont wrote the following essay for Business Week *in 1981.*

The nuclear power industry has been virtually stopped in the U.S. because   1
of fear. This is true despite the fact that for more than 20 years the commercial nuclear industry has operated under unprecedented public health scrutiny and that to date there have been no radiation-related injuries (let alone deaths) suffered by any member of the public. The accident at Three Mile Island was a financial disaster, but the health protections built into the plant worked. The independent Presidential commission established to investigate the accident concluded that the only negative health effect was "mental stress," or fear.

My interest in the curious paradox of widespread fear of nuclear power   2
despite credible evidence of safety was stimulated in part by my frustrations from more than 13 years of trying to encourage people to fear using illegal drugs such as heroin and marijuana. It has been as puzzling to me that 500,000 people shoot heroin into their veins voluntarily and that 23 million otherwise reasonably rational people regularly suck marijuana smoke into their lungs as it has been that nearly half of all Americans fear nuclear power so much they would rather import oil or suffer the consequences of burning more coal to make electricity.

The paradoxes.

My professional experience with unconscious motivations for human behav-   3
ior has helped me begin to understand these paradoxes. Before getting to the explanation, however, let me extend the paradox a bit further.

How is it possible to explain that despite massive public education, 50 million   4
American cigarette smokers have not been scared out of their habit, which takes the lives of more than 350,000 smokers a year? Or that more than 80% of Americans do not wear seat belts although 50,000 U.S. highway deaths, more

than 500,000 crippling injuries, and nearly 30 million traffic accidents occur on our roads each year?

Similar paradoxes exist in the public's feelings toward driving a car vs. flying in an airplane. Nearly 30 million Americans are afraid to fly while few fear the automobile—even though automobile accidents are the leading cause of death for every age group from 1 to 40 in the U.S., and commercial air travel in America took only 13 lives in 1980. The answer is found in our attitudes toward risk, which are rooted in three simple psychological perceptions—all irrational—that govern risk assessment.

The first and most important consideration is whether the individual thinks he controls the risk. Many recreational activities are quite dangerous. Skydiving, skiing, and skateboarding are obvious examples. And it is far more dangerous to ride a bicycle around the block once a week than it is to live next to a nuclear power plant. As anyone who has ever had an automobile accident knows, the driver does not control his risk—or he would not be in the accident. But this risk is denied by the person who anticipates driving a car or skiing down a slope because he thinks he does control his risk. The same illusion often protects the cigarette smoker from fear. He has been manipulated by peer and commercial pressures and by the pharmacology of nicotine addiction, but he thinks he can stop or cut down if he needs to. Therefore he is not fearful. This particular factor—the location of control of the risk—is exaggerated further for some people when the "they" who control the risk are big, impersonal, and often mistrusted institutions. Thus, fear of nuclear power is exaggerated in part because the risk is perceived to be controlled by "big utilities" and by "remote bureaucracies" such as the Nuclear Regulatory Commission.

The second major variable in risk assessment involves the question of whether the hazard shows up as one big event—an airplane crash, for example—or whether it occurs in separate, individual events scattered over time and space, such as automobile accidents or cigarette-related deaths. Single, big events are feared excessively. Multiple, separate dangers are more easily denied. Here the role of the media is particularly important. Compare the news value of 130 people dying in an airplane crash once a year with the news value of the 130 automobile-related deaths that now occur every day in the U.S. Imagine the public fear if all 350,000 American cigarette smokers who die each year died together in one place at one time.

The third element in risk assessment is whether the risk is familiar or unfamiliar. Familiar dangers, almost no matter what the relative danger involved, are hard to fear, while unfamiliar threats are almost impossible not to fear. For many people, cars and cigarettes are hard to fear, while airplanes and nuclear power plants are hard not to fear. The siting of nuclear power plants far from urban centers ensures this unfamiliarity, as do the regulations that restrict public visiting to nuclear installations.

When these three principles of risk assessment are put together, one realizes that the deck is stacked against nuclear power. The risk of nuclear power, as perceived in the public mind, is controlled by someone else; it is thought of as related to one massive accident, such as TMI; and it is unfamiliar.

'What is' vs. 'What if.'

It is not surprising, then, that many energy experts are paranoid about media   10
coverage and political handling of nuclear power. By contrast, consider how
those same three irrational psychological principles protect the alcohol,
tobacco, and automobile industries from political and media outrage over
the hundreds of thousands of preventable deaths caused each year by their
products.

If these distortions in risk assessment were simply quirks of the public   11
psyche, they would be interesting but hardly worthy of serious concern. But
the facts are otherwise. These distortions are built into daily political and
economic decisions, with far reaching implications for the nation's health and
economy. Contrast the preoccupation with—and cost of—further improving
the safety of nuclear power with the American inability either to require the
wearing of seat belts or to develop mandatory passive restraints in cars. Or
consider our unwillingness to discourage cigarette smoking in the light of our
expensive and destructive preoccupation with nuclear waste management.

These same principles are affecting the national debate over many drugs   12
and chemicals. Critics often point out that the risks involved have been identified in only a few cases and that an unknown danger of cancer and/or birth
defects—the two most emotionally potent health fears of our generation—may
be hanging over us.

There are several ways we can overcome our fears. The first is to separate   13
the "what is" from the "what if." We need to recognize, for example, that we
have more than 20 years of experience with nuclear power plants to study.
Rather than being endlessly preoccupied with what could happen, let us talk
about what has happened in terms of the public health effects of commercial
nuclear power. We can also begin to think more clearly about what our overall
health dangers are. We should indeed focus attention on cancer and birth
defects, since with the information we have today many cases are preventable.
The public should know that the U.S. has not experienced a rise in the rates of
either cancer or birth defects in recent decades. Aside from the tragic rise in
lung cancer rates (secondary to cigarette smoking), cancer rates are generally
level or headed slightly downward. When cancer and birth defects are discussed, let us consider all preventable causes and put each in proper perspective. When we do that, we will find that many risks are the result of lifestyle
decisions that individuals make every day, particularly decisions related to diet
and use of alcohol, tobacco, and illegal drugs.

Looking at facts.

We are likely to come to the uncomfortable conclusion, when we meet our   14
health "enemies," that "they is us." This is not to say that industry should not
have a role in improving health, but we need to put this into perspective. The
number one cause of preventable cancer is not nuclear power; it is cigarette
smoking.

Finally, it is vital that health agencies and the media reflect more clearly the full facts and not exploit, or simply reflect, the irrational fears of the public. This is particularly important when an industry (such as the nuclear industry or the chemical industry) is attacked as a health threat, since defenses from the involved industry tend to be dismissed as "biased" even when they are right. Public health agencies and the media have an affirmative responsibility to get the facts and educate the public about their fears.   15

Editors and reporters must become educated about what the dangers to public health really are, especially the dangers that are potentially controllable. If the media are to do more than reflect the common distortions in risk assessment, they will have to overcome their own limitations. Meanwhile, we should get off their backs. They do not cause nuclear fears; they are victims of the same irrationality as the rest of us.   16

Confronting necessity.

During the last four years, I have extended my study of fear to my clinical practice of psychiatry: I direct the Phobia Program of Washington to help people over the ultimate irrational fears. I have learned that only by repeated exposure to the feared situation can the phobic person overcome his fear. When considering fear of nuclear power, this principle leads to the conclusion that far more people need to visit nuclear power plants, see them in operation, and talk with their operators. People, especially young people, need to be able to measure radiation and learn about its effects through hands-on use of radiation detection devices. The new requirements for all nuclear power plants to have documented emergency plans that include informing the public within 5 mi. of the plants can be used to educate millions of people.   17

I have also learned that phobic people, like most of the rest of us, can overcome their fears when confronted with necessity. The phobic woman who cannot drive will do so when her child needs to get to the emergency room. The phobic man who cannot speak at a business meeting will speak if he concludes that his job depends on it. This helps explain why France, which lacks oil, gas, and coal, has done such a good job in overcoming public fear of nuclear power: Most Frenchmen know they have no choice if the lights are to go on when they pull the switches. This principle also explains courage: The courageous person acts out of what he considers necessity. ("I carried the child out of the burning building because I couldn't see anything else to do.") And when we tell a friend how courageous he or she is in facing a serious illness or operation, the most common response is, "What choice did I have?"   18

Maybe necessity will provide the route through which nuclear fear will subside in the U.S. When most Americans conclude that they need nuclear generation of electricity, they will face their fear and overcome it. But, as I have also learned, phobic people will seldom face their fears unless they feel they must. This leads to the opposite conclusion: If a nation thinks it can get by without nuclear power, it may try simply to avoid facing the fear, however irrational or expensive the fear may be.   19

QUESTIONS FOR MEANING

1. Du Pont writes that "nearly half of all Americans fear nuclear power so much they would rather import oil or suffer the consequences of burning more coal to make electricity." This implies that importing oil and burning coal also involve risks—risks that may be greater than the risk presented by nuclear energy. What is there to fear about importing oil or burning more coal?
2. What are the three psychological perceptions that govern the way people assess risk? Why are these perceptions "irrational"? Can you give an example of rational fear?
3. Why is it that people fear nuclear energy more than smoking cigarettes or driving cars?
4. Why does Du Pont believe that there is no need to fear nuclear power? How does he believe we can overcome our fears? Is his advice practical?
5. According to Du Pont, how does the media encourage irrational fear? Why does it do this? What should it be doing?
6. Vocabulary: unprecedented (1), credible (2), paradox (2), paranoid (10), quirks (11), and phobic (17).

QUESTIONS ABOUT STRATEGY

1. If you agree with Du Pont that smoking cigarettes, taking drugs, and driving cars are more dangerous than living near a nuclear power plant, would it logically follow that there is no reason to worry about living near a nuclear power plant? Does Du Pont make a convincing case, or is he ignoring the question?
2. How does Du Pont establish his authority to write on this question? What information about himself does he provide? What effect does this information have on you?
3. Are there any major concerns about nuclear energy that Du Pont fails to address?
4. In paragraph 18 Du Pont argues that people accept whatever they preceive as a "necessity." Does this contradict anything else in the essay? Can you identify a necessary activity that Du Pont encourages us to fear?

BENJAMIN SPOCK

A Statement on Nuclear Energy

Benjamin Spock (b. 1903) is one of the world's best-known pediatricians. He began to practice medicine in 1929, when he received his M.D. from the Columbia University College of Physicians and Surgeons. But it was with the publication of The Common Sense Book of Baby and Child Care *in 1946 that "Dr. Spock" became a household word. Revised in several subsequent editions,* Baby and Child Care *has sold over 28 million copies and has been translated into thirty languages, including Catalan and Urdu. The author of several other books on child care, Spock was a prominent opponent of the war in Vietnam and, in 1968, was indicted by a federal grand jury for counseling American youths on how to avoid being drafted. Although he continued to write about children, Spock's opposition to the war led him to begin writing about his political beliefs. A member of the Committee for a Sane Nuclear Policy, Spock ran for president as the nominee of the People's Party in 1972. His opposition to nuclear energy in the following essay reflects his concern for the type of world our children will inherit.*

By coincidence I had this article on the dangers of nuclear power, espe-   1
cially to children, almost finished when the frightening accident occurred at the Three Mile Island nuclear power plant near Harrisburg, Pennsylvania, a few months ago.

In 1962 I joined the National Committee for a Sane Nuclear Policy because I   2
was convinced then that if the United States and the Soviet Union did not negotiate a nuclear weapons test ban treaty, more and more children around the world would die of cancer and leukemia or be born with mental and physical defects as a result of radiation from fallout. (This conviction has been borne out by a veritable epidemic of cancer in Utah as a result of bomb tests made in Nevada between 1951 and 1962.) As a pediatrician I saw this as a pediatrics issue, since children—born and unborn—are particularly susceptible to radiation. It was this and the horrible danger of nuclear war that led me to become an advocate of world disarmament, and later an opponent of the disastrous war in Vietnam.

Earlier, after the end of World War II, when our Government and people   3
were feeling anxious and guilty about having invented and used the atom bomb, the suggestion of "atoms for peace" was received with enthusiasm. The chairman of the Atomic Energy Commission promised that nuclear power would be limitless, safe, clean and "so cheap that it would not need to be metered."

As the years have passed all these promises have proved false. And many of   4
us have come to realize that nuclear power—on a smaller scale for peacetime use—is just as dangerous as nuclear weapons. Furthermore, the rising cost of nuclear power is mind-boggling.

As the supply of vital uranium is dwindling its cost is skyrocketing. The   5
frequency of breakdowns and of dangerous accidents in nuclear power plants has compelled more and more elaborate safeguards, and the price of a plant

has gone up 1,000 percent in 15 years. All this has caused a rapid escalation of the price of nuclear power, which is now almost as expensive as power made from oil or coal when the cost of the plant is taken into account.

There are five distinct dangers in nuclear power; the most horrible would be a complete "meltdown" caused by a failure of the cooling system. Highly lethal radioactive materials would melt through the containing walls and be dispersed into the ground and into the atmosphere. This might promptly kill 50,000 people downwind from the plant from radiation sickness, and many more in the succeeding 30 years from leukemia and cancer, especially in children. And the irradiation of the germ cells in the ovaries and testicles of exposed adults, children and unborn babies would produce mental and physical defects for endless generations. For when mutations are produced in the germ cells, they are passed on forever.   6

Most commentators spoke as if the Three Mile Island nuclear accident was the first serious such accident, but it wasn't. The worst near disasters were at Brown's Ferry, Alabama, in 1975 and at the Fermi Plant, near Detroit, in 1966. But every year there have been dozens of lesser accidents and malfunctions that were threatening. Many plants have been shut down for long periods for decontamination after accidents, for repairs and for improvements in the safety systems. Yet our nuclear-utilities and government officials have kept reassuring us that the plants are safe, pointing to the multiple safeguards. The revelations of the poor functioning of the staff of Three Mile Island and of the Nuclear Regulatory Commission showed how ill prepared and helpless are the people who are supposed to know what to do when a nuclear plant gets out of control.   7

There have been serious accidents in Canadian and European plants too. And in the Soviet Union in 1958 there was a truly major disaster at Kyshtym that devastated a large area; it is now so radioactive that it will have to be barred to occupancy for thousands of years. It presumably killed hundreds of people, though the Soviet Government never acknowledged the accident.   8

A second danger from nuclear power plants is the regular leakage of low-level radiation into the atmosphere and into the water in the ground. It is now known that low levels of radiation are harmful to at least small percentages of the exposed population, depending on the intensity of the exposure. Thousands of cases of leukemia and cancer are calculated to have been caused in the past by diagnostic x-rays and by atomic weapons tests. Whether the radiation leaking from power plants has already caused an increase in leukemia and cancer in downwind areas is still a matter of controversy among scientists.   9

A third danger is from the transportation of uranium to nuclear plants—and of wastes from power plants to burial sites—by railway, by highway and through city streets. The wastes contain many radioactive substances, but the worst by far is plutonium. An invisibly small amount of plutonium is enough to kill a person. One pound dispersed evenly into the lungs of the world's people would kill them all. Its poisonous effects will last for hundreds of thousands of years. The Government assures us that all necessary precautions are being taken. But the fact is that there have already been serious accidents involving radioactive materials on the highways.   10

A fourth danger—and a great one—is in the permanent disposal of lethal   11 nuclear wastes. (Now they are in temporary storage at the power plants where they were created, or in other temporary depositories.) Even the authorities, with all their optimism, admit that they have no solution. These corrosive mixtures in a relatively few-score years will eat through steel or concrete. If they are buried in deep caves or mines, they will work their way into the water supply. If they are dumped in steel drums into the ocean, which has already happened, they will, when they begin to leak, be ingested and progressively concentrated, as smaller fish are consumed by larger and larger fish, and eventually they will be eaten by human beings. To try to shoot the wastes into space would be prohibitively expensive. What moral right do we have to jeopardize the lives of our children, grandchildren and further descendents by creating a menace against which there is no known protection?

12   A fifth danger looms: the theft of nuclear materials, including plutonium, by terrorists. The experts agree that it would not be too difficult to steal the materials or to make a crude bomb.

13   Defenders of nuclear power answer their critics by saying, "But we need the power!"

14   My first answer is that we can surely find ways to get along without a type of power that threatens to kill us, to kill our children with leukemia and cancer and to produce deformities in our descendents till the end of time.

15   My second reply is that all the energy experts whose opinions I've read agree that America *wastes* half the energy it now consumes. One of the largest causes of waste is the insufficiency or absence of insulation in the walls of houses, especially in the houses of those who can't afford the cost of insulation.

16   Unnecessarily hot buildings in winter, unnecessarily cold buildings in summer, unnecessarily powerful cars, are other examples of energy waste.

17   Why is there such a strong bias in favor of nuclear power in certain industries and in the Federal Government despite the grave dangers it entails? The great oil companies now control the mining and processing of uranium, the source of nuclear power, and expect to profit from it long after the oil is gone. General Electric, Westinghouse and two other companies make practically all the nuclear power plant equipment, and hope to make a good thing of it. Many utility companies have planned to make an ever-increasing portion of their profits from nuclear power. The utilities in turn are largely owned and controlled by the most powerful banks in the country. So there is strong industrial and financial pressure for nuclear power. And since our Presidents, governors and legislators depend mainly on industry for their campaign funds, they are obligated to listen to industry's wishes.

18   Most of the staff of the Nuclear Regulatory Commission, who now make the decisions about safety, would no longer have their jobs if they finally concluded that nuclear power was too dangerous to be worth the risk. This being the case, most of them, naturally, are inclined to believe that the problems can be licked with a little more ingenuity and time. But a few who have become convinced that the dangers are too great to justify nuclear power expansion, at least for now, have resigned or have been forced out. Three nuclear engineers at General Electric resigned in 1976 for that reason.

19   James Schlesinger, the secretary of the Energy Department, who always

pushes nuclear energy as against "renewable" energy sources, was formerly head of the Atomic Energy Commission, the precursor of the Nuclear Regulatory Commission. Both commissions have been accused many times by scientists of cover-ups, silencing critical employees and distortions of the truth.

Our Energy Department spends huge sums subsidizing nuclear power. Instead it should be spending generously to encourage further research and more rapid development of power from the sun, from the winds, from the tides, from small dams, from "biomass" (manure, sewage, garbage, trash, crop residues, weeds, wood) that can be burned directly or converted to fuels such as methane gas or alcohol. These are renewable sources of energy, in contrast to oil and coal. (Coal involves serious environmental problems.)   20

Actually our Government is spending only piddling sums to develop renewable energies. The main reasons are that the sun and the winds and the tides don't promise big profits to big industries and they don't make contributions to political parties.   21

So it is up to ordinary citizens to tackle the job of stopping the construction of more nuclear power plants and later dismantling those already built. This will take a long time and persistent effort.   22

You can—and should, if you agree—write letters to ... your senators and representatives, not once but every time you are reminded of the dangers. Some people don't write because they worry about how to express a letter or how to address it. Don't worry; the official may not even read your letter, but someone will count it and report on its contents. Just show how you feel. Address letters to the White House or the Energy Department or to the Senate or House of Representatives—or, better still, to all four—Washington, D.C.   23

Vote in coming elections for candidates who promise to work against nuclear power. Join a local antinuclear group and contribute to it.   24

Participate in demonstrations if you can overcome your shyness. This is a particularly effective way to spread the word and to show the depth of your convictions, as was shown by the spiraling numbers of participators at four successive demonstrations at Seabrook, New Hampshire, over a two-year period—18 at the first demonstration, 180 at the second, 2,400 at the third and 20,000 at the fourth, and as was shown by the participation of an estimated 100,000 people in an anti-nuclear-energy demonstration in Washington, D.C., shortly after the dangerous accident at Three Mile Island plant.   25

QUESTIONS FOR MEANING

1. Spock claims that nuclear testing has caused cancer, leukemia, and mental and physical birth defects. What evidence does he provide to link nuclear testing with nuclear power? If testing nuclear weapons is dangerous, does it necessarily follow that nuclear power plants are dangerous?

2. Why has nuclear power become increasingly expensive? In discussing this aspect of his subject, does Spock provide any evidence that an opponent could use against him?

3. According to Spock, what are the five distinct dangers of nuclear power? Is there any pattern to the order in which he discusses them?

4. The breakdown of the nuclear power plant at Three Mile Island occurred while Spock was finishing this essay. He alludes to it in paragraphs 1 and 7, but argues that this was neither the first nor the worst nuclear accident. What has been the worst accident?
5. What explanation does Spock give for the government's support of nuclear power? Does this explanation make sense to you?
6. What alternatives to nuclear power does Spock advocate? Are you persuaded that these alternatives are worth pursuing?
7. Vocabulary: escalation (5), corrosive (11), entails (17), ingenuity (18), and piddling (21).

QUESTIONS ABOUT STRATEGY

1. Where does Spock anticipate the opposition? Are there any counterarguments that he ignores?
2. Identify the concession in paragraph 9. To what extent does this concession weaken Spock's argument?
3. In paragraphs 15 and 16, Spock argues for a greater conservation of energy, complaining that Americans waste half the energy we consume. This was in 1979. Is this argument still valid today, or have we learned to conserve the resources we have?
4. What is the function of paragraphs 22–25? Do these paragraphs provide an effective conclusion to the essay? Consider paragraph 25 in particular.

ROGER STARR
The Case for Nuclear Energy

Roger Starr (b. 1918) graduated from Yale in 1939. He is the author of The Living
End *(1966),* Urban Choices *(1968),* Housing and the Money Market *(1975),*
America's Housing Challenge *(1978), and* The Rise and Fall of New York City
*(1985). He was executive director of the Citizens' Housing and Planning Council of
New York from 1958 to 1973, and he has lectured at City College, Pratt Institute, and
the New School for Social Research. His essays have appeared in numerous
periodicals, including* The New Republic, Commentary, *and the* National Review.
The following defense of nuclear energy was originally published in the New York
Times, *where Starr has been a member of the editorial board since 1977.*

I write of nuclear power as a self-confessed coward in the face of all massive   1
concentrations of energy. Lightning frightens me. A surge in the wind's strength
makes me uneasy in an airplane. And I cannot stand at the base of a 200-foot
dam without thinking of the force of gravity stored up behind it, waiting to
sweep everything before it.

When I was 10 years old, I was leery of the two large tanks in which cooking   2
gas was stored not far from my home in uptown Manhattan. I had been instructed that playing with matches was bad, particularly near stoves; lighting
the oven was a hazardous chore reserved for adults. If an oven could go off with
a bang, I thought, what would exploding gas tanks do?

Yet it was clear that my mother, timorous in the face of other perils—deadly   3
poisoning by a lunch eaten elsewhere than Schrafft's, for example—did not
fear those gas tanks. And I, too, might have made my peace with them if I had
known what she knew, that they were an essential part of the basically benefi-
cent petroleum-energy system that produced hot cocoa on cold afternoons.
Now, sensing the approaching demise of that system, I am steeling myself for
its successor. Without broadened use of nuclear power, I see little long-range
hope for the achievement of decent living standards everywhere.

The Western world has become accustomed to the availability of cooking   4
gas. It has become even more accustomed to oil for home heating, gasoline for
automobiles, jet fuel for airplanes. Like the natives of some South Pacific islands
who have no word for fever because they are always in a feverish condition, we
have not recognized that we have been living in the Petroleum Age. We have
known no other.

During its time, which began early in the 19th century, the Petroleum Age   5
has revolutionized human existence. On the most basic level, the world's population has grown from about one billion to more than four billion. New standards have been established for physical comfort, health care, length of life,
human mobility, public knowledge and cultural achievement. Yet, today, just as
it is raising expectations in areas of the world where they were never felt before,
the Petroleum Age is coming to a close.

The process is gradual but inexorable. The Petroleum Age will die fitfully, 6
like a terminally ill patient who, nevertheless, has good days. There will be
occasional oil gluts, such as the one we are now experiencing, when economic
activity declines or when there is a temporary dip in demand. Inevitably, those
moments will bring on a new attack of public complacency. Nothing will alter
the essential facts, however. Petroleum is a finite resource. It is unlikely, as the
RAND Institute reports, that there will be any major new oil discoveries that
would change the overall supply picture.

Meanwhile, overall demand for oil will continue to increase. Populations will 7
continue to rise in the industrialized countries, whose citizens will not be content with stagnation or decline in their standards of living. The developing
countries will insist on economic development they cannot have without petroleum, and they will impose their requirements, not only by appeals to conscience and justice, but by terrorism or by boycott or by their refusal to produce
or export raw materials the industrialized nations require.

There are, to be sure, a variety of other reasons for the United States and its 8
European partners to seek alternatives to their current petroleum dependency.
The necessity to import much of our oil, for example, creates huge foreign-
exchange losses, fuels inflation and puts our national security at risk, making
us hostage to the Organization of Petroleum Exporting Countries. The very
cost of a gallon of gasoline must make us look for other energy sources. But
whatever strategies we adopt, they will involve major changes in the ways of
the industrialized nations.

What options do we have? They range from petroleum conservation to the 9
development of synthetic fuels to the increased use of solar power or coal or
nuclear energy.

Among our potential strategies, conservation seems most attractive to most 10
people because it seems to be free of hazard and to be based wholly on the
admirable notion of eliminating waste. One problem with that sentiment is a
confusion over the definition of waste.

Many Americans have winced at the accusation that, with 5 percent of the 11
world's population, the United States uses 30 percent of its total energy. Are
Americans hogs, using too much energy? Or, as seems to me more likely, does
the rest of the world use too little energy because it has not yet achieved a
standard of living that satisfies its people? Is a significant part of the energy
used by the United States truly wasted? Or is it not used to manufacture goods
or to raise agricultural products that the other nations of the world pay for with
their raw materials or with the goods they manufacture? Do the Japanese, for
instance, think America is wasting energy when it uses gasoline to operate the
automobiles the Japanese sell in this country? I doubt it.

Clearly, conservation needs to be defined more specifically. The goal should 12
be to cut down on the use of petroleum to produce power that can be produced
just as well from other, more abundant sources. This sounds easy. It isn't.

The biggest reduction would come from a change in that hungriest of gaso- 13
line gobblers, the automobile. Americans are shifting away from large, heavy
cars to those that can get 30 miles to a gallon. If all automobiles could be so

exchanged overnight, the saving would come to about an eighth of total American petroleum consumption, or about half of what is consumed by automobiles today, and that should enable the United States to reduce its imports of foreign oil by 25 percent.

The catch is that automobiles are not going to be changed overnight; it will   14
be years before all the low-mileage cars now on the road will be replaced. Thus, to achieve the 30-miles-a-gallon average, we would have to develop cars that can get 50 miles from a gallon. How many such cars, with their smaller size and carrying capacity and their increased liability to serious accidents, will Americans buy?

Another catch: The big American gas-guzzler has always been most popular   15
in long-distance driving, rather than stop-and-go city driving, and for good reason. Big cars carry in one trip what may take two trips in mini-compact cars. The moral is that automobile driving habits reflect living styles that will be difficult to change.

Some people imagine that railroad transportation can be made more attrac-   16
tive and lead people to use their cars less. Indeed, the Federal Government has made major efforts to stimulate intercity and suburban passenger rail service; thus far, the effect on automobile usage has been negligible. Meanwhile, many of our central cities served by public transit are losing population, which is making the transit systems less financially viable. And those leaving the cities for greener fields in the suburbs are creating ever bigger parking lots out there.

Residential and commercial buildings represent another rich vein for con-   17
servationists to tap. In 1980, the amount of energy used in buildings—much of it for heating, airconditioning and hot water—was about 50 percent greater than the amount that went into all forms of transportation, public and private. But buildings use less energy when they are well insulated. The National Association of Home Builders claims its members built homes in 1978 that could be operated with 35 percent less energy than homes built four years earlier.

About 37 percent of the energy used to heat homes and business buildings   18
is produced by burning oil on the premises. (Almost all other buildings are heated by natural gas or electricity.) A complete reconstruction of America's homes and business offices, using the latest insulation methods, could reduce the use of oil in America by a total of only about 10 percent. Moreover, it can't happen overnight. Builders produce no more than two million homes, even in a great building year. If, at a guess, there are 60 million oil-burning homes in America that could be better insulated, it would take at least 30 years of good building to replace those homes and reach the 10 percent saving on a nationwide basis. And that assumes that all the new buildings would be devoted to replacing the old—rather unlikely, I think, since a growing population will be using the old homes as well as the new.

Two other schemes have been put forward as ways to augment insulation-   19
based energy savings. One, called co-generation, is based on the fact that the process of generating electricity is inefficient, with as much as two-thirds of the energy escaping as wasted heat. Co-generation equipment enables a company or even a family to produce its own electricity on site and to use the redundant heat to warm or air-condition its buildings and to provide hot water. Yet if an

oil-burning co-generating plant replaces electricity produced in a coal or nuclear plant, it fails to save the strategic ingredient, petroleum.

The second proposal to augment insulation as a means of conserving oil is   20
the expanded use of solar power to heat water in tubing installed on the roofs of buildings. This purely local application of solar energy appears to be more practical for providing hot water for washing and laundry than for heating rooms and hallways; space heating is a cold-weather requirement, but that is manifest in the winter when the radiant heat on the roof is at its lowest point. Israel's extensive use of solar collectors on low-rise buildings in a hot climate saves 1.5 percent of the nation's oil, all of which must be imported.

Of course, some limited savings can be produced by better-insulated homes,   21
and only a profligate would overlook them. And examples can be found of houses in which solar techniques prove economical. But the International Institute for Applied Systems Analysis, funded with American and Russian money and located in Austria, estimates that the world will need between three and four times its present energy supply by 2030. Pipes on the roof won't do it.

In the natural course of events, politics—the concerted expression of people's desires—will determine how much conservation Americans will tolerate.   22
They will doubtless accept gentle reminders to return bottles or wear sweaters indoors. They are likely to have a different reaction when conservation demands the loss of a job, perhaps in the vacation or recreation trades as auto travel drops, or the loss of a hobby as the outboard motor becomes obsolete, or the shrinkage of such amenities as air-conditioning. Anyone who doubts the political unacceptability of energy conservation on a grand scale need only remember the defeat of gasoline rationing and the all-but-universal willingness to accept unfounded rumors that a conspiracy by the oil companies was responsible for the gasoline shortage.

To be sure, higher prices will continue to reduce the public's consumption   23
of oil and to stimulate engineers to invent more efficient machinery. But we desperately require the development of a national policy to provide an adequate substitute for petroleum and a long-term substitute for the energy it yields.

What about alternative energy sources, then, if conservation cannot do   24
the job?

An artificial petroleum fuel has already been invented: gasohol. Gasoline can   25
be stretched by at least 10 percent by diluting it with alcohol made from the fermentation and distillation of farm and forest products. Gasohol requires no monstrous chopping down of hills or digging of vast open coal pits, it involves few apparent dangers and it does not require investment on the scale of other substitute fuels.

Inevitably, there are caveats. Critics make the point that production of gas-   26
ohol—the planting and harvesting of lumber and crops and their transportation to a processing area and the processing itself—uses up more energy than the finished product releases when burned. Moreover, gasohol competes for the same natural resources needed for food and construction purposes.

Another and potentially more significant alternative to oil would be a "hard"   27
solar program, which would require massive, centralized installations as op-

posed to such "soft" solar applications as individual, rooftop collectors. The goal would be to gather enough energy to free vast quantities of pure hydrogen from sea water. As the space shuttle demonstrated, hydrogen releases great amounts of energy when burned; theoretically, it might take over where oil and gasoline leave off.

Such a program would be practicable only if free of the vagaries of climate.   28 The International Institute for Applied Systems conceives of elaborate concrete bases built near the equator to support movable mirrors, which would be geared to follow the sun. The hydrogen would be transported to population centers by pipeline or tanker.

The plan has some obvious snags. For example, tankers carrying liquefied   29 hydrogen under high pressure and at low temperature would be as welcome as measles in most of the world's ports. Of greater significance is the very size and cost of a solar-energy program big enough to take care of the world's future energy needs. The solar concentrating stations would consume during each year of their construction an amount of concrete equal to the total poured in 1975 throughout the world; the institute predicts that this program would involve more fatal on-the-job accidents a year than any other energy operation, including coal mining.

There are some fossil-fuel substitutes for oil, including the so-called tar   30 sands of Canada and the oil shales of the American West; both contain massive quantities of petroleum. The tars and shale can be mined, but no process for extracting the oil from them has been proved on a commercial scale. Immense quantities of water are needed, leading to major quarrels over environmental impact.

A third substitute is available. Coal can be made into a liquid fuel, as the   31 Germans proved in World War II. As is true for the tar sands and shale, coal liquefication requires lots of water and a huge expenditure of money and energy. Whether in liquefied form, or used—as many recommend—as a substitute for oil or natural gas to produce electricity, coal is not so simple as it seems. You don't just dig it out of the ground and burn it like waste paper. It is a bulky commodity, and it has more than its share of disadvantages as a fuel.

Railroad facilities and barge canals must be greatly expanded and pipelines   32 constructed to carry the coal in dry or slurry form thousands of miles. Underground mining is hazardous and expensive; open-pit, or strip, mining engenders stiff opposition because it threatens to scar the landscape—in the United States, some particularly beautiful Western landscapes would be an early target. Burned under electric-generating boilers, coal leaves behind vast tonnages of residue, and the gasses it releases upon burning are heavy with contaminants. Getting rid of coal's ashes—usually in the form of a fine powder, because coal must be pulverized before burning for maximum efficiency—is difficult. Expensive scrubbers must be installed in new plants that burn coal with a high sulfur content to prevent the creation of "acid rain." The huge quantities of carbon dioxide that would be released into the air by burning coal on a vastly expanded scale could raise further havoc with the earth's atmosphere.

While a serious program for replacing petroleum must involve conservation,   33 solar power and coal, it is on behalf of nuclear energy that I would argue most forcefully. Partly, I am responding to the gross popular underestimate of the contribution already made by nuclear power, which produces 11 percent of America's electric power and a higher percentage of European power. I am responding to the charge that nuclear power is formidably expensive. In fact, though nuclear plants are expensive to build, their operating costs over the long haul are low.

I am responding, also, to the fact that no other technology has remained   34
under attack as basically unsafe and unsound after 20 years during which it caused not a single, nonworker fatality. Those who fear nuclear power emphasize the accidents and mistakes in plant operation that have produced political opposition to its increased use. They point to the accident at Three Mile Island, involving a partial melt-down of the fuel core, as proof that much more serious damage is not only possible but likely. One enthusiastic enemy of nuclear power has written that the Three Mile Island event could have made one-half of the United States uninhabitable. Actually, the accident revealed the need for improved operator training, company supervision and Government regulation, but it also showed that the plant could withstand gross abuse without leakage of dangerous quantities of radioactive material. Its extra safety systems kept the melted fuel within the reactor vessel inside the containment building, just as they were designed to do.

Many people associate nuclear power with the atomic bomb and with fears   35
of damage to the genes, and thus to the future of the race. Although most reasonably well informed people now understand that a nuclear power plant cannot be made to explode, very few seem to know that the radioactive emissions from all the nuclear plants in the United States will cause fewer than one case of genetic damage a year. The radioactive discharges at the gates of a nuclear power station are so minor that, in one year, someone living next to a nuclear station would be exposed to no more extra radiation than on a single flight from New York to California and back, at altitudes partly above the atmosphere that filters out cosmic radiation. Similarly, the ambient radiation readings from the granite in St. Peter's Square in Rome are higher than the permitted radiation at the gates of a nuclear power plant.

Many opponents of nuclear power plants argue that they produce plutonium,   36
and that plutonium, after having been separated chemically from spent reactor fuel, can be used by a small, non-nuclear nation to make bombs and start a nuclear war. But trying to prevent energy-poor nations from turning to nuclear power for peaceful purposes is tough today, and it will get even harder as the oil supply gets tighter. Moreover, the bomb made by a small nation is very unlikely to start a major war. Such a nuclear holocaust is more likely to be started by a great power seeking to protect its access to petroleum and other resources. Thus, the availability of nuclear power for industrial purposes would probably continue to diminish the chances of nuclear war rather than to increase them.

Nuclear power has major advantages over the other petroleum substitutes   37
or augmenters. It is, for example, nonpolluting, producing no sulfur oxides to

create acid rain, no soot or dust to stimulate bronchial disorders and no industrial smog. It also leaves the landscape relatively untouched, avoiding the environmental consequences of coal mining because the quantities of nuclear fuel
needed are small. A nuclear plant is stocked with about 30 tons of fuel once a
year, drawn from about 100 or 200 times as much ore. In comparison, a typical
coal plant will burn about 3,000 tons of coal a day, meaning that more than 150
times as much material must be taken from the earth. Nuclear ore is processed
near the mine; thus, only 30 tons of fuel must be shipped each year to each
plant, while the figure for a coal plant is 900,000 tons.

Many people tremble at the possible health and environmental conse-   38
quences of the radiation released by wastes from atomic plants. Yet the quantity
of such wastes is small—the amount produced annually at a single plant could
be stored in a space equal to a normal coat closet. And improved procedures to
store the wastes are being developed; Sweden, for example, has reported considerable success with the storage of specially treated wastes in stable geologic
formations. Politically, the problem should, with improved public awareness, be
less troubling than the problems of storing the far greater quantities of ash,
solid and toxic waste that are the inevitable byproducts of an industrial society.

Taking into account the capital investment in scrubbers, the disposal costs   39
of ash and other wastes produced by burning coal and the mining and transportation costs of the bulk materials involved, generation of electricity from
uranium oxide is no more expensive than from coal. The initial investment in a
nuclear plant is very high, but operating costs are correspondingly low. In the
case of plants in operation, nuclear power is far cheaper than any other generating method, excluding only hydro power.

Perhaps, I, too, would have been happier as one of Robin Hood's merry men,   40
living in Sherwood Forest at a time when the woods themselves produced
enough available protein to keep our little band alive. But the choice is not open
to me. We live in an industrialized world. Even our bowmen hunters use weapons that reflect the high technology of plastics and metallurgy.

Consider an event that has yet to occur, a major nuclear accident in which   41
the reactor vessel and the containment building are breached, neither of which
happened at Three Mile Island. In a recent *Scientific American* article on the
probable results of such an accident, the authors conclude it would not have
involved either explosion or intense heat. They conclude that only one square
mile would, in any case, have been subject to a possibly lethal degree of radioactivity, and that sufficient warning could have been given to evacuate an area
of 1,800 square miles in which two rems of radioactivity would have been
reached. That number is less than half the allowable maximum limit of annual
radiation for a worker in a nuclear plant, and one two-hundredth of the amount
that might cause a fatality.

Of course dangers exist, but compared with the dangers of not proceeding   42
with development of nuclear power they seem to me on about the level of the
tanks of cooking gas of my youth. The gas tanks on 125th Street *could* have
blown up. Atomic containment may be breached, sometime, somewhere. But
while Americans fret about these possibilities, they seem oblivious to the certain dangers of a failure to meet the threat posed by the end of the Petroleum

Age. To maintain our own standard of living, to provide for a world that increasingly demands a chance to achieve that standard, we must accept the nuclear alternative.

QUESTIONS FOR MEANING

1. Schrafft's is a chain of restaurants in New York City. Judging from Starr's description of his childhood, what kind of a restaurant would you imagine Schrafft's to be?
2. What is the thesis of this essay? Where does Starr first state it? Where does he restate it?
3. What does Starr mean by the "Petroleum Age"? When did it begin, and why is it ending? What changes did it bring about in the United States and throughout the world?
4. How does Starr respond to the frequently made argument that Americans waste energy and consume too great a portion of the world's resources? Why does he believe that Americans will tolerate only limited types of energy conservation?
5. Why is Starr skeptical about the role solar energy can play in the world's economy? Why does he object to burning more coal?
6. According to Starr, what did the nuclear accident at Three Mile Island illustrate? How does Starr's view of this incident differ from that of opponents of nuclear power? Does Starr recognize that the accident revealed any shortcomings in the way nuclear power plants are operated?
7. Why does Starr believe that nuclear power can help reduce the risk of a major war? Does his reasoning seem plausible?
8. Vocabulary: timorous (3), inexorable (6), liability (14), profligate (21), caveats (26), vagaries (28), havoc (32), and ambient (35).

QUESTIONS ABOUT STRATEGY

1. What is the function of paragraphs 1–3? What point is Starr making in these paragraphs? What advantage is there in introducing childhood memories into an argument on nuclear power? Where in the essay does Starr return to the fears of his childhood?
2. Why does Starr discuss the advantages of nuclear power only after he has exposed the shortcomings of all the commonly proposed alternatives to it?
3. Starr makes an effort to respond to most of the arguments that are made by people opposed to nuclear power. Identify the points where Starr anticipates the opposition and evaluate separately each of his counterarguments. Which is the strongest and which is the weakest? Is there any argument that Starr has overlooked?
4. Consider the tone of paragraph 40. How would you describe it? Does it differ from the tone that prevails throughout most of the essay? If you were Starr's editor, would you urge him to revise this paragraph or to keep it as it is?

SUGGESTIONS FOR WRITING

1. Are you willing to live near a nuclear power plant? If you are, write an essay in defense of nuclear power that responds to the objections raised by Barry Commoner, Helen Caldicott, and Benjamin Spock.

2. The principal purpose of nuclear power plants is to generate electricity. Americans have grown increasingly conscious of the need to conserve heating oil and gasoline, but we may still be wasting electricity. If you believe that this is so, write an essay arguing on behalf of ways through which we can reduce our consumption of electricity.

3. Robert Du Pont argued that Americans have an irrational fear of nuclear power. If you believe that nuclear power deserves to be feared, write an essay that explains why.

4. In "The Case for Nuclear Energy," Roger Starr argued that there is no reasonable alternative to nuclear energy. If you believe that he is mistaken, write an argument on behalf of the alternative energy source in which you believe. But if you favor an alternative discussed by Starr, make sure that you respond to his objections.

5. Edward Teller argued that nuclear power plants are built to withstand earthquakes. Research the controversy surrounding the nuclear power plant at Diablo Canyon, California and argue whether or not that specific facility should be in use.

6. The problem of how to dispose of nuclear waste remains one of the most controversial issues in the discussion of nuclear power. Contrast the way Barry Commoner and Edward Teller address this problem and then argue on behalf of the writer who makes the most persuasive case. Be sure to reveal the limitations of the argument you reject.

7. Caldicott, Spock, and Starr all refer to the nuclear accident at Three Mile Island, Pennsylvania, but they draw different conclusions about what that accident revealed. Research what happened at Three Mile Island and then argue whether that accident—and the way in which it was handled—should make us more or less concerned about the safety of nuclear power.

8. Both Helen Caldicott and Benjamin Spock claim that there is a link between nuclear power and cancer. Is this true? Do a research paper focused on the health of the men and women who work in the nuclear industry.

Section 7

Higher Education: What's the Point?

THEODORE HESBURGH
The Moral Purpose of Higher Education

Theodore Hesburgh (b. 1917) is one of America's most prominent educators. Ordained a priest in 1943, Hesburgh returned to the University of Notre Dame, from which he had graduated in 1937. Hired as an assistant professor of religion in 1945, Hesburgh rose to become the University's president by 1952—a position that he still holds. A member of the U.S. Commission on Civil Rights from 1957 to 1972, Hesburgh has also served as a trustee of the Rockefeller Foundation, the Carnegie Foundation for the Advancement of Teaching, and the Chase Manhattan Bank. His many awards include the Presidential Medal of Freedom in 1964 and the Charles Evans Hughes Award from the National Conference of Christians and Jews in 1970. The following essay is drawn from The Hesburgh Papers: Higher Values in Higher Education *(1979), one of Hesburgh's many books.*

Somewhere, in that vague morass of rhetoric that has always characterized descriptions of liberal education, one always finds a mention of values. The true purists insist on intellectual values, but there have always been educators, particularly among founders of small liberal arts colleges in the nineteenth century, who likewise stressed moral values as one of the finest fruits of their educational process, especially if their colleges were inspired by a religious group. 1

I believe it to be a fairly obvious fact that we have come full circle in our secularized times. Today one hears all too little of intellectual values, and moral values seem to have become a lost cause in the educational process. I know educators of some renown who practically tell their students, "We don't care what you do around here as long as you do it quietly, avoid blatant scandal, and don't give the institution a bad name." 2

Part of this attitude is an overreaction to *in loco parentis*, which goes from eschewing responsibility for students' lives to just not caring how they live. It is assumed that how students live has no relation to their education, which is, in this view, solely an intellectual process. Those who espouse this view would 3

377

not necessarily deny that values are important in life. They just do not think that values form part of the higher education endeavor—if, indeed, they can be taught anyway.

Moral abdication or valuelessness seems to have become a sign of the times.   4
One might well describe the illness of modern society and its schooling as anomie, a rootlessness.

I would like to say right out that I do not consider this to be progress,   5
however modern and stylish it might be. The Greeks (not the fraternities!) were at their best when they insisted that excellence (*arete*) was at the heart of human activity at its noblest, certainly at the heart of education at its civilized best. John Gardner wrote a book on the subject which will best be remembered by his trenchant phrase: "Unless our philosophers and plumbers are committed to excellence, neither our pipes nor our arguments will hold water."

Do values really count in a liberal education? They have to count if you take   6
the word "liberal" at its face value. To be liberal, an education must somehow liberate a person actually to be what every person potentially is: free. Free to be and free to do. What?

Excuse me for making a list, but it is important. The first fruit of a liberal   7
education is to free a person from ignorance, which fundamentally means freedom to think, clearly and logically. Moreover, allied with this release from stupidity—nonthinking or poor thinking—is the freedom to communicate one's thoughts, preferably with clarity, style, and grace, certainly with more than the Neanderthal grunt. A liberal education should also enable a person to judge, which in itself presupposes the ability to evaluate: to prefer this to that, to say this is good and that is bad or, at least, this is better than that. To evaluate is to prefer, to discriminate, to choose, and each of these actions presupposes a sense of values. Liberal education should also enable a person to situate himself or herself within a given culture, religion, race, sex, and to appreciate what is valuable in the given situation, even as simple an evaluation as "black is beautiful." This, too, is a value judgment and a liberation from valuelessness, insecurity, and despair at times. Liberal education, by all of these value-laden processes, should confer a sense of peace, confidence, and assurance on the person thus educated and liberate him or her from the adriftness that characterizes so many in an age of anomie.

Lastly, a liberal education should enable a person to humanize everything   8
that he or she touches in life, which is to say that one is enabled not only to evaluate what one is or does, but that, in addition, one adds value consciously to relationships that might otherwise be banal or superficial or meaningless: relations to God, to one's fellow men, to one's wife or husband or children, to one's associates, one's neighborhood, one's country and world.

In this way, the list of what one expects of liberal education is really a list of   9
the very real values that alone can liberate a person from very real evils or nonvalues—stupidity, meaninglessness, inhumanity.

One might well ask at this juncture, "How are these values attained educa-   10
tionally?" Again, one is almost forced to make a list. Language and mathematics stress clarity, precision, and style if well taught; literature gives an insight into

that vast human arena of good and evil, love and hate, peace and violence as real living human options. History gives a vital record of mankind's success and failure, hopes and fears, the heights and the depths of human endeavors pursued with either heroism or depravity—but always depicting real virtue or the lack of it. Music and art purvey a sense of beauty seen or heard, a value to be preferred to ugliness or cacophony. The physical sciences are a symphony of world order, so often unsuccessfully sought by law, but already achieved by creation, a model challenging man's freedom and creativity. The social sciences show man at work, theoretically and practically, creating his world. Too often, social scientists in their quest for a physical scientist's objectivity underrate the influence of freedom—for good or for evil. While a social scientist must remain objective within the givens of his observable data, his best contribution comes when he invokes the values that make the data more meaningful, as Tocqueville does in commenting on the values of democracy in America, Barbara Ward in outlining the value of social justice in a very unjust world, Michael Harrington in commenting on the nonvalue of property. Again, it is the value judgments that ultimately bring the social sciences to life and make them more meaningful in liberating those who study them in the course of a liberal education.

One might ask where the physical sciences liberate, but, even here, the bursting knowledge of the physical sciences is really power to liberate mankind: from hunger, from ignorance and superstition, from grinding poverty and homelessness, all of the conditions that have made millions of persons less than human. But the price of this liberation is value: the value to use the power of science for the humanization rather than the destruction of mankind.   11

Value is simply central to all that is liberalizing in liberal education. Without value, it would be impossible to visualize liberal education as all that is good in both the intellectual and the moral order of human development and liberation. Along the same line of reasoning, President Robben Fleming of Michigan this year asked his faculty why, in the recent student revolution, it was the liberal arts students who so easily reverted to violence, intolerance, and illiberality. Could it not be that their actions demonstrated that liberal education has begun to fail in the most important of its functions: to liberate man from irrationality, valuelessness, and anomie?   12

But, one might legitimately ask, how are these great values transmitted in the process of liberal education? All that I have said thus far would indicate that the values are inherent in the teaching of the various disciplines that comprise a liberal education in the traditional sense. However, one should admit that it is quite possible to study all of these branches of knowledge, including those that explicitly treat of values, philosophy and theology, without emerging as a person who is both imbued with and seized by great liberating and humanizing values. I believe that all that this says is that the key and central factor in liberal education is the teacher-educator, his perception of his role, how he teaches, but particularly, how he lives and exemplifies the values inherent in what he teaches. Values are exemplified better than they are taught, which is to say that they are taught better by exemplification than by words.   13

I have long believed that a Christian university is worthless in our day unless   14
it conveys to all who study within it a deep sense of the dignity of the human
person, his nature and high destiny, his opportunities for seeking justice in a
very unjust world, his inherent nobility so needing to be realized, for one's self
and for others, whatever the obstacles. I would have to admit, even immodestly,
that whatever I have said on this subject has had a miniscule impression on the
members of our university compared to what I have tried to do to achieve
justice in our times. This really says that while value education is difficult, it is
practically impossible unless the word is buttressed by the deed.

If all this is true, it means that all those engaged in education today must   15
look to themselves first, to their moral commitments, to their lives, and to their
own values, which, for better or worse, will be reflected in the lives and attitudes
of those they seek to educate. There is nothing automatic about the liberal
education tradition. It can die if not fostered. And if it does die, the values that
sustain an individual and a nation are likely to die with it.

QUESTIONS FOR MEANING

1. What is the meaning of a "liberal education"? Where does Hesburgh define
   it? How does his definition compare with your own concept of a liberal
   education?
2. How do moral values differ from intellectual values? Hesburgh argues that
   both moral and intellectual values are no longer automatically a part of
   higher education. What other sorts of "value" do people expect an education to deliver today?
3. According to Hesburgh, what is the single most important factor in trans-
   mitting values?
4. What is the function of the social and physical sciences in a liberal education? How important are they compared to the humanities?
5. Vocabulary: morass (1), blatant (2), *in loco parentis* (3), espouse (3),
   abdication (4), anomie (4), Neanderthal (7), depravity (10), purvey (10),
   cacophony (10), exemplification (13), and buttressed (14).

QUESTIONS ABOUT STRATEGY

1. If you were to divide this essay into separate parts, where would you make
   your divisions? What would be the topic of each subsection?
2. How does the function of paragraphs 7–9 differ from that of 10–13?
3. In paragraph 14, Hesburgh narrows his focus to the role of a "Christian
   university." Was he wise to limit his argument this way? Or was this a
   mistake? Can state and other nonreligious universities and colleges assume
   the role of teaching values? Could such teaching be abused?
4. Does Hesburgh sound as if he has benefited from a liberal education? If
   so, why?

ROBERT C. SOLOMON
Culture Gives Us a Sense of Who We Are

*Philosopher and educator Robert C. Solomon (b. 1942) graduated from the
University of Pennsylvania in 1963, and received his Ph.D. from the University of
Michigan in 1967. He has taught at Princeton, the University of Southern
California, the University of Pittsburgh and, since 1972, the University of
Texas at Austin. His books include* From Rationalism to Existentialism *(1972),*
Phenomenology and Existentialism *(1972),* Nietzsche *(1973),* The Passions *(1976),*
Introducing Philosophy *(1977),* History and Human Nature: A Philosophical Review
of European History and Culture 1750–1850 *(1979), and* Above the Bottom Line
*(1983). In the following short essay, Solomon argues on behalf of culture, and
laments what he believes to be the limitations of the average college student.*

In our aggressively egalitarian society, "culture" has always been a suspect   1
word, suggesting the pretentions of an effete and foolish leisure class, like the
grand dames spoofed in Marx Brothers' films. But the pretentions of a self-
appointed cultural elite notwithstanding, "culture" actually refers to nothing
more objectionable than a system of shared symbols and examples that hold a
society together. Within a culture we are kindred spirits, simply because we
understand one another.

A recent and somewhat frightening Rockefeller Foundation study on the   2
state of the humanities in American life reported that the vast majority of even
our most educated citizens are ignorant of the common literature and history
that reinforce not only cultural identity but also moral choices. Doctors, lawyers
and business executives are in positions of great responsibility, but often have
little or no training in the ethical background that makes their critical choices
meaningful.

Across our society in general, we find ourselves increasingly fragmented,   3
split into factions and "generation gaps"—which now occur at two- or three-
year intervals—just because the once-automatic assumption of a shared
culture, something beyond shared highways, television programming and
economic worries, is no longer valid.

In our schools, according to the Rockefeller report, the problem lies largely   4
in what has recently been hailed as the "back to basics" movement, which
includes no cultural content whatsoever, just skills and techniques. Reading is
taught as a means of survival in the modern world, not as a source of pleasure
and of shared experience. The notion of "great books" is viewed by most educators as an archaic concept, relegated to the museum of old teaching devices,
such as the memorization in Greek of passages from Homer.

But are "great books" (and legends, poems, paintings and plays) indeed the   5
only conduit of culture, or have they been replaced by more accessible and
effortless media of transmission—television, for example, and films?

Films, to be sure, have entered into our cultural identity in an extremely   6
powerful way; indeed, it is not clear that a person who knows nothing of Bogart

or Chaplin, who has never seen (young) Brando or watched a Western could claim to be fully part of American culture. But these are classics, and they have some of the same virtue as great books; their symbols, characters and moral examples have been around long enough to span generations and segments of our population, and to provide a shared vocabulary, shared heroes and shared values. No such virtue is to be found in television series that disappear every two years (or less), films that survive but a season or "made-for-TV" movies with a lifetime of two hours minus commercial breaks.

"Television culture" is no culture at all, and it is no surprise that, when kids   7
change heroes with the season, their parents don't (and couldn't possibly) keep up with them. The symbolism of *Moby Dick* and *The Scarlet Letter*, however much we resented being force-fed them in school, is something we can all be expected to share. The inanities of *The Dukes of Hazzard*, viewed by no matter how many millions of people, will not replace them.

The same is true of our musical heritage. The Beatles are only a name to   8
most 12-year-olds. Beethoven, by contrast, continues to provide the musical themes we can assume (even if wrongly) that all of us have heard, time and time again. This isn't snobbery; it's continuity.

A professor recently wrote in the *Wall Street Journal* that he had mentioned   9
Socrates in class (at a rather prestigious liberal arts college) and had drawn blanks from more than half the students. My colleagues and I at the University of Texas swap stories about references that our students don't catch. Even allowing generous leeway for our own professional prejudices and misperceptions of what is important, the general picture is disturbing. We are becoming a culture without a culture, lacking fixed points of reference and a shared vocabulary.

It would be so easy, so inexpensive, to change all that; a reading list for high   10
school students; a little encouragement in the media; a bit more enlightenment in our college curricula.

With all of this in mind, I decided to see just what I could or could not assume   11
among my students, who are generally bright and better educated than average (given that they are taking philosophy courses, hardly an assumed interest among undergraduates these days). I gave them a name quiz, in effect, of some of the figures that, on most people's list, would rank among the most important and often referred to in Western culture. Following are some of the results, in terms of the percentage of students who recognized them:

Socrates, 87%; Louis XIV, 59%; Moses, 90%; Hawthorne, 42%; John   12
Milton, 35%; Trotsky, 47%; Donatello, 8%; Copernicus, 47%; Puccini, 11%; Charlemagne, 40%; Virginia Woolf, 25%; Estes Kefauver, 8%; Debussy, 14%; Giotto, 4%; Archduke Ferdinand, 21%; Lewis Carroll, 81%; Charles Dodgson, 5%; Thomas Aquinas, 68%; Spinoza, 19%; Moliere, 30%; Tchaikovsky, 81%; Darwin, 56%; Karl Marx, 65%; Faulkner, 43%; George Byron, 18%; Goethe, 42%; Raphael, 17%; Euripides, 8%; Homer, 39%; T.S. Eliot, 25%; Rodin, 24%; Mozart, 94%; Hitler, 97%; Wagner, 34%; Dante, 25%; Louis XVI, 25%; Kafka, 38%; Stravinsky, 57%; John Adams, 36%.

A friend who gave the same quiz to his English composition class got results   13
more than 50% lower on average.

I suppose that many people will think the quiz too hard, the names often too   14
obscure—but that, of course, is just the point. The students, interestingly
enough, did not feel this at all—not one of them. They "sort of recognized"
most of the names and felt somewhat embarrassed at not knowing exactly who
these people were. There was no sense that the quiz was a "trivia" contest (as
in, "What's the name of Dale Evans' horse?") and there were no accusations of
elitism or ethnocentrism. The simple fact was that they knew these names were
part of their culture, and in too many cases they knew that they weren't—but
should be—conversant with them. Maybe that, in itself, is encouraging.

QUESTIONS FOR MEANING

1. What does Solomon mean by "culture"? Where in his essay does he most
   clearly define it? What sort of people is he talking about when he asks us
   not to confuse culture with "the pretensions of a self-appointed cultural
   elite"?
2. Why does Solomon believe that culture is important?
3. What is a "classic," and why are classics an important part of culture?
4. Why can't television serve as a substitute for great books, music, or films?
5. How many of the names on Solomon's quiz are you able to identify? How
   does your class as a whole compare with the two classes described in this
   essay?
6. Vocabulary: effete (1), kindred (1), archaic (4), inanities (7), prestigious
   (9), ethnocentrism (14), and coversant (14).

QUESTIONS ABOUT STRATEGY

1. How would you describe Solomon's attitude toward students? Is he realistic and straightforward, or snobbish and overly critical? Be prepared to
   defend your answer by discussing the average student at your own school.
2. Does Solomon succeed in making his subject seem timely—something of
   immediate concern? If so, how?
3. Where does Solomon propose what he wants? Why does he do it at this
   point in the essay and not wait until the last paragraph? Should he be more
   specific? Would a more detailed proposal be out of place in a short essay of
   this sort?
4. Why does Solomon introduce the subject of "trivia" into his conclusion?
   What is the sentence about Dale Evans's horse meant to illustrate?

CAROLINE BIRD
Where College Fails Us

After working as a researcher for Newsweek *and* Fortune *magazines in the mid-1940s, Caroline Bird (b. 1915) went on to a successful career in public relations. Her many books reflect her interest in business and, in particular, the position of women in the business world. These books include* Born Female: The High Cost of Keeping Women Down *(1968),* Everything a Woman Needs to Know to Get Paid What She's Worth *(1973),* What Woman Want *(1978), and* The Two Paycheck Marriage *(1979). The following essay, which has appeared in many anthologies, is probably Bird's best-known work. Drawing upon her knowledge of the economy and her skills as a researcher, Bird makes a well-supported attack upon the much cherished notion that going to college leads to a good paying job.*

The case *for* college has been accepted without question for more than a   1
generation. All high school graduates ought to go, says Conventional Wisdom and statistical evidence, because college will help them earn more money, become "better" people, and learn to be more responsible citizens than those who don't go.

But college has never been able to work its magic for everyone. And now   2
that close to half our high school graduates are attending, those who don't fit the pattern are becoming more numerous, and more obvious. College graduates are selling shoes and driving taxis; college students sabotage each other's experiments and forge letters of recommendation in the intense competition for admission to graduate school. Others find no stimulation in their studies, and drop out—often encouraged by college administrators.

Some observers say the fault is with the young people themselves—they are   3
spoiled, stoned, overindulged, and expecting too much. But that's mass character assassination, and doesn't explain all campus unhappiness. Others blame the state of the world, and they are partly right. We've been told that young people have to go to college because our economy can't absorb an army of untrained eighteen-year-olds. But disillusioned graduates are learning that it can no longer absorb an army of trained twenty-two-year-olds, either.

Some adventuresome educators and campus watchers have openly begun   4
to suggest that college may not be the best, the proper, the only place for every young person after the completion of high school. We may have been looking at all those surveys and statistics upside down, it seems, and through the rosy glow of our own remembered college experiences. Perhaps college doesn't make people intelligent, ambitious, happy, liberal, or quick to learn new things—maybe it's just the other way around, and intelligent, ambitious, happy, liberal, and quick-learning people are merely the ones who have been attracted to college in the first place. And perhaps all those successful college graduates would have been successful whether they had gone to college or not. This is heresy to those of us who have been brought up to believe that if a little

schooling is good, more has to be much better. But contrary evidence is beginning to mount up.

The unhappiness and discontent of young people is nothing new, and problems of adolescence are always painfully intense. But while traveling around the country, speaking at colleges, and interviewing students at all kinds of schools—large and small, public and private—I was overwhelmed by the prevailing sadness. It was as visible on campuses in California as in Nebraska and Massachusetts. Too many young people are in college reluctantly, because everyone told them they ought to go, and there didn't seem to be anything better to do. Their elders sell them college because it's good for them. Some never learn to like it, and talk about their time in school as if it were a sentence to be served.

Students tell us the same thing college counselors tell us—they go because of pressure from parents and teachers, and stay because it seems to be an alternative to a far worse fate. It's "better" than the Army or a dead-end job, and it has to be pretty bad before it's any worse than staying at home.

College graduates say that they don't want to work "just" for the money: They want work that matters. They want to help people and save the world. But the numbers are stacked against them. Not only are there not enough jobs in world-saving fields, but in the current slowdown it has become evident that there never were, and probably never will be, enough jobs requiring higher education to go around.

Students who tell their advisers they want to help people, for example, are often directed to psychology. This year the Department of Labor estimates that there will be 4,300 new jobs for psychologists, while colleges will award 58,430 bachelor's degrees in psychology.

Sociology has become a favorite major on socially conscious campuses, but graduates find that social reform is hardly a paying occupation. Male sociologists from the University of Wisconsin reported as gainfully employed a year after graduation included a legal assistant, sports editor, truck unloader, Peace Corps worker, publications director, and a stockboy—but no sociologist per se. The highest paid worked for the post office.

Publishing, writing, and journalism are presumably the vocational goal of a large proportion of the 104,000 majors in Communications and Letters expected to graduate in 1975. The outlook for them is grim. All of the daily newspapers in the country combined are expected to hire a total of 2,600 reporters this year. Radio and television stations may hire a total of 500 announcers, most of them in local radio stations. Nonpublishing organizations will need 1,100 technical writers, and public-relations activities another 4,400. Even if new graduates could get all these jobs (they can't, of course), over 90,000 of them will have to find something less glamorous to do.

Other fields most popular with college graduates are also pathetically small. Only 1,900 foresters a year will be needed during this decade, although schools of forestry are expected to continue graduating twice that many. Some will get sub-professional jobs as forestry aides. Schools of architecture are expected to turn out twice as many as will be needed, and while all sorts of people want to design things, the Department of Labor forecasts that there will be jobs for only 400 new industrial designers a year. As for anthropologists, only 400 will be needed every year in the 1970s to take care of all the college courses, public-health research, community surveys, museums, and all the archaeological digs on every continent. (For these jobs graduate work in anthropology is required.)

Many popular occupations may seem to be growing fast without necessarily   12 offering employment to very many. "Recreation work" is always cited as an expanding field, but it will need relatively few workers who require more special training than life guards. "Urban planning" has exploded in the media, so the U.S. Department of Labor doubled its estimate of the number of jobs to be filled every year in the 1970s—to a big, fat 800. A mere 200 oceanographers a year will be able to do all the exploring of "inner space"—and all that exciting underwater diving you see demonstrated on television—for the entire decade of the 1970s.

Whatever college graduates *want* to do, most of them are going to wind up   13 doing what *there is* to do. During the next few years, according to the Labor Department, the biggest demand will be for stenographers and secretaries, followed by retail-trade salesworkers, hospital attendants, bookkeepers, build-ing custodians, registered nurses, foremen, kindergarten and elementary-school teachers, receptionists, cooks, cosmetologists, private-household work-ers, manufacturing inspectors, and industrial machinery repairmen. These are the jobs which will eventually absorb the surplus archaeologists, urban plan-ners, oceanographers, sociologists, editors, and college professors.

Vocationalism is the new look on campus because of the discouraging job   14 market faced by the generalists. Students have been opting for medicine and law in droves. If all those who check "doctor" as their career goal succeed in getting their MDs, we'll immediately have ten times the target ratio of doctors for the population of the United States. Law schools are already graduating twice as many new lawyers every year as the Department of Labor thinks we will need, and the oversupply grows annually.

Specialists often find themselves at the mercy of shifts in demand, and the   15 narrower the vocational training, the more risky the long-term prospects. En-gineers are the classic example of the "Yo-Yo" effect in supply and demand. Today's shortage is apt to produce a big crop of engineering graduates after the need has crested, and teachers face the same squeeze.

Worse than that, when the specialists turn up for work, they often find that   16 they have learned a lot of things in classrooms that they will never use, that they will have to learn a lot of things on the job that they were never taught, and that most of what they have learned is less likely to "come in handy later" than to fade from memory. One disillusioned architecture student, who had already designed and built houses, said, "It's the degree you need, not every-thing you learn getting it."

A diploma saves the employer the cost of screening candidates and gives   17 him a predictable product: He can assume that those who have survived the four-year ordeal have learned how to manage themselves. They have learned how to budget their time, meet deadlines, set priorities, cope with impersonal

authority, follow instructions, and stick with a task that may be tiresome without direct supervision.

The employer is also betting that it will be cheaper and easier to train the   18
college graduate because he has demonstrated his ability to learn. But if the
diploma serves only to identify those who are talented in the art of schoolwork,
it becomes, in the words of Harvard's Christopher Jencks, "a hell of an expensive aptitude test." It is unfair to the candidates because they themselves must
bear the cost of the screening—the cost of college. Candidates without the
funds, the academic temperament, or the patience for the four-year obstacle
race are ruled out, no matter how well they may perform on the job. But if
"everyone" has a diploma, employers will have to find another way to choose
employees, and it will become an empty credential.

(Screening by diploma may in fact already be illegal. The 1971 ruling of the   19
Supreme Court in *Griggs* v. *Duke Power Co.* contended that an employer
cannot demand a qualification which systematically excludes an entire class of
applicants, unless that qualification reliably predicts success on the job. The
requiring of a high school diploma was outlawed in the *Griggs* case, and this
could extend to a college diploma.)

The bill for four years at an Ivy League college is currently climbing toward   20
$25,000; at a state university, a degree will cost the student and his family about
$10,000 (with taxpayers making up the difference).

Not many families can afford these sums, and when they look for financial   21
aid, they discover that someone else will decide how much they will actually
have to pay. The College Scholarship Service, which establishes a family's degree of need for most colleges, is guided by noble principles: uniformity of
sacrifice, need rather than merit. But families vary in their willingness to "sacrifice" as much as the bureaucracy of the CSS thinks they ought to. This is
particularly true of middle-income parents, whose children account for the bulk
of the country's college students. Some have begun to rebel against this attempt
to enforce the same values and priorities on all. "In some families, a college
education competes with a second car, a color television, or a trip to Europe—
and it's possible that college may lose," one financial-aid officer recently
told me.

Quite so. College is worth more to some middle-income families than to   22
others. It is chilling to consider the undercurrent of resentment that families
who "give up everything" must feel toward their college-age children, or the
burden of guilt children must bear every time they goof off or receive less than
top grades in their courses.

The decline in return for a college degree within the last generation has been   23
substantial. In the 1950s, a Princeton student could pay his expenses for the
school year—eating club and all—on less than $3,000. When he graduated, he
entered a job market which provided a comfortable margin over the earnings
of his agemates who had not been to college. To be precise, a freshman entering
Princeton in 1956, the earliest year for which the Census has attempted to
project lifetime earnings, could expect to realize a 12.5 percent return on his
investment. A freshman entering in 1972, with the cost nearing $6,000 annually,

could expect to realize only 9.3 percent, less than might be available in the money market. This calculation was made with the help of a banker and his computer, comparing college as an investment in future earnings with other investments available in the booming money market of 1974, and concluded that in strictly financial terms, college is not always the best investment a young person can make.

I postulated a young man (the figures are different with a young woman, but   24
the principle is the same) whose rich uncle would give him, in cash, the total cost of four years at Princeton—$34,181. (The total includes what the young man would earn if he went to work instead of to college right after high school.) If he did not spend the money on Princeton, but put it in the savings bank at 7.5 percent interest compounded daily, he would have, at retirement age sixty-four, more than five times as much as the $199,000 extra he could expect to earn between twenty-two and sixty as a college man rather than a mere high school graduate. And with all that money accumulating in the bank, he could invest in something with a higher return than a diploma. At age twenty-eight, when his nest egg had reached $73,113, he could buy a liquor store, which would return him well over 20 percent on his investment, as long as he was willing to mind the store. He might get a bit fidgety sitting there, but he'd have to be dim-witted to lose money on a liquor store, and right now we're talking only about dollars.

If the young man went to a public college rather than Princeton, the invest-   25
ment would be lower, and the payoff higher, of course, because other people— the taxpayers—put up part of the capital for him. But the difference in return between an investment in public and private colleges is minimized because the biggest part of the investment in either case is the money a student might earn if he went to work, not to college—in economic terms, his "foregone income." That he bears himself.

Rates of return and dollar signs on education are a fascinating brain teaser,   26
and, obviously, there is a certain unreality to the game. But the same unreality extends to the traditional calculations that have always been used to convince taxpayers that college is a worthwhile investment.

The ultimate defense of college has always been that while it may not teach   27
you anything vocationally useful, it will somehow make you a better person, able to do anything better, and those who make it through the process are initiated into the "fellowship of educated men and women." In a study intended to probe what graduates seven years out of college thought their colleges should have done for them, the Carnegie Commission found that most alumni expected the "development of my abilities to think and express myself." But if such respected educational psychologists as Bruner and Piaget are right, specific learning skills have to be acquired very early in life, perhaps even before formal schooling begins.

So, when pressed, liberal-arts defenders speak instead about something   28
more encompassing, and more elusive. "College changed me inside," one graduate told us fervently. The authors of a Carnegie Commission report, who

obviously struggled for a definition, concluded that one of the common threads in the perceptions of a liberal education is that it provides "an integrated view of the world which can serve as an inner guide." More simply, alumni say that college should have "helped me to formulate the values and goals of my life."

In theory, a student is taught to develop these values and goals himself, but in practice, it doesn't work quite that way. All but the wayward and the saintly take their sense of the good, the true, and the beautiful from the people around them. When we speak of students acquiring "values" in college, we often mean that they will acquire the values—and sometimes that means only the tastes—of their professors. The values of professors may be "higher" than many students will encounter elsewhere, but they may not be relevant to situations in which students find themselves in college and later.   29

Of all the forms in which ideas are disseminated, the college professor lecturing a class is the slowest and most expensive. You don't have to go to college to read the great books or learn about the great ideas of Western Man. Today you can find them everywhere—in paperbacks, in the public libraries, in museums, in public lectures, in adult-education courses, in abridged, summarized, or adapted form in magazines, films, and television. The problem is no longer one of access to broadening ideas; the problem is the other way around: how to choose among the many courses of action proposed to us, how to edit the stimulations that pour into our eyes and ears every waking hour. A college experience that piles option on option and stimulation on stimulation merely adds to the contemporary nightmare.   30

What students and graduates say that they did learn on campus comes under the heading of personal, rather than intellectual, development. Again and again I was told that the real value of college is learning to get along with others, to practice social skills, to "sort out my head," and these have nothing to do with curriculum.   31

For whatever impact the academic experience used to have on college students, the sheer size of many undergraduate classes in the 1970s dilutes faculty-student dialogue, and, more often than not, they are taught by teachers who were hired when colleges were faced with a shortage of qualified instructors, during their years of expansion and when the big rise in academic pay attracted the mediocre and the less than dedicated.   32

On the social side, colleges are withdrawing from responsibility for feeding, housing, policing, and protecting students at a time when the environment of college may be the most important service it could render. College officials are reluctant to "intervene" in the personal lives of the students. They no longer expect to take over from parents, but often insist that students—who have, most often, never lived away from home before—take full adult responsibility for their plans, achievements, and behavior.   33

Most college students do not live in the plush, comfortable country-clublike surroundings their parents envisage, or, in some cases, remember. Open dorms, particularly when they are coeducational, are noisy, usually overcrowded, and often messy. Some students desert the institutional "zoos" (their own word for   34 dorms) and move into run-down, overpriced apartments. Bulletin boards in student centers are littered with notices of apartments to share and the drift of conversation suggests that a lot of money is dissipated in scrounging for food and shelter.

Taxpayers now provide more than half of the astronomical sums that are   35
spent on higher education. But less than half of today's high school graduates go on, raising a new question of equity: Is it fair to make all the taxpayers pay for the minority who actually go to college? We decided long ago that it is fair for childless adults to pay school taxes because everyone, parents and nonparents alike, profits by a literate population. Does the same reasoning hold true for state-supported higher education? There is no conclusive evidence on either side.

Young people cannot be expected to go to college for the general good of   36
mankind. They may be more altruistic than their elders, but no great numbers are going to spend four years at hard intellectual labor, let alone tens of thousands of family dollars, for "the advancement of human capability in society at large," one of the many purposes invoked by the Carnegie Commission report. Nor do any considerable number of them want to go to college to beat the Russians to Jupiter, improve the national defense, increase the Gross National Product, lower the crime rate, improve automobile safety, or create a market for the arts—all of which have been suggested at one time or other as benefits taxpayers get for supporting higher education.

One sociologist said that you don't have to have a reason for going to college   37
because it's an institution. His definition of an institution is something everyone subscribed to without question. The burden of proof is not on why you should go to college, but why anyone thinks there might be a reason for not going. The implication—and some educators express it quite frankly—is that an eighteen-year-old high school graduate is still too young and confused to know what he wants to do, let alone what is good for him.

Mother knows best, in other words.   38

It had always been comfortable for students to believe that authorities, like   39
Mother, or outside specialists, like educators, could determine what was best for them. However, specialists and authorities no longer enjoy the credibility former generations accorded them. Patients talk back to doctors and are not struck suddenly dead. Clients question the lawyer's bills and sometimes get them reduced. It is no longer self-evident that all adolescents must study a fixed curriculum that was constructed at a time when all educated men could agree on precisely what it was that made them educated.

The same with college. If high school graduates don't want to continue their   40
education, or don't want to continue it right away, they may perceive more clearly than their elders that college is not for them.

College is an ideal place for those young adults who love learning for its own   41
sake, who would rather read than eat, and who like nothing better than writing research papers. But they are a minority, even at the prestigious colleges, which recruit and attract the intellectually oriented.

The rest of our high school graduates need to look at college more closely   42
and critically, to examine it as a consumer product, and decide if the cost in
dollars, in time, in continued dependency, and in future returns, is worth the
very large investment each student—and his family—must make.

QUESTIONS FOR MEANING

1. What does Bird see as the principal failure of college education? Why is
   college a "four year ordeal," and a "four year obstacle race"? Who should
   go to college, and who should not?
2. What risks does Bird concede to be in choosing a vocational education?
3. How do values differ from taste (paragraph 29)?
4. What does Bird mean when she demands that college should be examined
   as "a consumer product"?
5. How does Bird characterize the average college teacher? Is her appraisal
   justified by your own experience, or does it seem unfair?
6. Bird argues that college dorms are "noisy, usually overcrowded, and often
   messy," a far cry from the "country-clublike surroundings" many parents
   imagine. Is she right? What is your own dorm like? Are you getting good
   value for your money? Does Bird overlook any advantages to living in a
   dorm?
7. Have colleges changed in the ten years since this essay was written? What
   would Bird think of the school you attend?
8. Does Bird ever reveal what will happen to the thousands of high school
   graduates she would discourage from going to college? What do you think
   would happen if college attendance was suddenly reduced by half?
9. Vocabulary: pathetically (11), postulated (24), integrated (28), abridged
   (30), envisage (34), dissipated (34), altruistic (36), and credibility (39).

QUESTIONS ABOUT STRATEGY

1. In her opening paragraph, Bird introduces the three main arguments which
   people usually advance on behalf of going to college. If you study her essay,
   you will find that she responds to each of these arguments in the order in
   which she introduces them. This helps make her argument seem well-
   organized. But are there any arguments for college education that she
   overlooks?
2. Why does Bird put quotation marks around "better" in paragraph 1?
3. Was this essay originally intended for an audience of students or an audience of college graduates? Could someone understand Bird's argument
   before going to college, or is a college education necessary to understand
   what Bird is saying? If the latter is true, how does this affect the credibility
   of the argument? Define Bird's audience. Then explain what you think she
   was trying to accomplish with this essay.

4. Bird uses many statistics to strengthen her argument. Does she reveal where she got them? Are you impressed by the various numbers she cites concerning job placement and the value of a college education as an investment? How vital are these numbers to the argument as a whole? Would you take Bird seriously without them?
5. What is the function of paragraphs 24–25? How useful is this example?
6. In paragraphs 38–40, Bird rejects the argument that many high school graduates are too young and confused to know what to do with their lives— and the implied argument that college gives them the time to "grow up." When you graduated from high school, how many of your friends had clear career goals? Now that you are in college, do your fellow students seem more mature? Do you agree with this aspect of Bird's argument?

NORMAN COUSINS
How to Make People Smaller Than They Are

For over thirty years, Norman Cousins (b. 1915) was one of the most influential editors in this country. After working as an editor for the New York Evening Post *and* Current History, *Cousins joined the* Saturday Review *in 1940. It is with this magazine that he is most readily identified. As executive editor of the* Review *from 1942 to 1971, and again from 1975 to 1978, Cousins was in a position to champion numerous liberal causes, including the importance of education. Almost paralyzed with a serious disease in the mid-1960s, Cousins was given only a few months to live, but he fought his way back to health through a remarkable effort of will, which he describes in one of his best known books,* Anatomy of an Illness as Perceived by the Patient: Reflections on Healing and Regeneration *(1979). In his long career, Cousins has been awarded nearly fifty honorary doctorates. He is now Professor of Medical Humanities at UCLA. Cousins has been a strong advocate of culture, as can be seen in the following essay, one of his last columns as editor of the* Saturday Review.*

Three months ago in this space we wrote about the costly retreat from the   1
humanities on all the levels of American education. Since that time, we have had occasion to visit a number of campuses and have been troubled to find that the general situation is even more serious than we had thought. It has become apparent to us that one of the biggest problems confronting American education today is the increasing vocationalization of our colleges and universities. Throughout the country, schools are under pressure to become job-training centers and employment agencies.

The pressure comes mainly from two sources. One is the growing determi-   2
nation of many citizens to reduce taxes—understandable and even commendable in itself, but irrational and irresponsible when connected to the reduction
or dismantling of vital public services. The second source of pressure comes
from parents and students who tend to scorn courses of study that do not teach
people how to become attractive to employers in a rapidly tightening job
market.

It is absurd to believe that the development of skills does not also require   3
the systematic development of the human mind. Education is being measured
more by the size of the benefits the individual can extract from society than by
the extent to which the individual can come into possession of his or her full
powers. The result is that the life-giving juices are in danger of being drained
out of education.

Emphasis on "practicalities" is being characterized by the subordination of   4
words to numbers. History is seen not as essential experience to be transmitted
to new generations, but as abstractions that carry dank odors. Art is regarded
as something that calls for indulgence or patronage and that has no place
among the practical realities. Political science is viewed more as a specialized
subject for people who want to go into politics than as an opportunity for
citizens to develop a knowledgeable relationship with the systems by which
human societies are governed. Finally, literature and philosophy are assigned
the role of add-ons—intellectual adornments that have nothing to do with
"genuine" education.

Instead of trying to shrink the liberal arts, the American people ought to be   5
putting pressure on colleges and universities to increase the ratio of the humanities to the sciences. Most serious studies of medical-school curricula in
recent years have called attention to the stark gaps in the liberal education of
medical students. The experts agree that the schools shouldn't leave it up to
students to close those gaps.

The irony of the emphasis being placed on careers is that nothing is more   6
valuable for anyone who has had a professional or vocational education than to
be able to deal with abstractions or complexities, or to feel comfortable with
subtleties of thought or language, or to think sequentially. The doctor who
knows only disease is at a disadvantage alongside the doctor who knows at
least as much about people as he does about pathological organisms. The
lawyer who argues in court from a narrow legal base is no match for the lawyer
who can connect legal precedents to historical experience and who employs
wide-ranging intellectual resources. The business executive whose competence in general management is bolstered by an artistic ability to deal with
people is of prime value to his company. For the technologist, the engineering
of consent can be just as important as the engineering of moving parts. In all
these respects, the liberal arts have much to offer. Just in terms of career
preparation, therefore, a student is shortchanging himself by shortcutting the
humanities.

But even if it could be demonstrated that the humanities contribute nothing   7
directly to a job, they would still be an essential part of the educational equip-

ment of any person who wants to come to terms with life. The humanities would be expendable only if human beings didn't have to make decisions that affect their lives and the lives of others; if the human past never existed or had nothing to tell us about the present; if thought processes were irrelevant to the achievement of purpose; if creativity was beyond the human mind and had nothing to do with the joy of living; if human relationships were random aspects of life; if human beings never had to cope with panic or pain, or if they never had to anticipate the connection between cause and effect; if all the mysteries of mind and nature were fully plumbed; and if no special demands arose from the accident of being born a human being instead of a hen or a hog.

Finally, there would be good reason to eliminate the humanities if a free   8
society were not absolutely dependent on a functioning citizenry. If the main purpose of a university is job training, then the underlying philosophy of our government has little meaning. The debates that went into the making of American society concerned not just institutions or governing principles but the capacity of humans to sustain those institutions. Whatever the disagreements were over other issues at the American Constitutional Convention, the fundamental question sensed by everyone, a question that lay over the entire assembly, was whether the people themselves would understand what it meant to hold the ultimate power of society, and whether they had enough of a sense of history and destiny to know where they had been and where they ought to be going.

Jefferson was prouder of having been the founder of the University of Virginia than of having been President of the United States. He knew that the   9
educated and developed mind was the best assurance that a political system could be made to work—a system based on the informed consent of the governed. If this idea fails, then all the saved tax dollars in the world will not be enough to prevent the nation from turning on itself.

QUESTIONS FOR MEANING

1. According to Cousins, what are the two main sources of pressure for changes in the nature of American higher education?
2. How should the quality of an education be measured? How do many people tend to measure it? Explain the distinction Cousins draws in paragraph 3, and ask yourself if Cousins would approve of the education you are receiving.
3. One of the unfortunate signs of modern education, as Cousins sees it, is "the subordination of words to numbers." He lists several disciplines that no longer enjoy the respect they once inspired. Are these disciplines responsible in any way for their own decline? What are the "numbers" courses that now seem more serious and practical?
4. Cousins argues that doctors, lawyers, and business executives have an advantage if they had been broadly educated and not just narrowly trained. Would you like to go to a doctor who had majored in English or history as an undergraduate? Would you feel more or less confidence in him or her?

5. What does Cousins mean by "an artistic ability to deal with people"? Define this ability and explain how it can be gained through a college education. Is this something that comes from studying the liberal arts, or are there other sources as well—sources outside of school?

QUESTIONS ABOUT STRATEGY

1. Consider the title of this essay. What does it tell you about Cousins's conception of human nature?
2. What premise underlies Cousins's argument? Where does he state it? Are you persuaded that a liberal education satisfies the principle the premise involves?
3. Why does Cousins use "we" in his opening sentence? What does this tell you about how he sees himself when writing for the magazine in which this essay was originally published?
4. In paragraphs 6–8, Cousins advances three arguments on behalf of the humanities. Why are they arranged in the order in which he has them?
5. Most of paragraph 7 is a long sentence linked together with semicolons. What stylistic device enables Cousins to write such a long sentence, and what do you think motivated him to do it?
6. How effective is this argument? Does Cousins respond to your own needs and concerns, or does he write over them—obsessed with an ideal that you do not share?

LEWIS THOMAS
How to Fix the Premedical Curriculum

A graduate of Princeton and Harvard Medical School, Lewis Thomas (b. 1913) has taught at Cornell, Johns Hopkins, Tulane, the University of Minnesota, New York University, and Yale. Since 1973, he has been president and chief executive officer of the Memorial Sloan–Kettering Cancer Center in New York City. He has served as a trustee for Rockefeller University, Mt. Sinai School of Medicine, the Guggenheim Foundation, the Menninger Foundation, and the Kennedy Institute at Georgetown University. The author of more than two hundred articles for scholarly journals and medical textbooks, Thomas is best known for "Notes of a Biology Watcher," a column he has written for the New England Journal of Medicine *since 1971. When a collection of these essays was published as* The Lives of a Cell, *it won a National Book Award in 1974. Since then, Thomas has published three more books,* The Medusa and the Snail *(1979),* The Youngest Scientist *(1983), and* Late Night Thoughts on Listening to Mahler's Ninth Symphony *(1983). "How to Reform the Premedical Curriculum" reveals the two characteristics that distinguish almost all of his work: a clear style and a provocative point of view.*

The influence of the modern medical school on liberal-arts education in this country over the last decade has been baleful and malign, nothing less. The admission policies of the medical schools are at the root of the trouble. If something is not done quickly to change these, all the joy of going to college will have been destroyed, not just for that growing majority of undergraduate students who draw breath only to become doctors, but for everyone else, all the students, and all the faculty as well. 1

The medical schools used to say they wanted applicants as broadly educated as possible, and they used to mean it. The first two years of medical school were given over entirely to the basic biomedical sciences, and almost all entering students got their first close glimpse of science in those years. Three chemistry courses, physics, and some sort of biology were all that were required from the colleges. Students were encouraged by the rhetoric of medical-school catalogues to major in such nonscience disciplines as history, English, philosophy. Not many did so; almost all premedical students in recent generations have had their majors in chemistry or biology. But anyway, they were authorized to spread around in other fields if they wished. 2

There is still some talk in medical deans' offices about the need for general culture, but nobody really means it, and certainly the premedical students don't believe it. They concentrate on science. 3

They concentrate on science with a fury, and they live for grades. If there are courses in the humanities that can be taken without risk to class standing they will line up for these, but they will not get into anything tough except science. The so-called social sciences have become extremely popular as stand-ins for traditional learning. 4

The atmosphere of the liberal-arts college is being poisoned by premedical   5
students. It is not the fault of the students, who do not start out as a necessarily
bad lot. They behave as they do in the firm belief that if they behave any
otherwise they won't get into medical school.

I have a suggestion, requiring for its implementation the following announce-   6
ment from the deans of all the medical schools: henceforth, any applicant who
is self-labeled as a "premed," distinguishable by his course selection from his
classmates, will have his dossier placed in the third stack of three. Membership
in a "premedical society" will, by itself, be grounds for rejection. Any college
possessing something called a "premedical curriculum," or maintaining offices
for people called "premedical advisers," will be excluded from recognition by
the medical schools.

Now as to grades and class standing. There is obviously no way of ignoring   7
these as criteria for acceptance, but it is the grades *in general* that should be
weighed. And, since so much of the medical-school curriculum is, or ought to
be, narrowly concerned with biomedical science, more attention should be paid
to the success of students in other, nonscience disciplines before they are
admitted, in order to assure the scope of intellect needed for a physician's
work.

Hence, if there are to be MCAT tests, the science part ought to be made the   8
briefest, and weigh the least. A knowledge of literature and languages ought to
be the major test, and the scariest. History should be tested, with rigor.

The best thing would be to get rid of the MCATs, once and for all, and rely   9
instead, wholly, on the judgment of the college faculties.

You could do this if there were some central, core discipline, universal within   10
the curricula of all the colleges, which could be used for evaluating the free
range of a student's mind, his tenacity and resolve, his innate capacity for the
understanding of human beings, and his affection for the human condition. For
this purpose, I propose that classical Greek be restored as the centerpiece of
undergraduate education. The loss of Homeric and Attic Greek from American
college life was one of this century's disasters. Putting it back where it once
was would quickly make up for the dispiriting impact which generations of
spotty Greek in translation have inflicted on modern thought. The capacity to
read Homer's language closely enough to sense the terrifying poetry in some of
the lines could serve as a shrewd test for the qualities of mind and character
needed in a physician.

If everyone had to master Greek, the college students aspiring to medical   11
school would be placed on the same footing as everyone else, and their identi-
fiability as a separate group would be blurred, to everyone's advantage. Moreover, the currently depressing drift on some campuses toward special courses
for prelaw students, and even prebusiness students, might be inhibited before
more damage is done.

Latin should be put back as well, but not if it is handled, as it ought to be, by   12
the secondary schools. If Horace has been absorbed prior to college, so much
for Latin. But Greek is a proper discipline for the college mind.

English, history, the literature of at least two foreign languages, and philos-   13

ophy should come near the top of the list, just below Classics, as basic requirements, and applicants for medical school should be told that their grades in
these courses will count more than anything else.

Students should know that if they take summer work as volunteers in the   14
local community hospital, as ward aides or laboratory assistants, this will not
necessarily be held against them, but neither will it help.

Finally, the colleges should have much more of a say about who goes on to   15
medical school. If they know, as they should, the students who are generally
bright and also respected, this judgment should carry the heaviest weight for
admission. If they elect to use criteria other than numerical class standing for
recommending applicants, this evaluation should hold.

The first and most obvious beneficiaries of this new policy would be the   16
college students themselves. There would no longer be, anywhere where they
could be recognized as a coherent group, the "premeds," that most detestable
of all cliques eating away at the heart of the college. Next to benefit would be
the college faculties, once again in possession of the destiny of their own
curriculum, for better or worse. And next in line, but perhaps benefiting the
most of all, are the basic-science faculties of the medical schools, who would
once again be facing classrooms of students who are ready to be startled and
excited by a totally new and unfamiliar body of knowledge, eager to learn,
unpreoccupied by the notions of relevance that are paralyzing the minds of
today's first-year medical students already so surfeited by science that they
want to start practicing psychiatry in the first trimester of the first year.

Society would be the ultimate beneficiary. We could look forward to a gen-   17
eration of doctors who have learned as much as anyone can learn, in our
colleges and universities, about how human beings have always lived out their
lives. Over the bedrock of knowledge about our civilization, the medical schools
could then construct as solid a structure of medical science as can be built, but
the bedrock would always be there, holding everything else upright.

QUESTIONS FOR MEANING

1. According to Lewis Thomas, what is a major cause of the decline in liberal
   arts education? Do you know anything about the nature of American medical schools? Can you explain the relationship between admission requirements for medical school (and other graduate schools) and the courses
   college students take? Do college admission policies have a similar effect
   on the high school curriculum?
2. What do the social sciences include, and what is Lewis Thomas's opinion of
   them? Can you explain why someone might hold this opinion? What do you
   think of the social sciences, in terms of the classes that you have taken?
3. Thomas describes "premeds" as "that most detestable of all cliques eating
   away at the heart of the college." What is a clique, and do premedical
   students usually amount to one? Why would anyone find future doctors
   "detestable"? Are there any other cliques "eating away at the heart" of
   college as you've experienced it so far?

4. How can poetry be terrifying? Why should physicians be able to understand such poetry?

5. Why does Thomas believe that medical schools should be especially concerned with the grades applicants have achieved in such nonscience courses as English?

6. What are the three benefits that Thomas believes would result from his proposed reforms?

7. Vocabulary: malign (1), innate (10), beneficiaries (16), coherent (16), and surfeited (16).

QUESTIONS ABOUT STRATEGY

1. Thomas argues for a major change in the undergraduate curriculum, calling not simply for more courses in the humanities, but specifically for the reintroduction of Greek and Latin as basic courses for all students. Is he serious about this? Or is he simply trying to startle his audience? Would he settle for less than he asks for? How can you tell?

2. Consider the point of view of this essay. Could you tell it was written by a physician? What is a physician supposed to sound like? Should writers try to sound like people expect them to sound, or is there ever an advantage in writing in another voice?

3. Does Thomas exaggerate at any points in his essay? If so, is the exaggeration deliberate or unintentional? If deliberate, why did Thomas choose to exaggerate? If the exaggeration is unintended, what effect does this have upon you as a reader?

4. Did Thomas write this essay for a general audience, or primarily for an audience of physicians? Be prepared to explain your answer and to comment on how these different audiences would probably respond to Thomas's argument.

CARRIE TUHY
So Who Needs College?

The debate over the purpose of higher education took on new urgency in the 1980s,
when unemployment began to rise after a decade of high inflation that had
significantly increased the cost of a college education. Many college graduates in the
early 1980s found it difficult to find jobs within their chosen fields. The number of
majors in subjects like English, history, and philosophy continued to decline as
students turned to majors like business and computer science that seemed more
"practical." For many students, job training became more important than general
education. Vocational schools began to attract an increasing number of students
who might otherwise have gone to a college or university. The advantages of
vocational training are considered in the following essay by Carrie Tuhy, a staff
writer for Money *magazine.*

Career seekers, the want ads are trying to tell you something. Despite the   1
highest unemployment rate since 1941, Sunday papers across America are
thick with job postings for specialized skills. Employers seem unable to find
enough qualified people for such positions as bank teller, commercial artist,
computer programmer, data processor, electronics technician, medical technologist, nurse, office manager, salesperson and secretary. Fewer and fewer
classified ads stipulate college as a requirement.

The message is clear: even a severe recession hasn't caused a labor surplus   2
in certain occupations. But the message goes deeper. In good times as well as
bad, a bachelor's degree is becoming less valuable for some careers. As students
head off to college this month, they and their parents may wonder whether the
diploma is still worth its price in tuition, room, board and four years of forgone
income.

The majority of openings, now and for the economic recovery that could be   3
getting under way, require types of skills more likely to be acquired in a technical or trade school or on the job than on an ivied campus. Technical school
graduates are routinely landing jobs with higher starting pay than newly minted
bachelors of arts can command. A computer programmer fresh from a six-
month course can earn up to $14,000 a year while an English major is rewriting
his résumé for the umpteenth time. Clearly, the $5,000 certificate of technical
competence is gaining on the $50,000 sheepskin.

While graduates of four-year colleges still have a small financial edge, that   4
advantage is narrowing. In the 1960s, beginning salaries for college men started
an average of 24% higher than for the work force as a whole. That differential
is now down to 5%. Projections of the lifetime return on an investment in a
college education are still more disillusioning. The foremost specialist in such
estimates, Richard Freeman of the National Bureau of Economic Research,
predicts that the class of '82 will realize only 6% or 7% a year on its education
costs in the form of higher earnings compared with the 11% return projected

for the class of '62. Concludes Finis Welch, an economist at UCLA: "A college degree today is not a ticket to a high-paying job or an insurance policy against unemployment." . . .

In fact, going to college may even be a hindrance for some people with   5 extraordinary talent or ambition. They often feel that college bottles up their drive. Still, you shouldn't overlook educational values that cannot be measured in dollars. Pursuing a bachelor's degree can stretch the mind, help a young person gain maturity and generally enrich anyone's life. Indisputably too, college remains essential in preparing for the professions and advantageous in getting interviews for some occupations. You may not need a B.A. to do the work of an advertising copywriter, broker or journalist—to cite some conspicuous examples—but a diploma still helps you to get in the door. Degreeless applicants may have to start lower or fight harder to enter such fields, and they may be passed over for promotions, particularly to management levels.

Conversely, doors stand wide open to rewarding careers, especially in technical fields, for those with the right nonacademic training. Trade and technical schools are quickly outgrowing their matchbook-cover image—DRAW THIS DOG AND EARN BIG MONEY! Despite the continuing shabby practices of a few institutions, most of the nation's 7,000 private vocational schools for high school graduates competently provide training for all manner of careers from actor to X-ray technician.   6

The emphasis in vocational education is switching from training blue-collar   7 factory hands and brown-collar repairmen to preparing gray-collar technicians. Also, high-tech companies with a vested interest in a competent work force have taken it upon themselves to educate people in specialized skills. The list of those companies starts with AT&T, IBM and Xerox but goes on to include such somewhat smaller firms as Bell & Howell, Control Data and Wang. One of several courses sponsored by Bell & Howell's DeVry Institute of Technology in Chicago trains technicians to build product prototypes by following engineering drawings; the course takes 20 months and leads to jobs starting at $18,000 a year.

Profit-making trade schools are flourishing even as university enrollments   8 dwindle. One of the country's largest commercial schools, National Education Corp. (NEC), based in Newport Beach, Calif., has more than 100,000 students in 70 branches. Graduates repair jets (average starting salary: $15,000), manage radio stations ($30,000), write computer programs and design microprocessor chips (both $12,000).

Fees are often substantial at a high-tech school, but because the training is   9 condensed it costs far less than getting a university degree. A six-month course in computers at NEC's National Institute of Technology costs $5,000; a two-year program in electronics engineering is $7,900. Says Wayne Gilpin, president of the institute, with a touch of braggadocio: "Our students may not be able to quote Byron, but they are technically sharp. They can sit alongside four-year graduates from Purdue and MIT."

Trade school students should face the fact that they won't sit beside many   10 of those Purdue and MIT graduates. Electrical engineers, for example, can get jobs researching and developing new technology at salaries ranging from $23,000 to $30,000, while technicians are more likely to work at repairing those creations at $18,000 to $22,000.

Even so, bright people can advance surprisingly far on trade school training. One example: Ronald Billodeaux, now 29, who completed an electronics course at Little Rock's United Electronics (now called Arkansas College of Technology) and got a job maintaining equipment for Geophysical Services Inc., a Texas Instruments subsidiary that provides exploration data for oil companies. Over the years, Billodeaux helped search for oil in Africa, South America and Australia. Last year the company wanted to move him to London to oversee Middle Eastern and African operations, but he balked at further travel. Almost immediately, Mobil hired him away as a supervisor to scout oil prospects in the Gulf of Mexico.   11

Two-year community colleges and private junior colleges offer vocational training at a considerably lower cost than private technical schools do. Tuition averages $500 a year for such job-oriented studies as auto mechanics, data processing, police science and real estate sales. Says Roger Yarrington, until recently executive director of the American Association of Junior and Community Colleges: "The use of these schools has shifted from university preparation to job preparation." But community colleges, with their multitude of majors, may not have the resources to give as thorough and up-to-date training as you can get at single-subject technical schools. NEC, for example, is spending more than $1 million this year on new equipment.   12

What is most valuable in vocational education—whether at a community college or a technical school—is hands-on training. In choosing a program, you should ask about not only the school's resources but also about the time devoted to learning by doing and the companies that hire the most students. Then query those companies' personnel managers on how they rate the school's courses.   13

Employers say the best preparation combines study with work alongside people in the field. At the Fashion Institute of Design and Merchandising, a California junior college with branches in San Francisco and Los Angeles, Constance Bennett, 23, spent her second year working as an intern at Hang Ten, a sportswear manufacturer. The experience serves her well in her present job at Koret of North America, a San Francisco sportswear company. During a 21-month course at the Culinary Institute of America in Hyde Park, N.Y., the Harvard of *haute cuisine*, students get experience in some of the nation's best-known kitchens. John Doherty, 24, spent more than a quarter of his course at the Waldorf Astoria in New York City. After graduation in 1978, he was hired as a cook there; he has since risen to second in command of a kitchen with 170 cooks.   14

The best deal, of course, is getting paid to learn a skill. Competition for apprenticeships is always stiff, and a slack economy has cut the number of openings. But as business revives, so will the need for trainees. Along with the standard apprenticeships for plumbers, pipefitters and carpenters, there are programs in hundreds of occupations including biomedical equipment technician, film and video editor, recording engineer, meteorologist and chef. Frank   15

Ruta, 24, learned to cook and run a kitchen in a three-year apprenticeship arranged by the American Culinary Federation. Instead of forking out more than $13,000 to attend the Culinary Institute of America, he hired on at the Lemon Tree, a restaurant in his home town of McKeesport, Pa., at $3.25 an hour and got a 25¢ raise every six months. Ruta learned to cook well enough to satisfy a range of tastes, in politics as well as palates. As personal chef to the First Family, he has served the Carters and the Reagans.

The Labor Department's Bureau of Apprenticeship and Training supervises   16
programs in some 500 trades. Thirty years ago, federal regulation was aimed against racism, favoritism and exploitation in handing out job assignments. Today the bureau mainly monitors wages: apprentices at first average about $6 an hour, 40% to 50% of skilled workers' pay. State agencies with information about apprenticeships are listed in phone directories; look under "state government" for the employment security administration.

However, some of the most respected employer-sponsored programs, such   17
as those run by Kodak, General Electric and Westinghouse, are not listed with government offices. You can find them by asking major employers in your chosen field. Apprenticeships are investments of time rather than money; it takes five years to qualify as a journeyman machinist—only a year less than it usually requires to earn a bachelor's degree and an M.B.A. Though apprentices start with no job guarantee, a company that spends up to six years training a person is likely to keep him.

Even without training, high school graduates sometimes can land worth-   18
while jobs in marketing, retailing and a few other fields. Continental Illinois National Bank in Chicago occasionally hires promising teenagers as trainees at $10,000 a year. In five years, they can rise to loan service representative at $27,000—a position and a salary few people fresh from a liberal arts college would qualify for in less than two or three years.

In some government-regulated sales fields—particularly real estate, securi-   19
ties and insurance—a mere office clerk can impress the boss by passing the licensing exam. Judith Briles, 36, started as a secretary in a brokerage house with just a high school diploma and a housewife's experience. She quickly learned the business and got a stockbroker's license. After 10 years in the field, she was earning $150,000 a year in commissions at E.F. Hutton in San Jose.

Only after opening her own investment advisory company in 1978 did she   20
go to college—to hone her management skills. At Pepperdine University in Malibu, Calif., she took an entrance exam to determine how much her life's experience should count toward her degree. It counted a lot. In two years of part-time study, she bypassed a bachelor's degree and won an M.B.A.

QUESTIONS FOR MEANING

1. What does Tuhy mean by "sheepskin" in paragraph 3?
2. According to this argument, what is the principal advantage of technical training over general education? What is the principal career risk in choosing an education of this sort?

3. Why does Tuhy prefer private technical schools to community colleges that offer technical training?
4. How can you go about evaluating a vocational education program? What is the most important aspect in such programs? How can you determine the likelihood of getting a job upon completing your studies at a school you are considering attending?
5. Vocabulary: stipulate (1), braggadocio (9), and hone (20).

QUESTIONS ABOUT STRATEGY

1. What sort of tone does Tuhy adopt toward the various people she describes in her essay? What does this reveal about her values? Why doesn't she describe anyone who has paid for a vocational education and then been unable to find work?
2. This article was originally written for *Money* magazine. Assuming that Tuhy had a good sense of the audience she was writing for, what sort of people read this magazine?
3. Where does Tuhy concede that vocational education has its limitations? Why does she have an obligation to remind her readers that this is so?
4. Tuhy concludes her argument with one final example. Is this a good way to bring an essay to a close? Is the example strong enough to justify concluding without further commentary?

DAVID G. WINTER, ABIGAIL J. STEWART, AND DAVID C. McCLELLAND

Grading the Effects of a Liberal Arts Education

It is easy to generalize about education but hard to prove that some forms of education are more valuable than others. Advocates of the liberal arts have traditionally argued that the study of history, literature, and philosophy, together with the study of science, mathematics, and at least one foreign language, is of greater value than an education devoted exclusively to job training. Assumptions of this sort can be found in the essays by Hesburgh, Solomon, Cousins, and Thomas. In 1978, a team of psychologists put these assumptions to the test by conducting a study designed to determine if a liberal arts education yields specific skills that can be measured and compared to the abilities of students who have undergone other types of education.

David G. Winter (b. 1939) is a former Rhodes Scholar with a Ph.D. in psychology from Harvard. A contributor to numerous journals, he is the author of The Power Motive *(1973) and* The Don Juan Legend *(1975). He is married to Abigail J. Stewart (b. 1949), who teaches psychology at Boston University. Her principal research interests include personality and adaptation to stress. A graduate of Wesleyan University, Stewart has a M.Sc. from the London School of Economics and a Ph.D. from Harvard—where David C. McClelland (b. 1917) has taught since 1956. His books include* The Roots of Consciousness *(1964),* The Drinking Man *(1971),* Power: The Inner Experience *(1975), and* The Achieving Society *(1976). For his research in psychology, McClelland has been awarded fellowships and grants from the Guggenheim, Carnegie, and Ford Foundations, the National Institute of Mental Health, and the U.S. State Department.*

For more than 2,000 years, a liberal education has been the ideal of the West—for the brightest, if not for all, students. The tradition goes back to Plato, who argued in *The Republic* that leadership should be entrusted to the philosopher—"a lover not of a part of wisdom only, but of the whole ... able to distinguish the idea from the objects which participate in the idea." More recently, in a World War II–era treatise, a Harvard University committee concluded that a liberal education best prepared an individual to become "an expert in the general art of the free man and the citizen." The report, which led to the introduction of Harvard's general education curriculum, concluded, "The fruit of education is intelligence in action. The aim is mastery of life." 1

In recent years, the fruit has spoiled and such high-sounding rhetoric has been increasingly challenged. Critics have charged that liberal arts education is elitist education, based on undefined and empty shibboleths. Caroline Bird, social critic and author, argues in *The Case Against College* that the liberal arts are a religion, "the established religion of the ruling class." Bird writes, "The exalted language, the universalistic setting, the ultimate value, the inability to define, the appeal to personal witness ... these are all the familiar modes of religious discourse." 2

Students in the 1960s charged that such traditional liberal arts courses as   3
"Western Thought and Institutions" and "Contemporary Civilization" were eth-
nocentric and imperialistic. Other students found little stimulation in a curriculum that emphasized learning to both formulate ideas and engage in rational
discourse. They preferred, instead, to express themselves in experience and
action; they favored feeling over thought, the nonverbal over the verbal, the
concrete over the abstract. In the inflationary, job-scarce economy of the 1970s,
many students argue that the liberal arts curriculum is "irrelevant" because it
neither prepares them for careers nor teaches them marketable skills. In its
present form, moreover, liberal arts education is expensive education.

Partly in response to these charges and, more immediately to faculty discon-   4
tent, Harvard recently approved a redesigning of the liberal arts program. Faculty had complained that the growing numbers and varieties of courses had
"eroded the purpose of the existing general education program." Students, they
felt, could use any number of courses to satisfy the university's minimal requirements, making those requirements meaningless. The new core curriculum will
require students to take eight courses carefully distributed among five basic
areas of knowledge.* The Harvard plan proposed to give students "a critical
appreciation of the ways in which we gain knowledge and understanding of
ourselves." Plausible as this credo may be, it rests on rhetoric and not solid
research evidence—like curriculum innovations of the 1960s.

In an era of educational accounting and educational accountability, it would   5
be helpful to have a way of determining what the essential and most valuable
"core" of a university education is and what is peripheral and mere tradition.
What are the actual effects of a liberal education, this most persistent of Western ideals? It is sobering to realize that we have little firm evidence.

Against this background, we recently designed and carried out a new study   6
to get some of the evidence. Our findings suggest that liberal arts education
does, in fact, change students more or less as Plato envisioned, so that the
durability of this educational ideal in Western civilization may not be unde-
served. In our research, liberal education appears to promote increases in
conceptual and social-emotional sophistication. Thus, according to a number
of new tests we developed, students trained in the liberal arts are better able
to formulate valid concepts, analyze arguments, define themselves, and orient
themselves maturely to their world. The liberal arts education in at least one
college also seems to increase the leadership motivation pattern—a desire for
power, tempered by self-control.

The precise content of a liberal education remains unclear. Is it the study of   7
certain "core" disciplines or bodies of knowledge—courses in Western civilization or modern literature, or a particular set of "Great Books"? Does it require
a multidisciplinary approach, as, for example, in courses entitled "Science and
Responsibility" or "Freedom and Authority in the Modern Novel"? Many professors argue that the essence is not *what* is learned, but *how* it is taught—
with an emphasis on concepts rather than facts, on independent inquiry rather

---

*These are (1) letters and arts; (2) history; (3) social and philosophical analysis; (4) science and mathematics;
(5) foreign languages and cultures.

than learning by rote. Some educators, perhaps half-facetiously, contend that liberal arts include everything that is not of obvious practical or vocational use!

The Harvard committee during World War II theorized that general educa- 8 tion fostered four traits of mind: thinking effectively, communicating thought, making relevant judgments, and discriminating among values. Some 33 years later, the committee headed by present dean Henry Rosovsky characterized the goals of the liberally educated person in similarly luxuriant language: to "think and write clearly and effectively"; to have "some understanding of, and experience in thinking about, moral and ethical problems"; and to use experiences in the context of "other cultures and other times."

Still, these traits and skills remain largely unmeasured and ignored by psy- 9 chologists who, even when they study "thinking," focus on much more elemental and simple processes. Most of the abundant research on the effects of higher education have focused on changes in personality, values, and beliefs. Even here, the conclusions are largely equivocal: many college "effects" are due to the process by which the students were chosen in the first place and not to the changes that occur during college. Studies have shown, for instance, that attitudes are stabilized as much as they are altered during college.

We started our study from two fundamental premises: first, that the evidence 10 to date was probably more a reflection of the testing procedures used than of the efficacy of higher education; and, second, that new tests should be modeled on what university students actually do rather than on what researchers can easily score. If liberal education teaches articulate formation of complex concepts, then student research subjects should be asked to form concepts from complex material and then scored on how well they articulate them, rather than being asked to choose the "best" of five concepts by putting a check mark in one of the boxes. In more formal terms, tests of the effects of education should be *operant* tests that require operating on material and making up answers, rather than *respondent* tests that merely ask for choices from among precoded alternatives.

Any study of the effects of higher education has the difficult task of distin- 11 guishing educational effects from simple maturational effects. In order to have some control over the effects of maturation, therefore, we tested students who were receiving three different *kinds* of higher education:

1. A traditional four-year liberal arts education at a prestigious Eastern U.S. 12 institution. By any definition, students attending this school enjoy a curriculum that is considered liberal arts. It is a well-endowed, private college with a tradition of scholarly excellence, an eminent faculty, and great prestige. Its students, drawn from this country and abroad, must satisfy very competitive admissions standards. The college accepts 20 percent of all applicants. Approximately two-thirds of its students are men and one-third women. The curriculum emphasizes broad, interdisciplinary survey courses in the sciences, humanities, and social sciences, and individualized scholarship at all stages of the college career.

2. A four-year undergraduate program for training teachers and other 13 professionals. The offerings at this state-controlled institution have been expanded in recent years to include such general and career programs as law

enforcement and health education. The college's students, drawn from a large metropolitan area, must pass moderately competitive admissions standards; about one-half of those who apply are accepted. The student body is about evenly divided between men and women.

3. A two-year community college that offers career programs in data pro-   14
cessing, electronics, nursing, secretarial skills, and business administration. A publicly controlled institution, our community college is situated in a city and draws most of its students from nearby suburbs. It has a relatively nonselective admissions policy, accepting about 70 percent of those who apply. The student body is 60 percent male.

We administered three kinds of tests to a total of 414 students, half men and   15
half women, drawn from the first-year and last-year classes of the three colleges. We controlled statistically for intelligence and social class, to eliminate differences in performance based on these two characteristics. By comparing the test scores of first- and last-year students at each school, we hoped to determine the degree and nature of any changes brought about by the educational programs. By evaluating all three schools together, we hoped to find out whether the liberal arts school has a unique impact on its students.

With our new Test of Thematic Analysis, we examined the students' abilities   16
to create and express sophisticated concepts (see box, pages 410–11). We asked them to read two groups of brief, imaginative stories and then to describe the differences between the two in any way they liked. We awarded positive values to their work when they perceived characteristics of both story groups that could sensibly be compared and contrasted, used examples and qualifications to strengthen their arguments, legitimately redefined aspects of stories to support their theses, and found general categories to group apparently unrelated elements. When they compared unlike things or used affective and subjective phrasing such as "It makes the reader nervous" or "It left me satisfied," we awarded negative values.

At all three institutions, last-year students scored higher than first-year   17
students, but seniors at the liberal arts college far outdistanced their counterparts at the teachers' and community colleges.

Thus, a typical freshman at any of the schools might describe the differences   18
between the two groups of stories in rather wandering terms: "Group B stories are more exciting than Group A stories. They were about nasty leaders and I don't like that. Group B stories show people as not trusting each other." A typical final-year student at our liberal arts college might put what is essentially the same contrast in these terms: "Both groups of stories involve relations to authority. In Group A, authority is either accepted or actively rejected; while Group B stories involve moderate suspicion of authority. While story A-4, an animal fable, might seem an exception to the rule, it does, in fact, fit if one considers the phrase 'king of the beasts' as representing symbolic authority."

Liberal education, then, seems to affect the way in which people marshal,   19
organize, and "operate" on facts. These processes are spontaneous, self-initiated, and active, and are the same ones called for by an essay assignment to "compare and contrast the Renaissance and the Reformation," or an examination question asking, "What are the essential differences between normal

and malignant cells?" We believe these processes are more central to a liberal education than learning simple concepts and memorizing detailed facts. Indeed, we gave the students an adaptation of a standard reading-comprehension test and found that none of the three schools significantly affected the ability to learn and remember isolated facts.

As another means of probing the conceptual processes and reasoning abilities of the three groups of students, Abigail Stewart devised an Analysis of Argument test. The test first quotes an extreme, unpopular, and rather badly argued position on a controversial issue. Students must attack this position and support their own stance with reasoned argument. Again, the quality of the attacks improved from first to final year at all three schools, but more so at our liberal arts institution. Thus, a typical first-year student would dispute a series of facts: "X is wrong when he says that ..." A final-year attack focused on a more abstract, general principle, such as faulty logic: "X's arguments all derive from a confusion of association with causation." 20

In the second step of Stewart's test, students switched sides and had to defend the position they had formerly attacked. Most floundered and simply substituted a blank endorsement for a blanket attack. Only our final-year liberal arts students were able to craft a limited, qualified endorsement of a position they had opposed. They could respond: "While there are flaws in X's whole line of reasoning, it must be admitted that some of his particular claims and examples are true." In other words, the liberally educated students were better able to argue both sides of a question, but with integrity and intelligence rather than by simply espousing the other point of view uncritically. 21

The other changes in student ability unique to, or more pronounced at, the liberal arts college involved measures in the Thematic Apperception Test (TAT), a "projective" test that clinicians have used for over 40 years to assess personality. Subjects see a series of vague and ambiguous pictures—a man wearing the uniform of a ship's captain talking with a man in a business suit, for example, or two women in lab coats using equipment such as a test tube—and must tell or write stories about the pictures. Researchers may use any number of scoring systems to analyze the results, depending on the personality characteristics that interest them. We were looking for three elements in the responses: self-definition, maturity of adaptation to the environment, and the leadership motivation pattern. 22

A story that scores high in self-definition uses causal words such as "because" and "in order to," and portrays characters who take actions for reasons, for example: "After being miserable for a while, the woman in the picture will realize that her love affair won't work and will leave." Low-scoring stories portray ineffective actions, events with no apparent causes, and characters who experience intense feelings in response to others' actions, but who are unable to act themselves: "The man and woman pictured will try desperately to establish a love relationship, but will end up feeling only more alone." In a number of studies, people who score high in self-definition act instrumentally (that is, effectively and constructively), often in ways that go beyond ascribed roles. Self-defining women, for example, tend to seek careers as well as marriage, and in many different ways are not limited by traditional sex roles. Thus, self- 23

TESTING ONE, TWO, THREE SETS OF STUDENTS

In the Test of Thematic Analysis—a measure of complex concept formation—students were asked to compare and contrast two groups of brief stories, labeled A and B. Below are sample stories taken from each group, followed by typical responses written by a final-year student at each of the three colleges in our study.

Researchers scored answers in terms of the sophistication shown in the analysis and in the writing. Subjective opinions, based on emotional reactions to stories, and comparisons between totally dissimilar events or ideas were scored negatively. Statements supported by specific examples and parallel comparisons were considered evidence of complex reasoning and were scored positively. The liberal arts students—especially seniors—scored significantly higher on this test than did their counterparts at the other two schools.

Group A Story

It is a trial and the people are lawyers.

They are all involved in various machinations against the others in the trial which is to reveal graft.

All the trust that each put in someone else has been shattered by the letter which reveals the various plots and subplots taking place during the trial.

They will all be thrown in jail.

Group B Story

They are all politicians at a debate. One of them just got a special-delivery letter from a colleague not able to attend.

The man who wrote the letter is held in high esteem by the others.

They are all depending on the person who wrote the letter and now he has disappointed them.

They will seek a new "leader," someone to respect more than the others and to look to him for guidance.

Senior at the Liberal Arts College

"In each of the stories there are two major relationships: that among the figures described and (usually implicitly [*qualification*, scored +1]) that between the group in the picture and the writer of the story [*overarching issue*,

definition is associated with an instrumental, effective style of translating thought into action. When compared with the teachers' and community colleges, the liberal arts college produced unique and significant gains in student self-definition.

Maturity of adaptation to the environment refers to success in developing characteristics that personality theorists have identified as representing the

24

followed by a *parallel comparison* between the two groups, both scored + 1].
In Group A, each writer feels that self-interest divides the figures from one
another and that what they are doing is either criminal—hence to his own
disadvantage—or at least not helpful to him. In Group B, each writer conceives
of a cooperative relationship among the figures in the picture and thinks of
them as performing a service which may benefit him (*e.g.*, medical progress,
newscasting [*examples*, scored + 1]) or is at least in itself worthwhile [*sub-
suming alternatives*, scored + 1]—thoughtful speaking on controversial issues, leadership for those who feel they need it."

Senior at the Teachers' College

"Whoever wrote Group A does not have a very positive image of man. In all
four stories, man is dishonest, out for himself, arrogant, materialistic and all
the uncomplimentary character defects I can think of. But I must admit they
make for more interesting reading [*subjective reaction*, scored − 1]. Everyone
is manipulating everyone else for his own benefit . . . .

"Group B is very factual but rather cut and dry—no human emotions involved whatsoever ["apples and oranges," *nonparallel comparison* with
Group A, scored − 1]. I personally enjoy reading stories which include people's
feelings, reactions and emotions; showing both their human weaknesses and
their great strengths."

Sophomore (final year) at the Community College

"It seems to be that in the stories in Group A, in every case, each story makes
the reader have a bad feeling [*affective reaction*, scored − 1]. The people in
the higher positions such as lawyers or politicians are generally men who
should be respected. In the stories, however, they come across as cheaters,
liars, men out to better themselves and cheat the people. The people who trust
them and are more or less considered 'good people,' who come out of the
stories in a disillusioned way but also appear as the ones who the reader should
'root' for to win in the end.

"In Group B stories, there is an element of togetherness and cooperation of
the people in the stories ["apples and oranges," *nonparallel comparison* with
Group A, scored − 1]. I as the reader came out of these stories with an easier
feeling and with more respect for the people involved [*subjective reaction*,
scored − 1]."

highest levels of personality growth or maturity. Drawing on the ideas of Freud
and Erik Erickson, who described the "stages" of development, Steward recently worked out a TAT measure of this adaptation. As we expected, students
at all three institutions showed higher stages of adaptation over time, but those
at the liberal arts college showed larger, more significant gains. In terms of
particular scoring categories from the Stewart measure, this means that stu-

dents, our liberal arts students in particular: (1) see authority in complex, versus simplistic, pro and con terms; (2) view other people as differentiated beings in their own right, rather than as simple means of gratifying their (the students') desires; (3) integrate both joy and sorrow into their moods; (4) are able to work without falling victim to passivity, self-doubt, or anxiety about failure.

Seniors at the teachers' and community colleges scored higher than fresh-   25
men in both maturity of adaptation and self-definition, suggesting that almost any kind of higher education, or even just physical and social maturation, has some influence on these variables. But for all measures, the gains at the liberal arts college were significantly greater.

It appears that the liberal arts college also fosters a unique pattern of moti-   26
vation in its students: strong concern for power and weak concern for affiliation, combined with high self-control or ability to inhibit activity. Thus, the final-year liberal arts students wrote more TAT stories with the following combination of characteristics: (1) one character has an impact (or tries to) on another; (2) activity is restrained or inhibited—as indicated by the use of such words as "not" or "cannot"; and (3) characters do not show concern with establishing and maintaining warm, friendly relations with others.

David McClelland, of Harvard, has called this set of characteristics the lead-   27
ership or "imperial" motive pattern. In a series of experiments, McClelland has demonstrated that it is usually found in individuals who are considered effec-tive leaders—managers who have a talent for creating in their subordinates such qualities as high morale, a sense of responsibility, organizational clarity, and "team spirit." For, while the qualities of an imperial motive suggest that a person is not compassionate, they generally dictate that he will be fair, treating others in an impartial manner that subordinates seem to appreciate.

The present study of only three colleges limits inference and further specu-   28
lation. We must study other liberal arts schools to discover whether they have the same impact on the students as the liberal arts college discussed here. The issue will likely be complex. Indeed, data we recently collected from another college similar to the liberal arts school we examined suggest that liberal edu-cation there increases self-definition, but decreases maturity and has little or no effect on the imperial pattern.

When we know more about what causes the kinds of changes in students   29
detailed here, then our research can contribute to shaping educational policy. But who can say, from the evidence now at hand, that the effects of liberal education at our liberal arts college, or anywhere else, are caused by course requirements at all? It may be that the worth of an education at any school is determined more by faculty quality, library facilities, the size of the endowment, or even by the self-fulfilling anticipations and beliefs of faculty and students. We are currently seeking answers to these questions, taking our new test procedures to students at more than 15 different post-secondary-school insti-tutions. During the next year or two, we hope to point to specific qualities of liberal arts colleges that leave their particular imprints on the students.

Still, the changes unique to, or enhanced by, attendance at our liberal arts   30 college do establish at least a prima-facie case for education in the liberal arts. The pious goals and extravagant language of liberal arts educators must yet be analyzed, broken down into specific skills. With tests to measure student abilities in these skills, we can determine whether liberal arts education is doing what its proponents claim and how its performance can be improved.

QUESTIONS FOR MEANING

1. In what paragraphs do the authors state the thesis of their argument by summarizing the results of their research?
2. What specific abilities did liberal arts students prove to master, excelling students in the other two schools involved in this study?
3. What types of courses constitute the "liberal arts," and how are such courses usually best taught? What is the advantage of this type of teaching? Have you ever taken a course that was taught this way? What did you like or dislike about it?
4. What two premises determined the way in which the authors of this study went about conducting their research?
5. Explain the differences between operant and respondent testing. Can you give examples of these tests from your own experience in school?
6. What variables did the authors need to consider in analyzing their data? What steps did they take to make sure they were making fair comparisons?
7. In evaluating student responses to their Test of Thematic Analysis, what strengths and weaknesses were the researchers looking for? Explain in your own words why points were awarded and subtracted.
8. In the Analysis of Argument test, why were the essays of liberal arts students considered the strongest and most sophisticated?
9. What do the authors mean by "self-definition" in paragraphs 22 and 23?
10. Vocabulary: shibboleths (2), imperialistic (3), plausible (4), credo (4), innovations (4), peripheral (5), rote (7), facetiously (7), equivocal (9), eminent (12), floundered (21), affiliation (26), and prima-facie (30).

QUESTIONS ABOUT STRATEGY

1. In paragraphs 2 and 3, the authors summarize the main objections to liberal arts education. What advantage is there to doing this so early in their essay?
2. Do the authors explain their tests clearly? Do they tell you enough about them so that you can understand what the tests were designed to reveal? Similarly, how clearly do they report the results of their tests?
3. Where do the authors caution their readers, pointing out that their conclusions are only tentative and subject to further research? Do they provide any evidence to suggest that their initial results may be disputable?
4. Although their research supported the value of a liberal arts education, do the authors have any reservations about the liberal arts—or liberal arts educators? Consider the tone they adopt when discussing faculty and students at liberal arts schools.

5. Judging from this essay, what type of education do you think the authors had? Do you think they have any biases that may have affected their research? Can you point to anything in the essay that suggests that this may have been the case?

SUGGESTIONS FOR WRITING

1. Both Caroline Bird and Carrie Tuhy question the value of a college education as a means of securing a good job. How do you think your education will affect your own career? If you believe that a college education is essential for employment in your chosen field, write an essay designed to prove that this is so.

2. Write a defense for one course that you believe all students should take, regardless of their major.

3. Evaluate the basic degree requirements at your school. Will they give you the sort of knowledge that Hesburgh, Solomon, Cousins, and Thomas recommend? Are there too many requirements? Can requirements be satisfied with courses that offer little substance? If you believe that the degree requirements should be changed in some way, write an essay explaining and supporting your view.

4. Write an essay arguing on behalf of learning a foreign language.

5. Did your high school give you an adequate preparation for college? If you are finding college more difficult than it should be, and believe that this is because your high school education was weak, write an essay describing what was wrong at your school. Argue on behalf of a necessary reform.

6. Writing ten years ago, Caroline Bird commented on the large number of students graduating from American colleges and argued that the economy could not absorb so many graduates. Every year since then, our colleges and universities have continued to produce hundreds of thousands of new graduates. Write an essay that will argue one of the following propositions: (1) College entrance requirements should be made more rigorous and selective so that degrees will carry more prestige; or (2) the government has a responsibility to insure that everyone in the country, regardless of background, has access to higher education.

7. Do you learn anything important in college outside of the classroom that could not be learned elsewhere? If so, write an essay identifying this knowledge and arguing on behalf of its importance.

8. Consider the length of a college education. Are four years too little or too much?

9. How does the reading you do as a class assignment differ from the reading you do on your own? Write an essay in defense of reading that will explain why it is important to discuss what one has read.

10. What is the relationship between higher education and freedom? Write an essay explaining how knowledge can make one free.

11. If you are planning to drop out of college, or to take at least a semester off, write an argument that will justify your decision. Assume that you are writing for an audience that believes that you should remain in school.

Section 8
Literary Criticism: What Does a Poem Mean?

Stopping by Woods on a Snowy Evening

Whose woods these are I think I know.
His house is in the village though;
He will not see me stopping here
To watch his woods fill up with snow.

My little horse must think it queer
To stop without a farmhouse near
Between the woods and frozen lake
The darkest evening of the year.

He gives his harness bells a shake
To ask if there is some mistake.
The only other sound's the sweep
Of easy wind and downy flake.

The woods are lovely, dark and deep.
But I have promises to keep,
And miles to go before I sleep
And miles to go before I sleep.

Robert Frost

The ~~steaming horses~~ think it queer

            how   *must*
The ~~little~~ ~~my~~ ~~horse~~ ~~begins~~ to think it queer

To
~~We~~ stop with not a farm house near

                the woods an a frozen
Between a ~~forest and a~~ lake

The darkest evening of the year

She
        her
~~He~~ gives harness bells a shake

To ask if there is some mistake

                        the
The only other sounds the sweep

                    downy
Of easy wind and ~~falling~~ flake.

The woods are lovely dark and deep

But I have promises to keep

~~That bid me ~~not~~ give the reins a shake~~

And miles to go before I sleep

And miles to go before I sleep

JOHN HOLMES

On Frost's "Stopping by Woods on a Snowy Evening"

Poet and educator John Holmes (1904–1962) graduated from Tufts College in 1929.
He taught briefly at Lafayette College in Pennsylvania before returning to Tufts in
1934, where he taught poetry until his death twenty-eight years later. He was
poetry critic for the Boston Evening Transcript, *and a reviewer for the* New York
Times *and the* Atlantic Monthly. *His many books include* Address to the Living
(1937), The Poet's Work *(1939),* Fair Warning *(1939),* Map of My Country *(1943),*
The Symbols *(1955),* Writing Poetry *(1960), and* The Fortune Teller *(1961). His*
explication of "Stopping By Woods on a Snowy Evening" was originally published
in 1943. It demonstrates what an intelligent reader can learn from studying a
poet's revisions.

This facsimile is a reproduction of the last three stanzas of "Stopping by   1
Woods on a Snowy Evening" as Robert Frost worked it out. We know from the
poet that he had just written the long poem, "New Hampshire," in one all-night
unbroken stretch of composition, and that he then turned a page of his work-
book and wrote this short poem without stopping. This fact has interesting
implications. "New Hampshire" is a discourse in the idiomatic blank verse that
is so peculiarly Frost's own style—the rhythms of natural speech matched to
the strict but inconspicuous iambic pentameter, the beat always discernible
but never formal. It is reasonable to suppose that after the hours spent in
writing the long poem, in its loosened but never loose manner, he was ready,
unconsciously, for a poem in strict pattern. He had also obviously had in his
head for some time the incident on which the short poem was to be based, as
well as the use he wished to make of it. He committed himself, as he has said,
to the four-stress iambic line and to the *aaba* rime-scheme, in the first stanza,
which he wrote rapidly and did not revise. He knew what he had seen, and he
knew how he wanted to write it.

> Whose woods these are I think I know.
> His house is in the village though;
> He will not see me stopping here
> To watch his woods fill up with snow.

"That went off so easily I was tempted into the added difficulty of picking up   2
my 3 for my 1-2-4 to go on with in the second stanza. I was amused and scared
at what that got me into," Frost says. The facsimile shows what it got him into,
how he got out of it, and how he achieved the poem as it meant itself to be
written.

It began with what was the actual experience of stopping at night by some   3
dark woods in winter, and the fact that there were two horses. He remembered

what he saw then. "The steaming horses think it queer." But the poem needs truth more than fact, and he cancels the line, and begins again, "The horse begins to think it queer," but doesn't like the word "begins," needing in the allowed space a word that will particularize the horse, so writes "The little horse must think it queer." Now he runs into a grammatical difficulty, which must somehow be solved before he gets on into the poem he already feels sure of. "I launched into the construction 'My little horse must think it queer that we should stop.' I didn't like omitting the 'that' and I had no room for 'should.' I had the luck to get out of it with the infinitive." This groping and warming-up has a kind of impatience, an urgency to get on with the poem, but not until all the parts are right. At this point the poet knew and did not know how the poem would end. He knew the feel, and the sense, and almost everything about the form—certainly enough to know when he got off the track.

Whether he revised the third line here or later we cannot know. But we can see in several places in this poem his changes toward particularization. The line "Between a forest and a lake" is a notation, and "Between the woods and frozen lake" is a finished line of poetry. "A forest" is too big, too vague, but "the woods" is definite, and bounded; you get lost in a forest, but you can walk through and out of the woods, and probably you know who owns it—Vermonters do, as he has said in the first stanza. "A lake" has not the specific condition or picture of "frozen lake." This sort of revision, or what Frost calls, "touching up," is what makes a poem—this, plus the first inspiration. Either one, without the other, is unlikely to make a good poem.   4

The next stanza comes easier, because the rime-scheme has been determined, and one unexpected obstacle has been overcome. But once more there is a delay, as the poet makes a decision as to the "he" or "she"—and the more important and more interesting one about the falling snow. In writing "downy flake" for "fall of flake" the gain is great not only for accuracy of feeling and fact, but also for the music of the lines. The simple alliteration in "fall of flake" is canceled in favor of the word, one word, "downy," which blends with the vowel-chords a poet half-consciously makes and modulates as he goes. In this instance, it half-chimes with "sounds" and adds a rounder, fuller, and yet quieter tone.   5

Now the carry-over rime is "sweep," a fortunate one, really, and important to the final solution of the rime-scheme. It is not too much to assume, knowing all we know about the circumstances of the writing of this poem—the all-night composition of "New Hampshire," and the sudden urge to catch and shape still another saved idea—that the darker, more confident, more rapid strokes of the pen show the poet's growing excitement. The end is in sight. The thing he believed could happen will happen, surely now, and he must hurry to get it onto the page. This is the real moment of power, and any poet's greatest satisfaction.   6

"The woods are lovely dark and deep / But I have promises to keep." The first two lines of the last stanza come fast, and flow beautifully, the crest of the poem's emotion and its music. We cannot know whether he had held them in his head, or had swept up to and into them as he felt the destined pattern fulfilling itself.   7

Then, with success in sight, there comes an awkward and unexpected stum-   8
ble. He writes, "That bid me give the reins a shake," which may have been the
fact and the action. But the rime is wrong. Not only has the rime been used in
the previous stanza, but so has the image of the horse shaking his head and
reins. Things are moving fast now, no doubt impatiently, but certainly with
determination, shown in the heavy black lines of abrupt cancellation. He strikes
out "me give the reins a shake," and writes above it, so the line will read, "That
bid me on, and there are miles," and then the whole thing comes through! Of
course! "Miles to go . . ."

That's what it was supposed to be—the feeling of silence and dark, almost   9
overpowering the man, but the necessity of going on. "And miles to go before I
sleep." Then the triumph in the whole thing, the only right and perfect last line,
solving the problem of the carried-over rime, keeping the half-tranced state,
and the dark, and the solitude, and man's great effort to be responsible man . . .
the repetition of that line.

"Stopping by Woods on a Snowy Evening" can be studied as perfected struc-   10
ture, with the photostat manuscript to show that art is not, though it must
always appear to be, effortless. It can be thought of as a picture: the whites,
grays, and blacks of the masses and areas of lake, field, and woods, with the tiny
figure of the man in the sleigh, and the horse. And it can be thought of as a
statement of man's everlasting responsibility to man; though the dark and
nothingness tempt him to surrender, he will not give in.

QUESTIONS FOR MEANING

1. What is the connection between "Stopping by Woods on a Snowy Evening"
   and the long poem "New Hampshire"?
2. Do you understand what Holmes means by "blank verse," "iambic pentameter," and "rime-scheme"? Identify any other vocabulary that seems peculiar to the analysis of poetry. If you have never studied poetry before, how
   can you find out what these terms mean?
3. Explain what Holmes means in paragraph 3 when he writes, "the poem
   needs truth more than fact."
4. According to Holmes, what are the two essential steps in the process of
   writing poetry?
5. What theme or themes does Holmes find in this poem?
6. Vocabulary: facsimile (1), idiomatic (1), inconspicuous (1), discernible (1),
   and modulates (5).

QUESTIONS ABOUT STRATEGY

1. Why was it useful for Holmes to reproduce a partial facsimile of the original
   manuscript of "Stopping by Woods on a Snowy Evening"? If he had been
   unable to do so, what sort of changes would he have had to make in his
   essay?

2. How can studying the manuscript version of a poem help us to better understand the finished version? Explain why Frost deleted "steaming" and why two horses were turned into one "little" horse. Explain also why Frost changed "a forest" to "the woods" and "a lake" to "frozen lake." Do you agree with Holmes's interpretation of these changes? Could the changes mean anything else?
3. What does this essay reveal about the nature of literary criticism? Does it matter if critics work inductively or deductively? Would either approach be equally convincing?

EARL DANIELS
Misreading Poetry

Earl Daniels (1893–1970) was a teacher, critic, and poet. He graduated from Clark University in 1914 and served in the Army during World War I. After the war, he returned to school—receiving his A.M. from the University of Chicago in 1922 and his Ph.D. from Harvard in 1926. His poetry was published in Harper's, America, *and* New Masses. *But Daniels is remembered principally for his long association with Colgate University, where he taught from 1930 to 1961. After his retirement, he gave to Colgate a library of over four thousand books, including manuscripts and first editions. "Misreading Poetry" is an editor's title for an excerpt from the introductory chapter of* The Art of Reading Poetry, *a college textbook first published in 1941.*

If you are one of those taught to approach the presence of the poem in quest   1
of vital lesson, of profound comment on man and the universe, the answer is, *Don't.* Here should be no halfway measures, no reducing the urge to philosophy by half, no gradual tapering-off. You may, after all, rest comfortable in the assurance that if philosophy and morals are present in any vital way, they will make themselves felt without your conscious searching for them, insistent on their share in your awareness of the complete poem.

The way of a group of college freshmen with ... ["Stopping by Woods on a   2
Snowy Evening"] illustrates how deadly this concern about morals may be....

Here are some interpretations by freshmen who were supposed to be better-   3
than-average students.

a) In this poem the underlying thought seems to be that of suicide .... The last four lines of the poem indicate that the person decides he has more work to do on earth before he dies in order to fulfill a promise of some kind.

b) A man who has promised to leave town after committing some crime, and has been told "to get going and don't stop." The line, "The darkest evening of the year," might mean the disgrace he has brought on himself; and, "I have promises to keep," may mean he has promised to get out of the country.

c) If he didn't mention that the owner of the woods lived in the village, I would say he was talking about the life he has yet to live before he meets his Maker.

d) It deals with the thought of eternal rest .... But then the subject is brought back to reality with the thought of the things he has yet to do, and the rest of his life he has yet to spend.

e) It may represent one who is tired of life's hardships, and is tempted to drop by the wayside in some secluded retreat, but who must press on since he has many years of work ahead and many obligations to fulfill before such rest may be his.

f) Almost every day we find ourselves faced with the lures of temptation. We realize that we ought to keep on our way, yet the temptation to stay where all is peaceful and quiet is often too great for us to resist. While we are here in college we are often tempted to do the easiest thing. That is, to neglect our studies and to run around and have a good time. However we know that there are promises to be kept and obligations to be filled. We have been sent here by our parents for the purpose of receiving an education, and there is no doubt that our duty is to do all in our power to take advantage of this opportunity.

g) I am a college man. I am taking a pre-med course. I am away from home. I am open to temptations that college may offer me. Am I to take advantage of their owner's absence to sit and gaze in his woods—to take advantage of being away from my parents to stop by the wayside and admire the beautiful sirens? Or, am I to be a second Ulysses and have sufficient will power to overcome these temptations? Am I to stop where there is "easy wind and downy flake"—to sit back in my chair, just to dream and forget all hardships? Or am I to heed the impatience of the horse and the warning of the harness bell—to awaken to my will calling for me to go on? True, it is dark now, and I cannot see well, but do I not remember the vows that I have made—to go through at all costs? Yes, I must go through those long miles of roads rougher than *I* can imagine, before *I* call for time out.

Comments *f* and *g* are especially nauseous misunderstandings, and they represent the cardinal sin of personal application. To make a poem mean privately, to ourselves alone, to look first for directions about *our* life and *our* problems—no going wrong can be more abysmally bad. Like the old hocus-pocus magic-formula way in which the Bible used to be consulted, you put your question, open the book at random, drop an equally random finger on the page, and there you are—provided you are ingenious enough in twisting words to meet special situations and personal needs. The method is equally unintelligent with the Bible and with poetry, and to resort to it is to proclaim oneself part of an intellectual underworld of superstition and ignorance. The poet's message, so far as he has a message for the individual, is a message to the individual not in his private and peculiar selfhood, but in his representative capacity as a normal human being, as a man; it is part of the universality of the poet's speaking.

If facile talk about appreciation, concern with peripheral things, and preoccupation with morals and the meaning of life are heresies, what is sound doctrine in the reading of poetry? What is orthodox? What is a right approach to Frost's poem, or to any poem? The simple, natural approach, the easiest way. What is obvious in "Stopping by Woods on a Snowy Evening" is that the poet has had a perfectly everyday experience. On a snow-filled winter's afternoon, he has come to a patch of woodland; for no reason, save that he simply and unashamedly likes to, he has stopped, just to watch the woods fill up with snow. That is the experience, the start of the poem, which, from such an unassuming start, got itself written because *the poet enjoyed the experience*, remembered it, and something made him want to try to put it in words, *just for fun: the poem is a record of experience to be shared with a reader*, who must take it at this simple face value if he is to read the poem as it should be read. Most poems probably begin much like this. And if someone says, "It may never have happened to Frost; he may have imagined it all," the answer is that in literature and the arts there is no essential difference between experience in actuality and experience in imagination; both are the stuff of poems, in the broadest sense of the term, *experience*. It is really very little a reader's business whether a writer is using memory or imagination, so long as the reality of the result is not affected. Frost may, indeed, have imagined it all, so far as we have a right to know, or care.

But why should a poet want to share experience, if he has nothing "impor-   6
tant" to say, no "lesson" to teach, if he is not intent on "improving society," and "bettering the conditions of the human race"? Like so many facts, this is a mystery, hid in elemental human nature. Men do act this way: human nature prompts them to want to tell others what has happened to them. All conversation is built on that ancient formula, "Have you heard this one?" The questioner hopes "this one" has not been heard, so that he can go on and tell his story, enjoy sharing his experience.

The woman in the [following] parable is a case in point. She had lost her   7
money. It is not significant that she went on an orgy of spring cleaning, turning the house upside down, or that she fould her money. But when she found it, and this is the important thing, her next move was to give a party, inviting friends and neighbors for miles around, just that they might rejoice with her because she had found what had been lost: in other words, that they might share her experience. So the poet, though tangibilities like money may not be involved. Something emotionally stirring has happened, and he makes a poem, which is his invitation to his friends and neighbors to rejoice with him. How ungracious of the friends and neighbors of the woman, if they had hunted for lessons in the experience, emphasized, perhaps, the moral that in the future she must be more careful about her money, suggested it was all an illustration of the guidance of a good providence, enabling her to recover her fortune—or any other testimony a dyed-in-the-wool moralist might strain to discover. They had been invited to a party; the woman didn't want lessons; she wanted them to have a good time with her. No less ungracious is the reader who would deduce moral teaching from "Stopping by Woods on a Snowy Evening," and from many other poems, when what the poet wants is that we should have a good time at his party, along with him, because he, in the first place, had a good time with his experience. Such sharing is the request every good poet makes of his readers, and it leads straight to an idea at the heart of all poetry, the irrefragable cornerstone on which poetry rests. That idea ... is that *poetry, reduced to its simplest, is only experience*. Experience moved the poet; he enjoyed it, and wanted to put it down on paper, as experience and nothing else, partly because writing is a self-contained action which is fun for the writer, partly because he wanted the reader to enjoy the experience with him. If we are to learn to read, we must begin with elemental, irreducible facts like this.

QUESTIONS FOR MEANING

1. Consider the student interpretations of "Stopping by Woods on a Snowy Evening" that Daniels reports. Of interpretations *a* through *e*, which is the most and least intelligent? Explain why Daniels objects to *f* and *g*. What does he mean when he protests against "twisting words to meet special situations and personal needs"?

2. According to Daniels, how *should* we read poetry?
3. How does Daniels define "experience"?
4. Does Daniels imply that poetry is without moral content, and that writing poetry is always fun? How do you know if a poem is profound—and that the poet has asked us to do more than have "a good time at his party"?
5. Vocabulary: abysmally (4), ingenious (4), facile (5), heresies (5), orthodox (5), tangibilities (7), irrefragable (7), and irreducible (7).

QUESTIONS ABOUT STRATEGY

1. Is Daniels fair to students? Are the student interpretations that he reports reasonably representative of how "better-than-average" college freshmen respond to "Stopping by Woods on a Snowy Evening"?
2. Why does Daniels emphasize that reading poetry should be fun? What has he assumed about his audience?
3. Explain the parable in paragraph 7 and the point it is meant to illustrate.

JOHN CIARDI

Robert Frost: The Way to the Poem

The son of Italian immigrants, John Ciardi (b. 1916) taught English at Harvard from 1946 to 1953 and at Rutgers from 1953 to 1961, when he gave up teaching in order to be a full-time writer and poet. His many volumes of poetry include Homeward to America *(1940),* Other Skies *(1947),* Live Another Day *(1949),* If I Marry You: A Sheaf of Love Poems *(1958), and* In the Stoneworks *(1961). He is also the author of* How Does a Poem Mean?—*a highly respected book of criticism on the nature of poetry—and a fine translation of Dante's* Divine Comedy. *A fellow of the American Academy of Arts and Letters, Ciardi has won many awards, most notably the Prix de Rome (1956–1957). As poetry editor for the* Saturday Review *from 1956 to 1972, he was in a position not only to encourage new poets but also to challenge conventional ideas about well-known poems. His columns were frequently controversial, as can be seen from the letters inspired by the following essay on Frost. At a time when many readers liked to see Frost as a grandfatherly nature poet, a sort of literary Norman Rockwell, Ciardi was one of the first critics to emphasize the element of despair that can be found in much of Frost's work.*

The School System has much to say these days of the virtue of reading widely, and not enough about the virtues of reading less but in depth. There are any number of reading lists for poetry, but there is not enough talk about individual poems. Poetry, finally, is one poem at a time. To read any one poem carefully is the ideal preparation for reading another. Only a poem can illustrate how poetry works.   1

Above, therefore, is a poem ["Stopping by Woods on a Snowy Evening"]—one of the master lyrics of the English language, and almost certainly the best-known poem by an American poet. What happens in it?—which is to say, not *what* does it mean, but *how* does it mean? How does it go about being a human reenactment of a human experience? The author—perhaps the thousandth reader would need to be told—is Robert Frost.   2

Even the TV audience can see that this poem begins as a seemingly-simple narration of a seemingly-simple incident but ends by suggesting meanings far beyond anything specifically referred to in the narrative. And even readers with only the most casual interest in poetry might be made to note the additional fact that, though the poem suggests those larger meanings, it is very careful never to abandon its pretense to being simple narration. There is duplicity at work. The poet pretends to be talking about one thing, and all the while he is talking about many others.   3

Many readers are forever unable to accept the poet's essential duplicity. It is almost safe to say that a poem is never about what it seems to be about. As much could be said of the proverb. The bird in the hand, the rolling stone, the stitch in time never (except by an artful double-deception) intend any sort of statement about birds, stones, or sewing. The incident of this poem, one must conclude, is at root a metaphor.   4

Duplicity aside, this poem's movement from the specific to the general illus-   5
trates one of the basic formulas of all poetry. Such a grand poem as Arnold's
"Dover Beach" and such lesser, though unfortunately better known, poems as
Longfellow's "The Village Blacksmith" and Holmes's "The Chambered Nautilus"
are built on the same progression. In these three poems, however, the generalization is markedly set apart from the specific narration, and even seems additional to the telling rather than intrinsic to it. It is this sense of division one has
in mind in speaking of "a tacked-on moral."

There is nothing wrong-in-itself with a tacked-on moral. Frost, in fact, makes   6
excellent use of the device at times. In this poem, however, Frost is careful to
let the whatever-the-moral-is grow out of the poem itself. When the action ends
the poem ends. There is no epilogue and no explanation. Everything pretends
to be about the narrated incident. And that pretense sets the basic tone of the
poem's performance of itself.

The dramatic force of that performance is best observable, I believe, as a   7
progression in three scenes.

In scene one, which coincides with stanza one, a man—a New England   8
man—is driving his sleigh somewhere at night. It is snowing, and as the man
passes a dark patch of woods he stops to watch the snow descend into the
darkness. We know, moreover, that the man is familiar with these parts (he
knows who owns the woods and where the owner lives), and we know that no
one has seen him stop. As scene one forms itself in the theatre of the mind's-
eye, therefore, it serves to establish some as yet unspecified relation between
the man and the woods.

It is necessary, however, to stop here for a long parenthesis: Even so simple   9
an opening statement raises any number of questions. It is impossible to address all the questions that rise from the poem stanza by stanza, but two that
arise from stanza one illustrate the sort of thing one might well ask of the poem
detail by detail.

Why, for example, does the man not say what errand he is on? What is the   10
force of leaving the errand generalized? He might just as well have told us that
he was going to the general store, or returning from it with a jug of molasses he
had promised to bring Aunt Harriet and two suits of long underwear he had
promised to bring the hired man. Frost, moreover, can handle homely detail to
great effect. He preferred to leave his motive generalized. Why?

And why, on the other hand, does he say so much about knowing the absent   11
owner of the woods and where he lives? Is it simply that one set of details
happened-in whereas another did not? To speak of things "happening-in" is to
assault the integrity of a poem. Poetry cannot be discussed meaningfully unless
one can assume that everything in the poem—every last comma and variant
spelling—is in it by the poet's specific act of choice. Only bad poets allow into
their poems what is haphazard or cheaply chosen.

The errand, I will venture a bit brashly for lack of space, is left generalized in   12
order the more aptly to suggest *any* errand in life and, therefore, life itself. The
owner is there because he is one of the forces of the poem. Let it do to say that

the force he represents is the village of mankind (that village at the edge of winter) from which the poet finds himself separated (has separated himself?) in his moment by the woods (and to which, he recalls finally, he has promises to keep). The owner is he-who-lives-in-his-village-house, thereby locked away from the poet's awareness of the-time-the-snow-tells as it engulfs and obliterates the world the village man allows himself to believe he "owns." Thus, the owner is a representative of an order of reality from which the poet has divided himself for the moment, though to a certain extent he ends by reuniting with it. Scene one, therefore, establishes not only a relation between the man and the woods, but the fact that the man's relation begins with his separation (though momentarily) from mankind.

End parenthesis one, begin parenthesis two.   13

Still considering the first scene as a kind of dramatic performance of forces,   14
one must note that the poet has meticulously matched the simplicity of his language to the pretended simplicity of the narrative. Clearly, the man stopped because the beauty of the scene moved him, but he neither tells us that the scene is beautiful nor that he is moved. A bad writer, always ready to overdo, might have written: "The vastness gripped me, filling my spirit with the slow steady sinking of the snow's crystalline perfection into the glimmerless profundities of the hushed primeval wood." Frost's avoidance of such a spate illustrates two principles of good writing. The first, he has stated himself in "The Mowing": "Anything *more* than the truth would have seemed too weak" (italics mine). Understatement is one of the basic sources of power in English poetry. The second principle is to let the action speak for itself. A good novelist does not tell us that a given character is good or bad (at least not since the passing of the Dickens tradition): he shows us the character in action and then, watching him, we know. Poetry, too, has fictional obligations: even when the characters are ideas and metaphors rather than people, they must be *characterized in action*. A poem does not *talk about* ideas; it *enacts* them. The force of the poem's performance, in fact, is precisely to act out (and thereby to make us act out empathically, that is, to *feel out*, that is, *to identify with*) the speaker and why he stopped. The man is the principal actor in this little "drama of why" and in scene one he is the only character, though as noted, he is somehow related to the absent owner.

End second parenthesis.   15

In scene two (stanzas two and three) a *foil* is introduced. In fiction and   16
drama, a foil is a character who "plays against" a more important character. By presenting a different point of view or an opposed set of motives, the foil moves the more important character to react in ways that might not have found expression without such opposition. The more important character is thus more fully revealed—to the reader and to himself. The foil here is the horse.

The horse forces the question. Why did the man stop? Until it occurs to him   17
that his "little horse must think it queer" he had not asked himself for reasons. He had simply stopped. But the man finds himself faced with the question he imagines the horse to be asking: what *is* there to stop for out there in the cold,

away from bin and stall (house and village and mankind?) and all that any self-respecting beast could value on such a night? In sensing that other view, the man is forced to examine his own more deeply.

In stanza two the question arises only as a feeling within the man. In stanza   18
three, however (still scene two), the horse acts. He gives his harness bells a shake. "What's wrong?" he seems to say. "What are we waiting for?"

By now, obviously, the horse—without losing its identity as horse—has also   19
become a symbol. A symbol is something that stands for something else. Whatever that something else may be, it certainly begins as that order of life that does not understand why a man stops in the wintry middle of nowhere to watch the snow come down. (Can one fail to sense by now that the dark and the snowfall symbolize a death-wish, however momentary, *i.e.*, that hunger for final rest and surrender that a man may feel, but not a beast?)

So by the end of scene two the performance has given dramatic force to   20
three elements that work upon the man. There is his relation to the world of the owner. There is his relation to the brute world of the horse. And there is that third presence of the unownable world, the movement of the all-engulfing snow across all the orders of life, the man's, the owner's, and the horse's—with the difference that the man knows of that second dark-within-the-dark of which the horse cannot, and the owner will not, know.

The man ends scene two with all these forces working upon him simulta-   21
neously. He feels himself moved to a decision. And he feels a last call from the darkness: "the sweep / Of easy wind and downy flake." It would be so easy and so downy to go into the woods and let himself be covered over.

But scene three (stanza four) produces a fourth force. This fourth force can   22
be given many names. It is certainly better, in fact, to give it many names than to attempt to limit it to one. It is social obligation, or personal commitment, or duty, or just the realization that a man cannot indulge a mood forever. All of these and more. But, finally, he has a simple decision to make. He may go into the woods and let the darkness and the snow swallow him from the world of beast and man. Or he must move on. And unless he is going to stop here forever, it is time to remember that he has a long way to go and that he had best be getting there. (So there is something to be said for the horse, too.)

Then and only then, his question driven more and more deeply into himself   23
by these cross-forces, does the man venture a comment on what attracted him "The woods are lovely, dark and deep." His mood lingers over the thought of that lovely dark-and-deep (as do the very syllables in which he phrases the thought), but the final decision is to put off the mood and move on. He has his man's way to go and his man's obligations to tend to before he can yield. He has miles to go before his sleep. He repeats that thought and the performance ends.

But why the repetition? The first time Frost says "And miles to go before I   24
sleep," there can be little doubt that the primary meaning is: "I have a long way to go before I get to bed tonight." The second time he says it, however, "miles to go" and "sleep" are suddenly transformed into symbols. What are those "something-elses" the symbols stand for? Hundreds of people have tried to ask

Mr. Frost that question and he has always turned it away. He has turned it away *because he cannot answer it.* He could answer some part of it. But some part is not enough.

For a symbol is like a rock dropped into a pool: it sends out ripples in all directions, and the ripples are in motion. Who can say where the last ripple disappears? One may have a sense that he knows the approximate center point of the ripples, the point at which the stone struck the water. Yet even then he has trouble marking it surely. How does one make a mark on water? Oh very well—the center point of that second "miles to go" is probably approximately in the neighborhood of being close to meaning, perhaps, "the road of life"; and the second "before I sleep" is maybe that close to meaning "before I take my final rest," the rest in darkness that seemed so temptingly dark-and-deep for the moment of the mood. But the ripples continue to move and the light to change on the water, and the longer one watches the more changes he sees. Such shifting-and-being-at-the-same-instant is of the very sparkle and life of poetry. One experiences it as one experiences life, for everytime he looks at an experience he sees something new, and he sees it change as he watches it. And that sense of continuity in fluidity is one of the primary kinds of knowledge, one of man's basic ways of knowing, and one that only the arts can teach, poetry foremost among them.

Frost himself certainly did not ask what that repeated last line meant. It came to him and he received it. He "felt right" about it. And what he "felt right" about was in no sense a "meaning" that, say, an essay could apprehend, but an act of experience that could be fully presented only by the dramatic enactment of forces which is the performance of the poem.

Now look at the poem in another way. Did Frost know what he was going to do when he began? Considering the poem simply as an act of skill, as a piece of juggling, one cannot fail to respond to the magnificent turn at the end where, with one flip, seven of the simplest words in the language suddenly dazzle full of never-ending waves of thought and feeling. Or, more precisely, of felt-thought. Certainly an equivalent stunt by a juggler—could there be an equivalent—would bring the house down. Was it to cap his performance with that grand stunt that Frost wrote the poem?

Far from it. The obvious fact is that *Frost could not have known he was going to write those lines until he wrote them.* Then a second fact must be registered: *he wrote them because, for the fun of it, he had got himself into trouble.*

Frost, like every good poet, began by playing a game with himself. The most usual way of writing a four line stanza with four feet to the line is to rhyme the third line with the first, and the fourth line with the second. Even that much rhyme is so difficult in English that many poets and almost all of the anonymous ballad makers do not bother to rhyme the first and third lines at all, settling for two rhymes in four lines as good enough. For English is a rhyme-poor language. In Italian and in French, for example, so many words end with the same sounds that rhyming is relatively easy—so easy that many modern French and Italian poets do not bother to rhyme at all. English, being a more agglomerate language, has far more final sounds, hence fewer of them rhyme. When an Italian poet writes a line ending with "vita" (life) he has literally hundreds of rhyme choices available. When an English poet writes "life" at the end of a line he can summon "strife, wife, knife, fife, rife," and then he is in trouble. Now "life-strife" and "life-rife" and "life-wife" seem to offer a combination of possible ideas that can be related by more than just the rhyme. Inevitably, therefore, the poets have had to work and rework these combinations until the sparkle has gone out of them. The reader is normally tired of such rhyme-led associations. When he encounters "life-strife" he is certainly entitled to suspect that the poet did not really want to say "strife"—that had there been in English such a word as, say, "hife," meaning "infinite peace and harmony," the poet would as gladly have used that word instead of "strife." Thus, the reader feels that the writing is haphazard, that the rhyme is making the poet say things he does not really feel, and which, therefore, the reader does not feel except as boredom. One likes to see the rhymes fall into place, but he must end with the belief that it is the poet who is deciding what is said and not the rhyme scheme that is forcing the saying.

So rhyme is a kind of game, and an especially difficult one in English. As in every game, the fun of the rhyme is to set one's difficulties high and then to meet them skillfully. As Frost himself once defined freedom, it consists of "moving easy in harness."   30

In "Stopping by Woods on a Snowy Evening" Frost took a long chance. He decided to rhyme not two lines in each stanza, but three. Not even Frost could have sustained that much rhyme in a long poem (as Dante, for example, with the advantage of writing in Italian, sustained triple rhyme for thousands of lines in "The Divine Comedy"). Frost would have known instantly, therefore, when he took the original chance, that he was going to write a short poem. He would have had that much foretaste of it.   31

So the first stanza emerged rhymed a-a-b-a. And with the sure sense that this was to be a short poem, Frost decided to take an additional chance and to redouble: in English three rhymes in four lines is more than enough; there is no need to rhyme the fourth line. For the fun of it, however, Frost set himself to pick up that loose rhyme and to weave it into the pattern, thereby accepting the all but impossible burden of quadruple rhyme.   32

The miracle is that it worked. Despite the enormous freight of rhyme, the poem not only came out as a neat pattern, but managed to do so with no sense of strain. Every word and every rhyme falls into place as naturally and as inevitably as if there were no rhyme restricting the poet's choices.   33

That ease-in-difficulty is certainly inseparable from the success of the poem's performance. One watches the skill-man juggle three balls, then four, then five, and every addition makes the trick more wonderful. But unless he makes the hard trick seem as easy as an easy trick, then all is lost.   34

The real point, however, is not only that Frost took on a hard rhyme-trick and made it seem easy. It is rather as if the juggler, carried away, had tossed up one more ball than he could really handle, and then amazed himself by actually handling it. So with the real triumph of this poem. Frost could not have known   35 what a stunning effect his repetition of the last line was going to produce. He could not even know he was going to repeat the line. He simply found himself up against a difficulty he almost certainly had not forseen and he had to improvise to meet it. For in picking up the rhyme from the third line of stanza one and carrying it over into stanza two, he had created an endless chain-link form within which each stanza left a hook sticking out for the next stanza to hang on. So by stanza four, feeling the poem rounding to its end, Frost had to do something about that extra rhyme.

He might have tucked it back into a third line rhyming with the *know-* 36 *though-snow* of stanza one. He could thus have rounded the poem out to the mathematical symmetry of using each rhyme four times. But though such a device might be defensible in theory, a rhyme repeated after eleven lines is so far from its original rhyme sound that its feeling as rhyme must certainly be lost. And what good is theory if the reader is not moved by the writing?

It must have been in some such quandary that the final repetition suggested 37 itself—a suggestion born of the very difficulties the poet had let himself in for. So there is that point beyond mere ease in handling a hard thing, the point at which the very difficulty offers the poet the opportunity to do better than he knew he could. What, aside from having that happen to oneself, could be more self-delighting than to participate in its happening by one's reader-identification with the poem?

And by now a further point will have suggested itself: that the human-insight 38 of the poem and the technicalities of its poetic artifice are inseparable. Each feeds the other. That interplay is the poem's meaning, a matter not of WHAT DOES IT MEAN, for no one can ever say entirely what a good poem means, but of HOW DOES IT MEAN, a process one can come much closer to discussing.

There is a necessary epilogue. Mr. Frost has often discussed this poem on 39 the platform, or more usually in the course of a long-evening-after a talk. Time and again I have heard him say that he just wrote it off, that it just came to him, and that he set it down as it came.

Once at Bread Loaf, however, I heard him add one very essential piece to 40 the discussion of how it "just came." One night, he said, he had sat down after supper to work at a long piece of blank verse. The piece never worked out, but Mr. Frost found himself so absorbed in it that, when next he looked up, dawn was at his window. He rose, crossed to the window, stood looking out for a few minutes, and *then* it was that "Stopping by Woods" suddenly "just came," so that all he had to do was cross the room and write it down.

Robert Frost is the sort of artist who hides his traces. I know of no Frost 41 worksheets anywhere. If someone has raided his wastebasket in secret, it is possible that such worksheets exist somewhere, but Frost would not willingly allow anything but the finished product to leave him. Almost certainly, therefore, no one will ever know what was in that piece of unsuccessful blank verse he had been working at with such concentration, but I for one would stake my life that could that worksheet be uncovered, it would be found to contain the germinal stuff of "Stopping by Woods"; that what was a-simmer in him all night without finding its proper form, suddenly, when he let his still-occupied mind look away, came at him from a different direction, offered itself in a different form, and that finding that form exactly right the impulse proceeded to marry itself to the new shape in one of the most miraculous performances of English lyricism.

And that, too—whether or not one can accept so hypothetical a discussion—is part of HOW the poem means. It means that marriage to the perfect form, the poem's shapen declaration of itself, its moment's monument fixed beyond all possibility of change. And thus, finally, in every truly good poem, "How does it mean?" must always be answered "Triumphantly." Whatever the poem "is about," *how* it means is always how Genesis means: the word become a form, and the form become a thing, and—when the becoming is true—the thing become a part of the knowledge and experience of the race forever.

Letters to the Editor of the *Saturday Review*

Finding Each Other

The article "Robert Frost: The Way to the Poem," by John Ciardi (*SR* Apr. 12), is one of the most excellent pieces of explication I have had an opportunity to read. It is simple, thorough, and clear, and at the same time provocative of response to the deepest and most far-reaching values in poetry. The essay, just as it is, would be a boon to many students and teachers who together are seeking to find each other as they attend to a poem.

Joseph H. Jenkins.

Petersburg, Va.

Poking And Picking

Robert Frost's miracle, "Stopping by Woods on a Snowy Evening," comprises four stanzas, sixteen lines, 108 words. John Ciardi's analysis of it runs to ten full columns. This flushes an old question: Does such probing, poking, and picking really lead "The Way to the Poem"?

William L. Hassett.

Des Moines, Ia.

Critical Absurdity

I have just discovered, by way of John Ciardi's analysis of Robert Frost's poem, "Stopping by Woods on a Snowy Evening," that this charmingly simple, eloquent, lyrical little poem, long one of my favorites, is supposedly fraught with duplicity of meaning and symbolism, including a disguised death-wish, and that it is not at all about what it seems to be about.

This is really a new high in critical absurdity. If the presentation of this leading, cover-featured article were not so obviously straight-faced, I would have considered this a nice parody of much present-day "criticism." Who is Mr. Ciardi trying to kid? Or is he himself merely kidded? I am sure Mr. Frost must be highly amused or shaking his head in amazement at the awesome proportions his innocent poetic images have assumed ("By now, obviously, the horse has also become a symbol").

Mrs. Beverly Travers.

New Orleans, La.

Enhance A Rainbow

It seems to us that when a poet uses the skill Frost employs in creating a mood, sharing an experience, one should accept it as given, without further analysis. One does not enhance a rainbow by subjecting it to a spectrometric analysis.

John G. Gosselink.

Hartford City, Ind.

No Death-Wish

I was a little shocked when I read Ciardi's interpretation of the dark and snow-fall in Frost's "Stopping by Woods on a Snowy Evening" as a death-wish. I suppose every person must interpret poems like this in terms of his own experience. To me, it seems to say that there is a certain deep satisfaction in stopping to lose oneself in the contemplation of beauty. The experience itself is significant in that it brings the individual into a sense of relationship to basic reality. But one cannot escape too long into these subjective experiences. There is work to do; obligations must be met; one cannot spend his whole life escaping from these practical realities.

J. Josephine Leamer.

Gardiner, Mont.

Superfluous Info

I am used to most magazines pointing out the obvious, but when *SR* tells me that a symbol stands for something else (John Ciardi's article on Robert Frost), I am really hurt. Chances are, if I thought a symbol was something other than something else, I wouldn't be reading *SR* or any other magazine.

Marjorie Duryic.

Everett, Wash.

Simple Narrative

Why Mr. Ciardi had to pick such, as he himself states, "a simple narrative" to expound upon I'll never know. If one thought of poetry as Mr. C does, the joy of just reading beautiful poetry would be gone completely. One would begin to spend all his time searching for symbols and such.

H. Clay Barnard.

Sausalito, Calif.

Penetrating Analysis

I have just finished reading John Ciardi's penetrating analysis of Robert Frost's familiar lyric. This is distinguished service in the cause of criticism. More articles like this and we *will* develop a poetry-reading America.

Sister Mary Denise, RSM.

Dallas, Pa.

Its Essence

Through the years I've read "Stopping by Woods on a Snowy Evening" many times and felt that with each reading I had extracted its meaning to the point where I felt certain that there was no more it could tell me. John Ciardi has exposed new and deeper meanings to me and, as an excellent teacher, has dissected and made clear its very essence.

Lloyd Rodnick.

Detroit, Mich.

Heavy Limbs

Ciardi has some very interesting ideas. But wouldn't it be better to develop them in a separate essay? It seems to me that the literary woods is too full of heavy limbs falling upon little delicate branches.

Gary Thornburg.

Losantville, Ind.

No Discords

Ciardi's calm, cleanly developed, and illuminating article on Frost's poem surely is a savory example of what his readers have clamored for all these months. In this essay one finds all of Mr. Ciardi's inspiring adherence to principles and none of those bubonic symptoms which many of his readers have denounced. Personally, I am pleased to find also fewer coinings of discordant and sometimes hideous compounds, an indulgence that often spoils the point of what Mr. Ciardi has to say.

Earl Clendenon.

Chicago, Ill.

Frost's Analyst?

The business of equating this poem with all the current philosophical symbols that are in Ciardi's mind is, of course, Ciardi's privilege. But why should he speak as Frost's analyst?

Harvey Parker.

Vista, Calif.

Pedantic Reparation

Ciardi very pedantically makes complete reparation for last year's storm-provoking criticism of Anne Morrow Lindbergh's delicate and deep poetry. Many college and high-school teachers will be able to use such an exhaustive analysis in the classroom.

Joseph A. McNulty.

Philadelphia, Pa.

Self-Anointed Thor

After reading Ciardi's uncomprehending, clinical, anti-poetical "appreciation" of my friend Robert Frost's great lyric, I was so moved, in sundry unprintable ways, that I thought to write Robert: the essay reminded me throughout of a humorless pathologist slicing away with his microtome at a biopsy.

However, what I wanted to say "just came to me" and I simply "wrote it down"—on a Remington Noiseless which I use for all composition, including poetry. It took twenty minutes, from gag to madrigal—some twenty more to add an effort to refute Mr. Ciardi's contention that English is a knobby tongue to rhyme—and I forward the result to you, in the hope that you might print it as one (largely commercial) writer's testament that, to some of us, things do come, we do just write them down, and we know enough English to find little trouble in double-rhyming a ballad, even in what Mr. Ciardi regards as the difficult scheme of Frost's poem. I also felt J.C. should learn that "know," "here," "lake," and "sweep" hardly baffle an idle versifier—and Robert's variation of the ballad form is not beyond the reach even of typewriter poets like me.

Mr. Ciardi, neo-master of critique, finds it easy to demolish the avowedly amateur verses of Anne Lindbergh with his little mechanic's hammer; but he did not realize that when he undertook to acclaim a true poet his implement might bounce from the granite with predictable damage to the self-anointed Thor. Ciardi must be all Ph.D., and of the new academic sub-species.

Philip Wylie.

Miami, Fla.

Stopping to Write a Friend on a Thick Night

In this week's *Saturday Review*
The first bit, Robert, deals with you.
At least, its author, John Ciardi
Tears a poem of yours in two

And shreds the halves. His toy lombard, he
Loads with treacle praise, and lardy,
Salutes your metaphor and tmesis
And fires again to call you hardy.

Art, to him, is just its pieces,
The obvious, his noblest thesis—
Who even calls down holocaust
On his own tongue—the mangling Jesus!

Your blanket snow's thus double-crossed
By one who should be blanket-tossed
And he has miles to go to Frost
And years to learn it's Frost he lost.

JOHN CIARDI
Letter to Letter-Writers

I have never known a magazine with *SR's* knack for calling forth Letters to   43
the Editor. No one writing for *SR* need suffer from a sense that his ideas have
disappeared into the void: he will hear from the readers. I have been hearing of
late, and the charge this time, made by some readers, is that I have despoiled a
great poem in my analysis of Robert Frost's "Stopping By Woods on a Snowy
Evening" (*SR* Apr. 12).

The Frost article was self-declaredly an effort at close analysis. I believe the   44
poem to be much deeper than its surfaces, and I set out to ask what sort of
human behavior it is that presents a surface of such simplicity while stirring
such depths of multiple responses. It may be that I analyzed badly, but the
more general charge seems to be that all analysis is inimical to poetry, and that
general charge is certainly worth a closer look.

A number of readers seem to have been offended by the fact that the analysis   45
was longer than the poem, which, as one reader put it, "comprises four stanzas,
sixteen lines, 108 words" (rather technical analysis, that sort of word-counting),
whereas my article ran to "ten full columns."

A first clear assumption in this reader's mind is the assertion that an analysis   46
must not be longer than what it analyzes. I can see no way of defending that
assumption. If there is to be any analysis at all, it is in the nature of things that
the analysis be longer than the poem or the passage it analyzes. One hundred
and eight words will hardly do simply to describe the stanzaic form and rhyme
scheme of the poem, without any consideration of the nature of the rhyme
problem. Analysis and the poem are simply enough tortoise and hare. The
difference from the fable is that the poetic hare does not lie down and sleep.
The unfabled tortoise, however, may still hope to crawl after and, in some sense,
to mark the way the hare went.

The second assumption is that analysis obscures ("does not lead the way   47
to") a poem, and amounts in fact to mere "probing, poking, and picking." The
charge as made is not specifically against my article but against all analysis.
The question may, therefore, be simply located: should poetry be talked about
at all?

A number of readers clearly take the position that it must not be. "One   48
should accept it (the experience of the poem) as given, without further analysis," asserts one reader. "One does not enhance a rainbow by subjecting it to
spectrometric analysis." An unwavering position and an interesting figure of
speech. I am drawn to that rainbow and fascinated by this use of the word
"enhance." By "spectrometric analysis" I take the gentleman to mean "investigating the physical nature of" but said, of course, with an overtone of disdain at
the idea of seeing "beauty" meaningfully through any "instrument." That disdain aside, however, one may certainly ask why detailed knowledge of the
physical phenomena that produce a rainbow should "unenhance" the rainbow's
emotional value. Is speculation into the nature of things to be taken as a destruction of nature?

Two years ago, looking down on Rome from the Gianiculum, I saw two   49
complete rainbows in the sky at once, not just pieces of rainbows but complete
arcs with both ends of each arc visible at once in a great bridge above the city.
And in what way did it hurt me as part of my instant delight to register some
sense of the angle at which the sun had to hit the atmosphere in order to
produce such a prodigy? I must insist on remaining among those who are willing
to learn about rainbows.

Such disdain seems to be shared by many of our readers. Mr. Philip Wylie, a   50
man described to me as an author, filed the strongest, or at least the longest, of
the recent objections. My "implement," as he sees it, bounces "from the granite
(of the poem) with predictable damage to the self-anointed Thor. Ciardi must
be all Ph.D., and of the new academic sub-species."

Not exactly factual, since I do not own a Ph.D., but fair enough: giving lumps   51
is a time-honored literary game and anyone with a typewriter may play. Mr.
Wylie's indignation is largely against my way of dealing with Mr. Frost's poem,
and that is a charge I must waive—he may be right, he may be wrong; no score.
One part of his charge, however, is a more general anger at the idea that anyone
should go into a detailed analysis of the rhyme scheme of a poem that "just
came" to the poet. Once again the basic charge is that poetry is damaged by
analysis. One should "just let it come."

Many others have joined Mr. Wylie in his defense of the untouchable-   52
spontaneous. "Get your big clumsy feet off that miracle," says one reader I find
myself especially drawn to. "What good do you think you do," writes another,
"when you tear apart a thing as lovely as Mr. Frost's poem?" Another: "A
dissecting kit belongs in the laboratory, not the library." And still another: "If
one thought of poetry as Mr. C does, the joy of just reading beautiful poetry
would be gone completely. One would begin to spend all his time dealing with
symbols and such."

I must, parenthetically, reject some of the terms of that last letter. "Begin to   53
spend *all* his time," is the writer's idea: that "all" is no part of mine. I shall pass
the sneer contained in the phrase "symbols and such." But I cannot accept the
responsibility for defending myself when misquoted. One reader, for example,
accuses me of stating that a poem "is not at all about what it seems to be about."
I can only reply that those are his terms, not mine, and that I have no thought
of defending them.

It is that "all" in the first quotation, however, that locates the central misun-   54
derstanding. "Once one begins to analyze," the assumption runs, "he begins to
spend all of his time 'merely analyzing' and the analysis not only takes the place
of the poem but leads to the poem's destruction."

Were there no misconception involved, this reader's anger would certainly   55
be justified. What is misconceived is the idea that the analysis is intended to
take the place of the poem. Far from it. One takes a poem apart only in order to
put it back together again with greater understanding. The poem itself is the
thing. A good poem is a hanging gull on a day of perfect winds. We sit below
and watch it own the air it rides: a miracle from nature. There it hangs on
infallible wings. But suppose one is interested in the theory of flight (as the gull

itself, to be sure, need not be) and suppose one notices that the gull's wings can perform miracles in the air because they have a particular curvature and a particular sort of leading and trailing edge. And suppose he further notices that the gull's tail feathers have a great deal to do with that seemingly effortless mastery. Does that man cease to see the gull? Does he see nothing but diagrams of airflow and lift to the total damnation of all gulls? Or does he see the gull not only as the miracle of a perfect thing, but as the perfect thing in the enmarveling system of what encloses it?

The point involves the whole nature of perception. Do we "see" with our eyes? I must believe that it is the mind that sees, and that the eyes are only the windows we see through. We see with the patterns of what we know. Let any layman look into a tide-pool and list what he sees there. Then let him call an imaginative biologist and ask the biologist what he sees. The layman will have seen things, but the biologist will see systems, and the things in place in those systems.   56

He will also see many things simultaneously. A basic necessity to all poetic communication is what I have called *fluency* in an earlier article in these pages. Fluency is the ability to receive more than one meaning, impression, stimulus— call it what you please—at the same time. Analysis must always fumble and be long-winded because it must consider those multiple impressions doggedly and one by one. If such itemized dealing accurately locates true elements of the poem, the itemization will have served its purpose, and that purpose must certainly be defended as one that has summoned some of the best minds of all ages. What analysis does, though laboriously, is to establish patterns one may see with.   57

But there then remains the reader's work. It is up to him, guided by the analysis, to read the poem with the fluency it requires, and which analysis does not hope to achieve. Certainly, whatever is said here, poetry will be talked about and must be talked about. The one point of such talk, however, is to lead the reader more richly to the threshold of the poem. Over that threshold he must take himself. And I, for one, must suspect that if he refuses to carry anything as cumbersome as detail across that threshold, he will never furnish the house of his own mind.   58

QUESTIONS FOR MEANING

1. Explain the distinction that Ciardi makes between *how* a poem means and *what* a poem means. Paraphrase paragraphs 2, 38, and 42.
2. In paragraphs 3, 4, and 5, what does Ciardi mean by "duplicity"?
3. What is the topic statement of paragraph 11? Is this the premise that underlines Ciardi's approach to poetry?
4. According to Ciardi, what two principles are essential to writing good poetry?
5. Explain what Ciardi means by "foil" in paragraph 16.
6. Why does Ciardi believe that the horse in the poem is a symbol? Where does he define what he means by "symbol"?

7. What are the four dramatic forces that Ciardi identifies in "Stopping by Woods on a Snowy Evening"?
8. How does Ciardi explain Frost's decision to end his poem by repeating, "And miles to go before I sleep"? What technical problems did this decision solve for Frost, and why does Ciardi consider it a brilliant solution? What is the significance of the repetition?
9. Summarize the objections to Ciardi's essay that appear in the letters it inspired. What bothered people the most? Which is the best letter and which the silliest?
10. In responding to his critics, what did Ciardi identify as the major issue in the controversy over his interpretation of the poem? What is his response to this question? Had he anticipated it at any point in his original essay?
11. Explain what Ciardi means by "fluency" in the last two paragraphs of his "Letter to Letter Writers."
12. Vocabulary: epilogue (6), integrity (11), brashly (12), obliterates (12), spate (14), emphatically (14), haphazard (29), quandary (37), artifice (38), germinal (41), lyricism (41), despoiled (43), inimical (44), disdain (48), prodigy (49), indignation (51), and waive (51).

QUESTIONS ABOUT STRATEGY

1. What is the function of paragraph 1? How does it serve to prepare readers for the essay that follows?
2. Why are paragraphs 9 through 15 parenthetical to the primary purpose of Ciardi's essay?
3. Does Ciardi make any claims that he fails to support?
4. How useful is the analogy in paragraph 25? Did it help you to understand the nature of poetry?
5. Several of his critics complained that Ciardi's essay is too long. Do you agree? If so, what would you cut? How does Ciardi himself respond to this charge?
6. Which of Ciardi's critics makes an ad hominem argument? In responding to criticism, does Ciardi ever resort to sarcasm?
7. How effectively has Ciardi answered his critics? If you were amused by any of the letters to the editor, was Ciardi's rebuttal strong enough to win back your confidence in him?

HERBERT R. COURSEN, JR.

The Ghost of Christmas Past: "Stopping by Woods on a Snowy Evening"

Herbert R. Coursen, Jr. (b. 1932), graduated from Amherst College in 1954 and received his Ph.D. from the University of Connecticut in 1965. Since 1964 he has taught English at Bowdoin College, where he is now Professor of Creative Writing and Shakespeare. A former fighter pilot in the U.S. Air Force, Coursen has published in periodicals as diverse as Studies in Philology *and* Sports Illustrated. *He is the author of several works of criticism, including* The Rarer Action: Hamlet's Mousetrap *(1969),* Shaping the Self: Style and Technique in the Narrative *(1975), and* Christian Ritual and the World of Shakespeare *(1976). He has also written a novel,* After the War *(1980), and many volumes of poetry, including* Storm in April *(1973),* Fears in the Night *(1976), and* Walking Away *(1977). The following essay on Frost was first published in December 1962. As you read it, you should be prepared to smile.*

Much ink has spilled on many pages in exegesis of this little poem. Actually, critical jottings have only obscured what has lain beneath critical noses all these years. To say that the poem means merely that a man stops one night to observe a snowfall, or that the poem contrasts the mundane desire for creature comfort with the sweep of aesthetic appreciation, or that it renders worldly responsibilities paramount, or that it reveals the speaker's latent death-wish is to miss the point rather badly. Lacking has been that mind simple enough to see what is *really* there. 1

The first line ("Whose woods these are I think I know") shows that the speaker has paused aside a woods of whose ownership he is fairly sure. So much for paraphrase. Uncertainty vanishes with the next two lines ("His house is in the village though; / He will not see me stopping here"). The speaker knows (a) where the owner's home is located, and (b) that the owner won't be out at the woods tonight. Two questions arise immediately: (a) how does the speaker know? and (b) how does the speaker know? As will be made manifest, only one answer exists to each question. 2

The subsequent two quatrains force more questions to pop up. On auditing the first two lines of the second quatrain ("My little horse must think it queer / To stop without a farmhouse near"), we must ask, "Why does the little 'horse' think oddly of the proceedings?" We must ask also if this *is*, as the speaker claims, the "darkest evening of the year." The calendar date of this occurrence (or lack of occurrence) by an unspecified patch of trees is essential to an apprehension of the poem's true meaning. In the third quatrain, we hear "harness bells" shook. Is the auditory image really an allusion? Then there is the 3 question of the "horse's" identity. Is this really Equus Caballus? This question links itself to that of the *driver's* identity and reiterates the problem of the animal's untoward attitude toward this evidently unscheduled stop.

The questions have piled up unanswered as we reach the final quatrain and   4 approach the ultimate series of poetic mysteries to be resolved. Clearly, all of the questions asked thus far (save possibly the one about the "horse's" identity) are ones which any normal reader, granted the training in close analysis provided by a survey course in English Literature during his sophomore year in college, might ask. After some extraneous imagery ("The woods are lovely, dark and deep" has either been established or is easily adduced from the dramatic situation), the final three lines hold out the key with which the poem's essence may be released. What, to ask two more questions, are the "promises" which the speaker must "keep," and why are the last two lines so redundant about the distance he must cover before he tumbles into bed? Obviously, the obligations are important, the distance great.

Now, if we swing back to one of the previous questions, the poem will begin   5 to unravel. The "darkest evening of the year" in New England is December 21st, a date near that on which the western world celebrates Christmas. It may be that December 21st *is* the date of the poem, or (and with poets this seems more likely) that this is the closest the poet can come to Christmas without giving it all away. Who has "promises to keep" at or near this date, and who must traverse much territory to fulfill these promises? Yes, and who but St. Nick would know the location of *each* home? Only he would know who had "just settled down for a long winter's nap" (the poem's third line—"He will not see me stopping here"—is clearly a veiled allusion) and would not be out inspecting his acreage this night. The unusual phrase "fill up with snow," in the poem's fourth line, is a transfer of Santa's occupational preoccupation to the countryside; he is mulling the filling of countless stockings hung above countless fireplaces by countless careful children. "Harness bells," of course, allude to "Sleighing Song," a popular Christmas tune of the time the poem was written in which the refrain "Jingle Bells! Jingle Bells!" appears; thus again are we put on the Christmas track. The "little horse," like the date, is another attempt at poetic obfuscation. Although the "rein-reindeer" ambiguity has been eliminated from the poem's final version, probably because too obvious, we may speculate that the animal is really a reindeer disguised as a horse by the poet's desire for obscurity, a desire which we must concede has been fulfilled up to now.

The animal is clearly concerned, like the faithful Rudolph—another possible   6 allusion (post facto, hence unconscious)—lest his master fail to complete his mission. Seeing no farmhouse in the second quatrain, but pulling a load of presents, no wonder the little beast wonders! It takes him a full two quatrains to rouse his driver to remember all the empty stockings which hang ahead. And Santa does so reluctantly at that, poor soul, as he ponders the myriad farmhouses and villages which spread between him and his own "winter's nap." The modern St. Nick, lonely and overworked, tosses no "Happy Christmas to all and to all a good night!" into the precipitation. He merely shrugs his shoulders and resignedly plods away.

QUESTIONS FOR MEANING

1. What interpretations of the poem does Coursen reject?
2. On what "evidence" does Coursen base his claim that "Stopping By Woods on a Snowy Evening" is about an overworked Santa Claus? Could anyone take this argument seriously?
3. Identify the allusion in the essay's title. What famous writer wrote about "the Ghost of Christmas Past"?
4. Vocabulary: exegesis (1), mundane (1), aesthetic (1), paramount (1), latent (1), quatrains (3), auditing (3), apprehension (3), auditory (3), reiterates (3), extraneous (4), adduced (4), traverse (5), obfuscation (5), and myriad (6).

QUESTIONS ABOUT STRATEGY

1. At what point in this essay did you first become aware that you were reading a parody? Rereading the essay, can you find any clues that you originally overlooked?
2. How does Coursen's diction contribute to the essay's humor? Can you identify any comic shifts in style?
3. How does Coursen account for discrepancies between his thesis and the language of the poem itself?
4. What is the point of this essay? Is Coursen ridiculing the nature of literary criticism, or is he simply making a good-humored joke? How would you describe his tone?

WILLIAM H. SHURR

Once More to the "Woods": A New Point of Entry into Frost's Most Famous Poem

Born in Evanston, Illinois, William H. Shurr (b. 1932) attended Loyola University in Chicago, where he graduated in 1955, but remained to continue his study of philosophy and theology. He received his Ph.D. from the University of North Carolina at Chapel Hill in 1968, and has taught English at Washington State University and the University of Tennessee. His books include Prose and Poetry of England *(1965) and* The Mystery of Iniquity: Melville as Poet 1857–91 *(1972). His essay on Frost was first published in the* New England Quarterly *in 1974. As you read it, you should be careful to note the way in which Shurr draws upon earlier critics and incorporates their views into his essay while still advancing a thesis of his own.*

"Stopping by Woods on a Snowy Evening" may be the best-known poem ever   1
written by an American. It is surely one of the most commented upon—so much so that readers, critics, and the author himself frequently pleaded for a moratorium to criticism. Only the promise of a truly new "point of entry" can justify still another expenditure of effort, readers' and writer's, on the subject. The argument that follows presents a new interpretation of the poem based on a study of Frost's specific diction and its provenance. The interpretation thus established generates two insights: that Frost, in this poem, is responding negatively to one of the most profound and typical elements in the American experience; and that several other early poems, which Frost was always careful to popularize, can now be linked to a coherent series of statements. This cluster of poems documents a significant moment of change in the evolution of Frost's consciousness and of American consciousness generally.

Commentary on Robert Frost's "Stopping by Woods on a Snowy Evening" is   2
already extensive enough for us to determine something like a *stemma* of critical traditions. The most common interpretation, thematically, has been that the poem is an ethical statement concerning social commitments and obligations to which a man must listen. This obvious view responds to the attention-soliciting repetition with which the poem ends. Louis Untermeyer was one of the earliest to put this interpretation into writing. Reginald Cook, Robert Doyle, D.J. Lepore, and Stanley Poss have continued to accept this reading as adequate.[1]

[1]See Louis Untermeyer's *Come In* (New York, 1943), later amplified and published as *The Pocket Book of Robert Frost's Poems* (New York, 1956), 192. Reginald L. Cook, *The Dimensions of Robert Frost* (New York, 1958). John Robert Doyle, *The Poetry of Robert Frost: An Analysis* (Johannesburg, Witwatersrand, and New York, 1965), 195. D.J. Lepore, "Setting and/or Statement," *English Journal*, LV, 624–626. Stanley Poss, "Low Skies, Some Clearing, Local Frost," *New England Quarterly*, XLI, 438–442.

The second major tradition of interpretation was strikingly stated by John   3
Ciardi in his 1958 article in *The Saturday Review:* "Can one fail to sense by
now that the dark and snowfall symbolize a deathwish, however momentary,
i.e., that hunger for final rest and surrender that a man may feel, but not a
beast?" The insight had been anticipated a decade earlier by Wellek and Warren
in *Theory of Literature*, where *sleep* was seen as a "natural symbol" for *death*.
It continues as a tradition in Leonard Unger and William Van O'Connor, in John
Lynen, Lawrance Thompson, and James Armstrong. Lloyd Dendinger, more
recently, has seen the lure of death operating thematically in the poem, but
proposes the "lure of wilderness" typical in American letters as even more basic
to the poem.[2] One must note however that Frost objected strongly to Ciardi's
thesis: "That's all right, but it's hardly a death poem."[3]

These two interpretations can stand together. Ciardi conflated them in his   4
Saturday Review article by saying that the speaker in the poem is finally
recalled from the attractive power of the death wish by his sense of belonging
to the world of man; the social side of his nature prevails over the psychic lure
of the depths.

A third tradition of interpretation can be discerned in which the "dark   5
woods" stand out as the central symbol to be explicated. Robert Langbaum
used the terminology of theological existentialism when he analyzed the poem
as a "momentary insight into the nonhuman otherness of nature." John Ogilvie
rightly discerned that imagery of the dark woods is pervasive in Frost's early
poetry; for him the woods symbol implied the poet's desire for isolation and his
need to explore the inner self. George Nitchie, surveying the whole range of
Frost's poetry, read this poem as a "yearning back to Eden ... an imagined
withdrawal from the complicated world we all know into a mysterious loveliness
symbolized by woods or darkness."[4] One finds a vagueness in all of these readings, as if they were not based on sufficient evidence to make the readings
definite or persuasive.

Finally, one may mention a fourth tradition of interpreting the poem. This is   6
a blatant allegorization, particularly of the first stanza. I know whose woods
these are; He made them; His house is in the village; the village church. This
makes the poem a religious allegory of a fairly simpleminded type. If done with
some irony it could take its place beside the successful spoof of symbol hunting

[2]John Ciardi, "Robert Frost: The Way to the Poem," *Saturday Review*, 40 (April 12, 1958), 15ff. Rene Wellek and
Austin Warren, *Theory of Literature* (New York, 1949, 1955); the passage relevant to Frost can be found on
194–195 of the first edition and 179 of the second edition. Leonard Unger and William Van O'Connor, *Poems for
Study* (New York, 1953), 600. John F. Lynen, *The Pastoral Art of Robert Frost* (New Haven: Yale Univ. Press,
1960). Lawrance Thompson, *Fire and Ice: The Art and Thought of Robert Frost* (New York, 1961), 27. James
Armstrong, "The 'Death Wish' in 'Stopping by Woods,'" *College English*, XXV, 440–445. Lloyd N. Dendinger, "The
Irrational Appeal of Frost's Dark Deep Woods," *Southern Review*, II, 822–829.

[3]Quoted in Louis Mertins, *Robert Frost: Life and Talks–Walking* (Norman, 1965), 371.

[4]Robert Langbaum, "The New Nature Poetry," *American Scholar*, XXVIII, 323–340. John T. Ogilvie, "From
Woods to Stars: A Pattern of Imagery in Robert Frost's Poetry," *South Atlantic Quarterly*, LVIII, 64–76. George
W. Nitchie, *Human Values in the Poetry of Robert Frost* (Durham, 1960).

generally, Herbert Coursen's "proof" that the speaker is really Santa Claus and that he must get on with the distribution of toys he has promised to all good children.[5] But the allegory is presented seriously. Although I have not seen this tradition in print, each year students have assured me that it was the quasi-official interpretation whenever they came 'round, dutifully, almost ritually, to "doing" the poem again in secondary school English classes. The curious thing about this interpretation is that it bears some similarity to the one which I am about to propose. Allegory is too blunt an instrument to use for analysis here, but there is convincing evidence that the poem is the record of a religious experience; or, since it is more precise to be more general here, say rather that the poem is a record of the mind's encounter with transcendence. Emerson achieved it, and on very nearly the same New England ground. His experience is joyfully recorded in the first chapter of *Nature*. In the first two paragraphs he lays down two conditions for this experience, "solitude" and "reverence"—conditions which are also prominent in the poem by Frost. The experience itself is recorded thus:

> In the woods, is perpetual youth . . . . In the woods, we return to reason and faith. There I feel that nothing can befall me in life—no disgrace, no calamity (leaving me my eyes), which nature cannot repair. Standing on the bare ground,—my head bathed by the blithe air, and uplifted into infinite space,—all mean egotism vanishes. I become a transparent eye-ball. I am nothing. I see all. The currents of the Universal Being circulate through me; I am part or particle of God.

The notion of "transparence" is repeated frequently in the essay, for example in Chapter 6: "If the Reason be stimulated to more earnest vision, outlines and surfaces become transparent, and are no longer seen; causes and spirits are seen through them."[6] In similar woodland circumstances Frost's mind also threatens to become transparent, but his reaction is different. As he later told a questioner, "I thought it was about time I was getting the hell out of there."[7]   7

An analysis of the structure of Frost's poem shows that line 13, "The woods are lovely, dark and deep," is central. From the first line, irrelevancies tug at his attention: the curious question of the *ownership* of these woods (Emerson would have dismissed the question by asserting that nobody owns the landscape), the sudden attention to the trivial subject of the horse's response to a pause in their journey, and finally the abrupt shift to auditory sensation in the analysis of the sound of snow falling. In other words, there is only one assertion in the poem about the subject most under consideration: "The woods are lovely, dark and deep." All of Frost's attention to the actual woods is concentrated here; it is here that the subject itself is finally able to gain ascendancy over the side issues which attempt to snag the mind on its route towards this center. A   8

[5]"The Ghost of Christmas Past: 'Stopping by Woods on a Snowy Evening.'" *College English*, XXII, 236ff.

[6]I quote from the splendid edition of *Nature* by Merton M. Sealts, Jr., and Alfred R. Ferguson (New York, 1969), 8, 24.

[7]Quoted in Mertins, 304.

major effect with which criticism of the poem must concern itself is the tension created by the actual subject of the poem and the speaker's resistance to it for three-fourths of the poem. When the assertion is finally made, its diction assumes supreme importance.

The speculation that this resistance is primarily to the lure of death is finally   9 inadequate. Whatever associations with death the words "sleep" and "dark" may have, they also are appropriate to another area of experience to be set forth in a moment. A more problematical aspect of the death-wish interpretation is the existence in the poem of a concrete symbol of death, a symbol which is not at the center of focus. If death appears in the poem, it is represented by the "frozen lake" mentioned almost casually in line 7. This symbol takes its meaning from well-documented facts in Frost's life. Frost's early obsession with suicide usually took the form of death by drowning, and according to his family the lake of this poem was between the Frost farm and the nearest town of West Derry, a drive which the poet often had to take.[8] This information underlines the statement of the poem that while the speaker may feel caught between the lure of death and *something else* ("Between the woods and frozen lake"), it is the something else represented by the woods that mainly occupies his attention. If *lake* is associated in his mind with *death*, what then, does the more central assertion about the *woods* mean?

The "new point of entry" mentioned in my title, and which brings many of   10 these materials together, involves a climactic phrase from a poem by Henry Vaughan, "The Night." The phrase reads "A deep but dazzling darkness." It will be seen to have immediate correspondences with line 13 of Frost's poem, "The woods are lovely, *dark* and *deep*," prepared for earlier by "The *darkest* evening of the year" in line 8. Vaughan's poem works in the tradition of mystical theology which conceives of the soul's ascent to God as a passage through various well-defined stages of illumination until the final stage is reached in which the brightness is so intense that the seeker's senses and mind are blanked out, as it were by overstimulation. When the soul is wrapped in this dark night or cloud of unknowing, it knows, paradoxically, that it has arrived at the right place, at its spiritual center. The night becomes luminous, a deep but dazzling darkness which is God. One of the traditional sources for this notion of Divine Darkness is Dionysius the Areopagite, in his *De Mystica Theologia* (I, i):

> As for thee, dear Timothy, I counsel that in the earnest exercise of mystical contemplation thou leave the senses and the operations of the intellect and all things that the senses or the intellect can perceive, and all things in this world of nothingness or that world of being: and that, thine understanding being laid to rest, thou ascend (so far as thou mayest) towards union with Him whom neither being nor understanding can contain. For by the unceasing and absolute renunciation of thyself and all things, thou shalt in pureness cast all things aside, and be released from all, and so shalt be led upwards to the Ray of that Divine Darkness which exceedeth all existence.

[8]See Lawrance Thompson, *Robert Frost: The Early Years, 1874–1915* (New York, 1966), 548.

Throughout his poem, Vaughan works with these same paradoxes of darkness and vision and the finding of oneself in the total abandonment of the self. His final stanza reads:

> There is in God (some say)
> A deep, but dazzling darkness; As men here
> Say it is late and dusky, because they
>   See not all clear;
>   O for that night! where I in him
>   Might live invisible and dim.

The stanza sketches two alternative responses possible for one who approaches this kind of night. The practical New Englander (Frost) may say, equivalently, "it is late and dusky," and escape back to the brightly lit interior of home and family. The Anglican mystic (Vaughan) stays with the experience and relishes the slow and dangerous knowledge it provides.

    The question of biography must remain subsidiary to literary analysis, but there is much in Frost's early life to explain his resistance to this kind of experience. His mother, always something of a religious fanatic, was a devoted Swedenborgian during Frost's early boyhood. Among the stories she told the children were those of the Biblical Samuel, Joan of Arc, and Swedenborg himself, all of whom were granted direct auditory communication from the supernatural world. His mother encouraged the sensitive young boy to develop his own gifts of second sight and second hearing. When he actually began hearing the sound of voices from another world, "he almost scared himself out of his wits,"[9] a phrase that corresponds with Frost's own later statement of his desire to get "the hell out of there" when something similar seemed about to occur. 11

    The question remains, of course, whether Frost knew this passage from Vaughan. The answer can be a confident 'yes," merely on the basis of Frost's well-known competence in the documents of his trade. But we can come closer. No fewer than three writers must have thrust Vaughan's lines upon his attention with new freshness, shortly before Frost came to write his own poem. The year before, Herbert J.C. Grierson published his famous anthology *Metaphysical Lyrics and Poems of the Seventeenth Century*.[10] The volume, which included Vaughan's "The Night," was to start a renascence of interest in the Metaphysical Poets. T.S. Eliot, that same year, wrote his essay on the Metaphysical Poets as a review of this book, and published it the first of many times in the London *Times* Literary Supplement (October 20, 1921). Frost was very much aware of what Eliot was doing, as he would be for several years to come. He could hardly have ignored a book of poems that was promising to revise the official history of English letters. But a second book was also available which put Vaughan's poem explicitly in the mystical tradition and in the context of 12

---

[9]Thompson, *Robert Frost*, 36.

[10]The book was published by Oxford University Press in 1921. It is from this edition that I have cited Vaughan's "The Night" above.

"Divine Darkness" literature. This was Evelyn Underhill's *Mysticism*, a sensitively written book full of marvelous quotations, so popular that it went through twelve editions between 1911 and 1930. Miss Underhill's emphasis was on the Anglican mystical tradition, in which Eliot (again) was becoming so totally interested. Miss Underhill cites the final stanza of Vaughan's "The Night" on the same page that she quotes the passage from Dionysius the Areopagite introduced above.

In the absence of actual records, it always seems tendentious to propose 13 "probable" sources for a particular literary work. But the question of sources is not crucial in this instance. A more fertile source of investigation (as in the case of the Freudian criticism which posits a death wish here) is the more general question of *provenance:* analogous areas of human experience where similar diction is employed. The three authors mentioned above provide, then, a possible source for Frost's diction, and a certain analogue to both experience and diction. Frost, in the central statement of this poem, employs the vocabulary characteristic of this same kind of mysticism.

A well-known source of Frost's early thought provides a still richer trove of 14 analogues. This is William James. Frost already knew the writings of the noted psychologist when he sought admission to Harvard as a special student in 1897. James was on leave of absence when Frost was there, but one of his professors used James's shorter *Psychology* as his text. Frost used this text, as well as James's *Talks to Teachers on Psychology*, when he was a teacher at the Plymouth Normal School in 1911–1912.[11] Frost himself said in 1932, "The most valuable teacher I had at Harvard I never had .... He was William James. His books meant a great deal to me."[12]

In James's *The Varieties of Religious Experience* (1902), Frost would have 15 found the same vocabulary of mysticism used by Vaughan, though not the citation from the poet himself. In Lectures XVI and XVII, for example, James quotes from Henry Suso, German mystic of the fourteenth century, on the state of the soul in mystical rapture, "lost in the stillness of the glorious *dazzling obscurity* and of the naked simple unity. It is in this modeless *where* that the highest bliss is to be found." A night-time experience, close to Frost's in "Stopping by Woods," is also quoted: "The perfect stillness of the night was thrilled by a more solemn silence. The darkness held a presence that was all the more felt because it was not seen. I could not any more have doubted that *He* was there than that I was. Indeed, I felt myself to be, if possible, the less real of the two." To select a final citation, among many that relate to the vocabulary of Frost's poem, James quotes St. Teresa of Avila on the mystic's sense of nothingness, the threat of abandonment of one's being. The metaphors of wakefulness and sleep are especially pertinent: "In the orison of union, the soul is fully awake as regards God, but wholly asleep as regards things of this world and in respect of herself. During the short time the union lasts, she is as it were

---

[11]Thompson, *Robert Frost: The Early Years*; see 231–232, 239–241, 372.

[12]Lawrance Thompson, *Robert Frost: The Years of Triumph, 1915–1938* (New York, 1970), 643.

deprived of every feeling, and even if she would, she could not think of any single thing."[13] The provenance of Frost's imagery is, now, quite clear. The words and images do not characterize Freud's descriptions of the death-wish; they are found, however, throughout a large range of literature which attempts to describe a particular kind of mystical experience, an encounter with the Absolute in which man's own sense of selfhood is threatened with annihilation.

This kind of imagery, for this kind of terrifying experience of transcendent being, is deeply rooted in the human mind. In Greek mythology, high in the genealogy of the pre-divine entities, Sleep is the child of Night. One step further back, according to Hesiod's *Theogony*, is the father of Night, Chaos, the formlessness from which everything originates. Both Sleep and Night are mentioned in Frost's poem, as is also, by the implications of my argument, the Father of them all. One must point out, for those who espouse the death-wish interpretation, that Erebus is *another* child of Chaos, the sister of Sleep, and represents in mythological thought a distinctly different approach to the origin of all being. If we can reduce the statements of Frost's speaker here to mythological thought-patterns, they fall clearly into line with what I have been proposing. Frost's repeated line at the end of the poem, "And miles to go before I sleep," emphasizes his preference for other things, other "promises" he has made to himself, before he is ready to face this Night which exposes the sleeper to the infinite abandonment of forms, Chaos. 16

What all of these considerations lead to is the conclusion that "Stopping by Woods" is a decisive poem in the mental development of Robert Frost. It clearly describes the goal of a road not taken. This is the road of the holy man, whose goal is absorption in transcendent being. In determining the parameters of his genius Frost came upon this area, as is clearly shown by the vocabulary of this poem. Where the earlier Transcendentalists found in this experience the goal of their desires, Frost's later American draws the line and retreats. The poem is a statement of resistance to a particular kind of experience which the speaker finds radically uncongenial. Frost is on territory too personally threatening to cultivate as his own field of creative endeavor.[14] 17

Frost has several poems which verge upon the edge of this same emblematical night, where one knows that one will lose himself, and where the mystic trusts he will finally find himself and a total transforming wisdom as well. This cluster of poems has its own dramatic structure. We may sketch it lightly, with some well-known poems, to show the general curve; many more poems could be plotted along the points on this graph. The poems chosen are the ones Frost came back to again and again in his public readings. Several years earlier, in "An Old Man's Winter Night," the subject of the poem is vaguely troubled by a sense of presences in the night. But because of aloneness and feeble old age he is unable to confront them directly: "One aged man—one man—can't keep a 18

---

[13]*The Varieties of Religious Experience* was published in New York by Longmans, Green and Co., 1902; I quote from the edition published in New York by the New American Library of World Literature, 1958, 322, 67, 313.

[14]Eban Bass has recently discerned a grouping of Frost's poems which he calls the "poetry of fear." He finds, though, that the fear remains enigmatic. See *American Literature*, XLIII, 603–615.

house, / A farm, a countryside . . . ." Here is the beginning of the fear that will develop of the formlessness that lies outside of artificially established human boundaries. Another poem from the same volume (*Mountain Interlude*, 1916) confirms Frost's own preferences for the earthly and the particular. The famous "Birches" expresses a conscious choice of one direction over another as proper for human cultivation: "Earth's the right place for love:"[15]

> I'd like to go by climbing a birch-tree,
> And climb black branches up a snow-white trunk
> *Toward* heaven, till the tree could bear no more,
> But dipped its top and set me down again.

In other words, there is an unwillingness to cope with the experience of transcendence expressed several years before the moment in July, 1922, when "Stopping by Woods on a Snowy Evening" was written. A few years later, in *West-Running Brook* (1928), Frost printed "Acquainted with the Night." The speaker is again alone, again it is night. He feels totally isolated in a lifeless city and a loveless universe. A sign of the powerful feeling locked in this poem is the fact that it is held together by a tight terza rima, a form unusual in Frost. Panic, caused by a perception of limitlessness, is very close to the surface. Again, in "Desert Places" (1936), in a setting similar to that of "Stopping by Woods," the speaker has a sense of a universe that is no longer inhabited, whether these be the vast interstellar spaces or his own spaces "so much nearer home." In these poems the reason for his earlier rejection of the transcendent experience is developed: it is as if acceptance would have set him loose to wander in total isolation in the infinite formlessness of the universe. A final note to the explanation of Frost's resistance to the transcendent experience, as he recorded it in "Stopping by Woods," is stated in "Design" (from *A Further Range*, 1936). This is another closely knit poem, a well-designed sonnet more tightly unified by the use of only three rhymes. The "design" or providence which brings the moth and the dimpled spider together on the diseased flower is probably the "design of *darkness* to appall." The negative vastness that tenants the universe probably shapes things malevolently. One who perceived transcendence in this way could hardly be expected to cry, with Henry Vaughan, "O for the night . . . ."[16]

QUESTIONS FOR MEANING

1. How does Shurr justify writing this essay? What are the two new insights into the poem that he claims to offer?

---

[15]A similar reading of "Birches" is offered by Anna K. Juhnke, "Religion in Robert Frost's Poetry: The Play for Self-Possession," *American Literature*, XXXVI, 153–164.

[16]Some other poems of Frost that might be considered as part of this same cluster are "A Passing Glimpse," "Beeches," and "For Once, Then, Something,"—all of which state a choice of a circumscribed area of poetic inquiry in place of a limitless one. "Come In" is also interesting as a definite refusal to enter the dark woods.

2. What are the four traditional approaches to "Stopping by Woods on a Snowy Evening" that Shurr rejects? Why does he find these interpretations to be inadequate?
3. What does Shurr mean in paragraph 6 when he states that "Stopping by Woods on a Snowy Evening" is "a record of the mind's encounter with transcendence"?
4. Who was Ralph Waldo Emerson, and what was his experience in "the woods"?
5. What support does Shurr offer for his claim that Frost must have been familiar with "The Night" by Henry Vaughan?
6. Explain the concept of "Divine Darkness" discussed in paragraphs 10 and 15.
7. Who were the Transcendentalists, alluded to in paragraph 17?
8. In what sense is "Stopping by Woods on a Snowy Evening" a religious poem? According to Shurr, what is it that Frost rejects in this poem? Has he rejected God?
9. Vocabulary: moratorium (1), expenditure (1), provenance (1), *stemma* (2), conflated (4), psychic (4), theological (5), existentialism (5), ascendancy (8), paradoxically (10), subsidiary (11), tendentious (13), analogues (14), pertinent (15), orison (15), espouse (16), uncongenial (17), emblematical (18), terza rima (18), and malevolently (18).

QUESTIONS ABOUT STRATEGY

1. Why does Shurr begin his essay by summarizing earlier interpretations of the poem?
2. How good is Shurr's research? Does he convince you that he has made a thorough study of the poem and the criticism it has inspired?
3. Why is it important for Shurr to link Frost to Emerson and James—and not just to Henry Vaughan?
4. Why does Shurr conclude his argument by comparing "Stopping by Woods on a Snowy Evening" with several other poems by Frost?

N. ARTHUR BLEAU
Robert Frost's Favorite Poem

As the essays in this unit have revealed, literary criticism is often argumentative. Critics often disagree about the meaning of literature, and the greatest controversy is frequently provoked by the most familiar poems and stories. Many critics would argue that a work of art has a life of its own that is independent of the author's intentions. But to know something of the circumstances under which a work is composed can sometimes help us to understand it. In forming your own judgment of "Stopping by Woods on a Snowy Evening," you may want to consider the following postscript: a narrative account of a conversation between Frost and one of his many admirers.

Robert Frost revealed his favorite poem to me. Furthermore, he gave me a glimpse into his personal life that exposed the mettle of the man. I cherish the memory of that conversation, and vividly recall his description of the circumstances leading to the composition of his favorite work. 1

We were in my hometown—Brunswick, Maine. It was the fall of 1947, and Bowdoin College was presenting its annual literary institute for students and the public. Mr. Frost had lectured there the previous season; and being well received, he was invited for a return engagement. 2

I attended the great poet's prior lecture and wasn't about to miss his encore—even though I was quartered 110 miles north at the University of Maine. At the appointed time, I was seated and eagerly awaiting his entrance—armed with a book of his poems and unaware of what was about to occur. 3

He came on strong with a simple eloquence that blended with his stature, bushy white hair, matching eyebrows, and well-seasoned features. His topics ranged from meter to the meticulous selection of a word and its varying interpretations. He then read a few of his poems to accentuate his message. 4

At the conclusion of the presentation, Mr. Frost asked if anyone had questions. I promptly raised my hand. There were three other questioners, and their inquiries were answered before he acknowledged me. I asked, "Mr. Frost, what is your favorite poem?" He quickly replied, "They're all my favorites. It's difficult to single out one over another!" 5

"But, Mr. Frost," I persisted, "surely there must be one or two of your poems which have a special meaning to you—that recall some incident perhaps." He then astonished me by declaring the session concluded; whereupon, he turned to me and said, "Young man, you may come up to the podium if you like." I was there in an instant. 6

We were alone except for one man who was serving as Mr. Frost's host. He remained in the background shadows of the stage. The poet leaned casually against the lectern—beckoning me to come closer. We were side by side leaning on the lectern as he leafed the pages of the book. 7

"You know—in answer to your question—there is one poem which comes readily to mind; and I guess I'd have to call it my favorite," he droned in a 8 pensive manner. "I'd have to say 'Stopping by Woods on a Snowy Evening' is that poem. Do you recall in the lecture I pointed out the importance of the line 'The darkest evening of the year'?" I acknowledged that I did, and he continued his thoughtful recollection of a time many years before. "Well—the darkest evening of the year is on December twenty-second—which is the shortest day of the year—just before Christmas."

I wish I could have recorded the words as he reflectively meted out his story, but this is essentially what he said.   9

The family was living on a farm. It was a bleak time both weatherwise and financially. Times were hard, and Christmas was coming. It wasn't going to be a very good Christmas unless he did something. So—he hitched up the wagon filled with produce from the farm and started the long trek into town.   10

When he finally arrived, there was no market for his goods. Times were hard for everybody. After exhausting every possibility, he finally accepted the fact that there would be no sale. There would be no exchange for him to get a few simple presents for his children's Christmas.   11

As he headed home, evening descended. It had started to snow, and his heart grew heavier with each step of the horse in the gradually increasing accumulation. He had dropped the reins and given the horse its head. It knew the way. The horse was going more slowly as they approached home. It was sensing his despair. There is an unspoken communication between a man and his horse, you know.   12

Around the next bend in the road, near the woods, they would come into view of the house. He knew the family was anxiously awaiting him. How could he face them? What could he possibly say or do to spare them the disappointment he felt?   13

They entered the sweep of the bend. The horse slowed down and then stopped. It knew what he had to do. He had to cry, and he did. I recall the very words he spoke. "I just sat there and bawled like a baby"—until there were no more tears.   14

The horse shook its harness. The bells jingled. They sounded cheerier. He was ready to face his family. It would be a poor Christmas, but Christmas is a time of love. They had an abundance of love, and it would see them through that Christmas and the rest of those hard times. Not a word was spoken, but the horse knew he was ready and resumed the journey homeward.   15

The poem was composed some time later, he related. How much later I do not know, but he confided that these were the circumstances which eventually inspired what he acknowledged to be his favorite poem.   16

I was completely enthralled and, with youthful audacity, asked him to tell me about his next favorite poem. He smiled relaxedly and readily replied, "That would have to be 'Mending Wall.' Good fences do make good neighbors, you know! We always looked forward to getting together and walking the lines— each on his own side replacing the stones the winter frost had tumbled. As we moved along, we'd discuss the things each had experienced during the winter— and also what was ahead of us. It was a sign of spring!"   17

The enchantment was broken at that moment by Mr. Frost's host, who had   18
materialized behind us to remind him of his schedule. He nodded agreement
that it was time to depart, turned to me and with a smile extended his hand. I
grasped it, and returned his firm grip as I expressed my gratitude. He then
strode off to join his host, who had already reached the door at the back of the
stage. I stood there watching him disappear from sight.

I've often wondered why he suddenly changed his mind and decided to   19
answer my initial question by confiding his memoir in such detail. Perhaps no
one had ever asked him; or perhaps I happened to pose it at the opportune
time. Then again—perhaps the story was meant to be related, remembered
and revealed sometime in the future. I don't know, but I'm glad he did—so that
I can share it with you.

A Note by Lesley Frost

For many years I have assumed that my father's explanation to me, given   20
sometime in the forties, I think, of the circumstances round and about his
writing "Stopping by Woods" was the only one he gave (of course, excepting to
my mother), and since he expressed the hope that it need not be repeated,
fearing pity (pity, he said, was the *last* thing he wanted or needed), I have left
it at that. Now, in 1977, I find there was at least one other to whom he vouchsafed the honor of hearing the truth of how it all was that Xmas eve when "the
little horse" (Eunice) slows the sleigh at a point between woods, a hundred
yards or so north of our farm on the Wyndham Road. And since Arthur Bleau's
moving account is so closely, word for word, as I heard it, it would give me
particular reason to hope it might be published. I would like to add my own
remembrance of words used in the telling to me: "A man has as much right as
a woman to a good cry now and again. The snow gave me its shelter; the horse
understood and gave me the time." (Incidentally, my father had a liking for
certain Old English words. *Bawl* was one of them. Instead of "Stop crying," it
was "Oh, come now, quit bawling." Mr. Bleau is right to say my father bawled
like a baby.)

QUESTIONS FOR MEANING

1. Summarize the experience that led Frost to write "Stopping by Woods on
   a Snowy Evening."
2. Of the various critics included in this section, who would be the most likely
   to use Bleau's testimony to reinforce his own interpretation of the poem?
3. Does the biographical information reported in this essay change your own
   perception of the poem?
4. What does this essay reveal about N. Arthur Bleau? What was he like in
   1947? What was he like thirty years later?
5. Vocabulary: mettle (1), accentuate (4), droned (8), pensive (8), meted (9),
   enthralled (17), audacity (17), and opportune (19).

QUESTIONS ABOUT STRATEGY

1. How important is the note by Leslie Frost supporting the substance of Bleau's report? Would you take Bleau seriously without this reinforcement? If so, why? If not, why not?
2. Leslie Frost describes Bleau's essay as "moving." Do you agree? How would you describe the style and pace of this essay? How good is Bleau's writing?
3. What is the function of paragraph 9? Why does it come at this point, after Bleau has already quoted Frost in paragraphs 6 and 8?

SUGGESTIONS FOR WRITING

1. Write an explication of "Stopping by Woods on a Snowy Evening," drawing upon at least three of the essays in this unit.
2. Explicate one of the following poems. Do research if you wish, but make sure your interpretation explains the language of the poem you have chosen and not just the feelings it has inspired within you.

The Night

> Through that pure virgin shrine,
> That sacred veil drawn o'er Thy glorious noon,
> That men might look and live, as glowworms shine,
>   And face the moon,
> 5 Wise Nicodemus saw such light
> As made him know his God by night.
>
>   Most blest believer he!
> Who in that land of darkness and blind eyes
> Thy long-expected healing wings could see,
> 10   When Thou didst rise!
> And, what can never more be done,
> Did at midnight speak with the Sun!
>
>   O who will tell me where
> He found Thee at that dead and silent hour?
> 15 What hallowed solitary ground did bear
>   So rare a flower,
> Within whose sacred leaves did lie
> The fulness of the Deity?
>
>   No mercy-seat of gold,
> 20 No dead and dusty cherub, nor carved stone,
> But His own living works did my Lord hold
>   And lodge alone;
> Where trees and herbs did watch and peep
> And wonder, while the Jews did sleep.

25   Dear night! this world's defeat;
     The stop to busy fools; care's check and curb;
     The day of spirits; my soul's calm retreat
              Which none disturb!
        Christ's progress, and His prayer time;
30   The hours to which high heaven doth chime;

        God's silent, searching flight;
     When my Lord's head is filled with dew, and all
     His locks are wet with the clear drops of night;
              His still, soft call;
35   His knocking time; the soul's dumb watch,
        When spirits their fair kindred catch.

        Were all my loud, evil days
     Calm and unhaunted as is thy dark tent,
     Whose peace but by some angel's wing or voice
40   Is seldom rent,
        Then I in heaven all the long year
        Would keep, and never wander here.

        But living where the sun
     Doth all things wake, and where all mix and tire
45   Themselves and others, I consent and run
              To every mire,
        And by this world's ill-guiding light,
        Err more than I can do by night.

        There is in God, some say,
50   A deep but dazzling darkness, as men here
     Say it is late and dusky, because they
              See not all clear.
        O for that night! where I in Him
        Might live invisible and dim!

                                    Henry Vaughan
                                    1622–1695

A Bird Came Down the Walk

     A Bird came down the Walk—
     He did not know I saw—
     He bit an Angleworm in halves
     And ate the fellow, raw,

5   And then he drank a Dew
     From a convenient Grass—
     And then hopped sidewise to the Wall
     To let a Beetle pass—

He glanced with rapid eyes
10   That hurried all around—
They looked like frightened Beads, I thought—
He stirred his Velvet Head

Like one in danger, Cautious,
I offered him a Crumb
15   And he unrolled his feathers
And rowed him softer home—

Than Oars divide the Ocean,
Too silver for a seam—
Or Butterflies, off Banks of Noon
20   Leap, plashless as they swim.

Emily Dickinson
1830–1886

The Sick Rose

O Rose, thou art sick.
The invisible worm
That flies in the night
In the howling storm

5   Has found out thy bed
Of crimson joy,
And his dark secret love
Does thy life destroy.

William Blake
1757–1827

Dover Beach

The sea is calm tonight.
The tide is full, the moon lies fair
Upon the straits; on the French coast the light
Gleams and is gone; the cliffs of England stand,
5   Glimmering and vast, out in the tranquil bay.
Come to the window, sweet is the night-air!
Only, from the long line of spray
Where the sea meets the moon-blanched land,
Listen! you hear the grating roar
10   Of pebbles which the waves draw back, and fling,
At their return, up the high strand,

Begin, and cease, and then again begin,
With tremulous cadence slow, and bring
The eternal note of sadness in.

15   Sophocles long ago
Heard it on the Aegean, and it brought
Into his mind the turbid ebb and flow
Of human misery; we
Find also in the sound a thought,
20   Hearing it by this distant northern sea.

The Sea of Faith
Was once, too, at the full, and round earth's shore
Lay like the folds of a bright girdle furled.
But now I only hear
25   Its melancholy, long, withdrawing roar,
Retreating, to the breath
Of the night-wind, down the vast edges drear
And naked shingles of the world.

Ah, love, let us be true
30   To one another! for the world, which seems
To lie before us like a land of dreams,
So various, so beautiful, so new,
Hath really neither joy, nor love, nor light,
Nor certitude, nor peace, nor help for pain;
35   And we are here as on a darkling plain
Swept with confused alarms of struggle and flight,
Where ignorant armies clash by night.

Matthew Arnold
1822–1888

Section 9
Some Classic Arguments

PLATO
The Allegory of the Cave

One of the most important thinkers in the history of Western civilization, Plato (c. 428–348 B.C.) grew up in Athens during the difficult years of the Peloponnesian War. He was the student of Socrates, and it is through Plato that Socratic thought has been passed down to us. Socrates is the principal figure in Plato's early dialogues—discussing with the young such questions as "What should men live for?" and "What is the nature of virtue?" Plato devoted his life to answering questions of this sort and teaching others to understand them. In 387 B.C., he founded his Academy, the world's first university, where he taught the future rulers of numerous Greek states. The Academy survived for almost a thousand years, before closing in A.D. 529.

Plato's major works include the Gorgias, Meno, Phaedo, Symposium, Republic, *and* Phaedrus. *In each of these works, Plato insists upon two ideas that are fundamental to his philosophy. He believed that man has an immortal soul existing separately from the body both before birth and after death. Also, he believed that the physical world consists only of appearances; truth consists of ideas that can be discovered and understood only through systematic thought.*

"The Allegory of the Cave" is taken from The Republic, *which is Plato's greatest work. It is written in the form of a dialogue. The speaker is Socrates, and his "audience" is Glaucon, Plato's brother. But the dialogue should be regarded as a literary device, rather than an actual conversation. Its ultimate audience consists of everyone who wants to think seriously about the nature of truth, justice, and wisdom.*

Next, said I, here is a parable to illustrate the degrees in which our nature 1 may be enlightened or unenlightened. Imagine the condition of men living in a sort of cavernous chamber underground, with an entrance open to the light and a long passage all down the cave. Here they have been from childhood, chained by the leg and also by the neck, so that they cannot move and can see only what is in front of them, because the chains will not let them turn their heads. At some distance higher up is the light of a fire burning behind them;

and between the prisoners and the fire is a track with a parapet built along it, like the screen at a puppet-show, which hides the performers while they show their puppets over the top.

I see, said he.   2

Now behind this parapet imagine persons carrying along various artificial   3
objects, including figures of men and animals in wood or stone or other mate-rials, which project above the parapet. Naturally, some of these persons will be talking, others silent.

It is a strange picture, he said, and a strange sort of prisoners.   4

Like ourselves, I replied; for in the first place prisoners so confined would   5
have seen nothing of themselves or of one another, except the shadows thrown by the fire-light on the wall of the Cave facing them, would they?

Not if all their lives they had been prevented from moving their heads.   6

And they would have seen as little of the objects carried past.   7

Of course.   8

Now, if they could talk to one another, would they not suppose that their   9
words referred only to those passing shadows which they saw?

Necessarily.   10

And suppose their prison had an echo from the wall facing them? When one   11
of the people crossing behind them spoke, they could only suppose that the sound came from the shadow passing before their eyes.

No doubt.   12

In every way, then, such prisoners would recognize as reality nothing but   13
the shadows of those artificial objects.

Inevitably.   14

Now consider what would happen if their release from the chains and the   15
healing of their unwisdom should come about in this way. Suppose one of them set free and forced suddenly to stand up, turn his head, and walk with eyes lifted to the light; all these movements would be painful, and he would be too dazzled to make out the objects whose shadows he had been used to see. What do you think he would say, if someone told him that what he had formerly seen was meaningless illusion, but now, being somewhat nearer to reality and turned towards more real objects, he was getting a truer view? Suppose further that he were shown the various objects being carried by and were made to say, in reply to questions, what each of them was. Would he not be perplexed and believe the objects now shown him to be not so real as what he formerly saw?

Yes, not nearly so real.   16

And if he were forced to look at the fire-light itself, would not his eyes ache,   17
so that he would try to escape and turn back to the things which he could see distinctly, convinced that they really were clearer than these other objects now being shown to him?

Yes.   18

And suppose someone were to drag him away forcibly up the steep and   19
rugged ascent and not let him go until he had hauled him out into the sunlight, would he not suffer pain and vexation at such treatment, and, when he had

come out into the light, find his eyes so full of its radiance that he could not see a single one of the things that he was now told were real?

Certainly he would not see them all at once.   20

He would need, then, to grow accustomed before he could see things in that   21
upper world. At first it would be easiest to make out shadows, and then the images of men and things reflected in water, and later on the things themselves. After that, it would be easier to watch the heavenly bodies and the sky itself by night, looking at the light of the moon and stars rather than the Sun and the Sun's light in the day-time.

Yes, surely.   22

Last of all, he would be able to look at the Sun and contemplate its nature,   23
not as it appears when reflected in water or any alien medium, but as it is in itself in its own domain.

No doubt.   24

And now he would begin to draw the conclusion that it is the Sun that   25
produces the seasons and the course of the year and controls everything in the visible world, and moreover is in a way the cause of all that he and his companions used to see.

Clearly he would come at last to that conclusion.   26

Then if he called to mind his fellow prisoners and what passed for wisdom   27
in his former dwelling-place, he would surely think himself happy in the change and be sorry for them. They may have had a practice of honouring and commending one another, with prizes for the man who had the keenest eye for the passing shadows and the best memory for the order in which they followed or accompanied one another, so that he could make a good guess as to which was going to come next. Would our released prisoner be likely to covet those prizes or to envy the men exalted to honour and power in the Cave? Would he not feel like Homer's Achilles, that he would far sooner 'be on earth as a hired servant in the house of a landless man' or endure anything rather than go back to his old beliefs and live in the old way?

Yes, he would prefer any fate to such a life.   28

Now imagine what would happen if he went down again to take his former   29
seat in the Cave. Coming suddenly out of the sunlight, his eyes would be filled with darkness. He might be required once more to deliver his opinion on those shadows, in competition with the prisoners who had never been released, while his eyesight was still dim and unsteady; and it might take some time to become used to the darkness. They would laugh at him and say that he had gone up only to come back with his sight ruined; it was worth no one's while even to attempt the ascent. If they could lay hands on the man who was trying to set them free and lead them up, they would kill him.

Yes, they would.   30

Every feature in this parable, my dear Glaucon, is meant to fit our earlier   31
analysis. The prison dwelling corresponds to the region revealed to us through the sense of sight, and the fire-light within it to the power of the Sun. The ascent to see the things in the upper world you may take as standing for the

upward journey of the soul into the region of the intelligible; then you will be in possession of what I surmise, since that is what you wish to be told. Heaven knows whether it is true; but this, at any rate, is how it appears to me. In the world of knowledge, the last thing to be perceived and only with great difficulty is the essential Form of Goodness. Once it is perceived, the conclusion must follow that, for all things, this is the cause of whatever is right and good; in the visible world it gives birth to light and to the lord of light, while it is itself sovereign in the intelligible world and the parent of intelligence and truth. Without having had a vision of this Form no one can act with wisdom, either in his own life or in matters of state.

So far as I can understand, I share your belief.   32

Then you may also agree that it is no wonder if those who have reached this   33
height are reluctant to manage the affairs of men. Their souls long to spend all their time in that upper world—naturally enough, if here once more our parable holds true. Nor, again, is it at all strange that one who comes from the contemplation of divine things to the miseries of human life should appear awkward and ridiculous when, with eyes still dazed and not yet accustomed to the darkness, he is compelled, in a law-court or elsewhere, to dispute about the shadows of justice or the images that cast those shadows, and to wrangle over the notions of what is right in the minds of men who have never beheld Justice itself.

It is not at all strange.   34

No; a sensible man will remember that the eyes may be confused in two   35
ways—by a change from light to darkness or from darkness to light; and he will recognize that the same thing happens to the soul. When he sees it troubled and unable to discern anything clearly, instead of laughing thoughtlessly, he will ask whether, coming from a brighter existence, its unaccustomed vision is obscured by the darkness, in which case he will think its condition enviable and its life a happy one; or whether, emerging from the depths of ignorance, it is dazzled by excess of light. If so, he will rather feel sorry for it; or, if he were inclined to laugh, that would be less ridiculous than to laugh at the soul which has come down from the light.

That is a fair statement.   36

If this is true, then, we must conclude that education is not what it is said to   37
be by some, who profess to put knowledge into a soul which does not possess it, as if they could put sight into blind eyes. On the contrary, our own account signifies that the soul of every man does possess the power of learning the truth and the organ to see it with; and that, just as one might have to turn the whole body round in order that the eye should see light instead of darkness, so the entire soul must be turned away from this changing world, until its eye can bear to contemplate reality and that supreme splendour which we have called the Good. Hence there may well be an art whose aim would be to effect this very thing, the conversion of the soul, in the readiest way; not to put the power of sight into the soul's eye, which already has it, but to ensure that, instead of looking in the wrong direction, it is turned the way it ought to be.

Yes, it may well be so.   38

It looks, then, as though wisdom were different from those ordinary virtues,   39
as they are called, which are not far removed from bodily qualities, in that they
can be produced by habituation and exercise in a soul which has not possessed
them from the first. Wisdom, it seems, is certainly the virtue of some diviner
faculty, which never loses its power, though its use for good or harm depends
on the direction towards which it is turned. You must have noticed in dishonest
men with a reputation for sagacity the shrewd glance of a narrow intelligence
piercing the objects to which it is directed. There is nothing wrong with their
power of vision, but it has been forced into the service of evil, so that the keener
its sight, the more harm it works.

Quite true.   40

And yet if the growth of a nature like this had been pruned from earliest   41
childhood, cleared of those clinging overgrowths which come of gluttony and
all luxurious pleasure and, like leaden weights charged with affinity to this
mortal world, hang upon the soul, bending its vision downwards; if, freed from
these, the soul were turned round towards true reality, then this same power
in these very men would see the truth as keenly as the objects it is turned to
now.

Yes, very likely.   42

Is it not also likely, or indeed certain after what has been said, that a state   43
can never be properly governed either by the uneducated who know nothing
of truth or by men who are allowed to spend all their days in the pursuit of
culture? The ignorant have no single mark before their eyes at which they must
aim in all the conduct of their own lives and of affairs of state; and the others
will not engage in action if they can help it, dreaming that, while still alive, they
have been translated to the Islands of the Blest.

Quite true.   44

It is for us, then, as founders of a commonwealth, to bring compulsion to   45
bear on the noblest natures. They must be made to climb the ascent to the
vision of Goodness, which we called the highest object of knowledge; and, when
they have looked upon it long enough, they must not be allowed, as they now
are, to remain on the heights, refusing to come down again to the prisoners or
to take any part in their labours and rewards, however much or little these may
be worth.

Shall we not be doing them an injustice, if we force on them a worse life than   46
they might have?

You have forgotten again, my friend, that the law is not concerned to make   47
any one class specially happy, but to ensure the welfare of the commonwealth
as a whole. By persuasion or constraint it will unite the citizens in harmony,
making them share whatever benefits each class can contribute to the common
good; and its purpose in forming men of that spirit was not that each should be
left to go his own way, but that they should be instrumental in binding the
community into one.

True, I had forgotten.   48

You will see, then, Glaucon, that there will be no real injustice in compelling   49
our philosophers to watch over and care for the other citizens. We can fairly
tell them that their compeers in other states may quite reasonably refuse to

collaborate: there they have sprung up, like a self-sown plant, in despite of their country's institutions; no one has fostered their growth, and they cannot be expected to show gratitude for a care they have never received. 'But,' we shall say, 'it is not so with you. We have brought you into existence for your country's sake as well as for your own, to be like leaders and king-bees in a hive; you have been better and more thoroughly educated than those others and hence you are more capable of playing your part both as men of thought and as men of action. You must go down, then, each in his turn, to live with the rest and let your eyes grow accustomed to the darkness. You will then see a thousand times better than those who live there always; you will recognize every image for what it is and know what it represents, because you have seen justice, beauty, and goodness in their reality; and so you and we shall find life in our common-wealth no mere dream, as it is in most existing states, where men live fighting one another about shadows and quarrelling for power, as if that were a great prize; whereas in truth government can be at its best and free from dissension only where the destined rulers are least desirous of holding office.'

Quite true.   50

Then will our pupils refuse to listen and to take their turns at sharing in the   51
work of the community, though they may live together for most of their time in a purer air?

No; it is a fair demand, and they are fair-minded men. No doubt, unlike any   52
ruler of the present day, they will think of holding power as an unavoidable necessity.

Yes, my friend; for the truth is that you can have a well-governed society   53
only if you can discover for your future rulers a better way of life than being in office; then only will power be in the hands of men who are rich, not in gold, but in the wealth that brings happiness, a good and wise life. All goes wrong when, starved for lack of anything good in their own lives, men turn to public affairs hoping to snatch from thence the happiness they hunger for. They set about fighting for power, and this internecine conflict ruins them and their country. The life of true philosophy is the only one that looks down upon offices of state; and access to power must be confined to men who are not in love with it; otherwise rivals will start fighting. So whom else can you compel to undertake the guardianship of the commonwealth, if not those who, besides understand-ing best the principles of government, enjoy a nobler life than the politician's and look for rewards of a different kind?

There is indeed no other choice.   54

QUESTIONS FOR MEANING

1. Describe the cave and the situation of the men who live within it. What must be done before anyone can leave the cave?
2. According to Plato, the men in the cave see only the moving shadows of artificial objects that are paraded before them. What activities do people pursue today that involve watching artificial images move across a screen? If you spent a lifetime watching such images, would you mistake the artifi-cial for the real?

3. Having escaped from the cave, why would anyone want to return to it?
4. In paragraph 29, Plato claims that the men in the cave would kill someone who returned from the upper world in order to teach them the truth. What reason did Plato have for making this claim?
5. What does "The Allegory of the Cave" reveal about the importance of education? Why is education necessary before one can leave the cave? How does Plato perceive the nature of education?
6. What types of people should be excluded from government in an ideal republic? Why would it be necessary to force philosophers to rule, and why does Plato believe that making such men rule against their will is ethically defensible?
7. If philosophers are attuned to a higher "reality" than the men and women they govern, how can they understand the problems of the people they rule?
8. What would Plato think of American politics?
9. Vocabulary: parapet (1), perplexed (15), vexation (19), surmise (31), affinity (41), and collaborate (49).

QUESTIONS ABOUT STRATEGY

1. What assumptions about human nature underlie Plato's allegory? What assumptions does he make about the nature of government? If you were to summarize Plato's argument and put it into deductive form, what would be your premise?
2. How effective is the use of dialogue as a method for developing an argument? Is it hard to follow?
3. What role does Glaucon serve? Why does he usually agree rather than ask difficult questions?
4. What is the function of paragraph 31?

NICCOLÒ MACHIAVELLI
Should Princes Tell the Truth?

Historian, playwright, poet, and political philosopher, Niccolò Machiavelli (1469–1527) lived in Florence during the turbulence of the Italian Renaissance. From 1498 to 1512, he served in the Chancellery of the Florentine Republic and held the position of secretary for the committee in charge of diplomatic relations and military operations. In fulfilling his responsibilities, Machiavelli traveled to France, Germany, and elsewhere in Italy—giving him the opportunity to observe numerous rulers and the strategies they used to maintain and extend their power. When the Florentine Republic collapsed in 1512 and the Medici returned to power, Machiavelli was dismissed from office, tortured, and temporarily exiled. He retired to an estate not far from Florence and devoted himself to writing the books for which he is now remembered: The Prince *(1513),* The Discourses *(1519),* The Art of War *(1519–1520), and the* Florentine History *(1525). Of these works the most famous is* The Prince.*

In writing The Prince, *Machiavelli set out to define the rules of politics as he understood them. His work became a handbook on how to acquire and maintain power. Machiavelli's experience taught him that successful rulers are not troubled by questions of ethics. He observed that it is better to be feared than to be loved. As the following excerpt reveals, he believed that virtues such as honesty are irrelevant to the successful pursuit of power. The amorality of Machiavelli's book continues to disturb many readers, and its shrewd observations on the nature of politics have made the author's name synonymous with craftiness and intrigue.*

How laudable it is for a prince to keep good faith and live with integrity, and not with astuteness, every one knows. Still the experience of our times shows those princes to have done great things who have had little regard for good faith, and have been able by astuteness to confuse men's brains, and who have ultimately overcome those who have made loyalty their foundation. 1

You must know, then, that there are two methods of fighting, the one by law, the other by force: the first method is that of men, the second of beasts; but as the first method is often insufficient, one must have recourse to the second. It is therefore necessary for a prince to know well how to use both the beast and the man. This was covertly taught to rulers by ancient writers, who relate how Achilles and many others of those ancient princes were given to Chiron the centaur to be brought up and educated under his discipline. The parable of this semi-animal, semi-human teacher is meant to indicate that a prince must know how to use both natures, and that the one without the other is not durable. 2

A prince being thus obliged to know well how to act as a beast must imitate the fox and the lion, for the lion cannot protect himself from traps, and the fox cannot defend himself from wolves. One must therefore be a fox to recognise traps, and a lion to frighten wolves. Those that wish to be only lions do not understand this. Therefore, a prudent ruler ought not to keep faith when by so doing it would be against his interest, and when the reasons which made him 3 bind himself no longer exist. If men were all good, this precept would not be a good one; but as they are bad, and would not observe their faith with you, so you are not bound to keep faith with them. Nor have legitimate grounds ever failed a prince who wished to show colourable excuse for the non-fulfilment of his promise. Of this one could furnish an infinite number of modern examples, and show how many times peace has been broken, and how many promises rendered worthless by the faithlessness of princes, and those that have been best able to imitate the fox have succeeded best. But it is necessary to be able to disguise this character well, and to be a great feigner and dissembler; and men are so simple and so ready to obey present necessities, that one who deceives will always find those who allow themselves to be deceived.

I will only mention one modern instance. Alexander VI did nothing else but   4
deceive men, he thought of nothing else, and found the occasion for it; no man was ever more able to give assurances, or affirmed things with stronger oaths, and no man observed them less; however, he always succeeded in his deceptions, as he well knew this aspect of things.

It is not, therefore, necessary for a prince to have all the above-named   5
qualities, but it is very necessary to seem to have them. I would even be bold to say that to possess them and always to observe them is dangerous, but to appear to possess them is useful. Thus it is well to seem merciful, faithful, humane, sincere, religious, and also to be so; but you must have the mind so disposed that when it is needful to be otherwise you may be able to change to the opposite qualities. And it must be understood that a prince, and especially a new prince, cannot observe all those things which are considered good in men, being often obliged, in order to maintain the state, to act against faith, against charity, against humanity, and against religion. And, therefore, he must have a mind disposed to adapt itself according to the wind, and as the variations of fortune dictate, and, as I said before, not deviate from what is good, if possible, but be able to do evil if constrained.

A prince must take great care that nothing goes out of his mouth which is   6
not full of the above-named five qualities, and, to see and hear him, he should seem to be all mercy, faith, integrity, humanity, and religion. And nothing is more necessary than to seem to have this last quality, for men in general judge more by the eyes than by the hands, for every one can see, but very few have to feel. Everybody sees what you appear to be, few feel what you are, and those few will not dare to oppose themselves to the many, who have the majesty of the state to defend them; and in the actions of men, and especially of princes, from which there is no appeal, the end justifies the means. Let a prince therefore aim at conquering and maintaining the state, and the means will always be judged honourable and praised by every one, for the vulgar is always taken by appearances and the issue of the event; and the world consists only of the vulgar, and the few who are not vulgar are isolated when the many have a rallying point in the prince. A certain prince of the present time, whom it is well not to name, never does anything but preach peace and good faith, but he is really a great enemy to both, and either of them, had he observed them, would have lost him state or reputation on many occasions.

QUESTIONS FOR MEANING

1. What are the two methods of fighting cited by Machiavelli. Why is it important for princes to master both?
2. Machiavelli insists that princes must be both "lions" and "foxes." Explain what he means by this.
3. Under what circumstances should princes break their word?
4. Why is it useful for princes "to seem merciful, faithful, humane, sincere, religious, and also to be so"?
5. In paragraph 6 Machiavelli observes, "men in general judge more by the eyes than by the hands, for every one can see, but very few have to feel." What does this mean? Describe Machiavelli's opinion of the average man.

QUESTIONS ABOUT STRATEGY

1. What premise underlies Machiavelli's argument, and where does he first state it?
2. Consider the tone of this essay. What sort of assumptions has Machiavelli made about his audience?
3. Machiavelli mentions Alexander VI by name in paragraph 4, but refuses to identify the prince he alludes to in paragraph 6. What does this reveal?
4. How would you characterize Machiavelli's point of view? Is it cynical or realistic?

ANDREW MARVELL
To His Coy Mistress

*Andrew Marvell (1621–1678) was a Puritan patriot and political writer who is
now remembered for writing a book of poetry that was published after his death. He
graduated from Trinity College, Cambridge, in 1639, and after the death of his
father in 1641, he spent several years traveling in Europe, presumably as a tutor.
Upon his return to England, he became tutor to a ward of Oliver Cromwell, the man
who ruled England during the period between the execution of Charles I in 1649
and the restoration of the monarchy in 1660. Through his connection with
Cromwell, Marvell became assistant Latin Secretary for the Council of State, but he
was not seriously involved in government until 1658, when he was elected to
Parliament. He served in Parliament for the next twenty years, and his political
experience led him to write a number of prose satires on government and religion.
Claiming that Marvell owed her money at the time of his death in 1678, his
housekeeper went through his private papers, gathered together the miscellaneous
poems that Marvell had written for his own pleasure, and arranged for their
publication in 1681.*

*The seventeenth century was a great age for English poetry, and Marvell cannot
be said to rank with Shakespeare, Milton, or Donne. However, a few of his poems
are so very fine that they have won for him an honored place in the history of
literature. Of these poems the most famous is "To His Coy Mistress," an argument
in the form of a poem.*

To His Coy Mistress

Had we but world enough, and time,
This coyness, lady, were no crime.
We would sit down, and think which way
To walk, and pass our long love's day.
5   Thou by the Indian Ganges' side
Should'st rubies find: I by the tide
Of Humber would complain. I would
Love you ten years before the Flood,
And you should, if you please, refuse
10   Till the conversion of the Jews.
My vegetable love should grow
Vaster than empires, and more slow.
An hundred years should go to praise
Thine eyes, and on thy forehead gaze:
15   Two hundred to adore each breast:
But thirty thousand to the rest.
An age at least to every part,
And the last age should show your heart.
For, lady, you deserve this state,
20   Nor would I love at lower rate.

But at my back I always hear
Time's winged chariot hurrying near;
And yonder all before us lie
Deserts of vast eternity.
25   Thy beauty shall no more be found,
Nor in thy marble vault shall sound
My echoing song; then worms shall try
That long preserved virginity,
And your quaint honor turn to dust,
30   And into ashes all my lust.
The grave's a fine and private place,
But none, I think, do there embrace.
                    Now therefore, while the youthful hue
Sits on thy skin like morning dew,
35   And while thy willing soul transpires
At every pore with instant fires,
Now let us sport us while we may;
And now, like am'rous birds of prey,
Rather at once our time devour,
40   Than languish in his slow-chapt power,
Let us roll all our strength, and all
Our sweetness, up into one ball;
And tear our pleasures with rough strife
Thorough the iron gates of life.
45   Thus, though we cannot make our sun
Stand still, yet we will make him run.

Andrew Marvell

QUESTIONS FOR MEANING

1. What do we learn from the title of this poem? In the seventeenth century, "mistress" was a synonym for "sweetheart." But what does Marvell mean by "coy"?
2. What kind of woman inspired this poem? Identify the lines that reveal her character.
3. How does the poet feel about this woman? Does he love her? Is this a love poem?
4. What is the poet urging this woman to do? Under what circumstances would he be willing to spend more time pleading with her? Why is this not possible?
5. Why does the poet describe his feelings as a "vegetable love"? What are the implications of this phrase?
6. What is the "marble vault" referred to in line 26?
7. Identify the references to "Ganges" (line 5), "Humber" (line 7), and "the Flood" (line 8). What does Marvell mean by "Time's winged chariot" (line 22) and "the iron gates of life" (line 44)?
8. Explain the last two lines of the poem. Is the sun a figure of speech? How is it possible to make it "run" when we lack the power to make it stand still?

QUESTIONS ABOUT STRATEGY

1. This poem is divided into three sections. Consider separately the tone of each. How do they differ?
2. Summarize the argument of this poem in three sentences, one for each section. Is the conclusion valid, or does it rest upon a questionable premise?
3. What role does humor play in the poem? What serious emotions does the poet invoke in order to make his argument more persuasive?
4. How does Marvell use rhyme as a device for advancing his argument?

JONATHAN SWIFT

A Modest Proposal

For Preventing the Children of Poor People in Ireland from Being a Burden to Their Parents or Country, and for Making Them Beneficial to the Public

Jonathan Swift (1667–1745) was a clergyman, poet, wit, and satirist. Born in Ireland as a member of the Protestant ruling class, Swift attended Trinity College in Dublin before settling in England in 1689. For the next ten years, he was a member of the household of Sir William Temple at Moor Park, Surrey. It was there that Swift met Esther Johnson, the "Stella" to whom he later wrote a famous series of letters known as Journal to Stella *(1710–1713). Although he was ordained a priest in the Church of Ireland in 1695, and made frequent trips to Ireland, Swift's ambition always brought him back to England. His reputation as a writer grew rapidly after the publication of his first major work,* A Tale of a Tub, *in 1704. He became a writer on behalf of the ruling Tory party, and was appointed Dean of St. Patrick's Cathedral in Dublin as a reward for his services. When the Tories fell from power in 1714, Swift retired to Ireland, where he remained for the rest of his life, except for brief visits to England in 1726 and 1727. It was in Ireland that he wrote* Gulliver's Travels *(1726), which is widely recognized as one of the masterpieces of English literature, and "A Modest Proposal" (1729), one of the greatest of all essays.*

Ruled as an English colony and subject to numerous repressive laws, Ireland in Swift's time was a desperately poor country. Swift wrote "A Modest Proposal" in order to expose the plight of Ireland and the unfair policies under which it suffered. As you read it, you will find that Swift's proposal for solving the problem of poverty is anything but "modest." Even when we know that we are reading satire, this brilliant and bitter essay retains the power to shock all but the most careless of readers.

It is a melancholy object to those who walk through this great town or travel in the country, when they see the streets, the roads, and cabin doors, crowded with beggars of the female sex, followed by three, four, or six children, all in rags and importuning every passenger for an alms. These mothers, instead of being able to work for their honest livelihood, are forced to employ all their time in strolling to beg sustenance for their helpless infants, who, as they grow up, either turn thieves for want of work, or leave their dear native country to fight for the Pretender in Spain, or sell themselves to the Barbados. 1

I think it is agreed by all parties that this prodigious number of children in the arms, or on the backs, or at the heels of their mothers, and frequently of their fathers, is in the present deplorable state of the kingdom a very great additional grievance; and therefore whoever could find out a fair, cheap, and easy method of making these children sound, useful members of the commonwealth would deserve so well of the public as to have his statue set up for a preserver of the nation. 2

But my intention is very far from being confined to provide only for the   3
children of professed beggars; it is of a much greater extent, and shall take in
the whole number of infants at a certain age who are born of parents in effect
as little able to support them as those who demand our charity in the streets.

As to my own part, having turned my thoughts for many years upon this   4
important subject, and maturely weighed the several schemes of other projec-
tors, I have always found them grossly mistaken in their computation. It is true,
a child just dropped from its dam may be supported by her milk for a solar year,
with little other nourishment; at most not above the value of two shillings,
which the mother may certainly get, or the value in scraps, by her lawful
occupation of begging; and it is exactly at one year that I propose to provide for
them in such a manner as instead of being a charge upon their parents or the
parish, or wanting food and raiment for the rest of their lives, they shall on
the contrary contribute to the feeding, and partly to the clothing, of many
thousands.

There is likewise another great advantage in my scheme, that it will prevent   5
those voluntary abortions, and that horrid practice of women murdering their
bastard children, alas, too frequent among us, sacrificing the poor innocent
babes, I doubt, more to avoid the expense than the shame, which would move
tears and pity in the most savage and inhuman breast.

The number of souls in this kingdom being usually reckoned one million and   6
a half, of these I calculate there may be about two hundred thousand couples
whose wives are breeders; from which number I subtract thirty thousand couples who are able to maintain their own children, although I apprehend there
cannot be so many under the present distress of the kingdom; but this being
granted, there will remain an hundred and seventy thousand breeders. I again
subtract fifty thousand for those women who miscarry, or whose children die
by accident or disease within the year. There only remain an hundred and
twenty thousand children of poor parents annually born. The question therefore is, how this number shall be reared and provided for, which, as I have
already said, under the present situation of affairs, is utterly impossible by all
the methods hitherto proposed. For we can neither employ them in handicraft
or agriculture; we neither build houses (I mean in the country) nor cultivate
land. They can very seldom pick up a livelihood by stealing till they arrive at six
years old, except where they are of towardly parts; although I confess they
learn the rudiments much earlier, during which time they can however be
looked upon only as probationers, as I have been informed by a principal gentleman in the country of Cavan, who protested to me that he never knew above
one or two instances under the age of six, even in a part of the kingdom so
renowned for the quickest proficiency in that art.

I am assured by our merchants that a boy or a girl before twelve years old is   7
no salable commodity; and even when they come to this age they will not yield
above three pounds, or three pounds and half a crown at most on the Exchange; which cannot turn to account either to the parents or the kingdom, the
charge of nutriment and rags having been at least four times that value.

I shall now therefore humbly propose my own thoughts, which I hope will   8
not be liable to the least objection.

I have been assured by a very knowing American of my acquaintance in London, that a young healthy child well nursed is at a year old a most delicious, nourishing, and wholesome food, whether stewed, roasted, baked, or boiled; and I make no doubt that it will equally serve in a fricassee or a ragout.   9

I do therefore humbly offer it to public consideration that of the hundred and twenty thousand children, already computed, twenty thousand may be reserved for breed, whereof only one fourth part to be males, which is more than we allow to sheep, black cattle, or swine; and my reason is that these children are seldom the fruits of marriage, a circumstance not much regarded by our savages, therefore one male will be sufficient to serve four females. That the remaining hundred thousand may at a year old be offered in sale to the persons of quality and fortune through the kingdom, always advising the mother to let them suck plentifully in the last month, so as to render them plump and fat for a good table. A child will make two dishes at an entertainment for friends; and when the family dines alone, the fore or hind quarter will make a reasonable dish, and seasoned with a little pepper or salt will be very good boiled on the fourth day, especially in winter.   10

I have reckoned upon a medium that a child just born will weigh twelve pounds, and in a solar year if tolerably nursed increaseth to twenty-eight pounds.   11

I grant this food will be somewhat dear, and therefore very proper for land-lords, who, as they have already devoured most of the parents, seem to have the best title to the children.   12

Infant's flesh will be in season throughout the year, but more plentiful in March, and a little before and after. For we are told by a grave author, an eminent French physician, that fish being a prolific diet, there are more children born in Roman Catholic countries about nine months after Lent than at any other season; therefore, reckoning a year after Lent, the markets will be more glutted than usual, because the number of popish infants is at least three to one in this kingdom; and therefore it will have one other collateral advantage, by lessening the number of Papists among us.   13

I have already computed the charge of nursing a beggar's child (in which list I reckon all cottagers, laborers, and four-fifths of the farmers) to be about two shillings per annum, rags included; and I believe no gentleman would repine to give ten shillings for the carcass of a good fat child, which, as I have said, will make four dishes of excellent nutritive meat, when he hath only some particular friend or his own family to dine with him. Thus the squire will learn to be a good landlord, and grow popular among the tenants; the mother will have eight shillings net profit, and be fit for work till she produces another child.   14

Those who are more thrifty (as I must confess the times require) may flay the carcass; the skin of which artificially dressed will make admirable gloves for ladies, and summer boots for fine gentlemen.   15

As to our city of Dublin, shambles may be appointed for this purpose in the most convenient parts of it, and butchers we may be assured will not be want-ing; although I rather recommend buying the children alive, and dressing them hot from the knife as we do roasting pigs.   16

A very worthy person, a true lover of his country, and whose virtues I highly   17 esteem, was lately pleased in discoursing on this matter to offer a refinement upon my scheme. He said that many gentlemen of his kingdom, having of late destroyed their deer, he conceived that the want of venison might be well supplied by the bodies of young lads and maidens, not exceeding fourteen years of age nor under twelve, so great a number of both sexes in every county being now ready to starve for want of work and service; and these to be disposed of by their parents, if alive, or otherwise by their nearest relations. But with due deference to so excellent a friend and so deserving a patriot, I cannot be altogether in his sentiments; for as to the males, my American acquaintance assured me from frequent experience that their flesh was generally tough and lean, like that of our schoolboys, by continual exercise, and their taste disagreeable; and to fatten them would not answer the charge. Then as to the females, it would, I think with humble submission, be a loss to the public, because they soon would become breeders themselves; and besides, it is not improbable that some scrupulous people might be apt to censure such a practice (although indeed very unjustly) as a little bordering upon cruelty; which, I confess, hath always been with me the strongest objection against any project, how well soever intended.

But in order to justify my friend, he confessed that this expedient was put   18
into his head by the famous Psalmanazar, a native of the island Formosa, who came from thence to London above twenty years ago, and in conversation told my friend that in his country when any young person happened to be put to death, the executioner sold the carcass to persons of quality as a prime dainty; and that in his time the body of a plump girl of fifteen, who was crucified for an attempt to poison the emperor, was sold to his Imperial Majesty's prime minister of state, and other great mandarins of the court, in joints from the gibbet, at four hundred crowns. Neither indeed can I deny that if the same use were made of several plump young girls in this town, who without one single groat to their fortunes cannot stir abroad without a chair, and appear at the playhouse and assemblies in foreign fineries which they never will pay for, the kingdom would not be the worse.

Some persons of a desponding spirit are in great concern about that vast   19
number of poor people who are aged, diseased, or maimed, and I have been desired to employ my thoughts what course may be taken to ease the nation of so grievous an encumbrance. But I am not in the least pain upon that matter, because it is very well known that they are every day dying and rotting by cold and famine, and filth and vermin, as fast as can be reasonably expected. And as to the younger laborers, they are now in almost as hopeful a condition. They cannot get work, and consequently pine away for want of nourishment to a degree that if any time they are accidentally hired to common labor, they have not strength to perform it; and thus the country and themselves are happily delivered from the evils to come.

I have too long digressed, and therefore shall return to my subject. I think   20
the advantages by the proposal which I have made are obvious and many, as well as of the highest importance.

For first, as I have already observed, it would greatly lessen the number of   21

Papists, with whom we are yearly overrun, being the principal breeders of the nation as well as our most dangerous enemies; and who stay at home on purpose to deliver the kingdom to the Pretender, hoping to take their advantage by the absence of so many good Protestants, who have chosen rather to leave their country than to stay at home and pay tithes against their conscience to an Episcopal curate.

Secondly, the poorer tenants will have something valuable of their own, 22 which by law may be made liable to distress, and help to pay their landlord's rent, their corn and cattle being already seized and money a thing unknown.

Thirdly, whereas the maintenance of an hundred thousand children, from 23 two years old and upwards, cannot be computed at less than ten shillings a piece per annum, the nation's stock will be thereby increased fifty thousand pounds per annum, besides the profit of a new dish introduced to the tables of all gentlemen of fortune in the kingdom who have any refinement in taste. And the money will circulate among ourselves, the goods being entirely of our own growth and manufacture.

Fourthly, the constant breeders, besides the gain of eight shillings sterling 24 per annum by the sale of their children, will be rid of the charge of maintaining them after the first year.

Fifthly, this food would likewise bring great custom to taverns, where the 25 vintners will certainly be so prudent as to procure the best receipts for dressing it to perfection, and consequently have their houses frequented by all the fine gentlemen, who justly value themselves upon their knowledge in good eating; and a skillful cook, who understands how to oblige his guests, will contrive to make it as expensive as they please.

Sixthly, this would be a great inducement to marriage, which all wise nations 26 have either encouraged by rewards or enforced by laws and penalties. It would increase the care and tenderness of mothers toward their children, when they were sure of a settlement for life to the poor babes, provided in some sort by the public, to their annual profit instead of expense. We should see an honest emulation among the married women, which of them could bring the fattest child to the market. Men would become as fond of their wives during the time of their pregnancy as they are now of their mares in foal, their cows in calf, or sows when they are ready to farrow; nor offer to beat or kick them (as is too frequent a practice) for fear of a miscarriage.

Many other advantages might be enumerated. For instance, the addition of 27 some thousand carcasses in our exportation of barreled beef, the propagation of swine's flesh, and improvements in the art of making good bacon, so much wanted among us by the great destruction of pigs, too frequent at our tables, which are no way comparable in taste or magnificence to a well-grown, fat, yearling child, which roasted whole will make a considerable figure at a lord mayor's feast or any other public entertainment. But this and many others I omit, being studious of brevity.

Supposing that one thousand families in this city would be constant cus- 28 tomers for infants' flesh, besides others who might have it at merry meetings, particularly weddings and christenings, I compute that Dublin would take off annually about twenty thousand carcasses, and the rest of the kingdom (where probably they will be sold somewhat cheaper) the remaining eighty thousand.

I can think of no one objection that will possibly be raised against this proposal, unless it should be urged that the number of people will be thereby much lessened in the kingdom. This I freely own, and it was indeed one principal design in offering it to the world. I desire the reader will observe, that I calculate my remedy for this one individual kingdom of Ireland and for no other that ever was, is, or I think ever can be upon earth. Therefore let no man talk to me of other expedients: of taxing our absentees at five shillings a pound: of using neither clothes nor household furniture except what is of our own growth and manufacture: of utterly rejecting the materials and instruments that promote foreign luxury: of curing the expensiveness of pride, vanity, idleness, and gaming in our women: of introducing a vein of parsimony, prudence, and temperance: of learning to love our country, in the want of which we differ even from Laplanders and the inhabitants of Topinamboo: of quitting our animosities and factions, nor acting any longer like the Jews, who were murdering one another at the very moment their city was taken: of being a little cautious not to sell our country and conscience for nothing: of teaching landlords to have at least one degree of mercy toward their tenants: lastly, of putting a spirit of honesty, industry, and skill into our shopkeepers; who, if a resolution could now be taken to buy only our native goods, would immediately unite to cheat and exact upon us in the price, the measure, and the goodness, nor could ever yet be brought to make one fair proposal of just dealing, though often and earnestly invited to it. 29

Therefore I repeat, let no man talk to me of these and the like expedients, till he hath at least some glimpse of hope that there will ever be some hearty and sincere attempt to put them in practice. 30

But as to myself, having been wearied out for many years with offering vain, idle, visionary thoughts, and at length utterly despairing of success, I fortunately fell upon this proposal, which, as it is wholly new, so it hath something solid and real, of no expense and little trouble, full in our own power, and whereby we can incur no danger in disobliging England. For this kind of commodity will not bear exportation, the flesh being of too tender a consistence to admit a long continuance in salt, although perhaps I could name a country which would be glad to eat up our whole nation without it. 31

After all, I am not so violently bent upon my own opinion as to reject any offer proposed by wise men, which shall be found equally innocent, cheap, easy, and effectual. But before something of that kind shall be advanced in contradiction to my scheme, and offering a better, I desire the author or authors will be pleased maturely to consider two points. First, as things now stand, how they will be able to find food and raiment for an hundred thousand useless mouths and backs. And secondly, there being a round million of creatures in human figure throughout this kingdom, whose sole subsistence put into a common stock would leave them in debt two millions of pounds sterling, adding those who are beggars by profession to the bulk of farmers, cottagers, and laborers, with their wives and children who are beggars in effect; I desire those politicians 32 who dislike my overture, and may perhaps be so bold to attempt an answer, that they will first ask the parents of these mortals whether they would not at this day think it a great happiness to have been sold for food at a year old in this manner I prescribe, and thereby have avoided such a perpetual scene of misfortunes as they have since gone through by the oppression of landlords, the impossibility of paying rent without money or trade, the want of common sustenance, with neither house nor clothes to cover them from the inclemencies of the weather, and the most inevitable prospect of entailing the like or greater miseries upon their breed forever.

I profess, in the sincerity of my heart, that I have not the least personal   33
interest in endeavoring to promote this necessary work, having no other motive than the public good of my country, by advancing our trade, providing for infants, relieving the poor, and giving some pleasure to the rich. I have no children by which I can propose to get a single penny; the youngest being nine years old, and my wife past childbearing.

QUESTIONS FOR MEANING

1. What do we learn in this essay about the condition of Ireland in Swift's time, and how Ireland was viewed by England? Does Swift provide any clue about what has caused the poverty he describes?
2. What specific "advantages" does Swift cite on behalf of his proposal?
3. Why does Swift limit his proposal to infants? On what grounds does he exclude older children from consideration as marketable commodities? Why does he claim that we need not worry about the elderly?
4. What does this essay reveal about the relations between Catholics and Protestants in the eighteenth century?
5. Where in the essay does Swift tell us what he really wants? What serious reforms does he propose in order to improve conditions in Ireland?
6. Vocabulary: importuning (1), sustenance (1), prodigious (2), rudiments (6), ragout (9), collateral (13), desponding (19), inducement (26), emulation (26), propagation (27), parsimony (29) and incur (31).

QUESTIONS ABOUT STRATEGY

1. How does Swift present himself in this essay? Many readers have taken this essay seriously and come away convinced that Swift was heartless and cruel. Why is it possible for some readers to be deceived in this way? What devices does Swift employ in order to create the illusion that he is serious? How does this strategy benefit the essay?
2. Does the language of the first few paragraphs contain any hint of irony? At what point in the essay did it first become clear to you that Swift is writing tongue in cheek?
3. Where in the essay does Swift pretend to anticipate objections that might be raised against his proposal? How does he dispose of these objections?

4. How does the style of this essay contrast with its subject matter? How does this contrast contribute to the force of the essay as a whole?
5. What is the function of the concluding paragraph?
6. What is the premise of this essay if we take its argument at face value? When we realize that Swift is writing ironically, what underlying premise begins to emerge?
7. What advantage is there in writing ironically? Why do you think Swift chose to treat his subject in this manner?

THOMAS JEFFERSON
The Declaration of Independence

Thomas Jefferson (1743–1826) was the third president of the United States and one of the most talented men ever to hold that office. A farmer, architect, writer, and scientist, Jefferson entered politics in 1769 as a member of the Virginia House of Burgesses. In 1775, he was a member of Virginia's delegation to the Second Continental Congress. He was governor of Virginia from 1779 to 1781, represented the United States in Europe from 1784 to 1789, and was elected to the first of two terms as president in 1801. Of all his many accomplishments, Jefferson himself was most proud of having founded the University of Virginia in 1819.

Although the Continental Congress had delegated the responsibility for writing a declaration of independence to a committee that included Benjamin Franklin and John Adams as well as Jefferson, it was Jefferson who undertook the actual composition. His colleagues respected him as the best writer among them. Jefferson wrote at least two, and possibly three, drafts during the seventeen days allowed for the assignment. His work was reviewed by the other members of the committee, but they made only minor revisions—mainly in the first two paragraphs. When it came to adopting the declaration, Congress was harder to please. After lengthy and spirited debate, Congress made twenty-four changes and deleted over three hundred words. Nevertheless, "The Declaration of Independence," as approved by Congress on July 4, 1776, is almost entirely the work of Jefferson. In addition to being an eloquent example of eighteenth-century prose, it is a clear example of deductive reasoning.

When in the Course of human events, it becomes necessary for one people to dissolve the political bands which have connected them with another, and to assume among the powers of the earth, the separate and equal station to which the Laws of Nature and of Nature's God entitle them, a decent respect to the opinions of mankind requires that they should declare the causes which impel them to the separation.   1

We hold these truths to be self-evident, that all men are created equal, that they are endowed by their Creator with certain unalienable Rights, that among these are Life, Liberty and the pursuit of Happiness. That to secure these rights, Governments are instituted among Men, deriving their just powers from the consent of the governed, That whenever any Form of Government becomes destructive of these ends it is the Right of the People to alter or to abolish it, and to institute new Government, laying its foundation on such principles and organizing its powers in such form, as to them shall seem most likely to effect their Safety and Happiness. Prudence, indeed, will dictate that Governments long established should not be changed for light and transient causes; and accordingly all experience has shewn, that mankind are more disposed to suffer, while evils are sufferable, than to right themselves by abolishing the forms to which they are accustomed. But when a long train of abuses and usurpations, pursuing invariably the same Object evinces a design to reduce them under   2 absolute Despotism, it is their right, it is their duty, to throw off such Government, and to provide new Guards for their future security. Such has been the patient sufferance of these Colonies; and such is now the necessity which constrains them to alter their former Systems of Government. The history of the present King of Great Britain is a history of repeated injuries and usurpations, all having in direct object the establishment of an absolute Tyranny over these States. To prove this, let Facts be submitted to a candid world.

He has refused his Assent to Laws, the most wholesome and necessary for the public good. 3

He has forbidden his Governors to pass Laws of immediate and pressing importance, unless suspended in their operation till his Assent should be obtained; and when so suspended, he has utterly neglected to attend to them. He has refused to pass other Laws for the accommodation of large districts of people, unless those people would relinquish the right of Representation in the Legislature, a right inestimable to them and formidable to tyrants only. 4

He has called together legislative bodies at places unusual, uncomfortable, and distant from the depository of their public Records, for the sole purpose of fatiguing them into compliance with his measures. 5

He has dissolved Representative Houses repeatedly, for opposing with manly firmness his invasions on the rights of the people. 6

He has refused for a long time, after such dissolutions, to cause others to be elected; whereby the Legislative powers, incapable of Annihilation, have returned to the People at large for their exercise; the State remaining in the mean time exposed to all the dangers of invasion from without, and convulsions within. 7

He has endeavoured to prevent the population of these States; for that purpose obstructing the Laws for Naturalization of Foreigners; refusing to pass others to encourage their migrations hither, and raising the conditions of new Appropriations of Lands. 8

He has obstructed the Administration of Justice, by refusing his Assent to Laws for establishing Judiciary powers. 9

He has made Judges dependent on his Will alone, for the tenure of their offices, and the amount and payment of their salaries. 10

He has erected a multitude of New Offices, and sent hither swarms of Officers to harass our People, and eat out their substance. 11

He has kept among us, in times of peace, standing Armies without the Consent of our legislatures. 12

He has affected to render the Military independent of and superior to the Civil power. 13

He had combined with others to subject us to a jurisdiction foreign to our constitution, and unacknowledged by our laws; giving his Assent to their Acts of pretended Legislation: 14

For Quartering large bodies of armed troops among us: 15

For protecting them, by a mock Trial, from punishment for any Murders which they should commit on the Inhabitants of these States: 16

For cutting off our Trade with all parts of the world: 17

For imposing Taxes on us without our Consent: 18

For depriving us in many cases of the benefits of Trial by Jury: 19

For transporting us beyond Seas to be tried for pretended offences: 20

For abolishing the free System of English Laws in a neighbouring Province,   21
establishing therin an Arbitrary government, and enlarging its Boundaries so
as to render it at once an example and fit instrument for introducing the same
absolute rule into these Colonies:

For taking away our Charters, abolishing our most valuable Laws, and alter-   22
ing fundamentally the Forms of our Governments:

For suspending our own Legislatures, and declaring themselves invested   23
with power to legislate for us in all cases whatsoever.

He has abdicated Government here, by declaring us out of his Protection   24
and waging War against us.

He has plundered our seas, ravaged our Coasts, burnt our towns, and de-   25
stroyed the Lives of our people.

He is at this time transporting large Armies of foreign Mercenaries to com-   26
pleat the works of death, desolation and tyranny, already begun with circumstances of Cruelty & perfidy scarcely paralleled in the most barbarous ages, and
totally unworthy the Head of a civilized nation.

He has constrained our fellow Citizens taken Captive on the high Seas to   27
bear Arms against their Country, to become the executioners of their friends
and Brethren, or to fall themselves by their Hands.

He has excited domestic insurrections amongst us, and has endeavoured to   28
bring on the inhabitants of our frontiers, the merciless Indian Savages, whose
known rule of warfare, is an undistinguished destruction of all ages, sexes and
conditions.

In every stage of these Oppressions We have Petitioned for Redress in the   29
most humble terms: Our repeated Petitions have been answered only by repeated injury. A Prince, whose character is thus marked by every act which
may define a Tyrant, is unfit to be the ruler of a free people.

Nor have We been wanting in attentions to our Brittish brethren. We have   30
warned them from time to time of attempts by their legislature to extend an
unwarrantable jurisdiction over us. We have reminded them of the circumstances of our emigration and settlement here. We have appealed to their native
justice and magnanimity, and we have conjured them by the ties of our common
kindred to disavow these usurpations, which, would inevitably interrupt our
connections and correspondence. They too have been deaf to the voice of
Justice and of consanguinity. We must, therefore, acquiesce in the necessity,
which denounces our Separation, and hold them, as we hold the rest of mankind, Enemies in War, in Peace Friends.

We, therefore, the Representatives of the united States of America, in Gen-   31
eral Congress, Assembled, appealing to the Supreme Judge of the world for the
rectitude of our intentions, do, in the Name, and by Authority of the good
People of these Colonies, solemnly publish and declare, That these United
Colonies are, and of Right ought to be Free and Independent States; that they
are Absolved from all Allegiance to the British Crown, and that all political

connection between them and the State of Great Britain, is and ought to be totally dissolved; and that as Free and Independent States, they have full Power to levy War, conclude Peace, contract Alliances, establish Commerce, and to do all other Acts and Things which Independent States may of right do. And for the support of this Declaration, with a firm reliance on the protection of divine Providence, we mutually pledge to each other our Lives, our Fortunes and our sacred Honor.

John Hancock

Button Gwinnett	James Wilson
Lyman Hall	Geo. Ross
Geo Walton.	Caesar Rodney
Wm. Hooper	Geo Read
Joseph Hewes,	Tho M:Kean
John Penn	Wm. Floyd
Edward Rutledge.	Phil. Livingston
Thos. Heyward Junr.	Frans. Lewis
Thomas Lynch Junr.	Lewis Morris
Arthur Middleton	Richd. Stockton
Samuel Chase	Jno Witherspoon
Wm. Paca	Fras. Hopkinson
Thos. Stone	John Hart
Charles Carroll of Carrollton	Abra Clark
George Wythe	Josiah Bartlett
Richard Henry Lee	Wm: Whipple
Th: Jefferson	Saml. Adams
Benja. Harrison	John Adams
Thos. Nelson jr.	Robt. Treat Paine
Francis Lightfoot Lee	Elbridge Gerry
Carter Braxton	Step. Hopkins
Robt. Morris	William Ellery
Benjamin Rush	Roger Sherman
Benja. Franklin	Saml. Huntington
John Morton	Wm. Williams
Geo Clymer	Oliver Wolcott
Jas. Smith.	Matthew Thornton
Geo. Taylor	

QUESTIONS FOR MEANING

1. What was the purpose of "The Declaration of Independence"? What reason does Jefferson himself give for writing it?
2. In paragraph 1, what does Jefferson mean by "the Laws of Nature and of Nature's God"?

3. Paragraphs 3–28 are devoted to enumerating a list of grievances against King George III. Which of these are the most important? Are any of them relatively trivial? Taken together do they justify Jefferson's description of George III as "A Prince, whose character is thus marked by every act which may define a Tyrant"?

4. How would you summarize Jefferson's conception of the relationship between people and government?

5. How does Jefferson characterize his fellow Americans? At what points does he put the colonists in a favorable light?

6. What does Jefferson mean by "the Supreme Judge of the world"? Why does he express "a firm reliance on the protection of a divine Providence"?

7. Vocabulary: transient (2), evinces (2), usurpations (2), candid (2), annihilation (7), render (13), perfidy (26), unwarrantable (30), consanguinity (30), acquiesce (30), and rectitude (31).

QUESTIONS ABOUT STRATEGY

1. In paragraph 2, why does Jefferson declare certain truths to be "self-evident"? Paraphrase this paragraph and explain the purpose it serves in Jefferson's argument.

2. In evaluating "The Declaration of Independence" as an argument, what is more important: the general "truths" outlined in the second paragraph, or the specific accusations listed in the paragraphs that follow? If you were to write a counterargument to "The Declaration of Independence," on what points would you concentrate? Where is it most vulnerable?

3. Jefferson is often cited as a man of great culture and liberal values. Are there any points of "The Declaration of Independence" that now seem illiberal?

4. Does Jefferson use any loaded terms? He was forced to delete exaggerated language from his first two drafts of "The Declaration." Do you see any exaggerations that Congress failed to catch?

5. For what sort of audience did Jefferson write "The Declaration of Independence"? Is it directed primarily to the American people, the British government, or the world in general?

MARY WOLLSTONECRAFT
The Playthings of Tyrants

An English writer of Irish extraction, Mary Wollstonecraft (1759–1797) was an early advocate of women's rights. After working as a governess and a publisher's assistant, she went to France in 1792 in order to witness the French Revolution. She lived there with an American, Captain Gilbert Imlay, and had a child by him in 1794. Her relationship with Imlay broke down soon afterwards, and, in 1795, Wollstonecraft tried to commit suicide by drowning herself. She was rescued, however, and returned to London, where she became a member of a group of radical writers that included Thomas Paine, William Blake, and William Godwin. Wollstonecraft became pregnant by Godwin in 1796, and they were married the following year. Their child, Mary (1797–1851), would eventually win fame as the author of Frankenstein. *Wollstonecraft died only eleven days after Mary's birth.*

Wollstonecraft's fame rests upon one work, A Vindication of the Rights of Women *(1792). Although she had written about the need for educated women several years earlier in* Thoughts on the Education of Daughters *(1787), she makes a stronger and better-reasoned argument in her* Vindication. *"The Playthings of Tyrants" is an editor's title for an excerpt from the second chapter, "The Prevailing Opinion of a Sexual Character Discussed." As the excerpt suggests, Wollstonecraft was not especially interested in securing political rights for women. Her object was to emancipate women from the roles imposed upon them by men and to urge women to think for themselves.*

To account for, and excuse the tyranny of man, many ingenious arguments have been brought forward to prove, that the two sexes, in the acquirement of virtue, ought to aim at attaining a very different character: or, to speak explicitly, women are not allowed to have sufficient strength of mind to acquire what really deserves the name of virtue. Yet it should seem, allowing them to have souls, that there is but one way appointed by Providence to lead *mankind* to either virtue or happiness.

If then women are not a swarm of ephemeron triflers, why should they be kept in ignorance under the specious name of innocence? Men complain, and with reason, of the follies and caprices of our sex, when they do not keenly satirize our headstrong passions and groveling vices.—Behold, I should answer, the natural effect of ignorance! The mind will ever be unstable that has only prejudices to rest on, and the current will run with destructive fury when there are no barriers to break its force. Women are told from their infancy, and taught by the example of their mothers, that a little knowledge of human weakness, justly termed cunning, softness of temper, *outward* obedience, and a scrupulous attention to a puerile kind of propriety, will obtain for them the protection of man; and should they be beautiful, every thing else is needless, for, at least, twenty years of their lives.

Thus Milton describes our first frail mother; though when he tells us that women are formed for softness and sweet attractive grace, I cannot comprehend his meaning, unless, in the true Mahometan strain, he meant to deprive us of souls, and insinuate that we were beings only designed by sweet attractive grace, and docile blind obedience, to gratify the senses of man when he can no longer soar on the wing of contemplation.

How grossly do they insult us who thus advise us only to render ourselves   4
gentle, domestic brutes! For instance, the winning softness so warmly, and frequently, recommended, that governs by obeying. What childish expressions, and how insignificant is the being—can it be an immortal one? who will condescend to govern by such sinister methods! 'Certainly,' says Lord Bacon, 'man is of kin to the beasts by his body; and if he be not of kin to God by his spirit, he is a base and ignoble creature!' Men, indeed, appear to me to act in a very unphilosophical manner when they try to secure the good conduct of women by attempting to keep them always in a state of childhood. Rousseau was more consistent when he wished to stop the progress of reason in both sexes, for if men eat of the tree of knowledge, women will come in for a taste; but, from the imperfect cultivation which their understandings now receive, they only attain a knowledge of evil.

Children, I grant, should be innocent; but when the epithet is applied to men,   5
or women, it is but a civil term for weakness. For if it be allowed that women were destined by Providence to acquire human virtues, and by the exercise of their understandings, that stability of character which is the firmest ground to rest our future hopes upon, they must be permitted to turn to the fountain of light, and not forced to shape their course by the twinkling of a mere satellite. Milton, I grant, was of a very different opinion; for he only bends to the indefeasible right of beauty, though it would be difficult to render two passages which I now mean to contrast, consistent. But into similar inconsistencies are great men often led by their senses.

> 'To whom thus Eve with *perfect beauty* adorn'd.
> 'My Author and Disposer, what thou bidst
> '*Unargued* I obey; So God ordains;
> 'God is *thy law, thou mine*: to know no more
> 'Is Woman's *happiest* knowledge and her *praise*.'

These are exactly the arguments that I have used to children; but I have   6
added, your reason is now gaining strength, and, till it arrives at some degree of maturity, you must look up to me for advice—then you ought to *think*, and only rely on God.

Yet in the following lines Milton seems to coincide with me; when he makes   7
Adam thus expostulate with his Maker.

> 'Hast thou not made me here thy substitute,
> 'And these inferior far beneath me set?
> 'Among *unequals* what society
> 'Can sort, what harmony or true delight?
> 'Which must be mutual, in proportion due

'Giv'n and receiv'd; but in *disparity*
'The one intense, the other still remiss
'Cannot well suit with either, but soon prove
'Tedious alike: of *fellowship* I speak
'Such as I seek, fit to participate
'All rational delight—'

In treating, therefore, of the manners of women, let us, disregarding sensual   8
arguments, trace what we should endeavour to make them in order to co-
operate, if the expression be not too bold, with the supreme Being.

By individual education, I mean, for the sense of the word is not precisely   9
defined, such an attention to a child as will slowly sharpen the senses, form the
temper, regulate the passions as they begin to ferment, and set the understanding to work before the body arrives at maturity; so that the man may only have
to proceed, not to begin, the important task of learning to think and reason.

To prevent any misconstruction, I must add, that I do not believe that a   10
private education can work the wonders which some sanguine writers have
attributed to it. Men and women must be educated, in a great degree, by the
opinions and manners of the society they live in. In every age there has been a
stream of popular opinion that has carried all before it, and given a family
character, as it were, to the century. It may then fairly be inferred, that, till
society be differently constituted, much cannot be expected from education. It
is, however, sufficient for my present purpose to assert, that, whatever effect
circumstances have on the abilities, every being may become virtuous by the
exercise of its own reason; for if but one being was created with vicious inclinations, that is positively bad, what can save us from atheism? or if we worship
a God, is not that God a devil?

Consequently, the most perfect education, in my opinion, is such an exercise   11
of the understanding as is best calculated to strengthen the body and form the
heart. Or, in other words, to enable the individual to attain such habits of virtue
as will render it independent. In fact, it is a farce to call any being virtuous
whose virtues do not result from the exercise of its own reason. This was
Rousseau's opinion respecting men: I extend it to women, and confidently
assert that they have been drawn out of their sphere by false refinement, and
not by an endeavour to acquire masculine qualities. Still the regal homage
which they receive is so intoxicating, that till the manners of the times are
changed, and formed on more reasonable principles, it may be impossible to
convince them that the illegitimate power, which they obtain, by degrading
themselves, is a curse, and that they must return to nature and equality, if they
wish to secure the placid satisfaction that unsophisticated affections impart.
But for this epoch we must wait—wait, perhaps, till kings and nobles, enlightened by reason, and, preferring the real dignity of man to childish state, throw
off their gaudy hereditary trappings: and if then women do not resign the
arbitrary power of beauty—they will prove that they have *less* mind than
man . . . .

Many are the causes that, in the present corrupt state of society, contribute   12
to enslave women by cramping their understandings and sharpening their senses. One, perhaps, that silently does more mischief than all the rest, is their disregard of order.

To do every thing in an orderly manner, is a most important precept, which   13
women, who, generally speaking, receive only a disorderly kind of education, seldom attend to with that degree of exactness that men, who from their infancy are broken into method, observe. This negligent kind of guess-work, for what other epithet can be used to point out the random exertions of a sort of instinctive common sense, never brought to the test of reason? prevents their generalizing matters of fact—so they do to-day, what they did yesterday, merely because they did it yesterday.

This contempt of the understanding in early life has more baneful conse-   14
quences than is commonly supposed; for the little knowledge which women of strong minds attain, is, from various circumstances, of a more desultory kind than the knowledge of men, and it is acquired more by sheer observations on real life, than from comparing what has been individually observed with the results of experience generalized by speculation. Led by their dependent situation and domestic employments more into society, what they learn is rather by snatches; and as learning is with them, in general, only a secondary thing, they do not pursue any one branch with that persevering ardour necessary to give vigour to the faculties, and clearness to the judgment. In the present state of society, a little learning is required to support the character of a gentleman; and boys are obliged to submit to a few years of discipline. But in the education of women, the cultivation of the understanding is always subordinate to the acquirement of some corporeal accomplishment; even while enervated by confinement and false notions of modesty, the body is prevented from attaining that grace and beauty which relaxed half-formed limbs never exhibit. Besides, in youth their faculties are not brought forward by emulation; and having no serious scientific study, if they have natural sagacity it is turned too soon on life and manners. They dwell on effects, and modifications, without tracing them back to causes; and complicated rules to adjust behaviour are a weak substitute for simple principles.

As a proof that education gives this appearance of weakness to females, we   15
may instance the example of military men, who are, like them, sent into the world before their minds have been stored with knowledge or fortified by principles. The consequences are similar; soldiers acquire a little superficial knowledge, snatched from the muddy current of conversation, and, from continually mixing with society, they gain, what is termed a knowledge of the world; and this acquaintance with manners and customs has frequently been confounded with a knowledge of the human heart. But can the crude fruit of casual observation, never brought to the test of judgment, formed by comparing speculation and experience, deserve such a distinction? Soldiers, as well as women, practice the minor virtues with punctilious politeness. Where is then the sexual difference, when the education has been the same? All the difference that I can

discern, arises from the superior advantage of liberty, which enables the former to see more of life.

It is wandering from my present subject, perhaps, to make a political remark; but, as it was produced naturally by the train of my reflections, I shall not pass it silently over. 16

Standing armies can never consist of resolute, robust men; they may be well disciplined machines, but they will seldom contain men under the influence of strong passions, or with very vigorous faculties. And as for any depth of understanding, I will venture to affirm, that it is as rarely to be found in the army as amongst women; and the cause, I maintain, is the same. It may be further observed, that officers are also particularly attentive to their persons, fond of dancing, crowded rooms, adventures, and ridicule. Like the *fair* sex, the business of their lives is gallantry.—They were taught to please, and they only live to please. Yet they do not lose their rank in the distinction of sexes, for they are still reckoned superior to women, though in what their superiority consists, beyond what I have just mentioned, it is difficult to discover. 17

The great misfortune is this, that they both acquire manners before morals, and a knowledge of life before they have, from reflection, any acquaintance with the grand ideal outline of human nature. The consequence is natural; satisfied with common nature, they become a prey to prejudices, and taking all their opinions on credit, they blindly submit to authority. So that, if they have any sense, it is a kind of instinctive glance, that catches proportions, and decides with respect to manners; but fails when arguments are to be pursued below the surface, or opinions analyzed. 18

May not the same remark be applied to women? Nay, the argument may be carried still further, for they are both thrown out of a useful station by the unnatural distinctions established in civilized life. Riches and hereditary honours have made cyphers of women to give consequence to the numerical figure; and idleness has produced a mixture of gallantry and despotism into society, which leads the very men who are the slaves of their mistresses to tyrannize over their sisters, wives, and daughters. This is only keeping them in rank and file, it is true. Strengthen the female mind by enlarging it, and there will be an end to blind obedience; but, as blind obedience is ever sought for by power, tyrants and sensualists are in the right when they endeavor to keep women in the dark, because the former only want slaves, and the latter a play-thing. The sensualist, indeed, has been the most dangerous of tyrants, and women have been duped by their lovers, as princes by their ministers, whilst dreaming that they reigned over them. 19

QUESTIONS FOR MEANING

1. What's wrong with treating women as children and expecting "blind obedience"?
2. What causes does Wollstonecraft cite for the degradation of women? On what grounds does she defend their "follies" and "vices"?

3. What does Wollstonecraft mean by "false refinement" in paragraph 11? Explain why she believes it is dangerous to acquire "manners before morals."

4. Where in her essay does Wollstonecraft define the sort of education she believes women should receive? Why does she object to educating women privately in their homes?

5. Wollstonecraft was perceived as a radical by her contemporaries, and relatively few people took her ideas seriously. Looking back upon her work after almost two hundred years, can you find any traditional values that Wollstonecraft accepted without question? Could you argue that she was conservative in some ways?

6. Explain why "the sensualist" has been "the most dangerous of tyrants."

7. Vocabulary: ephemeron (2), specious (2), caprices (2), puerile (2), propriety (2), insinuate (3), docile (3), sanguine (10), desultory (14), corporeal (14), enervated (14), sagacity (14), punctilious (15) and cyphers (19).

QUESTIONS ABOUT STRATEGY

1. What is the premise of this argument? Where does Wollstonecraft first state it, and where is it restated?

2. What is the function of the last sentence in the second paragraph?

3. Why does Wollstonecraft quote John Milton and Francis Bacon? What do these quotations contribute to her argument?

4. Comment on the analogy Wollstonecraft makes between women and soldiers. What type of soldiers did she have in mind? Is her analogy valid?

5. Do you think Wollstonecraft wrote this argument primarily for men or for women? What kind of an audience could she have expected in the eighteenth century?

KARL MARX AND FRIEDERICH ENGELS
The Communist Manifesto

Karl Marx (1818–1883) was a German social scientist and political philosopher who believed that history is determined by economics. Originally intending to teach, Marx studied at the University of Berlin, receiving his Ph.D. in 1841. But, in 1842, he abandoned academics in order to become editor of the Rheinische Zeitung, *an influential newspaper published in Cologne. His editorials led the government to close the paper within a year, and Marx went into exile—first in France and Belgium, and eventually in England, where he spent the last thirty-three years of his life.*

It was in 1843 that Marx met Friederich Engels (1820–1895), the son of a wealthy German industrialist with business interests in England. The two men discovered that they shared the same political beliefs, and they worked together closely for the next forty years. It was not until 1867 that Marx was able to publish the first volume of Das Kapital, *his most important work. The second and third volumes were published after his death, completed by Engels, who worked from the extensive notes that Marx left behind him.* Das Kapital, *or* Capital, *provided the theoretical basis for what is variously known as "Marxism" or "Communism." It is an indictment of nineteenth-century capitalism that predicts a proletarian revolution in which the workers would take over the means of production and distribute goods according to needs, creating an ideal society in which the state would wither away.*

But Marx and Engels had outlined their views long before the publication of Das Kapital. *In 1848, they published a pamphlet called* The Communist Manifesto. *It was written during a period of great political unrest. Within months of its publication, revolutions broke out in several European countries. Most of the revolutions of 1848 were quickly aborted, but "the specter of Communism" has continued to haunt the world. Here are the first few pages of this classic argument.*

A specter is haunting Europe—the specter of Communism. All the Powers of old Europe have entered into a holy alliance to exorcise this specter; Pope and Czar, Metternich and Guizot, French Radicals and German police-spies.   1

Where is the party in opposition that has not been decried as communistic by its opponents in power? Where the Opposition that has not hurled back the branding reproach of Communism against the more advanced opposition parties, as well as against its reactionary adversaries?   2

Two things result from this fact.   3

I. Communism is already acknowledged by all European Powers to be itself a Power.   4

II. It is high time that Communists should openly, in the face of the whole world, publish their views, their aims, their tendencies, and meet this nursery tale of the specter of Communism with a Manifesto of the party itself.   5

To this end, Communists of various nationalities have assembled in London and sketched the following Manifesto, to be published in the English, French, German, Italian, Flemish and Danish languages.   6

Bourgeois and Proletarians*

The history of all hitherto existing society is the history of class struggles.   7

Freeman and slave, patrician and plebeian, lord and serf, guild-master and   8
journeyman, in a word, oppressor and oppressed, stood in constant opposition
to one another, carried on uninterrupted, now hidden, now open fight, a fight
that each time ended, either in a revolutionary re-constitution of society at
large, or in the common ruin of the contending classes.

In the earlier epochs of history we find almost everywhere a complicated   9
arrangement of society into various orders, a manifold gradation of social rank.
In ancient Rome we have patricians, knights, plebians, slaves; in the Middle
Ages, feudal lords, vassals, guild-masters, journeymen, apprentices, serfs; in
almost all of these classes, again, subordinate gradations.

The modern bourgeois society that has sprouted from the ruins of feudal   10
society, has not done away with class antagonisms. It has but established new
classes, new conditions of oppression, new forms of struggle in place of the old
ones.

Our epoch, the epoch of the bourgeoisie, possesses, however, this distinctive   11
feature; it has simplified the class antagonisms. Society as a whole is more and
more splitting up into two great hostile camps, into two great classes directly
facing each other: Bourgeoisie and Proletariat.

From the serfs of the Middle Ages sprang the chartered burghers of the   12
earliest towns. From these burgesses the first elements of the bourgeoisie were
developed.

The discovery of America, the rounding of the Cape, opened up fresh ground   13
for the rising bourgeoisie. The East Indian and Chinese markets, the coloniza-
tion of America, trade with the colonies, the increase in the means of exchange
and in commodities generally, gave to commerce, to navigation, to industry, an
impulse never before known, and thereby, to the revolutionary element in the
tottering feudal society, a rapid development.

The feudal system of industry, under which industrial production was mo-   14
nopolized by closed guilds, now no longer sufficed for the growing wants of the
new market. The manufacturing system took its place. The guild-masters were
pushed on one side by the manufacturing middle-class: division of labor between the different corporate guilds vanished in the face of division of labor in
each single workshop.

Meantime the markets kept ever growing, the demand ever rising. Even   15
manufacture no longer sufficed. Thereupon, steam and machinery revolutionized industrial production. The place of manufacture was taken by the giant,
Modern Industry, the place of the industrial middle-class, by industrial million-
aires, the leaders of whole industrial armies, the modern bourgeois.

Modern industry has established the world market, for which the discovery   16
of America paved the way. This market has given an immense development to

---

* By bourgeoisie is meant the class of modern Capitalists, owners of the means of social production and employers
of wage labor. By proletariat, the class of modern wage laborers who, having no means of production of their own,
are reduced to selling their labor-power in order to live. [Marx's note]

commerce, to navigation, to communication by land. This development has, in its turn, reacted on the extension of industry; and in proportion as industry, commerce, navigation, railways extended, in the same proportion the bourgeoisie developed, increased its capital, and pushed into the background every class handed down from the Middle Ages.

We see, therefore, how the modern bourgeoisie is itself the product of a long   17
course of development, a series of revolutions in the modes of production and of exchange.

Each step in the development of the bourgeoisie was accompanied by a   18
corresponding political advance of that class. An oppressed class under the sway of the feudal nobility, an armed and self-governing association in the medieval commune, here independent urban republic (as in Italy and Germany), there taxable "third estate" of the monarchy (as in France), afterwards, in the period of manufacture proper, serving either the semi-fuedal or the absolute monarchy as a counterpoise against nobility, and, in fact, corner stone of the great monarchies in general, the bourgeoisie has at last, since the establishment of Modern Industry and of the world-market, conquered for itself, in the modern representative State, exclusive political sway. The executive of the modern State is but a committee for managing the common affairs of the whole bourgeoisie.

The bourgeoisie, historically, has played a most revolutionary part.   19

The bourgeoisie, wherever it has got the upper hand, has put an end to all   20
feudal, patriarchal, idyllic relations. It has pitilessly torn asunder the motley feudal ties that bound man to his "natural superiors," and has left no other nexus between man and man than naked self-interest, than callous "cash payment." It has drowned the most heavenly ecstasies of religious fervor, of chivalrous enthusiasm, of Philistine sentimentalism, in the icy water of egotistical calculation. It has resolved personal worth into exchange value, and in place of the numberless indefeasible chartered freedoms, has set up that single, unconscionable freedom—Free Trade. In one word, for exploitation, veiled by religious and political illusions, it has substituted naked, shameless, direct, brutal exploitation.

The bourgeoisie has stripped of its halo every occupation hitherto honored   21
and looked up to with reverent awe. It has converted the physician, the lawyer, the priest, the poet, the man of science, into its paid wage laborers.

The bourgeoisie has torn away from the family its sentimental veil, and has   22
reduced the family relation to a mere money relation.

The bourgeoisie has disclosed how it came to pass that the brutal display of   23
vigor in the Middle Ages, which reactionists so much admire, found its fitting complement in the most slothful indolence. It has been the first to show what man's activity can bring about. It has accomplished wonders far surpassing Egyptian pyramids, Roman aqueducts and Gothic cathedrals; it has conducted expeditions that put in the shade all former Exoduses of nations and crusades.

The bourgeoisie cannot exist without constantly revolutionizing the instru-   24
ments of production, and thereby the relations of production, and with them the whole relations of society. Conservation of the old modes of production in

unaltered form was, on the contrary, the first condition of existence for all earlier industrial classes. Constant revolutionizing of production, uninterrupted disturbance of all social conditions, everlasting uncertainty and agitation distinguish the bourgeois epoch from all earlier ones. All fixed, fast frozen relations, with their train of ancient and venerable prejudices and opinions, are swept away, all new formed ones become antiquated before they can ossify. All that is solid melts into the air, all that is holy is profaned, and man is at last compelled to face with sober senses, his real conditions of life, and his relations with his kind.

The need of a constantly expanding market for its products chases the   25 bourgeoisie over the whole surface of the globe. It must nestle everywhere, settle everywhere, establish connections everywhere.

The bourgeoisie has through its exploitation of the world-market given a   26 cosmopolitan character to production and consumption in every country. To the great chagrin of reactionists, it has drawn from under the feet of industry the national ground on which it stood. All old-established national industries have been destroyed or are daily being destroyed. They are dislodged by new industries, whose introduction becomes a life and death question for all civilized nations, by industries that no longer work up indigenous raw material, but raw material drawn from the remotest zones; industries whose products are consumed, not only at home, but in every quarter of the globe. In place of the old wants, satisfied by the productions of the country, we find new wants, requiring for their satisfaction the products of distant lands and climes. In place of the old local and national seclusion and self-sufficiency, we have intercourse in every direction, universal interdependence of nations. And as in material, so also in intellectual production. The intellectual creations of individual nations become common property. National onesidedness and narrowmindedness become more and more impossible, and from the numerous national and local literatures there arises a world-literature.

The bourgeoisie, by the rapid improvement of all instruments of production,   27 by the immensely facilitated means of communication, draws all, even the most barbarian nations into civilization. The cheap prices of its commodities are the heavy artillery with which it batters down all Chinese walls, with which it forces the barbarians' intensely obstinate hatred of foreigners to capitulate. It compels all nations, on pain of extinction, to adopt the bourgeois mode of production; it compels them to introduce what it calls civilization into their midst, i.e., to become bourgeois themselves. In a word, it creates a world after its own image.

The bourgeoisie has subjected the country to the rule of the towns. It has   28 created enormous cities, has greatly increased the urban population as compared with the rural and has thus rescued a considerable part of the population from the idiocy of rural life. Just as it has made the country dependent on the towns, so it has made barbarian and semi-barbarian countries dependent on civilized ones, nations of peasants on nations of bourgeois, the East on the West.

The bourgeoisie keeps more and more doing away with the scattered state   29 of the population, of the means of production, and of property. It has agglomerated population, centralized means of production, and has concentrated property in a few hands. The necessary consequence of this was political centralization. Independent, or but loosely connected provinces, with separate interests, laws, governments, and systems of taxation, became lumped together in one nation, with one government, one code of laws, one national class interest, one frontier and one customs tariff.

The bourgeoisie, during its rule of scarce one hundred years, has created [30] more massive and more colossal productive forces than have all preceding generations together. Subjection of Nature's forces to man, machinery, application of chemistry to industry and agriculture, steam-navigation, railways, electric telegraphs, clearing of whole continents for cultivation, canalization of rivers, whole populations conjured out of the ground—what earlier century had even a presentiment that such productive forces slumbered in the lap of social labor?

We see then: the means of production and of exchange on whose foundation [31] the bourgeoisie built itself up, were generated in feudal society. At a certain stage in the development of these means of production and of exchange, the conditions under which feudal society produced and exchanged, the feudal organization of agriculture and manufacturing industry, in one word, the feudal relations of property became no longer compatible with the already developed productive forces; they became so many fetters. They had to burst asunder; they were burst asunder.

Into their places stepped free competition, accompanied by social and polit- [32] ical constitution adapted to it, and by economical and political sway of the bourgeois class.

A similar movement is going on before our own eyes. Modern bourgeois [33] society with its relations of production, of exchange and of property, a society that has conjured up such gigantic means of production and of exchange, is like the sorcerer, who is no longer able to control the powers of the nether world whom he has called up by his spells. For many a decade past, the history of industry and commerce is but the history of the revolt of modern productive forces against modern conditions of production, against the property relations that are the conditions for the existence of the bourgeoisie and of its rule. It is enough to mention the commercial crises that by their periodical return put on its trial, each time more threateningly, the existence of the entire bourgeois society. In these crises a great part not only of the existing products, but also of the previously created productive forces, are periodically destroyed. In these crises there breaks out an epidemic that, in all earlier epochs, would have seemed an absurdity—the epidemic of overproduction. Society suddenly finds itself put back into a state of momentary barbarism; it appears as if a famine, a universal war of devastation, had cut off the supply of every means of subsistence; industry and commerce seem to be destroyed; and why? Because there is too much civilization, too much means of subsistence, too much industry, too much commerce. The productive forces at the disposal of society no longer tend to further the development of the conditions of the bourgeois property; on the contrary, they have become too powerful for these conditions by which they are fettered, and as soon as they overcome these fetters they bring disorder into the whole of bourgeois society, endanger the existence of bourgeois property. The conditions of bourgeois society are too narrow to comprise the wealth created by them. And how does the bourgeoisie get over these crises? On the one hand by enforced destruction of a mass of productive forces; on the other, by the conquest of new markets, and by the more thorough exploitation of the old ones. That is to say, by paving the way for more extensive and more destructive crises, and by diminishing the means whereby crises are prevented.

The weapons with which the bourgeoisie felled feudalism to the ground are now turned against the bourgeoisie itself. 34

But not only has the bourgeoisie forged the weapons that bring death to itself; it has also called into existence the men who are to wield those weapons—the modern working class—the proletarians. 35

In proportion as the bourgeoisie, i.e., capital, is developed, in the same proportion is the proletariat, the modern working class, developed, a class of laborers who live only so long as they find work, and who find work only so long as their labor increases capital. These laborers, who must sell themselves piecemeal, are a commodity, like every other article of commerce, and are consequently exposed to all the vicissitudes of competition, to all the fluctuations of the market. 36

Owing to the extensive use of machinery and to division of labor, the work of the proletarians has lost all individual character, and, consequently, all charm for the workman. He becomes an appendage of the machine, and it is only the most simple, most monotonous and most easily acquired knack that is required of him. Hence, the cost of production of a workman is restricted almost entirely to the means of subsistence that he requires for his maintenance, and for the propagation of his race. But the price of a commodity, and also of labor, is equal to its cost of production. In proportion, therefore, as the repulsiveness of the work increases the wage decreases. Nay more, in proportion as the use of machinery and division of labor increases, in the same proportion the burden of toil increases, whether by prolongation of the working hours, by increase of the work enacted in a given time, or by increased speed of the machinery, etc. 37

Modern industry has converted the little workshop of the patriarchal master into the great factory of the industrial capitalist. Masses of laborers, crowded into factories, are organized like soldiers. As privates of the industrial army they are placed under the command of a perfect hierarchy of officers and sergeants. Not only are they the slaves of the bourgeois class and of the bourgeois state, they are daily and hourly enslaved by the machine, by the overlooker, and, above all, by the individual bourgeois manufacturer himself. The more openly this depotism proclaims gain to be its end and aim, the more petty, the more hateful and the more embittering it is. 38

The less the skill and exertion or strength implied in manual labor, in other words, the more modern industry becomes developed, the more is the labor of men superseded by that of women. Differences of age and sex have no longer any distinctive social validity for the working class. All are instruments of labor, more or less expensive to use, according to their age and sex. 39

No sooner is the exploitation of the laborer by the manufacturer, so far at an 40 end, that he receives his wages in cash, than he is set upon by the other portions of the bourgeoisie, the landlord, the shopkeeper, the pawnbroker, etc.

The lower strata of the middle class—the small trades-people, shopkeepers   41
and retired tradesmen generally, the handicraftsmen and peasants—all these sink gradually into the proletariat, partly because their diminutive capital does not suffice for the scale on which Modern Industry is carried on, and is swamped in the competition with the large capitalists, partly because their specialized skill is rendered worthless by new methods of production. Thus the proletariat is recruited from all classes of the population.

The proletariat goes through various stages of development. With its birth   42
begins its struggle with the bourgeoisie. At first the contest is carried on by individual laborers, then by the workpeople of a factory, then by the operatives of one trade, in one locality, against the individual bourgeois who directly exploits them. They direct their attacks not against the bourgeois conditions of production, but against the instruments of production themselves; they destroy imported wares that compete with their labor, they smash to pieces machinery, they set factories ablaze, they seek to restore by force the vanished status of the workman of the Middle Ages.

At this stage the laborers still form an incoherent mass scattered over the   43
whole country, and broken up by their mutual competition. If anywhere they unite to form more compact bodies, this is not yet the consequence of their own active union, but of the union of the bourgeoisie, which class, in order to attain its own political ends, is compelled to set the whole proletariat in motion, and is moreover yet, for a time, able to do so. At this stage, therefore, the proletarians do not fight their enemies, but the enemies of their enemies, the remnants of absolute monarchy, the landowners, the non-industrial bourgeois, the petty bourgeoisie. Thus the whole historical movement is concentrated in the hands of the bourgeoisie, every victory so obtained is a victory for the bourgeoisie.

But with the development of industry the proletariat not only increases in   44
number; it becomes concentrated in greater masses, its strength grows and it feels that strength more. The various interests and conditions of life within the ranks of the proletariat are more and more equalized, in proportion as machinery obliterates all distinctions of labor, and nearly everywhere reduces wages to the same low level. The growing competition among the bourgeois, and the resulting commercial crisis, make the wages of the workers even more fluctuating. The unceasing improvement of machinery, ever more rapidly developing, makes their livelihood more and more precarious; the collisions between individual workmen and individual bourgeois take more and more the character of collisions between two classes. Thereupon the workers begin to form combinations (Trades' Unions) against the bourgeois; they club together in order to keep up the rate of wages; they found permanent associations in order to make provision beforehand for these occasional revolts. Here and there the contest breaks out into riots.

Now and then the workers are victorious, but only for a time. The real fruit   45
of their battle lies not in the immediate result but in the ever-expanding union

of workers. This union is helped on by the improved means of communication that are created by modern industry, and that places the workers of different localities in contact with one another. It was just this contact that was needed to centralize the numerous local struggles, all of the same character, into one national struggle between classes. But every class struggle is a political struggle. And that union, to attain which the burghers of the Middle Ages with their miserable highways, required centuries, the modern proletarians, thanks to railways, achieve in a few years.

This organization of the proletarians into a class, and consequently into a   46
political party, is continually being upset again by the competition between the workers themselves. But it ever rises up again, stronger, firmer, mightier. It compels legislative recognition of particular interests of the workers by taking advantage of the divisions among the bourgeoisie itself. Thus the ten hours' bill in England was carried.

Altogether collisions between the classes of the old society further, in many   47
ways, the course of development of the proletariat. The bourgeoisie finds itself involved in a constant battle. At first with the aristocracy; later on, with those portions of the bourgeoisie itself whose interests have become antagonistic to the progress of industry; at all times, with the bourgeoisie of foreign countries. In all these battles it sees itself compelled to appeal to the proletariat, to ask for its help, and thus, to drag it into the political arena. The bourgeoisie itself, therefore, supplies the proletariat with its own elements of political and general education; in other words, it furnishes the proletariat with weapons for fighting the bourgeoisie.

Further, as we have already seen, entire sections of the ruling classes are, by   48
the advance of industry, precipitated into the proletariat, or are at least threatened in their conditions of existence. These also supply the proletariat with fresh elements of enlightenment and progress.

Finally, in times when the class-struggle nears the decisive hour, the process   49
of dissolution going on within the ruling class—in fact, within the whole range of an old society—assumes such a violent, glaring character that a small section of the ruling class cuts itself adrift and joins the revolutionary class, the class that holds the future in its hands. Just as, therefore, at an earlier period, a section of the nobility went over to the bourgeoisie, so now a portion of the bourgeoisie goes over to the proletariat, and in particular, a portion of the bourgeois ideologists, who have raised themselves to the level of comprehending theoretically the historical movements as a whole.

Of all the classes that stand face to face with the bourgeoisie today the   50
proletariat alone is a really revolutionary class. The other classes decay and finally disappear in the face of modern industry; the proletariat is its special and essential product.

The lower middle class, the small manufacturer, the shopkeeper, the artisan,   51
the peasant, all these fight against the bourgeoisie, to save from extinction their existence as fractions of the middle class. They are therefore not revolutionary, but conservative. Nay, more; they are reactionary, for they try to roll back the wheel of history. If by chance they are revolutionary, they are so only in view of

their impending transfer into the proletariat; they thus defend not their present, but their future interests; they desert their own standpoint to place themselves at that of the proletariat.

The "dangerous class," the social scum, that passively rotting mass thrown   52
off by the lowest layers of old society, may, here and there, be swept into the movement by a proletarian revolution; its conditions of life, however, prepare it far more for the part of a bribed tool of reactionary intrigue.

In the conditions of the proletariat, those of the old society at large are   53
already virtually swamped. The proletarian is without property; his relation to his wife and children has no longer anything in common with the bourgeois family relations; modern industrial labor, modern subjection to capital, the same in England as in France, in America as in Germany, has stripped him of every trace of national character. Law, morality, religion, are to him so many bourgeois prejudices, behind which lurk in ambush just as many bourgeois interests.

All the preceding classes that got the upper hand sought to fortify their   54
already acquired status by subjecting society at large to their conditions of appropriation. The proletarians cannot become masters of the productive forces of society, except by abolishing their own previous mode of appropriation, and thereby also every other previous mode of appropriation. They have nothing of their own to secure and to fortify; their mission is to destroy all previous securities for and insurances of individual property.

All previous historical movements were movements of minorities, or in the   55
interest of minorities. The proletarian movement is the self-conscious, independent movement of the immense majority. The proletariat, the lowest stratum of our present society, cannot stir, cannot raise itself up without the whole superincumbent strata of official society being sprung into the air.

Though not in substance, yet in form, the struggle of the proletariat with the   56
bourgeoisie is at first a national struggle. The proletariat of each country must, of course, first of all settle matters with its own bourgeoisie.

In depicting the most general phases of the development of the proletariat,   57
we traced the more or less veiled civil war, raging within existing society, up to the point where that war breaks out into open revolution, and where the violent overthrow of the bourgeoisie, lays the foundations for the sway of the proletariat.

Hitherto every form of society has been based, as we have already seen, on   58
the antagonism of oppressing and oppressed classes. But in order to oppress a class, certain conditions must be assured to it under which it can, at least, continue its slavish existence. The serf, in the period of serfdom, raised himself to membership in the commune, just as the petty bourgeois, under the yoke of feudal absolutism managed to develop into a bourgeois. The modern laborer, on the contrary, instead of rising with the progress of industry, sinks deeper and deeper below the conditions of existence of his own class. He becomes a pauper, and pauperism develops more rapidly than population and wealth. And here it becomes evident that the bourgeoisie is unfit any longer to be the ruling class in society, and to impose its conditions of existence upon society as an over-riding law. It is unfit to rule, because it is incompetent to assure an exist-

ence to its slave within his slavery, because it cannot help letting him sink into such a state that it has to feed him, instead of being fed by him. Society can no longer live under this bourgeoisie; in other words, its existence is no longer compatible with society.

The essential condition for the existence, and for the sway of the bourgeois class, is the formation and augmentation of capital; the condition for capital is wage labor. Wage labor rests exclusively on competition between the laborers. The advance of industry, whose involuntary promoter is the bourgeoisie, replaces the isolation of the laborers, due to competition, by their involuntary combination, due to association. The development of Modern Industry, therefore, cuts from under its feet the very foundation on which the bourgeoisie produces and appropriates products. What the bourgeoisie therefore produces, above all, are its own grave diggers. Its fall and the victory of the proletariat are equally inevitable. 59

QUESTIONS FOR MEANING

1. Comment on the authors' claim in paragraph 7 that the "history of all hitherto existing society is the history of class struggles." What does this mean?
2. In paragraph 11, the authors write: "Society as a whole is more and more splitting up into two great hostile camps, into two great classes directly facing each other: Bourgeoisie and Proletariat." Has history proven them right? How would you describe class relations within the United States? Can American history be seen in Marxist terms?
3. Explain the distinction in paragraph 14 between the feudal and manufacturing systems of industry.
4. Do Marx and Engels concede that modern industry has accomplished anything admirable? Do they credit the bourgeoisie with any virtues?
5. Why do Marx and Engels believe that the bourgeoisie is unfit to rule? Why do they believe that the rise of the proletariat is inevitable?
6. What do Marx and Engels mean when they claim "there is too much civilization, too much means of subsistence, too much industry, too much commerce"? Paraphrase paragraph 33.
7. What is "the social scum" that Marx and Engels dismiss in paragraph 52? Why do they believe this class is dangerous?
8. Vocabulary: exorcise (1), patrician (8), plebeian (8), vassals (9), patriarchal (20), nexus (20), slothful (23), indigenous (26), agglomerated (29), presentiment (30), vicissitudes (36), diminutive (41), obliterates (44), precarious (44), and augmentation (59).

QUESTIONS ABOUT STRATEGY

1. Why do Marx and Engels open their manifesto by describing Communism as "a specter"? Explain what they mean by this and how it serves as an introduction to the political analysis that follows.

2. In interpreting history entirely in economic terms, are there any major conflicts that Marx and Engels overlook?
3. What is the function of paragraphs 31 and 32?
4. Can you point to anything in this work that reveals that Marx and Engels were writing for an international audience?
5. What parts of this essay are the strongest? Where do Marx and Engels make the most sense?
6. Can you identify any exaggerations in *The Communist Manifesto*? If you were to write a rebuttal, are there any claims that you could prove to be oversimplified?
7. Is this "manifesto" an argument or an exhortation? Is it designed to convince readers who have no political opinions, or to rally the men and women who are already committed to revolution? What is its purpose?

MARGARET SANGER
The Cause of War

A pioneering advocate of birth control, Margaret Sanger (1883–1966) was one of eleven children. She studied nursing and worked as an obstetrical nurse in the tenements of Manhattan's Lower East Side. She became convinced of the importance of birth control in 1912, when a young woman died in her arms after a self-induced abortion. Sanger went to Europe in 1913 to study contraception, and she is credited with having coined the phrase "birth control." Upon her return to the United States, she founded a magazine, **Woman Rebel,** *in which she could publish her views. In 1916, she was jailed for opening a birth-control clinic in New York, the first of many times she would be imprisoned for her work. She founded the National Birth Control League in 1917, an organization which eventually became the Planned Parenthood Federation of America. By the time Sanger was elected the first president of the International Planned Parenthood Federation in 1952, her views had come to be widely accepted.*

A lecturer and a writer, Sanger published several books. The following essay is drawn from **Woman and the New Race** *(1920). Writing at a time when Europe had not yet recovered from the horrors of the First World War, Sanger argued that the underlying cause of the war was excessive population growth. Although most historians would argue that the war had multiple causes, Sanger makes a strong case on behalf of her view.*

In every nation of militaristic tendencies we find the reactionaries demanding a higher and still higher birth rate. Their plea is, first, that great armies are needed to *defend* the country from its possible enemies; second, that a huge population is required to assure the country its proper place among the powers of the world. At bottom the two pleas are the same. 1

As soon as the country becomes overpopulated, these reactionaries proclaim loudly its moral right to expand. They point to the huge population, which in the name of patriotism they have previously demanded should be brought into being. Again pleading patriotism, they declare that it is the moral right of the nation to take by force such room as it needs. Then comes war—usually against some nation supposed to be less well prepared than the aggressor. 2

Diplomats make it their business to conceal the facts, and politicians violently denounce the politicians of other countries. There is a long beating of tom-toms by the press and all other agencies for influencing public opinion. Facts are distorted and lies invented until the common people cannot get at the truth. Yet, when the war is over, if not before, we always find that "a place in the sun," "a path to the sea," "a route to India" or something of the sort is at the bottom of the trouble. These are merely other names for expansion. 3

The "need of expansion" is only another name for overpopulation. One supreme example is sufficient to drive home this truth. That the Great War, from the horror of which we are just beginning to emerge, had its source in overpopulation is too evident to be denied by any serious student of current history. 4

For the past one hundred years most of the nations of Europe have been   5
piling up terrific debts to humanity by the encouragement of unlimited numbers. The rulers of these nations and their militarists have constantly called
upon the people to breed, breed, breed! Large populations meant more people
to produce wealth, more people to pay taxes, more trade for the merchants,
more soldiers to protect the wealth. But more people also meant need of greater
food supplies, an urgent and natural need for expansion.

As shown by C.V. Drysdale's famous "War Map of Europe," the great conflict   6
began among the high birth rate countries—Germany, with its rate of 31.7,
Austria-Hungary with 33.7 and 36.7, respectively, Russia with 45.4, Serbia with
38.6. Italy with her 38.7 came in, as the world is now well informed through the
publication of secret treaties by the Soviet government of Russia, upon the
promise of territory held by Austria. England, owing to her small home area, is
cramped with her comparatively low birth rate of 26.3. France, among the
belligerents, is conspicuous for her low birth rate of 19.9, but stood in the way
of expansion of high birth rate Germany. Nearly all of the persistently neutral
countries—Holland, Denmark, Norway, Sweden and Switzerland have low birth
rates, the average being a little over 26.

Owing to the part Germany played in the war, a survey of her birth statistics   7
is decidedly illuminating. The increase in the German birth rate up to 1876 was
great. Though it began to decline then, the decline was not sufficient to offset
the tremendous increase of the previous years. There were more millions to
produce children, so while the average number of births per thousand was
somewhat smaller, the net increase in population was still huge. From
41,000,000 in 1871, the year the Empire was founded, the German population
grew to approximately 67,000,000 in 1918. Meanwhile her food supply increased only a very small percent. In 1910, Russia had a birth rate even higher
than Germany's had ever been—a little less than 48 per thousand. When czarist
Russia wanted an outlet to the Mediterranean by way of Constantinople, she
was thinking of her increasing population. Germany was thinking of her increasing population when she spoke as with one voice of a "place in the sun." . . .

The militaristic claim for Germany's right to new territory was simply a claim   8
to the right of life and food for the German babies—the same right that a chick
claims to burst its shell. If there had not been other millions of people claiming
the same right, there would have been no war. But there *were* other millions.

The German rulers and leaders pointed out the fact that expansion meant   9
more business for German merchants, more work for German workmen at
better wages, and more opportunities for Germans abroad. They also pointed
out that lack of expansion meant crowding and crushing at home, hard times,
heavy burdens, lack of opportunity for Germans, and what not. In this way, they
gave the people of the Empire a startling and true picture of what would happen
from overcrowding. Once they realized the facts, the majority of Germans
naturally welcomed the so-called war of defense.

The argument was sound. Once the German mothers had submitted to the   10
plea for overbreeding, it was inevitable that imperialistic Germany should make
war. Once the battalions of unwanted babies came into existence—babies

whom the mothers did not want but which they bore as a "patriotic duty"—it was too late to avoid international conflict. The great crime of imperialistic Germany was its high birth rate.

It has always been so. Behind all war has been the pressure of population.   11
"Historians," says Huxley, "point to the greed and ambition of rulers, the reckless turbulence of the ruled, to the debasing effects of wealth and luxury, and to the devastating wars which have formed a great part of the occupation of mankind, as the causes of the decay of states and the foundering of old civilizations, and thereby point their story with a moral. But beneath all this superficial turmoil lay the deep-seated impulse given by unlimited multiplication."

Robert Thomas Malthus, formulator of the doctrine which bears his name,   12
pointed out, in the closing years of the eighteenth century, the relation of overpopulation to war. He showed that mankind tends to increase faster than the food supply. He demonstrated that were it not for the more common diseases, for plague, famine, floods and wars, human beings would crowd each other to such an extent that the misery would be even greater than it now is. These he described as "natural checks," pointing out that as long as no other checks are employed, such disasters are unavoidable. If we do not exercise sufficient judgment to regulate the birth rate, we encounter disease, starvation and war.

Both Darwin and John Stuart Mill recognized, by inference at least, the fact   13
that so-called "natural checks"—and among them war—will operate if some sort of limitation is not employed. In his *Origin of Species*, Darwin says: "There is no exception to the rule that every organic being naturally increases at so high a rate, if not destroyed, that the earth would soon be covered by the progeny of a single pair." Elsewhere he observes that we do not permit helpless human beings to die off, but we create philanthropies and charities, build asylums and hospitals and keep the medical profession busy preserving those who could not otherwise survive. John Stuart Mill, supporting the views of Malthus, speaks to exactly the same effect in regard to the multiplying power of organic beings, among them humanity. In other words, let countries become overpopulated and war is inevitable. It follows as daylight follows the sunrise.

When Charles Bradlaugh and Mrs. Annie Besant were on trial in England in   14
1877 for publishing information concerning contraceptives, Mrs. Besant put the case bluntly to the court and the jury:

"I have no doubt that if natural checks were allowed to operate right through   15
the human as they do in the animal world, a better result would follow. Among the brutes, the weaker are driven to the wall, the diseased fall out in the race of life. The old brutes, when feeble or sickly, are killed. If men insisted that those who were sickly should be allowed to die without help of medicine or science, if those who are weak were put upon one side and crushed, if those who were old and useless were killed, if those who were not capable of providing food for themselves were allowed to starve, if all this were done, the struggle for existence among men would be as real as it is among brutes and would doubtless result in the production of a higher race of men.

"But are you willing to do that or to allow it to be done?"   16

We are not willing to let it be done. Mother hearts cling to children, no matter   17
how diseased, misshapen and miserable. Sons and daughters hold fast to parents, no matter how helpless. We do not allow the weak to depart; neither do
we cease to bring more weak and helpless beings into the world. Among the
dire results is war, which kills off, not the weak and the helpless, but the strong
and the fit.

What shall be done? We have our choice of one of three policies. We may   18
abandon our science and leave the weak and diseased to die, or kill them, as
the brutes do. Or we may go on overpopulating the earth and have our famines
and our wars while the earth exists. Or we can accept the third, sane, sensible,
moral and practicable plan of birth control. We can refuse to bring weak, the
helpless and the unwanted children into the world. We can refuse to overcrowd
families, nations and the earth. There are these ways to meet the situation, and
only these three ways.

The world will never abandon its preventive and curative science; it may be   19
expected to elevate and extend it beyond our present imagination. The efforts
to do away with famine and the opposition to war are growing by leaps and
bounds. Upon these efforts are largely based our modern social revolutions.

There remains only the third expedient—birth control, the real cure for war.   20
This fact was called to the attention of the Peace Conference in Paris, in 1919,
by the Malthusian League, which adopted the following resolution at its annual
general meeting in London in June of that year:

"The Malthusian League desires to point out that the proposed scheme for   21
the League of Nations has neglected to take account of the important questions
of *the pressure of population*, which *causes the great international economic competition* and rivalry, and of the *increase of population*, which is
put forward as a justification for *claiming increase of territory*. It, therefore,
wishes to put on record its belief that the League of Nations will only be able to
fulfill its aim *when it adds a clause* to the following effect:

"'That each Nation desiring to enter into the League of Nations shall pledge   22
itself *so to restrict its birth rate* that its people shall be able to live in comfort
in their own dominions without need for territorial expansion, and that it
shall recognize that *increase of population shall not justify* a demand either
for increase of territory or for the compulsion of other Nations to admit its
emigrants; so that when all Nations in the League have shown their ability to
live on their own resources without international rivalry, they will be in a
position to fuse into an international federation, and territorial boundaries will
then have little significance.'"

As a matter of course, the Peace Conference paid no attention to the reso-   23
lution, for, as pointed out by Frank A. Vanderlip, the American financier, that
conference not only ignored the economic factors of the world situation, but
seemed unaware that Europe had produced more people than its fields could
feed. So the resolution amounted to so much propaganda and nothing more.

This remedy can be applied only by woman and she will apply it. She must   24
and will see past the call of pretended patriotism and of glory of empire and
perceive what is true and what is false in these things. She will discover what

base uses the militarist and the exploiter make of the idealism of peoples. Under the clamor of the press, permeating the ravings of the jingoes, she will hear the voice of Napoleon, the archtype of the militarists of all nations, calling for "fodder for cannon."

"Woman is given to us that she may bear children," said he. "Woman is our   25 property, we are not hers, because she produces children for us—we do not yield any to her. She is, therefore, our possession as the fruit tree is that of the gardener."

That is what the imperialist is *thinking* when he speaks of the glory of the   26 empire and the prestige of the nation. Every country has its appeal—its shibboleth—ready for the lips of the imperialist. German rulers pointed to the comfort of the workers, to old-age pensions, maternal benefits and minimum wage regulations, and other material benefits, when they wished to inspire soldiers for the Fatherland. England's strongest argument, perhaps, was a certain phase of liberty which she guarantees her subjects, and the protection afforded them wherever they may go. France and the United States, too, have their appeals to the idealism of democracy—appeals which the politicians of both countries know well how to use, though the peoples of both lands are beginning to awake to the fact that their countries have been living on the glories of their revolutions and traditions, rather than the substance of freedom. Behind the boast of old-age pensions, material benefits and wage regulations, behind the bombast concerning liberty in this country and tyranny in that, behind all the slogans and shibboleths coined out of the ideals of the peoples for the uses of imperialism, woman must and will see the iron hand of that same imperialism, condemning women to breed and men to die for the will of the rulers.

Upon woman the burden and the horrors of war are heaviest. Her heart is   27 the hardest wrung when the husband or the son comes home to be buried or to live a shattered wreck. Upon her devolve the extra tasks of filling out the ranks of workers in the war industries, in addition to caring for the children and replenishing the war-diminished population. Hers is the crushing weight and the sickening of soul. And it is out of her womb that those things proceed. When she sees what lies behind the glory and the horror, the boasting and the burden, and gets the vision, the human perspective, she will end war. She will kill war by the simple process of starving it to death. For she will refuse longer to produce the human food upon which the monster feeds.

QUESTIONS FOR MEANING

1. According to Sanger, what motives have led governments to encourage population growth?
2. From an evolutionary point of view, why is war unacceptable as a "natural check" upon population growth?
3. What are the three policies that Sanger believes nations must inevitably chose among? Are there any alternatives that she overlooks?

4. The Second World War began less than twenty years after the publication of this essay. Do you know anything about the conditions under which that war began which could be used as evidence to support Sanger's thesis that "militarists" and "reactionaries" favor high birth rates?
5. Vocabulary: belligerents (6), conspicuous (6), turbulence (11), debasing (11), foundering (11), inference (13), progeny (13), base (24), jingoes (24), and bombast (26).

QUESTIONS ABOUT STRATEGY

1. Is Sanger ever guilty of oversimplification? Can you think of any causes of war that have nothing to do with population?
2. How useful are the statistics cited in paragraphs 6 and 7?
3. Of the various quotations that Sanger includes in her essay, which is the most effective?
4. How would you describe the tone of this essay? Is it suitable for the subject?
5. Do you detect any bias in this essay? Does Sanger ever seem to suggest that World War I was caused by one country in particular? Is such an implication historically valid?

GEORGE ORWELL
Politics and the English Language

*George Orwell was the pseudonym adopted by Eric Arthur Blair (1903–1950) upon
the publication of his first book,* Down and Out in Paris and London *(1933). Born the
son of a British civil servant in India, he distinguished himself at an early age by
winning a King's scholarship to Eton, where he studied between 1917 and 1921.
Deciding not to go on to a university, he joined the Indian Imperial Police, and
served in Burma from 1922 to 1927—an experience upon which he drew for his
novel,* Burmese Days *(1935), and essays like "Shooting an Elephant" and "A
Hanging." During the 1930s Orwell published two more novels,* A Clergyman's
Daughter *(1935) and* Keep the Aspidistra Flying *(1936), but most of his income
came from writing book reviews and political journalism. Throughout these years,
Orwell thought of himself as a socialist, but he was basically a libertarian who could
not reconcile himself to the regimentation of party politics. With* The Road to Wigan
Pier *(1937) and* Homage to Catalonia *(1938), Orwell's work becomes increasingly
political. His two most famous books,* Animal Farm *(1945) and* Nineteen Eighty-
Four *(1949), reveal his conviction that social revolutions eventually lead to the
subjugation of the individual by an all-powerful and faceless state.*

*Orwell is a writer who makes readers think, but he is also one of the best stylists
in our century. His many essays are written with simplicity, clarity, and grace.
Orwell cared deeply about the importance of language, and in "Politics and the
English Language" he offers a brilliant analysis of the many ways in which
language can be abused. This is an essay that every writer should read.*

Most people who bother with the matter at all would admit that the English   1
language is in a bad way, but it is generally assumed that we cannot by conscious action do anything about it. Our civilization is decadent and our language—so the argument runs—must inevitably share in the general collapse.
It follows that any struggle against the abuse of language is a sentimental
archaism, like preferring candles to electric light or hansom cabs to aeroplanes.
Underneath this lies the half-conscious belief that language is a natural growth
and not an instrument which we shape for our own purposes.

Now, it is clear that the decline of a language must ultimately have political   2
and economic causes: it is not due simply to the bad influence of this or that
individual writer. But an effect can become a cause, reinforcing the original
cause and producing the same effect in an intensified form, and so on indefinitely. A man may take to drink because he feels himself to be a failure, and
then fail all the more completely because he drinks. It is rather the same thing
that is happening to the English language. It becomes ugly and inaccurate
because our thoughts are foolish, but the slovenliness of our language makes it
easier for us to have foolish thoughts. The point is that the process is reversible.
Modern English, especially written English, is full of bad habits which spread
by imitation and which can be avoided if one is willing to take the necessary

trouble. If one gets rid of these habits one can think more clearly, and to think clearly is a necessary first step towards political regeneration: so that the fight against bad English is not frivolous and is not the exclusive concern of professional writers. I will come back to this presently, and I hope that by that time the meaning of what I have said here will have become clearer. Meanwhile, here are five specimens of the English language as it is now habitually written.

These five passages have not been picked out because they are especially   3 bad—I could have quoted far worse if I had chosen—but because they illustrate various of the mental vices from which we now suffer. They are a little below the average, but are fairly representative samples. I number them so that I can refer back to them when necessary:

(1) I am not, indeed, sure whether it is not true to say that the Milton who once seemed not unlike a seventeenth-century Shelley had not become, out of an experience ever more bitter in each year, more alien[*sic*] to the founder of that Jesuit sect which nothing could induce him to tolerate.

Professor Harold Laski (Essay in *Freedom of Expression*).

(2) Above all, we cannot play ducks and drakes with a native battery of idioms which prescribes such egregious collocations of vocables as the Basic *put up with* for *tolerate* or *put at a loss* for *bewilder*.

Professor Lancelot Hogben (*Interglossa*).

(3) On the one side we have the free personality: by definition it is not neurotic, for it has neither conflict nor dream. Its desires, such as they are, are transparent, for they are just what institutional approval keeps in the forefront of consciousness; another institutional pattern would alter their number and intensity; there is little in them that is natural, irreducible, or culturally dangerous. But *on the other side*, the social bond itself is nothing but the mutual reflection of these self-secure integrities. Recall the definition of love. Is not this the very picture of a small academic? Where is there a place in this hall of mirrors for either personality or fraternity?

Essay on psychology in *Politics* (New York).

(4) All the "best people" from the gentlemen's clubs, and all the frantic fascist captains, united in common hatred of Socialism and bestial horror of the rising tide of the mass revolutionary movement, have turned to acts of provocation, to foul incendiarism, to medieval legends of poisoned wells, to legalize their own destruction of proletarian organizations, and rouse the agitated petty-bourgeoisie to chauvinistic fervor on behalf of the fight against the revolutionary way out of the crisis.

Communist pamphlet.

(5) If a new spirit *is* to be infused into this old country, there is one thorny and contentious reform which must be tackled, and that is the humanization and galvanization of the B.B.C. Timidity here will bespeak cancer and atrophy of the soul. The heart of Britain may be sound and of strong beat, for instance, but the British lion's roar at present is like that of Bottom in Shakespeare's *Midsummer*

Night's Dream—as gentle as any sucking dove. A virile new Britain cannot continue indefinitely to be traduced in the eyes or rather ears, of the world by the effete languors of Langham Place, brazenly masquerading as "standard English." When the Voice of Britain is heard at nine o'clock, better far and infinitely less ludicrous to hear aitches honestly dropped than the present priggish, inflated, inhibited, school-ma 'amish arch braying of blameless bashful mewing maidens!

Letter in *Tribune.*

Each of these passages has faults of its own, but, quite apart from avoidable   4
ugliness, two qualities are common to all of them. The first is staleness of imagery: the other is lack of precision. The writer either has a meaning and cannot express it, or he inadvertently says something else, or he is almost indifferent as to whether his words mean anything or not. The mixture of vagueness and sheer incompetence is the most marked characteristic of modern English prose, and especially of any kind of political writing. As soon as certain topics are raised, the concrete melts into the abstract and no one seems to think of turns of speech that are not hackneyed: prose consists less and less of *words* chosen for the sake of their meaning, and more and more of *phrases* tacked together like the sections of a prefabricated hen-house. I list below, with notes and examples, various of the tricks by means of which the work of prose-construction is habitually dodged:

Dying Metaphors

A newly invented metaphor assists thought by evoking a visual image, while   5
on the other hand a metaphor which is technically "dead" (e.g., *iron resolution*) has in effect reverted to being an ordinary word and can generally be used without loss of vividness. But in between these two classes there is a huge dump of worn-out metaphors which have lost all evocative power and are merely used because they save people the trouble of inventing phrases for themselves. Examples are: *Ring the changes on, take up the cudgels for, toe the line, ride roughshod over, stand shoulder to shoulder with, play into the hands of, no axe to grind, grist to the mill, fishing in troubled waters, on the order of the day, Achilles' heel, swan song, hotbed.* Many of these are used without knowledge of their meaning (what is a "rift," for instance?), and incompatible metaphors are frequently mixed, a sure sign that the writer is not interested in what he is saying. Some metaphors now current have been twisted out of their original meaning without those who use them even being aware of the fact. For example, *toe the line* is sometimes written *tow the line*. Another example is *the hammer and the anvil*, now always used with the implication that the anvil gets the worst of it. In real life it is always the anvil that breaks the hammer, never the other way about: a writer who stopped to think what he was saying would be aware of this, and would avoid perverting the original phrase.

Operators or Verbal False Limbs

These save the trouble of picking out appropriate verbs and nouns, and at   6
the same time pad each sentence with extra syllables which give it an appearance of symmetry. Characteristic phrases are: *render inoperative, militate
against, make contact with, be subjected to, give rise to, give grounds for,
have the effect of, play a leading part (role) in, make itself felt, take effect,
exhibit a tendency to, serve the purpose of, etc., etc.* The keynote is the
elimination of simple verbs. Instead of being a single word, such as *break, stop,
spoil, mend, kill,* a verb becomes a *phrase*, made up of a noun or adjective
tacked on to some general-purpose verb such as *prove, serve, form, play,
render.* In addition, the passive voice is wherever possible used in preference
to the active, and noun constructions are used instead of gerunds (*by examination of* instead of *by examining*). The range of verbs is further cut down by
means of the *-ize* and *de-* formation, and the banal statements are given an
appearance of profundity by means of the *not un-* formation. Simple conjunc-
tions and prepositions are replaced by such phrases as *with respect to, having
regard to, the fact that, by dint of, in view of, in the interests of, on the
hypothesis that*; and the ends of sentences are saved from anticlimax by such
resounding commonplaces as *greatly to be desired, cannot be left out of
account, a development to be expected in the near future, deserving of
serious consideration, brought to a satisfactory conclusion,* and so on and
so forth.

Pretentious Diction

Words like *phenomenon, element, individual* (as noun), *objective, cate-*   7
*gorical, effective, virtual, basic, primary, promote, constitute, exhibit, ex-
ploit, utilize, eliminate, liquidate,* are used to dress up simple statements and
give an air of scientific impartiality to biased judgments. Adjectives like *epoch-
making, epic, historic, unforgettable, triumphant, age-old, inevitable,
inexorable, veritable,* are used to dignify the sordid processes of international
politics, while writing that aims at glorifying war usually takes on an archaic
color, its characteristic words being: *realm, throne, chariot, mailed fist, tri-
dent, sword, shield, buckler, banner, jackboot, clarion.* Foreign words and
expressions such as *cul de sac, ancien régime, deus ex machina, mutatis
mutandis, status quo, gleichshaltung, weltanschauung,* are used to give an
air of culture and elegance. Except for the useful abbreviations *i.e., e.g.,* and
etc., there is no real need for any of the hundreds of foreign phrases now
current in English. Bad writers, and especially scientific, political and sociological writers, are nearly always haunted by the notion that Latin or Greek words

---

[1]An interesting illustration of this is the way in which the English flower names which were in use till very recently
are being ousted by Greek ones, *snapdragon* becoming *antirrhinum, forget-me-not* becoming *myosotis,* etc.
It is hard to see any practical reason for this change of fashion: it is probably due to an instinctive turning-away
from the more homely word and a vague feeling that the Greek word is scientific.

are grander than Saxon ones, and unnecessary words like *expedite, amelio-rate, predict, extraneous, deracinated, clandestine, subaqueous* and hundreds of others constantly gain ground from their Anglo-Saxon opposite numbers.[1] The jargon peculiar to Marxist writing (*hyena, hangman, cannibal, petty bourgeois, these gentry, lackey, flunkey, mad dog, White Guard*, etc.) consists largely of words and phrases translated from Russian, German or French; but the normal way of coining a new word is to use a Latin or Greek root with the appropriate affix and, where necessary, the *-ize* formation. It is often easier to make up words of this kind (*deregionalize, impermissible, extramarital, nonfragmentatory* and so forth) than to think up the English words that will cover one's meaning. The result, in general, is an increase in slovenliness and vagueness.

Meaningless Words

In certain kinds of writing, particularly in art criticism and literary criticism, it is normal to come across long passages which are almost completely lacking in meaning.[2] Words like *romantic, plastic, values, human, dead, sentimental, natural, vitality*, as used in art criticism, are strictly meaningless in the sense that they not only do not point to any discoverable object, but are hardly ever expected to do so by the reader. When one critic writes, "The outstanding feature of Mr. X's work is its living quality," while another writes, "The imme-diately striking thing about Mr. X's work is its peculiar deadness," the reader accepts this as a simple difference of opinion. If words like *black* and *white* were involved, instead of the jargon words *dead* and *living*, he would see at once that language was being used in an improper way. Many political words are similarly abused. The word *Fascism* has now no meaning except in so far as it signifies "something not desirable." The words *democracy, socialism, freedom, patriotic, realistic, justice*, have each of them several different meanings which cannot be reconciled with one another. In the case of a word like *democracy*, not only is there no agreed definition, but the attempt to make one is resisted from all sides. It is almost universally felt that when we call a country democratic we are praising it: consequently the defenders of every kind of regime claim that it is a democracy, and fear that they might have to stop using the word if it were tied down to any one meaning. Words of this kind are often used in a consciously dishonest way. That is, the person who uses them has his own private definition, but allows his hearer to think he means something quite different. Statements like *Marshal Pétain was a true patriot, The Soviet Press is the freest in the world, The Catholic Church is opposed to persecution*, are almost always made with intent to deceive. Other words

8

[2]Example: "Comfort's catholicity of perception and image, strangely Whitmanesque in range, almost the exact opposite in aesthetic compulsion, continues to evoke that trembling atmospheric accumulative hinting at a cruel, an inexorably serene timelessness . . . Wrey Gardiner scores by aiming at simple bull's-eyes with precision. Only they are not so simple, and through this contented sadness runs more than the surface bitter-sweet of resigna-tion." (*Poetry Quarterly*.)

used in variable meanings, in most cases more or less dishonestly, are: *class, totalitarian, science, progressive, reactionary, bourgeois, equality.*

Now that I have made this catalogue of swindles and perversions, let me give   9
another example of the kind of writing that they lead to. This time it must of its nature be an imaginary one. I am going to translate a passage of good English into modern English of the worst sort. Here is a well-known verse from *Ecclesiastes:*

> I returned and saw under the sun, that the race is not to the swift, nor the battle to the strong, neither yet bread to the wise, nor yet riches to men of understanding, nor yet favor to men of skill; but time and chance happeneth to them all.

Here it is in modern English:

> Objective consideration of contemporary phenomena compels the conclusion that success or failure in competitive activities exhibits no tendency to be commensurate with innate capacity, but that a considerable element of the unpredictable must invariably be taken into account.

This is a parody, but not a very gross one. Exhibit (3), above, for instance,   10
contains several patches of the same kind of English. It will be seen that I have not made a full translation. The beginning and ending of the sentence follow the original meaning fairly closely, but in the middle the concrete illustrations—race, battle, bread—dissolve into the vague phrase "success or failure in competitive activities." This had to be so, because no modern writer of the kind I am discussing—no one capable of using phrases like "objective consideration of contemporary phenomena"—would ever tabulate his thoughts in that precise and detailed way. The whole tendency of modern prose is away from concreteness. Now analyze these two sentences a little more closely. The first contains forty-nine words but only sixty syllables, and all its words are those of everyday life. The second contains thirty-eight words of ninety syllables: eighteen of its words are from Latin roots, and one from Greek. The first sentence contains six vivid images, and only one phrase ("time and chance") that could be called vague. The second contains not a single fresh, arresting phrase, and in spite of its ninety syllables it gives only a shortened version of the meaning contained in the first. Yet without a doubt it is the second kind of sentence that is gaining ground in modern English. I do not want to exaggerate. This kind of writing is not yet universal, and outcrops of simplicity will occur here and there in the worst-written page. Still, if you or I were told to write a few lines on the uncertainty of human fortunes, we should probably come much nearer to my imaginary sentence than to the one from *Ecclesiastes.*

As I have tried to show, modern writing at its worst does not consist in   11
picking out words for the sake of their meaning and inventing images in order

to make the meaning clearer. It consists in gumming together long strips of words which have already been set in order by someone else, and making the results presentable by sheer humbug. The attraction of this way of writing is that it is easy. It is easier—even quicker once you have the habit—to say *In my opinion it is a not unjustifiable assumption that* than to say *I think*. If you use ready-made phrases, you not only don't have to hunt about for words; you also don't have to bother with the rhythms of your sentences, since these phrases are generally so arranged as to be more or less euphonious. When you are composing in a hurry—when you are dictating to a stenographer, for instance, or making a public speech—it is natural to fall into a pretentious, Latinized style. Tags like *a consideration which we should do well to bear in mind* or *a conclusion to which all of us would readily assent* will save many a sentence from coming down with a bump. By using stale metaphors, similes and idioms, you save much mental effort, at the cost of leaving your meaning vague, not only for your reader but for yourself. This is the significance of mixed metaphors. The sole aim of a metaphor is to call up a visual image. When these images clash—as in *The Fascist octopus has sung its swan song, the jackboot is thrown into the melting pot*—it can be taken as certain that the writer is not seeing a mental image of the objects he is naming; in other words he is not really thinking. Look again at the examples I gave at the beginning of this essay. Professor Laski (1) uses five negatives in fifty-three words. One of these is superfluous, making nonsense of the whole passage, and in addition there is the slip *alien* for akin, making further nonsense, and several avoidable pieces of clumsiness which increase the general vagueness. Professor Hogben (2) plays ducks and drakes with a battery which is able to write prescriptions, and, while disapproving of the every-day phrase *put up with*, is unwilling to look *egregious* up in the dictionary and see what it means. (3), if one takes an uncharitable attitude towards it, is simply meaningless: probably one could work out its intended meaning by reading the whole of the article in which it occurs. In (4), the writer knows more or less what he wants to say, but an accumulation of stale phrases chokes him like tea leaves blocking a sink. In (5), words and meaning have almost parted company. People who write in this manner usually have a general emotional meaning—they dislike one thing and want to express solidarity with another—but they are not interested in the detail of what they are saying. A scrupulous writer, in every sentence that he writes, will ask himself at least four questions, thus: What am I trying to say? What words will express it? What image or idiom will make it clearer? Is this image fresh enough to have an effect? And he will probably ask himself two more: Could I put it more shortly? Have I said anything that is avoidably ugly? But you are not obliged to go to all this trouble. You can shirk it by simply throwing your mind open and letting the ready-made phrases come crowding in. They will construct your sentences for you—even think your thoughts for you, to a certain extent—and at need they will perform the important service of partially concealing your meaning even from yourself. It is at this point that the special connection between politics and the debasement of language becomes clear.

In our time it is broadly true that political writing is bad writing. Where it is   12
not true, it will generally be found that the writer is some kind of rebel, expressing his private opinions and not a "party line." Orthodoxy, of whatever color,
seems to demand a lifeless, imitative style. The political dialects to be found in
pamphlets, leading articles, manifestos, White Papers and the speeches of
under-secretaries do, of course, vary from party to party, but they are all alike
in that one almost never finds in them a fresh, vivid, home-made turn of speech.
When one watches some tired hack on the platform mechanically repeating the
familiar phrases—*bestial atrocities, iron heel, bloodstained tyranny, free
peoples of the world, stand shoulder to shoulder*—one often has a curious
feeling that one is not watching a live human being but some kind of dummy;
a feeling which suddenly becomes stronger at moments when the light catches
the speaker's spectacles and turns them into blank discs which seem to have
no eyes behind them. And this is not altogether fanciful. A speaker who uses
that kind of phraseology has gone some distance towards turning himself into
a machine. The appropriate noises are coming out of his larynx, but his brain is
not involved as it would be if he were choosing his words for himself. If the
speech he is making is one that he is accustomed to make over and over again,
he may be almost unconscious of what he is saying, as one is when one utters
the responses in church. And this reduced state of consciousness, if not indispensable, is at any rate favorable to political conformity.

In our time, political speech and writing are largely the defense of the inde-   13
fensible. Things like the continuance of British rule in India, the Russian purges
and deportations, the dropping of the atom bombs on Japan, can indeed be
defended, but only by arguments which are too brutal for most people to face,
and which do not square with the professed aims of political parties. Thus
political language has to consist largely of euphemism, question-begging and
sheer cloudy vagueness. Defenseless villages are bombarded from the air, the
inhabitants driven out into the countryside, the cattle machine-gunned, the huts
set on fire with incendiary bullets: this is called *pacification*. Millions of peasants are robbed of their farms and sent trudging along the roads with no more
than they can carry: this is called *transfer of population* or *rectification of
frontiers*. People are imprisoned for years without trial, or shot in the back of
the neck or sent to die of scurvy in Arctic lumber camps: this is called *elimination of unreliable elements*. Such phraseology is needed if one wants to
name things without calling up mental pictures of them. Consider for instance
some comfortable English professor defending Russian totalitarianism. He cannot say outright, "I believe in killing off your opponents when you can get good
results by doing so." Probably, therefore, he will say something like this:

"While freely conceding that the Soviet régime exhibits certain features   14
which the humanitarian may be inclined to deplore, we must, I think, agree that
a certain curtailment of the right to political opposition is an unavoidable
concomitant of transitional periods, and that the rigors which the Russian
people have been called upon to undergo have been amply justified in the
sphere of concrete achievement."

The inflated style is itself a kind of euphemism. A mass of Latin words fall   15 upon the facts like soft snow, blurring the outlines and covering up all the details. The great enemy of clear language is insincerity. When there is a gap between one's real and one's declared aims, one turns as it were instinctively to long words and exhausted idioms, like a cuttlefish squirting out ink. In our age there is no such thing as "keeping out of politics." All issues are political issues, and politics itself is a mass of lies, evasions, folly, hatred and schizophrenia. When the general atmosphere is bad, language must suffer. I should expect to find—this is a guess which I have not sufficient knowledge to verify—that the German, Russian and Italian languages have all deteriorated in the last ten or fifteen years, as a result of dictatorship.

But if thought corrupts language, language can also corrupt thought. A bad   16 usage can spread by tradition and imitation, even among people who should and do know better. The debased language that I have been discussing is in some ways very convenient. Phrases like *a not unjustifiable assumption, leaves much to be desired, would serve no good purpose, a consideration which we should do well to bear in mind*, are a continuous temptation, a packet of aspirins always at one's elbow. Look back through this essay, and for certain you will find that I have again and again committed the very faults I am protesting against. By this morning's post I have received a pamphlet dealing with conditions in Germany. The author tells me that he "felt impelled" to write it. I open it at random, and here is almost the first sentence that I see: "(The Allies) have an opportunity not only of achieving a radical transformation of Germany's social and political structure in such a way as to avoid a nationalistic reaction in Germany itself, but at the same time of laying the foundations of a co-operative and unified Europe." You see, he "feels impelled" to write—feels, presumably, that he has something new to say—and yet his words, like cavalry horses answer the bugle, group themselves automatically into the familiar dreary pattern. This invasion of one's mind by ready-made phrases (*lay the foundations, achieve a radical transformation*) can only be prevented if one is constantly on guard against them, and every such phrase anaesthetizes a portion of one's brain.

I said earlier that the decadence of our language is probably curable. Those   17 who deny this would argue, if they produced an argument at all, that language merely reflects existing social conditions, and that we cannot influence its development by any direct tinkering with words and constructions. So far as the general tone or spirit of a language goes, this may be true, but it is not true in detail. Silly words and expressions have often disappeared, not through any evolutionary process but owing to the conscious action of a minority. Two recent examples were *explore every avenue* and *leave no stone unturned*, which were killed by the jeers of a few journalists. There is a long list of flyblown metaphors which could similarly be got rid of if enough people would interest themselves in the job; and it should also be possible to laugh the *not un-*formation out of existence,[3] to reduce the amount of Latin and Greek in the

[3]One can cure oneself of the *not un-* formation by memorizing this sentence: *A not unblack dog was chasing a not unsmall rabbit across a not ungreen field.*

average sentence, to drive out foreign phrases and strayed scientific words, and, in general, to make pretentiousness unfashionable. But all these are minor points. The defense of the English language implies more than this, and perhaps it is best to start by saying what it does *not* imply.

To begin with it has nothing to do with archaism, with the salvaging of   18
obsolete words and turns of speech, or with the setting up of a "standard English" which must never be departed from. On the contrary, it is especially concerned with the scrapping of every word or idiom which has outworn its usefulness. It has nothing to do with correct grammar and syntax, which are of no importance so long as one makes one's meaning clear, or with the avoidance of Americanisms, or with having what is called a "good'prose style." On the other hand it is not concerned with fake simplicity and the attempt to make written English colloquial. Nor does it even imply in every case preferring the Saxon word to the Latin one, though it does imply using the fewest and shortest words that will cover one's meaning. What is above all needed is to let the meaning choose the word, and not the other way about. In prose, the worst thing one can do with words is to surrender to them. When you think of a concrete object, you think wordlessly, and then, if you want to describe the thing you have been visualizing you probably hunt about till you find the exact words that seem to fit. When you think of something abstract you are more inclined to use words from the start, and unless you make a conscious effort to prevent it, the existing dialect will come rushing in and do the job for you, at the expense of blurring or even changing your meaning. Probably it is better to put off using words as long as possible and get one's meaning as clear as one can through pictures or sensations. Afterwards one can choose—not simply *accept*—the phrases that will best cover the meaning, and then switch round and decide what impression one's words are likely to make on another person. This last effort of the mind cuts out all stale or mixed images, all prefabricated phrases, needless repetitions, and humbug and vagueness generally. But one can often be in doubt about the effect of a word or a phrase, and one needs rules that one can rely on when instinct fails. I think the following rules will cover most cases:

   (i)   Never use a metaphor, simile or other figure of speech which you are used to seeing in print.
   (ii) Never use a long word where a short one will do.
   (iii) If it is possible to cut a word out, always cut it out.
   (iv) Never use the passive where you can use the active.
   (v)   Never use a foreign phrase, a scientific word or a jargon word if you can think of an everyday English equivalent.
   (vi) Break any of these rules sooner than say anything outright barbarous.

These rules sound elementary, and so they are, but they demand a deep change in attitude in anyone who has grown used to writing in the style now fashionable. One could keep all of them and still write bad English, but one could not write the kind of stuff that I quoted in those five specimens at the beginning of this article.

I have not here been considering the literary use of language, but merely   19
language as an instrument for expressing and not for concealing or preventing
thought. Stuart Chase and others have come near to claiming that all abstract
words are meaningless, and have used this as a pretext for advocating a kind of
political quietism. Since you don't know what Fascism is, how can you struggle
against Fascism? One need not swallow such absurdities as this, but one ought
to recognize that the present political chaos is connected with the decay of
language, and that one can probably bring about some improvement by starting
at the verbal end. If you simplify your English, you are freed from the worst
follies of orthodoxy. You cannot speak any of the necessary dialects, and when
you make a stupid remark its stupidity will be obvious, even to yourself. Political
language—and with variations this is true of all political parties, from Conservatives to Anarchists—is designed to make lies sound truthful and murder
respectable, and to give an appearance of solidity to pure wind. One cannot
change this all in a moment, but one can at least change one's own habits, and
from time to time one can even, if one jeers loudly enough, send some worn-
out and useless phrase—some *jackboot, Achilles' heel, hotbed, melting pot,
acid test, veritable inferno* or other lump of verbal refuse—into the dustbin
where it belongs.

QUESTIONS FOR MEANING

1. Why should language concern everyone, and not just English teachers and
   professional writers? Explain what Orwell means by his claim that language
   can corrupt thought.
2. Many people believe that they sound "educated" by using big words and
   abstract phrases, and so "rain" becomes "precipitation" (or *shower activity*) and libraries become learning resource centers. Why does Orwell prefer simple, concrete language?
3. Why do people write badly? What causes does Orwell identify in his essay?
4. Explain in your own words what is wrong with each of the five writing
   samples that Orwell includes in paragraph 3.
5. What does Orwell mean by "verbal false limbs"?
6. Almost forty years have passed since Orwell first published this essay, and
   some of the phrases he ridicules have fallen from general use. Demonstrate
   that you understand what Orwell is complaining about by citing contemporary examples of pretentious diction, meaningless words, and political
   double-talk.
7. What is the connection between politics and language?
8. Orwell's fourth rule for writing well is, "Never use the passive where you
   can use the active." Explain the difference between the passive and active
   voice, and give at least one example of each.
9. Why is Orwell's sixth rule important?
10. Vocabulary: archaism (1), slovenliness (2), regeneration (2), frivolous (2),
    egregious (3), metaphor (5), evocative (5), banal (6), euphonious (11),
    idioms (11), scrupulous (11), purges (13), euphemism (13), concomitant
    (14), and colloquial (18).

QUESTIONS ABOUT STRATEGY

1. What point is Orwell emphasizing in his first two paragraphs, and why is it important to establish this point early in the essay?

2. Comment on Orwell's use of analogy in paragraph 2. How does the comparison between drinking and writing help to clarify Orwell's point?

3. How would you describe Orwell's own style? Does he ever violate his own standards?

4. Orwell protested against the use of "dying metaphors." Can you find examples of figurative language in this essay that are fresh and original?

5. What is the function of paragraph 9? Orwell writes that it is "a parody, but not a very gross one." What does he mean by this, and what is he trying to accomplish by contrasting "modern English" with a verse from the King James version of the Bible?

6. Orwell writes, "Political language . . . is designed to make lies sound truthful and murder respectable, and give an appearance of solidity to pure wind." As writing, this sentence is admirably clear. But is it fair? Do you agree with Orwell about the language of politics, or do you think he weakens his case through overstatement?

MARTIN LUTHER KING, JR.
Letter From Birmingham Jail

Martin Luther King, Jr. (1929–1968) was the most important leader of the movement to secure civil rights for black Americans during the mid-twentieth century. Ordained a Baptist minister in his father's church in Atlanta, King went on to receive a Ph.D. from Boston University in 1955. Two years later, he became the founder and director of the Southern Christian Leadership Conference, an organization he continued to lead until his assassination in 1968. He first came to national attention by organizing a boycott of the buses in Montgomery, Alabama (1955–1956)—a campaign that he recounts in Stride Toward Freedom: The Montgomery Story *(1958). His other books include* The Measure of a Man *(1959),* Why We Can't Wait *(1963), and* Where Do We Go From Here: Chaos or Community? *(1967). An advocate of nonviolence, King was jailed fourteen times in the course of his work for civil rights. His efforts helped secure the passage of the Civil Rights Bill in 1963, and, during the last years of his life, he was the recipient of many awards, most notably the Nobel Peace Prize in 1964.*

"Letter from Birmingham Jail" was written in 1963, when King was jailed for eight days as the result of his campaign against segregation in Birmingham, Alabama. In it, King responds to white clergymen who had criticized his work and blamed him for breaking the law. But "Letter from Birmingham Jail" is much more than a rebuttal of criticism. It is a well-reasoned and carefully argued defense of civil disobedience as a means of securing civil liberties.

April 16, 1963

My Dear Fellow Clergymen:

While confined here in the Birmingham city jail, I came across your recent statement calling my present activities "unwise and untimely." Seldom do I pause to answer criticism of my work and ideas. If I sought to answer all the criticisms that cross my desk, my secretaries would have little time for anything other than such correspondence in the course of the day, and I would have no time for constructive work. But since I feel that you are men of genuine good will and that your criticisms are sincerely set forth, I want to try to answer your statement in what I hope will be patient and reasonable terms. 1

I think I should indicate why I am here in Birmingham, since you have been influenced by the view which argues against "outsiders coming in." I have the honor of serving as president of the Southern Christian Leadership Conference, an organization operating in every southern state, with headquarters in Atlanta, Georgia. We have some eighty-five affiliated organizations across the South, and one of them is the Alabama Christian Movement for Human Rights. Frequently we share staff, educational, and financial resources with our affiliates. Several months ago the affiliate here in Birmingham asked us to be on call to engage in a nonviolent direct-action program if such were deemed necessary. We readily consented, and when the hour came we lived up to our promise. So I, along with several members of my staff, am here because I was invited here. I am here because I have organizational ties here. 2

But more basically, I am in Birmingham because injustice is here. Just as the   3
prophets of the eighth century B.C. left their villages and carried their "thus
saith the Lord" far beyond the boundaries of their home towns, and just as the
Apostle Paul left his village of Tarsus and carried the gospel of Jesus Christ to
the far corners of the Greco-Roman world, so am I compelled to carry the
gospel of freedom beyond my own home town. Like Paul, I must constantly
respond to the Macedonian call for aid.

Moreover, I am cognizant of the interrelatedness of all communities and   4
states. I cannot sit idly by in Atlanta and not be concerned about what happens
in Birmingham. Injustice anywhere is a threat to justice everywhere. We are
caught in an inescapable network of mutuality, tied in a single garment of
destiny. Whatever affects one directly, affects all indirectly. Never again can we
afford to live with the narrow, provincial, "outside agitator" idea. Anyone who
lives inside the United States can never be considered an outsider anywhere
within its bounds.

You deplore the demonstrations taking place in Birmingham. But your state-   5
ment, I am sorry to say, fails to express a similar concern for the conditions that
brought about the demonstrations. I am sure that none of you would want to
rest content with the superficial kind of social analysis that deals merely with
effects and does not grapple with underlying causes. It is unfortunate that
demonstrations are taking place in Birmingham, but it is even more unfortunate that the city's white power structure left the Negro community with no
alternative.

In any nonviolent campaign there are four basic steps: collection of the facts   6
to determine whether injustices exist; negotiation; self-purification; and direct
action. We have gone through all these steps in Birmingham. There can be no
gainsaying the fact that racial injustice engulfs this community. Birmingham is
probably the most thoroughly segregated city in the United States. Its ugly
record of brutality is widely known. Negroes have experienced grossly unjust
treatment in courts. There have been more unsolved bombings of Negro homes
and churches in Birmingham than in any other city in the nation. These are the
hard, brutal facts of the case. On the basis of these conditions, Negro leaders
sought to negotiate with the city fathers. But the latter consistently refused to
engage in good-faith negotiation.

Then, last September, came the opportunity to talk with leaders of Birming-   7
ham's economic community. In the course of the negotiations, certain promises
were made by the merchants—for example, to remove the stores' humiliating
racial signs. On the basis of these promises, the Reverend Fred Shuttlesworth
and the leaders of the Alabama Christian Movement for Human Rights agreed
to a moratorium on all demonstrations. As the weeks and months went by, we
realized that we were the victims of a broken promise. A few signs, briefly
removed, returned; the others remained.

As in so many past experiences, our hopes had been blasted, and the shadow   8
of deep disappointment settled upon us. We had no alternative except to prepare for direct action, whereby we would present our very bodies as means of
laying our case before the conscience of the local and the national community.

Mindful of the difficulties involved, we decided to undertake a process of self-purification. We began a series of workshops on nonviolence, and we repeatedly asked ourselves: "Are you able to accept blows without retaliating?" "Are you able to endure the ordeal of jail?" We decided to schedule our direct-action program for the Easter season, realizing that except for Christmas, this is the main shopping period of the year. Knowing that a strong economic-withdrawal program would be the by-product of direct action, we felt that this would be the best time to bring pressure to bear on the merchants for the needed change.

9   Then it occurred to us that Birmingham's mayoral election was coming up in March, and we speedily decided to postpone action until after election day. When we discovered that the Commissioner of Public Safety, Eugene "Bull" Connor, had piled up enough votes to be in the run-off, we decided again to postpone action until the day after the run-off so that the demonstrations could not be used to cloud the issues. Like many others, we waited to see Mr. Connor defeated, and to this end we endured postponement after postponement. Having aided in this community need, we felt that our direct-action program could be delayed no longer.

10   You may well ask, "Why direct action? Why sit-ins, marches, and so forth? Isn't negotiation a better path?" You are quite right in calling for negotiation. Indeed, this is the very purpose of direct action. Nonviolent direct action seeks to create such a crisis and foster such a tension that a community which has constantly refused to negotiate is forced to confront the issue. It seeks so to dramatize the issue that it can no longer be ignored. My citing the creation of tension as part of the work of the nonviolent-resister may sound rather shocking. But I must confess that I am not afraid of the word "tension." I have earnestly opposed violent tension, but there is a type of constructive, nonviolent tension which is necessary for growth. Just as Socrates felt that it was necessary to create a tension in the mind so that individuals could rise from the bondage of myths and half-truths to the unfettered realm of creative analysis and objective appraisal, so must we see the need for nonviolent gadflies to create the kind of tension in society that will help men rise from the dark depths of prejudice and racism to the majestic heights of understanding and brotherhood.

11   The purpose of our direct-action program is to create a situation so crisis-packed that it will inevitably open the door to negotiation. I therefore concur with you in your call for negotiation. Too long has our beloved Southland been bogged down in a tragic effort to live in monologue rather than dialogue.

12   One of the basic points in your statement is that the action that I and my associates have taken in Birmingham is untimely. Some have asked: "Why didn't you give the new city administration time to act?" The only answer that I can give to this query is that the new Birmingham administration must be prodded about as much as the outgoing one, before it will act. We are sadly mistaken if we feel that the election of Albert Boutwell as mayor will bring the millennium to Birmingham. While Mr. Boutwell is a much more gentle person than Mr. Connor, they are both segregationists, dedicated to maintenance of the status quo. I have hoped that Mr. Boutwell will be reasonable enough to see the futility

of massive resistance to desegregation. But he will not see this without pressure from devotees of civil rights. My friends, I must say to you that we have not made a single gain in civil rights without determined legal and nonviolent pressure. Lamentably, it is an historical fact that privileged groups seldom give up their privileges voluntarily. Individuals may see the moral light and voluntarily give up their unjust posture; but, as Reinhold Niebuhr has reminded us, groups tend to be more immoral than individuals.

We know through painful experience that freedom is never voluntarily given   13
by the oppressor; it must be demanded by the oppressed. Frankly, I have yet to engage in a direct-action campaign that was "well timed" in the view of those who have not suffered unduly from the disease of segregation. For years now I have heard the word "Wait!" It rings in the ear of every Negro with piercing familiarity. This "Wait" has almost always meant "Never." We must come to see, with one of our distinguished jurists, that "justice too long delayed is justice denied."

We have waited for more than 340 years for our constitutional and God-   14
given rights. The nations of Asia and Africa are moving with jetlike speed toward gaining political independence, but we still creep at horse-and-buggy pace toward gaining a cup of coffee at a lunch counter. Perhaps it is easy for those who have never felt the stinging darts of segregation to say, "Wait." But when you have seen vicious mobs lynch your mothers and fathers at will and drown your sisters and brothers at whim; when you have seen hate-filled policemen curse, kick, and even kill your black brothers and sisters; when you see the vast majority of your twenty million Negro brothers smothering in an airtight cage of poverty in the midst of an affluent society; when you suddenly find your tongue twisted and your speech stammering as you seek to explain to your six-year-old daughter why she can't go to the public amusement park that has just been advertised on television, and see tears welling up in her eyes when she is told that Funtown is closed to colored children, and see ominous clouds of inferiority beginning to form in her little mental sky, and see her beginning to distort her personality by developing an unconscious bitterness toward white people; when you have to concoct an answer for a five-year-old son who is asking, "Daddy, why do white people treat colored people so mean?"; when you take a cross-country drive and find it necessary to sleep night after night in the uncomfortable corners of your automobile because no motel will accept you; when you are humiliated day in and day out by nagging signs reading "white" and "colored"; when your first name becomes "nigger," your middle name becomes "boy" (however old you are) and your last name becomes "John," and your wife and mother are never given the respected title "Mrs."; when you are harried by day and haunted by night by the fact that you are a Negro, living constantly at tiptoe stance, never quite knowing what to expect next, and are plagued with inner fears and outer resentments; when you are forever fighting a degenerating sense of "nobodiness"—then you will understand why we find it difficult to wait. There comes a time when the cup of endurance runs over, and men are no longer willing to be plunged into the

abyss of despair. I hope, sirs, you can understand our legitimate and unavoidable impatience.

You express a great deal of anxiety over our willingness to break laws. This is certainly a legitimate concern. Since we so diligently urge people to obey the Supreme Court's decision of 1954 outlawing segregation in the public schools, at first glance it may seem rather paradoxical for us consciously to break laws. One may well ask: "How can you advocate breaking some laws and obeying others?" The answer lies in the fact that there are two types of laws; just and unjust. I would be the first to advocate obeying just laws. One has not only a legal but a moral responsibility to obey just laws. Conversely, one has a moral responsibility to disobey unjust laws. I would agree with St. Augustine that "an unjust law is no law at all."   15

Now, what is the difference between the two? How does one determine whether a law is just or unjust? A just law is a man-made code that squares with the moral law or the law of God. An unjust law is a code that is out of harmony with the moral law. To put it in the terms of St. Thomas Aquinas: An unjust law is a human law that is not rooted in eternal law and natural law. Any law that uplifts human personality is just. Any law that degrades human personality is unjust. All segregation statues are unjust because segregation distorts the soul and damages the personality. It gives the segregator a false sense of superiority and the segregated a false sense of inferiority. Segregation, to use the terminology of the Jewish philosopher Martin Buber, substitutes an "I-it" relationship for an "I-thou" relationship and ends up relegating persons to the status of things. Hence segregation is not only politically, economically, and sociologically unsound, it is morally wrong and sinful. Paul Tillich has said that sin is separation. Is not segregation an existential expression of man's tragic separation, his awful estrangement, his terrible sinfulness? Thus it is that I can urge men to obey the 1954 decision of the Supreme Court, for it is morally right; and I can urge them to disobey segregation ordinances, for they are morally wrong.   16

Let us consider a more concrete example of just and unjust laws. An unjust law is a code that a numerical or power majority group compels a minority group to obey but does not make binding on itself. This is *difference* made legal. By the same token, a just law is a code that a majority compels a minority to follow and that it is willing to follow itself. This is *sameness* made legal.   17

Let me give another explanation. A law is unjust if it is inflicted on a minority that, as a result of being denied the right to vote, had no part in enacting or devising the law. Who can say that the legislature of Alabama which set up that state's segregation laws was democratically elected? Throughout Alabama all sorts of devious methods are used to prevent Negroes from becoming registered voters, and there are some counties in which, even though Negroes constitute a majority of the population, not a single Negro is registered. Can any law enacted under such circumstances be considered democratically structured?   18

Sometimes a law is just on its face and unjust in its application. For instance,   19

I have been arrested on a charge of parading without a permit. Now, there is nothing wrong in having an ordinance which requires a permit for a parade. But such an ordinance becomes unjust when it is used to maintain segregation and to deny citizens the First-Amendment privilege of peaceful assembly and protest.

I hope you are able to see the distinction I am trying to point out. In no sense do I advocate evading or defying the law, as would the rabid segregationist. That would lead to anarchy. One who breaks an unjust law must do so openly, lovingly, and with a willingness to accept the penalty. I submit that an individual who breaks a law that conscience tells him is unjust, and who willingly accepts the penalty of imprisonment in order to arouse the conscience of the community over its injustice, is in reality expressing the highest respect for law.   20

Of course, there is nothing new about this kind of civil disobedience. It was evidenced sublimely in the refusal of Shadrach, Meshach, and Abednego to obey the laws of Nebuchadnezzar, on the ground that a higher moral law was at stake. It was practiced superbly by the early Christians, who were willing to face hungry lions and the excruciating pain of chopping blocks rather than submit to certain unjust laws of the Roman Empire. To a degree, academic freedom is a reality today because Socrates practiced civil disobedience. In our own nation, the Boston Tea Party represented a massive act of civil disobedience.   21

We should never forget that everything Adolf Hitler did in Germany was "legal" and everything the Hungarian freedom fighters did in Hungary was "illegal." It was "illegal" to aid and comfort a Jew in Hitler's Germany. Even so, I am sure that, had I lived in Germany at the time, I would have aided and comforted my Jewish brothers. If today I lived in a Communist country where certain principles dear to the Christian faith are suppressed, I would openly advocate disobeying that country's anti-religious laws.   22

I must make two honest confessions to you, my Christian and Jewish brothers. First, I must confess that over the past few years I have been gravely disappointed with the white moderate. I have almost reached the regrettable conclusion that the Negro's great stumbling block in his stride toward freedom is not the White Citizen's Counciler or the Ku Klux Klanner, but the white moderate, who is more devoted to "order" than to justice; who prefers a negative peace which is the absence of tension to a positive peace which is the presence of justice; who constantly says, "I agree with you in the goal you seek, but I cannot agree with your methods of direct action"; who paternalistically believes he can set the timetable for another man's freedom; who lives by a mythical concept of time and who constantly advises the Negro to wait for a "more convenient season." Shallow understanding from people of good will is more frustrating than absolute misunderstanding from people of ill will. Lukewarm acceptance is much more bewildering than outright rejection.   23

I had hoped that the white moderate would understand that law and order exist for the purpose of establishing justice and that when they fail in this purpose they become the dangerously structured dams that block the flow of social progress. I had hoped that the white moderate would understand that   24 the present tension in the South is a necessary phase of the transition from an obnoxious negative peace, in which the Negro passively accepted his unjust plight, to a substantive and positive peace, in which all men will respect the dignity and worth of human personality. Actually, we who engage in nonviolent direct action are not the creators of tension. We merely bring to the surface the hidden tension that is already alive. We bring it out in the open, where it can be seen and dealt with. Like a boil that can never be cured so long as it is covered up but must be opened with all its ugliness to the natural medicines of air and light, injustice must be exposed, with all the tension its exposure creates, to the light of human conscience and the air of national opinion, before it can be cured.

In your statement you assert that our actions, even though peaceful, must   25 be condemned because they precipitate violence. But is this a logical assertion? Isn't this like condemning a robbed man because his possession of money precipitated the evil act of robbery? Isn't this like condemning Socrates because his unswerving commitment to truth and his philosophical inquiries precipitated the act by the misguided populace in which they made him drink hemlock? Isn't this like condemning Jesus because his unique God-consciousness and never-ceasing devotion to God's will precipitated the evil act of crucifixion? We must come to see that, as the federal courts have consistently affirmed, it is wrong to urge an individual to cease his efforts to gain his basic constitutional rights because the quest may precipitate violence. Society must protect the robbed and punish the robber.

I had also hoped that the white moderate would reject the myth concerning   26 time in relation to the struggle for freedom. I have just received a letter from a white brother in Texas. He writes: "All Christians know that the colored people will receive equal rights eventually, but it is possible that you are in too great a religious hurry. It has taken Christianity almost two thousand years to accomplish what it has. The teachings of Christ take time to come to earth." Such an attitude stems from a tragic misconception of time, from the strangely irrational notion that there is something in the very flow of time that will inevitably cure all ills. Actually, time itself is neutral; it can be used either destructively or constructively. More and more I feel that the people of ill will have used time much more effectively than have the people of good will. We will have to repent in this generation not merely for the hateful words and actions of the bad people, but for the appalling silence of the good people. Human progress never rolls in on wheels of inevitability; it comes through the tireless efforts of men willing to be co-workers with God, and without this hard work, time itself becomes an ally of the forces of social stagnation. We must use time creatively, in the knowledge that the time is always ripe to do right. Now is the time to make real the promise of democracy and transform our pending national elegy into a creative psalm of brotherhood. Now is the time to lift our national policy from the quicksand of racial injustice to the solid rock of human dignity.

You speak of our activity in Birmingham as extreme. At first I was rather   27 disappointed that fellow clergymen would see my nonviolent efforts as those of an extremist. I began thinking about the fact that I stand in the middle of two opposing forces in the Negro community. One is a force of complacency, made up in part of Negroes who, as a result of long years of oppression, are so drained of self-respect and a sense of "somebodiness" that they have adjusted to segregation; and in part of a few middle-class Negroes who, because of a degree of academic and economic security and because in some ways they profit by segregation, have become insensitive to the problems of the masses. The other force is one of bitterness and hatred, and it comes perilously close to advocating violence. It is expressed in the various black nationalist groups that are springing up across the nation, the largest and best-known being Elijah Muhammad's Muslim movement. Nourished by the Negro's frustration over the continued existence of racial discrimination, this movement is made up of people who have lost faith in America, who have absolutely repudiated Christianity, and who have concluded that the white man is an incorrigible "devil."

I have tried to stand between these two forces, saying that we need emulate   28
neither the "do-nothingism" of the complacent nor the hatred and despair of the black nationalist. For there is the more excellent way of love and nonviolent protest. I am grateful to God that, through the influence of the Negro church, the way of nonviolence became an integral part of our struggle.

If this philosophy had not emerged, by now many streets of the South would,   29
I am convinced, be flowing with blood. And I am further convinced that if our white brothers dismiss as "rabble-rousers" and "outside agitators" those of us who employ nonviolent direct action, and if they refuse to support our nonviolent efforts, millions of Negroes will, out of frustration and despair, seek solace and security in black-nationalist ideologies—a development that would inevitably lead to a frightening racial nightmare.

Oppressed people cannot remain oppressed forever. The yearning for free-   30
dom eventually manifests itself, and that is what has happened to the American Negro. Something within has reminded him of his birthright of freedom, and something without has reminded him that it can be gained. Consciously or unconsciously, he has been caught up by the *Zeitgeist*, and with his black brothers of Africa and his brown and yellow brothers of Asia, South America, and the Caribbean, the United States Negro is moving with a sense of great urgency toward the promised land of racial justice. If one recognizes this vital urge that has engulfed the Negro community, one should readily understand why public demonstrations are taking place. The Negro has many pent-up resentments and latent frustrations, and he must release them. So let him march; let him make prayer pilgrimages to the city hall; let him go on freedom rides—and try to understand why he must do so. If his repressed emotions are not released in nonviolent ways, they will seek expression through violence; this is not a threat but a fact of history. So I have not said to my people, "Get rid of your discontent." Rather, I have tried to say that this normal and healthy discontent can be channeled into the creative outlet of nonviolent direct action. And now this approach is being termed extremist.

But though I was initially disappointed at being categorized as an extremist,   31
as I continued to think about the matter I gradually gained a measure of satis-

faction from the label. Was not Jesus an extremist for love: "Love your enemies, bless them that curse you, do good to them that hate you, and pray for them which despitefully use you, and persecute you." Was not Amos an extremist for justice: "Let justice roll down like waters and righteousness like an everflowing stream." Was not Paul an extremist for the Christian gospel: "I bear in my body the marks of the Lord Jesus." Was not Martin Luther an extremist: "Here I stand; I cannot do otherwise, so help me God." And John Bunyan: "I will stay in jail to the end of my days before I make a butchery of my conscience." And Abraham Lincoln: "This nation cannot survive half slave and half free." And Thomas Jefferson: "We hold these truths to be self-evident, that all men are created equal ...." So the question is not whether we will be extremists, but what kind of extremists we will be. Will we be extremists for hate or for love? Will we be extremists for the preservation of injustice or for the extension of justice? In that dramatic scene on Calvary's hill three men were crucified. We must never forget that all three were crucified for the same crime—the crime of extremism. Two were extremists for immorality, and thus fell below their environment. The other, Jesus Christ, was an extremist for love, truth, and goodness, and thereby rose above his environment. Perhaps the South, the nation, and the world are in dire need of creative extremists.

I had hoped that the white moderate would see this need. Perhaps I was too 32 optimistic; perhaps I expected too much. I suppose I should have realized that few members of the oppressor race can understand the deep groans and passionate yearnings of the oppressed race, and still fewer have the vision to see that injustice must be rooted out by strong, persistent, and determined action. I am thankful, however, that some of our white brothers in the South have grasped the meaning of this social revolution and committed themselves to it. They are still all too few in quantity, but they are big in quality. Some—such as Ralph McGill, Lillian Smith, Harry Golden, James McBride Dabbs, Ann Braden, and Sarah Patton Boyle—have written about our struggle in eloquent and prophetic terms. Others have marched with us down nameless streets of the South. They have languished in filthy, roach-infested jails, suffering the abuse and brutality of policemen who view them as "dirty nigger-lovers." Unlike so many of their moderate brothers and sisters, they have recognized the urgency of the moment and sensed the need for powerful "action" antidotes to combat the disease of segregation.

Let me take note of my other major disappointment. I have been so greatly 33 disappointed with the white church and its leadership. Of course, there are some notable exceptions. I am not unmindful of the fact that each of you has taken some significant stands on this issue. I commend you, Reverend Stallings, for your Christian stand on this past Sunday, in welcoming Negroes to your worship service on a nonsegregated basis. I commend the Catholic leaders of this state for integrating Spring Hill College several years ago.

But despite these notable exceptions, I must honestly reiterate that I have 34 been disappointed with the church. I do not say this as one of those negative critics who can always find something wrong with the church. I say this as a minister of the gospel, who loves the church; who was nurtured in its bosom; who has been sustained by its spiritual blessings and who will remain true to it as long as the cord of life shall lengthen.

When I was suddenly catapulted into the leadership of the bus protest in   35
Montgomery, Alabama, a few years ago, I felt we would be supported by the white church. I felt that the white ministers, priests, and rabbis of the South would be among our strongest allies. Instead, some have been outright opponents, refusing to understand the freedom movement and misrepresenting its leaders; all too many others have been more cautious than courageous and have remained silent behind the anesthetizing security of stained-glass windows.

In spite of my shattered dreams, I came to Birmingham with the hope that   36
the white religious leadership of this community would see the justice of our cause and, with deep moral concern, would serve as the channel through which our just grievances could reach the power structure. I had hoped that each of you would understand. But again I have been disappointed.

There was a time when the church was very powerful—in the time when   37
the early Christians rejoiced at being deemed worthy to suffer for what they believed. In those days the church was not merely a thermometer that recorded the ideas and principles of popular opinion; it was a thermostat that transformed the mores of society. Whenever the early Christians entered a town, the people in power became disturbed and immediately sought to convict the Christians for being "disturbers of the peace" and "outside agitators." But the Christians pressed on, in the conviction that they were "a colony of heaven," called to obey God rather than man. Small in number, they were big in commitment. They were too God-intoxicated to be "astronomically intimidated." By their effort and example they brought an end to such ancient evils as infanticide and gladiatorial contests.

Things are different now. So often the contemporary church is a weak,   38
ineffectual voice with an uncertain sound. So often it is an archdefender of the status quo. Far from being disturbed by the presence of the church, the power structure of the average community is consoled by the church's silent—and often even vocal—sanction of things as they are.

But the judgment of God is upon the church as never before. If today's   39
church does not recapture the sacrificial spirit of the early church, it will lose its authenticity, forfeit the loyalty of millions, and be dismissed as an irrelevant social club with no meaning for the twentieth century. Every day I meet young people whose disappointment with the church has turned into outright disgust.

Perhaps I have once again been too optimistic. Is organized religion too   40
inextricably bound to the status quo to save our nation and the world? Perhaps I must turn my faith to the inner spiritual church, the church within the church, as the true *ekklesia* and the hope of the world. But again I am thankful to God that some noble souls from the ranks of organized religion have broken loose from the paralyzing chains of conformity and joined us as active partners in the

struggle for freedom. They have left their secure congregations and walked the streets of Albany, Georgia, with us. They have gone down the highways of the South on torturous rides for freedom. Yes, they have gone to jail with us. Some have been dismissed from their churches, have lost the support of their bishops and fellow ministers. But they have acted in the faith that right defeated is stronger than evil triumphant. Their witness has been the spiritual salt that has preserved the true meaning of the gospel in these troubled times. They have carved a tunnel of hope through the dark mountain of disappointment.

I hope the church as a whole will meet the challenge of this decisive hour.   41
But even if the church does not come to the aid of justice, I have no despair about the future. I have no fear about the outcome of our struggle in Birmingham, even if our motives are at present misunderstood. We will reach the goal of freedom in Birmingham and all over the nation, because the goal of America is freedom. Abused and scorned though we may be, our destiny is tied up with America's destiny. Before the pilgrims landed at Plymouth, we were here. Before the pen of Jefferson etched the majestic words of the Declaration of Independence across the pages of history, we were here. For more than two centuries our forebears labored in this country without wages; they made cotton king; they built the homes of their masters while suffering gross injustice and shameful humiliation—and yet out of a bottomless vitality they continued to thrive and develop. If the inexpressible cruelties of slavery could not stop us, the opposition we now face will surely fail. We will win our freedom because the sacred heritage of our nation and the eternal will of God are embodied in our echoing demands.

Before closing I feel impelled to mention one other point in your statement   42
that has troubled me profoundly. You warmly commended the Birmingham police force for keeping "order" and "preventing violence." I doubt that you would have so warmly commended the police force if you had seen its dogs sinking their teeth into unarmed, nonviolent Negroes. I doubt that you would so quickly commend the policemen if you were to observe their ugly and inhumane treatment of Negroes here in the city jail; if you were to watch them push and curse old Negro women and young Negro girls; if you were to see them slap and kick old Negro men and young boys; if you were to observe them, as they did on two occasions, refuse to give us food because we wanted to sing our grace together. I cannot join you in your praise of the Birmingham police department.

It is true that the police have exercised a degree of discipline in handling the   43
demonstrators. In this sense they have conducted themselves rather "nonviolently" in public. But for what purpose? To preserve the evil system of segregation. Over the past few years I have consistently preached that nonviolence demands that the means we use must be as pure as the ends we seek. I have tried to make clear that it is wrong to use immoral means to attain moral ends. But now I must affirm that it is just as wrong, or perhaps even more so, to use moral means to preserve immoral ends. Perhaps Mr. Connor and his policemen have been rather nonviolent in public, as was Chief Pritchett in Albany, Georgia,

but they have used the moral means of nonviolence to maintain the immoral end of racial injustice. As T.S. Eliot has said, "The last temptation is the greatest treason: To do the right deed for the wrong reason."

I wish you had commended the Negro sit-inners and demonstrators of Birmingham for their sublime courage, their willingness to suffer, and their amazing discipline in the midst of great provocation. One day the South will recognize its real heroes. They will be the James Merediths, with the noble sense of purpose that enables them to face jeering and hostile mobs, and with the agonizing loneliness that characterizes the life of the pioneer. They will be old, oppressed, battered Negro women, symbolized in a seventy-two-year-old woman in Montgomery, Alabama, who rose up with a sense of dignity and with her people decided not to ride segregated buses, and who responded with ungrammatical profundity to one who inquired about her weariness: "My feets is tired, but my soul is at rest." They will be the young high school and college students, the young ministers of the gospel and a host of their elders, courageously and nonviolently sitting in at lunch counters and willingly going to jail for conscience' sake. One day the South will know that when these disinherited children of God sat down at lunch counters, they were in reality standing up for what is best in the American dream and for the most sacred values in our Judeo-Christian heritage, thereby bringing our nation back to those great wells of democracy which were dug deep by the founding fathers in their formulation of the Constitution and the Declaration of Independence.

Never before have I written so long a letter. I'm afraid it is much too long to take your precious time. I can assure you that it would have been much shorter if I had been writing from a comfortable desk, but what else can one do when he is alone in a narrow jail cell, other than write long letters, think long thoughts, and pray long prayers?

If I have said anything in this letter that overstates the truth and indicates an unreasonable impatience, I beg you to forgive me. If I have said anything that understates the truth and indicates my having a patience that allows me to settle for anything less than brotherhood, I beg God to forgive me.

I hope this letter finds you strong in the faith. I also hope that circumstances will soon make it possible for me to meet each of you, not as an integrationist or a civil-rights leader but as a fellow clergyman and a Christian brother. Let us all hope that the dark clouds of racial prejudice will soon pass away and the deep fog of misunderstanding will be lifted from our fear-drenched communities, and in some not too distant tomorrow the radiant stars of love and brotherhood will shine over our great nation with all their scintillating beauty.

Yours for the cause of Peace and Brotherhood,

Martin Luther King, Jr.

QUESTIONS FOR MEANING

1. What reason does King give for writing this letter? What justification does he provide for its length? How do these explanations work to his advantage?

2. One of the many charges brought against King at the time of his arrest was that he was an "outsider" who had no business in Birmingham. How does King defend himself? What three reasons does he cite in order to justify his presence in Birmingham?

3. King also responds to the criticism that his campaign for civil rights was "untimely." What is his defense against this charge?

4. What does King mean by nonviolent "direct-action"? What sort of activities did he lead people to pursue? Identify the four basic steps to a direct-action campaign and explain what such campaigns were meant to accomplish.

5. Why did King believe that a direct-action campaign was necessary in Birmingham? Why did the black community in Birmingham turn to King? What problems were they facing, and what methods had they already tried before deciding upon direct-action?

6. What was the 1954 Supreme Court decision that King refers to in paragraph 16? Why was King able to charge that the "rabid segregationist" breaks the law?

7. King's critics charged that he obeyed the law selectively. He answers by arguing there is a difference between just and unjust laws, and that moral law requires men and women to break unjust laws that are imposed upon them. How can you tell the difference between laws that you should honor, and laws that you should break? What is King's definition of an unjust law, and what historical examples does he give to illustrate situations in which unjust laws have to be broken?

8. What does King mean when he complains of the "anesthetizing security of stained-glass windows"? How can churches make men and women feel falsely secure?

QUESTIONS ABOUT STRATEGY

1. Why did King address his letter to fellow clergymen? Why was he disappointed in them, and what did he expect his letter to accomplish?

2. Is there anything in the substance of this letter that reveals it was written for an audience familiar with the Bible and modern theology? Do you think King intended this letter to be read only by clergymen? Can you point to anything that suggests King may have really written for a larger, more general audience?

3. How does King characterize himself in this letter? What sort of a man does he seem to be, and what role does his presentation of himself play in his argument? How does he establish that he is someone worth listening to— and that it is important to listen to what he has to say?

4. *Ekklesia* is Greek for assembly, congregation, or church. Why does King use this word in paragraph 40 instead of simply saying "the church"?

5. Martin Luther King had much experience as a preacher when he wrote this famous letter. Is there anything about its style that reminds you of oratory? How effective would this letter be if delivered as a speech?

BETTY FRIEDAN
The Importance of Work

Betty Friedan (b. 1921) was one of the founders of the National Organization of Women, serving as NOW's first president between 1966 and 1970. Born in Peoria, Illinois, and educated at Smith College, the University of California, and the University of Iowa, Friedan has lectured at more than fifty universities and institutes. Her essays have appeared in numerous periodicals, including the Saturday Review, Harper's, McCall's, Redbook, Good Housekeeping, *and the* Ladies' Home Journal. *Her books include* It Changed My Life *(1976) and* The Second Stage *(1981). The following essay is drawn from the book that made her famous,* The Feminine Mystique *(1963).*

A quarter of a century has now passed since Friedan published this book, and the leadership of the woman's movement has passed to a younger generation. But if the development of that movement could be traced back to the publication of a single work, it would have to be The Feminine Mystique. *Friedan believed that women needed to escape from the roles they had assumed as wives and mothers, and if her ideas no longer seem as bold as they once were, it is because she anticipated most of the concerns that would dominate the analysis of male/female relations during the 1970s and 1980s. "The Importance of Work" is an editor's title for the concluding pages of Friedan's book, an excerpt that reveals Friedan's conviction that women need to enter the mainstream of the American workforce—not simply as typists and file clerks, but as the full equals of men.*

The question of how a person can most fully realize his own capacities and thus achieve identity has become an important concern of the philosophers and the social and psychological thinkers of our time—and for good reason. Thinkers of other times put forth the idea that people were, to a great extent, defined by the work they did. The work that a man had to do to eat, to stay alive, to meet the physical necessities of his environment, dictated his identity. And in this sense, when work is seen merely as a means of survival, human identity was dictated by biology.   1

But today the problem of human identity has changed. For the work that defined man's place in society and his sense of himself has also changed man's world. Work, and the advance of knowledge, has lessened man's dependence on his environment; his biology and the work he must do for biological survival are no longer sufficient to define his identity. This can be most clearly seen in our own abundant society; men no longer need to work all day to eat. They have an unprecedented freedom to choose the kind of work they will do; they also have an unprecedented amount of time apart from the hours and days that must actually be spent in making a living. And suddenly one realizes the significance of today's identity crisis—for women, and increasingly, for men. One sees the human significance of work—not merely as the means of biological survival, but as the giver of self and the transcender of self, as the creator of human identity and human evolution.   2

For "self-realization" or "self-fulfillment" or "identity" does not come from   3 looking into a mirror in rapt contemplation of one's own image. Those who have most fully realized themselves, in a sense that can be recognized by the human mind even though it cannot be clearly defined, have done so in the service of a human purpose larger than themselves. Men from varying disciplines have used different words for this mysterious process from which comes the sense of self. The religious mystics, the philosophers, Marx, Freud—all had different names for it: man finds himself by losing himself; man is defined by his relation to the means of production; the ego, the self, grows through understanding and mastering reality—through work and love.

The identity crisis, which has been noted by Erik Erikson and others in   4
recent years in the American man, seems to occur for lack of, and be cured by finding, the work, or cause, or purpose that evokes his own creativity. Some never find it, for it does not come from busy-work or punching a time clock. It does not come from just making a living, working by formula, finding a secure spot as an organization man. The very argument, by Riesman and others, that man no longer finds identity in the work defined as a paycheck job, assumes that identity for man comes through creative work of his own that contributes to the human community: the core of the self becomes aware, becomes real, and grows through work that carries forward human society.

Work, the shopworn staple of the economists, has become the new frontier   5
of psychology. Psychiatrists have long used "occupational therapy" with patients in mental hospitals; they have recently discovered that to be of real psychological value, it must be not just "therapy," but real work, serving a real purpose in the community. And work can now be seen as the key to the problem that has no name. The identity crisis of American women began a century ago, as more and more of the work important to the world, more and more of the work that used their human abilities and through which they were able to find self-realization, was taken from them.

Until, and even into, the last century, strong, capable women were needed   6
to pioneer our new land; with their husbands, they ran the farms and plantations and Western homesteads. These women were respected and self-respecting members of a society whose pioneering purpose centered in the home. Strength and independence, responsibility and self-confidence, self-discipline and courage, freedom and equality were part of the American character for both men and women, in all the first generations. The women who came by steerage from Ireland, Italy, Russia, and Poland worked beside their husbands in the sweatshops and the laundries, learned the new language, and saved to send their sons and daughters to college. Women were never quite as "feminine," or held in as much contempt, in America as they were in Europe. American women seemed to European travelers, long before our time, less passive, childlike, and feminine than their own wives in France or Germany or England. By an accident of history, American women shared in the work of society longer, and grew with the men. Grade- and high-school education for boys and girls alike was almost always the rule; and in the West, where women shared the pioneering work the longest, even the universities were coeducational from the beginning.

The identity crisis for women did not begin in America until the fire and   7 strength and ability of the pioneer women were no longer needed, no longer used, in the middle-class homes of the Eastern and Midwestern cities, when the pioneering was done and men began to build the new society in industries and professions outside the home But the daughters of the pioneer women had grown too used to freedom and work to be content with leisure and passive femininity.

It was not an American, but a South African woman, Mrs. Olive Schreiner, who warned at the turn of the century that the quality and quantity of women's functions in the social universe were decreasing as fast as civilization was advancing; that if women did not win back their right to a full share of honored and useful work, woman's mind and muscle would weaken in a parasitic state; her offspring, male and female, would weaken progressively, and civilization itself would deteriorate.   8

The feminists saw clearly that education and the right to participate in the more advanced work of society were women's greatest needs. They fought for and won the rights to new, fully human identity for women. But how very few of their daughters and granddaughters have chosen to use their education and their abilities for any large creative purpose, for responsible work in society? How many of them have been deceived, or have deceived themselves, into clinging to the outgrown, childlike femininity of "Occupation: housewife"?   9

It was not a minor matter, their mistaken choice. We now know that the same range of potential ability exists for women as for men. Women, as well as men, can only find their identity in work that uses their full capacities. A woman cannot find her identity through others—her husband, her children. She cannot find it in the dull routine of housework. As thinkers of every age have said, it is only when a human being faces squarely the fact that he can forfeit his own life, that he becomes truly aware of himself, and begins to take his existence seriously. Sometimes this awareness comes only at the moment of death. Sometimes it comes from a more subtle facing of death: the death of self in passive conformity, in meaningless work. The feminine mystique prescribes just such a living death for women. Faced with the slow death of self, the American woman must begin to take her life seriously.   10

"We measure ourselves by many standards," said the great American psychologist William James, nearly a century ago. "Our strength and our intelligence, our wealth and even our good luck, are things which warm our heart and make us feel ourselves a match for life. But deeper than all such things, and able to suffice unto itself without them, is the sense of the amount of effort which we can put forth."   11

If women do not put forth, finally, that effort to become all that they have it in them to become, they will forfeit their own humanity. A woman today who has no goal, no purpose, no ambition patterning her days into the future, making her stretch and grow beyond that small score of years in which her body can fill its biological function, is committing a kind of suicide. For that future half a century after the child-bearing years are over is a fact that an American woman cannot deny. Nor can she deny that as a housewife, the world is indeed rushing past her door while she just sits and watches. The terror she feels is real, if she has no place in that world.   12

The feminine mystique has succeeded in burying millions of American   13
women alive. There is no way for these women to break out of their comfortable
concentration camps except by finally putting forth an effort—that human
effort which reaches beyond biology, beyond the narrow walls of home, to help
shape the future. Only by such a personal commitment to the future can American women break out of the housewife trap and truly find fulfillment as wives
and mothers—by fulfilling their own unique possibilities as separate human
beings.

QUESTIONS FOR MEANING

1. In her opening paragraph, Friedan writes, "when work is seen merely as a
   means of survival, human identity was dictated by biology." What does this
   mean?
2. Does Friedan believe that all types of work are equally satisfying? Where
   does she define the type of work that has "human significance"?
3. According to Friedan, what is the historical explanation for the identity
   crisis many American women suffered in recent decades?
4. What's wrong with "Occupation: housewife"? Why does Friedan believe
   that women cannot find fulfillment simply by being wives and mothers?
5. Explain Friedan's allusion to "feminists" in paragraph 9. Who were the early
   feminists, and what did they accomplish?
6. Although you have been given only the last few pages of Friedan's book,
   can you construct a definition for what she means by "the feminine mystique"?
7. Vocabulary: transcender (2), rapt (3), mystics (3), parasitic (8), deteriorate (8), and forfeit (10).

QUESTIONS ABOUT STRATEGY

1. What is the premise that underlies Friedan's argument on behalf of meaningful careers for women?
2. Why does Friedan discuss women within the context of pyschological
   "identity"? Why is it important for her to link the needs of women with the
   needs of men?
3. Comment on Friedan's use of quotation. She refers, for support, to four
   men (Marx, Freud, Erik Erikson, and William James) and to only one
   woman, Olive Schreiner. Does her reliance upon male authorities help or
   hurt her argument?
4. When Friedan declares that housewives are "committing a kind of suicide"
   trapped within homes that are "comfortable concentration camps," is she
   drawing her work together with a forceful conclusion or weakening it
   through exaggeration?

SUGGESTIONS FOR WRITING

1. Defend or attack Plato's claim that "government can be at its best and free from dissension only where the destined rulers are least desirous of holding office."
2. Identify a modern politician who governs according to Machiavellian principles. Be careful not to make groundless accusations. Do research if necessary to write an argument that will include specific evidence.
3. Write a dialogue between Plato and Machiavelli on the question of how a republic should be ruled.
4. Respond to Marvell by writing an argument in defense of chastity.
5. Using "A Modest Proposal" as your model, write a satirical essay proposing a "solution" to a contemporary social problem other than poverty.
6. Write a counterargument to Jefferson, a "Declaration of Continued Dependence" from the point of view of George III.
7. Drawing upon the work of Mary Wollstonecraft, Margaret Sanger, and Betty Friedan, write a "Declaration of Independence for Women."
8. Marx and Engels predicted that communism would triumph in advanced industrialized nations with large proletariats. But Russia was primarily an agricultural country at the time of the Russian Revolution, and Marxism now seems to appeal principally to agricultural nations in Africa, Asia, and Central America. Defend or attack *The Communist Manifesto* in the light of twentieth-century history.
9. Do a research paper on birth control in Mexico, India, or China.
10. Analyze a speech by a contemporary politician, using the criteria of George Orwell.
11. Drawing upon "Letter from Birmingham Jail," defend an illegal act that you would be willing to commit in order to fight for something in which you strongly believe.

PART 3

A Guide to Research and Documentation

Writing may be hard work, but it's much easier when you have something to write about. If forced to write about an unfamiliar subject, even the best writers can find themselves drifting into wordiness, repetition, and vague generalizations. The great advantage of research is that it gives you the material for writing. You need to organize this material and determine its worth before you can write a good research paper. You also need to know how to handle the mechanics of a research paper, since this is the most formal type of writing that most students are expected to do. There are strict conventions that must be observed when you draw upon the work of others. But these conventions can be mastered easily by anyone willing to take the trouble. There is nothing especially difficult about writing a research paper if you approach it as a process that begins long before the assignment is due.

Your instructor may allow you to choose your own subject for research. Or you may be required to work on a subject that has been assigned to you. But in either case, there are two basic points that you need to remember when undertaking a research paper: 1) A graceful style cannot compensate for a failure to do thorough research. Even if you are an excellent writer, your paper will be superficial if your research has been superficial. 2) Although research is essential to the process of writing a research paper, there is more to the research paper than research alone. You can spend months investigating your subject, but your essay will be a failure if it consists of nothing more than one quotation after another. You should remember that you are a writer as well as an investigator, and your own thoughts and interpretations are ultimately as important as the research itself. You may occasionally have an assignment that requires nothing more than reporting on a technical question such as "How is gasoline refined?" or "How do eagles mate?" But most research papers require that the writer have a thesis and a point of view about the subject under consideration. Unless specifically instructed otherwise, you should think of the research paper as an extended form of argument—an argument which is supported by evidence you have discovered through research.

There are two types of research: primary and secondary. *Primary research* requires firsthand experimentation or analysis. This is the sort of research that is done in scientific laboratories and scholarly archives. Research of this sort is seldom expected of college students, although, if you interview someone, you are doing a type of primary research. An undergraduate research paper is usually confined to *secondary research*, which means the examination of what other people have already published on a given subject. In order to do this type of research efficiently, you must know where to look. And this means that you must be familiar with the resources that are available to you in your library and develop a strategy for using these resources effectively.

GETTING STARTED

Your primary goal in preliminary research is to get your subject in focus. This usually means narrowing your topic down. A clear focus is essential if your paper is to have depth and coherence. A ten-page paper on "The Question of Race in *Huckleberry Finn*" is likely to be much more thoughtful than one of that length on "Mark Twain: America's Favorite Writer." Moreover, the clearer your focus, the easier your research will be. When you know what you are looking for, you know what you need to read and what you can afford to pass over. This will keep you from feeling overwhelmed as your research progresses.

Different instructors make different assignments, and you should always be certain that you have understood what your instructor expects of you. But if you have been asked to write a fixed number of pages on a subject of your own choice, a good rule to follow is to narrow your subject as much as possible without narrowing yourself out of the library. Don't put yourself in the position of aimlessly reading dozens of books on an unnecessarily broad subject. On the other hand, don't make your subject so obscure that you will be unable to find enough material to write a paper of the length required.

If you know very little about your subject, you may want to begin your research by reading whatever can be found in a general encyclopedia, such as the *Encyclopedia Britannica* or the *Encyclopedia Americana*. Encyclopedias contain the basic background information that other works may assume you already possess. Within the reference rooms of most libraries, you can also find special encyclopedias and dictionaries for major fields such as art, biography, economics, education, history, law, literature, medicine, music, philosophy, and psychology. Do some preliminary reading in an encyclopedia if doing so will make you feel more comfortable with your subject, but do not spend a lot of time reading in the library at this early stage in your research. Although the reference room may be a good place to begin your work, it has a great disadvantage: The books in this room are seldom allowed to circulate. Your first day in the library should be devoted primarily to finding out what types of material are going to be available to you in the days ahead.

LOOKING FOR BOOKS

One of the first steps in your search strategy should be to go through the drawers of the card catalog. Never assume that your topic is so new, or so specialized, that the library will not have books on it. The card catalogs of most libraries include two or three cards for every book the library owns. This allows you to locate books in a variety of ways, depending upon how much you already know. You may be looking for books by a particular author, so libraries provide *author cards*. You may know the title of a book but not know who wrote it, so libraries also provide *title cards*. In many libraries, these two types of card are filed together in one catalog known as the *author/title catalog*. But when beginning a research paper, you may not know the names of any authors or titles of works within your subject. For this reason, books are also filed under subject headings.

The *subject catalog* is usually separate from the author/title catalog. Large subjects, like American history, are broken down into numerous subcategories. If you have chosen a large subject and are unsure about how to narrow it down, it is often useful to consult the subject catalog. Not only will you be able to see how professional indexers have divided the subject into manageable components, but you will also be able to see how many books are available within each subdivision.

When using the subject catalog, you should always begin your search under the most specific heading you can think of and then consult broader subjects only if it is necessary to do so. You can usually assume that the library has at least one book on the subject you are investigating. Your goal is to find it. Do not give up easily, and remember that you will often find it necessary to consider alternative headings under which the material you need may be catalogued. Books on the Civil War may be listed under "War Between the States," and books on nuclear energy may be listed under "Atomic Energy." Sometimes you will find a card that will direct you to the correct subject heading, just as the yellow pages in a telephone directory may tell you to "See Grocers–Retail" if you look up "Super Markets." But you may have to rely upon your own ingenuity. If you are sure that the library must have books on your subject and that you are simply unable to find the correct subject heading, ask a librarian for help.

Most American libraries use one of two systems for classifying the books in their collections: the Dewey Decimal system and the Library of Congress system. If you understand how these systems work, you can save valuable time in the library by knowing where to look for material when you are already working in the stacks.

The Dewey Decimal system classifies books numerically:

000–099	General Works
100–199	Philosophy
200–299	Religion
300–399	Social Sciences

400–499	Language
500–599	Natural Sciences
600–699	Technology
700–799	Fine Arts
800–899	Literature
900–999	History and Geography

These major divisions are subdivided by ten in order to identify specializations within each general field. For example, within the 800–899 category for literature, American literature is found between 810 and 819, English literature between 820 and 829, German literature between 830 and 839—and so forth. Specific numbers narrow these areas further, so that 811 represents American poetry, for example, and 812 American drama. Additional numbers after the decimal point enable catalogers to classify books more precisely: 812.54 would indicate an American play written since 1945. In order to distinguish individual books from others that are similar, an additional number is usually placed beneath the Dewey number. Most libraries that use the Dewey Decimal system combine it with one of three systems for providing what is called an "author mark." These systems (Cutter two-figure, Cutter three-figure, and Cutter-Sanborn) all work according to the same principle. Librarians consult a reference table which provides a numerical representation for the first four to six letters of every conceivable last name. The first letter of the author's last name is placed immediately before this number, and the first letter of the first significant word in the title is placed after the number. Here is a complete call number for *Cat on a Hot Tin Roof*, by the American playwright Tennessee Williams:

812.54
W675c

Although the Dewey Decimal system remains the most widely used system for the classification of books in American libraries, many university libraries prefer to use the Library of Congress system, which uses the alphabet to distinguish twenty-one major categories as opposed to Dewey's ten:

A	General Works
B	Philosophy, Psychology, and Religion
C	General History
D	Foreign History
E-F	American History (North and South)
G	Geography and Anthropology
H	Social Sciences

J	Political Science
K	Law
L	Education
M	Music
N	Fine Arts
P	Language and Literature
Q	Science
R	Medicine
S	Agriculture
T	Technology
U	Military Science
V	Naval Science
Z	Bibliography and Library Science

Each of these categories can be subdivided through additional letters and numbers. PR, for example, indicates English literature, and PS indicates American. The complete entry will usually involve three lines. Unless you are planning to become a librarian, you will not find it necessary to memorize the complete code. But whether you are using Dewey or the Library of Congress, *always be sure to copy down the complete call number for any book you wish to find.* If you leave out part of the number you may find yourself wandering in the stacks and unable to find the book you want.

The call number always appears in the upper left hand corner of the author, title, and subject cards. Figure 1 (p. 544) shows four sample cards for the same book, using the Library of Congress system. Each card has a different heading but otherwise contains the same information: the title of the book and the author (in this case two coeditors), the city of publication, the publisher, the date of publication, the length of the introduction, the number of pages, the size of the book (24 cm.) and the presence of a bibliography and an index.

There is no foolproof method for determining the quality of a book from a catalog card. The best way to judge a book is always to read it. But a catalog card can reveal some useful clues if you know how to find them. Consider, for example, the date of publication. There is no reason to assume that new books are always better than old books, but unless you are researching a historical or literary topic you should be careful not to rely heavily upon material that may be out of date. Consider also the length of the book. A book with 300 pages is likely to provide more information than a book half that size. A book with a bibliography may help you to find more material. Finally, you might also consider the reputation of the publisher. Any conclusions that you draw at this point should be tentative. But some books are better than others, and it is your responsibility as a researcher to evaluate the material that you use. If you are fortunate enough to find several books on your subject, select the books that seem the most substantial.

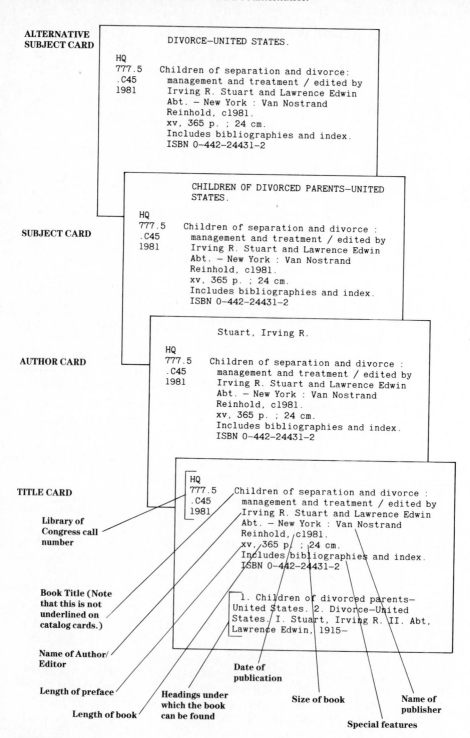

ALTERNATIVE SUBJECT CARD

DIVORCE—UNITED STATES.

HQ
777.5   Children of separation and divorce:
.C45   management and treatment / edited by
1981   Irving R. Stuart and Lawrence Edwin
           Abt. — New York : Van Nostrand
           Reinhold, c1981.
           xv, 365 p. ; 24 cm.
           Includes bibliographies and index.
           ISBN 0-442-24431-2

CHILDREN OF DIVORCED PARENTS—UNITED
STATES.

HQ
777.5   Children of separation and divorce :
.C45   management and treatment / edited by
1981   Irving R. Stuart and Lawrence Edwin
           Abt. — New York : Van Nostrand
           Reinhold, c1981.
           xv, 365 p. ; 24 cm.
           Includes bibliographies and index.
           ISBN 0-442-24431-2

SUBJECT CARD

Stuart, Irving R.

HQ
777.5   Children of separation and divorce :
.C45   management and treatment / edited by
1981   Irving R. Stuart and Lawrence Edwin
           Abt. — New York : Van Nostrand
           Reinhold, c1981.
           xv, 365 p. ; 24 cm.
           Includes bibliographies and index.
           ISBN 0-442-24431-2

AUTHOR CARD

HQ
777.5   Children of separation and divorce :
.C45   management and treatment / edited by
1981   Irving R. Stuart and Lawrence Edwin
           Abt. — New York : Van Nostrand
           Reinhold, c1981.
           xv, 365 p. ; 24 cm.
           Includes bibliographies and index.
           ISBN 0-442-24431-2

           1. Children of divorced parents—
           United States. 2. Divorce—United
           States. I. Stuart, Irving R. II. Abt,
           Lawrence Edwin, 1915—

TITLE CARD

Library of
Congress call
number

Book Title (Note
that this is not
underlined on
catalog cards.)

Name of Author/
Editor

Length of preface

Length of book

Headings under
which the book
can be found

Date of
publication

Size of book

Name of
publisher

Special features

FIGURE 1

ALTERNATIVES TO THE CARD CATALOG

Because of the great amount of material being published, many libraries are now using systems that allow for material to be recorded in less space than a card catalog requires. When looking for books, you may need to use some type of microform—which means printed material which has been reduced in size through microphotography. Libraries that use microform provide researchers with special readers that magnify the material in question—whether it is available on microfilm or microfiche, which means a flat sheet of microfilm.

Increasing numbers of libraries are also now using computers to either supplement or replace their card catalogs. In addition to recording material in their own collections, these libraries usually subscribe to one or more data-base services which link individual libraries with computerized lists of material available throughout the United States and Canada. The most commonly used bibliographic networks are BRS (Bibliographical Retrieval Services), DIALOG (operated by Lockheed Information Systems), ERIC (Educational Research Information Center), RLIN (Research Libraries Information Network), and OCLC (Online Computer Library Center). Some libraries provide students with direct access to computers; other libraries restrict the use of the computer to librarians. Usually there is a fee (sometimes a substantial one) for a computer search.

Searching for material with the assistance of a computer requires a research strategy which is similar to the one you must use in order to locate material through a card catalog. You must be able to supply the computer with an important piece of information—either a specific book title, an author's name, or a subject heading. And as with a card catalog, you must use the correct subject heading in order to get results.

USING PERIODICAL INDEXES

A good researcher wants to be aware of the latest developments in his or her field. A scholarly book may be several years in the making; publication may be delayed, and another year or two pass before the book is purchased and cataloged by your library. You may also need to obtain detailed information on a particular subtopic that is discussed only briefly in the books that are available to you. Therefore, you will often need to turn to periodicals after searching for books. "Periodicals" means magazines, newspapers, and scholarly journals: material that is published "periodically." And there are numerous indexes to help you find literature of this sort.

The best known of these is the *Readers' Guide to Periodical Literature*, which has been published since 1900. It covers 150 magazines and journals, indexing material by subject and by author. The limitation of the *Readers' Guide* is that it covers only popular, mass-circulation periodicals. The articles you find on most subjects will often be relatively short and general.

Begin your search for periodical literature with the *Readers' Guide* if you wish. But most college libraries have a variety of specialized indexes that will lead you to more substantial material. Almost every field has its own index. Detailed lists of such indexes and other reference books can be found in *Guide to Reference Books* by Eugene P. Sheehy and *American Reference Books Annual*, edited by Janet H. Littlefield. Among the specialized indexes most frequently used are:

The *Applied Science and Technology Index*

The *Art Index*

The *Biological and Agricultural Index*

The *Business Periodicals Index*

The *Education Index*

The *Humanities Index*

Index to Legal Periodicals

Index Medicus (for medicine)

The *Music Index*

The *Philosopher's Index*

The *Science Citation Index*

The *Social Sciences Index*

Anyone doing research in literature should also be familiar with the *MLA International Bibliography* (which appears annually and includes both books and articles written about English, American, and foreign language literature), and also with the *Essay and General Literature Index*, which indexes essays and articles which have appeared in books rather than in journals.

Although there is occasionally some overlapping from one index to another, you need to realize that each of these indexes covers different periodicals. The references that you find in one will usually be entirely different from the references you find in another. This is worth remembering for two reasons: (1) You should not get easily discouraged when searching for periodical literature. If you cannot locate any material in the last few years of one index, then you should try another index that sounds as if it might include references to your subject. (2) Many subjects of general interest will be found in more than one index, and if you consult more than one index, you are increasing the likelihood of being exposed to different points of view.

You may choose to do a research paper on one of the subjects discussed in Part Two of this book. But in order for you to see how different indexes lead to different types of material, let us take an example from outside of the book—pretending that you have decided to do a paper on divorce. This is a very broad subject, as you realize when you look it up in the *Readers' Guide*. See Figure 2 (p. 547) for an example. The list of articles under "Divorce" lacks a clear focus. It ranges as broadly as the subject itself. But the "See also" directs you to four related subjects. "Children of divorced parents" sounds promising. Perhaps you could do your paper on ways to minimize the effects of divorce upon children. This is still a big subject, but it is much more manageable than "Divorce," and as your reading progresses you may find ways of narrowing the topic further. Figure 3 (p. 548) shows what you will find when looking up "Children of divorced parents." It looks as if there is plenty of material on this subtopic, but

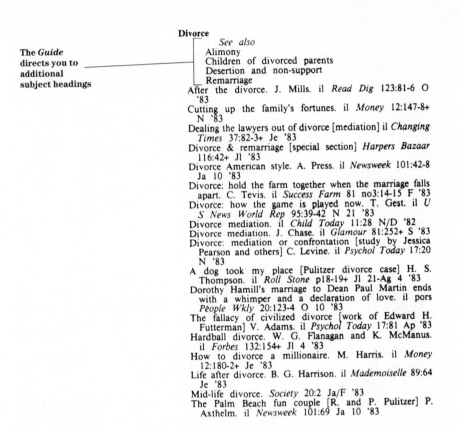

The *Guide* directs you to additional subject headings

Divorce

See also
Alimony
Children of divorced parents
Desertion and non-support
Remarriage

After the divorce. J. Mills. il *Read Dig* 123:81-6 O '83
Cutting up the family's fortunes. il *Money* 12:147-8+ N '83
Dealing the lawyers out of divorce [mediation] il *Changing Times* 37:82-3+ Je '83
Divorce & remarriage [special section] *Harpers Bazaar* 116:42+ Jl '83
Divorce American style. A. Press. il *Newsweek* 101:42-8 Ja 10 '83
Divorce: hold the farm together when the marriage falls apart. C. Tevis. il *Success Farm* 81 no3:14-15 F '83
Divorce: how the game is played now. T. Gest. il *U S News World Rep* 95:39-42 N 21 '83
Divorce mediation. il *Child Today* 11:28 N/D '82
Divorce mediation. J. Chase. il *Glamour* 81:252+ S '83
Divorce: mediation or confrontation [study by Jessica Pearson and others] C. Levine. il *Psychol Today* 17:20 N '83
A dog took my place [Pulitzer divorce case] H. S. Thompson. il *Roll Stone* p18-19+ Jl 21-Ag 4 '83
Dorothy Hamill's marriage to Dean Paul Martin ends with a whimper and a declaration of love. il pors *People Wkly* 20:123-4 O 10 '83
The fallacy of civilized divorce [work of Edward H. Futterman] V. Adams. il *Psychol Today* 17:81 Ap '83
Hardball divorce. W. G. Flanagan and K. McManus. il *Forbes* 132:154+ Jl 4 '83
How to divorce a millionaire. M. Harris. il *Money* 12:180-2+ Je '83
Life after divorce. B. G. Harrison. il *Mademoiselle* 89:64 Je '83
Mid-life divorce. *Society* 20:2 Ja/F '83
The Palm Beach fun couple [R. and P. Pulitzer] P. Axthelm. il *Newsweek* 101:69 Ja 10 '83

FIGURE 2
Sample page from *Readers' Guide*

looking closer you realize that three of the articles are only one page long, and your thesis may not be taken seriously if you base your argument upon material drawn from *Readers' Digest, Mademoiselle*, and *Seventeen*. You decide to continue your search elsewhere, grateful that the *Readers' Guide* has at least helped you to narrow your topic.

Since the *Social Sciences Index* includes material on sociology, education, and psychology (and other related fields) you decide that it would probably include references to articles on the children of divorced parents. See Figure 4 (p. 549). Reading over the list of citations from the *Social Sciences Index*, you can see that it directs you to material that looks substantial. Of the first three articles, two are thirteen pages long, and another is fourteen. All three of these articles include bibliographies, as do several others. And by using periodicals like *Child Development* and the *American Journal of Psychology*, you should be able to write with more authority than had you stayed with articles

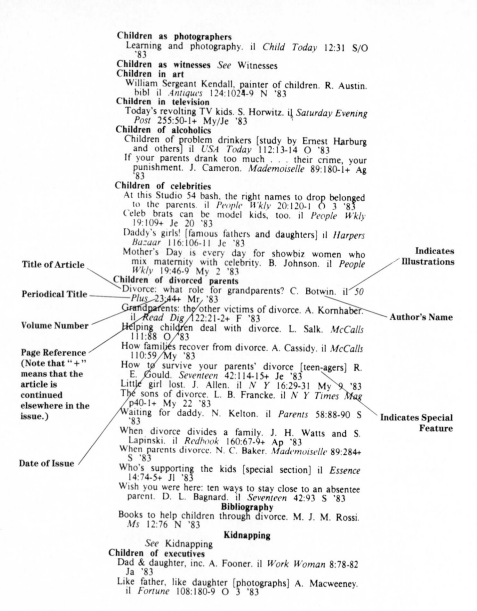

Children as photographers
Learning and photography. il *Child Today* 12:31 S/O '83
Children as witnesses *See* Witnesses
Children in art
William Sergeant Kendall, painter of children. R. Austin. bibl il *Antiques* 124:1024-9 N '83
Children in television
Today's revolting TV kids. S. Horwitz. il *Saturday Evening Post* 255:50-1+ My/Je '83
Children of alcoholics
Children of problem drinkers [study by Ernest Harburg and others] il *USA Today* 112:13-14 O '83
If your parents drank too much . . . their crime, your punishment. J. Cameron. *Mademoiselle* 89:180-1+ Ag '83
Children of celebrities
At this Studio 54 bash, the right names to drop belonged to the parents. il *People Wkly* 20:120-1 O 3 '83
Celeb brats can be model kids, too. il *People Wkly* 19:109+ Je 20 '83
Daddy's girls! [famous fathers and daughters] il *Harpers Bazaar* 116:106-11 Je '83
Mother's Day is every day for showbiz women who mix maternity with celebrity. B. Johnson. il *People Wkly* 19:46-9 My 2 '83
Children of divorced parents
Divorce: what role for grandparents? C. Botwin. il *50 Plus* 23:44+ Mr '83
Grandparents: the other victims of divorce. A. Kornhaber. il *Read Dig* 122:21-2+ F '83
Helping children deal with divorce. L. Salk. *McCalls* 111:88 O '83
How families recover from divorce. A. Cassidy. il *McCalls* 110:59 My '83
How to survive your parents' divorce [teen-agers] R. E. Gould. *Seventeen* 42:114-15+ Je '83
Little girl lost. J. Allen. il *N Y* 16:29-31 My 9 '83
The sons of divorce. L. B. Francke. il *N Y Times Mag* p40-1+ My 22 '83
Waiting for daddy. N. Kelton. il *Parents* 58:88-90 S '83
When divorce divides a family. J. H. Watts and S. Lapinski. il *Redbook* 160:67-9+ Ap '83
When parents divorce. N. C. Baker. *Mademoiselle* 89:284+ S '83
Who's supporting the kids [special section] il *Essence* 14:74-5+ Jl '83
Wish you were here: ten ways to stay close to an absentee parent. D. L. Bagnard. il *Seventeen* 42:93 S '83
Bibliography
Books to help children through divorce. M. J. M. Rossi. *Ms* 12:76 N '83
Kidnapping
See Kidnapping
Children of executives
Dad & daughter, inc. A. Fooner. il *Work Woman* 8:78-82 Ja '83
Like father, like daughter [photographs] A. Macweeney. il *Fortune* 108:180-9 O 3 '83

Labels (left): Title of Article · Periodical Title · Volume Number · Page Reference (Note that "+" means that the article is continued elsewhere in the issue.) · Date of Issue

Labels (right): Indicates Illustrations · Author's Name · Indicates Special Feature

FIGURE 3

Sample page from *Readers' Guide*

drawn exclusively from the *Readers' Guide*. These articles are going to be more difficult to read than articles in popular magazines. But you can overcome this difficulty through proper preparation: Do not try to read articles in scholarly journals until you have completed preliminary reading in encyclopedias, books, and magazines.

Continuing your search, you should be able to find additional material in the

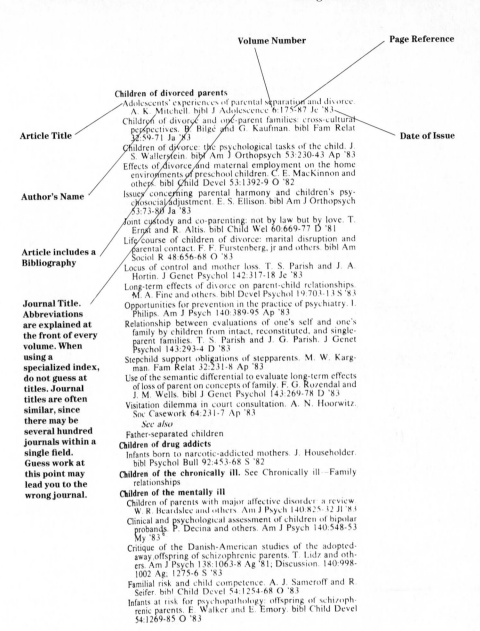

Volume Number

Page Reference

Children of divorced parents
Adolescents' experiences of parental separation and divorce. A. K. Mitchell. bibl J Adolescence 6:175-87 Je '83

Article Title

Children of divorce and one-parent families: cross-cultural perspectives. B. Bilgé and G. Kaufman. bibl Fam Relat 32:59-71 Ja '83

Date of Issue

Children of divorce: the psychological tasks of the child. J. S. Wallerstein. bibl Am J Orthopsych 53:230-43 Ap '83

Effects of divorce and maternal employment on the home environments of preschool children. C. E. MacKinnon and others. bibl Child Devel 53:1392-9 O '82

Author's Name

Issues concerning parental harmony and children's psychosocial adjustment. E. S. Ellison. bibl Am J Orthopsych 53:73-80 Ja '83

Joint custody and co-parenting: not by law but by love. T. Ernst and R. Altis. bibl Child Wel 60:669-77 D '81

Life course of children of divorce: marital disruption and parental contact. F. F. Furstenberg, jr and others. bibl Am Sociol R 48:656-68 O '83

Article includes a Bibliography

Locus of control and mother loss. T. S. Parish and J. A. Hortin. J Genet Psychol 142:317-18 Je '83

Long-term effects of divorce on parent-child relationships. M. A. Fine and others. bibl Child Devel 19:703-13 S '83

Opportunities for prevention in the practice of psychiatry. I. Philips. Am J Psych 140:389-95 Ap '83

**Journal Title.
Abbreviations
are explained at
the front of every
volume. When
using a
specialized index,
do not guess at
titles. Journal
titles are often
similar, since
there may be
several hundred
journals within a
single field.
Guess work at
this point may
lead you to the
wrong journal.**

Relationship between evaluations of one's self and one's family by children from intact, reconstituted, and single-parent families. T. S. Parish and J. G. Parish. J Genet Psychol 143:293-4 D '83

Stepchild support obligations of stepparents. M. W. Kargman. Fam Relat 32:231-8 Ap '83

Use of the semantic differential to evaluate long-term effects of loss of parent on concepts of family. F. G. Rozendal and J. M. Wells. bibl J Genet Psychol 143:269-78 D '83

Visitation dilemma in court consultation. A. N. Hoorwitz. Soc Casework 64:231-7 Ap '83
        See also
    Father-separated children
Children of drug addicts
    Infants born to narcotic-addicted mothers. J. Householder. bibl Psychol Bull 92:453-68 S '82
Children of the chronically ill. See Chronically ill—Family relationships
Children of the mentally ill
    Children of parents with major affective disorder: a review. W. R. Beardslee and others. Am J Psych 140:825-32 Jl '83
    Clinical and psychological assessment of children of bipolar probands. P. Decina and others. Am J Psych 140:548-53 My '83
    Critique of the Danish-American studies of the adopted-away offspring of schizophrenic parents. T. Lidz and others. Am J Psych 138:1063-8 Ag '81; Discussion. 140:998-1002 Ag; 1275-6 S '83
    Familial risk and child competence. A. J. Sameroff and R. Seifer. bibl Child Devel 54:1254-68 O '83
    Infants at risk for psychopathology: offspring of schizophrenic parents. E. Walker and E. Emory. bibl Child Devel 54:1269-85 O '83

FIGURE 4
Sample page from *Social Sciences Index*

Education Index (since teachers are involved with children) and the *Index to Legal Periodicals* (since lawyers are involved with divorce). The articles would be different, but the form of the citations would be similar, just as the citations in the *Social Sciences Index* are similar to those in the *Readers' Guide*.

DIVORCE, Separations and Annulments — Cont

number of marriages rose 2%, to 2.5 million (S), Mr 16,16:6

Jamie Talan article on difficulty of arranging wedding ceremonies in cases where parents of bride or groom are divorced; drawing (M), Ap 3,XXI,10:3

Detroit, Mich, resident Vickie Alex files suit in Wayne County Circuit Court charging that her husband Joseph did not tell her he had herpes before they were married in Sept 1982; is seeking $100,000 in damages; husband filed for divorce on Feb 8 in separate suit and denies charges in new suit (S), Ap 11,II,8:3

Republic Insurance Group of Dallas to offer program intended to guarantee flow of child-support or alimony payments in event of default; program is available only through lawyers representing parties in divorce and arrangement can be made only during original negotiation or renegotiation of divorce; details of how program operates (M), Ap 12,IV,23:2

Article on Rhode Island schoolteacher Paul W Lataille, who has been jailed for failing to pay $15,000 in savings, legal fees and alimony that his wife was awarded in divorce judgment; Family Court Judge William Goldberg has vowed to keep Lataille in jail for contempt of court until he pays; Lataille's lawyer Mitchell S Riffkin comments (M), Ap 17,I,23:1

Linda Bird Francke article on studies showing that boys tend to be more handicapped by divorce of their parents than girls; drawing (L), My 22,VI,p40

NYS Assembly, 124-14, approves Assemblywoman May W Newburger's bill directing divorce courts to distribute property equally; Sen approval doubted (S), My 29,I,39:2

Michigan Appeals Court upholds Jan 1982 judgment governing divorce of Ann M Woodworth and Michael G Woodworth in which Ingham County Circuit Court Judge James Kallman ruled husband's law degree was marital property and therefore wife was entitled to share of his future earnings; Kallman had ordered Michael to pay Ann $2,000 annually for 10 years as her share of degree (S), Je 8,I,14:5

Joseph Cardinal Bernardin of Chicago becomes highest-ranking Roman Catholic prelate to celebrate mass for divorced and separated church members (S), Je 27,I,10:6

Bill that is designed to help Orthodox Jews who want to remarry within faith passes both houses of NYS Legislature; under bill, NYS cannot grant civil divorce until party suing for divorce swears he has removed any barriers to remarriage (S), Je 27,II,4:3

Letter by Rabbi Bernard M Zlotowitz and Albert Vorspan urges Gov Cuomo to veto bill passed by New York State Legislature; holds it would involve state in religion, Jl 18,I,14:5

Joan Gelman (Hers column) comment on social 'stresses' of children from intact homes who do not enjoy 'benefits' of competitive bidding by divorced parents wooing their young; drawing (S), Ag 4,III,2:1

NYS Gov Cuomo signs into law bill under which Jewish husbands who refuse to grant their wives divorces under Jewish religious law will be barred from obtaining civil divorces (M), Ag 10,II,7:1

Judge Linda Thomas of Family Court divorces 108 people at once, Dallas, Texas; all are clients of lawyer Averil Sweitzer (S), Ag 21,I,22:6

Georgia Dullea column Relationships discusses lawyer-client relationships in divorce cases; drawing (M), Ag 22,II,10:1

Article on program begun by child and adolescent out-patient division of Westchester division of New York Hospital-Cornell Medical Center to help families in first years of marital separation or those who are considering divorce; photo (M), S 4,XXII,18:3

Article on benefits to children of divorced parents of not breaking ties with relatives of noncustodial parent (M), S 5,I,29:1

Note that the *New York Times Index* gives you a one sentence summary of each article, rather than article titles. "drawing" tells you the article is illustrated. (L) means that this is a long article. The date of issue is May 22 (of 1983, the year of the volume consulted). "VI" means that the article is in section number six—on page 40 in this case.

Short article on your subject

Medium length article on your subject.

FIGURE 5

Sample page from the *New York Times Index*

USING A NEWSPAPER INDEX

There are indexes available for the *Wall Street Journal* and the *Christian Science Monitor*, and, since 1972, the *Newspaper Index* has provided information on articles in the *Chicago Tribune*, the *Los Angeles Times*, the *New Orleans Times-Picayune*, and the *Washington Post*. But if your library has an index for any one newspaper, it is most likely to be the *New York Times Index*, which has been published since 1913. Figure 5 (p. 550) is an example of what you would find if you consulted this index for your paper on the children of divorced parents. This is only part of the list of articles on divorce in one year of the *New York Times*. Several of the articles look as if they would be worth reading, but you may decide that you already have enough material on children and divorce without searching further. Bear in mind that the *New York Times* is especially useful when researching historical events or very contemporary topics that have only recently made news.

USING ABSTRACTING SERVICES

There is one other type of print resource usually available in a college library and that is an *abstract*, which means a summary of an article or book (see page 207). Among the most important abstracting services are:

Abstracts in Anthropology
Biological Abstracts
Chemical Abstracts
Historical Abstracts
Physics Abstracts
Psychological Abstracts
Sociological Abstracts
Women Studies Abstracts

These abstracts are organized in different ways, and when you decide that you need to use an abstract, you can find instructions on how to proceed in the front of any volume. If you run into difficulties, remember that you can always ask a librarian for help. But here is an example of what you would find if you looked up "Divorce" in *Psychological Abstracts*—which is divided into two parts, the subject index being separate from the actual summaries. Figure 6 (p. 552) shows what you will find when consulting the subject index for "Divorce." The most important entry in the subject index is the number which appears at the end of each citation. This is not a page number. It is the number of the article being summarized. Article summaries can be found in numerical order, either at the front of the volume containing the subject index or in a separate

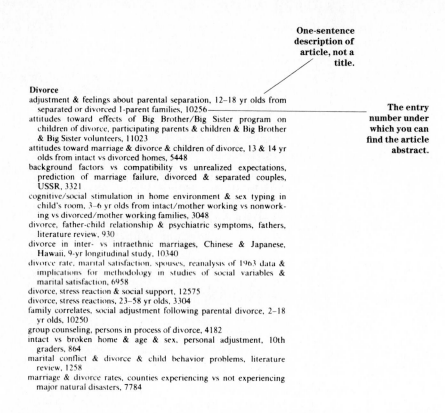

One-sentence
description of
article, not a
title.

The entry
number under
which you can
find the article
abstract.

Divorce
adjustment & feelings about parental separation, 12–18 yr olds from separated or divorced 1-parent families, 10256

attitudes toward effects of Big Brother/Big Sister program on children of divorce, participating parents & children & Big Brother & Big Sister volunteers, 11023

attitudes toward marriage & divorce & children of divorce, 13 & 14 yr olds from intact vs divorced homes, 5448

background factors vs compatibility vs unrealized expectations, prediction of marriage failure, divorced & separated couples, USSR, 3321

cognitive/social stimulation in home environment & sex typing in child's room, 3–6 yr olds from intact/mother working vs nonworking vs divorced/mother working families, 3048

divorce, father-child relationship & psychiatric symptoms, fathers, literature review, 930

divorce in inter- vs intraethnic marriages, Chinese & Japanese, Hawaii, 9-yr longitudinal study, 10340

divorce rate, marital satisfaction, spouses, reanalysis of 1963 data & implications for methodology in studies of social variables & marital satisfaction, 6958

divorce, stress reaction & social support, 12575

divorce, stress reactions, 23–58 yr olds, 3304

family correlates, social adjustment following parental divorce, 2–18 yr olds, 10250

group counseling, persons in process of divorce, 4182

intact vs broken home & age & sex, personal adjustment, 10th graders, 864

marital conflict & divorce & child behavior problems, literature review, 1258

marriage & divorce rates, counties experiencing vs not experiencing major natural disasters, 7784

FIGURE 6
Sample page from subject index of *Psychological Abstracts*

volume (which will be shelved beside it) depending upon how your library decides to bind them. Figure 7 (p. 553) shows a partial page of summaries, including one of the articles found in the subject index: 10250. Note that it is only at this point that you learn the author of the article, the title of the article, and the journal, volume, date, and pages where it can be found.

Abstracts can be cumbersome to use, especially at first. But they offer an obvious advantage. Sometimes it is hard to tell from a title alone if an article will be useful, and a summary can help you to decide whether or not you want to read the entire article. A good rule to follow with abstracts is that if you can't understand the summary, you probably won't understand the article. And there is one other point to remember when using abstracting services. Many of them are international in scope. Just because the article summary is written in English does not mean that this is true of the article itself. But if an article is written in a foreign language, that will be indicated—as in numbers 10251 and 10252.

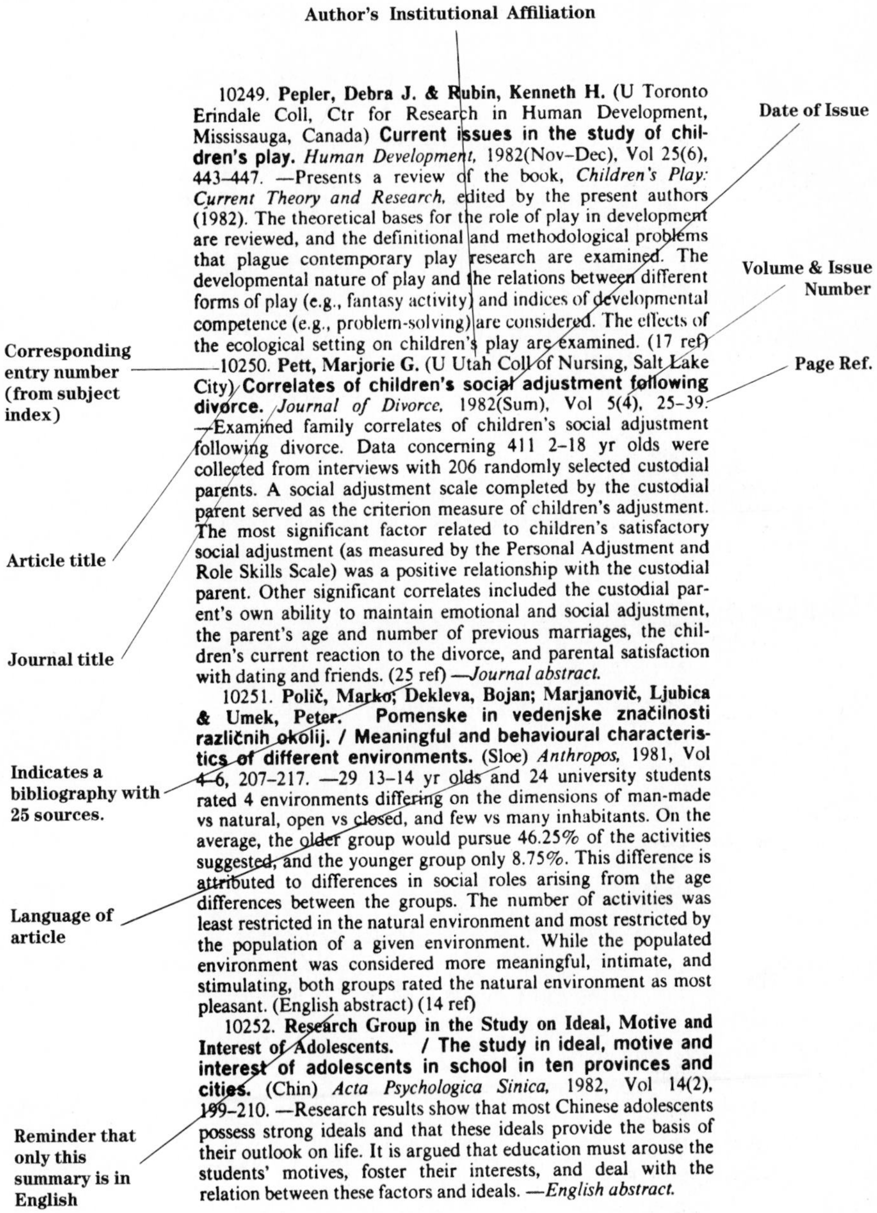

Author's Institutional Affiliation

Date of Issue

Volume & Issue Number

Page Ref.

Corresponding entry number (from subject index)

Article title

Journal title

Indicates a bibliography with 25 sources.

Language of article

Reminder that only this summary is in English

10249. **Pepler, Debra J. & Rubin, Kenneth H.** (U Toronto Erindale Coll, Ctr for Research in Human Development, Mississauga, Canada) **Current issues in the study of children's play.** *Human Development,* 1982(Nov–Dec), Vol 25(6), 443–447. —Presents a review of the book, *Children's Play: Current Theory and Research,* edited by the present authors (1982). The theoretical bases for the role of play in development are reviewed, and the definitional and methodological problems that plague contemporary play research are examined. The developmental nature of play and the relations between different forms of play (e.g., fantasy activity) and indices of developmental competence (e.g., problem-solving) are considered. The effects of the ecological setting on children's play are examined. (17 ref)

10250. **Pett, Marjorie G.** (U Utah Coll of Nursing, Salt Lake City) **Correlates of children's social adjustment following divorce.** *Journal of Divorce,* 1982(Sum), Vol 5(4), 25–39. —Examined family correlates of children's social adjustment following divorce. Data concerning 411 2–18 yr olds were collected from interviews with 206 randomly selected custodial parents. A social adjustment scale completed by the custodial parent served as the criterion measure of children's adjustment. The most significant factor related to children's satisfactory social adjustment (as measured by the Personal Adjustment and Role Skills Scale) was a positive relationship with the custodial parent. Other significant correlates included the custodial parent's own ability to maintain emotional and social adjustment, the parent's age and number of previous marriages, the children's current reaction to the divorce, and parental satisfaction with dating and friends. (25 ref) —*Journal abstract.*

10251. **Polič, Marko; Dekleva, Bojan; Marjanovič, Ljubica & Umek, Peter. Pomenske in vedenjske značilnosti različnih okolij. / Meaningful and behavioural characteristics of different environments.** (Sloe) *Anthropos,* 1981, Vol 4–6, 207–217. —29 13–14 yr olds and 24 university students rated 4 environments differing on the dimensions of man-made vs natural, open vs closed, and few vs many inhabitants. On the average, the older group would pursue 46.25% of the activities suggested, and the younger group only 8.75%. This difference is attributed to differences in social roles arising from the age differences between the groups. The number of activities was least restricted in the natural environment and most restricted by the population of a given environment. While the populated environment was considered more meaningful, intimate, and stimulating, both groups rated the natural environment as most pleasant. (English abstract) (14 ref)

10252. **Research Group in the Study on Ideal, Motive and Interest of Adolescents. / The study in ideal, motive and interest of adolescents in school in ten provinces and cities.** (Chin) *Acta Psychologica Sinica,* 1982, Vol 14(2), 199–210. —Research results show that most Chinese adolescents possess strong ideals and that these ideals provide the basis of their outlook on life. It is argued that education must arouse the students' motives, foster their interests, and deal with the relation between these factors and ideals. —*English abstract.*

FIGURE 7
Sample page of summaries from *Psychological Abstracts*

COMPILING A PRELIMINARY BIBLIOGRAPHY

As you begin locating sources of possible value for your paper, you should be careful to record certain essential information about the books and articles you have discovered. You will need this information in order to compose a preliminary bibliography. For books, you need to record the full title, the full name of the author or authors, the city of publication, the publisher, and the date of publication. If you are using a particular part of a book, be sure to record the pages in question. And if you are using an article or a story included in an anthology edited by someone else than the author of the material you are using, make the distinction between the author and the title of the selection and the editor and title of the book as a whole. When you have located articles in periodicals, record the author(s) of the article, the title of the article, the title of the journal in which it was published, the volume number, the issue number (if there is one), the date of the issue, and the pages between which the article can be found.

The easiest way to compile a preliminary bibliography is to use a set of 3 × 5 note cards, recording separate sources on separate cards. This involves a little more trouble than jotting references down on whatever paper you have at hand, but it will be to your ultimate advantage. As your research progresses, you can easily eliminate any sources that you were unable to obtain—or that you have rejected as inappropriate for one reason or another. And by using this method, you will later find it easier to arrange your sources in the order in which they should appear in the formal typewritten bibliography which will be included at the end of your finished paper. But whatever method you use, be sure to keep accurate notes. No one enjoys discovering a failure to record an important reference—especially if this discovery comes after the paper is written and shortly before it must be handed in.

GOING OUTSIDE THE LIBRARY

A good college library should give you all the resources you need for most research papers, especially in introductory courses. But you may occasionally find it necessary to look beyond the library where you normally work. If you live in or near a city, there may be several other libraries that you can use. If this is not the case, remember that most libraries also provide an interlibrary loan service which allows you to request a book or a journal article that your own library does not possess. When a library offers interlibrary loan, you will be asked to provide bibliographical information about the material you are requesting. Librarians will then do the work of locating and securing a copy of the book or article for you. You should ask for material only if you are reasonably certain that it would be an important asset for you, and that an equivalent resource is not already available in your own library. You should also realize that interlibrary loan usually takes approximately two weeks, and sometimes longer. It is of no use to the student who defers his or her research to the week before the paper is due.

On some topics, you may want to interview people with expertise in that subject area. Interviews are usually inappropriate for literary and scientific papers, but they can be helpful for work in the social sciences. If writing a paper on the effects of divorce upon children, you might decide to interview both parents and children. But unless your instructor has encouraged you to do some interviews, you should check to make sure that interviews are acceptable for your assignment. Remember also that interviews need to be planned ahead, and you should have a list of questions before you go. But don't feel compelled to adhere rigidly to the questions you prepared in advance. A good interviewer listens carefully and knows how to ask a follow-up question that is inspired by a provocative response to an earlier question. Do not get so caught up in an interview, however, that you forget to take careful notes. (If you want to use a tape recorder, courtesy demands that you ask permission to do so when you arrange for the interview.) Since you will need to include the interview in your bibliography, record the date of the interview and the full name of the person you have interviewed.

TAKING NOTES

If you have never done a research paper before, you would be wise to take notes on 3 × 5 note cards. Note-taking is essential to research. Unfortunately, few researchers can tell in advance exactly what material they will want to include in their final paper. Especially during the early stages of your research, you may record information that will later seem unnecessary when you have become more expert on your subject and have a clear thesis. So you will probably have to discard some of your notes when you are ready to write your paper.

The advantage of the note card system is that it allows for flexibility when you are ready to move from research to composition. The odds are against discovering material in the exact order in which you will want to use it. By spreading your note cards out on a desk or table, you can study how they best fit together. You can arrange and rearrange note cards until you have them in a meaningful sequence. This system only works, however, when you have the self-restraint to limit yourself to recording one fact, one idea, or one quotation to a card. This means that many of your cards will have a lot of empty space that you may be tempted to fill. Don't. As soon as you decide to put two ideas on the same card, you have made an editorial decision that you may later regret. The cost of a set of note cards is minimal compared to the amount of time you must invest in doing a good research paper.

Sorting your note cards is also one of the easiest ways to determine if you have enough material to write a good paper. If your notes fall into a half-dozen different categories, your research might lack focus. In this case you should do some more research, concentrating on the category that interests you the most. If, on the other hand, your notes fall into a clear pattern, you may be ready to start writing. Of course, the point at which you move from research into writing will depend not only on your notes but also on the length of the paper you have in mind: Long papers usually involve more research than short papers. But if you classify your notes every few days during the process of doing your research, you will be in a position to judge when you have taken as many notes as you will need.

AVOIDING SELECTIVE RESEARCH

Although your research should have a clear focus, and you may have a tentative thesis in mind, you should formulate your final thesis only after your research is complete. Your research strategy should be designed to answer a question that you have posed to yourself, such as "How does divorce affect children?" This is very different from starting your research with your thesis predetermined. A student who is morally opposed to divorce may be tempted to take notes only from sources that discuss the harmful effects of divorce—rejecting as irrelevant any source that suggests that divorce can sometimes benefit children. Research, in this case, is not leading to greater knowledge or understanding. On the contrary, it is being used to reinforce personal beliefs that may border on prejudice.

We have seen that "anticipating the opposition" is important even in short essays of opinion. It is no less important in the research paper. Almost any topic worth investigating will yield up facts and ideas that could support different conclusions. The readings assembled in this book have demonstrated that it is possible to defend or attack gun control, capital punishment, censorship, abortion, nuclear power, and animal experimentation—among other issues. As you may have already observed, some of the most opinionated people are also the most ignorant. Well-educated men and women are usually aware of how most problems are complex, and this is because they have been exposed to different points of view during their education. Good students remember this when they are doing research. They allow their reading to influence their thought, and not their thoughts to determine their reading. Your own research may ultimately support a belief that you already hold, but it could just as easily lead you to realize that you were misinformed. When taking notes, you should remember the question that you have posed for yourself so that you do not waste time recording information that is not relevant to the question. But you should not be tempted to overlook material that directly concerns your question just because you don't agree with what this material says. If you have a good reason to reject the conclusion of someone else's work, your paper will be stronger if you recognize that this disagreement exists and then demonstrate why you favor one position over another.

ORGANIZING YOUR PAPER

If you have used the note card system, you may be able to dispense with an outline and compose your first draft by working directly from your notes—assuming that you have sorted them carefully and arranged them into an easily understandable sequence. But many writers find it useful to outline the ideas they plan to cover. Students who lack experience in writing long papers are especially likely to benefit from taking the trouble to prepare an outline before attempting to write.

If you decide to outline your paper, you should use the standard format for a formal outline:

I. Major idea
    A. Supporting idea
        1. Minor idea
            a. Supporting detail
            b. Supporting detail
        2. Minor idea
    B. Supporting idea
II. Major idea

And so forth. Subdivisions only make sense when there are at least two categories—otherwise there would be no need to subdivide. So Roman numeral I usually implies the existence of Roman numeral II, and supporting idea "A" implies the existence of supporting idea "B". A good outline is usually parallel, with each part in balance with the others.

An outline may consist of complete sentences or simply of topics, but follow consistently whichever system you choose. (For an example of a topic outline, see page 574.) The extent to which you benefit from an outline is usually determined by the amount of effort you devote to preparing it. The more developed your outline, the more likely you are to have thought your essay through and considered how it can be best organized. Your outline may show you that you have much to say about one part of your paper and little about another. This could result in a lopsided paper if the parts should be of equal importance. In this case, your outline may lead you to do some additional research in order to obtain more information for the part of the paper that looks as if it is going to be weak. Or you may decide to rethink your essay and draft another outline, narrowing your paper to the discussion of the part that had most interested you. Either of these decisions would make it easier for you to write a well-organized paper by reducing the risk of introducing ideas you could not pursue.

You should remember that an outline is not an end in itself; it is only a device to help you write a good paper. You can rewrite an outline much more easily than you can rewrite a paper, so do not think of an outline as some sort of fixed contract which you must honor at all cost. Be prepared to rework any outline that does not help you to write better.

AVOIDING PLAGIARISM

Plagiarism is the worst form of dishonest writing. As mentioned in Part One, you are guilty of plagiarism if you take someone else's words or ideas without giving adequate acknowledgment.

The most obvious form of plagiarism is to submit someone else's essay as your own. No one does this accidently. Another form of plagiarism is to copy long passages from a book or article and to pretend that the words are your own. Once again, anyone doing this is almost certain to know that he or she is cheating.

But students sometimes plagiarize without intending to do so. The most common form of plagiarism is an inadequate paraphrase. Some students will read a passage in a book, change the wording, and then convince themselves that they have transformed the material into their own work. You must always remember that it is important to give credit to the *ideas* of others, as well as their words. If you take most of the information another writer has provided, and repeat it in essentially the same pattern, you are only an insignificant half-step away from copying the material word for word. Here is an example:

ORIGINAL SOURCE:

Hawthorne's political ordeal, the death of his mother—and whatever guilt he may have harbored on either score—afforded him an understanding of the secret psychological springs of guilt. *The Scarlet Letter* is the book of a changed man. Its deeper insights have nothing to do with orthodox morality or religion—or the universal or allegorical applications of a moral. The greatness of the book is related to its sometimes fitful characterizations of human nature and the author's almost uncanny intuitions: his realization of the bond between psychological malaise and physical illness, the nearly perfect, if sinister, outlining of the psychological techniques Chillingsworth deployed against his victim.

PLAGIARISM:

Nathaniel Hawthorne understood the psychological sources of guilt. His experience in politics and the death of his mother brought him deep insights that don't have anything to do with formal religion or morality. The greatness of *The Scarlet Letter* comes from its characters and the author's brilliant intuitions: his perception of the link between psychological and physical illness and his almost perfect description of the way Roger Chillingsworth persecuted his victim.

This student has simplified the original material, changing some of its wording. But he is clearly guilty of plagiarism. Pretending to offer his own analysis of *The Scarlet Letter*, he owes all of his ideas to another writer who is unacknowledged. Even the organization of the passage has been followed. This "paraphrase" would still be considered a plagiarism even if it ended with a reference to the original source (p. 307 of *Nathaniel Hawthorne in His Times*, by James R. Mellow). A reference or footnote would not reveal the full extent to which this student is indebted to his source. Here is an acceptable version:

PARAPHRASE:

As James R. Mellow has argued in *Nathaniel Hawthorne In His Times, The Scarlet Letter* reveals a profound understanding of guilt. It is a great novel because of its insight into human nature—not because of some moral about adultery. The most interesting character is probably Roger Chillingsworth because of the way he was able to make Rev. Dimmesdale suffer (307).

This student has not only made a greater effort to paraphrase the original material, but he has also introduced it with a reference to the writer who inspired it. The introductory reference to Mellow, coupled with the subsequent page reference, "brackets" the passage—showing us that Mellow deserves the credit for the ideas in between the two references. And additional bibliographical information about this source is provided by the list of works cited which is included at the end of the paper. Turning to the bibliography we find:

Mellow, James. *Nathaniel Hawthorne In His Times.* Boston: Houghton, 1980.

One final caution: It is possible to subconsciously remember a piece of someone else's phrasing and inadvertently repeat it. You would be guilty of plagiarism if the words in question embody a critically important idea or reflect a distinctive style or turn of phrase. When you revise your rough draft, be on the lookout for such unintended quotations; if you use them, show who deserves the credit for them.

ORGANIZING YOUR FINAL BIBLIOGRAPHY

The form of your final bibliography will vary, depending upon the subject of your paper and the requirements of your instructor. Students in the humanities are usually asked to follow the form of the Modern Language Association (MLA) or that recommended by *The Chicago Manual of Style.* Students in the social sciences are often expected to follow the format of the American Psychological Association (APA). And students in the natural sciences are usually required to use either a parenthetical system resembling that of the APA or else a system that involves numbering their sources. Make sure that you understand the requirements of your instructor, and remember that you can consult a specific manual in your field if you run into problems. Here is a list of manuals that can be found in many college libraries:

American Institute of Physics. Publication Board. *Style Manual for Guidance in the Preparation of Papers.* 3rd ed. New York: American Inst. of Physics, 1978.

American Chemical Society. *American Chemical Society Style Guide and Handbook.* Washington: American Chemical Soc., 1985.

American Mathematical Society. *A Manual for Authors of Mathematical Papers.* 7th ed. Providence: American Mathematical Soc., 1980.

American Psychological Association. *Publication Manual of the American Psychological Association.* 3rd ed. Washington: American Psychological Assn., 1983.

The Chicago Manual of Style. 13th ed. Chicago: University of Chicago Press, 1982.

Council of Biology Editors. Style Manual Committee. *CBE Style Manual: A Guide for Authors, Editors, and Publishers in the Biological Sciences.* 5th ed. Bethesda: Council of Biology Editors, 1983.

Gibaldi, Joseph and Walter S. Achtert. *MLA Handbook for Writers of Research Papers.* 2nd ed. New York: Modern Language Assn., 1984.

Harvard Law Review. *A Uniform System of Citation.* 12th ed. Cambridge: Harvard Law Review Assn., 1976.

International Steering Committee of Medical Journal Editors. "Uniform Requirements for Manuscripts Submitted to Biomedical Journals." *Annals of Internal Medicine* 96 (June): 766–71.

A detailed discussion of all of these styles is beyond the range of this chapter. But the following pages provide model entries for the most frequently used styles.

WORKS CITED IN MLA STYLE

In an MLA style bibliography, the works cited are arranged in alphabetical order determined by the author's last name. MLA style requires that the author's first name be given. Every important word in the titles of books, articles, and journals is capitalized. The titles of books, journals, and newspapers are all underlined (italicized). The titles of articles, stories, and poems appear within quotation marks. Second and subsequent lines are indented five spaces (leave five spaces blank). Here are some examples:

A. Book with One Author

```
Bate, Walter Jackson.   Coleridge.   New York: Macmillan, 1968.
```

B. Book with Two or Three Authors

```
Gilbert, Sandra M. and Susan Gubar.   The Madwoman in the Attic: The
    Woman Writer and the Nineteenth-Century Literary Imagination.
    New Haven: Yale UP, 1979.
```

Note that the subtitle is included, set off from the main title by a colon. The second author's name is not inverted, and abbreviations are used for "University Press" in order to provide a shortened form of the publisher's name. For books with three authors, put commas after the names of the first two authors; separate the second two authors with a comma followed by "and."

C. An Edited Book

```
Garner, Helen, ed.   A Book of Religious Verse.   New York: Oxford UP,
    1972.
```

D. A Book with More Than Three Authors or Editors

```
Clark, Donald, et al., eds.  English Literature.  New York:
     Macmillan, 1960.
```

Give the name of the first author or editor only, and add the abbreviation "et al." (Latin for *et alii,* "and others"**).**

E. A Revised Edition

```
Smart, William.  Eight Modern Essayists.  3rd ed.  New York: St.
     Martin's, 1980.
```

F. A Work in an Anthology

```
Levin, Harry.  "The Language of the Outlaw."  Joyce: A Collection of
     Critical Essays.  Ed. William M. Chace.  Englewood Cliffs:
     Prentice, 1974.  113-129.
```

Note that a period comes after the title of the selection but before the second quotation marks. A period is also used to separate the date of publication from the pages between which the selection can be found. No abbreviation is used before the page reference.

G. A Translated Book

```
Camus, Albert.  Notebooks 1935-1942.  Trans. Philip Thody.  New
     York: Knopf, 1963.
```

H. A Work in More Than One Volume

```
Daiches, David.  A Critical History of English Literature.  2 vols.
     New York: Ronald P, 1960.
```

If the work has been published over several years, give the inclusive dates.

I. An Introduction, Preface, Foreword, or Afterword

```
Schorer, Mark.  Afterword.  Babbitt.  By Sinclair Lewis.  New York:
     Signet-NAL, 1961.  320-327.
```

J. Journal Article with One Author

```
Beidler, Peter G. "What Can You do with an English Major?"  College
     English 47 (1985):  39-42.
```

The volume number comes after the journal title without any intervening punctuation. The year of publication is included within parentheses after the volume number. A colon separates the year of publication and the page reference.

K. Journal Article Paginated Anew in Each Issue

```
Aronson, Arnold. "American Scenography."  Drama Review 28.2 (1984):
     2-22.
```

In this case, the issue number is included immediately after the volume number, and the two are separated by a period without any intervening space.

L. An Article from a Magazine Published Monthly

```
Owen, David.   "I Spied on the Twelfth Grade."  Esquire Mar. 1981:
     72-78.
```

Instead of citing the volume number, give the month and year of the issue. Abbreviate the month.

M. An Article from a Magazine Issued Weekly

```
Gallant, Mavis.   "Overhead in a Balloon."  New Yorker 2 July 1984:
     34-44.
```

The form is the same as for an article in a magazine that is issued monthly, but you add the date immediately before the month. Although months are usually abbreviated, an exception is made for May, June, and July.

N. An Article from a Daily Newspaper

```
Robinson, Karen.   "The Line to Privacy is Unlisted."  Milwaukee
     Journal 26 March 1985, sunrise ed., sec. 2: 2.
```

If more than one edition is available on the date in question, specify the edition immediately after the date. If the city of publication is not part of the newspaper's name, identify the city in brackets after the newspaper title. If the article is unsigned, begin the citation with the title of the article; alphabetize the article under its title, passing over small words like "a" and "the."

O. Editorial

```
Lewis, Anthony.   "The Wasted Country."  Editorial.  New York Times
     21 March 1985, natl. ed., sec. 1: 27.
```

Editorials are identified as such in between the title of the article and the title of the newspaper or magazine.

P. Interviews

```
Fox, Cynthia.    Personal interview.    16 Jan. 1982.
```

If you interview someone, alphabetize the interview under the name of the person interviewed.

REFERENCES IN APA STYLE

In APA style, the reference list is arranged alphabetically, the order being determined by the author's last name. The date of publication is emphasized by placing it within parentheses immediately after the author's name. If a second or third line is necessary, such lines should be indented three spaces (leave three spaces blank).

A. Book with One Author

```
Gardner, H. (1975).    The shattered mind.    New York: Knopf.
```

Note that the author's first name is indicated only by an initial. Only the first letter of the first word in the title is capitalized. The name of the publisher, Alfred A. Knopf, is given in shortened form. A period comes after the parenthesis surrounding the date of publication, and also after the title and publisher.

B. Book with Two Authors or More

```
Jencks, C. & Riesman, D. (1968).    The academic revolution.    Garden
    City: Doubleday.
```

An ampersand is used to separate the names of two authors. When there are three or more authors, separate their names with commas and put an ampersand immediately before the last author's name.

C. Edited Book

```
Bottomore, T. & Nisbet R. (Eds.). (1978).    A history of sociological
    analysis.    New York: Basic.
```

Give the names of all editors, no matter how many there are. The abbreviation for editors is "Eds."; it should be included within parentheses between the names of the editors and the date of publication. A single editor is identified as such by "Ed." in parentheses.

D. Article or Chapter in an Edited Book

```
Rickman, J. (1940).   On the nature of ugliness and the creative
    impulse.   In H. Ruitenbeek (Ed.), The creative imagination (pp.
    97—121).   Chicago: Quadrangle.
```

Do not invert the editor's name when it is not in the author's position. Do not put the title of the article or chapter in quotation marks. Use a comma to separate the editor from the title of the edited book. The pages between which the material can be found appear within parentheses immediately after the book title. Use "p." for page and "pp." for pages.

E. Translated Book

```
Beauvoir, S. de. (1972).   The coming of age (P. O'Brian, Trans.).
    New York: Putnam's.
```

Within parentheses immediately after the book title, give the translator's name followed by a comma and the abbreviation "Trans." Put a period after the parentheses.

F. Revised Edition of a Book

```
Samuelson, P.A. (1980).   Economics (11th ed.).   New York: McGraw.
```

The edition is identified immediately after the title. Note that edition is abbreviated "ed." and should not be confused with "Ed." for editor.

G. Book with a Corporate Author

```
American Medical Association.   (1982).   Family medical guide.   New
    York: Random.
```

H. Multivolume Book

```
Jones, E. (1953—57).   The life and work of Sigmund Freud (Vol. 2).
    New York: Basic.
```

The volume number is included within parentheses immediately after the title. When a multivolume book is published over a number of years, list the years between which it was published.

I. Journal Article with One Author

```
Cornell, S.  (1985).  Crisis and response in Indian—White relations:
    1960—1984.  Social Problems, 32, 44—59.
```

Put a comma after the journal title and then give the volume and page numbers. Abbreviations are not used for "volume" and "page". In order to distinguish between the numbers, underline the volume number and put a comma between it and the page numbers.

J. Journal Article with Up to Six Authors

```
Korner, A., Zeanah, C.H., Linden, J., Berkowitz, R., Kraemer, H., &
    Agras, W.S. (1985). The relations between neonatal and later
    activity and temperament. Child Development, 56, 38–52.
```

K. Journal Article Paginated Anew in Each Issue

```
Kupfer, D.J. & Reynolds, C.F. (1983). Sleep disorders. Hospital
    Practice, 18 (2), 101–119.
```

When each issue of a journal begins with page 1, you need to include the issue number in parentheses immediately after the underlined volume number.

L. Article from a Magazine Issued Monthly

```
McDermott, J. (1983, November). Robots are taking a hand in our
    affairs. Smithsonian, pp. 60–69.
```

Within parentheses immediately after the author, include the month of issue after the year of publication. Use "p." or "pp." in front of the page number(s). Do not include the volume number. Follow the same form for an article in a magazine issued on a specific day, but add the date after the month:

```
Greenfield, M. (1984, June 11). The whole world is listening.
    Newsweek, p. 88.
```

M. Article from a Newspaper

```
Pollack, R.F. (1985, March 14). A wrong way to see the aged. New
    York Times, Part 1, p. 27.
```

Place the exact date of issue within parentheses immediately after the author. After the newspaper title, specify the section and page numbers.

THE NUMBERED SYSTEM

In a numbered system the bibliography may be arranged in alphabetical order (determined by the authors' last names) or in the order in which the works are cited within the paper itself. Once this sequence is established, the items are assigned numbers in consecutive order beginning with 1, and these numbers are used as citations within the paper. There are many variations on the particular form of the bibliographical entries; authors of scientific papers should adopt the style recommended by the journal for which they are writing. But here are examples of two frequently used forms:

A. Biology

1. Ferris, F.G.; Beveridge, T. J. Functions of bacterial cell surface structures. Bioscience. 35:172–177; 1985.
2. Lewis, A. E. Biostatistics. New York: Reinhold; 1966.

Note that neither journal nor book titles are underlined. Quotation marks are not used for article titles. The year of publication appears at the end of the citation, and it is preceded by a semicolon.

B. Chemistry

(1) Silverman, M. P. J. Chem. Ed. 1984, 62, pp. 112–114.
(2) Bard, A. J. Chemical Equilibrium; Harper & Row: New York, 1966; pp. 17–28.

Note that journal titles are abbreviated, and article titles are not included.

For an example of a numbered system in use, see the essay by Shirley K. Bell (pp. 300–304).

DOCUMENTING YOUR SOURCES

"Documenting your sources" means revealing the source of the information you report. You must provide documentation for:

1. any direct quotation
2. any idea that has come from someone else's work
3. any fact or statistic that is not widely known

The traditional way to document a source is to footnote it. Strictly speaking, a "footnote" appears at the foot of the page, and an "endnote" appears at the end of the paper. But "footnote" has become a generic term covering both forms. Most writers prefer to keep their notes on a separate page since doing so is easier than remembering to save adequate space for notes on the bottom of each page. Footnotes used for documentation would include the same information as a bibliographical reference with the addition of a specific page reference. The precise form of such notes varies, depending upon the style manual being followed. Here is how a documentary footnote would look in MLA style:

A. Bibliographic Form

Manchester, William. <u>American Caesar: Douglas MacArthur 1880–1964</u>.
Boston: Little, 1978.

B. Note Form

[1] William Manchester, <u>American Caesar: Douglas MacArthur 1880–1964</u> (Boston: Little, 1978) 65.

The indentation is reversed, the author's name is not inverted, and the publishing data are included within parentheses. Also, the author is separated from the title by a comma rather than a period. A subsequent reference to the same work would follow a shortened form:

[5] Manchester, 182.

If more than one work by this same author is cited, then a shortened form of the title would also be included:

[7] Manchester, <u>Caesar</u> 228.

Documentary footnotes require what many authorities now regard as unnecessary repetition, since the author's full name and the publishing data are already included in the bibliography. And many readers object to being obliged to turn frequently to another page if they want to check the notes. Some writers still use notes for documentation purposes. (You can find examples of such notes in the essays by Sissela Bok and Peter Singer in Part Two.) But both the MLA and APA (and also the influential University of Chicago Press, in *The Chicago Manual of Style*) now urge writers to provide their documentation parenthetically within the work itself, reserving numbered notes for additional explanation or discussion that is important but cannot be included within the actual text without a loss of focus. Notes used for providing additional information are called *content* notes. (The essays by Bok and Singer also include content notes, as do the essays by Ernest van den Haag and Edward Teller elsewhere in Part Two.)

PARENTHETICAL DOCUMENTATION: THE MLA AUTHOR/WORK STYLE

In 1984 the Modern Language Association adopted parenthetical documentation to take the place of endnote or footnote citations. In MLA form, the author's name is followed by a page reference. It is not necessary to repeat within the parentheses information that is already provided within the text.

A.   A Work by a Single Author

Henry James often identified wickedness with sexual duplicity (Kazin 227).

or

Alfred Kazin has argued that Henry James identified wickedness with sexual duplicity (227).

There is no punctuation between the author's name and the page reference when both are cited parenthetically. Note also that the abbreviation "p." or "pp." is not used before the page reference.

B.   A Work with More Than One Author

According to Cleanth Brooks and Robert Penn Warren, "indirection is an essential part of the method of poetry" (573).

or

Although this sonnet may seem obscure, its meaning becomes clearer when we realize "indirection is an essential part of the method of poetry" (Brooks and Warren 573).

Note that when a sentence ends with a quotation, the parenthetical reference comes before the final punctuation mark. Note also that the ampersand is not used in MLA style. When referring to a work by more than three authors, you should follow the guidelines for bibliographic entries and list only the first author's name followed by "et al.":

Comley et al. have produced a fine anthology.

C.   A Work with a Corporate Author

When a corporate author has a long name, you should include it within the text rather than within parentheses. For example:

In 1980 the Council on Environmental Quality reported that there is growing evidence of ground water contamination throughout the United States (81).

rather than

There is growing evidence of ground water contamination throughout the United States (Council on Environmental Quality 81).

Although both of these forms are technically correct, the first is pre-

ferred because it is easier to read. Long parenthetical references are unnecessarily intrusive, interrupting the flow of ideas.

D. A Work with More Than One Volume

When you wish to cite a specific part of a multivolume work, include the volume number between the author and the page reference:

As Jacques Barzun has argued, "the only hope of true culture is to make classifications broad and criticism particular" (2: 340).

Note that the volume number is given in an arabic numeral, and a space separates the colon and the page reference. The abbreviation "vol." is not used unless you wish to cite the entire volume: (Barzun, vol. 2).

E. More Than One Work by the Same Author

If you cite more than one work by the same author, you need to make your references distinct. You can do so by putting a comma after the author's name and then adding a shortened form of the title: (Hardy, *Mayor*, 179). But your paper will be easier to read if you include either the author or the title directly in the text:

Twain's late work reflects a low opinion of human nature. But when Satan complains that all men are cowards (<u>Stranger</u> 184), he is only echoing Col. Sherburn's speech in <u>Huckleberry Finn</u> (123–124).

F. A Quotation Within a Cited Work

If you want to use a quotation which you have discovered in another book, your reference must show that you acquired this material secondhand and that you have not consulted the original source. Use the abbreviation "qtd. in" (for "quoted in") to make the distinction between the author of the passage being quoted and the author of the work in which you found this passage:

In 1835 Thomas Macaulay declared the British to be "the acknowledged leaders of the human race" (qtd. in Davis 231).

G. A Quotation of Poetry

Identify line numbers when you quote poetry, but do not use the abbreviations "l." or "ll." These abbreviations can easily be confused with numbers. Write "line" or "lines" in your first citation of poetry; subsequent citations should include only the line numbers. Quotations of three lines or less should be included directly into the text of your paper. Separate the lines with a slash (/), leaving an extra space both before and after the slash:

```
Yeats returned to this theme in "The Second Coming": "The best lack
all conviction, while the worst / Are full of passionate intensity"
(7-8).
```

Each line of longer quotations should begin on a new line, indented ten spaces from the margin.

PARENTHETICAL DOCUMENTATION: THE APA AUTHOR/YEAR STYLE

The APA requires that in-text documentation identifies the author of the work being referred to and the year in which this work was published. This information should be provided parenthetically, although it is not necessary to repeat any information that has already been provided directly in the sentence.

A. One Work by a Single Author

```
It has been argued that fairy tales can play a vital role in child
development (Bettelheim, 1975).
```

or

```
Bettelheim (1975) argued that fairy tales can play a vital role in
child development.
```

or

```
In 1975 Bruno Bettelheim argued that fairy tales can play a vital role
in child development.
```

If the reference is to a specific chapter or page, that information should also be included. For example:

```
(Bettelheim, 1975, p., 126)
(Bettelheim, 1975, chap. 6)
```

Note that the abbreviations for page and chapter emphasize the distinction between the year of publication and the part of the work being referred to.

B. A Work with More than One Author

If a work has two authors, you should mention the names of both authors every time a reference is made to this work:

In a recent study of children (Walker & Emory, 1983) it was argued
that . . . .

or

More recently, Walker and Emory (1983) have argued that . . . .

Note that the ampersand is used only within parentheses.

Scientific papers often have multiple authors because of the amount
of research involved. In the first reference to a work with up to six
authors, you should identify each of the authors:

Hodges, McKnew, Cytryn, Stern, and Kline (1982) have shown . . . .

Subsequent references to the same work should use an abbreviated
form:

Hodges et al. (1982) also questioned . . . .

If a work has six authors or more, this abbreviated form should be
used even in the first reference. If confusion is possible because you
refer to more than one work by the first author, list as many authors
as necessary to distinguish between the two works.

C. A Work with a Corporate Author

When a work has a corporate author, your first reference should
include the full name of the corporation, committee, agency, or institution involved. For example:

(United States Fish and Wildlife Service [USFWS], 1984)

Subsequent references to the same source can be abbreviated:

(USFWS, 1984)

D. A Reference to More Than One Work

When the same citation refers to two or more sources, the works
should be listed alphabetically according to the author's name and
separated with semicolons:

(Pepler & Rubin, 1982; Schesinger, 1982; Young, 1984)

If you are referring to more than one work by the same author(s), list
the works in the order in which they were published.

```
The validity of this type of testing has been established during the
last three years (Collins, 1983, 1985).
```

If you refer to more than one work by the same author published in the same year, distinguish individual works by identifying them as "a," "b," "c," etc.:

```
These findings have been questioned by Walker (1983a, 1983b).
```

RULES TO REMEMBER

Whether you document your sources by using traditional footnotes or one of the recommended systems for parenthetical references, you should remember the following rules:

1. Every source cited in a reference should have a corresponding entry in the bibliography.
2. Be consistent. Don't shift from the author/year system to the author/work system in the middle of your paper.
3. Try to vary the introductions you use for quotations and paraphrases and make sure that the material in question has been incorporated smoothly into your text. Read your first draft aloud in order to be better able to judge its readability.
4. When you mention authorities by name, try to identify who they are so that your audience can evaluate the source. (For example: "According to William Bennett, Chairman of the National Endowment for the Humanities, funding for the arts next year will....") But do not insult the intelligence of your audience by identifying well-known figures.
5. If in doubt about whether to document a source, you would probably be wise to err on the side of caution by going ahead and documenting it. But be careful not to overdocument your paper. A paper that is composed of one reference after another usually lacks synthesis and interpretation.

OTHER POINTS OF MECHANICS

Unless instructed otherwise, you should be guided by the following rules when preparing your final draft:

1. Research papers should be typed. Use nonerasable 8½-by-11 inch white, 20-pound paper. Type on one side of each page only. Double-space all lines, leaving a margin of one inch on all sides.
2. In the upper left corner of page 1, or on a separate title page, include the following information: your name, your instructor's name, the course and section number, and the date the essay is submitted.

3. Beginning on page 2, number each page in the upper right corner, ½ inch from the top.

4. Long quotations (anything more than four lines) should be set off from the rest of the text. Begin a new line, indenting ten spaces to form the left margin for the quotation. The indentation means that you are quoting, so additional quotation marks are unnecessary in this case.

5. In order to avoid the charge of "padding," you should try to edit long quotations whenever possible. Use the ellipsis (...) to indicate that you have omitted a word or phrase within a sentence. Leave a space before and after each period. Begin with a fourth period with no space before it when the ellipsis comes at the end of a sentence (....).

6. Make sure that edited quotations are still grammatical and clear. If the addition of an extra word or two would help make the quotation more easily understandable, you can make an editorial interpolation enclosing the inserted material within square brackets [   ]. If your typewriter does not have brackets, you can draw them in by hand.

7. Proofread your paper carefully. The research paper should be the product of many hours of work, and it should not look as if written in haste. Typographical errors or careless mistakes in spelling or grammar can cause your audience to lose confidence in you. If your instructor allows ink corrections, make them as neatly as you can. Retype any page that has numerous or lengthy corrections.

8. Use a paper clip to bind your work together. This allows your instructor to easily separate the pages of your paper if he or she wishes to do so.

IN CONCLUSION

The readings assembled in Part Two have demonstrated the importance of research in the world beyond the classroom. Extensive research is readily apparent in the articles by van den Haag, Burger, Gallistel, Mayo, Singer, Bok, Bell, Teller, Bird, and Shurr. But research also supports the arguments of Kates, Bruck, Hentoff, Kaminer, FitzGerald, and Commoner—among others. None of these works could have been written if their authors had not taken the trouble to become well-informed on their chosen subjects.

Having studied these essays, you should be familiar with the way experienced writers use content notes to clarify various points in their arguments. Individual essays have also demonstrated the major documentation styles: Deborah Mayo and C.R. Gallistel use the APA author/year system, and as noted earlier, the essay by Shirley K. Bell provides an example of a numbered system. Sissela Bok's essay demonstrates the *Chicago Manual of Style* system for documentary footnotes, and Andrew Rowan's essay demonstrates the *Chicago Manual* system for parenthetical documentation. For an example of the MLA author/work style, study the following student paper.

Richard Kaufman
Professor Molinaro
English 102, sec. 14
May 7, 1985

The Case for Robert Cohn:
The Unsung Hero of <u>The Sun Also Rises</u>

I.   Introduction
    A. What most critics think of Robert Cohn
       1. Quotation from Allen Tate
       2. Quotation from Leon Seltzer
       3. Quotation from Robert Cochran
       4. Quotation from Earl Rovit
    B. The historical background of the book
       1. The friends with whom Hemingway traveled to Spain
       in 1925
          a. Lady Duff Twysden and her companion Pat Guthrie
          b. Bill Smith, a boyhood friend of Hemingway's
       2. Harold Loeb, the model for Robert Cohn
          a. Loeb's biographical background
          b. Hemingway's feelings towards Loeb
II.   How other characters in the book view Cohn
    A. Bill's point of view
       1. The importance of Cohn's religion
       2. Evidence that Bill is anti-Semitic
    B. Jake's point of view
       1. Positive information about Cohn provided by Jake
       2. Evaluation of negative details provided by Jake
III. My own view of Cohn
    A. Cohn as an idealist
       1. Evidence that he wants his life to be worthwhile
       2. Evidence that he is capable of falling seriously in
       love
    B. Cynicism the cause of other characters' resentment of
    Cohn
       1. Jake's and Bill's ridicule of romantic love
       2. Mike's relationship with Brett

    C. Critics who ridicule Cohn for being in love
       1. Quotation from Sheridan Baker
       2. Quotation from Mark Spilka
    D. Evidence from the book that shows Cohn's critics to be
       wrong
       1. Jake's speech to Brett about behaving badly
       2. Comparison of Cohn with Pedro Romero and other
         characters

IV.   Conclusion
    A. Cohn's role in the book
       1. The significance of his status as an outsider
       2. Cohn's effect upon other characters
    B. Final Statement

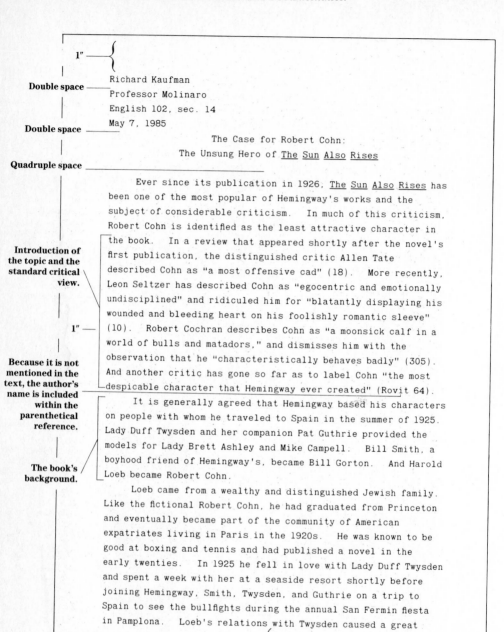

Double space

Richard Kaufman
Professor Molinaro
English 102, sec. 14
May 7, 1985

Double space

The Case for Robert Cohn:
The Unsung Hero of The Sun Also Rises

Quadruple space

Introduction of the topic and the standard critical view.

Ever since its publication in 1926, The Sun Also Rises has been one of the most popular of Hemingway's works and the subject of considerable criticism.   In much of this criticism, Robert Cohn is identified as the least attractive character in the book.   In a review that appeared shortly after the novel's first publication, the distinguished critic Allen Tate described Cohn as "a most offensive cad" (18).   More recently, Leon Seltzer has described Cohn as "egocentric and emotionally undisciplined" and ridiculed him for "blatantly displaying his wounded and bleeding heart on his foolishly romantic sleeve" (10).   Robert Cochran describes Cohn as "a moonsick calf in a world of bulls and matadors," and dismisses him with the observation that he "characteristically behaves badly" (305). And another critic has gone so far as to label Cohn "the most despicable character that Hemingway ever created" (Rovit 64).

Because it is not mentioned in the text, the author's name is included within the parenthetical reference.

It is generally agreed that Hemingway based his characters on people with whom he traveled to Spain in the summer of 1925. Lady Duff Twysden and her companion Pat Guthrie provided the models for Lady Brett Ashley and Mike Campell.   Bill Smith, a boyhood friend of Hemingway's, became Bill Gorton.   And Harold Loeb became Robert Cohn.

The book's background.

Loeb came from a wealthy and distinguished Jewish family. Like the fictional Robert Cohn, he had graduated from Princeton and eventually became part of the community of American expatriates living in Paris in the 1920s.   He was known to be good at boxing and tennis and had published a novel in the early twenties.   In 1925 he fell in love with Lady Duff Twysden and spent a week with her at a seaside resort shortly before joining Hemingway, Smith, Twysden, and Guthrie on a trip to Spain to see the bullfights during the annual San Fermin fiesta in Pamplona.   Loeb's relations with Twysden caused a great

Kaufman 2

⎱— ½"

deal of ill feeling.   After several days of building tension,
Hemingway and Loeb quarreled.   (They left a restaurant
intending to have a fist fight, but unlike Jake and Cohn they did
not actually come to blows.)

        But if Hemingway had reason to resent Loeb, he also took
trouble to remain on good terms with him.   On the morning after
the quarrel, Hemingway sent Loeb a note of apology, the heart
of which reads as follows:

> I was terribly tight and nasty to you last night and
> I dont [sic] want you to go away with that nasty
> insulting lousiness as the last thing of the fiestas.
> I wish I could wipe out all the mean-ness [sic] and I
> suppose I cant [sic] but this is to let you know that
> I'm thoroly [sic] ashamed of the way I acted and the
> stinking, unjust uncalled for things I said.
> (Letters 166)

Hemingway may have remembered that the publication of his first
book, In Our Time, had recently been arranged for through
Loeb's intervention with his own publisher.   And there is
reason to believe that Hemingway may have been jealous of Loeb.
Sheridan Baker has described Loeb as "the Princeton man . . .
who could outplay Hemingway at tennis and outbox his twitching
eye, who had beaten him to publication and then too fortunately
helped him--had run off with the most desirable woman in Paris"
(41).   So if the original model for Robert Cohn was a man who
was worthy of some respect, it may be that his fictional
counterpart is something more than a fool.

        At least part of Hemingway's resentment of Loeb can be
traced to anti-Semitism.   Discussing The Sun Also Rises while
he was still working on it, Hemingway is reported to have told
a friend, "I'm putting everyone in it and that kike Loeb is the
villain" (qtd. in C. Baker 154).   Cohn's religion is
emphasized throughout the novel.   It is, for example, one of
the first things the reader is told about him: "No one had ever
made him feel he was a Jew, and hence any different from
anybody else, until he went to Princeton" (4).   The

Student adds [sic] to a quotation in order to indicate that the errors are part of the quotation and have not been made in transcription.

Student introduces his own thesis.

An indirect source for a quotation. Author's first initial is included to distinguish him from another writer with the same last name.

Student begins to cite evidence from the book in support of his thesis.

Kaufman 3

implication of this line is that a "Jew" <u>is</u> "different from anybody else." Many readers come to like Bill Gorton, but it is Bill who complains about Cohn's "Jewish superiority," (162) refers to Cohn as "That kike!" (164) and sarcastically asks Jake, "Haven't you got some more Jewish friends you could bring along?" (101) Bearing these remarks in mind, an unbiased reader should try to appraise Cohn more objectively.   The victim of prejudice, Cohn may be more admirable than the other characters in the novel were able to recognize.

There are many positive references to Cohn within the novel that are frequently overlooked.   After describing Cohn's boxing career at Princeton, Jake remarks, "I mistrust all frank and simple people, especially when their stories hold together" (4).   The implication is that Cohn is "frank" and "simple" and honest about his background.   These are undeniably attractive qualities.   Jake also comments that Cohn was "a nice boy, a friendly boy, and very shy" (4) when he went off to college——a description that is at odds with attempts to portray Cohn as egoistic and self-centered.   Several chapters later, Jake returns to the subject of Robert Cohn, offering a detailed description which is worth quoting at length:

> Somehow I feel I have not shown Robert Cohn clearly.
> The reason is that until he fell in love with Brett,
> I never heard him make one remark that would in any
> way detach him from other people.   He was nice to
> watch on the tennis-court, he had a good body, and he
> kept it in shape; he handled his cards well at
> bridge, and he had a funny sort of undergraduate
> quality about him.   If he were in a crowd nothing he
> said stood out.   He wore what used to be called polo
> shirts at school, and may be called that still, but
> he was not professionally youthful.   I do not
> believe he thought about clothes very much.
> Externally he had been formed at Princeton.
> Internally he had been moulded by the two women who
> had trained him.   He had a nice, boyish sort of

This is an unusually long quotation to be included in a research paper, but it is acceptable because it describes the character who is the subject of the paper. Quotation marks are not used because the passage is begun on a new line and indented ten spaces.

Kaufman 4

> cheerfulness that had never been trained out of him,
> and I probably have not brought that out.   He loved
> to win at tennis. . . .   On the other hand, he was
> not angry at being beaten.   When he fell in love
> with Brett his tennis game went all to pieces.
> People beat him who had never had a chance with him.
> He was very nice about it. (45)

The worst that is said about Cohn in this passage is that he did
not make clever remarks that would have made him stand out in a
crowd--and that he had been "trained" by the two women with
whom he had lived.   Neither of these observations is
especially damaging, although they do convey a sense that Cohn
was weak in some ways.   These two details aside, the rest of
the passage is positive.   The reader learns that Cohn had a
good body and kept it in shape and that he seemed young even
though he was not "professionally youthful"--which means he
did not work at seeming young.   Some critics have condemned
Cohn because he did not like to fish and was upset when he saw
horses gored at a bullfight (Ross 522; Cochran 305).   But to
value fishing and bullfighting over tennis, boxing, and bridge is
to judge Cohn by an arbitrary standard.   The point to grasp is
that Cohn is good at some games; they just don't happen to be
the games that Jake and Bill most like.   It's not as if Cohn
was entirely inept; there's nothing ridiculous about being good
at tennis and bridge.   Nor is there anything wrong about
dressing casually.   That Cohn did not fuss about his clothing
shows a commendable lack of pretension.   Most importantly, the
passage as a whole suggests that Cohn was "nice."   Surely a
character with a "nice, boyish sort of cheerfulness" is a
welcome relief within a novel full of characters who are
anything but nice.   And critics who emphasize Cohn's failings
should at least give him credit for being a good loser on the
tennis court.

But Cohn's greatest virtue has nothing to do with clothing
or sports.   He is an admirable character because he is an
idealist who expects more from life than sitting around getting

Student provides analysis of the quotation.

A summary of other views, cited within the same parenthetical reference.

Kaufman 5

drunk.   Consider the following conversation between Cohn and
Jake:

> "Listen, Jake. . . . .Don't you ever get the
> feeling that all your life is going by and you're not
> taking advantage of it?   Do you realize you've lived
> nearly half the time you have to live already?"

Quotation marks are used despite indentation because dialogue is involved.

> "Yes, every once in a while."
> "Do you know that in about thirty-five years
> more we'll be dead?"
> "What the hell, Robert," I said.   "What the
> hell."
> "I'm serious."
> "It's one thing I don't worry about," I said.
> "You ought to." (11)

It may not be sophisticated to be so earnest about life, but
people can be too sophisticated for their own good.   Cohn
should be admired for thinking about his future and wanting to
make something of his life.

The worst charge that can be brought against Cohn is that
he shows bad judgment by falling in love with Brett Ashley——who
is superficial, promiscuous, and manipulative.   But the other
characters in the novel do not blame Cohn for loving Brett;
they blame him for <u>revealing</u> that he loves her——as if adults
should know better than to be open about how they feel.
Waiting at the Pamplona station for Brett's train, Jake
observes:

> I have never seen a man in civil life as nervous as
> Robert Cohn——nor as eager.   I was enjoying it.   It
> was lousy to enjoy it, but I felt lousy.   Cohn had a
> wonderful quality of bringing out the worst in
> anybody. (98)

Jake has a good reason for feeling "lousy."   He is impotent as
the result of a war wound and incapable of feeling the
excitement with which Cohn anticipates Brett's arrival.
Contemptuous of Cohn's open display of feeling, Jake seems to
believe that love is somehow ridiculous.   Thinking over the

Kaufman 6

entire situation, Jake concludes:

> That damn Cohn.   He should have hit somebody the
> first time he was insulted, and then gone away.   He
> was so sure that Brett loved him.   He was going to
> stay, and true love would conquer all. (199)

The reference to "true love" is distinctly sarcastic, as if no
one could truly be in love.   Bill seems to share Jake's belief
that Cohn's devotion to Brett is foolish, as if fidelity were a
breach of good taste.   After Cohn fights with Pedro Romero and
unsuccessfully tries to take Brett away with him, Bill dryly
comments: "Wanted to make an honest woman of her, I imagine.
Damned touching scene" (201).   And Mike Campbell seems as
resentfully impotent as Jake Barnes.   He spends most of the
novel getting drunk and trying to overlook Brett's affairs with
other men.   He objects to her affairs with Cohn and Romero not
because she was being unfaithful to him, but because she was
being unfaithful to their social class: No one is ever allowed
to lose sight of the fact that Cohn is a Jew and Romero a
bullfighter.   After a scene in which he embarrasses everyone by
savagely ridiculing Cohn, Mike defends his behavior on grounds
that are worth noting, complaining that Cohn had joined a party
"where he damned well wasn't wanted" and then "hung around
Brett and just <u>looked</u> at her" (143).   The implication seems to
be that Mike wouldn't have minded Cohn doing more than just
"looking" and that he would have respected Cohn more if he had
been more aggressive.

Most critics have agreed with Mike's appraisal of Cohn's
behavior, as if love has no place in modern fiction.   According
to Sheridan Baker, Cohn is an "unrealist still living by
Victorian mottoes, springing to arms over imaginary insults to
a nonexistent lady. . ." (44).   Mark Spilka is a little more
sympathetic to Cohn.   But in an often cited essay, Spilka
argues that Cohn's predicament reveals the death of romantic
love:

> Cohn's romanticism explains his key position in the
> parable.   He is the last chivalric hero, the last

Student cites criticism with which he disagrees.

Kaufman 7

defender of an outworn faith, and his function is to
illustrate its present folly--to show us through the
absurdity of his behavior, that romantic love is
dead, that one of the great guiding codes of the past
no longer operates. (129)

But a conversation between Jake and Brett suggests that Cohn is
not "the last chivalric hero":

"Everybody behaves badly," I said, "Give them
the proper chance."

"You wouldn't behave badly," Brett looked at
me.

"I'd be as big an ass as Cohn," I said. (181)

"Behaving badly," according to Brett and her friends, means
being serious and unwilling to treat life like a joke. Cohn
"behaves badly" by being seriously in love with Brett and
unwilling to pretend otherwise. Jake is smart enough to
realize that Cohn is only being human. Given the right
circumstances, "everybody" could act like Cohn--even the
world-weary Jake. And it is worth remembering that of all the
characters in the book, Jake comes closest to being Hemingway's
own counterpart. So Jake's recognition that he himself could
be like Cohn is significant.

In defense of Robert Cohn, it should also be noted that he
shares a number of qualities with Pedro Romero, a character who
is generally admired. They are both "fighters": Cohn is a
boxer, and Romero a bullfighter. They drink only moderately.
They have little sense of humor. And they both love Brett.
Romero is even more old-fashioned than Cohn; it is Romero,
after all, who expects Brett to grow her hair longer in order
to be more "womanly" (242). Comparing the two men, one critic
concludes that Cohn is "sadly incapable of the self-sufficient
manhood of Romero" (S. Baker 44). But this is not clearly
established by what actually happens in the book. There may
be something ridiculous in the fist fight between Cohn and Romero
over Brett, but surely Cohn deserves at least some credit for
being strong enough to knock the younger man down. When Cohn

**First initial is
used to
distinguish the
author from
another writer
with the same
last name.**

Kaufman 8

bends down to shake hands with his opponent, Romero hits him in the face.   Is this a "manly" act?   And is Romero really all that "self-sufficient"?   He can't even get dressed by himself, but has to rely upon a group of attendants who follow him almost everywhere.   And as far as self-sufficiency goes, it is Romero, not Cohn, who actually wants to <u>marry</u> Brett.

Much has been made of the fact that Cohn breaks down and cries after his fight with Romero, but his misery seems genuine. Jake reports that Cohn was "crying without making any noise" (194)—a fact that rescues Cohn from seeming merely pathetic. It is to their discredit that the other characters in the novel see Cohn's pain as still another reason to turn against him. As Robert W. Lewis has argued in <u>Hemingway</u> <u>on</u> <u>Love</u>, "they hate him because he suffers" (24).   This is in part because his unhappiness is spoiling their party, but it may also be because Cohn's capacity for suffering underscores their own want of feeling.

Robert Cohn provides a standard against which all the other characters can be measured.   It is for this reason that he occupies such a central position in the book: The first two words of the novel are "Robert Cohn," and Hemingway devotes the entire first chapter to describing him.   The other characters eventually unite against him.   Cohn is an "outsider" who can't fit into their circumscribed little world of parties and deceit. He makes them feel bad by revealing their own shortcomings. They cannot forgive him for being different.   "Do you think you belong here among us?"   Mike demands, "People who are out to have a good time?" (177)

If life was meant to be nothing more than having "a good time," then Mike could be excused for telling Cohn, "Go away. Go away, for God's sake. Take that sad Jewish face away" (177). But it may be "for God's sake" that Cohn remains where he is, surrounded by people who know not what they do.   He makes them question their values—or lack of values—and tells them truths they need to hear.   After Jake has brought Brett and Romero together, Cohn calls him a "damned pimp" (190).   Jake

Student begins to move towards his conclusion, revealing why Cohn is an important character.

cannot forgive this because he knows that it is true.   And it
may very well be Cohn's "sad Jewish face" that eventually leads
Brett to decide, "I'm not going to be one of those bitches that
ruins children" (243).   Her decision to leave the nineteen
year old Romero represents something of a moral victory, as her
subsequent conversation with Jake reveals:

> "You know it makes one feel rather good
> deciding not to be a bitch."
> "Yes."
> "It's sort of what we have instead of God."
> "Some people have God," I said.   "Quite a
> lot." (245)

It is impossible to judge whether or not Robert Cohn is
one of the many people who still "have God" to guide them and
are not just dependent on whatever code of social behavior
happens to be momentarily fashionable.   But this much at least
is clear: It's good to be an outsider when the insiders are
corrupt.   Robert Cohn is the most attractive character in The
Sun Also Rises precisely because he doesn't fit in to a world
that is not worth fitting in with.

WORKS CITED

Baker, Carlos.   Ernest Hemingway: A Life Story. New York:
        Scribner's, 1969.

Baker, Sheridan.   "Jake Barnes and Spring Torrents." Studies
        in The Sun Also Rises.   Ed. William White.   Columbus:
        Merrill, 1969.   37–52.

Castillo-Puche, José.   Hemingway in Spain.   Trans. Helen R.
        Lane.   Garden City: Doubleday, 1974.

Cochran, Robert W.   "Circularity in The Sun Also Rises."
        Modern Fiction Studies 14 (1968): 297–305.

Hemingway, Ernest.   Ernest Hemingway: Selected Letters 1917–
        1961.   Ed. Carlos Baker.   New York: Scribner's, 1981.

---.   The Sun Also Rises.   New York: Scribner's, 1926.

Lewis, Robert W.   Hemingway on Love. 1965.   New York: Haskell,
        1973.

Nelson, Gerald B., and Glory Jones.   Hemingway: Life and
        Works.   New York: Facts On File, 1984.

Ross, Morton L.   "Bill Gorton, The Preacher in The Sun Also
        Rises." Modern Fiction Studies 18 (1972–73): 517–527.

Rovit, Earl.   "The Sun Also Rises: An Essay in Applied
        Principles." Studies in The Sun Also Rises.   Ed. William
        White.   Columbus: Merrill, 1969.   58–72.

Seltzer, Leon F.   "The Opportunity of Impotence: Count
        Mippipopolous in The Sun Also Rises." Renascence 21
        (1978): 3–14.

Spilka, Mark.   "The Death of Love in The Sun Also Rises."
        Hemingway: A Collection of Critical Essays.   Ed. Robert
        P. Weeks.   Englewood Cliffs: Prentice, 1962.   127–138.

Sprague, Claire.   "The Sun Also Rises: Its 'Clear Financial
        Basis'." American Quarterly 21 (1969): 259–266.

Tate, Allen.   "Hard-Boiled." Studies in The Sun Also Rises.
        Ed. William White.   Columbus: Merrill, 1969. 17–19.

Five spaces

Student cites two works by same author. Three hyphens followed by a period are used instead of repeating the author's name.

Glossary of Useful Terms

ad hominem argument: An argument that makes a personal attack upon an opponent instead of addressing itself to the issue that is under dispute.

allusion: An informal reference that an audience is expected to understand without explanation.

analogy: A comparison that works on more than one level, usually between something familiar and something abstract.

anticipating the opposition: The process through which a writer or speaker imagines the most likely counterarguments that could be raised against his or her position.

audience: Whoever will read what you write. Your audience may consist of a single individual (such as one of your instructors), a particular group of people (such as English majors), or a larger and more general group of people (such as "the American people"). Good writers have a clear sense of audience, which means that they never lose sight of whomever they are writing for.

authority: A reliable source that helps support an argument. It is important to cite authorities who will be recognized as legitimate by your opponents. This means turning to people with good credentials in whatever area is under consideration: If you are arguing about the economy, cite a prominent economist as an authority—not the teller at your local bank.

begging the question: An argument that assumes as already agreed upon whatever it should be devoted to proving.

bibliography: A list of works on a particular subject. One type of bibliography is the list of works cited that appears at the end of a research paper, scholarly article, or book. Another type of bibliography is a work in itself—a compilation of all known sources on a subject. An annotated bibliography is a bibliography that includes a brief description of each of the sources cited.

bogus claim: An unreliable or false promise; a questionable statement that is unsupported by reliable evidence or legitimate authority.

cliché: A worn-out expression; any group of words that are frequently and automatically used together. In "the real world" of "today's society," writers should avoid clichés because they are a type of instant language that make writing seem "as dead as a doornail."

concession: Any point in an opposing argument that you are willing to recognize as valid. In argumentation, concessions help to diffuse the opposition by demonstrating that you are fair-minded.

connotation and denotation: Connotation consists of the associations inspired by a word, whereas denotation describes its literal, dictionary definition.

deduction: The type of reasoning through which a general observation leads to a specific conclusion.

diction: Word choice. Having good diction means more than having a good vocabulary; it means using language appropriately by using the right word in the right place. In a famous essay on James Fenimore Cooper, Mark Twain ridiculed Cooper for describing an Indian carrying the "fragments" of a deer that he had killed with an arrow. It would have taken an arrow equipped with an explosive warhead to break a deer into "fragments," a word that is best used for describing small pieces—not the carcass of a large animal. Twain was criticizing Cooper's diction. Bad diction, which means any misuse of words, can also take the form of writing the sort of gobbledegook that George Orwell ridiculed in "Politics and the English Language" (see page 509).

documentation: The data that writers supply in order to reveal the source of the information they have reported.

equivocation: The deliberate use of vague, ambiguous language in order to mislead others. In writing, equivocation often takes the form of using abstract words in order to obscure meaning.

evidence: The experience, examples, or facts that support an argument. Good writers are careful to offer evidence for whatever they are claiming.

focus: The particular aspect of a subject upon which a writer decides to concentrate. Many things can be said about most subjects. Having a clear focus means narrowing a subject down so that it can be discussed without loss of direction. If you digress from your subject and begin to ramble, you have probably lost your focus.

generalization: Argumentative writing demands a certain amount of generalization. After citing several pieces of evidence, a writer may then form a conclusion that seems generally acceptable. Another writer may successfully base an entire argument upon an idea that is generally held to be true. Generalization becomes a problem only when it is easily disputable. You have overgeneralized if someone can think of exceptions to what you have claimed. Be wary of words like "all" and "every" since they increase the likelihood of overgeneralization.

hyperbole: A deliberate exaggeration for dramatic effect.

hypothesis: A theory that guides your research. A hypothesis is a conditional thesis that is subject to change as evidence accumulates.

induction: The type of reasoning through which specific observations lead to a generally acceptable conclusion.

irony: A manner of speech or writing in which one's meaning is the opposite of what one has said.

jargon: A specialized vocabulary that is usually abstract and limited to a particular field, hence difficult to understand for those outside the field.

loaded term: A word or phrase that is considered an unfair type of persuasion because it is either slanted or gratuitous within its context.

metaphor: A comparison in which two unlike things are declared to be the same. For example: "The Lord is my shepherd."

meter: The rhythm of poetry, in which stressed syllables occur in a pattern with regular intervals. In the analysis of poetry, meter is measured by a unit called a "foot," which usually consists of between two or three syllables of which at least one is stressed.

non sequitur: Latin for "it does not follow"; a logical fallacy in which a writer bases a claim upon an unrelated point.

paradox: A statement or situation which appears to be contradictory but is nevertheless true. For example: "Conspicuous by his absence."

paraphrase: Restating someone's words in order to demonstrate that you have understood them correctly or in order to make them more easily understandable.

personification: Giving human qualities to nonhuman objects. For example: "The sofa smiled at me, inviting me to sit down."

persuasion: A rhetorical strategy designed to make an audience undertake a specific action. Although there are many different types of persuasion, most involve an appeal to feeling that would not be part of a strictly logical argument.

plagiarism: Taking someone's words or ideas without giving adequate acknowledgment.

point of view: The attitude with which a writer approaches a subject. Good writers maintain a consistent point of view within each individual work.

post hoc, ergo propter hoc: Latin for "after this, therefore because of this"; a logical fallacy in which precedence is confused with causation.

premise: The underlying value or belief which one assumes as a given truth at the beginning of an argument.

rhetorical question: A question which is asked for dramatic effect, without expectation of a response.

rime scheme (or "rhyme"):   A fixed pattern of rimes that occurs throughout a poem.

simile: A direct comparison between two unlike things which includes such words as "like," "as," or "than." For example: "My love is like a red, red rose."

stereotype: An unthinking generalization, especially of a group of people in which all the members of the group are assumed to share the same traits. For example: the "dumb jock" is a stereotype of high school and college athletes.

style: The combination of diction and sentence structure that characterizes the manner in which a writer writes. Good writers have a distinctive style, which is to say their work can be readily identified as their own.

summary: A brief and unbiased recapitulation of previously stated ideas.

syllogism: A three-stage form of deductive reasoning through which a general truth yields a specific conclusion.

thesis: The central idea of an argument; the point that an argument seeks to prove. In a unified essay, every paragraph helps to advance the thesis.

tone: The way a writer sounds when discussing a particular subject. Whereas point of view establishes a writer's attitude toward his or her subject, tone refers to the voice he or she adopts in conveying this point of view to an audience. For example: One can write with an angry, sarcastic, humorous, or dispassionate tone when discussing a subject about which one has a negative point of view.

topic sentence: The sentence that defines the function of a paragraph; the single most important sentence in each paragraph.

transition: A link or bridge between topics that enables a writer to move smoothly from one subtopic to another so that every paragraph is clearly related to the paragraphs that surround it.

Author-Title Index

Copyrights and Acknowledgments